74-1612

MARXIST ECONOMIC THEORY

Volume One

MARXIST ECONOMIC THEORY

Volume One

by

ERNEST MANDEL

TRANSLATED BY

BRIAN PEARCE

 NEW YORK AND LONDON

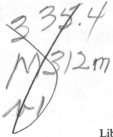

Published in the United States 1968
by Monthly Review Press
116 West 14th Street,
New York, N.Y. 10011

Library of Congress Catalog Card Number: 68-13658

Throughout this book the term
billion refers to a *thousand million.*

PREFACE TO ENGLISH EDITION

THE manuscript of the French original of this work was completed in 1960, and the French edition appeared in the spring of 1962. The English edition thus reaches the reader seven years after the completion of the French manuscript. The author would have liked to bring the documentation of the book up to date and embody in it the conclusions of a number of important works which have been published since 1960, but he has not had the time to do this. He has confined himself to rewriting Chapter 15, devoted to the Soviet economy, so as to be able to include in it a critical analysis of the important changes that have taken place during the period which has elapsed. He has made slight amendments to some other chapters and extended some of the series of statistics given. Nevertheless, the English edition constitutes a revised and corrected edition, as compared with the original one, more especially because of the corrections which have been made to printers' errors and mistakes in the references.

ERNEST MANDEL

CONTENTS OF VOLUME I

INTRODUCTION

CHAPTER ONE

LABOUR, NECESSARY PRODUCT, SURPLUS PRODUCT

CHAPTER TWO

EXCHANGE, COMMODITY, VALUE

CHAPTER NINE

AGRICULTURE

CHAPTER TEN

REPRODUCTION AND GROWTH OF THE NATIONAL INCOME

CHAPTER ELEVEN

PERIODICAL CRISES

INTRODUCTION

THE attitude of the academic world towards Marxist economic theory is ruled by a strange paradox. Half a century ago, this theory was the subject of increasing theoretical interest and of fervent discussions in university circles, but it was said to lack all practical significance: a socialist economy "is impracticable", said the economists.[1] Today nobody denies that Marxist theory is capable of inspiring, and not unsuccessfully, the economic policy of states both large and small; but in academic circles it now meets only with indifference or contempt.* If it sometimes figures as the subject of more thorough studies, this happens not for its own sake but in so far as it is a sub-branch of the new "science" called "sovietology", or is included within a still stranger discipline, "marxology"...

Whoever regards as valid the Marxist method of investigation and the mass of results which it has produced—and the writer is unreservedly of that opinion—might obviously retort that there is nothing to be surprised at here. Is not academic science "in the service of the ruling class"? Is not the capitalist world "engaged in a fight to the death" with the "socialist camp"? Is not Marxist theory an essential weapon of this "camp"? Are not the servants of capitalism obliged to discredit systematically whatever is of service to their class foes? From this standpoint the discredit cast upon Marxism in the West is merely a manifestation of the class struggle itself, indirectly confirming the validity of the Marxist propositions. This method of reasoning runs the risk of producing the sort of dialogue between people who are impervious to each other's arguments which is what the exchange of "technical" invective between Marxist and psychoanalysts amounts to.

We shall not, of course, deny that there is a grain of truth in these allegations; but only a grain! If we consider objectively the entire realm in which ideas are shaped and defended, we shall not be able to deny that a fair number of cynics and careerists are to be met therein, people who sell their pens and their brains to the highest

---

* J. M. Keynes describes Marx's *Capital* as "an obsolete economic textbook ... not only scientifically erroneous but without interest or application for the modern world."[2] A. A. Berle, Jr., considers that Marx's political economy is outworn and refuted.[3] François Perroux declares that "none of the 'chronic tendencies' [of capitalism, revealed by Marx] is logically demonstrable or can be proved by resort to scientific observation."[4] Raymond Aron writes: "Marxism no longer holds any place in the culture of the West, even in France and Italy, where an important section of the intelligentsia openly supports Stalinism. It would be vain to seek an economist worthy of the name who could be described as a Marxist in the strict sense of the word."[5] And so on.

13

bidder, or who subtly modify the direction taken by their thought if it risks prejudicing their promotion. It must further be added that for some decades now the Soviet Union, in possession of increasing material power, itself also wields an influence of the same sort.

No Marxist worthy of the name, faithful to the great scientific tradition of Marx himself, would be capable, however, of reducing the problem of the evolution of ideas to mere matters of corruption, whether direct (working through personal interest) or indirect (working through the pressure of the surrounding milieu). Marx and Engels emphasised more than once that the history of ideas follows its own dialectic, that ideas evolve on the basis of data bequeathed by one generation to another, and by the clash of competing schools of thought (cf. Engels's letter to Franz Mehring, 14th July, 1893). The social determination of this process operates essentially on material provided in this manner, with its own contradictions and possibilities of "explosion" in different directions.

Commenting on Marx's *Theorien über den Mehrwert* [Theories of Surplus Value], which were to have constituted Volume IV of *Capital*, Rudolph Hilferding correctly stressed that what we have here is a study of the dialectical evolution of ideas in accordance with their own logic and their internal contradictions *(Selbstentwicklung der national-ökonomischen Wissenschaft)*. Marx did not bring in the social factor except as the explanation of this evolution in the last analysis, and not at all as its immediate explanation.[6]

Now, Marxist tradition sums up the evolution of bourgeois political economy, that is, of "official" or "academic" political economy, in three stages, each of which coincides with a stage in the evolution of capitalism. In the stage when the bourgeoisie is rising to the position of ruling class, political economy undertakes to master economic reality, and we have the working out of the theory of labour-value, from William Petty to Ricardo. Then comes the stage when the bourgeoisie is involved in an even more acute class struggle with the proletariat, without, however, having finally eliminated the former ruling classes: this is the period when the range of possibilities contained in the inherent contradictions of the bourgeois theory of labour-value is wide open, so that we have the birth of the Marxist school, on the one hand, and that of the various post-Ricardian schools of bourgeois economic thought, on the other. Lastly, in the third stage, the bourgeoisie, having finally consolidated its ruling position, has no other struggle to wage than a defensive one against the proletariat. This is the period of the decline of bourgeois political economy. It ceases to be scientific and becomes merely apologetic. The theory of labour-value is replaced, first by "vulgar (eclectic) economics", and then by the marginalist school or by mixed schools which synthesise eclecticism and marginalism.

When one analyses the evolution of official economic thought during the last thirty years, one perceives, however, that this schema is not complete. Since the great crisis of 1929–1933 a *fourth* stage in the evolution of bourgeois political economy can easily be discerned: the stage of *purely pragmatic theory.* Mere apologetics is an effective device only so long as the system is threatened in the theoretical sphere alone. It becomes absurdly inadequate as soon as the system is in danger of collapsing in practice.

From that moment on, political economy throws overboard most of its purely academic concerns, in order to become *a technique for the practical consolidation of capitalism.* This is in fact the function it has fulfilled since the "Keynesian revolution" and the working out of the various techniques of econometry.*

Here we touch upon one of the roots of the indifference shown nowadays by "official" economists towards Marxism. In their minds, Marxism appears as just one of the schools of "the old political economy" which were centred on problems of micro-economics and were content to "reason in the abstract", without offering any recipes for increasing the volume of employment or remedying a deficit in the balance of payments. More than that, the only contemporary economists who accord Marx an honourable place in the history of economic ideas are precisely those who see him as an ancestor of the macro-economic theories now fashionable.† Some Marxists too try to show that Marx's merit consists above all in his having "foreshadowed" Keynes, the theory of economic cycles and the calculation of the national income . . .

But though interest in "pure" economic problems detached from immediate practical concerns has undeniably diminished in our times, marked as they have been by tremendous social upheavals,[11] those who claim to be Marxists are themselves partly responsible for the decline in interest in Marxist economic theory. The fact is that, for nearly fifty years, they have been content to repeat Marx's teaching, in summaries of *Capital* which have increasingly lost contact with contemporary reality. Here we touch upon the second root of the paradox mentioned at the beginning: the inability of the Marxists to repeat in the second half of the twentieth century the work that Marx carried through in the nineteenth.

This inability is due above all to political causes. It results from the subordinate position in which theory was kept in the U.S.S.R. and in the Communist Parties during the Stalin era. Theory was then the handmaid of day-to-day politics, just as in the Middle Ages philosophy was the handmaid of theology. From this situation, theory suffered

* See Chapter 18, the paragraphs: "The Keynesian revolution" and "Econometry, or the Triumph of pragmatism."

† Notably, Schumpeter,[7] Henri Guitton,[8] Condliffe,[9] Alvin Hansen,[10] etc.

a distortion towards pragmatism and apologetics which especially showed itself in economic theory. As the Stalin era was also marked by a ban on independent theoretical research, a sterile dogmatism was laid down on top of this apologetical distortion, thus forming a structure which is repulsive to the young generations both in the East and in the West. Thinking which has been stopped and distorted for 25 years* does not get back into its stride otherwise than slowly, especially if the social conditions which, in the last analysis, have caused this stoppage have not been fundamentally abolished.

Moreover, there is a secondary reason for this cessation of development in Marxist economic thought, not only in the U.S.S.R. and in the parties connected with it but also in the West, in all the Marxist schools which have remained independent of the Soviet Union. This derives from a misunderstanding regarding the Marxist method itself.

In a famous passage in his introduction to the *Contribution To The Critique Of Political Economy*, Marx explains the method that a scientific exposition of political economy must follow—proceeding from the abstract so as to reconstitute the concrete.[13] Popularisers without number have been inspired by this passage, as also by the structure of the three volumes of *Capital*, to renew again and again, in abridged and often unsatisfactory form, the economic explanations which Marx elaborated last century.

Now, *one ought not to confuse method of presentation with origin of knowledge*. While Marx insists on the fact that the concrete cannot be understood without first being analysed into the abstract relationships which make it up, he equally stresses that these relationships themselves cannot be the outcome of a mere brilliant intuition or superior capacity for abstraction; they must emerge from the study of empirical data, the raw material of every science. To grasp what Marx's opinion really was, it is enough to put beside the passage on method in the introduction to the *Contribution To The Critique Of Political Economy* the following text from the second edition of *Capital*:

"Of course the method of presentation must differ in form from that of inquiry. *The latter has to appropriate the material in detail*, to analyse its different forms of development, to trace out their inner connexion. *Only after this work is done* can the actual movement be adequately described. If this is done successfully, if the life of the

* "In our country no fundamental creative work has been done in Marxism-Leninism. Most of our theoreticians busy themselves with turning over and over again old quotations, formulas and theses. What is a science without creative work? It is not so much science as scholasticism, a pupils' exercise, not a science; for science is above all creation, creation of something new and not repetition of what is old."[12]

subject-matter is ideally reflected as in a mirror, then it may appear as if we had before us a mere *a priori* construction." [Emphasis ours.][14]

It is thus apparent that a presentation which, in the middle of the twentieth century, restricts itself to summarising, more or less accurately, the chapters of *Capital*, written in the last century, is definitely insufficient, first and foremost from the standpoint of the Marxist method itself. Still less valid, of course, are the numerous peremptory declarations made by critics of Marxism, according to which the latter is out of date "because it relies on the data of the science of last century".

The scientifically correct position is obviously that which *endeavours to start from the empirical data of the science of today in order to examine whether or not the essence of Marx's economic propositions remains valid.** This is the method we have tried to follow in this book.

We must therefore issue a warning. The reader who expects to find numerous quotations from Marx and Engels or their chief disciples will close this book disappointed. Unlike all the writers of Marxist economic textbooks, we have *strictly abstained* (with very few exceptions) from quoting the sacred texts or interpreting these quotations. As against that, we quote abundantly from the chief economists, economic historians, ethnologists, anthropologists, sociologists and psychologists of our times, in so far as they express opinions on phenomena relating to the economic activity, past, present or future, of human societies. What we seek to show is that it is possible, on the basis of the scientific data of contemporary science, to reconstitute the whole economic system of Karl Marx. Furthermore, we seek to show that only Marx's economic teaching makes possible this synthesis of the totality of human knowledge, and above all a synthesis of economic history and economic theory, just as it alone makes possible a harmonious integration of micro-economic and macro-economic analysis.

The great superiority of the Marxist method compared with other schools of economic thought in fact consists of this dynamic synthesis

---

* Several writers, notably François Perroux, have frequently declared that the laws of capitalist development discovered by Marx have never been demonstrated by observation or by means of statistical data (see quotation *supra*). We try in this book to show that this is not so—making our point of departure, of course, Marx's own laws of development and not those which have been falsely attributed to him (such as that of "absolute impoverishment", of the permanent decline of real wages, or other such notions). We are curious to know whether the official economists will be able to refute the material we have brought together in this connexion, or if they will go on declaring dismissively that "Marx is out of date", thus revealing the same lack of scientific rigour as the pseudo-Marxists who confine themselves to repeating figures and examples from the last century.

of economic history and economic theory which it alone makes possible. Marxist economic theory ought not to be regarded as a completed outcome of past investigation but rather as the summation of a method, of the results obtained by using this method, and of results which are continually subject to re-examination. Such non-Marxist writers as Joseph Schumpeter and Joan Robinson have voiced their nostalgia for this synthesis.[15] Marxism alone has been able to achieve it. The Marxist method is morever inconceivable except as an *integration* of dialectical rationalism with empirical (and practical) grasping of the facts.*

The method must therefore be genetico-evolutionary, critical, materialistic and dialectical. *Genetico-evolutionary*, because the secret of no "category" can be discovered without study both of its origin and its evolution, which is nothing else but the development of its inner contradictions, that is to say, the revelation of its true nature.† *Critical*, because no "category" ought to be "taken for granted", neither the categories "society", "labour", and "necessary product" (subsistence) nor the categories "commodity", "exchange", "money" and "capital" whose secrets Marx himself revealed. In order to do this we have generally relied on the very profound though fragmentary remarks which are scattered through Marx's writings. Sometimes, however, we have had to proceed from scratch.

In any case, critical, genetico-evolutionary study of these "fundamental categories" has brought us face to face with anthropology, sociology and social psychology. So as not to put the reader off, and not to interrupt the logical course of the demonstration, we have put the bulk of this analysis in the penultimate chapter instead of the

---

* Cf. Marx in his letter to Engels dated 1st February, 1858. "He [Lassalle] will learn to his cost that to bring a science by criticism to the point where it can be dialectically presented is an altogether different thing from applying an abstract ready-made system of logic to mere inklings of such a system."[16]

† Cf. Hilferding: "What distinguishes Marx from all his predecessors is the social theory which underlies his system, the materialist conception of history. Not only because it implies understanding the fact that economic categories are equally historical categories; this understanding by itself is not yet the essential thing; but rather because it is only by revealing the law-governed nature of social life that one can reveal and show the mechanism of evolution, [that one can show] how economic categories are born, change and pass away, and how all that happens."[17] Here still, of course, there is conflict between the origin of knowledge and the method of its presentation. Before fully grasping the significance of a category in the phase in which it first appears one needs to have analysed it in its mature form. This is why Marx deliberately abandons the genetico-evolutionary method of presentation in the first chapters of *Capital*. Once, however, in possession of the key to the mystery, the contemporary researcher who wants to re-examine the validity of a category in the face of fresh empirical data has every reason to go over its evolution, starting from the beginning.

first.* An obvious dialectical temptation exists, moreover, to study the category of labour in the light of socialist society rather than in that of primitive society. Is it not in its negation, or rather in its surpassing, in the negation of its negation, that the nature of a phenomenon is seen in its full brilliance and richness?

Finally, the method is *materialistic* and *dialectical*, since the ultimate secret of any economic category is not to be found in men's heads; it is in every instance to be found in the social relations which men have been obliged to establish among themselves in the production of their material life. And this life, together with these relations, is examined both as an indissoluble entity and as a contradictory entity which evolves under the pressure of its own contradictions.

An objection will doubtless be urged against the method which the author has followed and the results to which it has led. It will be said that though he has certainly based himself on empirical data of contemporary science, he has done this selectively. He has chosen the data which fit into "his" preconceived system, and not *all* the data. He has interpreted *some* facts but not *the* facts.

This objection is valid only to the extent that the author has indeed tried to get away from the childish obsession for "writing history with *all* the details", that obsession which Anatole France ridicules so wittily in *Le Livre de mon Ami*. The task is not merely impossible in the material sense—several men's lives would be needed to read all the books and all the sources, in all the languages of the world, which relate to the economic activity of mankind—it is also quite pointless.

At the level of the various disciplines, valid syntheses have been worked out. The Marxist who wants to study the conclusions that are to be deduced from the primitive ways in which land was held in mediaeval France need not consult a lot of sources for this purpose; he can rely sufficiently on such works as Marc Bloch's *Les Caractères Originaux de l'Historie Rurale Française*.

It is moreover obvious that selecting one's facts is characteristic of every science, the natural sciences no less than the social sciences.†

---

* See Chapter 17, paragraphs: "Alienated labour, free labour, withering away of labour", "Social revolution, economic revolution and psychological revolution", and "Man's limitations?"

† "Science is not a set of facts but a way of giving order, and therefore giving unity and intelligibility to the facts of nature," declares Dr. Bronowski, chairman of the British Association.[18] "Unless I am seriously mistaken, the prevailing view among statisticians is that the theory to be tested determines the statistical procedure to be adopted . . . It is logically impossible, except by accident, to bring the testing of theories into the problem as one proceeds along the road, as a sort of by-product of a more general examination of facts," says the economist Metzler.[19] And the economists Edey and Peacock stress that "the facts with which we are concerned in most fields of knowledge are many in number and exhibit great complexity in their relationships one with

What is anti-scientific is not the unavoidable choice of "significant facts", it is the deliberate suppression (or falsification) of experiments and observations, so as to "deny" phenomena which do not fit into the schema. We have tried to avoid all subjectivism of that sort.

It remains true that the attempt we have made to "de-Westernise" the material, except that relating to nineteenth-century capitalism, *that is to say, to discover the common features of pre-capitalist economic categories in all the civilisations which have reached the stage of developed international trade,* may seem rash. We have neither the knowledge of languages nor the knowledge of history needed for success in undertaking such a task. Nevertheless, it is indispensable, both because the public to which Marxism appeals today is no longer essentially a Western public, and also because the popularisers of Marxism have brought a tremendous confusion into this sphere with their theory of the "successive stages" that society is supposed to have passed through, or must necessarily pass through, in all parts of the world, a theory which was explicitly repudiated by Marx himself (see especially his letters to the *Otechestvennie Zapiski*, November 1877, and to Vera Zasulich, 8th March, 1881.[21]*

This is therefore merely an attempt, at once a draft which calls for many corrections and an invitation to the younger generations of Marxists, in Tokyo and Lima, in London and Bombay, and (why not?) in Moscow, New York, Peking and Paris, to catch the ball in flight and carry to completion by team work what an individual's efforts can obviously no longer accomplish. If this work succeeds in causing such consequences, even if in the form of criticisms, the author will have fully achieved his aim, for he has not tried to reformulate or discover eternal truths, but only to show the amazing relevance of living Marxism. It is by collective synthesis of the empirical data of universal science that this aim will be attained, far more than by way of exegesis or apologetics.

ERNEST MANDEL

another. To know in detail all the facts relating to a particular study and to be able to trace their individual relationships would be normally impossible for any person, however industrious. It seems to be the natural reaction of the human mind in such circumstances to classify, with varying degrees of precision depending upon the man and the nature of the problem, the relevant facts and relationships into a sufficiently small number of categories for them to be comprehended and considered together, after which they can be used as a basis for judgments about the nature of the world and its inhabitants; and, perhaps, for purposes of prediction."[20]

* It must be noted, however, that, starting a few years ago, some historians in the Chinese People's Republic have seriously questioned this non-Marxist dogma of world-wide "successive stages", and, in particular, have returned to Marx's ideas regarding "Asiatic society".

REFERENCES

1. E. Lippincott, introduction to: Oskar Lange and Fred M. Taylor: *On the Economic Theory of Socialism*, p. 3.
2. J. M. Keynes, *Essays in Persuasion*, p. 300.
3. A. A. Berle, Jnr.: *The XXth Century Capitalist Revolution*, pp. 13-24.
4. Fr. Perroux: *Le Capitalisme*, p. 109.
5. Raymond Aron: *L'Opium des Intellectuels*, p. 115.
6. R. Hilferding: *Aus der Vorgeschichte der Marxschen Oekonomie*, in *Die Neue Zeit*, Vol. XXIX, pt. 2, p. 574.
7. J. Schumpeter: *History of Economic Analysis*, p. 391.
8. Henri Guitton: *Les Fluctuations économiques*, pp. 329-32.
9. J. B. Condliffe: *The Commerce of Nations*, p. 241.
10. Alvin Hansen: *Readings in Business Cycles and National Income Theories*, p. 129.
11. Paul M. Sweezy: *The Theory of Capitalist Development*, p. 209.
12. Mikoyan at the 20th Congress of the C.P.S.U. *Die Presse der Sowjet-Union*, 1956, Vol. XXIII, p. 559.
13. K. Marx: *Zur Kritik der politischen Oekonomie*, ed. Kautsky, p. xxxvi.
14. K. Marx: *Das Kapital*, Vol. I, p. xvii.
15. J. Schumpeter: op. cit., p. 4; Joan Robinson: *The Accumulation of Capital*, p. 56.
16. K. Marx-F. Engels: *Briefwechsel*, II, p. 243.
17. R. Hilferding: op. cit., p. 626.
18. *Manchester Guardian*, 8 September 1955.
19. *Social Research*, September 1947, p. 375.
20. H. C. Edey and A. T. Peacock: *National Income and Social Accounting*, p. 155.
21. K. Marx-F. Engels: *Selected Correspondence* (1953), pp. 379, 412.
22. See especially articles by Fan Wen-lan and Jiang Quan in *Neue Chinesische Geschichtswissenschaft—Zeitschift für Geschichtswissenschaft*, Sonderheft 7, Jahrgang, 1959.

CHAPTER ONE

LABOUR, NECESSARY PRODUCT, SURPLUS PRODUCT

Labour, society, communication, language, consciousness, humanity
MAN alone, of all species, is unable to survive by adapting himself to the natural environment, but has instead to try to bend this environment to his own needs.[1] Labour, an activity at once conscious and social, born of the possibility of communication and of spontaneous mutual aid between the members of this species, is the means whereby man acts upon his natural environment.

The other animal species adapt themselves to a particular environment through development of specialised organs. Man's specialised organs, a hand with an opposable thumb and a developed nervous system, do not give him the means of directly obtaining his food in a particular natural environment. But they enable him to use tools and, through the development of language, to construct a social organisation which ensures the survival of the human race in an indefinite number of different natural environments.* Labour, social organisation, language, consciousness, are thus the distinctive characteristics of man, inseparably linked each with the others and mutually determining one another.

The tools without which man cannot produce, that is, in the first place, obtain the food needed for the survival of the species, appear at first as artificial prolongations of his natural organs. "Man needs tools to make up for the inadequacy of his physiological equipment."[3] At the dawn of mankind, these tools were very crude: sticks, chipped stones, sharpened pieces of bone and horn. In fact, prehistory and ethnology classify the primitive peoples in accordance with the raw materials from which they make their chief tools. This classification usually begins with the epoch of chipped stone, though among the prehistoric inhabitants of North America an age of bone seems to have preceded the stone age properly so called.

---

* "A creature which has become perfectly adapted to its environment, an animal whose whole capacity and vital force is concentrated and expended in succeeding here and now, has nothing left over with which to respond to any radical change . . . It can therefore beat all competitors in the special field but equally on the other hand should that field change it must become extinct. It is this success of efficiency which seems to account for the extinction of an enormous number of species."[2]

Production techniques emerge progressively from the continual repetition of the same work-movements. The most important technical discovery in human prehistory was undoubtedly that of the production and maintenance of fire. Though there are no longer any primitive tribes which were ignorant of fire before their contact with external civilisation,* innumerable myths and legends testify to an age without fire, followed by a period in which man did not yet know how to keep it going.

Sir James Frazer brought together the myths about the origin of fire of nearly two hundred primitive peoples. All show the great importance at the dawn of mankind of the discovery of a technique for generating fire and conserving it.[5]

Necessary Product

It is by labour that men satisfy their basic needs. Food, drink, rest, protection against inclemencies and excesses of cold or heat, ensuring the survival of the species by procreation, exercise for the muscles—these are the most elementary needs, according to the ethnologist Malinowski. All these needs are satisfied *socially*, that is to say, not by a purely physiological activity, by single combat between the individual and the forces of nature, but by activity which results from mutual relations established between the members of a human group.[6]

The more primitive a people the bigger is the share of its labour, and indeed of its entire existence, absorbed by seeking and producing food.[7]

The most primitive methods of food production are the gathering of wild fruit, the catching of harmless little animals, and elementary forms of hunting and fishing. A people living at this primitive stage, such as the aborigines of Australia or, better, the primitive inhabitants of Tasmania, who completely disappeared three-quarters of a century ago, know neither permanent dwellings nor domestic animals (except sometimes the dog), neither weaving of clothes nor making of containers for food. They have to traverse a very extensive territory in order to gather together sufficient food. Only the old men who are physically incapable of constant movement may be to some extent released from direct gathering of food, so as to busy themselves with making tools. The majority of the most backward communities that still survive today, such as the inhabitants of the Andaman Islands in the Indian Ocean, the Fuegians and Botocudos of Latin America, the Pigmies in Central Africa and Indonesia, the Kubu savages in Malaya, lead lives similar to those of the Australian aborigines.[8]

---

* In the sixteenth century the explorer Magellan came upon communities in the Mariana Islands in the Pacific who did not know fire. In the eighteenth century, Steller and Krasheninnikov visited the Kamchadales, inhabiting the Kamchatka Peninsula, who also were ignorant of fire.[4]

If it be accepted that mankind has been in existence for a million years, at least 980,000 years of that period were spent in a state of extreme poverty. Famine was a permanent threat to the survival of the species. The average production of food was inadequate to meet the average need for consumption. The keeping of reserves of food was unknown. Infrequent periods of plenty and good luck led to substantial wasting of food.

"The Bushmen, Australians, Veddahs of Ceylon and Fuegians hardly ever hoard for the future. The Central Australians want all their food at once, so as to have a good gorge; then they are resigned to 'go one big fella hungry' . . . When they move they leave their stone utensils lying about. If they need more they make them . . . A single tool is enough, until it wears out, for a Papuan; he has no idea of providing a successor before-hand . . . Insecurity prevented hoarding all through the primitive time. Periods of repletion and of semi-starvation regularly succeeded one another."[9]

This "improvidence" is not due to intellectual shortcomings in primitive man. It is rather the result of thousands of years of insecurity and endemic famine, which urged him to gorge himself to the full whenever opportunity occurred, and which did not allow him to work out a technique for hoarding food. Production as a whole provides the *necessary product*, that is to say, food, clothing, the community's dwelling-place, and a more or less stable stock of tools serving to produce these good things. There is no permanent surplus.

Beginning of the social division of labour

So long as an adequate supply of food is not ensured, men cannot devote themselves consistently to any other economic activity than the production of food. One of the first explorers of Central America, Cabeza de Vaca, encountered Indian tribes who knew how to make straw rugs for their dwellings but never undertook this work.

"They wish to give their full time to getting food, since when otherwise occupied they are pinched with hunger."[10]

Since all the men devote themselves to producing food, no true social division of labour, no specialisation into different *crafts*, can occur. For certain peoples it is quite incomprehensible that everybody should not be able to make all the objects in current use. The Indians of Central Brazil were always asking the German explorer Karl von der Steiner whether he had made his trousers, his mosquito-net and many other things himself. They were very surprised when he told them that he had not.[11]

Even at this level of social evolution there are individuals gifted with a special aptitude for a particular kind of work. But the economic situation, that is to say, the lack of a permanent reserve of foodstuffs, does not yet permit them to exercise these special aptitudes exclusively.

Describing the activities of the islanders of Tikopia, in the Solomon archipelago in the Pacific, Raymond Firth writes:

"Every Tikopia man is an agriculturist and a fisherman, and to some extent a worker in wood; every woman weeds plantations, uses her scoop net on the reef, beats bark-cloth and plaits mats. Such specialisation as exists is the development of extra capacity in a craft and not the practice of the craft to the exclusion of others."[12]

What is true of comparatively advanced society, where agriculture is already known, is even truer of a still more primitive society.

But the social organisation described by Raymond Firth reveals at the same time the existence of a rudimentary division of labour that can be observed at all the stages of mankind's economic development: *the division of labour between the sexes.* Among the most primitive peoples, the men devote themselves to hunting, the women gather fruit and harmless little animals. Among communities which have developed a little, certain of the techniques acquired are employed exclusively either by the men or by the women. The women undertake those activities which can be carried on near the dwelling-place: maintaining the fire, spinning, weaving, pottery-making, etc. The men go further out, hunting larger game, and work up basic raw materials into tools, using wood, stone, ivory, horns and bones.

The absence of such a division of labour as would lead to the formation of specialised crafts prevents the working out of techniques requiring a long apprenticeship and special knowledge, though it makes possible a more harmonious development of the body and of human activity. Those peoples who do not know as yet the division of labour, but who have been able to overcome famine and the worst epidemics, thanks to favourable natural conditions (Polynesians, some North American Indians before the white conquest, etc.), have developed a human type admired by modern civilised man.

First appearance of a social surplus product

The slow accumulation of inventions, discoveries and knowledge makes it possible to increase the production of food while reducing the physical effort needed from the producers. This is the first sign of an *increase in productivity of labour*. The invention of the bow and arrow, along with that of the harpoon, makes it possible to improve the technique of hunting and fishing and thus to regularise mankind's supply of foodstuffs. Henceforth, these activities become more important than the gathering of wild fruit, which is now nothing more than a supplementary economic activity. The skins and hair of animals regularly caught, along with their horns, bones and tusks, become raw material which man possesses the leisure to work up. The discovery of particularly rich hunting-grounds or fishing-beaches makes possible transition from the nomadic state to that of hunters or fishermen who are semi-settled (with seasonal alternation of dwelling-place) or even completely settled. This is the position with communities such as the Minkopies (inhabiting the shores of the Andaman Islands), the Klamath (Indians of the Californian coast), some tribes in Malaya, etc.[13] The transition to a settled way of life, whether temporary or permanent, made possible by the development of the productivity of labour, in turn makes it possible to increase the latter. It now becomes feasible to accumulate tools over and above the limited amount that a migratory community could carry with it.

Thus there gradually appears, alongside the product necessary for the survival of the community, a first permanent surplus, a first form of *social surplus product*. Its essential function is to make possible the formation of food reserves, so as to prevent or at least to mitigate the periodical return of famine. Through thousands of years primitive peoples tried to solve the problem of storing food. Numerous tribes found the solution only through contact with higher civilisations. Thus, those communities which have remained nomadic hunters and who as a rule do not produce any regular surplus, are all ignorant of salt, the most effective material for keeping meat.[14]*

The second original function of the social surplus product is to enable a more advanced division of labour to take place. From the moment that the tribe has more or less permanent reserves of food at its disposition, some of its members can devote a more considerable part of their time to producing objects which are not for eating: tools, ornaments, containers for food. What was previously just a personal inclination or talent for a certain technique now becomes a specialisation, the embryo of a craft.

The third original function of the social surplus is to make possible a more rapid increase of population. Conditions of semi-famine practically limit the population of any tribe to able-bodied men and women. The tribe cannot keep alive more than a minimum of small children. Most primitive peoples know about and extensively apply artificial birth-control, which is absolutely indispensable because of the inadequate food supply.[15] Only a limited number of sick or disabled people can be looked after and kept alive. Infanticide is commonly practised. Prisoners of war are usually killed, if not eaten. All these efforts to restrict the growth of population do not show that primitive man is innately cruel, but testify rather to an effort to avoid a greater danger, the disappearance of the entire people for lack of food.

From the moment, however, when a more or less permanent food

---

* Before the discovery of the preservative functions of salt, a discovery which was decisive for the establishment of permanent reserves of protein, a wide variety of methods were used to preserve meat. It was dried, smoked, kept in bamboo vacuum containers, etc. All these methods have been found inadequate for long-term preservation.

reserve makes its appearance, a new equilibrium between the food available and the number of the population can be achieved. Births increase, and with them the number of children surviving infancy. Sick people and the aged can live longer, increasing the average age of the tribe. The density of the population on a given territory will increase with the productivity of labour, and this is an excellent index of economic and social progress.[16] With the growth of the population and the specialisation of its labour the productive forces at mankind's disposal are increased. The appearance of a social surplus is an essential condition for this increase.

The neolithic revolution

The formation of a permanent surplus of foodstuffs is the material basis for the carrying through of the most important economic revolution man has known since his appearance on earth: the beginning of agriculture and of the domestication and rearing of animals. In accordance with the period of prehistory during which this revolution occurred, the period of polished stone, or neolithic period, it is known as the neolithic revolution.

Agriculture and cattle-raising presuppose the existence of a certain surplus of food, and this for two reasons. First, because their technique demands the utilisation of seed and animals for purposes not directly concerned with food consumption, so as to produce more plants and more meat at a later stage. Peoples who have lived for thousands of years on the brink of famine do not easily agree to diverting towards a more distant goal whatever is immediately edible, unless they possess other stocks of food.*

Besides, neither agriculture nor cattle-raising immediately produce the food needed for the tribe's existence, and a food reserve is needed to cover the period between seed-time and harvest. For these reasons, neither primitive agriculture nor cattle-raising could be adopted straight away as the principal production system of a people. They make their appearance by stages, being at first regarded as activities secondary to hunting and the gathering of fruit, and they long continue to be supplemented by these activities, even when they have become the basis of the people's livelihood.

It is generally thought that the raising of domestic animals (beginning: c. 10,000 B.C.) came later than the first attempts at systematic agriculture (beginning: c. 15,000 B.C.), though the two activities may appear simultaneously or, with certain peoples, the order of appearance may even be reversed.[18] The most primitive form of agriculture,

* "Agriculture calls for . . . an ascetic self-discipline which does not follow automatically from a knowledge of tools," Gehlen points out. The author wonders whether, for this reason, the first crops were perhaps protected by being exclusively devoted to religious purposes.[17]

still practised today by a number of peoples of Africa and Oceania, consists of scratching the surface of the soil with a pointed stick, or digging it with a hoe. Since the soil is rapidly exhausted by such methods of cultivation, it is necessary to leave the land thus worked, after a few years, and occupy fresh land. Several peoples, for example, the mountain tribes of India, acquire this fresh land for cultivation by burning the jungle, the ashes forming a natural fertiliser.[19]

The neolithic revolution brings the production of means of subsistence, for the first time since the dawn of mankind, under man's direct control: this is its main importance. The gathering of fruit, hunting and fishing are *passive* methods of providing food. They reduce, or, at least, maintain at a given level, the quantity of resources that nature puts at the disposal of man on a given territory. Agriculture and cattle-raising, however, are *active* methods of providing food, since they increase the natural resources available to mankind, and create new ones. With the same expenditure of labour, the amount of food at man's disposal can be increased tenfold. These methods thus constitute a tremendous increase in the social productivity of human labour.

The neolithic revolution also gives a powerful stimulus to the development of tools. By creating a *permanent surplus* it creates the possibility of a professional body of craftsmen.

"The preliminary condition for the formation of craft (technical) abilities is a certain amount of leisure which can be taken from the time devoted to producing means of subsistence."[20]

The beginning of agriculture and the raising of domestic animals leads, moreover, to the first great social division of labour: pastoral peoples appear alongside agricultural peoples.

Undoubtedly, the decisive progress due to the practice of agriculture must be ascribed to women. The example of the peoples who still exist as primitive agriculturists, as well as numberless myths and legends,* confirm that women, who in primitive society devote themselves to gathering fruit, and usually remain close to the dwelling-place, were the first to sow the seeds of the fruit they had collected, so as to facilitate the provision of food for the tribe. The women of the Indian Winnebago tribe were, moreover, compelled to *hide* the rice and maize destined for sowing, as otherwise the men would have eaten them. In close connexion with the development of agriculture by the women there appear, among numerous primitive agricultural peoples, religions based on the worship of goddesses of fertility.† The

---

* "The appellation *pasigadong*—the means of getting *gadong*, or food—is jocosely applied by the Batak to his wife . . ."[21]

† Cf. the following observation by Robert Graves: "The whole of neolithic Europe, to judge from surviving artifacts and myths, had a remarkably homogeneous system of religious ideas, based on worship of the many-titled Mother-goddess, who was also known in Syria and Libya. Ancient Europe had no

institution of the matriarchate, the existence of which can be shown among a number of peoples at the same level of social development, is also connected with the part played by women in the creation of agriculture. Sumner and Keller and Kritz Heichelheim[24] list a large number of proved instances of matriarchate among primitive agricultural peoples.

Co-operative organisation of labour

Hobhouse, Wheeler and Ginsberg studied the mode of production of all the primitive peoples who were still surviving at the beginning of the twentieth century. They found that all the tribes who know only a rudimentary form of agriculture and cattle-raising—and, *a fortiori*, all those peoples who have remained at a lower stage of economic development—are ignorant of the use of metals and possess only a very crude technique of pottery-making and weaving.

Archaeological data confirm those of ethnography. In the neolithic epoch we find in Europe only the crudest forms of pottery. In India, in North China, and in North and West Africa, we find traces of similar societies between the sixth and fifth millennia B.C.[25] The non-existence of advanced pottery or weaving indicates the absence of a fully separate body of craftsmen. The surplus that agriculture and cattle raising supplies to society does not yet make it possible to free the craftsman completely from the task of producing his own food.

Thus, even today, in the Chinese village of Taitou:

"None of the artisans . . . makes his living entirely from his trade . . . All the masons, carpenters, weavers, workers in the small foundry, the village schoolteacher, the crop watcher, and the several village officers work on their land with their families during the sowing and harvesting seasons or whenever they happen not to be engaged in their professional work."[26]

Just as at more primitive stages of economic development, society remains based on the co-operative organisation of labour. The community needs the labour of every one of its members. It does not yet produce a surplus sufficiently large for this to become private property without jeopardising the survival of the whole community. The customs and code of honour of the tribe are opposed to any *individual* accumu-

gods. The Great Goddess was regarded as immortal, changeless, and omnipotent; and the concept of fatherhood had not been introduced into religious thought. She took lovers, but for pleasure, not to provide her children with a father. Men feared, adored, and obeyed the matriarch; the hearth which she tended in a cave or hut being their earliest social centre, and motherhood their prime mystery."[22] The Indian writer Debiprasad Chattopadhyaya has made an extensive analysis of the relationships between the part played by women as the first cultivators of the soil, the matriarchate, and the magico-religious cult of goddesses of fertility, on the basis of the history and literature of his country.[23]

lation in excess of the average. Differences in individual productive skill are not reflected in distribution. Skill as such does not confer a right to the product of individual work, and the same applies to more diligent work.[27]

"Maori distribution," writes Bernard Mishkin, "was fundamentally dominated by one aim: to meet the needs of the community. No one could starve so long as anything remained in the community storehouses."[28]

Special institutions were developed—for instance, the ceremonial exchange of gifts and the organisation of feasts after the harvest—to ensure an equitable sharing of foodstuffs and other necessary products among all the members of the community. Describing the feasts organised among the Papuan people of Arapesh, Margaret Mead considers that this institution "is actually an effective measure against any one man's accumulating wealth disproportionate to the wealth accumulated by others."[29]

Georges Balandier writes to the same effect regarding the Bakongo tribes in Equatorial Africa:

"An institution like the one called *malaki* throws light on this ambiguous situation. At the start, it was in the nature of an annual feast (in the dry season) which extolled the unity of the kindred by honouring ancestors, and made possible the reinforcement of alliances . . . On this occasion, a quantity of good things which had been accumulated during the year were consumed collectively in a true atmosphere of rejoicing and celebration. Thrift operated, upheld by the heads of the kindreds, in the form of *renewal of relationships of consanguinity and alliance*. The *malaki* functions, by its regular periodicity and the amount of wealth needed for it, as one of the driving forces and regulators of the Bakongo economy . . . It testifies to a moment (hard to date) in economic evolution when the surplus of products presented men with new problems: their products came between them and distorted the system of personal relations."[30]

James Swann, describing the customs of the Indians of Cape Flattery (Washington State, U.S.A.), says that whoever has produced a plentiful supply of food, in whatever form, customarily invites a series of neighbours or members of his family to come and consume it with him. If an Indian has gathered sufficient stocks of food, he has to give a feast, which goes on until this stock is exhausted.[31] A society of this kind puts the accent on the quality of *social solidarity* and regards as immoral an attitude of economic competition and ambition for individual enrichment.

Solomon Asch, who has studied on the spot the customs of the Hopi Indians, observes:

"All individuals must be treated alike; no one must be superior and no one must be inferior. The person who is praised or who praises himself is automatically subject to resentment and to criticism . . . Most Hopi men refuse to be foremen . . . The play behaviour of children is equally instructive in this respect. From the same source I learned that the children, young and old, are never interested in keeping score during a game. They will play basket-ball by the hour without knowing who is winning or losing. They continue simply because they delight in the game itself . . ."[32]

The co-operative organisation of labour implies, on the one hand, the carrying-out in common of certain economic activities—building huts, hunting the larger animals, making paths, felling trees, breaking up new land—and, on the other, mutual aid between different families in daily life. The American anthropologist John H. Province has described such a work-system in the Siang Dyak tribe, who live in Borneo. All members of the tribe, including the witch-doctor, work alternately on their own paddy field and on that of another family. They all go hunting and firewood-collecting and all carry out domestic tasks.[33]

Margaret Mead describes a similar system prevailing among the Arapesh, a mountain people of New Guinea.[34] The co-operative organisation of labour in its pure form means that no adult holds back from participating in labour. It thus implies the absence of a "ruling class". The work is planned by the community in accordance with custom and with ancient rites based on a deep knowledge of the natural environment (climate, composition of the soil, habits of game, etc.). The chief, if there is one, is merely the embodiment of these rites and customs, the correct fulfilment of which he ensures.

Labour co-operation continues, as a rule, throughout the slow process, prolonged through hundreds (if not thousands) of years, of disintegration of the village community.[35] It must be stressed that the custom of carrying out tasks in common which is found very late in class-divided societies is doubtless the origin of *corvée*, that is, of unpaid extra work which is carried out on behalf of the State, the Temple, or the Lord. In the case of China, the evolution from one to the other is perfectly clear.

Melville J. Herskovits[36] mentions a very interesting transitional case in Dahomey. *Dókpwê*, communal work, is usually carried out for the benefit of every native household. But, contrary to tradition, and to official statements, a request for help from a relatively prosperous household is answered before one from a poor household. Furthermore, the head of the *dókpwê* has become a member of the ruling class. The Dahomeyans are, moreover, aware of the evolution which his taken place, and themselves told Herskovits the following:

"The *dókpwê* is an ancient institution. It existed before there were kings. In the olden times there were no chiefs and the *dókpwêgâ* [directing the communal work] was in command of the village. The male members of the village formed the *dókpwê* as today, and the cultivation of the ground was done communally. Later, with the coming of chiefs and kings, disputes arose as to their respective authority . . ."[37]

According to Nadel, in the Nigerian kingdom of Nupe, communal work, called *egbe*, is carried out first (and above all!) on the lands of the chiefs; Joseph Bourrilly mentions a similar evolution of the *touiza*, as co-operative work is called among the Berbers.[38]

Primitive occupation of the soil

At the moment when tribes start to practise agriculture they are usually organised on the basis of kinship. The oldest form of social organisation seems to be that of the *horde*, such as still exists among the aborigines of Australia.

"[A horde] is a body of persons who jointly possess, occupy and exploit a certain defined area of country. The rights of the horde over its territory can be briefly indicated by saying that no person who is not a member of the horde has the right to any animal, vegetable or mineral product from the territory except by invitation or consent of members of the horde."[39]

Later, the large family, the clan, the tribe as a confederation of clans, the confederation of related tribes, are the normal forms of organisation of the primitive peoples, at the moment when they begin to apply themselves to agriculture. It is therefore not surprising that the primitive occupation of the soil, and the establishment of one or other form of authority (ownership) over the latter, are first and foremost influenced by this predominant form of social organisation.

So long as the people concerned have not yet reached the stage of intensive agriculture, with manuring and irrigation, the occupation of the soil usually takes the form of occupation of a village by a large family, a group of men and women united by kinship. In Northern Rhodesia, Audrey I. Richards notes that the Bemba people "live in small communities, the average village consisting of 30 to 50 huts . . . Each village is a kinship unit under the rule of a headman . . ."[40]

Among the settled Berbers of Morocco, "the typical state is not the tribe but what we call, inaccurately enough, the fraction of a tribe [the large family] . . . All the members of the fraction say they are descended from the same ancestor, whose name they bear."[41] In the Slavonic countries of the sixth to ninth centuries the tribes "lived each with its own clans and on its own lands, each clan being its own master."[42]

Describing country life in mediaeval France, Marc Bloch concluded:

"To sum up, the village and its fields are the work of a very large group, perhaps . . . of a tribe or a clan; the *manses* (English *hides*, German *Hufe*) are the shares allotted to smaller sub-groups. What was this secondary collectivity, of which the *manse* formed the shell? Very probably, it was the family, as distinct from the clan . . . , a family still patriarchal in type, large enough to embrace several collateral couples. In England the word *hide* has as its Latin synonym *terra unius familiae* [the land of one family]."[43]

Speaking of agricultural life in Lorraine, Ch. Edmond Perrin confirms "that the *manse* was, in the beginning, the share of land cultivated by a single family, is proved sufficiently by the practices of the Merovingian period; in the seventh century, indeed . . . it was by head of family and not by *manse* that the obligations of tenants were calculated on the lands of the Church and of the Crown."[44]

It is thus the large family, the clan, that occupies the village, and the family strictly so called that builds the farm. Now, primitive agriculture was confronted above all by the problem of periodical clearing of new land, a task carried out in common by the entire village, as is testified by the example of those peoples who have remained to this day at the given stage of development, and as is celebrated in old Chinese songs. It is logical, within the framework of a co-operative organisation of labour, that the cultivable land, cleared communally, should remain common property and be redistributed periodically. Only the garden around the dwelling, cleared by the family alone, or the fruit tree they have planted, evolves towards the stage of private property.[45] *Garden* means, moreover, "enclosed place", that is, "field closed to others", in contrast to the fields which are common property and are not divided up by fences.*

The allotment and periodical redistribution of the cultivable land by drawing lots are confirmed by numerous pieces of historical and linguistic evidence. The cultivable lands in Lorraine were first called *sors* (lots); the lands distributed by lot in Old Testament Palestine were called *nahala* (lots), a word which later came to mean property, etc. The same is true of ancient Greece.[47]

When, with the development of more advanced agricultural methods, the cultivated area at last became stabilised and the collective clearing of new land ceased to play an important part in the life of the village, private property in land began to appear. Even then, however, so long as the village community had not been dissolved, the ancient communal ownership survived in various forms. A third of the village—over and above the houses and gardens, on the one hand, and the cultivable fields, on the other—made up essentially of pastures and woods, remained common property. The right to graze, that is, the

* When the T'ang dynasty came to power in China (A.D. 618), thanks to a peasants' revolt, it re-established the system of periodical redistribution of the cultivable land, but left the gardens (about one-fifth of all the land of each farm) as hereditary property of the peasant families.[46]

use of all the fields, before sowing began, by the cattle of all the
members of the community; the right to glean after the harvest; the
right to build and use mills or wells in common; the constitution of
the village as a unit collectively responsible for the payment of taxes;
the keeping up of customs of mutual aid; the right to set up new farms
on cleared portions of woodland; all these phenomena show that for
centuries a strong collective solidarity continues in village life, a
solidarity the roots of which lie deep in the communal ownership of
olden times.

It is not possible to list all the sources that confirm the existence of
this common ownership of the land among all civilised peoples, at a
certain phase of their agricultural evolution; we will briefly mention
some of the chief sources. The Japanese village community called the
mura is described by Yoshitomi. Yosoburo Takekoshi, in his monu-
mental work *Economic Aspects of the History of Civilisation in Japan*
describes the common ownership of the land in ancient times, with
division of the soil by lot. In Indonesia "the village community
represents the original community", writes Dr. J. H. Boeke. Wittfogel
has analysed the *tsing-tien* system of dividing the fields of the Chinese
villages into nine squares, and discovered there the village community
which has descended from the collective appropriation of the soil.[48]
The work of Professor Dyckmans on the ancient empire of the
Egyptian Pharaohs states explicitly that there the land was originally
clan property with periodical redistribution of the holdings. Professor
Jacques Pirenne says the same thing in his *History of Institutions and
Private Law in Ancient Egypt*.[49] M. Jacques Weulersse, describing the
agricultural system of the Arab people called the Alaouites, has
found among them even today traces of collective ownership, which
was formerly predominant throughout the Islamic world:

"Those villages are called *mouchaa* villages in which the whole of
the land belongs collectively to the whole village community. No
member of the latter possesses any land as his own, but only a right
in the entire territory. This right guarantees him a definite share of
the soil when the periodical redistribution of land takes place . . .
usually every three years."[50]

In respect of all Central and East Africa the semi-official *African
Survey* states that:

"It is true to say that throughout that part of Africa with which we
are concerned, there is a prevailing conception of the land as the
collective possession of the tribe or group."[51]

Speaking of the Polynesian economy of Tikopia, Raymond Firth
notes "the traditional ownership of orchards and garden plots by
kinship groups."[52]

Historical research confirms the existence of collective ownership
of the land in Homeric Greece, in the Germanic *Mark*, in the ancient

Aztec village, in the ancient Indian village of the time of the Buddhist writings; in the Inca village where the ploughed fields are called *Sapslpacha*, that is, "the land (*pacha*) which belongs to everyone"; in the villages of the Byzantine Empire, notably in Egypt, Syria, Thrace, Asia Minor and the Balkans, before the Slav colonisation; in ancient Russia, with its village community the *obshchina*; among the South Slavs, the Poles, the Hungarians, etc. In a study undertaken for the F.A.O., Sir Gerald Clausen confirms, furthermore, that everywhere, in the beginning, agriculture was carried on within the framework of an agrarian system based on communal ownership, with periodical redistribution of land.[53]

The cultivation of irrigated land, cradle of civilisation

Agriculture was initially clumsy and irregular; man did not know how to preserve the soil's fertility. The discovery of irrigation and of the effect of letting land lie fallow completely revolutionised agricultural technique.

The consequences of this revolution in agriculture were incalculable. The breeding of domestic animals and the first beginnings of agriculture had enabled men to take control of the means of subsistence. The systematic application of the practice of letting land lie fallow, and above all, of irrigation, linked with the use of draft animals, enabled mankind to guarantee itself permanently a substantial surplus of foodstuffs, dependent only on man's own work. Each seed sown in Mesopotamia was repaid a hundredfold at harvest-time.[54]

The existence of this permanent surplus of foodstuffs made it possible for craft techniques to become independent, specialised and perfected. Society was able to support thousands of men who no longer participated directly in the production of foodstuffs. The town could separate itself from the country. Civilisation was born.

Already the ancient Greeks of Homer's time regarded civilisation as the product of agriculture.[55] The Chinese of the classical epoch attributed the "invention" of agriculture, of trade and of civilisation, all to the mythical emperor Chen-Nung.[56] It is interesting to note that in Aztec tradition the origin of the people's prosperity is to be found in a communication received by the high priest in a dream, a communication "which ordered the Mexicans to dam a great river which flowed round the foot of the hill, so that the water spread over the plain."[57] Over and above these limited examples, the historian Heichelheim does not shrink from stating, with justification, that *agriculture has been the foundation of all civilisations down to modern capitalism*.[58] And the American Encyclopaedia of the Social Sciences says:

"History and archaeology have so far brought to light no great civilisation not largely dependent upon one of these three grains [wheat, maize and rice]."[59]

The transition to cultivation of the land by irrigation, and the appearance of town life, which resulted from it, occurred in several parts of the world where natural conditions made it possible. It is still difficult to determine to what extent this evolution took place among different peoples independently of each other; but this independence seems established as regards some of them. We find the development of agriculture by irrigation of the land, of a large permanent surplus of foodstuffs, of specialisation of crafts and of the rise of towns, successively in the valley of the Nile and in the valley of the Euphrates and Tigris in the fifth millennium B.C.; in the valley of the Hwang-ho in China, in Iran and on the island of Cyprus in the fourth millennium; in the valley of the Indus, in Central Asia and on the island of Crete in the third millennium; in mainland Greece, in Anatolia, in the Danube valley and in Sicily in the second millennium; in Italy and in Southern Arabia (the kingdom of Minea* and the Sabaean civilisation) in the first millennium B.C.; and in West Africa (civilisations of Ghana, Mali and Songhai in the valleys of the Niger and the Senegal) and also in America (in Mexico, Guatemala and Peru) in the first millennium A.D.

The metallurgical revolution

The agricultural revolution coincided broadly with the end of the age of polished stone. Men, released from the degrading servitude of hunger, were able to develop their innate qualities of curiosity and technical experimentation. They had long since learnt that it was possible to cook certain kinds of clay in the fire to make pots. By subjecting different kinds of stone to the fire they discovered metals, and then their wonderful capacity for being made into tools. The successive discovery of copper (sixth millennium B.C., in the valley of the Euphrates and Tigris and also in that of the Nile), of tin, then of the appropriate mixture of copper and tin called bronze (third millennium B.C., in Egypt, Mesopotamia, Iran and India), and at last of iron (c. 1300 B.C., among the Hittites, after a sporadic use of it among the coastal peoples of the Black Sea) constitute the most important stages in this technical revolution.

The effects of the metallurgical revolution were important first of all in the field of agriculture itself, which continued to be the basic economic activity of society. With the introduction of metal implements in agriculture, especially the plough with a metal share, the

---

* Etymologically, Minea means "spring water".[60] In the same period, Germany and Gaul were opened to civilisation thanks to the use of the fallow system.

employment of animal power for draft purposes became necessary, and the productivity of agricultural labour made a fresh leap forward. The use of the iron plough made possible extensive agriculture and the appearance of towns on the heavy soils of Europe in the eighth to seventh centuries B.C.[61] The introduction of metal tools in Japan in the eighth century A.D. made possible a considerable extension of the cultivated area and consequently a notable increase in the population.[62]

Thus was created the material condition for the rise of craft techniques and for the separation of town and country. The growth of population, made possible by the general increase in well-being,* provided the labour force. The increase in the surplus of foodstuffs supplied the means of subsistence for this urban labour-force. The metals themselves constituted the main raw material for the work of these craftsmen. At first essentially a technique of luxury and ornamentation, the metal-working craft later became specialised in the

* As for every species of life, this increase of the population is indeed the most objective index of progress. The geographer Ratzel[63] gives the following table of the density of population corresponding to the different ways of life at the beginning of this century. We have slightly simplified it:

	Inhabitants per square mile
Tribes of hunters, and of fishermen in the peripheral parts of the inhabited world (Eskimos)	·1–·3
Tribes of fishermen and hunters inhabiting steppe-land (Bushmen, Australian aborigines, Patagonians)	·1–1·5
Tribes of hunters with rudimentary agriculture (Dyaks, Papuans, Indian hill tribes, the poorest Negro tribes)	1–20
Tribes of fishermen settled on the coasts or river-banks (North-West American Indians, peoples of small Polynesian islands, etc.)	Up to 100
Nomadic shepherds	40–100
Agriculturists with beginnings of crafts and trade (Central Africa, Malay Archipelago)	100–300
Nomads with agriculture (Kordofan, Persia, Sennaar)	200–300
Peoples carrying on extensive agriculture (Moslem countries of Western Asia and the Sudan, Eastern European countries)	200–500
Tribes of fishermen carrying on agriculture (Pacific islands)	Up to 500
Regions carrying on intensive agriculture (peoples of Central Europe)	2,000
Regions of Southern Europe where intensive agriculture is carried on	4,000
Regions of India where irrigation agriculture is carried on	Over 10,000
Regions of Western Europe where large scale industry is carried on	Over 15,000

making of tools and weapons of all kinds. The crafts won final independence with the labour of the smith.*

Production and accumulation

Agriculture which can preserve and increase the fertility of the soil creates a permanent surplus of foodstuffs, a substantial *social surplus*. This surplus is not only the basis for the social division of labour, for the separation of the crafts from agriculture, of town from country. It is also the basis of the division of society into classes.

So long as society is too poor to be able to accumulate a permanent surplus, social inequality cannot develop on any great scale. To this day, in the countries of the Levant, whereas on the fertile land the property-right of lords has been established, taking from the peasant half and even more of his crop, on the mountain land "the crops are so poor that the land would not be able to bear the double burden of a share-cropper and a landlord."[65]

"Under primitive conditions it [slavery] does not exist. It has no economic basis at a time when a pair of hands can produce only as much and no more than one mouth consumes. It comes into being when the cumulative results of labour can be stored, or integrated into large works of construction."[66]

After examining the social institutions of 425 primitive tribes, Hobhouse, Wheeler and Ginsberg found that slavery was completely absent among peoples ignorant of agriculture and cattle-raising. They found the beginnings of slavery among one-third of the peoples who had reached the pastoral stage or the initial stage of agriculture, and a generalisation of slavery at the stage of fully developed agriculture. Thirty years later, C. Darryl Forde arrived at the same conclusions.[67]

As soon as a considerable surplus has been formed, the possibility appears for a part of society to give up productive labour, obtaining leisure at the expense of the remainder of society.† The use of

* In mediaeval Europe the smith appears as the first craftsman who works professionally for the market. The Latin word *faber* = "smith", and the German word *Schmied* = "smith" meant originally just "craftsman".[64] In Western and Central Europe, however, the Bronze Age did not see the appearance of an urban civilisation; only the iron plough created a plentiful surplus there. In Central America, on the other hand, the climatic conditions and the low density of population made possible a rise of civilisation already before metal tools came into use. These exceptions show, however, that the production and concentration of a large social surplus constitute indeed the condition for the appearance of civilisation. The differentiation of the natural environment inevitably entails differences in the methods of producing this surplus and differences as to the epoch in which different peoples attain to this.

† This is obviously only a *possibility*; it is equally possible that the leisure thus won may reduce the working time of all of the producers and be put to use for extra-economic activities by everyone. This seems to have been the

prisoners of war or captives of any kind as slaves (in Polynesia, slave means *Tangata-Taua* = "man obtained by war"[69]) constitutes one of the two most common forms in which society is first divided into classes. The other form of this same primitive division is the payment of an imposed tribute to part of society.

When advanced agriculture is carried on in a large number of small villages, each of them produces a surplus which, taken separately, is quite insufficient for the formation of a body of professional craftsmen, and still less sufficient for the foundation of towns.* The concentration of this surplus becomes the preliminary condition for its effective utilisation:

"The surplus produced by an individual family above the requirements of domestic consumption is liable to have been exceedingly small under a rural economy so backward that a large proportion of each season's calves had simply to be eaten. For a community to acquire any substantial quantity of foreign material a concentration of the surplus would be requisite. Historical testimony from the Bronze Age civilisations of the Ancient East and ethnographic evidence from Polynesia and North America show that one way of effecting this concentration is the institution of chieftainship, another the cult of a deity. Offerings made by each family of followers or votaries from its tiny surplus, the real chief or the representative of the imaginary god can accumulate quite a substantial surplus."[71]

Something which is at first voluntary and intermittent later becomes obligatory and regular. By the application of force, that is to say, by the organisation of the state, a social order is established which is founded on the surrender by the peasants of their surplus of foodstuffs to the new masters.†

Speaking of the most primitive peoples, Malinowski explains:

"These people have no centralised authority nor any tribal policies. Consequently they have no military force, no militia, no police; and they do not fight as between one tribe and another. Personal injuries are avenged by stealthy attacks on individuals, or by hand to hand

case among the Siane of New Guinea, among whom the replacement of their old stone axes by steel ones cut down the share of their working time devoted to the production of means of subsistence from 80 per cent to 50 per cent, according to Salisbury.[68]

* According to the American Assyriologist A. L. Oppenheim, the first Mesopotamian towns were only big villages, and retained a structure exactly the same as that of the village community.[70]

† In the Nigerian kingdom of Nupe, the rent paid to the chiefs is still called a gift, *kynta*, in the villages, whereas it is already called a tithe, *dzanka*, in the environs of the capital, Bida.[72] It is significant that the Arabic word *makhzen*, which means "government", comes from the verb *khazana*, "to accumulate", "to store", and that it has given us the French and Spanish words *magasin* and *almacén*!

fighting . . . War does not exist among them." C. Darryl Forde describes similarly the primitive clan communism, without hereditary chiefs, among the Tungus in North-East Siberia.[73]* Heichelheim notes, in contrast, the appearance of a state organisation in the first towns:

"The majority of the town population . . . lived from rents and tributes [that is, by appropriating the surplus product of agricultural labour]. Some belonged to the ruling class, princes, priests and nobles. The upper class had in its employ a large range of officials, agents, servants, tradesmen . . ."[75]

Beyond concentrating and accumulating the social surplus, these new possessing classes fulfilled other socially-necessary and progressive functions. They made possible the development of art, a product of the luxury crafts working for the new lords. They made possible the differentiation of the surplus product as a result of its accumulation, and the differentiation of the surplus product meant also the differentiation of production itself. They made possible, and to some extent themselves ensured in person, thanks to their leisure, the accumulation of techniques, knowledge and rules which guaranteed the maintenance and development of the productive forces of agriculture: astronomical and meteorological knowledge regulating the control of the waters, the approximate most favourable moment for starting the harvest, and in certain circumstances the forbidding of it: geometrical knowledge making possible the division of the fields; carrying out of works of initial cultivation made necessary by the growth of population, on a scale exceeding that of the power of a village or a group of villages; construction of canals, dykes and other hydrographical works essential for irrigation, etc.†

The technique of accumulation has been used to justify the appropriation of extensive material privileges. Even if it be historically indispensable, there is no reason to believe that it could not have been applied eventually by the collectivity itself. As for the privileges, they were in any case felt as exactions by the people who were the victims of them, and they inspired protests such as those of the peasant of the ancient Egyptian empire who speaks in the *Satire of the Crafts*.[77]

---

* Among the Nambikwara Indians the chief (*nilikande*: he who unites) enjoys an authority based on consent, and possesses no power of coercion. When Lévi-Strauss asked an Indian what were the privileges of the chief he received the same answer ("He's the first man to march off to war") as Montaigne had received in 1560—four centuries earlier!—to a similar question which he put to an American Indian.[74]

† 2,400 years ago, Kautilya, prime minister to the Indian King Maurya Chandragupta, explained in his work *Arthashastra* the origin of all civilisation as springing from the work of the peasantry: "For the fact that the villages supply their own needs and that men find their only pleasure [!] in the fields makes it possible to increase the King's treasury, merchandise [trade!], corn and moveable property."[76]

The Marxist category of "historical necessity" is moreover much more complex than popularisers commonly suppose. It includes, dialectically, both the accumulation of the social surplus which was carried out by the ancient ruling classes, and also the struggle of the peasants and slaves against these classes, a struggle without which the fight for emancipation waged by the modern proletariat would have been infinitely more difficult.

Is there an "economic surplus"?

The idea of a social surplus product, which is rooted in that of a permanent surplus of means of subsistence, is essential for Marxist economic analysis. Now, this idea has until recently been accepted not only by the majority of economists but, what is more significant, by all anthropologists, archaeologists, ethnologists and specialists in primitive economy. The numerous references to the work of these specialists which are scattered through the first chapters of this work testify that the empirical data of contemporary science confirm the validity of the basic hypotheses of Marxist economic analysis.

The only serious scientific attack directed against the ideas of economic surplus and social surplus product in pre-capitalist economy has been launched by Professor Harry W. Pearson, in a chapter of the collective work published under the editorship of Karl Polanyi, Conrad M. Arensberg and Pearson himself: *Trade and Market in the Early Empires*. It deserves refutation in detail.

Professor Pearson's criticisms can be summarised in five points:

1. The idea of "economic surplus" is a muddled one, since it in fact covers two different entities: the absolute surplus, in the physiological sense of the word, without which society cannot exist, and the relative surplus, which society has decided to form.

2. Now, an "economic surplus" in the absolute, biological, sense of the expression, does not exist. It is impossible to determine the minimum level of subsistence below which an individual would perish; it is impossible to determine this for society as a whole.[78] In any case, this level is so low that there is no proof that any human society has ever lived as a whole at this level.

3. As for the relative surplus, this is not the result of an economic evolution, in particular of the increase in the average productivity of labour. There are always and everywhere potential surpluses. The decisions to create or increase resources not assigned for consumption by the producers are social decisions which may be taken for quite non-economic reasons (religious, political, prestige).

4. There is "not a shred of evidence" to show that the appearance of "private property, barter, trade, division of labour, markets, money, commercial classes and exploitation" is due to the appearance of an economic surplus at crucial moments in the development of human

society. Such statements can be justified only by the assumption that "the logical course of economic development . . . is toward the market system of nineteenth-century western Europe."[79]

5. Furthermore, this whole conception is founded on the crudest materialism, which "bases social and economic development upon 'the narrow capacity of the human stomach'."[80] At every level of material existence, economic resources have been employed for non-economic ends.

Professor Pearson's argument proceeds from the distinction between "absolute surplus" and "relative surplus", a distinction which he has himself, of course, introduced into the discussion. To our knowledge, neither the physiocrats nor the British classical economists, nor, above all, Marx and Engels, ever regarded the "subsistence level" as an absolute biological notion. But one cannot thereby conclude that this idea has no definite historical significance in each specific instance, that one may arbitrarily reduce the level regarded as the minimum by a particular people at a particular time. For this reason it is wrong to state that every society possesses a potential source of surplus, regardless of an increase in the average productivity of labour.

True, no society can continue to exist if, after providing the most modest of livelihoods to its members, its production is inadequate to maintain the supply of tools. In this "absolute" sense of the word, no society reduced to the mere "biological" level of subsistence could survive. But so long as man *is not in control of* his means of subsistence—or in other words, so long as we are dealing with hordes, or primitive tribes who live by gathering fruit, hunting and fishing—this "surplus" is both precarious and extremely limited. The reason for this is quite simple: any exceptional increase in current production would not produce a "permanent surplus" but, on the contrary, a famine, upsetting the ecological balance of the inhabited area.

When Professor Pearson writes that no human society has ever lived at such a level of poverty he commits in reality a mistake similar to that for which he rightly blames the neo-classical economists. Just as the latter conceive all economic activity as a function of a market economy, Professor Pearson sees the entire economic past of humanity in the light of the economy of primitive peoples on the threshold of civilisation or already civilised, that is, of peoples who have already accomplished their "neolithic revolution" and are carrying on agriculture and cattle-raising. But when one considers that the period since that revolution occupies only a small fraction of the time that man has existed on the earth, when one recalls that hundreds, if not thousands, of primitive tribes have disappeared before reaching the stage of the neolithic revolution, in particular because they have not been able to solve the problem of subsistence in a modified natural environment, one realises how untenable this statement is.

Proof, both logical and empirical, shows the contrary, that the majority of human societies previous to the neolithic revolution* had to carry on a permanent struggle for subsistence; that they were obsessed by this struggle, which seemed never to reach a victorious conclusion, and that all the social institutions quoted by Professor Pearson in support of the opposite view (especially the important place held by magic and religion in these societies) had definitely economic *functions*, that is, were supposed to contribute precisely to the solution of the agonising problem of subsistence. "The universal occurrence of magical and religious practices in association with productive processes reveals . . . that anxiety with respect to food supply is universal."[81]

That is where the key importance of the neolithic revolution lies. For the first time in human prehistory, control over mankind's means of subsistence passes from nature to man. For the first time, henceforth, these means can be multiplied, if not without limit, then at least in a proportion quite unknown before. For this reason, an important fraction of society can be released from the need to contribute directly to the production of food. There are no archaeological or anthropological data to bring into question today this obvious proof of the connexion between the appearance of a *permanent and substantial surplus of food*, on the one hand, and, on the other, the separation of the crafts from agriculture and of town from country, and the division of society into classes.

True, the growth in the average productivity of labour creates only the *necessary material conditions* for social evolution and transformation. There is no economic automatism, independent of social forces.† Men make their own history; an existing society defends itself against forces of transformation. Primitive society defends its egalitarian structure. There must then be a social revolution to break up egalitarian primitive society and give birth to a society divided into classes. But this social revolution is not *possible* unless a level of productivity has been reached which enables part of society to release itself from material work. So long as this material condition, this potential surplus, does not exist, the social revolution in question is impossible.

Professor Pearson will retort that, after all, the decisive driving force has been social, the replacement of one "model" of social organ-

---

* Except tribes living in an exceptionally favourable natural environment, usually described as "developed hunters".

† See Chapter 2, paragraph: "Co-operatively organised society and society based on economy of labour-time."

isation by another.* We readily agree to this primacy of the social. But would a confederation of tribes of primitive hunters have been able to build the Roman Empire, or even the Babylon of Hammurabi? Would the Mesopotamian peasants have been able to create modern industry? To answer these questions is to appreciate the strategic role of the increase in the economic surplus and the social surplus product in human history, through the growth in the productivity of labour.

* George Dalton[82] has endeavoured to enlarge upon the ideas of Professor Pearson in this connection. He is obviously right in opposing the anachronistic use, in relation to a primitive society, of motives like the *unlimited* search for material means. He is also right in opposing the use, in this different social setting, of categories derived from a commodity or money economy. But he is wrong when he concludes that the shortage of material goods is a purely "ideological" notion, or that there is no rational economic explanation of the socio-economic conduct of primitive peoples. To allege that "transactions of material goods in primitive society are expressions of social obligations which have neither mechanisms nor meaning [!] of their own apart from the social ties and social situations they express"[83] is to forget that primitive people are obliged, after all, to keep themselves alive, no less than modern ones; that their survival demands a certain amount of production of material goods; that social organisation is not independent of the need to produce these material goods; that the economic motive, that is, the striving to ensure that a certain *limited* amount of production takes place is thus definitely present in this primitive society; and that if it is often difficult to analyse this socio-economic structure, nobody ought to declare it an impossible task from the outset, because this would make impossible the scientific study of the evolution of societies in general.

REFERENCES

1. J. Grahame Clark: *From Savagery to Civilisation*, p. 26; A. Gehlen: *Der Mensch*, p. 24.

2. G. Heard: *The Source of Civilisation*, pp. 66-67. See also Gehlen, op. cit., pp. 35, 91, etc.

3. Gordon Childe: *Man Makes Himself*, p. 49. Cf. also Prof. Oakley in *An Appraisal of Anthropology Today*, p. 235.

4. G. Renard: *Le Travail dans la Préhistoire*, p. 67; R. Furon, *Manuel de Préhistoire générale*, p. 174.

5. Sir James Frazer: *Myths of the Origin of Fire*.

6. B. Malinowski: *A Scientific Theory of Culture*, p. 95.

7. Raymond Firth: *Primitive Polynesian Economy*, pp. 37-38.

8. L. T. Hobhouse, G. C. Wheeler and M. Ginsberg: *Material Culture of the Simpler Peoples*, pp. 16-18.

9. W. G. Sumner and A. G. Keller: *The Science of Society*, Vol. I, pp. 163-4.

10. M. J. Herskovits: *The Economic Life of Primitive Peoples*, p. 48.

11. Kaj Birket-Smith: *Geschichte der Kultur*, pp. 143-4.

12. Raymond Firth: op. cit., pp. 112-13.

13. Heinrich Cunow: *Allgemeine Wirtschaftsgeschichte*, Vol. I, pp. 103-23; C. Darryl Forde: *Habitat, Economy and Society*, p. 374.

14. H. Cunow: op. cit., Vol. I, p. 95.

15. Raymond Firth: op. cit.; Cl. Lévi-Strauss: *Tristes Tropiques*, pp. 297-8.

16. Gordon Childe: op. cit., pp. 15-19.

17. A. Gehlen: op. cit., pp. 433-4.

18. Fritz Heichelheim: *Wirtschaftsgeschichte des Altertums*, p. 36; C. Darryl Forde: op. cit., p. 397. See in *Historia Mundi*, Vol II, pp. 66-80, the discussion of the present state of this question by Karl J. Narr.

19. L. T. Hobhouse: et al., op. cit., p. 22.

20. R. Thurwald: article *"Handwerk"* in *Reallexicon der Vorgeschichte*, Vol. V, pp. 98. These ideas are nowadays generally accepted by the specialists: see *An Appraisal of Anthropology Today*, pp. 40-41.

21. W. G. Sumner: et. al., op. cit., Vol. I, p. 134.

22. Robert Graves: *The Greek Myths*, p. 13, Vol. I, Penguin Books, revised edition 1960.

23. Debiprasad Chattopadhyaya: "Lokayata", People's Publishing House, 1959, pp. 251-65 and 273-92.

24. W. G. Sumner: et al., op. cit., Vol. III, pp. 1954 sqq.; F. Heichelheim; *Antike Wirtschaftsgeschichte*, Vol. II, p. 898. See also F. Kern: *Mutterrecht einst und jetzt*, in *Theologische Zeitschrift*, Basel, 6, 1950, and *Historia Mundi*, Vol. I, p. 389, and Vol. II, pp. 91-92, 94.

25. R. Furon: op. cit., passim.

26. Martin C. Yang: *A Chinese Village*, p. 27.

27. R. Firth: op. cit., p. 63.

28. Margaret Mead: *Co-operation and Competition among Primitive People*, p. 445.

29. Ibid., p. 29.

30. Georges Balandier: *"Structures sociales traditionnelles et changements economiques"*, in *Revue de l'Institut de Sociologie Solway*, U.L.B., No. 1, 1959, pp. 38-39.

31. *Smithsonian Contributions to Knowledge*, Vol. XVI.

32. Laura Thompson: *A Culture in Crisis*, pp. 94-95.

33. M. J. Herskovits: op. cit., pp. 72-77.

34. Margaret Mead: *Sex and Temperament*, pp. 26-27. See also the description by Jomo Kenyatta of communal work among the Kikuyu: *Facing Mount Kenya*.

35. *Les Populations aborigènes*, published by the International Labour Office, p. 225.

36. M. J. Herskovits: *Dahomey, An Ancient West African Kingdom*, Vol. I, p. 64.

37. Ibid., Vol. I, p. 65.

38. S. F. Nadel: *A Black Byzantium, The Kingdom of Nupe in Nigeria*, p. 49; Joseph Bourrilly: *Eléments d'ethnographie marocaine*, p. 139.

39. A. R. Radcliffe-Brown: *Structures and Functions in Primitive Society*, p. 33.

40. Audrey I. Richards: *Land, Labour and Diet in Northern Rhodesia*, p. 18.

41. Henri Terrasse: *Histoire du Maroc*, p. 28.

42. *The Russian Primary Chronicle*, trans. S. H. Cross (1930), p. 8.

43. Marc Bloch: *Les caractères originaux de l'histoire rurale française*, p. 163.
44. Ch. E. Perrin: *Recherches sur la seigneurie rurale en Lorraine*, p. 639.
45. C. Darryl Forde: op. cit., p. 375; René Grousset: *Histoire de la Chine*, p. 9.
46. Stefan Balazs: *Beiträge zur Wirtschaftsgeschichte der T'ang-Zeit*, in *Mitteilungen des Seminars für Orientalische Sprachen*, 1931–32.
47. See in particular J. Caesar: *De Bello Gallico*, Vol. IV, 21, 23; Perrin: op. cit., p. 629: *Old Testament*, Numbers 26, verses 55, 56, Joshua 18, verse 6, Micah 2, verse 5, etc.
48. M. Yoshitomi: *Etude sur l'histoire économique de l'ancien Japon*, p. 67; Yosoburo Takekoshi: *Economic Aspects of the History of the Civilisation of Japan*, pp. 26-27; J. H. Boeke: *Theorie der Indische Economie*, p. 30; K. A. Wittfogel: *Probleme chinesischer Wirtschaftsgeschichte*, p. 304. See also a recent Chinese publication, *An Outline History of China*, p. 19.
49. G. Dijckmans: *Histoire économique et sociale de l'Ancienne Egypte*, Vol. I, p. 128; Jacques Pirenne: *Histoire des Institutions et du Droit Privé de l'Ancienne Egypte*, Vol. I, p. 29.
50. Jacques Weulersse: *Le Pays des Alaouites*, p. 357.
51. *African Survey*, pp. 833-4 (1st and 2nd editions only).
52. R. Firth: op. cit., pp. 57-58.
53. G. Glotz: *Le Travail dans la Grèce antique*, pp. 14-15; J. Kulischer: *Wirtschaftsgeschichte des Mittelalters*, Vol. I, pp. 12-32; G. C. Vaillant: *The Aztecs of Mexico*, p. 113; *Cambridge History of India*, Vol. I, p. 200; H. Cunow: *Geschichte und Kultur des Inka-Reiches*, p. 138; M. V. Levtchenko: *Byzance*, p. 48; P. I. Lyastchenko: *History of the National Economy of Russia*, p. 70; Sir Gerald Clausen: *La Tenure Communautaire*, passim, pp. 23-25.
54. Gordon Childe: *What Happened in History*, p. 90.
55. G. Glotz: op. cit., p. 48.
56. Chen Huan-Chang: *The Economic Principles of Confucius*, p. 122.
57. Ramirez Ms.: *Histoire de l'Origine des Indiens*, p. 13.
58. F. Heichelheim: *Vormittelalterliche Geschichtsepochen*, pp. 163-4.
59. *Encylopaedia of Social Sciences*, Vol. I, article "Agriculture", p. 572.
60. P. K. Hitti: *History of the Arabs*, pp. 49-58.
61. F. Heichelheim: *Wirtschaftsgeschichte des Altertums*, Vol. I, p. 205.
62. M. Yoshitomi: op. cit., p. 208; Sir George Sansom: *A History of Japan to 1334*, p. 14.
63. Ratzel, *Anthropogeography*, Vol. II, pp. 264-5. (1st German edition, 1891).
64. J. Kulischer: op. cit., Vol. I, p. 71.
65. J. Weulersse: op. cit., p. 357.
66. B. Malinowski: *Freedom and Civilisation*, p. 301.
67. L. T. Hobhouse: et. al., op. cit., pp. 235-6; C. Darryl Forde: op. cit., p. 391.
68. Salisbury: *From Stone to Steel*, passim. Melbourne University Press, 1962.
69. H. Cunow, *Allgemeine Wirtschaftsgeschichte*, Vol. I, p. 411.
70. In Karl Polanyi et al., *Trade and Market in the Early Empires*, pp. 30-31.

71. Gordon Childe: *Scotland before the Scots*, p. 48.
72. S. F. Nadel: op. cit., p. 190.
73. B. Malinowski: *Freedom and Civilisation*, p. 278; C. Darryl Forde: op. cit., p. 359.
74. Cl. Lévi-Strauss: op. cit., p. 330.
75. F. Heichelheim: *Wirtschaftsgeschichte des Altertums*, Vol. I, p. 171.
76. *Kautilya's Arthashastra*, German trans. by J. J. Mayer, pp. 61-62.
77. G. Maspéro: *Histoire ancienne des peuples de l'Orient classique*, Vol. I, p. 331.
78. K. Polanyi: et al., op. cit., p. 324.
79. Ibid., p. 327.
80. Ibid., p. 325.
81. Marvin Harris: "The Economy has no surplus?", in: *American Anthropologist*, Vol. LXI, nr. 2, April 1959, p. 194.
82. George Dalton: "Economic Theory and Primitive Society", in: *American Anthropologist*, Vol. LXIII, nr. 1, February 1961, pp. 1-25.
83. Ibid., p. 21.

CHAPTER TWO

EXCHANGE, COMMODITY, VALUE

Simple exchange

THE conditions for occasional exchange were created by encounters between hordes gathering different fruits or hunting different animals. "Barter and trade develop in areas of contrasted produce, where bush and sea-coast, forest and plain, mountain and lowland, offer each other novelties and encourage the exchange of goods."[1]

Speaking of the Bemba people of Rhodesia, who trade very little, Audrey I. Richards notes that "the environmental conditions of the Bemba account to some extent for their poor development of trade, since conditions are, generally speaking, so uniform in this area that there is little reason for one district to exchange goods with another".[2]

The origin of exchange is thus to be found *outside* the primitive social unit, whether this be horde, clan or tribe. Within it there prevail originally mutual aid and labour co-operation, which exclude exchange. The service each person owes to the community is laid down by custom or religious rite; it varies with age and sex and with the system of consanguinity. But it does not depend on any expectation of a precise reciprocal payment, whereas *a measured reciprocal payment is what constitutes the essential characteristic of exchange.*

The measurement involved here is not necessarily an *exact* one. Indeed, it cannot be exact at the stage of simple exchange, which is casual and occasional. Hordes and tribes who know little about the nature, origins, conditions of production, or precise use of a product which they receive "in exchange" for another, inevitably let themselves be ruled by arbitrariness, caprice or mere chance in determining the conditions of such exchange. Exchange, the most precisely "measured" operation in modern economic life, was born in material conditions that excluded any possibility of precise measurement.

Simple exchange is casual and occasional exchange; it cannot form part of the normal mechanism of primitive life. It may result either from the chance appearance of surplus or from a sudden crisis in the primitive economy (famine).*

In either case, a primitive group which knows other groups are liv-

---

* Speaking of the Bachiga tribe in East Africa, May Mandelbaum Edel notes that "as a rule trade occurs only when it is necessary, as the result of a lean harvest, to eke out the food supply."[3]

ing nearby will try to establish exchange-relations, either by violent methods or by peaceful ones. This encounter between two occasional surpluses, varying in natural qualities, utility and *use-value*, creates the most usual conditions for a simple exchange transaction.

Silent barter and ceremonial gifts

When a primitive group regularly has a surplus of certain products, after meeting its own consumer needs, simple exchange can become developed exchange. This is no longer a casual exchange operation happening at exceptional moments, but a more or less regularised series of exchange operations.

The establishment of strict rules of exchange is only the culmination of a long transition which starts from a situation in which sporadic exchange takes place without any precise measurement. To the two ways of acquiring foreign products—simple exchange and war for plunder—there correspond two transitional forms of exchange among primitive groups: ceremonial gifts and silent barter.

Contacts between primitive groups not related by blood are hardly ever contacts between groups of equal strength. They imply relations near the brink of hostility, and this brink is quickly crossed.

Experience teaches the weaker groups that it is wisest to flee before the approach of formidable strangers. To the latter it teaches that if they decimate weaker groups whose products they want, this entails the risk of losing all chance of obtaining these products.* Thus conventionally regulated exchange-relations, known as silent barter, are established at the borderline of open hostility. The weaker group leaves its products for exchange in an uninhabited spot and goes away until the partner has left its own products in the same place.

Economic history is full of examples of this silent barter. The case of the relations between Moors and Negroes to the west of Gibraltar, mentioned by Herodotus, and that of the relations between Persian, Tartar and Greek merchants in South Russia with the inhabitants of the frozen steppes of North Russia, mentioned by the traveller Ibn Batuta, figure in the classical literature on the subject. Today, silent barter is to be found in several parts of the world: among the Chukchi tribes of Siberia, in their relations with the inhabitants of Alaska; among the *negritos* who live in the valleys in the north of the island of Luzon, in the Philippines, in their relations with the Christian inhabitants of the same area; among the Awatwa tribe, in Northern

---

* "The Mundugumor [headhunters of New Guinea] wander far afield not only in search of enemies to ambush, but in search of trade-acquaintances . . . From the emaciated, half-starved, rickety peoples who inhabit the eastern swamps, they buy cooking-pots, carrying baskets, mosquito-bags . . . They said they were careful not to kill all of them, for then there would be no makers of pots left alive."[4]

Rhodesia, in the relations between the inhabitants of the interior and those of the marshlands; in New Guinea, in the New Hebrides, in India, in Indonesia, etc.[5]

Silent barter, and still more the exchange operations which are derived from relations of open hostility, originate in contact between different primitive groups unconnected by ties of blood. Within the group, as we have seen, exchange relations are absent, in primitive conditions. Food and other primary necessities are not exchanged but shared.[6] What exists is a mere giving of gifts, presents (precious objects, talismans, ornaments) which are conventionally returned, just as today within a modern family, without any exact calculation of equivalent values.

However, when groups with a common ancestry grow large and spread themselves over a territory which is too extensive to be administered by a single leadership, they split into fragments. The exchange of presents, consisting of different products specially found in the respective territories on which these sub-groups live, is institutionalised, repeated periodically in a solemn manner, and becomes regular. The ceremony expresses the relations of real material interdependence which exist between these sub-groups, one being unable to live without the help of another, or else merely the existence of ties of blood.[7]

This institution of ceremonial exchange of gifts survives among primitive groups which have already reached the stage of individual agriculture but remain settled together in village communities. The difference between individual harvests within one and the same community, or between the harvests of a number of villages related by ties of blood, will be offset from time to time by exchange of gifts; numerous relations involving solemn exchange of gifts, the economic function of which appears today vague or even invisible, had a functional origin like this.

In his *Structures élementaires de la parenté*, Claude Lévi-Strauss has convincingly shown how these exchanges of presents, like exchanges of women, are integrated in economic life at this stage of social evolution, and how these two parallel circuits—which the primitive people regard as the same, the women being themselves considered as presents—are indispensable for *maintaining the social cohesion of the group*. The division of labour being still essentially the division of labour between the sexes, any disorganised choice of wives would lead to the weakening of certain groups, and even to their disappearance.

This is why the rules of reciprocity imply that a man "may not receive a wife from any other group than that from which he has the right to obtain one, because in the previous generation a sister or a daughter was lost; while a brother owes the outside world a sister (or a father owes a daughter), because in the previous generation a wife was acquired".[8]

"Exogamy," concludes Lévi-Strauss, "provides the only means of maintaining the group as a group, avoiding the endless break-up and separation that consanguine marriages would mean".[9]*

Among the Ozuitem Ibo of Southern Nigeria, the exchange of presents of food is explained by members of the tribe themselves as follows:

"The people of Ozuitem claim that in the past, before cassava was first introduced at the beginning of this century, there was often a severe food shortage in the three months (June-August) before the annual yam harvest. A long-established system of food transfers during this period is still practised whereby food gifts are made by those having available supplies on the understanding that money gifts will be made in return. Men are also under obligation to make food gifts to their wives and female kinsfolk which ultimately benefit the households of these women."[11]

The practice of ceremonial exchange may proceed beyond the limits of a single tribe and extend to several tribes or peoples inhabiting a particular region. Just as ceremonial exchange within a narrow group merely gives expression to the close bonds of solidarity and co-operation in labour, its extension to several tribes and peoples expresses an effort to stabilise peaceful relations of co-operation among them.[12]

"The tribute-missions began as the gestures of the princes of the countries of the Nanyang [south-east Asia] sending envoys to the Chinese capital with gratulatory or ceremonial messages to the Chinese court. They were always received as humble emissaries conveying the submission of their masters to the Sun of Heaven. They brought presents, of course, usually of native produce, and the emperor, out of the benevolence of his heart, bestowed presents upon them in return. It happened that these return presents were often more valuable than those brought from Java, Borneo or Malacca, as the case might be; but even if they were only of equal value it was clear that here ready established was an embryonic foreign trade."[13]

When individual economic activity—above all, agriculture—comes

---

* Lévi-Strauss argues against Frazer, who explains the exchange of women by the fact that primitive people were unable to pay any other "price" [sic] for them. He is right in blaming Frazer for supposing the existence in the past of "calculations" which are found only in much more "advanced" societies. But he is wrong when he concludes: "In exchange of women there is nothing like a reasoned solution to an economic problem . . . It is an act of primitive and indivisible consciousness . . ." Actually, Lévi-Strauss himself has shown what a vital economic role was played by women in primitive economy. The desire to regulate the "circulation of women" so as to ensure the maximum equality of opportunity to marry for all the able-bodied men thus fully corresponds to an *economic* need for social equilibrium.[10]

to take a more and more important place in the life of the village community, when relations of ceremonial exchange of presents and of silent barter become frequent and are regularised, increasingly numerous elements of *measurement*, of *calculation* of the presents exchanged are introduced into the community, so as to maintain its economic equilibrium. In the *desa*, the Indonesian village community, two forms of economic activity thus coexist: the *samba sinambat*, unpaid activity directed towards the satisfaction of vital needs, and the *toeloeng menseloeng*, activity directed towards the realisation of individual needs for which one has the right to expect a more or less equivalent counter-payment.[14] Schechter,[15] having examined most of the examples of ceremonial exchanging of presents, found that in the majority of cases the principle of equivalence, and so of precise measurement of the counter-payment, already plays a preponderant part. True, this is still a long way from a market economy, based on commodity production, but equivalence is generally accepted and even institutionalised, as appears in Hammurabi's code.[16]

Developed exchange

Silent barter and ceremonial gifts are transitional forms between simple exchange and generalised exchange, which can be included under the common heading of *developed exchange*.

Developed exchange results from an encounter between surpluses of different products which are no longer casual but habitual. Both silent barter and ceremonial gifts can take the form of developed exchange, and can also outgrow this form and appear as part of generalised exchange properly so called.

In primitive society in which the crafts have not yet won their independence, a *regional specialisation*, a regional division of labour, can appear in consequence of specific peculiarities of a given territory. The tribe occupying this territory may devote itself to a large extent to producing this speciality, and appear in the eyes of neighbouring tribes as a collective specialist. It will produce a considerable surplus of the goods in question, and exchange it against the special products of other tribes. Prehistory and ethnography show that *tools* and *ornaments* are the first products likely to spread in substantial quantity from a given centre of production, through operations of developed exchange.

Thus, before the colonial conquest of their country, the Gouro tribe of the Ivory Coast used to exchange with the people of the savannah mainly cola nuts, which they produced, for iron rods, called *sompe*, which they used both as raw material for making agricultural tools and weapons and as media of exchange. Cola and *sompe* were elements in a trade between the South and the North which was genuinely complementary, between two different geographical zones.[17] It should further be noted that, at the same time as they carried on this genuine trade, the Gouro kept up relations of ceremonial exchange of gifts with tribes, such as the Baoulé, whom they regarded as their kindred.[18]

Already in the old stone age, real workshops for the production of stone implements were organised, notably at Saint-Acheul and on the island of Bömlo, in South-West Norway. In the new stone age, real flint quarries existed in Egypt, Sicily, Portugal, France (Grand Pressigny), at Grime's Grave and Cissbury in England, at Obourg and Spienne in Belgium, in Sweden and in Poland (Eastern Galicia and Kielce district). On the island of Marua remains have been found of workshops producing stone implements which supplied the needs of a large part of New Guinea.[19] Heichelheim mentions a number of sources which seem to confirm the circulation of ornamental objects within a very wide radius, from the earliest times.[20]

With the progress of the productivity of labour and the formation of small regular surpluses among many neighbouring tribes and communities, this system of regional specialisation can expand into a regular network of exchange and lead to a true regional division of labour. In the Amazon basin, for instance, various tribes each have their own specialities: the Menimels are particularly well-known for their pottery, the Karahone produce especially virulent poisons, the Boro specialise in the making of rugs, ropes and pipes; the Nitoto excel in the making of hammocks.[21] Exchange becomes more and more regularised between these tribes, on the basis of these specialities.

For each of the tribes concerned, however, the making of special products constitutes only a supplementary and secondary activity in their economic life. The latter remains based essentially on fruit-gathering, hunting and fishing (with sometimes the beginning of some agriculture), that is, on looking for food. No craft specialisation yet exists within the tribe, where developed exchange is completely absent, except perhaps in the form of ceremonial gifts. Those who today are making pots must tomorrow go hunting or cultivate the land, if the tribe is to escape falling victim to famine.

Trade

With the neolithic revolution, the development of agriculture and the formation of permanent surpluses create the possibility of permanent exchange with peoples who have not yet acquired such surpluses, and exchange enters a new phase. Exchanges are no longer restricted to a few rare products which are the specialities of certain regions. They henceforth embrace all the products of a whole region; *local markets* make their appearance. Each tribe or each village continues to provide for its own needs to a large extent, but none is any longer entirely independent of a supply of foreign products.

"Many communities (in Southern Nigeria) dispose of a surplus of foodstuffs and other goods in daily use, such as pottery, matting and wooden utensils, which find their way through the multitude of local market places to purchasers in other communities . . . Thus, the Agoi forest villages on the slopes of the Oban hills . . . trade smoked bush meat to the markets of the villages close to the Cross river in which they purchase yams, some of which may have been grown not by the people of these villages but by the Ibo living several miles on the far side of the river. Similarly, pot-making villages, which are re-latively few and far between, are nearly all surplus producers, their wares being distributed over areas of a hundred square miles or more. Thus, though in general, the household, and still more the village community as a whole, is largely self-sufficient in food supplies and most other household needs, few, if any, are completely so."[22]

The system of *generalised exchange* coincides with the beginnings of professional crafts within the village or tribe. But this specialisa-tion is a specialisation within a *village community*. The craftsmen who increasingly give up agricultural work receive their food in reward for their services. Exchange within the village or the tribe thus remains *rudimentary*. This is the situation, for example, among the inhabitants of the Marquesa Islands in the Pacific, or among the Kafflitcho and Gougo tribes in East Africa. Some craftsmen have already become fully independent, others not yet. The craftsmen in the first category receive a certain quantity of food, clothing and ornaments every year from the village community, in reward for all their work. The crafts-men in the second category are helped by other members of the tribe in the work they have to do on the land which is to supply them with means of existence.[23] In neither case have we here exchange in the strict sense.

Generalised exchange between different villages, tribes and com-munities is carried on in a more or less collective way, by the pro-ducers themselves, by a section of the community (for example, the women*), or by representatives of the community. It is not yet in itself a specialised economic activity.

"In mediaeval Europe, as in agricultural areas of our own day, the average producer was able to dispose of the petty surpluses of his household (eggs, cheese, hens, vegetables, milk, cattle, and even grain) without the assistance of a professional trader. Similarly, wherever an industry happened to be organised in small handicraft units and goods

---

* In so far as it was women who first undertook the cultivation of the soil, it is understandable that they should have been the first to undertake the exchange of food surpluses in a regular way. According to Chinese tradition, women were the first to engage in trade. Quite recently, all trade was in the hands of the women among the following peoples: the Togo, Somali, Galla and Masai in Africa, the Tatars and Tibetans in Asia.[24] Forde, Scott and Nadel note the same phenomenon in Nigeria. In pre-Columbian Nicaragua, only the women were allowed to appear in the market-place.[25] Similarly, only women sold in the local market in the kingdom of Dahomey.

were made in small quantities, or to order, producers and consumers could deal with each other without the intervention of a trader. Not only the village smith and potter, but the urban butcher, baker and candlestick-maker themselves disposed of their produce."[26]

This situation changes with the metallurgical revolution. The first metals that man found how to use, copper and tin, are not found in all countries, nor, in particular, in those which, thanks to irrigation agriculture, saw the first rise of civilisation. The mines are located in certain well defined areas, especially in mountainous parts, where the metals in question may well have been used over a long period for purposes of decoration, without giving rise to a metallurgical revolution in the economic sense of the word.

In order to acquire these minerals, the agricultural peoples who possessed adequate food surpluses, techniques and leisure had to go and seek them where they were to be found, first, no doubt, by way of plunder, then later through normalised exchange.[27] Exchange over long distances, international exchange between regions separated by hundreds of miles, could no longer be a supplementary activity, alongside the work of the crafts and agriculture. A new division of labour took place, the carrying-out of exchange was separated from other economic activities: trade was born.

Among the primitive peoples, the metallurgical revolution caused the appearance of professional crafts to coincide with the generalisation of exchange. The first craftsmen wholly detached from agricultural work are *itinerant smiths* (they are still found among the Bantu of equatorial Africa and the Peuls in West Africa). Among these peoples, the metallurgical revolution, by making trade independent, separates it completely from the crafts, just as it separates the latter from agriculture.

It is interesting to observe that the two forms of exchange, generalised exchange which has not yet become a specialised activity, and specialised trade properly so called, are usually found together in agricultural regions. Thus, among the Indians of the Chorti tribe, in Guatemala, the peasants and craftsmen themselves go to the local market once a week, and to the cantonal market once a month, or once every two months, to sell their small surpluses. But the trader who imports products from outside the region itself is a professional trader. The same distinction is observed among the Nupe, in Nigeria.[28]

From the age of copper onward, trade developed, notably in the first pre-dynastic civilisation in Egypt; in the first, "pre-diluvian" civilisation in Mesopotamia; in the most ancient of the civilisations discovered on the site of Troy, in Asia Minor; in the Creto-Mycenaean civilisation in Greece; in the civilisation of the Aztecs in Mexico, before the Spanish conquest; in the ancient Chinese, Indian and Japanese civilisations, etc.

In a work of Chinese classical literature, the *Appendix to Con-fucius's Book of Changes*, it is reported that markets (that is, trade) were invented in the same period as the plough, i.e. at the same time as the important changes in agriculture which result from the metal-lurgical revolution.[29]

With the bronze age, the development of trade relations becomes the preliminary condition for the productive use of technical know-ledge. By a careful study of the deposits of copper and tin available in that period, Gordon Childe showed that in proportion as the Mediter-ranean peoples went over to the making of bronze objects they neces-sarily had to enter into international trade relations with a number of countries. From India to Scandinavia there are in fact only four regions where these two metals can be found together, namely, in the Caucasus, in Bohemia, in Spain, and in Cornwall.[30] However, the bronze age did not begin in any of these four regions.

The peoples who presided over the rise of the bronze age were obliged, in order to obtain these precious metals, to organise tremend-ous trading expeditions—in so far as they were not periodical raids, such as those which subjected the mines of the Sinai peninsula to Egypt from the time of the second dynasty.[31]* The wheeled chariot and the sailing ship were invented in the bronze age, and accompanied the progress of civilisation throughout the ancient world. Regular cara-vans linked Egypt with Mesopotamia across the Sinai peninsula, Palestine and Syria, and linked Mesopotamia with India across Iran, the north of Afghanistan and the Indus valley. From the bronze age onward, in a Europe which was still barbarous, extensive trade rela-tions were formed between the Baltic and the Mediterranean, the Danube valley, the Pannonian Plain and the British Isles.

When this international trade became stabilised and peaceful, it continued none the less to be a State matter, and was carried on at first through merchants who were State servants. A neutral entrepôt provided the meeting-place for the two nations.[32]

Production for use and production of commodities

Production in primitive societies is essentially production to meet needs. The producers work in order to satisfy the needs of their community, whether this be large (tribe or clan) or small (family). This is true of the peoples who are still at the stage of gathering their food and also of those who are already producing it in the strict sense

---

* China, where copper and tin are plentiful, was able to enter the bronze age very soon. Internal trade therefore developed *earlier and further* than external trade. The decisive role of the metallurgical revolution in the develop-ment of trade is thus confirmed by this exception, too. In America copper and tin are found on the high plateaux of Peru and were basic to the Inca civilisation.

of the word. The first empires built up on the basis of irrigation agriculture do not show any economic features fundamentally different from the latter. The kings or priests who centralise the surpluses use them to satisfy their own needs or those of the community as a whole. It is significant that the King of Babylon was called, in official inscriptions: "Peasant of Babylon", "Shepherd of Men", "Irrigator of the Fields". In Egypt, the Pharaoh and the governmental administration were called *Pr'o*, meaning the big household. In China, one of the legendary emperors who were supposed to have founded the nation was called Héou-tsi, millet-prince.[33] The whole of the economy appeared indeed like a great estate producing *use-values* to satisfy its needs.[34]

With the independent crafts a new kind of production appeared. Producers who were peasant-craftsmen living in a village community, brought to the market only the *surplus* of their production, that is, what was left over after the needs of their families and their community had been met. The specialist craftsmen detached from a community, the itinerant smith or potter, no longer produces use-values to meet his own needs. *The whole of his production is intended for exchange.* It is in exchange for the products of his labour that he will acquire the means of subsistence, clothing, etc., to meet the needs of his family and himself. The independent craftsman detached from the village community no longer produces anything but *exchange-values, commodities* destined for the market.

Someone who essentially produces use-values, intended to satisfy his own needs or those of his community, lives by the products of his own labour. Production and products, labour and products of labour, are identical for him, in practice as in his mind. In commodity production this unity is broken.

The producer of commodities no longer lives directly on the products of his own labour: on the contrary, he can live only if he *gets rid* of these products. *He lives,* as Glotz says of the Greek craftsmen of the Homeric age, *exclusively by his labour.* This is all the truer in that these first craftsmen went to the homes of their clients and received from them the raw material for their production.[35] It was the same in most societies when the first development of commodity production took place: notably in Egypt, in China, in Japan, in India and at the beginning of the European Middle Ages.[36]

Commodity production does not appear all at once or over the whole of society. After the crafts have become professional and some craftsmen have become commodity producers detached from the village community, the peasants and the remainder of the craftsmen may for centuries go on living as producers of use values. They will exchange only small surpluses of their products in order to acquire the few commodities which they need. These commodities consist essentially of *salt* and *iron* (or other metals). It was so in China, in mediaeval Europe, in mediaeval Russia,* in mediaeval Japan, in the Indian village community, in Africa, in pre-Columbian America, etc.[37]

Generalised and specialised exchange, trade, is at first restricted to the metals and ornaments (luxury products) more or less reserved for the State (king, prince, temple). But commodity production attains a higher level from the moment that it supplies both craft and agricultural products to trade. The invention of the wheel, for chariots, makes it possible to use the principle of rotation in pottery-making technique. The potter's wheel is the first tool that makes possible "mass production" of commodities exclusively intended for trade.

Ethnography shows in most cases that, while women are the first to make pottery so long as this is merely a domestic or village technique, men are the first to use the potter's wheel and become specialists working for the market.[38] As regards agricultural products transformed into commodities, these first appear when human communities are formed that are completely separated from production of means of subsistence, communities of craftsmen, merchants and administrators, that is, *urban communities*. According to Polanyi, it was probably in Lydia, and then later at Athens, that the first local markets for foodstuffs were established. We have the impression, however, that in China such markets were also in existence in the fifth century B.C., if not earlier.[39]

Co-operatively organised society and society based on economy of labour-time

In primitive society producing little or no surplus, the co-operative organisation of labour is based on custom and religious rites which serve to regulate the essential economic activities. In poorly-favoured regions, where food supplies are hard to come by, labour co-operation may mean incessant economic activity, carried to the limits of human strength. In regions better favoured by nature, such as the Pacific islands, production of the necessary product may take up relatively little of the time available, the rest being devoted to leisure pursuits.

As a rule, no community will voluntarily give up a substantial part of its leisure to work and produce more if it is not forced to by economic and social necessity.† Economic necessity means the need to obtain a bigger surplus of products so as to acquire, through ex-

---

* The old Russian word for a merchant engaged in internal trade, *prasol*, indicates trade in salt, though later on the name came to be the general word for any retail trader.

† "Despite the frequency of famines no Mkamba (a Negro tribe) thinks of ever sowing more than is necessary to carry him on to the next rains."[40]

change, goods needed for the well-being of society and which the community itself does not produce (certain kinds of food, salt, raw materials for making tools, ornaments for ritual use, etc.). Social necessity means that which compels the community regularly to give up a surplus to a centralising authority, either in the interests of the community (to carry out irrigation works, etc.) or as the result of a conquest which has forcibly imposed such a tribute.

These two necessities may be combined. Speaking of the Mojo and Baure tribes, which live in eastern Bolivia, Alfred Métraux writes: "So great was the desire for metal, which eased the daily struggle for life, that the Indians, lacking other commodities acceptable to the whites, soon turned into slavers . . ."[41]

In other words: the growth of the surplus product beyond narrow limits (food reserves) is not the result of an independent development of the economy. It results from the intervention of *outside pressures*, either economic (exchange) or social (appropriation of the surplus by a central power or a ruling class).*

So long as primitive society, co-operatively organised, does not know any division of labour other than that between the sexes, the rhythm of labour is fixed by custom and religious rites. When a more consistent division of labour has been established, the contribution to the community made by each producer has to be measurable by a common yardstick. Otherwise, labour co-operation would tend to break up through the emergence of privileged and unprivileged groups. This common measure of organisation cannot be other than *economy of labour-time*.

The village can be regarded as a big family. Its total annual production has to correspond more or less to its needs in means of subsistence, clothing, housing and tools. To avoid any imbalance between these different forms of production, to ensure that the peasants do not devote an excessive share of their time to producing pots or leather articles, while leaving part of their land uncultivated, it is necessary that the community compile a record of the amount of labour-time available and allot this labour-time first and foremost among the essential sectors of production, indispensable for the well-being of the community, while leaving everyone free to employ the rest of his time as he pleases.

Ethnography and economic history show that the village community which has experienced the beginning of a division of labour

---

* This does not contradict the proposition we were defending earlier, according to which the development of a ruling class presupposes the existence of a social surplus. Though a primary development of the surplus does precede any formation of a ruling class, the latter thereafter in turn brings about a major expansion of this surplus, and a fresh development of the productive forces.

does indeed organise its social life on the basis of an economy of labour-time. Primitive peoples consider that only labour is something "scarce", says Ruth Bunzel.[42] According to Boeke, the economy of the Indonesian *desa* (village community) is based on calculation of hours of labour expended.[43]

In the economy of the Japanese village, "the principle of exchange is people and days. Thus, if household A has two people at work on household B's field for two days, household B is expected to provide its equivalent on A's fields—this may be three people one day and one person another day or any other combination to equal two people working two days . . . When four or five families work together in one *kattari* group [team for transplanting rice], the figuring is on the same basis. This requires a book to check days and workers."[44]

Among the Negro tribe called Heh, peasants who order a spear from the smith (who is himself a peasant as well as a smith), work on the smith's land while he is making the spear.[45] In ancient India, in the Maurya epoch, labour and products of labour governed the rules of organisation of economic life.[46]

When the first forms of social subordination were established, with appropriation of the surplus by a privileged section of society, the reckoning of exploitation was also based on an economy of labour-time. Among the Incas, "tribute was to consist solely of labour, time and skill as a workman, artisan or soldier. All men were equal in this respect, he being held to be rich who had children to aid him in making up his appointed tribute, and he who had none being considered to be poor. Every craftsman who laboured in the service of the Inca, or of his *curaca* (superior), must be provided with all the raw materials, and his employment in this way must not exceed two or three months in the year."[47]

It was the same in Europe in the early Middle Ages, when a large section of the peasantry lived under serfdom. The villagers were governed by a strict economy of labour-time: three days a week, on the average, being spent in work in the lord's land, and three days on the serf's own land.*

Similarly, the serfs' wives had to work a fixed number of days in the workshops of the manor, spinning, weaving, sewing, etc. Each craftsman had his own field, in exchange for which he had to render specific services to the manor and to the other tenants.

The social organisation based on the economy of labour-time has left numerous traces, even in the language. In central Europe in the Middle Ages the most common unit of area is the *Tagewerk*, the area

---

* We read, for example, in the old laws of Bavaria, that the "serfs of the Church" have to spend three days a week in work on the demesne (of their lord) and that "they do three days' work for themselves." *Opera vero 3 dies in ebdomada in dominico operet, 3 vero sibi faciat.*[48]

that a man can plough in one day. In mediaeval English the word "acre" had the same meaning. In the Kabyle mountains, holdings are evaluated in terms of *zouija*, days of ploughing carried out with a plough drawn by two oxen. In France, the "carrucata" signified the amount of land a man can normally plough in a single day. The "pose", the Swiss unit of area, is similar in meaning.[49]

The extent to which the economy of labour-time regulated the whole of economic life emerges clearly from the description given by Dollinger of the disappearance of the serf day-workers.

"These exemptions from service [as day-worker] did not, of course, leave the serf idle: they implied that he received from his lord a holding which he cultivated for himself on his free days . . . Undoubtely, this holding was as a rule proportionate to the time at his disposal. The serf who had only one free day a week probably obtained a very small piece of land, whereas the one who had two or three days free might perhaps receive an entire *manse*."[50]

Analysing the mediaeval peasants' obligations as a whole, Marc Bloch came to the same conclusion:

"The peasants, or at least some of them, had to render to the lord every year a fixed number of manufactured products: wooden articles; fabrics; clothing; in the case of certain *manses* where, from generation to generation, the income from a skilled trade was accumulated, even metal tools. Sometimes the supply of raw material was, like the labour, at the expense of the tenant: this was probably usual in the case of wooden articles. But where fabrics were concerned, the materials were often provided by the lord: the peasant or his wife *gave only their time* [my emphasis, E.M.], their efforts and their skill."[51]

In many instances, the description of the peasants' dues takes forms which are interchangeable, in labour-time or in quantity of products. Thus, the dues owed to the lordship of St. Gall by the serf women are sometimes—as in the ancient *Lex Alemannorum*—indicated by the number of days of labour to be performed, and sometimes by the number of products to be produced during these days.[52] The Aztecs imposed on the other peoples of Mexico a tribute calculated in working days, in amount of craft products, or in area of land to be cultivated.[53] In Japan there were in the eighth century A.D. two kinds of non-agricultural obligatory labour, called *cho* and *yo*. The statute of Taiho fixed the amount of these two obligations both in length of labour-time (ten days), in quantity of cloth (26 *shaku*, i.e. approximately 10 yards) and in quantity of corn (1 *To*, i.e. approximately two bushels).[54] Thus, among the producers in a society of this kind, the length of time needed to produce a given commodity was quite clear. Similarly in Western Europe, when from the twelfth century onward direct cultivation of the manor was more and more replaced, on the

Continent, by leasehold farming, it was *half the crop* that had to be given to the lord in place of the classic three days of work each week. In China the chronicles of the Tang dynasty calculate exactly how much work has to be devoted to growing millet (283 days a year) and wheat (177 days), the land tax being payable in kind.[55] In the mediaeval commune, notes Espinas, there is a strict equivalence between the working day and the (quantitative) amount of the work to be done.[56]

We find this same economic accounting based on the duration of labour in Spanish America, at the time when the forced labour of the Indians was transformed into rent in kind, in the system of *repartimiento-encomienda*,[57] and also in Indonesia at the time of the introduction of the *cultuurstelsel*. The population had no longer to pay "land rent" but to plant one-fifth of its land with products to be sold to the Government: indigo, sugar, coffee, tobacco, etc. "If one had no land, one had to work 66 days a year on the Government's plantations."[58] In Vietnam, during the dead season of the year, loans are made which are repayable in working days: 1·5 piastres, to be repaid by ten days' work at the time when there is much to be done, etc.

Exchange-value of commodities

Now, generalised exchange, trade, appears only at a stage of social development marked by this economy of labour-time. Those peoples who have escaped the need to observe this economy are satisfied with a small surplus product and exchange which is merely rudimentary or ritual.* It follows that this exchange is guided by the same objective standard which underlies all social organisation, namely, *that the exchange-value of commodities is measured by the labour time needed to produce them.*

We observe the transition from a social organisation *consciously governed* by the economy of labour time to one with exchanges regulated half-consciously, half-objectively, by the same principle, in the case of the trading relations established in the Nilgiri Hills, in the South-West of the Indian peninsula, between four tribes: the Toda, Karumba, Badaga and Kota.

* This is why numerous primitive peoples whose development has been stopped before the appearance of petty commodity production do not exchange their products in accordance with objective standards or on the basis of an economy of labour-time. This fact has led many ethnologists to false conclusions as regards economic analysis. Margaret Mead records, however, that the inhabitants of Manua (Samoa), who practise ceremonial exchange of finely woven mats, had originally fixed an exchange value for these mats which corresponded to the labour-time spent on producing them. Later, this value was greatly increased. This Samoan people, like the inhabitants of many other Pacific islands, consists of emigrants who have come from inhospitable countries to countries of plenty, where exchange no longer plays an economically important role.[59]

The Toda are shepherds; the Karumba still live in the jungle; the Badaga are agriculturists; and the Kota are primarily craftsmen who are already acquainted with metal-working and make knives. They supply these knives to the three other tribes, together with pots and musical instruments needed for religious ceremonies. In exchange they receive from the Toda buffaloes and other cattle; from the Karumba, honey, wild fruits, and (magical) protection; and from the Badaga, wheat. But the Kota are not mere craftsmen; they themselves possess land which they cultivate. Religious rites determine the traditional quantity of wheat—the outcome of long experience—which must be exchanged for the metal utensils provided by the Kota smiths. "Should a Badaga wish more of these utensils, he would have to work in the field of the Kota iron-worker of whom he requested them, while they were being forged."[60]

In the same way, among the people of Dahomey, "the practice among the iron-workers, for example, is for one smith to buy a quantity of scrap iron and keep it until such time as it is his turn to benefit from the labour of his fellows, for whom he has been working in the meantime. When this time arrives, all the members of the craft of forgers convert the iron he has acquired into hoes, axes, bush-knives, and other saleable goods. The owner of the iron then is free to sell these implements, and to keep the proceeds gained from selling them. This money he will use for living expenses and the purchase of scrap iron, meanwhile working for his associates, until it is once more his turn to have the use of the combined labour-power of his craft of forgers."[61]

Exchange which is simple, occasional, ritual and without economic importance may well disregard strict equivalence. It is not the same with generalised exchange. Lack of an objective criterion of equivalence would prevent any regulation of exchange-relations. It would lead to disorganisation and the dissolution of any society which included a substantial number of commodity producers. The producers would give up the kinds of work in which they received less for their products than in other kinds of work. Strict relations of equivalence between the products and commodities being exchanged are therefore indispensable.

But a relation of equivalence between two products, two commodities, demands a common gauge, a common commensurable quality. The *use-value* of a commodity depends on the totality of its physical qualities, which determine its utility. The existence of this use-value is an indispensable condition for the appearance of an exchange-value; nobody will accept in exchange for his own product a commodity which has no utility, no use-value, for anyone. But the use-value of two commodities, expressed in their physical qualities, is incommensurable; one cannot measure with a common gauge the *weight* of corn, the *length* of cloth, the *volume* of pots, the *colour* of flowers. For reciprocal exchange between these products to be possible, a quality must be found which they all possess, which can be measured and expressed quantitatively, and which must be a *social quality*, acceptable to all members of society.

Now, the totality of the physical qualities of commodities which give them their use-value, is determined by the *specific labour* which has produced them; the labour of a weaver determines the dimensions, fineness and weight of the cloth; the labour of a potter determines the durability, shape and colour of the pot. But if these commodities are each the products of a specific kind of labour, they are also the products of *social human labour*, that is, of a part of the total labour time available to a particular society, and on the economy of which society is based, as we have just shown. This is the fact that makes commodities commensurable; it is this general human labour —called abstract labour because abstraction is made from its specific nature, just as when one adds together three apples, four pears and five bananas one has to abstract from their specific qualities so as to be left with merely twelve *fruits*—that is the basis of exchange value.* It is the measurement of this work—the duration of the labour-time needed to produce the commodity—that provides the measurement of exchange-value.

Petty commodity production

So long as independent craft work, trade, and division of society into classes have developed only slightly, commodity production occupies a relatively limited place in society. It is only when trade and town life have reached a certain stage of development, when they have created a *sufficiently extensive market*, that commodity production develops and becomes general in its turn, in the towns.[63] We then enter a period of history marked by the fact that commodity production has become general in the towns while production for use is slowly breaking up in the country. This commodity production carried on by

* Since the dawn of petty commodity production, about 3,000 B.C., all labour has been considered equivalent, regardless of its special character. On the tablets, inscribed in a Semitic language, found at Susa, the wages in the household of a prince are fixed uniformly at 60 *qua* of barley for the cook, the barber, the engraver of stones, the carpenter, the smith, the cobbler, the tailor, the cultivator, the shepherd and the donkey man.[62] At this early phase of the production of exchange-values, however, men were not able to arrive at the notion of "abstract labour"; the equivalence of different skilled trades was conceived as such. The idea of "abstract labour" could not arise until the appearance of the *mobility of labour-power* in the capitalist era. This implies not merely that one hour of the labour of a textile worker produces as much as one hour of the labour of a brickmaker, but also that these jobs have been *interchangeable* in large-scale industry. See also Chapter 5, section: "Human labour-power and machine production".

craftsmen who own their own means of production (tools) is called simple or petty commodity production. It became preponderant in periods of urban civilisation, notably in Antiquity, from the sixth century B.C., in Greece; about the eighth century A.D. in the Islamic world; and from the eleventh century A.D. in Western Europe, where it reached its most characteristic development in the Southern Netherlands and in Italy in the thirteenth to fifteenth centuries.

In petty commodity production, labour no longer results directly in satisfying the producer's needs; labour and product of labour are no longer identical for him. But the producer remains owner of the product of his labour; he gives it up only in order to acquire for himself the goods which will ensure his existence. The division of labour has already separated the producer from his product, but it does not yet oppress the former by means of the latter. Commodity production develops slowly within society, while production of use-values pure and simple is slowly shrinking.

The more production of commodities extends, the more necessary becomes exact reckoning in hours of labour. In primitive society where only a rudimentary division of labour exists, accounting is of vital importance for the community survival only as regards the essential kinds of work. Apart from them, as we have seen, it matters relatively little whether two hours or three are spent on producing a particular object. This is what explains the quite extensive freedom enjoyed by members of such societies, within the framework of strict rules which govern the activities that produce food. Herskovits has given a striking picture of this mixture of strict accounting and wide freedom in the cycle of production and consumption among the Talensi, a people living by fruit-gathering and agriculture in Ghana.[64]

Once, however, commodity production has become widespread within a primitive community, the reckoning of labour-time takes place more strictly. On the market where the products of the labour of different villages, even different regions, meet, exchange-values establish themselves henceforth in accordance with *social averages*. It is not the number of hours actually spent on making an object that determine its value, but the number of hours of labour necessary to make it in the average conditions of productivity of this society in this period. Commodities would indeed become incommensurable if their value were determined by the *actual* time spent, by chance, by each individual producer on producing them. "He [the mediaeval artisan] has to produce, in accordance with fixed conditions, cloth which is 'not personal but official, municipal'; his labour, one might say, is expressly objective not subjective."[65]

Since the value of commodities is established by the amount of labour *socially necessary* to produce them—that is, since this average becomes fixed by the experience of repeated acts of exchange, by the simultaneous appearance of products from several different producers competing with each other—producers who are clumsy, slow, or who employ out-of-date methods, are penalised. They receive in exchange for the labour-time they have individually given to society only an equivalent produced in a shorter length of time. Greater discipline and stricter labour accounting thus accompany the development of commodity production.*

With the development of petty commodity production, human labour begins to be differentiated according to quality. *Composite, skilled* labour separates off from simple labour. As the crafts, becoming more and more specialised, necessitate a more or less lengthy period of apprenticeship, the cost of which can on longer be borne, as in primitive societies, by the whole community, but has to be met by the apprentice's family or by himself personally, no one would devote himself to the prolonged apprenticeship to a craft if, in exchange for an hour of skilled labour, he were to receive the same equivalent as for an hour of unskilled labour. Skilled labour is regarded as composite labour, into which there enters not only the labour expended by the craftsman at the moment when he is producing something as a qualified man, but also part of his expenditure of unpaid labour in the days when he was an apprentice (social depreciation of the overhead costs of apprenticeship).

Law of value in petty commodity production

The *law of value* which regulates the exchange of commodities in accordance with the amount of abstract, simple, socially-necessary human labour they contain, at last begins to fulfil a supplementary function. Primitive society and the village community, with their rudimentary division of labour, were organised on the basis of *conscious* labour co-operation, in which custom, religious rites, the counsels of elders or elected administrators, determined the rhythm of production; on these being grafted in due course the unpaid labour or tribute to be surrendered to the possessing classes.

But when petty commodity production has developed, we have

* This is clearly seen in the petty commodity production of the Guatemala Indians of Panajachel, as described by Professor Sol Tax. Men, women and even small children are continually on the alert to make a few pence by trade. It is not surprising that exchanges and equivalences are strictly calculated in this society where, Professor Tax tells us, a woman who could not read or write was able to state almost to within a penny the exact cost of production of a carpet on which she had worked the whole of one day. Under conditions like this, if land is sometimes rented in exchange for unpaid labour, sometimes in exchange for a part of the harvest, and sometimes for a money rent, one must suppose that in each case strict equivalences have been worked out, which could only be based on labour-value.[66]

before us producers who are free from any subordination to a collective social organisation. Each producer, within the limits of his physical strength and his capacity to produce (tools, etc.), can produce as much as he likes. These producers are no longer producing use-values for the consumption of a closed community; they are now producing commodities for a market which is more or less extensive, more or less impersonal. The law of value, which co-ordinates exchanges on an objective basis and ensures only equivalents for each commodity exchanged thus *reorganises*, through successful exchanges and unsuccessful ones, the distribution among the different branches of production of the totality of hours of labour at society's disposal. Human labour in primitive societies was *directly social* labour. In petty commodity society, individual labour acquires its quality as social labour only *indirectly*, through the mechanism of exchange, by the operation of the law of value.*

If a craftsman produces more cloth than the market of his society can absorb, part of his production will remain unsold, not exchanged, which will show him that he spent too great a share of the labour-time at society's disposal on producing this cloth, or, in other words, that he wasted social labour time. This waste, in a consciously co-ordinated society, would have been realised in advance, by custom or the observations of other members of the community. On the market, the law of value reveals it only after the event, to the disadvantage of the producer, who does not receive an equivalent for part of his exertion and its products.

These rules nevertheless remain quite obvious at the beginning of the period of commodity production. The proof is to be seen in the fact that in the corporations of Antiquity and in those of China, of Byzantium, of the European and Arab Middle Ages, etc., fixed rules, known to all, laid down alike the labour-time to be devoted to the making of each object, the length of apprenticeship, its cost, and the equivalent normally to be asked for each commodity.[67]†

This obviousness merely gives expression to the fact that with petty commodity production we have reached only a transitional stage between a society consciously governed by labour co-operation, and a society in which the complete dissolution of community ties leaves no room for anything but "objective" laws, that is, laws which are blind, "natural", independent of men's will, as the regulators of economic activity.

* See, in Chapter 18, refutation of current criticisms of the labour theory of value.

† Nadel mentions that in the Kingdom of Nupe the value of commodities is broadly proportional to the labour time spent on producing them.[68]

REFERENCES

1. Hingston Quiggin: *A Survey of Primitive Money*, pp. 21-22.
2. Audrey I. Richards: *Land, Labour and Diet in Northern Rhodesia*, p. 222.
3. Margaret Mead: *Competition and Co-operation among Primitive People*, p. 134.
4. Margaret Mead: *Sex and Temperament*, pp. 170-1.
5. Thurwald: *L'économie primitive*, p. 201; article *"Handel"* in *Reallexicon der Vorgeschichte*, Vol. V, p. 74; Herskovits: *The Economic Life of Primitive People*, p. 160; Quiggin: op. cit., p. 11.
6. M. Mauss: *"Essai sur le don"* in *Sociologie et Anthropologie*, p. 214.
7. Polanyi: et al., op. cit., p. 88.
8. Cl. Lévi-Strauss: *Les Structures élémentaires de la parenté*, p. 168.
9. Ibid., p. 593.
10. Ibid. , pp. 178-180, 48-49.
11. C. Darryl Forde and R. Scott: *The Native Economics of Nigeria*, p. 68.
12. M. Mauss: op. cit., pp. 277-8.
13. Victor Purcell: *The Chinese in Southern Asia*, p. xxvii.
14. J. H. Boeke: *De Theorie der Indische Economie*, p. 39.
15. Schechter: The Law and Morals of Primitive Trade, in Herskovits: *Economic Life of Primitive People*.
16. Polanyi: et. al., op. cit., pp. 20, 269.
17. Claude Meillassoux: *Anthropologie économique des Gouro de Côte d'Ivoire*, pp. 267-9.
18. Ibid., pp. 266-7.
19. Heichelheim: *Wirtschaftsgeschichte des Altertums*, p. 21; Gordon Childe: *What Happened in History*, p. 61, and *Cambridge Economic History of Europe*, Vol. I, p. 4; J. Graham Clark: *L'Europe préhistorique*, pp. 363, 371; J. C. Van Eerde, *Inleiding tot de Volkenkunde van Ned. Indië*, p. 57.
20. Heichelheim: *Wirtschaftsgeschichte des Altertums*, Vol. I, pp. 26-27.
21. Herskovits: *The Economic Life of Primitive People*, p. 129.
22. Forde and Scott: op. cit., p. 43.
23. Herskovits: *The Economic Life of Primitive People*, p. 125; Thurwald: article *"Lohn"* in *Reallexicon der Vorgeschichte*, Vol. VII, pp. 308-9.
24. W. G. Sumner and A. G. Keller: *Science of Society*, Vol. IV, p. 46.
25. Forde and Scott: op. cit., p. 79; S. F. Nadel: *A Black Byzantium*, p. 254; *Histoire du Commerce*, Vol. IV, p. 148; Polanyi: et al., op. cit., pp. 178-83.
26. M. M. Postan: "Trade of Mediaeval Europe: the North", in *Cambridge Economic History of Europe*, Vol. II, pp. 168-9.
27. Gordon Childe: *Man Makes Himself*, pp. 120-2; *What Happened in History*, pp. 96-97.
28. Charles Wisdom: *The Chorti Indians of Guatemala*, pp. 24-25, 199; S. F. Nadel: op. cit., p. 321.
29. Chen Huan-Chang: *The Economic Principles of Confucius*, p. 122.
30. Gordon Childe: *The Bronze Age*, p. 8.

31.	G. Dijckmans: *Histoire économique et sociale de l'ancienne Egypte*, Vol. II, p. 226; Polanyi: et. al., op. cit., pp. 41 et. al.

32.	Polanyi: et al., op. cit., pp. 51-55. D. D. Kosambi, *An Introduction to the Study of Indian History*, p. 151, *et al.*

33.	Heichelheim: op. cit., Vol. I, p. 179; René Grousset: *Histoire de la Chine*, p. 9.

34.	Boeke: op. cit., p. 44.

35.	G. Glotz: *Le Travail dans la Grèce antique*, p. 53.

36.	Dijckmans: op. cit., Vol. II, p. 236; K. A. Wittfogel: *Wirtschaft und Gesellschaft Chinas*, p. 514; Yoshitomi: *Etude sur l'histoire économique de l'ancien Japon*, p. 203; G. B. Jathar and S. G. Beri: *Indian Economics*, p. 104; Josef Kulischer: *Allgemeine Wirtschaftsgeschichte des Mittelalters*, Vol. I., p. 75.

37.	Wittfogel: op. cit., p. 497; P. I. Lyashchenko: *History of the National Economy of Russia*, p. 162; M. Takizawa: *The Penetration of Money Economy in Japan*, p. 24; Jathar and Beri: op. cit., p. 103; Herskovits: op. cit., p. 187; Audrey I. Richards: op. cit., p. 22; Paul S. Martin: George L. Quimby and Donald Collier: *Indians Before Columbus*, p. 67.

38.	Gordon Childe: *What Happened in History*, p. 85.

39.	Polanyi: et al., op. cit., pp. 84-85; *An Outline History of China*, p. 28.

40.	Sumner and Keller: op. cit., Vol. IV, p. 53.

41.	Alfred Métraux, in: *Handbook of South American Indians*, Vol. III, p. 418.

42.	Ruth Bunzel: in Franz Boas, ed., *General Anthopology*, p. 346.

43.	Boeke: op. cit., p. 64.

44.	John Embree: *Mura, A Japanese Village*, pp. 100-1.

45.	Ralph Piddington: *An Introduction to Social Anthropology*, p. 275.

46.	Kautilya's *Arthashastra*: German trans. by J. J. Mayer, p. 147.

47.	John Collier: *The Indians of the Americas*, pp. 61-62.

48.	See other articles in the Polyptique of Saint Germain-des-Prés and the *descriptio villarum* of the Abbey of Lobbes.

49.	Joseph Bourrilly: *Eléments d'ethnographie marocaine*, pp. 137-8; Roger Grand and Raymond Delatouche: *L'Agriculture au moyen âge*, p. 79.

50.	P. Dollinger: *L'évolution des classes rurales en Bavière*, p. 270.

51.	Marc Bloch: *Caractères originaux de l'histoire rurale française*, p. 77.

52.	Herman Bikel: *Die Wirtschaftsverhältnisse des Klosters St. Gallen*, pp. 133-239.

53.	H. Cunow: *Wirtschaftsgeschichte*, Vol. I, pp. 270-1.

54.	Y. Takekoshi: *Economic Aspects of the History of the Civilisation of Japan*, Vol. I, p. 117.

55.	L. Génicot: *L'Economie rurale namuroise au bas moyen âge*, pp. 236-85; Grand and Delatouche: op. cit., pp. 105-35; Jacques Gernet: *Les aspects économiques du bouddhisme dans la société chinoise du Ve au Xe siecle*, p. 98.

56.	Georges Espinas: *Les Origines du capitalisme*, Vol. I, p. 140.

57.	Robert S. Chamberlain: "Castilian Backgrounds of the Repartimiento Encomienda", in *Contributions to American Anthropology*, Vol. V, pp. 25-26.

58. H. J. De Graaf: *Geschiedenis van Indonesië*, p. 406.
59. Margaret Mead: *Social Organization of Manua*, pp. 73-75, p. 65.
60. David Mandelbaum: "Notes on Fieldwork in India", in Herskovits: *Economic Life of Primitive Peoples*, pp. 136-7.
61. M. J. Herskovits: *Dahomey, an ancient West African Kingdom*, Vol. I, pp. 75-76.
62. Clement Huart and Louis Delaporte: *L'Iran antique*, p. 83.
63. Gordon Childe: *What Happened in History*, p. 156.
64. Herskovits: *Economic Life of Primitive Peoples*, pp. 248-51.
65. Espinas: op. cit., Vol. I, p. 142.
66. Sol Tax: *Penny Capitalism*, pp. 18, 15, 80.
67. Espinas: op. cit., Vol. I, pp. 118, 140-2.
68. Nadel: op. cit., p. 318.

CHAPTER THREE

MONEY, CAPITAL, SURPLUS-VALUE

Need for a universal equivalent

SIMPLE or developed exchange is carried out in the form of barter, that is, direct encounter between the products being exchanged. For primitive peoples, accustomed to exchanging the same products in accordance with procedures that were traditional and even ritual, barter created no economic "problem".[1]

It is different with generalised exchange and commerce. No longer is a single product, the tribe's surplus, exchanged for other products; a great number of a great variety of products are now exchanged for many other products. The relations of equivalence concern no longer just two products, or two categories of product, but an infinite variety of different goods. It is no longer the labour-time of the potter that is compared with that of the agriculturist; ten, twenty, thirty different crafts have to compare their respective productive efforts from time to time. In order that these exchanges may go on without interruption, the owners of the commodities must be able to get rid of their goods before they have had the luck to encounter purchasers who possess the products they themselves want to obtain in exchange for these goods. For exchanges to be carried out on the basis of equivalence, a commodity is needed in which all the others can express their respective exchange values. This function is fulfilled by the *universal equivalent* commodity.

The appearance of a universal equivalent, of money in all its forms, accompanies the generalisation of exchange and the beginnings of trade. The need for such an equivalent is obvious. Sir Samuel Baker tells of hearing country people shouting in the market-place of Unyoro, in Uganda:

"Milk to sell, for beads or salt! Salt to exchange for lance-heads! Coffee, coffee, going cheap, for red beads!"[2]

If the owners of salt do not want milk but red beads; if the owners of red beads do not want either salt or coffee but milk, none of these exchanges can take place, because there are no owners of commodities in proximity to one another here who are ready to exchange their goods reciprocally. What is characteristic of the universal equivalent is that it is a commodity for which *any other* commodity can be obtained. Suppose that salt became the universal equivalent. At once, the three operations could be carried through without difficulty. The trader will readily exchange his red pearls for salt, not because he wants to realise the use value of salt but because in exchange for salt, the universal equivalent, he can get the milk he wants.

The universal equivalent is thus itself a commodity; its own exchange-value is determined, like that of any other commodity, by the amount of labour socially necessary to produce it. It is in relation to this real exchange-value that all other commodities will henceforth express their own exchange-value. As a commodity, the universal equivalent also retains a use value which is determined by its natural qualities: when it has finished circulating, the salt ends up by being used for the salting of meat. But alongside its own natural, physical value, the universal equivalent commodity acquires a supplementary use value—that of facilitating the mutual exchange of other commodities, of being a means of circulation and a measure of value.

Thus, in Egypt in the days of the Ramassides, cattle served as universal equivalent, and

1 mat
5 measures of honey and } were equal in value to a bull.[3]
11 measures of oil

At the beginning of the second millennium B.C., in the reign of King Bilalama, silver had become the universal equivalent at Eshuna, in Mesopotamia. On the tax tablets discovered in 1947 at Tell Harmal, we find inscribed the following equivalences (converted into those of the metric system):

12 litres of sesame oil
300 litres of wheat
600 litres of salt } were equal in value to one shekel (about 8 grammes) of silver.
5 kilogrammes of wool
1 kilogramme of copper

In the Hittite code, 500 years earlier than that of King Bilalama, we find a long list of equivalences, from which we extract the following examples.

1 sheep
1 "zimittani" of butter
1 hide of a large ox
4 minas of copper } were equal in value to one shekel of silver.
20 lambskins
2 "pa" of wine
½ "zimittani" of good oil

3 goats were worth 2 shekels of silver.
1 divided robe was worth 3 shekels of silver.
1 large piece of cloth was worth 3 shekels of silver.
1 cart horse was worth 20 shekels of silver.[5]

What we have here is a real *price list*. The price is nothing but the exchange value of a commodity expressed in a definite quantity of the equivalent commodity. The universal equivalent has become money; price is the expression of exchange-value in money terms.

Evolution of the universal equivalent

Often, the commodities which were most commonly exchanged in a given region became, at the dawn of petty commodity production, the first universal equivalents. These commodities fall into two categories: the products which are of maximum importance for the people concerned (foodstuffs, tools, salt), and ornaments, which are among the first objects involved in any human exchange.

Those peoples who are engaged in both agriculture and cattle-raising usually choose as their universal equivalent either cattle, wheat or rice. Thus, Greeks and Romans adopted the ox as first universal equivalent down to the sixth and fifth centuries B.C. The Indians' word for their national currency, *rupee*, is derived from *rupa*, meaning a herd. The Iranians of the *Avesta* and the Germans of the *Lex Saxonum* also chose the ox as universal equivalent, which indicates the predominance of cattle-raising in the epoch when this happened. In North, East and South Africa, cattle, in the shape of camels, sheep, goats or cows, likewise constituted the universal equivalent among people who were essentially cattle-breeders. The horse played the same part among the Kirghiz, the buffalo in Annam and the sheep in Tibet.

In those cases where cultivation of the land was more important than cattle-raising at the time when the universal equivalent appeared, various products of the soil fulfilled this function. In ancient Japan, rice was for centuries the only universal equivalent. In China it was at first wheat and millet, later rice as well. In Mesopotamia it was wheat. In Egypt, wheat prepared as food, that is, loaves baked in a certain form, soon ousted the ox.

In India too, wheat took the place of the ox as universal equivalent from the fifth century B.C., and in the countryside it retained this function until the nineteenth century. In the Sudan, dates were for a long time used as universal equivalent. In Central America it was maize. In Newfoundland and in Iceland down to the fifteenth century, it was dried fish; in the Nicobar Islands, coconuts; among the primitive tribes of the Philippines, rice; and on the Hawaiian Islands, before Western penetration, salt fish.

The principal tools have also been used as universal equivalents: bronze or copper axes and bronze tripods in Crete; bronze vases in Laos; iron shovels and hoes in Central and East Africa; fish-hooks in the Solomon and Marshall Islands of the Pacific, etc. In China, the names of two of the oldest coins, "pu" and "tsian", meant originally "farming tool", and come from the names of bronze tools.[6] In Japan, in the seventh and eighth centuries A.D., iron shovels or hoes were the essential forms of movable wealth.[7]

The raw materials from which these tools were made could often in their turn, play the part of universal equivalent. Stone was the universal equivalent on the island of Yap, in the Pacific. In Homeric Greece, when bronze vases were beginning to be used as universal equivalent among the Achaeans of the mainland, the inhabitants of the island of Lemnos already regarded bronze, the metal, as itself the universal equivalent. Ingots and small sticks of iron have played the same role among the more advanced communities in Africa.

With the development of exchange, products of primary necessity, such as the chief foodstuffs or most important tools, may be replaced as universal equivalent by the local *commodity*, that is, the product chiefly bought or sold in relations with foreign traders. Thus we find as universal equivalents packets of compressed tea among the Tatars and Mongols of the nineteenth century; cocoa beans in Mexico in the time of the Aztecs; salt in Abyssinia, in West, Equatorial and East Africa, in Burma, in mediaeval Tibet and among some Indian tribes of North America; pelts in Canada down to the eighteenth century; white squirrel skins in Russia; hempen fabrics in mediaeval Japan; measures of cloth in certain communities of Western Europe in the Middle Ages, and so on. In China, a foot of cloth (*tch'e*) was worth a bushel (*che*) of grain and was used as universal equivalent, alongside wheat, millet and copper money, under the T'ang emperors.[8]

Ornaments, the first use of which may well have been magical,* were often used as universal equivalent in the early days of petty commodity production. Alongside utilitarian objects of bronze, small tripods of bronze thus made their appearance in the Creto-Mycenaean civilisation as universal equivalents. Bronze rings similarly come on the scene in Egypt. Jade fulfilled a similar function among the pre-Columbian Indians of Central America, and turquoises among the Pueblo Indians. Glass or enamel pearls were used for the same purpose in Egypt, and spread from there to Mediterranean Europe. They spread through Africa as a real currency.

The ornament which enjoyed the widest circulation as universal equivalent was the *cowrie* shell. From China and India these shells spread over the Pacific Islands, into Africa and Europe and even into the New World.

"Cowries surpass all other shell currencies in solidity and uniformity.

---

* The exchange of ornaments or other objects of value in a primitive society, as a magical phenomenon, also has an economic origin. In his *Essai sur le don*, Marcel Mauss explains that these objects "are regarded as replicas of inexhaustible instruments, creators of food, which the spirits have given to one's ancestors."[9]

They are fairly constant both in size and weight, and equal in these respects to foodstuffs such as kidney beans, broad beans, rice, wheat or barleycorns which provided the earliest units of weighing gold and silver."[10]

The precious metals as universal equivalent thus represent a coincidence of the object of primary necessity as universal equivalent and the ornament as universal equivalent. Copper, bronze, silver, gold have always served first of all as raw materials for the making of ornaments. Only with the progress of metal-working are these metals also used to make objects of primary necessity. As soon as this stage was reached, these metals played a vital part in the economy. At the same time they retained a religious, ritual, even magical significance, inherited from the era when they were used only to make ornaments. These factors facilitated the adoption of the precious metals as universal equivalent of all commodities.

Money

The development of international trade usually coincides with the metallurgical revolution. Metals are the chief objects of this trade. The need for a universal equivalent is felt more strongly now. It is not surprising that it should be precisely metals that are most often chosen to fulfil this function. At the start it is still objects made of metal that are used as universal equivalent, but if exchanges become frequent this means complications and extra costs.

In East Africa, iron hoes serve as universal equivalent. The tribes which live in areas rich in iron ore make these hoes, and exchange them for the products of other areas, and in the latter the local smiths often reforge them into weapons or ornaments.[11] In this way, they come to take as their universal equivalent *pure unwrought metal*, measured by weight. Hence the role of weighers of gold, who are synonymous with money-changers, bankers and usurers at the start of every money economy.

But it is tedious to weigh metal, whether or not in the form of ingots, whenever one makes an exchange. After a certain level of commercial development has been reached the State adopts the practice of stamping ingots of precious metal with a mark indicating their weight. Such officially weighed ingots appear from the third millennium B.C. in Mesopotamia and Egypt, and from the second millennium in Europe, in Crete and the Peloponnese, in the centres of the Creto-Mycenaean civilisation. Much later, about 700 B.C., the idea appears of adapting the form of the ingot to the needs of transport over long distances. The King of Lydia, who wanted to attract the trade of the Greek cities to the great entrepôts of his capital, Sardis, undertook the minting of small gold coins, each weighing only a few grammes. One of these coins, henceforth, could be used for the exchange against money of commodities of comparatively high value. The spread of trade was thus encouraged; peasants and small craftsmen could from now on sell their surpluses for money instead of having to barter.[12] This system of minting coins spread to the Persian Empire, to the Greek cities, and through these civilisations made its way throughout the world affected by their trade. In India and China it seems to have developed independently of Asia Minor. In China, metal coins were in circulation about 1,000 B.C. and were given official weights from 65 B.C. onward.[13]

If the precious metals established themselves everywhere as universal equivalents, this was because they possess a series of intrinsic qualities which merchants and administrators discovered empirically and which make them especially suitable for this purpose.

1. They are easily *transportable*: their high specific weight enables them to concentrate in a modest volume a quantity of metal representing a fairly large exchange-value. This value remains stable: comparatively few technical changes have occurred in the way they are produced, over several millennia.

2. They are *durable*, owing to their resistance to wear and tear, rust, etc.

3. They are easily *divisible*; and the fragments can be easily melted down into larger units.

4. They are easily *recognisable*, owing to specific physical qualities, and any counterfeiting can be detected fairly easily (by changes in weight).

However, while these intrinsic qualities of the precious metals predestine them, in a sense, for the role of universal equivalent as soon as trade has grown to a certain extent, their effective use as such remains dependent on their being produced in adequate quantity in a definite territory. As a rule, gold is produced before silver, and, at the start, even at lower cost. It was so in Egypt of the Pharaohs, in ancient India, in pre-Columbian America, etc.[14]

When the precious metals are hard to come by, other metals are normally employed as universal equivalent. In ancient Greece, before the gold mines of Laurium and Strymon were discovered, which brought riches first to Athens and then to the Kings of Macedonia, gold coins were very rare; silver, copper and sometimes even iron, were the most usual materials for coins. In Laconia, rich in iron, iron money predominated until the third century B.C. In China, where silver and gold are very rare, copper remained until the fifteenth century A.D. the metal base of the currency, and was sometimes replaced by iron. The same scarcity of gold and silver in Japan determined the use there of copper as the general measure of value, from the seventh to the seventeenth century A.D. Then the discovery of big deposits of gold and silver made it possible to mint plenty of coins from precious metals.[15] It is interesting to observe that even countries which possess great resources in precious metals do not usually start exploiting them until the development of trade really calls for a plentiful supply of currency made of these metals. This is easily explained by the fact that it is only at that stage that people apply themselves actively to looking for these deposits.*

So long as the universal equivalent consists of commodities which possess their own use-value—objects of primary necessity, ornaments, metallic raw materials—their new use-value, which is that of providing a universal equivalent for all other commodities, is only a subsidiary one, which may disappear when the purchaser of this special commodity wants to realise its natural use-value. It is otherwise with precious metals in the form of ingots bearing an official stamp, and later metal coins struck by a public authority. As soon as they appear, the use-value which is common and exclusive to this new commodity consists in its function as universal equivalent of the other commodities. For stamped ingots or minted coins to serve afresh as raw materials for the making of jewellery, they must first be melted down again, ceasing to exist as ingots or coins. We have thus arrived, at the end of the evolution of the universal equivalent, at a commodity which has no other use-value than that of serving as universal equivalent. This commodity is called *currency* or *money*.

Evolution of social wealth and different functions of money

A society which essentially produces use values has as its index of social wealth the accumulation of these same use-values. Among primitive peoples or in a primitive village community, the accumulation of foodstuffs is the best understood expression of wealth and the criterion of social prestige. Among pastoral peoples, social wealth is reckoned in cattle or horses; among agricultural peoples, in amount of wheat, rice, maize, etc. At the beginning of the seventeenth century in Japan, the wealth of the whole country and of each lord was still calculated in weight of rice (*koku* of rice). The accumulation of use values makes possible a concentration of wealth which should not be underestimated. A single family, that of the Tokugawa shoguns, possessed in those days 8 million *koku* of rice, out of 28 million *koku* which was the annual production of all Japan, i.e. a big proportion of the entire national income.[16]

With the spread of trade, the generalisation of exchange, the more and more current use of money, the latter becomes increasingly the main or even the only index of the wealth of individuals, families and nations. Its function is no longer merely to serve as universal equivalent in exchange transactions. Money fulfils at the same all the following functions:

* See on this subject, Chapter 4, as regards Western Europe.

1. It is the *universal equivalent,* i.e. it makes it possible to acquire all the commodities available on the market;

2. It is the *means of exchange,* i.e. it makes possible the circulation of commodities even between owners of commodities who do not want to realise the use-values of their respective commodities;

3. It is the *measure of value* and *gauge of prices.* The value of each commodity is expressed in a quantity, a particular weight of the precious metal, i.e. expressed in money. The price is nothing but this monetary expression of value. As such, *ideal money* can express the price of any commodity at all. To do this one need not *possess* a sum of money, it is enough to *name* it.

4. It is the universal *means of payment*: debts and fines owed to the State, the clergy or individuals, the counter-value of all commodities, services or payments, can be rendered by means of money, in contrast to primitive society in which there are special products for carrying out these different functions.*

Here, "ideal" money is of no use; coins that ring and weigh as they should are needed.

5. It is the *means of accumulating values* and the *means of forming hoards.* Every society needs to possess reserves to meet its requirements in case of natural disasters, such as epidemics, floods, harvest failures, earthquakes, fires, etc., or social disasters, such as wars, civil strife, etc. The original function of the social surplus is to constitute this reserve fund. In a society producing essentially use-values, these reserves consist of stored-up products.

In a society which is beginning to produce commodities on a large scale, it is precious metals, or metal coins, that are accumulated as hoards. In case of need, this hoard, a store of values and counter-values, makes it possible to obtain all the goods that are lacking, even if distant countries have to be applied to. The precious metals are indeed universally recognised as universal equivalents. Experience teaches the peoples that a metal reserve is much more reliable and less perishable than a reserve of wheat or of cattle.[18]

Circulation of commodities and circulation of money

In a society producing simple commodities, money serves as universal equivalent only in a fairly limited number of commercial transactions. Its function is above all to serve as a hoard. It is jealously kept by those who possess it and who utilise it, at most, for increasing or improving their personal consumption. "Down to the end of

---

* At the beginning of the era of petty commodity production, these different functions of money can be fulfilled by *different* products. Thus, in Babylon in Hammurabi's time, barley was the universal means of payment, silver the measure of value, gauge of prices and doubtless also means of accumulation, while as universal equivalent they used barley, wool, oil, silver, wheat, etc.[17]

the wars with Persia," says Glotz, "Greek society remained in the hoarding stage. Money was accumulated and not set to work."[19] It was the same in Western Europe in the early Middle Ages.[20] In fact, in a mode of production which is essentially based on co-operative organisation of labour within a patriarchal family and a village community, and on the individual work of the town craftsman, money, even when it circulates, is employed only for acquiring use-values. It remains a subordinate element, an *instrument of commodity circulation*. The latter takes place according to this diagram:

$$C^1 \quad - \quad M \quad - \quad C^2$$

Commodity   Money   Commodity

In the municipal market of the Chorti Indians, in Guatemala, a cabinet-maker appears, the possessor of some wooden chairs. He does not want to (or he cannot) realise the use-value of his commodity; on the contrary, he wants to get rid of it, that is, to realise its exchange-value. In order that this operation may take place, he must meet the possessor of a sum of money, M, who will be willing to realise the exchange value of the chairs. It is further necessary that this possessor of money be ready to get rid of his money because he wants to realise the use-value of the wooden chairs. Thus the sale of the chairs, $C^1 - M$, takes place to the satisfaction of both partners.

But the possessor of the wooden chairs wanted to sell his commodity so as to acquire another one, for example, some woven mats from Amatilla district which he needs for his home. Taking the money he has obtained by selling his chairs, he goes in search of a producer-possessor of woven mats, in order to buy them from him. If such a producer-possessor turns up in the municipal market, the purchasing transaction $M - C^2$ can as a rule take place. At the end of these two successive operations of sale and purchase, the cabinet-maker has, instead of a commodity which he did not want to realise the use-value of, a new commodity which is of use to him. Two commodities, the wooden chairs and the woven mats, have disappeared from the market because their use-value has been successively realised by two purchasers. On the other hand, the sum of money, M, has passed through the hands of three persons: from the purchaser of the chairs to the cabinet-maker, and from the cabinet-maker to the maker of woven mats. At the start of the era of petty commodity production, the last owner of this sum of money, the maker of woven mats, will in his turn be able to use this money for two purposes only: either to put it by as a reserve, a hoard, savings, against a rainy day; or to use it to buy some other commodity.

But when a society at the stage of petty commodity production makes contact with a more advanced trading civilisation, owners of money who want to make this possession of theirs "circulate", "work", "pay", appear alongside owners of commodities who merely want to get rid of these commodities in order to meet some needs. Thus, the professional traders among the Chorti visit a certain number of districts, often three or four between them, with a sum of money sufficient to buy all the surplus of the craftsmen they meet. This surplus they transport to the markets of the provincial capitals. They do not buy commodities in order to realise their use-values, like the small producers of chairs and woven mats. On the contrary, they buy commodities in order to *sell them again at a profit* to the inhabitants of the towns whose markets they visit.

The circulation of commodities, that is, the operations carried out successively by the owners of commodities in a society based on petty commodity production, consists in *selling in order to buy*, selling one's own products in order to buy products whose use-value one realises.

The circulation of money, that is, the operations carried out successively by the owners of *money capital* in a society in which professional trade already exists alongside petty commodity production, consists, on the contrary, in *buying in order to sell*, buying another's products so as to sell them again at a profit, that is, to increase by a *surplus-value* the money capital one possesses. *Capital is, by definition, any value that is increased by surplus-value.*

If we ask again the question we asked regarding the maker of woven mats—what will he do with the money he has just received from the cabinet-maker?—there are no longer two but three replies we can give, when it is a matter of the money increased by surplus-value which the Chorti professional trader has obtained at the conclusion of his activities and travels. He can, as before, use it simply to obtain what he needs to feed, clothe and house himself and his family, or to form a hoard. If he does either of these we have not left the limits of petty commodity production.

But he can also act in a different manner: he can use his money, increased by surplus-value, either wholly or in part, to go to other districts, buy other craft products, sell them again, dearer, in other markets, and find himself at the end of his transactions in possession of more money than he started with. In this case we have left the limits of petty commodity production strictly so called and entered the stage of the circulation of money, the *accumulation of money capital*, which takes place according to the formula:

$$M \quad — \quad C \quad — \quad M^1$$
Money   Commodity   Money + surplus value

The difference between the circulation of commodities, $C^1 — M — C^2$, and the circulation of money, $M — C — M^1$, consists then in this; in the circulation of commodities, the *equivalence* of the commodities C^1 and C^2 which are found at the extreme ends of the circulation process is the necessary condition for the two operations to be carried through. No simple producer of commodities can acquire commodities of a value higher than that of the commodities he has himself produced and sold. In the circulation of money, on the contrary, the appearance of a surplus-value ($M^1 - M$) is the necessary condition for circulation to take place: no owner of money-capital is going to "circulate" his money only to see come back to his pocket exactly the same amount which left it!

Surplus-value emerging from the circulation of commodities

Surplus-value has just appeared, then, in the course of the circulation of money. It seems, indeed, to be the essential aim of this circulation. But where has it come from?

In a society based on petty commodity production, the surplus-value obtained by owners of money comes either from *trade* or from usury. It is only when trade and usury have developed extensively that the possessing classes becomes conscious of the need to "make their money pay". The fifth century B.C. saw the rise of petty commodity production not only in ancient Greece but also in China. During this century, Chi-Jan, teacher of the great merchant, Fan-lin, instructed him in "the laws of accumulating capital" and explained to him that, above all, "one must not allow money to be idle".[21] Eighteen hundred years later, when petty commodity production had attained an unprecedented development in the empire of Islam, the historian Ibn Khaldun judiciously noted that "trade, regarded as a way of earning one's livelihood . . . consists in artful tricks performed in order to establish between the buying price and the selling price a difference from which one can make a profit".[22]

It was no different in Ancient Greece, in China in the classical epoch, or in mediaeval Europe. The Odyssey speaks of the Phoenicians, the typical trading people of antiquity, as "clever navigators, deceitful traders". The biographer of St. Godric of Finchale, who engaged in trade at the end of the eleventh century, explains that "he bought in various countries goods which he knew were scarce and therefore dearer elsewhere, and carried them into other regions where they were almost unknown to the inhabitants and therefore seemed to them more desirable than gold".[23]

In fact, large scale trade consisted in going to buy goods at low prices from peoples at a lower stage of economic development, or perhaps not even arrived yet at the stage of general exchange, and who for this reason sold their products very cheap. Then one went to sell these same goods at a much higher price wherever they were very scarce and in demand, where their real value (the labour-time needed to produce them) was unknown, where fashion made certain goods especially attractive, or, better still, where as a result of disasters, famines, etc., a particularly marked shortage of these goods prevailed.

The surplus-value of the traders in an epoch like this comes from their buying goods below their real value and selling them above this real value. There is nothing surprising in the fact that in these conditions Mercury, lord of trade, is also regarded as the king of thieves. It is not surprising that among the African people called the Hereros, "who have no words for 'buy' and 'sell' but merely for 'barter', a merchant in the European sense 'is always a deceiver' because he seeks to win something by exchange."[24] It is not surprising that the Navajo Indians always have the impression that an unusually rich man has obtained his wealth by dishonest means.[25] All folk wisdom repeats the same thing, in all the languages of the earth. As getting something cheap is the basis of this trader's profit, pure plundering and piracy are to be found at the cradle of surplus value.

"More typical still of repeated enrichment at the expense of others which is, so to speak, admitted, is the frankness with which Ulysses relates that he conducted nine piratical expeditions before the Trojan war, or the way he questions the shade of Agamemnon, asking him whether he fell in battle for his city or while he was 'stealing the oxen or the sheep of the State', as though there were little difference between these two activities."[26]

From the earliest times, "piracy is the first phase of trade. This is so true that from the end of the ninth century, when they stopped their plundering, they [the Norsemen] transformed themselves into traders."[27] We know that Aristotle still regarded piracy and highway robbery as legitimate ways of earning one's livelihood. Solon gave the law's protection to associations of pirates, just as the British and French monarchies did 2,000 years later in relation to privateers.[28] The Aztec merchants, combining the function of traders with that of conquerors, imposed tributes to be paid wherever they could, and provide a typical example of the inextricable ties linking the origins of trade with brigandage. Here are clearly revealed the origins of commercial surplus-value![29]

The trade-brigands called Varangians (the word *varyag* means in Slavonic "cattle-merchant"), men of Scandinavian origin who ravaged Russia from the eighth to the eleventh century of our era, are another typical example of the same phenomenon: "The trading and plundering parties of Norsemen-Swedes penetrated into Slavic territory. As merchants of the eighth and tenth centuries, they went there in quest both of trade and plunder. Robbery and conquest were alike a source of trade, with trade supplementing robbery."[30]

Trade and plundering are inextricably connected in the Sahara:
"The hostile tribes organised against their foes, and those protected

by the latter, plundering operations planned as real trading expeditions, which is why they have a place in this treatise. They were governed by customary law, which laid down in detail the role of the capitalists who financed the expedition, that of those who carried it into effect, and the profits of each, in proportion to his participation. It was a typical contract of a very ancient kind which was still in use, with the same features, thirty years ago, in Upper Mauretania as well as in the Sahara."[31]

This system makes possible an extremely rapid enrichment of a few merchants, or of the merchant class of a people. The profits are very high, often exceeding 1,000 per cent on a single transaction. In the fourteenth century merchants bought Tatar horses in the Crimea for one dinar and sold them in India for 25 or even sometimes 50 dinars, we are told by the great Arab traveller Ibn Batuta.[32] The Dutch East India Company bought spices in the seventeenth century for 7·5 cents a pound, in the Moluccas, and sold them in Holland for 300 cents.[33] Such differences between prices are possible only if the backward condition of a people implies that it is unaware of the exchange value of a commodity on the world market. The Phoenicians knew what they were doing when they regularly preferred to do business with barbarian peoples whom they could oppress politically.[34]

Under the Sung dynasty "the peoples of the North [of China] whose usual food was meat, cheese and milk, liked tea to drink. To get it they used to come and sell their horses on the 1st and 2nd of February and March. At the start, when exchanges of tea against horses began, they would offer a good horse for a dozen pounds of ordinary tea. The Chinese tea monopoly drew substantial profits from these transactions. Soon smuggling began, and the foreigners, informed as to prices, demanded ten times as much for their horses."[35]

However, a circulation of money which results in surplus-value that originated in this way is *sterile* from a global point of view; it does not increase the total wealth of human society.* It consists in fact of a *transfer* of wealth, pure and simple; what one gains the other loses, in absolute value. Social wealth remains unchanged.

Let us represent by C the value of a quantity of amber produced by the inhabitants of the Baltic coast; by M the price paid by the Phoenician merchants to the producers of amber; and by M^1 the

---

* At least from the static standpoint. From the historical point of view, the concentration of surplus-value obtained by plundering, direct or indirect, made possible a development of merchant capital and world trade which undoubtedly favoured the spread of culture and the growth of productive forces. It must also be stressed that the surplus-value of merchant and usurers' capital represents to some extent the appropriation by these new possessing classes of part of the agricultural surplus-product which was the income of the old possessing classes (of the Egyptian lord in the example which follows).

selling price obtained by these same Phoenicians in Egypt. Before these exchanges took place, the three partners possessed altogether the values $C + M + M^1$: C belonged to the Danes, M to the Phoenician merchants and M^1 to some rich Egyptian lord. When the exchanges have been completed, the Danes have M, the Egyptian lord has C, and the Phoenician merchants have M^1. The total of these three values is still $C + M + M^1$. Society has been neither enriched nor impoverished. A transfer of value has taken place, that is all.

The Danes have been impoverished by the difference in value between C and M and the Egyptian lord by the difference between M^1 and C, whereas the Phoenician merchants have enriched themselves by the difference in value between M^1 and M, which represents exactly their surplus-value (or the sum of the losses of value suffered by their two trading partners). It is always the same when surplus-value is acquired through the circulation of money: it is created at the expense of a partner, and does not lead to the enrichment of society as a whole.

It may be objected that the Danes have suffered no real impoverishment unless they are already living in a trading economy, and the very barbarism that causes them to accept this unequal exchange implies that they are unaware of this "loss of value". Moreover, this whole argument supposes a unified system of values, whereas in reality what we have before us are different civilisations, with different systems of production and different values, which touch only at their peripheries.

This objection is not valid if one regards exchange value as something *objective* and not subjective. It is precisely trade that unifies values by establishing international markets, in which nations at different levels of development may well participate. It is, furthermore, enough to study the history of certain peoples in certain periods to realise that the idea of impoverishment by *transfer of value* is an obvious reality (cf. West Africa from the sixteenth to the nineteenth century, etc.).

Surplus-value arising from commodity production

When petty commodity production is at its beginning, social wealth remains almost stationary, and the surplus grabbed by the owners of money may simply arise from an absolute impoverishment of the successive buyers and sellers. The history of Antiquity is to a large degree the history of the successive conquest of the hoards of various kingdoms and then their concentration, also by way of conquest, by the Kings of Persia and by Alexander the Great. "The new wealth with which imperialism enriched Babylonia and Egypt was really just loot, and represented no addition to the total supply of real wealth available to humanity . . ."[36] The increase of real social wealth in that period is chiefly a function of the increase in the productivity of agricultural labour and the spreading knowledge of craft techniques, both connected with the growth of population. As the agricultural and craft techniques concerned are fairly simple and do not require costly equipment, the expansion of trade in ancient times towards the barbarian parts of the world ended by introducing there the same conditions of production as at the centre, and so itself put an end to the inequality in levels of economic development which had made this trade profitable. One of the chief reasons for the blind alley which ancient merchant capital got into, and for the decline of the Roman empire, is to be found in this simple fact. In the same way, *usury*, while it is a frequent source of individual enrichment, does not in the least signify an enrichment of society as a whole, since it represents, even more clearly than pre-capitalist trade, a simple *transfer of values* from one person to another.

Now, when we examine the evolution of certain societies based on petty commodity production, such as Greece from the sixth to the third century B.C., China from the eight to the third century B.C., the Islamic world from the eighth to the twelfth century A.D., or Western Europe from the eleventh to the fifteenth century, we observe that enrichment of the entire society did in fact occur. This enrichment exceeded by far the increase in agricultural and craft production; nor was it the mere result of looting economically backward countries, since it involved the totality of the countries linked by trade relations. It could, then, have resulted only from a mass of *new values* making their appearance in money economy. How could the creation of new values occur during the circulation of money $M - C - M^1$?

We know already that value is only crystallised human labour. Money cannot, it would seem, create fresh values. But instead of buying commodities which he will sell for more than their value, the merchant can use his money to buy *a commodity which has, as its use-value, the quality of producing new values*: human labour-power.*

In the fifth and fourth centuries B.C. the purchase price of an adult male slave varied in Athens between 180 and 200 drachmas. Suppose a merchant buys such a slave. The average net daily income, after deduction of maintenance costs, obtainable from a slave amounts, according to Xenophon and Demosthenes, to an obolus a day, or allowing for holidays, 300 oboli or 50 drachmas a year.[37] After ten years' work this slave will thus have earned his master 500 drachmas,

* On this matter Aristotle and also the authorities of the Catholic Church, from the Council of Nicœa to St. Thomas Aquinas, had quite correct ideas, not as advocates of the labour theory of value but as representatives of an essentially natural economy which was defending itself against the dissolving invasion of money and usury.

or 300 drachmas of surplus value.* Buying a slave thus constitutes a source of surplus value of a special kind. This surplus value is not the result of a mere appropriation of existing values, a mere transfer of values from one pocket to another. It results from *the production of new values*, the appropriation and sale of which are the source of surplus value.

In fact, the biggest fortunes in Athens came from the employment or hiring-out of slaves for work in the mines. Possessing or hiring-out as many as 1,000 slaves, Kallias the Athenian was able to accumulate 200 talents, Nikias 100 talents.[40] At one obolus a day of net income produced by a slave, 100 talents (36,000 oboli) represents the income from 36,000 days worked by these slaves, without taking into account the recovery of the purchase price. The orator Demosthenes makes exactly the same calculation when he records the income received by his father, who owned two manufactories, one making furniture, with 20 slaves who each brought him, net, one obolus a day, and the other making swords and knives, with 30 slaves who each brought him, on the average, 1·5 oboli a day.[41]

The surplus value produced by a slave, leaving out of account the recovery of his purchase price, represents the difference between the value of the commodities he produces (and which his master appropriates) and the cost of production of these commodities (cost of raw material, overheads, including depreciation of tools, and maintenance costs of the slave himself). The figures quoted above show that this difference can be considerable. Otherwise, there would not have been the thousands of entrepreneurs and landowners that there were in the ancient world, ready to buy slaves in order to set them producing a large quantity of craft and agricultural products, the sale of which brought in a substantial surplus value to these slave-owners.

Two thousand years later there are no more slaves in Western Europe. Herr Fugger—like Messrs. Nikias and Kallias, a concession-holder and later owner of mines—does not buy slaves any more. He does not have to invest a small capital, outright, recoverable only over

---

* We do not know what the daily maintenance costs of a Greek slave amounted to. But De Castro records that in the British West Indies in the eighteenth century the food for a black slave for whom £50 had been paid cost only 25s. a *year*.[38] And Juan Leon Africano tells how, two centuries earlier, the Portuguese planters reduced to zero the maintenance costs of the slaves on Sao Thomé: "The slaves were compelled to work the whole week long for their masters, except Sunday: that day they worked for themselves, sowing millet, yams or sweet potatoes, and lots of vegetables, such as lettuces, cabbages, leeks and parsley. They kneaded cakes of millet flour; their drink was water or palm wine, and sometimes goats' milk; their only clothing was a cotton loin-cloth which they wove themselves. Thus, the masters had to pay nothing for the livelihood of their servants."[39]

a dozen years, in order to acquire a potential labour force.* He recruits *wage* workers in the villages of Bohemia and the Tyrol. He pays them by the week or by the day. This wage, while a little more than the value of the food given to the slaves of Messrs. Nikias and Kallias, is no more than the minimum necessary for the subsistence of the worker and his family.

The new value created by the workers whose labour power Herr Fugger buys by the day or by the week, must of course exceed the value their employer spends on their wages, or else he would not be interested in employing them. It must even be confessed that this difference was considerable, for, just like Messrs. Nikias and Kallias, Herr Fugger became the richest man of his age, to whom barons, dukes, princesses, kings, even the Emperor in person, owed real fortunes.

The individual enrichment of merchants and manufacturers by the exploitation of labour-power, whether it be servile, half-free or free, is achieved by transferring to the pockets of these entrepreneurs the *new values* created by this labour-power. It is an enrichment which is accompanied by an overall increase in social wealth.

The surplus value which makes its appearance in the circulation of money is thus not created in this circulation. It is the result either of the appropriation through trade or usury of a value belonging to others, or of the appropriation of new values created by the labour power which has been bought. In the latter case, the surplus value is nothing but *the difference between the value created by the worker and the cost of maintaining him*. The totality of the capital existing in the world is only the accumulated result of this dual appropriation, as was soon appreciated by sharp observers. Fifteen hundred years before Proudhon borrowed from the Chartist leader O'Brien his famous sally: "What is property? Theft!" the golden-mouthed bishop John Chrysostom told the rich merchants of Antioch: "You possess the results of theft, even if you are not yourselves the thieves."

Capital, surplus-value and social surplus product

Primitive man learns by long and painful experience how to avoid famines and guarantee himself regular nourishment which will enable him to increase the productivity of his labour and bring the production of the means of life under his own control. For this reason he produces a surplus in excess of his necessary product. "On the whole it may be said that capital in Tikopia is accumulated by surplus production over immediate requirements rather than by abstinence *per se*," states the anthropologist Raymond Firth.[48]

---

* A slave-owner, indeed, runs a risk. He buys only a *potential* labour force; slave labour has always involved an enormous wasting of human labour. The Roman writer Varro estimated that in his day 13 out of 45 of a slave's working days were a dead loss.

We do not intend to discuss at this point whether the word "capital" is correctly used here. But the historical survey we have carried out has made it possible for us to affirm that nowhere in the world have social enrichment, the generalisation of trade, primitive accumulation of money and the production of a growing mass of surplus value been the result of voluntary abstinence on the part of producers who thus make savings and become rich. Everywhere the generalisation of commodity production, the primitive accumulation of money capital and its circulation at a more rapid rate so as to obtain surplus value, have been the outcome of an appropriation, a *grabbing by one part of human society of the social surplus product which has been produced by the rest of this same society.* This appropriation may, indeed, be the result of an "abstinence", namely, that of the producers, reduced to subsistence level by the grabbers of the surplus product. Unfortunately, it has been the grabbers and not the unwilling heroes of this abstinence who have emerged enriched from the ordeal.

The growth of the productivity of labour is an indispensable condition for the appearance of capital and surplus value. Surplus value which has emerged from the process of production, as we have seen, represents only the difference between the product of labour and the cost of maintaining labour. So long as the product of labour is more or less equal to the cost of maintaining labour (that is, to the means of subsistence of the producer and his family), there is no objective basis for the lasting and organised exploitation of labour power. It is only when growth in the productivity of labour has made it possible to recognise such a difference, such a surplus product, that the struggle to appropriate it can break out.

While, however, capital is the historical result—not an automatic result, but arising in particular conditions that can be specifically defined—of growth in the productivity of human labour, it is not synonymous with the *means* that ensure such growth. This confusion is still made even by specialists who are well informed regarding the historical facts. Thus, for the historian Fritz Heichelheim the neolithic revolution, the transition to agriculture and cattle-raising, means the appearance of "capital, . . . that is, the creation of the first reliable way of transferring human work into something which gave rent for a longer time and even for the duration of generations".[44]

A peasant who had sown 1,000 seeds of wheat on the banks of the Euphrates harvested 100,000. But this 'rent' no more made a capitalist of him than striking a banana tree with a stick to make the fruit fall sooner makes an industrialist of a chimpanzee.

Each important technical invention represents an important saving of human labour for society, and each tool that makes it possible to produce at less cost can be regarded as a "store of accumulated labour" which brings in a more or less permanent "rent" in saving of labour. All this, however, relates only to the progress of the productivity of labour in *the production of use-values.**

Capital and surplus value do not appear until *exchange* and *money* have developed, and until an increased average productivity of labour is used no longer so as to enable *the whole of society* to achieve a saving in labour-time but so as to ensure for *one part of society* the products of this increased productivity, by subjecting the rest of society to a heavier burden of work. Capital is the culmination of the history of the appropriation of the social surplus product by one part of society at the expense of another, and not the culmination of the history of the saving of human labour accomplished for the benefit of human society as a whole.

Appropriation of the surplus value produced during the process of production assumes the existence of a market economy and the sale of commodities produced by producers who do not own the products of their labour. Surplus value, in this sense, is the *monetary form of the social surplus product*. In a society producing use values, the social surplus product which a possessing class appropriates is appropriated directly, either in the form of labour (*corvée*) or of products (land rent, tribute). In a society producing commodities, the social surplus product appropriated by the possessing class is indirectly appropriated, in the form of money, by the sale of commodities, from the results of which sale the costs of maintaining labour and the other costs of production have been deducted.

Like petty commodity production, capital developed originally within the pores of a society which was first and foremost engaged in producing use values. Surplus value appeared and developed in a society in which the social surplus product essentially retained the form of use-values. The entire history of capital, from its origins to its apotheosis in the capitalist mode of production, is the history of the slow disintegration of this fundamentally non-market economy, through the effect of trade, of usury, of money, of capital and of surplus value. Capital is embodied, in a non-trading society and in contrast to the old-established possessing classes, in a new class, the bourgeoisie. Capital is only a new social relation between producers and owners of capital, a relation which replaces the old social relations between small commodity producers, on the one hand, and

---

* It could be objected that this is merely a matter of definition. If so, it would be necessary to find *another expression* to indicate capital and surplus value which arise from commodity production and the circulation of money. The confusion consists in the simultaneous use of the same term, capital, for every technique of growth in the productivity of labour, on the one hand, and for specific social relations, based on exploitation, on the other. Etymology meets economics here, moreover, since H. Sée says that the word "capital" means originally only *a sum of money which is to be invested so as to earn interest.*[45]

between peasant producers and those who take the surplus product of agriculture, on the other.

The law of uneven development

The study of the origin and development of economic categories is necessarily a study of economic history, and an analysis of the economy of those peoples of our own day which have remained at stages of historical evolution long since left behind in the capitalist world. It actually isolates "pure" forms which in real life are combined, or have more or less degenerated. To reduce economic history to a series of "stages" or to the successive appearance of "categories" is to make it excessively mechanical, to the point of rendering it unrecognizable. But to eliminate from historical study any allusion to successive stages of economic organisation and any reference to the progressive appearance of these "categories" is to make it merely incomprehensible.

Marxism has often been compared to Darwinism, and the evolution of societies to that of species. Like any other comparison, this one includes points of resemblance and of difference. In biology, too, however, a *dialectical* conception of evolution is gradually taking the place of the mechanical, unilateral and linear conception.* The Marxist conception of economic and social change has no place for any fatalism or automatism. No phase of social organisation "must" necessarily succeed another.

Alongside linear progress there is progress by leaps. Economic evolution can lead to blind alleys or age-long stagnations, especially through excessive adaptation to a specific environment; that seems to have happened with the agricultural peoples of South-East Asia.[47] Moreover, Marxism would not be dialectical if it did not recognise, alongside societies which are progressing (from the standpoint of the average productivity of labour), societies in marked regression.[48]

The law of uneven development, which some have wished to restrict in application to the history of capitalism alone, or even merely to the imperialist phase of capitalism, is thus a universal law of human history. Nowhere in the world has there been a straight-line progressive evolution, starting from the first stages of fruit-gathering and ending with the most advanced capitalist (or socialist) industry. The peoples which reached the highest level of development of productive forces at the stage of food-gathering, hunting and fishing—the

---

* The idea of a straight-line progress from the anthropoid apes up to the emergence of man has now been dropped. Today it is supposed either that the anthropoid apes and man have simian-like ancestors in common, or that man is descended from an anthropoid ape less specialised than any of those that exist today. Thus, there has been progress combined with stagnation, retardation or proterogenesis.[46]

Eskimos, and, above all, the Indians of the North-West coast of America—did not invent agriculture. This first appeared in the well-watered valleys of Abyssinia, Anatolia, Afghanistan, Transcaucasia, and North-Western India.[49] But it was not there, either, that agriculture gave birth to civilisation, which is the child of irrigation.*

Agricultural civilisation reaches its most advanced phase in Egypt, Mesopotamia, India and China. It was not however, in these countries, but rather in Greece, at Rome, at Byzantium, and in mediaeval Europe (Italy and Flanders) that the progress of the productivity of labour culminated in the most advanced forms of crafts and trade within the framework of petty commodity production. And for petty commodity production to produce the industrial revolution and the capitalist mode of production, we have to move still further north, to England, a country which had long remained backward as regards crafts and trade, and which in the seventeenth century was still far from being the richest in the world or in Europe. Nor was it in Great Britain or in any other advanced capitalist country that capitalism was first overthrown, but in Russia, a typical backward country at the beginning of the twentieth century. May we venture a prophecy and say that it will not be in Russia, either, though this was the first country to introduce a planned economy based on socialisation of the chief means of production, that we shall first see the emergence of a completed socialist society, with the withering away of classes, commodities, money and the state?

* Gordon Childe, too, insists on the absence of any identical succession of stages passed through by the peoples in the neolithic epoch. "Evolution and differentiation go hand in hand," he concludes; but he also mentions a number of instances of convergence.[50] Is not evolution as a *combination of differentiation and convergence* an eminently *dialectical idea*?

REFERENCES

1. Hingston Quiggin: *A Survey of Primitive Money*, p. 5.
2. Sir Samuel Baker: *The Albert Nyanza* (1866), Vol. II, p. 182.
3. A. De Foville: *La Monnaie*, p. 9.
4. Jacques Lacour-Gayet: *"Le roi Bilalama et le juste prix"*; in *Revue des Deux Mondes*, 15th November, 1949.
5. Frédéric Hrozny: *Code Hittite*, p. 137.
6. Wang Yü-Chüan: *Early Chinese Coinage*, in *The American Numismatic Society*, p. 259.
7. Sir George Sansom: *A History of Japan to 1334*, p. 88.
8. Jacques Gernet: *Les Aspects économiques du bouddhisme dans la société chinoise du V⁰ au X⁰ siecle*, pp. 88-89.
9. M. Mauss: *"Essai sur le don"*, p. 221.
10. Hingston Quiggin: *A Survey of Primitive Money*, p. 26.
11. Ibid., p. 92.

12. Gordon Childe: *What Happened in History*, pp. 192-3.
13. Nancy Lee Swann: *Food and Money in China*, pp. 217-22.
14. Herman Kees: *Kulturgeschichte des Alten Orients*, Vol. I, *Aegypten*, pp. 103-29; Louis Renon and Jean Filliozat: *L'Inde classique*, p. 378; *Histoire du commerce*, Vol. III, p. 142.
15. Gustave Glotz: *Le Travail dans la Grèce antique*, pp. 278-84; K. A. Wittfogel: *Wirtschaft und Gesellschaft Chinas*, pp. 96-104; M. Takizawa: *The Penetration of Money Economy in Japan*, pp. 30-33.
16. Takizawa, p. 20.
17. K. Polanyi: et. al., *Trade and Market in the Early Empires*, p. 266.
18. Gordon Childe: op. cit., p. 155.
19. Glotz: op. cit., p. 20.
20. P. Boissonnade: *Le Travail dans l'Europe chrétienne du Moyen Age*, p. 196.
21. Chen Huan-Chang: *The Economic Principles of Confucius*, p. 457.
22. Ibn Khaldoun: *Prolégomènes*, Vol. II, p. 325.
23. J. Kulischer: *Allgemeine Wirtschaftsgeschichte*, Vol. I, p. 89.
24. W. G. Sumner and A. G. Keller: *Science of Society*, Vol. I, p. 155.
25. A. H. and D. C. Leighton: *The Navaho Door*, p. 18.
26. A. Andréadès: *Geschichte der Griechischen Staatswirtschaft*, Vol. I, p. 27.
27. H. Pirenne: *Le mouvement économique et social du moyen âge*, p. 24.
28. F. Heichelheim: *Wirtschaftsgeschichte des Altertums*, Vol. I, p. 262.
29. V. W. von Hagen: *The Aztec and Maya Papermakers*, p. 12; W. H. Prescott: *History of the Conquest of Mexico*, p. 85.
30. P. I. Lyashchenko: *History of the National Economy of Russia*, p. 77.
31. H. Labouret: in *Histoire du Commerce*, Vol. III, p. 76.
32. Ibn Batuta: *Voyages*, Vol. I—, pp. 324-7.
33. S. I. Rutgers: *Indonesië*, p. 57.
34. Heichelheim: op. cit., Vol. I, p. 230.
35. J. Bonmarchand: in *Histoire du Commerce*, Vol. III, p. 312.
36. Gordon Childe: op. cit., p. 159.
37. Pauly-Wissowa: *Handwörterbuch der Altertumswissenschaften*, Supplementband VI, pp. 916-17.
38. J. de Castro: *Géopolitique de la Faim*, p. 139.
39. R. P. Rinchon: *La Traite et l'esclavage des Congolais par les Européens*, p. 50.
40. Heichelheim: op. cit., Vol. I, p. 392.
41. Ibid., p. 381.
42. R. H. Barrow: *Slavery in the Roman Empire*, p. 78.
43. Raymond Firth: *Primitive Polynesian Economy*, p. 274.
44. Heichelheim: op. cit., Vol. I, pp. 35-36.
45. H. Sée: *Les Origines du Capitalisme*, p. 7.
46. A. Gehlen: *Der Mensch*, pp. 133-6.
47. *An Appraisal of Anthropology Today*, pp. 42-143 passim.

48. A typical instance is quoted by Cl. Lévi-Strauss, in *Anthropologie structurale*, p. 126.
49. *An Appraisal of Anthropology Today*, pp. 70-72; Ralph Linton: *The Tree of Culture*, pp. 53-57.
50. Gordon Childe: *Social Evolution*, pp. 166-8.

CHAPTER FOUR

THE DEVELOPMENT OF CAPITAL

Forms of agricultural surplus product

AGRICULTURAL surplus product is the basis of all surplus product and thereby of all civilisation. If society had to devote all its working time to producing the means of subsistence, no other specialised activity, whether craft, industrial, scientific or artistic, would be possible.

Agricultural surplus product can appear in society in three different forms. In the fourth century B.C. the Chinese philosopher Mencius already distinguished between these three essential forms of agricultural surplus product: surplus product in the form of work (labour services), in the form of products (use values), or in the form of money.[1] *

Agricultural surplus product supplied in the form of unpaid work or labour services makes its appearance at the dawn of every class society. At the beginning of the Middle Ages in Western Europe, the land of the village was divided into three shares: the lands which the peasants cultivated for their own needs; the lands which the lord exploited directly by means of the unpaid work of peasants who were obliged to render labour services; the common lands, woods, meadows, wastes, etc., which remained more or less freely at the disposal of the peasants and of the lord.[2] The peasant had to divide his working week between work on his own fields and work on the lord's land. The former, *necessary labour* from the social point of view, provided the product needed for the subsistence of the producers. The latter, *surplus labour* from the social point of view, provided the surplus product needed for the subsistence of the possessing classes not participating in production.

A system similar to this has operated in innumerable countries at different epochs of history. Under the feudal system which existed in the Hawaiian Islands before the coming of the whites, the peasant had to work one day in five on the lands exploited by the landowner.[3] In Mexico, before the agrarian reform, there existed "the custom of paying rents for small subsistence holdings by two or three days per week of unpaid labour on the estates".[4]

* It is interesting to note that this same Mencius regards labour services as the most advantageous form of surplus product from the standpoint of a state which seeks to protect the peasantry from the exactions of the landowners, because it gives the peasants the maximum guarantees of stability.

Alongside surplus product supplied as unpaid work there may appear surplus product paid in kind. The serfs of the Middle Ages in Western Europe had to provide the lords not only with labour services but also with rent in kind (in agricultural or craft products). Similarly, in the Hawaiian Islands, rent in kind had to be supplied, over and above labour services.[5]

In Japan rent in kind (*so*) existed alongside labour services (*etachi*).[6] In China rent in kind appeared alongside labour services and gradually took their place, except as regards large-scale works of public utility. In fact, payment of rent in kind, that is, of agricultural surplus product in the form of use values (wheat, rice, wine, cloth woven in the peasant's household, etc.) fairly soon in history became the predominant form of surplus product, and remained in being for thousands of years, with little modification. In the history of Egypt, agricultural surplus product retained this form of provision of goods in kind from the time of the Pharaohs down to the empire of Rome and Byzantium. Each year for seven centuries, as payment of rent, 20 million *modii* of wheat were sent to Italy, then 24 million *modii* to Byzantium, or about 12·5 per cent of the total production of Egypt.[7]

So long as agricultural surplus product retains this form of rent in kind, trade, money, capital exist only *in the pores of a natural economy*. The bulk of the producers, the peasants, hardly ever appear on the market, consuming as they do only what they themselves produce, after deducting the surplus product.

The progressive increase in agricultural production is taken by the lords, who sell it on the market. But, for the same reason, the bulk of the population is unable to buy the products of craftsmen working in the towns. These products thus remain chiefly luxury goods. The narrowness of the market severely limits the development of craft production.

This was how ancient Greece, the Roman empire, the empires of Byzantium and of Islam, with India, China and Japan down to recent centuries, actually lived. The often remarkable splendour that petty commodity production and international trade were capable of attaining within these societies should not conceal from us their basically agricultural character.[8] So long as agricultural surplus product retains the form of goods in kind, trade, money and capital could develop only superficially within such a society.

The transformation of agricultural surplus product from rent in kind to money rent turns the social situation thoroughly upside down. In order to pay his rent, the peasant is henceforth obliged to sell his products himself on the market. He leaves the condition of a natural and closed economy and enters an essentially money economy. Money, which renders possible the acquisition of an infinite variety of goods, allows an infinite range of needs to develop.[9] Economic life quits its centuries-long torpor and relative equilibrium and becomes dynamic, unbalanced, spasmodic. Production and consumption develop along with the unprecedented expansion of trade. Money penetrates everywhere, dissolves all traditional bonds, transforms all established relationships. Everything is given a price. A man's worth is no longer estimated otherwise than according to his income. Universal venality accompanies the triumph of money economy, as Saint Thomas Aquinas observed early on.[10] At the same time, money begins to conceal the real economic relationship, formerly transparent, between serfs and lords, between necessary and surplus labour. Landowners and tenants, employers and wage-earners, meet on the market as free owners of commodities, and the fiction of this "free exchange" hides the continuation of the old relationship of exploitation under its new money forms.*

The transformation of agricultural surplus product from rent in kind into money rent is not the inevitable result of the expansion of trade and money economy; it results from *the existing relation of forces between the classes.*

"The rise of money economy has not always been the great emancipating force which nineteenth-century historians believed it to have been. In the absence of a large reservoir of free landless labour and without the legal and political safeguards of the liberal state, the expansion of markets and the growth of production is as likely to lead to the increase of labour services as to their decline."[11]

"The development of exchange in the peasant economy, whether it served the local market directly, or more distant markets through merchant middlemen, led to the development of money rent. The development of exchange in the lord's economy, on the other hand, led to the growth of labour services . . ."[12]

The typical example in this connection is the evolution of village economy in eastern Europe, including eastern Germany, from the fifteenth and sixteenth centuries onward; there, labour services, with the attachment of the serf-peasants to the land, continually increased,† following the development of production of agricultural commodities for the international market, on the lord's estates.

For money rent to take the place of rent in kind, the extension of money economy must be accompanied by economic, social and political conditions (the role played by the central authority, leaning for

* If the serf was attached to the land, the land was also attached to the serf. "The land holds him and he holds the land," said Fustel de Coulanges. In "freeing" the serf, the market economy also enables the landowner to separate him from his means of subsistence. This dialectical aspect of economic freedom is usually overlooked by liberal critics of the mediaeval economy.

† Duke Ferdinand I of Silesia proclaimed in 1528: "No peasants or gardeners, nor the sons or daughters thereof, may leave their hereditary lord without his consent."[13]

support on the urban bourgeoisie) such that the landowners find themselves obliged to leave in the peasants' possession a substantial part of their increasing production.

Accumulation of use-values and accumulation of surplus-value

So long as the agricultural surplus product retains the form of rent in kind, the accumulation of wealth by the possessing classes takes place essentially in the form of accumulation of use values. Agriculture supplies as use values only foodstuffs, clothing, wood and stone for building houses. Thus, the possessing classes have no interest in developing agricultural production to an unlimited extent. Their own *consumption capacity* constitutes the ceiling of the development of the productive forces:

"Having no means, for lack of outlets, to produce for sale, he [the large-scale mediaeval landowner] has thus no need to worry about obtaining from his men and his land a surplus which would only be an encumbrance to him. Compelled to consume his reserves, in person, he restricts himself to keeping them within his needs."[14]

In the Hawaiian Islands, where the surplus product takes the form, almost exclusively, of foodstuffs, the "demands (of the landowners) were further restricted by the perishableness of much of the produce (fish, bananas, sweet potatoes, *poi*); and in the circumstance that there was no reason for the chiefs to take more than they could themselves use . . . And although the *alii* (feudal lords) prided themselves justly upon their fatness and stature—the women especially were proud of their bulk—there was a limit to their power of consumption."[15]

When exchange and trade begin to develop, the possessing classes have a new interest in increasing production. In exchange for the part of the agricultural surplus product which they do not manage to consume themselves, they can acquire luxury products, jewels, domestic utensils of great value and beauty which they hoard in order to obtain both social prestige and security in the event of disasters. The Odyssey lists such treasures accumulated in the hero's storehouse, the *thalamos*: jars of old wine and vases of scented oil, heaps of gold, bronze and iron, rare weapons, rich fabrics, delicately carved cups, etc.[16]

With the generalisation of exchange and trade, the possessing classes receive a fresh stimulus to develop production. In exchange for that part of the agricultural surplus product which they do not themselves consume, they can now acquire rare consumer goods from distant countries. Their needs multiply, their tastes become more refined. Hoards of incalculable value are accumulated.

No longer are wheat, wine, oil or precious metals in the raw state subject to hoarding. Precious stones and works of art from the hands of the most famous craftsmen (or artists) are alone worthy to enter the palaces of the great. Hitti thus describes the wealth accumulated by the Egyptian caliph Al-Mustansir (1035–1094): "Precious stones, crystal vases, inlaid gold plates, ivory and ebony inkstands, amber cups, phials of musk, steel mirrors, parasols with gold and silver sticks, chess-boards with gold and silver pawns, jewelled daggers and swords and embroidered fabrics manufactured at Dabiq and Damascus."[17]

More impressive still are these treasures of the Byzantine court of the ninth century:

"He [the Emperor Theophilus, who reigned from 829 to 842] loved pomp and magnificence: to enhance the splendour of his palace receptions, he ordered from his craftsmen marvels of goldsmiths' work and mechanical ingenuity: the Pentapyrgian, a famous golden cupboard where the crown jewels were displayed; the golden organs that played on the days when the Emperor held solemn audience; the golden plane-tree that rose beside the imperial throne and on which mechanical birds fluttered and sang; the golden lions lying at the prince's feet, which at certain moments got up, waved their tails and roared; and the golden griffins of mysterious aspect which seemed, as in the palaces of Asian kings, to watch over the Emperor's serenity."[18]

The Empire of China and that of the Moguls in India knew luxurious displays of the same order. One has only to think of the walls of the Taj Mahal, covered with precious stones.

After all, though, all these treasures constitute hoarded use values, unconsumable and unused for the development of the productive forces. The concentration of a considerable share of social wealth for the mere purpose of luxury and waste is thus an important cause of the stagnation and decadence of societies of this sort.

The transformation of agricultural surplus product from rent in kind into money rent does not necessarily change this situation. It gives the ruling classes easier access to the market and possession of wealth even more excessive than before. But the money they receive continues to be wasted on *unproductive consumption*. Under these conditions, the development of money economy, and the powerful stimulus which this gives to the needs of the ruling classes, may become the cause of exactions which prove unbearable to the working classes, a factor of impoverishment and ruin for large sections of society. This was the case in Japan, after the development of money economy in the eighteenth century.[19]

But the money that the original possessing classes thus waste in extravagant luxury ends by leaving their pockets and becoming concentrated in those of usurers, traders and manufacturers. It is this concentration of wealth, in the form of money, in the hands of a new bourgeois possessing class that completely changes social evolution. In the hands of the original possessing classes, all accumulated wealth, including money, was merely wealth in use values, or means of acquiring use values. The object of accumulation was consumption (and hoarding with a view to future consumption). In the hands of the bourgeois classes, *accumulated money becomes capital*.

Money is accumulated in order to bring in surplus value. The surplus value thus accumulated, after deduction of the minimum necessary for subsistence at a level "in accordance with rank", is in its turn capitalised, transformed into capital, in order to bring in further surplus value. Such an accumulation of values which bring in new values is, in the long run, impossible to achieve by mere periodical transfers of wealth from one country to another or from one class to another. Either the accumulation of capital kept within the limits of such a transfer ends by ceasing, because its sources inevitably must dry up, or else it finds a new way forward thanks to the *introduction of capital into production itself*, the ultimate culmination of money economy. This penetration of capital into the sphere of production creates the conditions for an unlimited advance of the productive forces. No longer do the limited consumer needs of the possessing class restrict the productive forces—the need to increase the value which accretes to capital, a need without any limits by its very nature, makes possible on the contrary the abolition of every restriction on their development.

Usurer's capital

The first form in which capital makes its appearance in an economy which is still basically natural, agricultural, producing use-values, is that of usurer's capital. Usurer's capital, the hoard accumulated by an institution or an individual, makes up for the inadequacy of social reserves. Hesiod tells how the peasants of ancient Greece, when in need, borrowed wheat from their better-off neighbours, paying it back later with something more added.[20] Usurer's capital appearing in this way in the form of use values was common, all through the centuries, in essentially agricultural civilisations (Babylon, Egypt, China, India, Japan). In Sumerian the term *mas* (interest) means literally "young animal" (*Tierjunges*) and clearly testifies to the origin of usurer's capital in loans in kind.

What usurer's capital in the form of loans in kind is in relation to the peasants, usurer's capital in the form of advances of money is in relation to the lords and the kings.* During the period of transition from natural to money economy, the essential function of the usurers in France was to advance money to the kings on the security of taxes which were still essentially paid in kind.[22] Wars, famine, other natural

---

* Cf. the development of usury in China by the Buddhist temples from the fifth century onward: usury in kind at the expense of the peasants, usury in money at the expense of the lords and rich officials.[21]

and social catastrophes, necessitate exceptionally large concentrations of money. The transformation of hoards of objects made of precious metal into usurer's capital, or the use of the merchant's capital of foreign merchants as usurer's capital, provide the chief sources of these concentrations.

When exchange has started to become general and has already created a big money sector in the economy, but when at the same time the bulk of the producers and of the possessing classes still receive their incomes in the form of use values, usurer's capital has its golden age. Lending money at usurious rates becomes the chief source of profit. The ancient Hindu epic the *Mahabharata* mentions usury first among the sources of wealth:

"By usury, agriculture, trade and cattle-breeding may you acquire the power of wealth, O King of Kings."[23]

All the religious and political vetos are powerless to prevent usurer's capital from undermining the social relationships of such an epoch. The indebtedness of the great, the ruin of the small, the expropriation of peasants fallen into debt, or their sale as slaves, the concentration of landed property—these are the traditional calamities that usurer's capital provokes in this phase of social development. Most social disturbances are in this phase revolts against these disintegrating consequences of usurer's capital. In Greece in the fifth and fourth centuries B.C., the slogan generally accepted by the people was: "Redistribution of land and cancellation of debts."[24] Rome in the days of the Republic, Chinese society in the period of decline of each dynasty, Byzantium and India at several epochs of their history present a spectacle in no way different.

In vain did the legislation of Solon in Athens, that of the *decemviri* in Rome or of the Chinese minister Wang An-shi under the Sung dynasty, in vain did the Agrarian Law in Byzantium endeavour to check this encroachment by usurer's capital. They succeeded only in delaying the outcome, without being able to change the general direction of development. Caesar undertook his war of plunder against Gaul in order to rid himself of a burden of debt. The Roman citizens had to pillage the whole Mediterranean world and accumulate enormous wealth before they could free themselves to some extent from the pressure of usurer's capital during the first centuries of the Empire. When this Empire broke up, usurer's capital lasted a long time after the disappearance of large-scale trade[25] and the complaints of writers about usurious rates of interest follow one another monotonously from century to century.*

---

* One of the reasons why serfdom and feudal economy spread was that the free peasants were unable to pay taxes and fines fixed in money terms, when money had become very rare and extremely dear in relation to agricultural products. In the sixth century an ox was worth 1 to 3 *solidi*, but a *wergeld*

During the Middle Ages, the need to protect a basically natural economy from the disintegrating effects of money economy and usurer's capital led the Catholic Church in Western Europe to condemn vigorously the lending of money at interest. Usurer's capital then appeared in a special form, in order to get round this prohibition: *the purchase of land rent*. In exchange for a lump sum of money, a landowner surrendered to the lender the annual income from his land until he had repaid the capital advanced. The land became in fact the lender's property, recoverable by the owner when he had discharged his debt.[28]*

This was only a special form of the loan upon security which remained, in mediaeval Europe as in India, China and Japan, the most favoured operation of usurer's capital in a natural economy which was slowly breaking up. The purchase of land rent which played an important part in mediaeval European economy shows clearly what is the source of the surplus value obtained by usurer's capital: *the transfer of the incomes of the lords (or of the peasants) to the usurers*. The accumulation of usurer's capital at the expense of the landowners is essentially a transfer of agricultural surplus product into the hands of the usurers.

When money economy becomes widespread, usurer's capital in the strict sense loses its preponderant position and retreats to the dark corners of society, where it survives for centuries at the expense of the small man. It is not that the big man has less need of money—on the contrary, he needs more than ever. But in the meantime trade has become the essential field of action and source of profit for capital. Credit and trade are combined; it is the epoch of the great Italian, Flemish and German merchant financiers which opens with the thirteenth and fourteenth centuries in Western Europe.

Merchant capital

The appearance of a native merchant class in the midst of a basically natural economy presumes a primitive accumulation of money capital. This comes from two main sources: piracy and brigandage, on the one hand; on the other, the appropriation of part of the agricultural surplus product or even of the peasant's necessary product.

It was by raids into foreign territory, operations of brigandage and piracy, that the first merchant navigators assembled their little starting

---

might amount to as much as 800.[26] The same factor played an important role in the development of feudalism in the Islamic world, in Japan and in Byzantium.[27] Cf. what has been said above about the possibilities of extension of a money economy.

* The same form of usury is to be found among the Ifugao people in the Philippines. Its origins go back to the *antichresis* practised in ancient Greece. It is also found in China in the epoch of the rise of the Buddhist monasteries.[29]

capital. From the earliest times, the origins of maritime trade have been mixed-up with piracy.[30]* Professor Takehoshi observes that the first accumulation of money-capital in Japan (in the fourteenth and fifteenth centuries) was obtained by pirates operating on the coasts of China and Korea:

"While the government of Japan strove to get money by foreign trade, the Japanese pirates employed the more direct method of pillage, and as their booty consisted of gold and silver, copper coins and other treasure, it is impossible to estimate the value of the wealth they brought to Kyushu, Shikoku and the maritime regions of the islands in the central provinces of Japan. Subsequently these plundered treasures injected new life into the whole country."[31]

The accumulation of money capital by the Italian merchants who dominated European economic life from the eleventh to the fifteenth centuries originated directly from the Crusades,[32] an enormous plundering enterprise if ever there was one.

"We know for instance, that in 1101 the Genoese helped the Crusaders to capture and sack Caesarea, a Palestinian seaport. They reserved rich prizes for their officers and remunerated the shipowners with 15 per cent of the loot. They distributed the remainder among 8,000 sailors and soldiers, each receiving 48 *solidi* and two pounds of pepper. Thus each of them was transformed into a petty capitalist."[33]

The mediaeval chronicler Geoffroi de Villehardouin reports the reply given by the Doge of Venice to the Western nobles' request for help in the Fourth Crusade (1202):

"We will supply *vuissiers* (transports for horses) to carry 4,500 horses and 9,000 squires, and ships for 4,500 knights and 20,000 sergeants of foot. And we will agree also to purvey food for these horses and men during nine months. This is what we undertake to do at the least, on condition that you pay us for each horse four marks and for each man two marks . . . The sum total of your payment will thus be 85,000 marks. And we will do more. We will add to the fleet 50 galleys for the love of God [!], if it be agreed that, so long as this contract continues, we shall have the half (and you the other half) of all the conquests that we make by land or sea."

Later, in the fifteenth and sixteenth centuries, the primitive accumulation of money capital by the Portuguese, Spanish, Dutch and English merchants was to have exactly the same source.

In an economy essentially based on petty commodity production,

* N. S. B. Gras, professor of economic history at the Business Administration school attached to Harvard University, feels obliged to refute vigorously[34] this universally recognised truth, which seems to him incompatible with the dignity of capital. Equally unfounded is Schumpeter's assertion[35] that Marx and the Marxists are unable to solve the problem of the primitive accumulation of capital because they have a theory of interest based on exploitation. See also our quotations in the preceding chapter.

retail trade and even wholesale trade in articles of prime necessity is at first strictly limited and regulated.[36] Hardly separated from the crafts, it cannot give rise to a substantial accumulation of merchant capital.[37] Only foreign trade, international trade, allows of such an accumulation. This trade essentially involves *luxury products* intended for the possessing classes. It is through this trade that the merchants appropriate part of the agricultural surplus product on which the landowning classes live. The rise of trade in the Middle Ages in Western Europe, trade in spices and Eastern products, as also trade in Flemish and Italian cloth, is the rise of a typical luxury trade.[38]

The same is true of every society in which merchant capital develops. The customs inspector of the Chinese province of Fukien, Chan Ju-kua, left a picture of China's trade in the twelfth and thirteenth centuries A.D. He lists forty-three articles imported—camphor, incense, myrrh, amber, tortoise-shell, bee's wax, even parrots, all articles of luxury, or spices.[39] Trade in the earliest period of Japanese history was exclusively luxury trade, observes Georges Bonmarchand.[40] Andreades notes that Byzantine exports were almost exclusively luxury products.[41] The trade of the Islamic empire at the height of its greatness was in the same way largely confined to luxury products. Lopez lists as follows the commodities entering into this trade:

" 'Egyptian' emeralds, turquoises from Nishapur, rubies from Yemen, pearls from the Persian Gulf, coral from North-West Africa and Sicily, and marble from Syria and Azerbaijan . . . great quantities of linen from Egypt, Yemen and South-western Persia, of cotton from Merv, Eastern Persia and Spain, of silk from Turkestan and the South Caspian area, of carpets from various regions of Persia, of leather work from Andalusia, of pottery from Khurasan and other provinces, of glass ware from the Syrian coast, and of iron ware from Farghana . . . the scent of Iraqian violet water, of Persian rose water, of Arabian incense and ambergris . . . Maghrebine and Spanish figs, Iraqian and African dates, Turkestanian melons, Tunisian olive oil, Persian, Yemenite and Palestinian sugar, saffron from North-western Persia, sturgeon from the lake of Van, 'edible earth' from Kuhistan, and . . . excellent wine from Iraq and Spain."[42]

Before the coming of the Dutch to Indonesia, the Chinese merchants brought to the great trading centre at Bantam porcelain, silk, damask, velvet, silk thread, gold thread, cloth of gold, spectacles, costly fans, drugs, mercury, etc., and bought spices, musk, ivory, shells and indigo —both sides of this trade consisting of luxury goods.[43]*

---

* Pre-Columbian America had reached the threshold of the appearance of merchant capital at the moment of the Spanish invasion. The embryonic international trade which had been established between the Incas and the Aztecs concerned metals and luxury articles: "The Incas sell the Aztecs metals and alloys, bronze, *tumbaga* (an alloy of copper and zinc) and especially com-

In order effectively to realise surplus-value at the expense of the noble purchasers, the traders in luxury goods had to ensure for themselves real monopolies at both the buying and the selling end. "Seeking no territorial hegemony, they [the Phoenicians and the Carthaginians] did not wish to penetrate into the interior [of Africa], since they had ensured by long experience that they dominated the peoples of the interior through cleverly arranged trading monopolies."[45] All mediaeval trade in luxuries was a monopoly trade. The prosperity of Byzantium was based for six centuries on its role as exclusive entrepôt for the silks and spices of the East. The loss of this monopoly to Venice sounded the knell of Byzantine power.

When the Italian cities dominated Mediterranean trade, they had in their turn obtained monopolies of trade with Egypt, the new entrepôt for Eastern spices, and with the peoples of the Black Sea coast. The trade in herrings, wheat and timber in the Baltic and the Black Sea was transformed in the same period into trade in which large amounts of capital were employed, thanks to the *de facto* monopolies established by the German merchants in Scandinavia and in the regions recently colonised in the East. But these monopolies were broken owing to the fierce competition between the merchant bourgeoisies of different cities, and also, especially, by Dutch competition. This competition enabled the sellers to raise their prices, and at the same time compelled the merchants to lower their selling prices, thus sharply reducing their profit margin.[46]

The capital accumulated by the big merchants who operate in a society based on petty commodity production thus cannot be continually reinvested in international trade itself. When merchant capital has spread itself sufficiently, it has to endeavour to restrict all farther expansion, on pain of itself destroying the monopolistic roots of its own profits. The merchants of a period like this end by investing a considerable part of their profits in other spheres: landed property, usury, large-scale international credit. Cicero[47] advises the wholesale merchant to invest his profits in landed property. The Talmud—the Jewish commentary on the Old Testament—gives the advice, in the third century A.D., that one-third of one's fortune should be invested in land, and one-third in trade and craft production, with the remaining third kept available as ready money.[48]

Matters were no different in ancient India, in China, in Japan and in Byzantium. In the eleventh and twelfth centuries the Jewish merchants possessed nearly one-third of the land in the County of Barcelona.[49] Gras records that the Norwegian prose treatise *The King's Looking-*

pounds of silver, gold and copper. The Aztecs give the Incas in exchange precious stones such as amethysts, emeralds and obsidians, and to an even greater extent the highly specialised work of their most famous corporations: weapons, dyes, cloth made of embroidered cotton, jewellery . . ."[44]

Glass, compiled about 1260, advises itinerant merchants to invest two-thirds of their high profits in land.[50] In the city of Genoa in the thirteenth century "even the greatest of the merchants . . . backed their commercial investments with very considerable investments in real estate . . . behind the group interested in commerce was another, far larger and infected only slightly or not at all with the adventurous spirit of the capitalist, which based its financial system directly upon the land."[51]

As for the great Italian and German merchants of the thirteenth, fourteenth, fifteenth and sixteenth centuries, the Bonsignori, Scotti, Peruzzi, Bardi, Medici, Fugger, Welser and Hochstätter, the capital they acquired through trade was used for large-scale credit operations, and a substantial part of the profit realised was employed in the purchase of landed property.

The commercial revolution

The expansion of trade from the eleventh century onward had speeded up the development of a money economy in Western Europe. But coins remained very scarce. After the end of the economic decline which accompanied the Hundred Years War, the shortage of coins became oppressive. Everywhere, old mines that had been abandoned since Roman times were reopened, or new mines were sought for.[52] The advance of the Turks and the convulsions which were occurring along the old trade routes in Central Asia stimulated efforts to break the Venetian monopoly of the spice trade. At last an unexpected success was obtained. The discovery of America, the plundering of Mexico and Peru, the circumnavigation of Africa, the establishment of a sea link with India, Indonesia, China and Japan, completely transformed economic life in Western Europe. This was the commercial revolution, the creation of a world commodity market, the most important change in the history of mankind since the metallurgical revolution.

The precious metals, whose cost of production had been stable for a thousand years, were suddenly shrunk in value by important technical revolutions (separation of silver from copper by means of lead; use of draining machinery; digging of improved shafts; use of the stamping-mill, etc.).[53] There ensued an important price revolution, the same quantity of silver being now the equivalent only of a smaller quantity of goods. From the countries where these methods of exploitation were first applied[54]—Bohemia, Saxony and Tyrol in the fifteenth century—this price revolution spread rapidly into Spain in the sixteenth century. The plundering of the treasures of Cuzco and the opening of the silver mines of Potosi reduced still further the cost of production of the precious metals, by the use of slave labour. Subsequently, the increase in prices spread all across Europe, where the new mass of precious metals found its way.

The ruination of the nobility and of the wage-earning classes was thus hastened. For the first time in human history, landed property lost the economic predominance it had possessed from the dawn of civilisation. The fall in real wages—particularly marked by the substitution of cheap potatoes for bread as the basic food of the people—became one of the main sources of the primitive accumulation of industrial capital between the sixteenth and eighteenth centuries.

"In England and France the vast discrepancy between prices and wages, born of the price revolution, deprived labourers of a large part of the incomes they had hitherto enjoyed, and diverted this wealth to the recipients of other distributive shares. As has been shown, rents, as well as wages, lagged behind prices; so landlords gained nothing from labour's loss." Labour's loss thus benefited the capitalist entrepreneurs only. Between 1500 and 1602 in England, the index of wages rose from 95 to 124 whereas the index of prices rose from 95 to 243![55]

As a result of Spain's adverse balance of trade, and of the stagnation and decline of its crafts, the bulk of these treasures of gold and silver which had been plundered or acquired by the enslavement of Indians and Negroes, ended up in the hands of the bourgeoisie of Western Europe, of Germany, France, the Netherlands and Great Britain. The supply of materials of war for the numerous dynastic conflicts which tore Europe apart during these three centuries was another important lever for the accumulation of commercial capital. The brothers Pâris, the biggest French capitalists of the eighteenth century, owed their wealth to war contracts. The appearance of the public debt,* of loans in the form of state bonds negotiable on the stock exchanges—first, those of Lyons and Antwerp, then that of Amsterdam, which remained predominant over a long period—constituted another lever of this primitive accumulation of capital, provided by the pillage of America and India.†

Like the primitive accumulation of merchant capital, the primitive accumulation of commercial capital took place first and foremost by way of brigandage and piracy. Scott[57] notes that about 1550 there was

---

* The British national debt rose from £16 million in 1701 to £146 million in 1760 and £580 million in 1801. The public debt of the Netherlands increased from 153 million florins in 1650 to 1,272 million in 1810.

† "The fairs which played so big a part when large-scale trade was still merely periodic in character, gradually lose their old importance, in proportion as static, urban trade develops. From the sixteenth century onward we see the establishment of the world stock exchanges . . . which will more and more completely replace them. In the fairs, financial transactions occurred only on the occasion and as a result of commercial transactions. On the stock exchanges commodities are no longer dealt with in kind, business being carried on only in the values which represent them."[56]

a marked shortage of capital in England. Within a few years, the pirate expeditions against the Spanish fleet, all of which were organised in the form of joint stock companies, changed the situation. Drake's first pirate undertaking, in the years 1577–1580, was launched with a capital of £5,000, to which Queen Elizabeth contributed. It brought in about £600,000 profit, half of which went to the Queen. Beard estimates that the pirates introduced some £12 million into England during the reign of Elizabeth. The frightful barbarism of the Spanish *conquistadores* in the Americas is notorious. In a period of fifty years they exterminated 15 million Indians, if we are to believe Bartholomé de las Casas, or 12 million according to more "conservative" critics. Densely populated regions like Haiti, Cuba, Nicaragua, the coast of Venezuela, were completely depopulated.[58] The primitive accumulation of Portuguese commercial capital in India was marked by "civilising" activities of the same sort:

"Vasco da Gama's second voyage (1502–1503), at the head of a veritable war fleet of 21 vessels, resulted in the replacement of the Egyptian-Venetian monopoly (of the spice trade) by a new monopoly. This was not established without bloody incidents. It was a kind of crusade [!] by merchants of pepper, cloves and cinnamon. It was punctuated by horrible atrocities; everything seemed permissible against the hated Moslems whom the Portuguese was surprised to meet again at the other end of the world, after having driven them out of the Algarve and fought them in Barbary. Arson and massacre, destruction of rich cities, ships burnt with their crews in them, prisoners slaughtered and their hands, noses and ears sent in mockery to the 'barbarian' kings, these were the exploits of the Knight of Christ; he left alive, after mutilating him in this way, only one Brahmin, who was given the task of conveying these horrid trophies to the local rulers."[59]

Hauser mentions in this passage that the new commercial expansion remained based on monopoly. It is therefore not to be wondered at that the Dutch merchants, whose profits depended on their monopoly of spices obtained through conquests in the Indonesian archipelago, went over to mass destruction of cinnamon trees in the small Islands of the Moluccas as soon as prices began to fall in Europe. The "Hongi voyages" to destroy these trees and massacre the population which for centuries had drawn their livelihood from growing them, set a sinister mark on the history of Dutch colonisation, which had, indeed, began in the same style, Admiral J. P. Coen not shrinking from the extermination of all the male inhabitants of the Banda Islands.[60]

The source of the surplus value obtained by pre-capitalist commercial capital is thus identical with the source of surplus value accumulated by usurer's capital and merchant capital. A remarkable illustration of this is to be found in the following table of the purchase prices and selling prices of the French East India Company in 1691:

	Purchase price £	Selling price £
White cotton cloth and muslin	327,000	1,267,000
Silks	32,000	97,000
Pepper (100,000 lb.)	27,000	101,000
Raw silk	58,000	111,000
Saltpetre	3,000	45,000
Cotton thread	9,000	28,000
Total, including some smaller items	487,000	1,700,000

Or a rate of profit of nearly 250 per cent, and this in "ordinary" trade! [61]

One of the pioneers of Dutch large-scale trade, Willem Wisselinx, wrote plainly enough in a pamphlet published at the beginning of the seventeenth century:

"The trade on the Guinea coast was, indeed, profitable to the country in two ways: first, commodities of great value were obtained there from people who as yet were ignorant of their true value [!]; secondly, these commodities were obtained in exchange for European goods of much smaller value."[62]

While the commercial revolution brought about a general increase in the price of goods, it nevertheless also caused a relative reduction in the prices of the luxury products of the East. Alongside a larger supply, an extension of the market and of needs thus occurred. What had originally been the privilege of a few noble families now entered into the ordinary consumption of all the possessing classes (sugar, tea, spices, tobacco, etc.). Trade in colonial products increased substantially and was soon monopolised by a few joint-stock companies: the *Oost-Indische Companie* in the Netherlands, the *East India Company* and the *Hudson Bay Company* in Great Britain, the *Compagnie des Indes Orientales* in France.

As in the dark centuries of the Middle Ages and at the dawn of trade in Antiquity, these companies combined the spice trade with the slave trade. Enormous profits were realised in this way. Between 1636 and 1645 the Dutch West India Company sold 23,000 Negroes for 6·7 million florins in all, or about 300 florins a head, whereas the goods given in exchange for each slave were worth no more than 50 florins. Between 1728 and 1760 ships sailing from Le Havre transported to the Antilles 203,000 slaves bought in Senegal, on the Gold Coast, at Loango, etc. The sale of these slaves brought in 203 million *livres*.[63] From 1783 to 1793 the slavers of Liverpool sold 300,000 slaves for

£15 million, a substantial slice of which went into the foundation of industrial enterprises.[64]

All the well-to-do classes of the population sought to share in the rain of gold from the plundering of the colonies. Kings, dukes, princes, judges and notaries tried to invest their money with the big traders so as to get regular interest, or bought shares or holdings in the colonial companies. Hochstätter, the Nuremburg banker, Fugger's great rival, must have received such investments to the value of more than £100 millon in the sixteenth century.[65] The New Royal African Company, which was engaged down to 1698 in the slave traffic, had partners so distinguished as the Duke of York and the Earl of Shaftesbury, as well as the latter's illustrious friend, the philosopher John Locke.[66]

The rise in prices impoverished those people who were living on fixed incomes. The public debt,* speculation and wholesale trade concentrated capital in the hands of the bourgeoisie. Basically, international trade remained luxury trade.[68] However, government orders and the growing needs of the well-to-do classes stimulated the production of non-agricultural commodities. Alongside trade in colonial products and precious metals, trade in craft and manufactured products became more extensive than in the Middle Ages. The English clothing industry, the Lyons silk industry, the metallurgical industry of Solingen, the textile industries of Leyden, Brittany and Westphalia, were already working for international markets, including those of the overseas colonies, and going beyond the stage of luxury manufacture. This extension of the market hastened the accumulation of capital by big merchants and created one of the conditions for the flowering of capitalist industry.

Domestic industry

In spite of the extension of large-scale international trade from the eleventh century onwards in Western Europe, the mode of production in the towns remained basically petty commodity production. Master craftsmen, working with a few journeymen, produced a quantity of certain products in a certain labour-time, and sold them directly to the public at prices fixed in advance. The census of a district of the city of Ypres, in Flanders, in 1431, revealed 704 people working at 161 different trades. In the enterprises of 155 different occupations there were only 17 hired journeymen. Altogether, more than half

---

* "We see appearing in France from the seventeenth century onward the tax-farmers who, in exchange for advances to the royal treasury, are given the right to collect a given tax . . . The profits they realise at the expense of the treasury are enormous . . . If Boulainvilliers is to be believed, between 1689 and 1708, out of an amount collected of one milliard *livres*, 266 millions remained in their hands."[67]

of the persons covered by the census were independent entrepreneurs.[69] The differences of social condition between master craftsmen and journeyman were limited; every journeyman, at the termination of his apprenticeship, had the chance to rise to the dignity of master.

This mode of production encountered, however, a number of contradictions. In the first place, contradictions inherent in the system itself; the progressive increase in the town population and in the number of craftsmen was not balanced by an extension of the market. It led to increasing competition between one town and another, to an accentuation of the protectionist tendencies of each town and to the development of protectionist tendencies in the craft corporations themselves, which endeavoured to close their doors against new mastercraftsmen. Apprentices had harder and harder conditions imposed on them as they strove to rise to the status of master. In fact, this rise soon became impossible. According to Hauser, this was the situation in France from 1580 onward.[70] Kulischer quotes numerous openly monopolistic declarations by craft corporations, from the fourteenth and fifteenth centuries.[71]

On the other hand, the craftsmen of Flanders and Italy who had begun by the twelfth century to work for markets wider than the mere urban market, ended by losing control of the products of their labour.[72] In order to carry his own products to a distant fair, a weaver or a brazier had to stop producing and could not start again until he returned. Inevitably, some of them, notably the richer ones who could provide themselves with a substitute at home, soon specialised in trade. At first they conveyed to the market their neighbours' products along with their own, simply as a favour. They ended by buying up directly the products of a large number of master craftsmen and undertaking the whole charge of selling them in distant parts. This system does not necessarily imply subordination of the craftsman to the merchant. But it promotes it, especially in the textile branch, in which numerous craft-guilds carry out one after the other a series of jobs on the same product, and thus find themselves at the end confronted by a single purchaser.[73] It was the same with the making of leather saddles in London, where the "saddlers" subordinated the secondary trades from the fourteenth and fifteenth centuries.[74]

This subordination was achieved by the thirteenth century in the Flemish clothing industry and in the Italian woollen and silk industries. The cloth merchant was still dealing with master-craftsmen, owners of their means of production. Wage-earners, in the strict sense, were an exception, elsewhere than in the Florentine woollen industry, where there were 20,000 day-workers by the middle of the fourteenth century.[75] But the master craftsmen had to buy their raw material from the cloth merchant, and were likewise obliged to sell him their finished products. "Having been able to sell at the highest prices, (the clothier) will insist on buying at the lowest prices."[76]* In his study of a great clothier of Douai at the end of the thirteenth century, Sire Jehan Boinebroke, Espinas notes that the clothiers were already tending to make the craftsmen lodge in houses belonging to themselves, and even beginning to buy means of production. The inevitable indebtedness of the craftsmen to the merchants provided a natural path to this subordination.†

The craftsmen did not accept without resistance a subordination like this, whether partial or complete. In the thirteenth and fourteenth centuries the Flemish and Italian communes were torn by violent class struggles which often ended with the victory of the craftsmen. But this could only intensify the decadence of urban petty commodity production, which had come to a blind alley. It often hastened this decline by protectionist measures. In order to escape from the strict regulations of the town guilds and the high wages of the craftsmen, the merchants began to put work out to craftsmen working at home in the country, who received raw material and means of production from the merchant entrepreneurs, and worked, no longer only *de facto* but also *de jure*, for a mere wage.

From the fifteenth century onward, this domestic industry spread to the countryside in Belgium, in Italy, in France and in Great Britain. The big merchants of Antwerp financed the "new draperies" of French Flanders and the carpet-making of Oudenarde and Brussels.[79] But progress remained slow. In the sixteenth century every English clothier still had to undergo a seven years' apprenticeship.[80] In the seventeenth century, in the Lyons silk industry, the merchant masters had no trades of their own, though they possessed the capital, supplied silk and patterns to the master-workers, and collected the finished product from them.[81]

In the mining industry, however, where large-scale costs of installation were inescapable, the commercial bourgeoisie succeeded more quickly in taking possession of the means of production.[82] At Liège, the chief coal-producing centre of the Continent, the independent associations of miners had almost completely disappeared by 1520, and been replaced by small capitalist enterprise, mostly belonging to merchants of the town. Most of the mining enterprises were transformed into joint-stock companies, the shares in which were bought by members of the well-to-do classes. The most important were taken over as

* The law, wherever it favoured the merchants, expressly granted them a selling monopoly. It was exceptional that in Venice a law of 1442 authorised weavers who had no apprentices or journeymen—and only these—to sell their products on the market.[77]

† It was inevitable only in so far as these clothiers, splendid embodiments of the capitalist spirit of money-making, squeezed and robbed the wretched producers in every imaginable way. Espinas paints a striking picture of this behaviour on the part of Jehan Boinebroke.[78]

concessions by rich commercial or banking families like the Fuggers.

The *Saigerhütten*, works where silver was separated from copper, in Saxony, Thuringia, Tyrol and Carinthia, were, through the cost of the installations and the concentration of wage-earning labour, the most important industrial enterprises of the sixteenth century. With them we have already passed from the realm of domestic industry to that of modern manufacture.[83] In the following century the richest Dutch merchants acquired immense fortunes by securing the monopoly of exploitation of the Emperor's mercury mines (the Deutz family) and the iron and copper mines in Sweden, combined with the manufacture of arms and munitions (the De Geer and Tripp families).[84]

It is interesting to note that this separation of the producers from their means of production by the merchant middlemen took place in a very similar way in other societies besides those of Western Europe. Bruno Lasker, basing himself on original fieldwork by Pieter H. W. Sitsen, describes the system operating in the countryside of Java:

"In the Central lands of East Java, the quasi-independent home workers always had credit accounts in the finishing business and could draw against it in an emergency . . . The *Bakul*, or middleman . . . was the real financier and manager of the cottage industry . . . Through their debts to him, which he encourages in every possible way . . . he keeps the nominally independent producers so dependent on him that he can take the better part of their earnings. For example, in the furniture industry of the region, more than half of the gross return went to the *bakuls* when Dr. Sitsen made his study in 1936."[85]

Raymond Firth discovered an identical system in Malaya, where "in Trengganu the system of borrowing cash or equipment has often crystallised into a financial relationship between fishermen and fish-buyers, especially those who cure for export."[86]

S. F. Nadel found a similar system in the domestic industry making glass beads at Bida, in Nigeria. In India the *mahajans* advance the raw material and the other products needed for domestic industry. The textile industry of Soochow, in China, seems to have been organised in the same way in the sixteenth and seventeenth centuries, according to the chronicles of the Ming dynasty.[87]

Domestic industry is the logical culmination of the subordination of petty commodity production to money capital, in a money economy in which production for distant markets has destroyed all possibility of giving a stable foundation to the existence of the small producer.

Manufacturing capital

Domestic industry separates the small commodity producer first from control of his product and then from his means of production. But production increases only slowly, parallel to the slow extension

of the market. The commercial bourgeoisie, like the merchant bourgeoisie before it, invests only a part of its capital and profits in domestic
industry. The greater part is devoted to trade itself, to speculation, to
the acquisition of landed property. The Fuggers, who began as mere
weavers in Augsburg, made their fortune in the international trade in
spices and fabrics, in which they continued after they had acquired
the concessions for Central Europe's silver mines and had built the
most important manufactories of their day. They ended by dedicating
themselves essentially to credit operations for the house of Habsburg,
which brought them to bankruptcy.

By the amount of labour it employed, domestic industry remained
the chief form of non-agricultural production between the sixteenth
and eighteenth centuries in Western Europe. Alongside it developed
another system of production which constituted a sort of bridge to the
modern big factory: the system of *manufacture*.

Manufacture means the assembling under one roof of workers who
work with means of production which are provided for them and with
raw material which is advanced to them. But instead of their being
paid for the total value of the finished product, after deduction of the
value of the raw material advanced and the cost of hiring the tools of
labour, as with domestic industry, the fiction of the selling of the
finished product to the entrepreneur is given up. The worker receives
no more than what he was already earning *de facto* under the system
of domestic industry: a mere wage.

This evolution can be followed step by step in the history of the
cloth industry of Leyden, which has been analysed in masterly fashion
by Posthumus. This industry was first organised on a craft basis. From
the end of the sixteenth century it spread to the countryside and the
merchants got the upper hand of the clothiers. The latter began to lose
ownership, first of the raw material and the finished product, then of
the means of production. Towards 1640 a fresh set of middlemen, the
reeders, inserted themselves between the merchants and the clothiers.
The stage of manufacture was reached, and around 1652 there is even
talk of "manufacturers"! [88]

The new system presented two advantages for the suppliers of
capital. On the one hand, they could do away with the overhead
charges arising from the need to maintain a large number of middlemen to collect the finished products, distribute the raw material, etc.
On the other, they could put a stop to the considerable embezzlement
of raw material which inevitably occurred in domestic industry, as a
means whereby the workers made up for inadequate wages. In manufactories the concentration of labour-power and its subjection to direct
and continuous supervision by capital has already reached an advanced
stage.

Manufacture also constitutes a considerable advance from the standpoint of the productivity of labour. In petty commodity production there is only a *social* division of labour between different crafts; *within* each craft, that is, during the process of production, division of labour hardly exists. Even when each craft is not completing a finished product, intended for direct consumption, as in the clothing or woollen industries, each craft does carry out one complete process of production: weaving, fulling, dyeing, etc.

Thanks to manufacture it becomes possible to *subdivide* each craft and each production process into an infinite number of labour operations, mechanised and simplified to the uttermost. This makes it possible at one and the same time to increase output, to increase the number of finished products completed in the same period of time, and to reduce the cost of production by substituting an unskilled labour-force of women, children, sick or old persons and even lunatics. This is the fact which appears as an entirely new social phenomenon, especially as regards the manufacture of textiles: the labour-force is largely composed of these wretched people. It is above all the low cost of such labour-power that makes it profitable to concentrate wage-earners in such numbers under one roof. One can compare the situation to some extent to the mines and large-scale state manufacturers in the ancient world, in China, India and elsewhere, in which slave or semi-slave labour predominates.

The utmost brutality, together with an amazing hypocrisy, were normally employed to compel these unfortunates to furnish a cheap supply of labour to young manufacturing capital.* In 1721 it was decided to set up a cloth manufactory in Graz "because hundreds of people are suffering from hunger and are idle". In order to provide the necessary labour-force, a suitable number of persons had to be "caught and locked up", from among the beggars who crowded the streets of the town. In Amsterdam, in 1695, on the proposal of the sheriffs, the municipal council considered "whether it was appropriate to seek a site for (the establishment) of a spinning mill where young girls could be employed so as to support themselves, along with other persons who were leading lives of idleness and beggary." As some merchants who wanted to set up woollen mills were offering favourable terms and as these worthy councillors considered that what was involved was a "very good and Christian work" [!], they authorised the Mayor to see to the putting of the scheme into effect.[90] Sombart[91] quotes numerous examples of the State's *compelling* the population to carry out veritable forced labour in manufactories,

---

* Already in the *arte di lana*, the Florentine woollen industry of the fourteenth century, where the wage-earner was tied to his employer by *debts*, a whole set of laws was introduced in order to compel him to do overtime. He was in particular forbidden by a law of 1371 to repay his debt in *money*; he had to do this in the form of *work*.[89]

notably in Spain, France, Holland, Germany, Switzerland, Austria, and, of course, England. In the countries where serfdom still existed, serfs were compelled to work in the manufactories, notably in Russia, in the copper manufactory in Tula.

The development of manufacture did not yet do away with manual labour as the preponderant means of production in industry: the greater part of the expenditure of manufacturing capital still went on wages. Nevertheless, manufacture developed most rapidly in the sectors in which costly apparatus had to be installed to an increasing extent. In the eighteenth century, in Rheims and Louviers, thousands of workers were already massed together in manufactories which had cost hundreds of thousands of *livres* to build.[92]

Leyden, which was the leading textile centre of Europe in the middle of the seventeenth century, saw its manufactories develop owing to the large-scale use of fulling-mills. The use of these mills was profitable, however, only on the basis of the employment of children or women as workers. For this reason, the entrepreneurs organised expeditions to places as far away as the Liège region to recruit labour.[93]

Creation of the modern proletariat

Alongside this broadening of the field of action of capital, which was steadily entering the sphere of production, from the sixteenth century onward a new social class came into existence, which had been present in the Middle Ages only in the form of a few uprooted "hire-lings" who wandered from town to town. This class originated from the cutting down of the retinues of the feudal lords, itself a result of the impoverishment of the latter by the price revolution. It originated also from the decay of the urban crafts since the merchant entre-preneurs had started to put out their orders to men working in the countryside. Its development was speeded up by deep-seated changes in the field where the great majority of the producers were still con-centrated: in agriculture.

In the mediaeval village the peasants' land was broken up into numerous plots. In order to work on these plots, the peasants had to have free access to the land separating them. This free access was linked with the right to gleaning and gathering straw, to free common pasture, the reservation of land for the benefit of new households, and compulsory rotation of crops, all of which were essential to the stability of a village economy based on the three-field system and marked with the imprint of the primitive village community.[94] At the same time, the common lands offered free amenities for pasturing cattle and collecting wood, both for fires and for building, etc.

From the fifteenth century onward, despite numerous governmental decrees and laws directed against this development, the landlords in England began to divide up the common lands and to rearrange the farmers' plots of land, so as to constitute farms for a single tenant. This movement was particularly encouraged by the rapid rise in the price of wool from the middle of the fifteenth century, which made sheep raising more profitable to the lords than cultivation of the soil.[95] But the practice of enclosure, of putting fences around fields, remained very sporadic until the eighteenth century.

It was then precipitated by a revolution in the agricultural mode of production itself: the abolition of fallow, transition from the three-field system to periodical cultivation of lucerne, turnips and fodder plants which restore the soil's productivity. This was a system of scientific agriculture, orginating in Flanders and Lombardy, which after several tentative attempts, now began to become general in England.[96] The agricultural surplus product increased markedly. The landlords, anxious to take this surplus for themselves, changed the system of tenancy, going over from long leases, which ensured a peasant family's tenancy for a century, to tenancies at will, or short leases, which implied a change of tenancy every nine years at most.[97]

From this resulted a large increase in ground rent, which hastened the expropriation of poor peasants and accompanied the enclosure movement, which was favoured also by the fact that with the ending of the three-field system the scattering of plots became burdensome to the cultivators. By about 1780 this movement had culminated in England in the quasi-liquidation of the class of independent peasants, who were replaced by big capitalist farmers working with wage labour. In France a similar movement for the break-up of the common lands occurred in the seventeenth and eighteenth centuries, but to a smaller extent,[98] until the French Revolution gave it a great impetus. Development followed similar lines to the French in Western Germany and Belgium.

The economic changes which, between the sixteenth and eighteenth centuries, created a mass of producers separated from their means of production in the towns, were thus accompanied by changes which in practice deprived part of the peasantry of land as a means of producing their means of life. In this way the *modern proletariat* appeared. This class was thus described, from the sixteenth century onward, by the entrepreneurs of Leyden:

"Poor and needy persons, many of whom have the charge and burden of wives and many children to support, and who have nothing but what they can get by the work of their hands."[99]

The ancestors of this proletariat were described already in 1247 as "those who earned money by the strength of their arms."[100] And in our own day, when the process of formation of the proletariat is being repeated among the backward peoples, they say in Malaya of a fisherman who has no net of his own (no means of production): "he has not a single thing; he only helps other people."[101] In other words, the separation of the producers from their means of production creates a class of proletarians who cannot live otherwise than by hiring out their strength, that is, by selling their labour-power, to the owners of capital, which enables the latter to secure for themselves the surplus-value produced by these producers.*

The Industrial Revolution

For capital to be able to penetrate into the sphere of industrial production, industry must be suddenly confronted with a market which is no longer stable but has expanded to the point where it seems ready to absorb a continuously increasing volume of products. The introduction of machinery into industry and transport, and the lowering of the cost of the products of large-scale factories resulting from this, have created such a market and signalised the definitive victory of the *capitalist mode of production*.

For thousands of years, the only two sources of power available for work were human power and the power of domestic animals. The ancient world was able to build the first machine which utilised another source of power: the water-mill. In the Roman mines, Archimedes' screw and Ctesibius's water-pump were used for draining purposes.[108] They were not widely employed, however, in agriculture. The Middle Ages inherited these machines, put them into general use from the tenth century onward, which resulted in a significant increase in the productivity of labour, and then received the windmill from the East.†

From the fifteenth century onward, a long series of small inventions and technical improvements increasingly transformed these machines, while still using water as the main source of power. Mills were built to make paper, to operate forge-hammers, to make silk, to pump out mines, to full cloth, to saw wood, etc.[104] Sombart lists about twenty different kinds of mills dating from that period.[105]

However, these technical improvements were only applied sporadically so long as economic and social conditions did not favour a large-scale flow of capital into industrial production. As mentioned above, it was above all in mining and metallurgy that progress was substantial, at the dawn of modern times. It was in the mines that the first kinds of railway were developed, to facilitate the carriage of coal.[106] The fifteenth century saw the building of the first blast furnace.[107] But the

---

* "The current analysis of the situation of the wage-earner points to its essential feature as being that labour is separated from and deprived of ownership of the means of production, and bases on this feature the difference between the wage-earner's situation and that of others."[102]

† In China, windmills were in use on a large scale in agriculture from the sixth century. As in Western Europe, they were the monopoly of rich landowners and of temples, and thus reinforced the exploitation of the peasants. In Europe windmills were the basis of the *banalités*, the additional burdens placed on the peasants which we also find in China.

development of these blast furnaces was hindered so long as the fuel they used was wood. In 1777 the use of the steam engine in the coal industry transformed the production process. It made possible a rapid increase in coal production and a reduction in prices which opened the way to the use of coke as fuel in blast furnaces. A few years later, about 1785, the making of iron by the puddling process again transformed the production process. The production of iron in England increased from 12,000 to 17,000 tons a year about 1750 to 68,000 in 1788, 244,000 tons in 1806 and 455,000 tons in 1823.[108]

The use of water power in the fulling mill and other mills, but still more and especially the invention of the mechanical loom, transformed the textile industry. At the same time, the expansion of Liverpool's maritime trade opened up to Lancashire overseas markets which seemed limitless. With the aid of new machines, the textile manufacturers produced their cottons at prices much lower than those of the craftsman and the domestic worker, and set out to conquer this immense market. Capital broke down first of all the internal customs barriers inherited from the feudal past: in 1776 by the formation of the United States, in 1795 in France, in 1800 in the United Kingdom, in 1816 in Prussia, in 1824 in Sweden and Norway, in 1834 by the creation of the Zollverein in Germany, in 1835 in Switzerland, in the 1850s in Russia and Austria-Hungary. Next, the world market was attacked. British exports of cotton grew from £5,915 in 1679 and £45,000 in 1751, to £200,354 in 1764, £19 million in 1830, £30 million in 1850, and £73 million in 1871.[109]

The iron and coal industries found enormous new outlets in the making and fuelling of steam engines. From 1825 onward, the building of railways made general this triumphal march of machine production and of the capitalist mode of production. By closely linking town and country they facilitated the penetration of commodities produced at low prices by big factories into the remotest corners of all countries. At the same time the building of railway lines constituted, for over half a century, the chief market for the products of heavy industry (coal, steel, metal products, etc.), first in Great Britain, then on the Continent, later in America and throughout the world.

Special features of capitalist development in Western Europe

Under petty commodity production the producer, master of his means of production and his products, can live only by selling these products in order to acquire the means of life. Under capitalist production, the producer separated from his means of production is no longer master of the products of his labour and can live only by selling, that is, by making a commodity of, his own labour-power, in exchange for a wage which enables him to acquire these means of life. The transition from petty commodity production to capitalist production properly so called is thus marked by two parallel phenomena: on the one hand, the *transformation of labour-power into a commodity*, and on the other, the *transformation of the means of production into capital*.* These two concomitant phenomena had never occurred on a large scale before they appeared, from the sixteenth century onward, and above all from the eighteenth century onward, in Western Europe, mainly in Great Britain.

Capital itself, in its primitive forms of usurer's capital and merchant capital, was, however, not at all a special feature of Western civilisation. Many civilisations which saw an advanced stage of petty commodity production saw with it a substantial flowering of capital: the ancient world, Byzantine society, the Mogul empire in India, the Islamic empire, China and Japan, to mention only the most important. The quantitative expansion of capital in these societies was in no way inferior to what occurred in mediaeval Europe.

In the middle of the fourteenth century King Edward III of England received 1,365,000 florins from the Florentine companies of the Bardi and the Peruzzi.[111] These were the richest bourgeois families of the West before the Fuggers. About the same period, a group of Karimi (Yemenite) merchants, who monopolised the spice trade with India in the Egypt of the Mamelukes, advanced 700,000 silver *dirhems* to some notables of Damascus, and then 400,000 gold *dinars* to the King of Yemen (coins which contained more pure metal than the European coins of the time).[112] In the ninth and tenth centuries, at the zenith of the Islamic empire, we find a number of merchants of Basra who have an *annual income* of over a million *dirhems*. A Baghdad jeweller, Ibn-al-Jassas, was still a rich man after 16,000 gold *dinars* of his had been confiscated.[113] In 144 B.C. the imperial prince Hsio, of Liang, died in China leaving 400,000 *catties* of gold (one *cattie* is about 600 grammes).[114] Why did this accumulation of usurer's and merchant capital not give birth to industrial capital in these various civilisations?

It was not that the forms of organisation lying between crafts in the strict sense and large-scale factories—the *Verlagssystem* of merchants putting out work to craftsmen, domestic industry, and manufacture—were unknown to these pre-capitalist civilisations. In Byzantium, real textile manufactories appeared, from the time of the Emperor Justinian, based, to be sure, on crafts and with a labour-force which, though concentrated in large establishments, remained in possession of its means of production.[115] But, already about the tenth century,

---

* This does not seem to be understood by Professor Sol Tax, who calls his work on the Guatemalan community of Panajachel *Penny Capitalism*. He examines the reasons for this definition, and discovers them above all in the "mental habit" of the natives of Panajachel to seek "maximum returns". In reality we have here a typical society where petty commodity production prevails, where neither the land nor labour-power have in practice become commodities.[116]

"the merchants of raw silk and the clothiers had a strong predominance over the other guilds, and some members of these two guilds were trying to rise above their colleagues and to become capitalist entrepreneurs. The guild of the dealers in raw silk . . . had brought under their control not only the impoverished silk spinners (*Katartarioi*) . . . but the whole guild of the *katartarioi*. As a matter of fact, a silk spinner could not sell the processed silk directly to the clothiers; he had to hand it over to a dealer in raw silk. Nor could he buy raw silk from the importers without the permission of the dealers . . . [and] he could buy only the quantity he could process in his own workshop . . . It is true that theoretically the dealers were forbidden to take over directly the spinning, or to do anything but buying and selling the raw material. But this prohibition . . . was practically nullified by the fact that a merchant of raw silk could hire workers, paying them in advance. It is hardly believable that these workers were employed just to assist him in buying and selling! "[116]

A no less impressive development of domestic industry and manufacture occurred in the Islamic empire. Over 1,000 workers are said to have been concentrated in the mercury mines of Moslem Spain. In Tinnis, the famous cloth-weaving town, domestic industry was in full operation from A.D. 815. The cloth merchants gave work to men and women for wages of half a dirhem a day.[117] China similarly had great mining and metal-working manufactories which employed slave labour, several centuries before our era. Rich entrepreneurs arose, especially in iron and copper working and in the exploitation of mercury and cinnabar.[118] Later, manufactories of porcelain and domestic textile work saw a great expansion, especially from the time of the Ming dynasty onward.[119] It was the same in India for a thousand years. Yet, nevertheless, the coexistence of these types of modern enterprise with a big accumulation of money capital did not result in the development of industrial capitalism.

Petty commodity production is already the production of commodities. But it is usually a production of commodities in the midst of production of use values. So long as the overwhelming majority of the population participates little or not at all in this commodity production, the latter inevitably remains restricted. Large-scale trade basically remains luxury trade. Faced with the narrow limits of this market, capital finds outlets more profitable than investment in production. This is what explains the fact that the manufactories and domestic industries of Byzantium, the Islamic world, China and India embraced almost exclusively luxury branches, unless they worked for State orders.

It was the penetration of money economy into the peasant economy, as a result of the changing of the agricultural surplus product from rent in kind, or labour services, to money rent that made possible a considerable expansion of commodity production in Western Europe, and so created the conditions for the flowering of industrial capitalism. Nowhere outside Western Europe did the agricultural surplus assume lastingly the form of money rent. Taxation in kind predominated in the Roman Empire and in Byzantium.[120] In the Islamic empire the land tax was paid partly in kind and partly in money, under the Abbasids, but soon afterwards rent in kind became preponderant again, and remained so in the Turkish period.[121] In India, land rent was generally paid in kind, except during a brief period of prosperity under the Moguls in the seventeenth century. In China, rent-tax in money, briefly general under the Mings towards the end of the fifteenth century, resumed the form of rent-tax in kind after the fall of this dynasty, to reappear definitely as tax-rent in money only in the seventeenth and eighteenth centuries in South China.[122]

Machine production, which alone enables the big factory to overcome the competition of domestic industry and the crafts, is the product of the application of natural science to production that, in turn, demands a ceaseless striving to economise human labour. The predominance of slave labour and the presence of an enormous mass of unproductive poor in the Roman Empire prevented any endeavour in this direction.* The significant comment of the Emperor Vespasian will be remembered, when he refused to allow the use of a mechanical crane: "I must feed my poor."[123]

As for the Islamic world, India, China and Japan, these were essentially agricultural civilisations, in which irrigation made possible the development of an extremely intensive agriculture which in turn led to a considerable growth of population. The competition of very cheap labour was to prevent for thousands of years any attempt to introduce machinery into the crafts. At the same time, the productive use of hydraulic power for non-agricultural purposes, the basis of the slow advance of machine production in Europe from the thirteenth to the eighteenth centuries, was much restricted in these agricultural civilisations because it came into conflict with the requirements of irrigation of the soil.†

* To this must be added the widespread contempt for manual labour, engendered by slavery and formulated in striking fashion by Xenophon in his *Economics*: "The arts which men call vulgar are generally held in low esteem and disdained by the state, and this for good reason. They utterly spoil the bodies both of the workers and their supervisors . . . And when men's bodies are exhausted, their souls become sick. *Further, these arts imply a total lack of leisure, and prevent men from leading a social and civic life.*"
This last observation is most pertinent.

† These installations (water mills and automatic milling), which were a source of very big incomes for great lay families and for important monasteries, became numerous in the T'ang epoch [*i.e. four or five centuries sooner than in Europe!*], at the time when large landed property was also developing. The imperial administration had to fight against this new abuse, because the

The accumulation of money capital, usurer's capital, merchant capital and commercial capital took place in Western Europe between the tenth and eighteenth centuries, in the hands of a bourgeois class which progressively freed itself from the control of the feudal classes and the state, and ended by subjecting the state to itself and using it to accelerate the accumulation of capital for its own advantage. The formation of the bourgeoisie as a class, with a clear consciousness of its interests, took place in the free communes of the Middle Ages, where the bourgeoisie underwent its apprenticeship to political struggle. The establishment of centralised modern states from the fifteenth century onward did not result from a crushing of the urban bourgeoisie but from a new ascent of this class, which broke through the narrow confines of commune politics to confront, as the Third Estate, the old ruling classes on the national level (Russia, Spain, and to some extent the Austria of the Habsburgs, were in this respect interesting exceptions, something that had significant consequences for the later history of capitalism in these countries).

In the other pre-capitalist civilisations, however, capital remained unchangingly under the arbitrary power of the despotic and all-powerful state. In Rome it was the landed nobility that, thanks to the booty obtained in its plundering wars, ended by entirely subjecting the free capital of the ancient world.[125] In ancient India, the state monopolies made the king himself the chief banker, manufacturer and wholesale trader. Rostovtsev notes that the imperial treasury was the chief usurer in Rome.[126] The predominance of state manufactories in Byzantium, where the imperial treasure concentrated in its coffers the greater part of the available capital, is as well known as the pitiless taxation that crushed craft and industrial production in the Islamic world.[127] In China, under each successive dynasty, the state strove to monopolise whole sectors of industry.[128]

The nascent bourgeoisie underwent a strange life-cycle in all these societies. Each new fabulous accumulation of profits was followed by brutal confiscations and persecutions. Bernard Lewis notes that even the Islamic cities of the Middle Ages knew only an ephemeral existence, with a prosperity which lasted no more than a century and was followed by a long and pitiless decay.[129] The fear of confiscation of their capital haunts the owners of movable property in all these societies. It causes the bourgeois to conceal their profits, to invest them in ten small enterprises rather than one big one, to prefer the hoarding of gold and precious stones to public enterprises, and the purchase

paddle-wheels obstructed the flow of the rivers and caused some of the irrigation water to be lost. Moreover, they caused the depositing of mud in the canals. Accordingly, special laws restricted the use of mills to certain seasons of the year." The author quotes decrees and texts from the eighth century relating to the restriction and destruction of mills.[124]

of landed property to the accumulation of capital. Instead of concentrating, a bourgeoisie like this disperses itself as it disperses its capital.
Instead of advancing towards autonomy and independence, it crouches
in fear and servility.[130] "Never," says Istvan Balazs, "did the Chinese
merchant class attain autonomy . . . the privileges of the big traders
were never won in struggle, but were stingily granted by the state. The
way of expressing their demands continues, for the merchant and the
rest of the *misera plebs*, to be the petition, the timid request humbly
submitted to the authorities."[131]*

Only in Japan, whose pirate merchants infested the China Sea and
the Philippines from the fourteenth century on, and accumulated
substantial capital while the state's authority was breaking down, did
the supremacy of the commercial and banking bourgeoisie over the
nobility, and then the development of manufacturing capital, make
it possible to repeat, starting in the eighteenth century, two centuries
late, the evolution of capitalism in Western Europe, independently of
the latter.†

The predominance of the absolute state in the non-European pre-
capitalist civilisations was itself no result of chance. It followed from
the conditions of irrigation agriculture, which necessitated a strict
administration and centralisation of the social surplus. Paradoxically,
it was the superior fertility of their soil and the greater growth of their
population that doomed these civilisations to stop midway in their
development. The much more primitive agriculture of mediaeval
Europe could not carry the weight of a density of population comparable to that of China or the Nile valley in prosperous periods. But
just for this reason it largely escaped the control of a centralising
state.‡

In the mediaeval towns the bourgeoisie was favoured by a weakened

---

* The idea that in China, as against mediaeval Europe, the towns were
subjected to the close supervision of the mandarins, whereas the villages
enjoyed extensive administrative autonomy, was, says Balazs "brilliantly
anticipated" by Max Weber. The author seems unaware that Marx expressed
the same view three quarters of a century earlier, and that he also clearly
defined the difference between Western and Oriental towns.[132]

† Even in Japan, however, the merchant Yodoya Tatsugoro, who had made
an immense fortune during the Kwambuu era (1661–1672), had all his property
confiscated "because he led too ostentatious a life."[133]

‡ It is interesting to note that in Black Africa the comparative abundance of
land, which made possible an infinite spread of primitive agriculture, proved
to be a barrier to the flowering of a black civilisation, except in the valleys of
the Senegal, Niger and Zambesi.[134] It would seem that the relationship between
land, water and population made possible the optimum combination *for
agriculture* in the ancient Asian civilisations, and the optimum *economic*
combination in Western Europe, starting in the sixteenth century. In this field
too there is a striking parallel between the particular conditions in which
agriculture developed in Japan (in contrast to the continent of Asia) and in
Western Europe.[135]

central power which had to lean upon its support in order to recover the prerogatives it had lost at the dawn of feudalism. At first, the advance of this bourgeoisie was slow and interrupted. Many a Western financier ended up like his Islamic, Chinese or Indian colleague, by having his fortune confiscated by the kings he helped. But from the fifteenth century this interruption became the exception instead of the rule. The superiority of movable wealth over landed property was finally established, and with it the subjection of the state to the golden chains of the public debt. The road was clear for an accumulation of capital without political obstacles. Modern capitalism could be born.

These special features of the economic development of Western Europe (and to a certain extent of Japan) do not mean that the flowering of the industrial revolution was not *possible* in other regions: they merely explain why the capitalist mode of production appeared *first* in Europe. Thereafter it was the violent intervention of Europe in the economies of other parts of the world that smashed the elements that would have made possible more rapid economic progress there, so preventing or holding back their advance. The contrast between Japan on the one hand and India and China on the other shows the decisive role played in the nineteenth century by the maintenance or loss of real political independence, for the acceleration or retardation of the industrial revolution.*

Capital and the capitalist mode of production

Capital can appear as soon as there is a minimum of commodity circulation and of money circulation. It is born and develops within the framework of a pre-capitalist mode of production (village community, petty commodity production). Whatever dissolving effects it has on such a society, these are limited by the fact that it does not change the basic mode of production, especially in the countryside. Loaded with debts, harried by his creditors or by tax-collectors, the pre-capitalist peasant always finds in the solidarity of other villagers a support which guarantees him at least a meagre pittance:

"The Ifugaos [natives of the Philippines] are partial capitalists. Their wealth is rice land. It is prepared with a enormous labour, limited in quantity, and belongs to a class of rich men . . . Through a system of usury, the rich become richer and the poor poorer. Still, the poor are not entirely destitute. Yam gardens are by definition not 'wealth', and cannot be permanently owned. Anyone may plant as much as he wishes, and manage to live after a fashion . . ."[136]

The development of the capitalist mode of production implies the generalisation of commodity production for the first time in mankind's history. This production no longer embraces merely luxury

* See Chapter 13 for numerous examples of economic regression caused by imperialism.

products, the surplus of foodstuffs or other goods of current consumption, metals, salt and other products indispensable for maintaining
and extending the social surplus product. Everything that is the object
of economic life, everything that is produced is henceforth a commodity: all foodstuffs, all consumer goods, all raw materials, all
means of production, including labour-power itself. Every outlet being
closed, the mass of dispossessed people who no longer have their own
tools are compelled to sell their labour-power in order to acquire the
means of life. The entire organisation of society is fashioned so as to
ensure to the owners of capital a regular and constant supply of wage
labour, so as to facilitate the uninterrupted productive use of their
capital.

During the process of its formation, industrial capital obtained, by
the methods described above, the parallel formation of the modern
proletariat. But when the capitalist mode of production had spread
throughout the world, it experienced a need for wage labour before
the primitive societies which it encountered were sufficiently disintegrated for this proletariat to be formed in the normal way. The intervention of state, law, religion and morality—if not of force pure and
simple—made it possible to recruit the unhappy slaves of the new
Moloch. The colonisers of Black Africa and Oceania repeated at the
end of the nineteenth century the procedures whereby their slave-
trading ancestors had assembled a mass of slave labour. This time,
however, it was no longer a matter of sending this labour over the
ocean to the plantations of the New World. It was on the spot, in
capitalist agricultural, mining or industrial enterprises that this labour
was employed to produce the surplus value indispensable to the life
of Capital.*

The disintegrating action of money economy on primitive communities has in all civilisations favoured the primitive accumulation
of usurer's capital and merchant capital. But it does not ensure by itself
the development of the capitalist mode of production, of industrial
capital.

However, the disintegrating action of money economy on primitive
communities already confronted with the capitalist mode of production becomes the chief force for the recruitment of a native proletariat
in the colonies. The introduction of an individual poll tax in money in
primitive areas which are still living in conditions of natural economy
has uprooted, in Africa and elsewhere, millions of natives from their
customary centres and has forced them to sell their labour-power, their
only resource, to get money. Where people do not find it necessary to
sell their labour-power in order to obtain the means of life, the capitalist state has resorted to this modern form of compulsion in order to

* See Chapter 9, section: "Landed property and the capitalist mode of
production."

supply proletarians to the bourgeoisies who are coming into existence in the colonies. For capitalism and the bourgeoisie are inconceivable without a proletariat. According to Alexander Hamilton, freedom is freedom to acquire wealth.[137] *But this freedom cannot be affirmed for one small part of society unless it be denied for the rest, even though this be the majority.*

REFERENCES

1. *Mong Dsi* (Mong Ko translated by Richard Wilhelm), pp. 51-52.

2. Boissonnade: *Le Travail dans l'Europe chrétienne du moyen âge*, pp. 99-107.

3. Theodore Morgan: *Hawaii, A Century of Economic Change*, p. 25.

4. International Labour Office: *Les Populations aborigènes*, p. 368.

5. Morgan: op. cit., p. 25.

6. Yoshitomi: *Etude sur l'histoire économique de l'ancien Japon*, pp. 139-40.

7. G. I. Bratianu: *Etudes byzantines d'histoire économique et sociale*, p. 133; A. Segré: *Essays in Byzantine Economic History*, p. 402.

8. F. Heichelheim: *Vormittelalterliche Geschichtsepochen*, pp. 163-4; J. C. Van Leur: *Eenige beschouwingen betreffende den Ouden Aziatischen Handel*, passim.

9. Gordon Childe: *What Happened in History*, p. 193.

10. E. Schreiber: *Die Volkswirtschaftlichen Anschauungen der Scholastik seit Thomas v. Aquino*, p. 23.

11. M. M. Postan: "Chronology of Labour Services", in *Transactions of the Royal Historical Society*, 4th Series, Vol. XX, 1937, pp. 192-3.

12. E. A. Kosminsky: "Services and Money Rents in the 13th Century", *Economic History Review*, Vol. V, 1934–5, No. 2, p. 43.

13. Günther Dessmann: *Geschichte der Schlesischen Agrarverfassung*, p. 58.

14. H. Pirenne: *Le mouvement économique et social au moyen âge*, p. 60.

15. Morgan: op. cit., p. 26.

16. Glotz: *Le Travail dans la Grèce antique*, p. 16.

17. P. K. Hitti: *History of the Arabs*, p. 626.

18. Ch. Diehl: *Les Figures byzantines*, Vol. I, pp. 147-8.

19. Takizawa: *The Penetration of Money Economy in Japan*, pp. 71-79; Hugh Barton: *Peasant Uprisings in Japan of the Tokugawa Period*, pp. 8-26.

20. *Handwörterbuch der Staatswissenschaften*, article by von Below on "Geschichte des Zinsfuss", Vol. VIII, p. 1017.

21. Jacques Gernet: *Les Aspects économiques du bouddhisme dans la société chinoise du Vᵉ au Xᵉ siecle*, p. 171.

22. H. Hauser: *Les Débuts du capitalisme*, p. 19.

23. *Mahabarata*, Vol. XII, pp. 62-69.

24. M. Rostovtzeff: *Social and Economic History of the Roman Empire*, p. 2.

25. R. S. Lopez: in *Cambridge Economic History of Europe*, Vol. II, p. 266.

26. J. Kulischer: *Allgemeine Wirtschaftsgeschichte*, Vol. I, p. 41.

27. F. Løkkegaard: *Islamic Taxation in the Classic Period*, pp. 66-68; Yoshitomi: op. cit., pp. 74-82, 131-5.

28. *Handwörterbuch der Staatswissenschaften*, art. cit.; Kulischer: op. cit., Vol. I, p. 336.

29. Paul Radin: *Social Anthropology*, p. 115; Gernet: op. cit., p. 131.

30. W. Sombart: *Der moderne Kapitalismus*, Vol. I, p. 116; Glotz: op. cit., pp. 63-67; A. Sapori: *Mercatores*, pp. 20-21; *Histoire du Commerce*, Vol. I, pp. 140-1 (Lacour-Gayet), etc.

31. Y. Takekoshi: *Economic Aspects of the History of the Civilisation of Japan*, Vol. I, p. 346.

32. Kulischer: op. cit., Vol. I, p. 275.

33. R. S. Lopez: op. cit., p. 306.

34. N. S. B. Gras: *Business and Capitalism*, p. 60.

35. J. Schumpeter: *Business Cycles*, Vol. I, p. 22.

36. K. Polanyi: et al., *Trade and Market in the Early Empires*, pp. 258-9, 269.

37. G. von Below: *Probleme der Wirtschaftsgeschichte*, pp. 307-8.

38. H. Pirenne: op. cit., p. 38.

39. Chan Ju-kua: *His Work on the Chinese and Arab Trade in the 12th and 13th Centuries*, pp. 191-239.

40. *Histoire du Commerce*: Vol. III, p. 397 (G. Boumarchand).

41. A. Andréadès: "The Economic Life of the Byzantine Empire", in *Byzantium*, p. 61.

42. R. S. Lopez: op. cit., p. 281.

43. S. I. Rutgers: *Indonesië*, p. 46.

44. *Histoire du Commerce:* Vol. IV, pp. 143, 149: cf. Polanyi: et al., op. cit., p. 115.

45. *Histoire du Commerce:* Vol. III, p. 34.

46. R. S. Lopez: op. cit., p. 46.

47. Cicero: *De Officiis*, Vol. I, pp. 150-1.

48. F. Heichelheim: *Wirtschaftsgeschichte des Altertums*, p. 709.

49. Abram Neumann: *Jews in Spain*, Vol. I, p. 164.

50. N. S. B. Gras: op. cit., pp. 38-39.

51. Margaret H. Cole: "The Investment of Wealth in 13th Century Genoa", in *Economic History Review*, Vol. VIII, 2nd May, 1938, p. 187.

52. H. Hauser and A. Renaudet: *Les Débuts de l'age moderne (Peuples et Civilisations*, Vol. VIII), pp. 52-53.

53. Robert C. West: *The Mining Community in Northern New Spain*, pp. 26 sqq.

54. K. Kautsky: *Die Vorläufer des neueren Sozialismus*, p. 201.

55. Earl J. Hamilton: "American Treasure and the Rise of Capitalism", *Economica*, November 1929, pp. 352, 355.

56. H. Sée: *Origines du capitalisme*, pp. 36-37.

57. W. R. Scott: *The Constitution and Finance of English, Scottish and Irish Joint Stock Companies, to 1720*, Vol. I, p. 17.

58. Barthélémi de las Casas: *Oeuvres*, Vol. I, pp. 9-10, 34-35, 75-76, etc.

59. H. Hauser and A. Renaudet: op. cit., p. 645.

60. H. T. Colenbrander: *Koloniale Geschiedenis*, Vol. II, pp. 117-229.

61. P. Kaeppelin: *La Compagnie des Indes Orientales*, p. 224.

62. Quoted in W. van Ravesteyn, Jnr.: *Onderzoekingen over de economische sociale ontwikkeling van Amsterdam gedurende de 16ᵉ eeuw*, p. 218.

63. Kulischer: op. cit., p. 265.

64. G. Lefebvre: et al., *La Révolution française* (*Peuples et Civilisations*, Vol. XIII), p. 349.

65. Hauser and Renaudet: op. cit., p. 349.

66. Kulischer: op. cit., Vol. II, p. 266.

67. Sée: op. cit., p. 92.

68. B. Nogaro and W. Oualid: *L'Evolution du commerce, du crédit et du transport depuis 150 ans*, p. 35.

69. H. Pirenne: *Histoire économique de l'Occident médiéval*, pp. 479-83.

70. Hauser: op. cit., pp. 34-36.

71. Kulischer: op. cit., Vol. I, p. 205; F. Vercauteren: *Luttes sociales à Liège*, pp. 102-3.

72. Sée: op. cit., pp. 15-17.

73. G. Espinas: *Les Origines du capitalisme*, Vol. I, p. 157.

74. Gras: op. cit., pp. 68-69.

75. Kulischer: op. cit., Vol. I, p. 218; A. Doren: *Italienische Wirtschafts-geschichte*, Vol. I, p. 502.

76. Espinas: op. cit., Vol. I, p. 153.

77. Doren: op. cit., Vol. I, p. 497.

78. Espinas: op. cit., Vol. I, pp. 175-6.

79. Pirenne: *Histoire économique de l'Occident médiéval*, pp. 637, 646-7.

80. Kulischer: op. cit., Vol. II, p. 116.

81. J. Dénian: *Histoire de Lyon et du Lyonnais*, p. 87.

82. Kulischer: op. cit., Vol. II, p. 135.

83. J. U. Nef: "Mining and metallurgy in mediaeval civilisation", in *Cambridge Economic History of Europe*, Vol. II, pp. 475-80.

84. Violet Barbour: *Capitalism in Amsterdam in the 17th Century*, pp. 35-39, 41, 109.

85. Bruno Lasker: *Human Bondage in Southeast Asia*, pp. 127-8.

86. Raymond Firth: *Malay Fishermen*, p. 60.

87. S. F. Nadel: *A Black Byzantium*, p. 283; Cl. Lévi-Strauss: *Tristes Tropiques*, p. 148; Fan Wen-Lan: *"Einige Probleme der chinesischen Geschichte"*, in *Neue chinesische Geschichtswissenschaft*, pp. 7-71.

88. N. W. Posthumus: *Bronnen tot de Geschiedenis van de Leidsche Laken-nijverheid*.

89. Kulischer: op. cit.

90. F. Mayer: *Anfänge des Handels und der Industrie in Oesterreich*, p. 64; Wagenaar: *Amsterdam in zijn Opkomst*.

91. Sombart: op. cit., Vol. I, pp. 814-17.

92. Sée: op. cit., pp. 139-40.

93. Posthumus: op. cit.

94. Marc Bloch: *Les Caractères originaux de l'histoire rurale française*, pp. 37-48.

95. N. S. B. Gras: *A History of Agriculture*, p. 161.
96. Ibid., pp. 170, 183.
97. P. Sagnac: *La Fin de l'ancien régime et la révolution américaine (Peuples et Civilisations*, Vol. XII), p. 57.
98. H. Sée, *Histoire économique de la France*, Vol. I, pp. 189-200.
99. Posthumus: op. cit., Vol. V, document 201.
100. *Acte* of 2nd February, 1247, Tailliar: *Recueil d'Actes*, quoted in G. Espinas: op. cit., Vol. I, p. 37, note I.
101. R. Firth: op. cit., p. 136.
102. Simiand: *Le Salaire*, Vol. I, p. 148.
103. Vitruvius: *De architecture*, Vol. X, pp. 6, 7.
104. Hauser: op. cit., pp. 8, 9, 11, 15; Pirenne: *Histoire de Belgique*, Vol. IV, p. 421.
105. Sombart: op. cit., 1, 2, pp. 485-7.
106. J. H. Clapham: *An Economic History of Modern Britain*, Vol. I, pp. 86-99.
107. J. U. Nef: "Mining and metallurgy in mediaeval civilisation", in *Cambridge Economic History of Europe*, Vol. II, pp. 464-6.
108. Kulischer: op. cit., Vol. II, p. 452.
109. Clapham: op. cit., pp. 249-50; A. P. Usher: *An Introduction to the Industrial History of England*, p. 305.
110. Sol Tax: *Penny Capitalism*, pp. 13, 14, 16.
111. Sapori: op. cit., pp. 50 sqq.
112. Fischel: *Studia arabica*, Vol. I, p. 77.
113. Hitti: op. cit., p. 344.
114. Lien Sheng-yang: *Money and Credit in China*, p. 4.
115. C. M. Macri: *L'organisation de l'économie urbaine dans Byzance sous la dynastie de Macédoine*, pp. 18-19.
116. R. S. Lopez: "Silk Industries in the Byzantine Empire", in *Speculum*, Vol. XX, No. 1, pp. 18-19.
117. A. Metz: *Die Renaissance des Islams*, pp. 417, 442-3.
118. Nancy Lee Swann: *Food and Money in China*, pp. 265, 405, et seq.
119. *An Outline History of China*, pp. 175-7; Helmut Wilhelm: *Gesellschaft und Staat in China*, p. 73; Du Shen: *"Die Diskussion über das Problem der Keime des Kapitalismus in China"*, in *Neue Chinesische Geschichtswissenschaft*, pp. 130-7.
120. Rostovtzeff: op. cit., p. 95; Bratianu: op. cit., p. 139.
121. A. von Kremer: *Kulturgeschichtliche Streifzüge auf dem Gebiete des Islams*, p. 77 (Eng. trans. by S. Khuda Bukhsh, in "Contributions to the History of Islamic Civilisation", edited by the same author, second edition, 1929, University of Calcutta.)
122. Chen Huan-Chang: *The Economic Principles of Confucius*, p. 656; Lien Sheng-yang: op. cit., p. 3.
123. Suetonius: *Lives of the Twelve Caesars*, Book 8, 18.
124. Gernet: op. cit., p. 141.
125. Heichelheim: *Wirtschaftsgeschichte des Altertums*, pp. 507-8, 565.
126. J. J. Mayer: introduction to translation of Kautilya's *Arthashastra*, pp. 77-78; Rostovtzeff: op. cit., p. 172.

127: A. Mazahéri: *La Vie quotidienne des Musulmans au moyen âge*, p. 117.

128. Wilhelm: op. cit., pp. 40-41, 73.

129. Bernard Lewis: "The Islamic Guilds", in *Economic History Review*, Vol. VIII, No. 1, November 1937, p. 20.

130. Fischel: *Jews in the Economic and Political Life of Mediaeval Islam*, pp. 13-14 et seq.; A. Bonné: *State and Economics in the Middle East*, p. 48.

131. E. Balazs: *Les Villes chinoises*, in *La Ville, Recueils de la Société Jean Bodin*, pp. 237-8.

132. See especially his letter to Engels, 14th June, 1853 (p. 420 of Vol. I of the "Correspondence" published by Bebel and Bernstein), the first article on the Spanish revolution, a number of passages in *Capital*, etc.

133. *Histoire du Commerce*, Vol. II, 486.

134. Basil Davidson: *The African Awakening*, pp. 40-41.

135. Cf. Sir George Sansom: *A History of Japan to 1334*, pp. 4, 235, etc.

136. R. F. Barton: *Ifugao Economics*, summarized by Ruth Bunzel: "The Economic Organization of Primitive Peoples", p. 336.

137. For Alexander Hamilton's opinion, see: *Propositions for a Constitution of Government and Speeches in the Federal Convention. (The Works of Alexander Hamilton*, Vol. I, pp. 347-428).

CHAPTER FIVE

THE CONTRADICTIONS OF CAPITALISM

Capital thirsting for surplus-value

THE owner of slaves distributed food among them and in return took the entire product of their labour. The feudal lord took the products of the unpaid work which his serfs were obliged to render him in the form of labour services. The capitalist buys the worker's labour-power for a wage which is less than the new value produced by this worker. In each of these varying forms the possessing classes take for themselves the social surplus product, the product of the surplus labour of the producers.

The contract made at Liège in 1634 between Antoine de Jelly, master-weaver, and Nicolas Cornélis, states bluntly that the latter will be paid "half of what he makes, the other half being the master's profit."*

The wage-worker creates new value while he expends his labour-power to produce commodities in his employer's factory. At a certain moment he will have produced new value exactly equivalent to what he receives as his wages. If he were to stop working at that moment he would not have produced any surplus value. But the employer does not mean that to happen. He does not want to do a favour, he wants to do business. He does not buy labour-power in order to keep it alive, he buys it as he buys any other commodity, in order to realise its use-value.[2] And the use-value of labour-power, from the capitalist's standpoint, is precisely its capacity to create surplus-value, to provide surplus labour over and above the labour needed to produce the equivalent of the wage paid for it. In order to be hired by an employer, a worker must work longer than is needed to produce this equivalent. In doing this he will create new value for which he will be paid nothing. He is creating surplus value, which is the difference between the value created by labour-power and the value of labour-power itself.

---

* Apologists for slavery did not fail to stress the analogy between this daily, weekly or monthly alienation of a man's labour-power and the alienation for life that is slavery: "It is not essentially repugnant to justice and reason that a man should surrender to another, even for his whole lifetime, the labour that every day a workman pledges to his employer, his master, provided that the inalienable [!] rights of man are safeguarded," wrote in 1742 the Dutch captain Elias Joannes.[1]

The capitalist's aim is to accumulate capital, to capitalise surplus value. The very nature of the circulation of money implies this aim. Industrial capital pursues this aim of accumulation even more, much more insatiably than usurer's capital or merchant capital. It produces for a free and anonymous market, *dominated by the laws of competition*. A capitalist is not alone in offering his products on this market to possible customers. Under the rule of competition, each industrialist tries to grab as large a share of the market as possible. To succeed, however, he must reduce his prices. There is only one way to reduce selling prices without threatening profit: to reduce the cost of production, the value of commodities, to curtail the labour-time socially necessary for producing them, to produce more commodities in the same length of time.

"Last year already the expansion of the enterprise, which took only a few months, enabled us to maintain the profit on our cement business at the expected level, despite the fact that competition considerably cut down the price of cement. This experience has confirmed us in our decision to make up for the increasing decline in prices which we foresee by an increase in the amount we produce," was proudly proclaimed by the annual report of a German cement-works in the nineteenth century.

In order to bring about such an increase in production, equipment must be improved, the process of production rationalised, the division of labour within the enterprise carried to a higher level. All of which demands an increase in capital. But the increase in capital can come, in the last analysis, only from an increase in the surplus-value capitalised. Under the lash of competition, the capitalist mode of production thus becomes the first mode of production in the history of mankind the essential aim of which appears to be *unlimited increase in production*, constant accumulation of capital by the capitalisation of the surplus value produced in the course of production itself.

The capitalist's thirst for surplus value is not the thirst for use-values and luxuries of the old possessing classes; only a limited part of surplus value is consumed unproductively in order to keep the capitalist alive. It is a thirst for surplus-value to capitalise, a thirst to accumulate capital: ". . . that whole system of appetites and values, with its deification of the life of snatching to hoard, and hoarding to snatch . . ."[3]

There is nothing irrational or mystical in this thirst. The old possessing classes, who took the social surplus product essentially in the form of use-values, were assured of being able to go on doing this so long as the social edifice remained standing which had this particular form of exploitation as its foundation. They could be affected only by natural disasters, wars or social revolutions, disasters against which they tried to provide by constituting big reserves. The predominant form in which capital first appears in history—usurer's and merchant capital—is characteristic of the same striving for *stability and security*. It is significant that the investments made by the bourgeois in the Middle Ages were calculated so as to guarantee stable incomes, regardless of fluctuations in money or prices.[4] The classical type of bourgeois in the historical epoch of the primitive accumulation of money capital, the miser, is haunted by this same thirst for security. It is not the *return* on his capital that he is worried about but its *existence*.

It is otherwise with the capitalist properly so called, the capitalist entrepreneur. Carrying on business for a market which is anonymous, unknown, undefined, his enterprises are dominated by risk and uncertainty. Today a deal has been successful, tomorrow another may fail to come off. It is not only the fact of competition, but the very fact of production which is *free from any overall social regulation***** that gives capitalist enterprise this aspect of uncertainty and that compels the capitalist to try and make the maximum profit on each separate deal, in face of the permanent danger that hangs over his business as a whole.

The landowner, the small commodity producer, the purchaser of ground-rents, all find in the certainty of their incomes an adequate reason for keeping their activities within given *limits*. The uncertainty of capitalist profit implies, on the contrary, the need for a continuous *expansion* of business, an expansion which in turn depends on maximum accumulation of capital, maximum realisation of profits. Thus there emerges the image of the capitalist, of whose mediaeval ancestor Georges Espinas has drawn this masterly portrait:

"To achieve the biggest possible gain while paying out the least possible amount in wages; to make the producers supply as much as possible while paying them as little as he can get away with, or even robbing them within the same limits; to draw to himself, to breathe in, to suck up, as it were, all he can take of the money which ought to go to the small employers (the producers) for the work which he alone can obtain for them and which they carry out for him alone— this is obviously the constant aim of the efforts of the 'capitalist' entrepreneur to secure the biggest profit he can, even at the expense of the utmost harm to the people in his employment. He is like a spider, in the centre of his web. To apply this 'sweating' system all means are good in his eyes, and every circumstance is favourable; he

---

* Such regulation existed for all the pre-capitalist crafts and even for the beginnings of the *Verlagssystem* (putting-out system) in several countries. In Carinthia and Styria in the middle of the fifteenth century "Duke Frederick III regulated afresh the way to be followed for iron, he fixed prices and taxes, restricted the number of forges and the amount of iron that each merchant could have, and laid down the terms of contracts (*Verläge*)."[5]

knows how to take advantage of everything; he cheats on materials, he violates agreements and steals from wages; business means other people's money."[6]

The lengthening of the working day

Thirst for surplus-value is thirst for surplus labour, for unpaid labour over and above the labour that produces the equivalent value of the worker's means of life. In order to get more surplus labour the capitalists can, in the first place, lengthen the working day to the utmost without increasing the daily wage. If we suppose that a worker produces the equivalent of his wages in 5 hours, then lengthening his working day from 10 to 12 hours without any increase in wages will increase the surplus labour from 5 to 7 hours a day, or by 40 per cent. This way of increasing surplus-value is called *increasing absolute surplus value*.

In every society where the obtaining of use values remains the basic aim of production, for both the producers and the exploiters, a constant lengthening of the working day must appear absurd. The limitation of needs and of markets imposes a limit no less narrow upon production. So long as the slavery of ancient times remained patriarchal, on estates which were self-sufficient, the lot of the slaves was quite tolerable, and was really little different from that of the poor relations of the estate-owning family. It was only when the slavery of ancient times became the basis of production for the market that barbarous treatment of slaves became general.[7]

In the Middle Ages, the communal laws placed strict limits on the working time of the craftsmen. In such laws we find, as a rule, besides prohibition of night work, also the stoppage of work on numerous religious holidays (saints' days) and at certain periods of the year. On the basis of a study of the by-laws of the small town of Guines, in Artois, Georges Espinas has estimated the number of actual working days in the mediaeval year at 240.[8] In the Bavarian mines there were in the sixteenth century between 99 and 190 holidays every year.[9] Hue concludes that, taking into account the numerous holidays, the average working week in the mines of the fifteenth century was 36 hours.[10]

As soon, however, as capitalist enterprise appears, a constant striving to lengthen the working day is to be observed. From the fourteenth century onward laws were passed in Great Britain to forbid too short a working day. English writing of the seventeenth and eighteenth centuries is full of complaints regarding the "idleness" of the workers, who, "if they earn in four days enough to provide food for a whole week, do not go to work for the three following days." All the leading bourgeois thinkers take part in this campaign: the Dutchman Jan De Witt, Spinoza's friend; William Petty, the father of

English classical political economy; Colbert, who speaks of the "idle people", etc. Sombart fills seven pages with quotations like this from the period under consideration.[11]

When the capitalist mode of production crosses the oceans and penetrates fresh continents, it finds itself up against the same natural resistance by the workers to the lengthening of their working day. In the seventeenth and eighteenth centuries the press of the virtuous Puritan colonists in North America resounded with complaints about the high cost of labour, "contrary to reason and equity". "'Tis the poor that make the rich," artlessly declared the *New York Weekly Journal*. In 1769 the *Maryland Gazette* complained that "the wages they receive for the labour of one day will support them (the workers) in intemperance for three days."[12] "The denunciations of the 'luxury, pride and sloth' of the English wage-earners of the seventeenth and eighteenth centuries are, indeed, almost exactly identical with those directed against African natives today."[13]

Alfred Bonné notes the amazement shown by Western observers when they behold poor Arabs who prefer to earn £1 a year as shepherds rather than £6 a month as factory hands.[14] Audrey I. Richards reports the same repugnance among the Negroes of Rhodesia: "Men who worked an intermittent three or four hours a day in their tribal reserves are now asked to do a regular eight to ten hours under white supervision on the big plantations or in industrial concerns."[15]

It was sufficient, however, to take advantage of the enormous mass of labour-power uprooted and unemployed as a result of the social and economic upheavals of the period between the fifteenth and eighteenth centuries to bring a pressure to bear on wages which brought them below subsistence level. In this way the bourgeoisie was able to advance from victory to victory in this "struggle against the idleness of the people".

From the eighteenth century onward we find that the normal working day in England is 13 or 14 hours.[16] In the English cotton mills the working week is between 75 and 80 hours in 1747; 72 hours in 1797; between 74 and 80 hours in 1804.[17] And since wages had fallen so low that every day without work was a day without food, Napoleon cuts a more generous figure than his minister Portalis when he rejects the latter's proposal to prohibit Sunday work: "Since the people eat every day they should be allowed [!] to work every day."[18]

The growth in the productivity and intensity of labour

However, absolute surplus-value cannot be increased without limit. Its natural limit is, first of all, the physical capacity of the workers. Capital is interested in exploiting but not in destroying the labour-power which constitutes its constant source of potential surplus labour.

Beyond a definite physical limit, the worker's capacity to produce declines rapidly towards zero.

Furthermore, the organisation of workers' resistance by the trade unions brought about from the middle of the nineteenth century the first regulation of the working day in the direction of laying down a maximum length. The legal limit of the working day was fixed first at 12, then at 10, and in the twentieth century at 8 hours, so as to give in some countries a 40-hour week; not without howls about economic ruin from the bourgeoisie at each reduction.*

Capital now falls back more and more upon a second way of increasing surplus-value. Instead of lengthening the working day, it tries to cut down the labour-time necessary to produce the equivalent of the worker's wages. Let us assume that with a working day of 10 hours, 4 hours are needed to create the amount of necessary value represented by the worker's wages. If this necessary labour can be cut from 4 to 2 hours, then surplus labour is increased from 6 to 8 hours, and exactly the same result is achieved as if the working day had been lengthened from 10 to 12 hours. This is what is called *increasing relative surplus value*.

The increase of relative surplus-value results essentially from *growth in the productivity of labour* thanks to the employment of new machinery, more rational methods of work, a more advanced division of labour, a better way of organising labour, etc.† Industrial capitalism has transformed economic life more than all the earlier modes of production put together. The fall in prices of articles of current consumption is clearly expressed in these figures:

In 1779 a certain quantity of No. 40 cotton thread cost 16s.

In 1784 it cost only 10s. 11d.

In 1799 it cost only 7s. 6d.

In 1812 it cost only 2s. 6d.

In 1830 it cost only 1s. 2·5d.[19]

No less eloquent is the following table, which relates to a slightly later period in the United States, where the triumphs of machine production occurred somewhat later than in Great Britain.

* These howls are to be compared to the well-known exclamation by the economist Senior: "Abolishing the last hour of work means abolishing profit."

† Surplus value is the difference between what is produced by labour-power and the cost of upkeep of this same labour-power. By gathering the workers together in factories and by introducing among them a more and more far-reaching division and co-operation of labour, capital increased their productivity (their production) even without changing the instruments of labour, and took the increased product for itself.

Labour-time necessary for making various articles (in thousands of minutes):

	Manual work		Machine work	
100 pairs men's shoes	1859	86·2	1895	9·2
100 pairs ladies' shoes	1859	61·5	1895	4·8
100 dozen collars	1855	81·0	1895	11·5
12 dozen shirts	1853	86·3	1894	11·3
100 dozen corn boxes	1865	6·5	1894	2·7
25,000 lb. soap	1839	25·9	1897	1·3
12 tables	1860	33·8	1894	5·0
50 doors	1857	83·1	1895	30·6
100,000 envelopes	1855	26·1	1896	1·9
Transporting 100 tons of coal	1859	7·2	1896	0·6[20]

By substantially reducing the value of all articles of primary necessity capital reduces the part of the worker's working day during which he is producing the equivalent of his wages. Also to be taken into account is the substitution of cheap articles for dear ones as consumer goods for the working classes—especially the substitution of potatoes for bread—together with a general deterioration in workers' food, housing and clothes, which facilitates the growth in relative surplus value.

Growth in absolute surplus value results, however, from *intensification of labour*, which is basically the same thing as lengthening the working day. The worker is obliged to expend in 10 hours of work the same productive effort as previously he expended in 13 or 14 hours. Such intensification can be brought about by various methods: speeding up the pace of work; speeding up the machinery; increasing the number of machines to be watched (e.g. of looms to be overlooked in textile mills), etc.

Particularly in the most recent phase of capitalist development, characterised by "scientific organisation of labour" (Taylor and Bedaux systems; piece-work; time and motion study, etc.), has the intensification of labour immensely increased the absolute surplus value obtained by capital. Georges Friedmann presents a striking picture of two methods used for this purpose by two great French motor-car firms, Berliet in Lyons and Citroën in Paris:

"Why has the Berliet works the reputation, in spite of the spacious beauty of its halls, of being a gaol? Because here they apply a simplified version of the Taylor method of rationalising labour, in which the time taken by a demonstrator, an 'ace' worker, serves as the criterion imposed on the mass of workers. He it is who fixes, watch in hand, the 'normal' production expected from a worker. He seems, when he is with each worker, to be adding up in an honest way the time needed for the processing of each item. In fact, if the worker's movements seem to him to be not quick or precise enough, he gives a practical demonstration, and his performance determines the norm expected in return for the basic wage . . . Add to this supervision in the technical sphere the disciplinary supervision of uniformed warders who patrol the factory all the time and go so far as to push open the doors of the toilets to check that the men squatting there are not smoking, even in workshops where the risk of fire is non-existent.

"At Citroën's the methods used are more subtle. The working teams are in rivalry one with another, the lads quarrel over travelling cranes, drills, pneumatic grinders, small tools. But the supervisors in white coats, whose task is to keep up the pace, are insistent, pressing, hearty. You would think that by saving time a worker was doing them a personal favour. But they are there, unremittingly on the back of the foreman, who in turn is on your back; they expect you to show an unheard-of quickness in your movements, as in a speeded-up motion picture."[21]

Capital which is as thirsty as this for every minute, every movement the worker makes, during the whole of the time that "belongs" to it— does this not provide the best illustration of the fact that profit, capitalist surplus-value, is nothing but the unpaid surplus labour of the worker?

We find a striking confirmation of this thirst for surplus labour in the fact that General Motors pays its workers in the United States not by the hour but by the fraction of ten minutes [!] of work they have actually performed.[22]

Daniel Bell sums up admirably the radical revolution that industrial capitalism has carried out in the idea of time: "In the various ways it has been expressed two modes of time have been dominant: time as a function of space, and time as *durée*. Time as a function of space follows the rhythm of the movement of the earth: a year is the curving ellipse around the sun; a day, the spin of the earth on its axis. The clock itself is round; and the hour, the sweep of a line in 360 degrees of space. But time, as the philosophers and novelists—and ordinary people—know it, is also artless. These are the psychological modes which encompass the differing perceptions: the dull moments and the swift moments, the bleak moments and the moments of bliss, the agony of time prolonged and of time eclipsed, of time recalled and time anticipated—in short, time not as a chronological function of space, but time felt as a function of experience.

"Utilitarian rationality [euphemism for industrial capitalism] knows little of time as *durée*. For it, and for modern industrial life, time and effort are hitched only to the clock-like, regular 'metric' beat. The modern factory is fundamentally a place of order in which stimulus and response, the rhythms of work, derive from a *mechanically imposed* sense of time and pace. No wonder, then, that Aldous Huxley can assert: 'Today, every efficient office, every up-to-date factory is

a *panoptical prison* in which the workers suffer . . . from the consciousness of being inside a machine."[23] [Emphasis ours.]

In his book *The Anatomy of Work*, Georges Friedmann quotes the
example of a British factory in which several operations have been
reduced to a duration of less than a minute.[25]* At the Ford works at
River Rouge the conveyor-belt allows less than two minutes for most
of the workers to carry out their task.[26] Some technicians have begun
to question the efficacy of this "speed-up".[27]

The picture of a contemporary factory that G. Friedmann and D.
Bell have given us in the passages quoted brings out also the *hierarchical structure* of the organisation of labour. So long as the producer
is himself owner of his means of production the question of a "workshop police" does not arise. It is to his own interest to observe a strict
economy of raw material. When domestic industry or the *Verlagssystem*
become general, we find that complaints become frequent, on the part
of the entrepreneurs, that the producers spoil, waste or steal the raw
material entrusted to them. This was one of the main reasons for
the establishment of manufactories, in which these workers worked
under the constant supervision of the entrepreneur.

The latter has become, from being a mere owner of money and head
of an enterprise with the aim of putting this capital to fruitful use, at
one and the same time the organiser of an exact technical process of
production and the *commander of a mass of wage-workers* who have
to be supervised. He is no longer master merely of his capital but
also of machines and men.

In order to perform this task effectively, he has to perfect the
organisation of labour, introduce intermediate rungs, group the
workers into teams under leaders, make use of foremen and workshop
managers, technicians and engineers. Alongside the purely technical
division of labour in the enterprise a *social hierarchic division of
labour* develops and becomes ever more thorough, *between those who
give orders and those who carry them out*.†

Human labour-power and machine production

Industrial capital finds its *raison d'être* and the essential source of
its power to increase surplus-value in the use of machinery. Capitalism
does not introduce new machines to increase the productivity of human
labour; that is only a by-product of the aims it pursues. The capitalist

---

* "In time study, work is divided into elements of the order of a second, or
a fifth of a second, while in motion study one goes down to one hundredth or
one two-hundredth of a second."[24]

† See the striking parallel which Professor P. Sargant Florence has drawn
between the hierarchy of the church, the pyramid of military ranks, and the
organisation of present-day factories.[28] Vance Packard has subsequently made
use of this parallel, too.[29]

introduces machinery to reduce his costs of production, so as to sell cheaper and beat his competitors. And it is not possible to reduce costs of production by means of machines unless the cost of these machines is itself *less* than the wages of the workers whom the machine replaces. The current expression used in English, "labour-saving machines", indicates only imperfectly the function of machines in the capitalist mode of production. To be bought by a capitalist enterprise a machine must *both save human labour and make profit*; it must be "labour-saving" and "profit-increasing". When a machine costs exactly as much as the *saving in wages* that it can achieve, it will doubtless not be bought, despite the fact that, even so, it may represent a substantial *saving in labour-time from the standpoint of society as a whole*. There we see a very important difference between the dynamics of a capitalist industry and those of a planned and socialised industry.

The cigarette industry was born in the United States in the 1860s. At first all the work was done by hand; a skilled worker could roll no more than 3,000 cigarettes in a working day of ten hours. In 1876 the wages cost was 96·4 cents per 1,000 cigarettes of a certain brand. One firm then offered a prize of 75,000 dollars for the invention of a cigarette-making machine. Bonsack came forward in 1881 with a rational machine which produced between 200 and 220 cigarettes a *minute* and cut wages costs from 96·4 to 2 cents [!] per 1,000 cigarettes. A single one of these machines could have produced all the cigarettes made by hand in the United States in 1875.[30]

A machine which saves wages throws producers out of production. The introduction of machines gives rise to unemployment, and does this so directly that the victims tried at first to destroy these machines which were condemning them to poverty (Luddite movement in Britain; similar movement in France, 1816–1825).* Between 1840 and 1843, as a result of the competition of the mechanised linen industry, the number of Flemish women spinning at home fell from 221,000 to 167,000.[32] In 1824–1825 the introduction of mechanical looms caused considerable unemployment in England, and wages were cut by 50 per cent.[33]

If they were to stand up to competition by large scale machinery the manual workers had to accept big reductions in wages. The weekly wages of hand weavers in Bolton fell from 25s. in 1800 to 9s. in 1820 and from 19s. 6d. in 1810 to 5s. 6d. in 1830.[34]

The unemployment of a mass of workers for whom there is no work because of competition by machines becomes a permanent institution

---

* In the centuries preceding the industrial revolution the public authorities often confiscated machines which condemned labour to unemployment. Thus, a machine for knitting stockings was forbidden, first in Britain and then in France, in the seventeenth century. In 1623 a machine for making needles, and about 1635 a windmill for sawing wood, were banned in England.[31]

of the capitalist mode of production.* This is the *industrial reserve army*, thanks to which the wage-earners are forced to accept as wages the bare cost of reproducing their labour-power. In the first phase of industrial capitalism, whatever the country in which the capitalist mode of production becomes established, the destruction of the crafts by large-scale industry gives rise to an acute problem of unemployment. Subsequently, other phenomena which we describe later on determine the scope and fluctuations of this unemployment.

Industry based on machinery does not merely transform a section of the producers into wretched unemployed. It devalues manual work in general and changes many skilled workers into unskilled or semi-skilled workers. In the epoch of the craft guilds, or that of domestic industry, every producer was in principle a skilled producer, with a thorough knowledge of his craft. The unskilled "hirelings" were a floating mass which lacked great importance, either numerically or economically. The skill of the producers at their trade was the chief condition for the success of any productive enterprise.

But the division of labour effected in manufacture, and then the general introduction of machinery, and finally the progress of semi-automation, simplify and mechanise to the utmost the work of the producers.[35] Their tasks, which no longer require any skill, are henceforth such that anybody can perform them. An apprenticeship of a few months enables anyone today to become a good worker on the conveyor belt. In the Ford works in the U.S.A., 75 to 80 per cent of the personnel in the production workshops can be trained in less than a fortnight; in one of the factories of the Western Electric trust the percentage of skilled workers has fallen to 10 per cent of the labour force.[36]

The sudden formation of great masses of unskilled producers gave rise, at the dawn of industrial capitalism, to the appearance of a mass of *migrant workers*, such as the navvies of Britain who dug canals and built the railways.[37] Capitalist industry, born amid vast human migrations within the modern nations, caused in its turn a series of such migrations on the national and international scale: massive emigration of Europeans to North and South America, Australia, South Africa, etc.; Indian emigration to the countries around the Indian Ocean, and emigration of Japanese and Chinese to the countries around the Pacific, etc.

---

* Today as previously, official political economy upholds the same view with great candour. The absence of any unemployment would enable the workers to raise wages "excessively" and provoke inflation. See the *Economist* of 20th August, 1955, and *L'Echo de la Bourse* of 15th December, 1959, which quotes these words, ascribed to ex-President Truman: "On the contrary, it is a good thing for economic hygiene that there should always be some spare labour looking for work."

Forms and evolution of wages

In the capitalist mode of production, labour-power has become a commodity.* Like that of any other commodity, the value of this labour-power is determined by the amount of labour socially necessary to produce it. The value of labour-power is thus the cost of reconstituting this labour-power *in a given social setting* (food, clothing, housing, etc.). Because the worker has only his labour-power to sell in order to buy what he and his family need to live, and because of the presence of the industrial reserve army, wages vary around a *subsistence minimum* (an idea we will define later) which maintains the worker in his condition as a proletarian:

"The workers cannot possess the economic means of improving their position. Industry is organised in such a way that, in order to win independence, the workers would need to have money. How could they get it? . . . As regards the wages that the clothier pays to the petty producers, these are obviously fixed and distributed with a view merely to enabling those who receive them to keep themselves alive, so as to go on working under the exploitation of the one who pays them and keeps them alive for his personal and exclusive profit, and not to enriching them so that they may free themselves bit by bit from their former masters, rise to the level of the latter, and eventually compete with them."[38]

This analysis of the wages received by the small craftsmen of the Middle Ages who did work put out to them by the merchant-masters applies to wages in all forms of civilisation. It is an extraordinarily stable phenomenon throughout the ages. Examining the wages of agricultural workers at Eshnuna, in Mesopotamia, at the beginning of the second millennium B.C., Jacques Lacour-Gayet comes to the conclusion that, "reckoned in terms of wheat these wages are very well comparable with those of our day. The amount of wheat they represent is about the same as that represented by a harvest-worker's wages nowadays."[39]

For ancient Greece, Fr. Heichelheim has worked out the vital minimum of a worker at Delos, in the time of Alexander the Great. It is made up of the *sitos* (basic food, bread), the *opsonion* (additional food), clothes and some small extras. In good years the wages rose a little above this minimum; in bad ones, the extra expenses and even the *opsonion* were practically eliminated.[40]

This characteristic situation in ancient Greece already contains potentially the elements of that fluctuation of wages which is to be

---

* Is it necessary to add, for the benefit of opponents whether ignorant or dishonest, that it is absurd to say that the Marxists degrade labour-power to the level of a commodity? They merely *recognise* that capitalism has carried out this degradation. The term "Labou˜ ˜˜change" is sufficient evidence of this.

found in country after country and age after age, allowing for differences in customs, manners, traditions and, above all, *relations of strength between sellers and buyers of labour-power*. At certain times, the *opsonion* and the extras may be fairly big and varied: at others they may disappear almost completely. The two elements, the historical and the physical ("absolute minimum"), nevertheless form integral parts of wages.

The evolution of real wages under the capitalist mode of production corresponds to a series of exact and complex laws. Contrary to what was supposed by Malthus, whose ideas were the foundation for the wages theory of Ricardo and Lassalle ("the iron law of wages"), there is no *demographic law* governing fluctuations in the supply and demand of labour-power ("the labour market"). What determine these fluctuations, in the last analysis, are *the laws of capital accumulation*.

This phenomenon is easiest to grasp in the *short-term fluctuations* during the capitalist production cycle,*, which leads industry out of stagnation and depression, through economic recovery and high conjuncture, towards boom and crisis. At the start of the cycle the mass of unemployed available on the "labour market" as a result of the previous crisis, exceeds the demand for labour caused by economic recovery. Wages will thus remain stable at a comparatively low level. (It is indeed the contradiction between these stable wages and an initial rise in selling prices that makes possible an increase in the profit margin. The rate of profit rises and this encourages recovery.) On the other hand, at the peak of the boom, if full employment is actually achieved (which is not at all a certainty, a point to which we shall return), the demand for labour greatly exceeds the supply, and the workers can bring pressure to bear to push wages up, the reduction in the rate of profit which results being one of the causes of the outbreak of crisis.

We find these laws again at work in *long-term fluctuations*. When the accumulation of capital is taking place at a pace slower than the increase in unemployment which it has itself caused, real wages remain stable or even tend to decline. We can say that in these circumstances the accumulation of capital is destroying more jobs (crafts, agricultural work, domestic work, jobs in enterprises which have been put out of business by competition) than it is creating. The industrial reserve army will then tend to grow over a long period, and there will be no full employment even in a boom period, so that the workers will be unable to win wage-increases in that situation (conditions which prevailed in Europe down to 1850–70 and which still prevail in most

---

* See Chapter 11, devoted to this problem.

colonial and semi-colonial countries).* We can also say that in this case industrial expansion is proceeding at a slower pace than the growth in productivity.

However, when the accumulation of capital is proceeding at a quicker pace than the growth in the unemployment it causes—when the industrial reserve army ceases to grow, and even tends to be absorbed back into employment, e.g. when large scale emigration occurs alongside hindrances to immigration—real wages will tend to rise slowly over a long period. This is likewise what happens when industrial expansion proceeds at a quicker pace than the growth of productivity.

In fact, it is not the *absolute level* of wages that matters to capital. The latter prefers, certainly, that wages should be as low as possible in its own enterprises—but it wants at the same time to see wages as high as possible paid in competing enterprises or by the employers of its customers! What matters to capital is the possibility of extracting more surplus labour, more unpaid labour, more surplus value, more profit from its workers. The growth in the productivity of labour, which makes possible the growth of relative surplus value, implies the possibility of a slow rise in real wages, if the industrial reserve army is limited, on condition that the equivalent of these increased real wages is produced in an ever shorter period of time, i.e. that wages rise less quickly than productivity.

One can indeed observe in history that real wages are generally highest in the countries which have known for some time a substantial growth in the productivity of labour, as compared with countries where this productivity has remained stagnant for a long time or has risen only slowly.

Nevertheless, the rise in real wages does not follow *automatically* from the rise in the productivity of labour. The latter only creates the *possibility* of such a rise, within the capitalist framework, provided profit is not threatened. For this potential increase to become actual, two interlinked conditions are needed: a favourable evolution of "relations of strength on the labour market" (i.e. predominance of the tendencies for the industrial reserve army to shrink over the tendencies for it to expand), and effective organisation (above all, trade union organisation) of the wage workers which enables them to abolish competition among themselves and so to take advantage of these "favourable market conditions".

Statistics and historical studies have shown that any theory that deduces the level of real wages directly from the relative level of productivity of labour, leaving out the two factors we have just mentioned, does not correspond to reality. Here, taken from a study by the International Federation of Metal Workers,[41] is the productivity

* See some concrete examples in Chapter 13.

(annual production of steel per employed worker) and the average wage (in Swiss francs) in a series of steel works in 1957:

	Annual production per worker tons	Annual profits per worker frs.	Annual cost of labour per worker frs.
U.S. Steel Corp.	110	6,800	30,000
Inland Steel Corp.	170	6,800	29,800
Youngtown Sheet	150	6,100	27,700
Average of 8 American firms	138	6,400	29,500
United Steel Ltd.	96	3,800	10,500
Colvilles Ltd.	115	3,500	8,700
Average of 8 British firms	100	3,400	±9,500
Yawata Iron & Steel	70	2,200	6,000
Nakayama	170	7,000	7,000
Fuji Iron & Steel	82	3,000	6,500
Average of 6 Japanese firms	76	3,100	6,000

The differences are obvious. The physical productivity of the British steel workers is 33 per cent higher than that of the Japanese, yet the financial productivity is only 10 per cent higher. On the other hand, the difference in the respective wages exceeds 50 per cent. Again, the American steel works enjoy a physical productivity 38 per cent higher than that of the British, and a financial productivity 80 per cent higher. But the American wages are more than three times the British. Between the U.S.A. and Japan the difference in productivity is two to one, while the difference in wages is *five* to one! And one Japanese steel works, Nakayama, has the same productivity as the Americans, whereas it pays wages which are only a *quarter* of American wages!

M. Madinier has convincingly shown in a recent work that the persistence of a wage differential of 20 per cent between the French provinces and Paris is explained essentially by the difference in trade union strength between the former and the latter.

It would be wrong, however, to regard trade union strength as an *independent* variable in the fixing of wages. This is because the possibility of overcoming competition among the workers does not exist—outside certain highly-skilled trades which enforce what is practically a *numerus clausus* in apprenticeships or other access to their ranks —unless the reserve army is no longer steadily increasing. Even in this favourable circumstance, the increase of wages comes up against an *institutional* barrier which is not at all a technical or "purely economic" one. Theoretically, a rise in real wages remains possible so long as the total amount paid in wages is less than the net national product. It then implies *a redistribution of incomes and a reallocation of resources* between the consumer goods sector and the production goods sector, two processes which may cause friction but which are nevertheless perfectly possible without giving rise to actual crisis or inflation. They merely require an *institutional* change, i.e. the disappearance of the power of capital, and in particular its power to stop investing when the rate of profit falls too low.

Under the capitalist régime, however, increases in wages come up against a certain barrier well before reaching either the physical or the economic one. When, as a result of full employment, wages increase faster than productivity, the rate of profit and even the rate of surplus value decline. And the risk of such a decline occurring quickly sets in motion the readaptation mechanisms of an economy based on profit: on the one hand, compensatory price increases, inflationary tendencies, fall in investment and reduction in employment; on the other, furious rationalisation and replacement of workers by machines. In both cases, unemployment reappears. As soon as this "barrier" is reached, the rise of real wages becomes impossible under the capitalist régime. This is why the most plain-spoken advocates of capitalism declare that it cannot exist in conditions of "over-employment", i.e. full employment.

How are we to explain, within the framework of the theory of labour-value, the increase in real wages which occurs in the circumstances described above?

The value of labour-power comprises not only the prices of the means of existence needed for its purely physical reconstitution (and the maintenance of the workers' children, i.e. the reproduction of labour-power). It also includes a moral and historical element, i.e. the prices of those commodities (and, later, of certain personal services) which the traditions of the given country have come to include in the subsistence minimum.* These needs depend on the comparative level of (past and present) civilisation, and thus, in the last analysis, on the average level of the productivity of labour over a certain period. So long as the pressure of the industrial reserve army prevents these needs being included in the calculation of the subsistence minimum, *wages, i.e. the price of labour-power, fall in reality below the value of labour-power*. When real wages are increased, the price of labour-power merely catches up with its value, which tends to rise with the overall rise in the level of civilisation.

We thus see that *the growth in the productivity of labour has a contradictory effect on wages*. To the extent that it reduces the value of the means of subsistence it tends to cut down, if not absolute wages then at least relative wages (the part of the working day during which the worker is producing the value-equivalent of his wages), and so to diminish the value of labour-power. To the extent that it reduces the value and price of many luxury products, develops mass produc-

---

* The influence of the "tradition" factor in the forming of wage-levels is strongly emphasised by Polanyi[42] and Joan Robinson.[43]

tion (often at the expense of quality!) and incorporates a number of new commodities* in the subsistence minimum, it tends, on the contrary, to increase the value of labour-power.

The accumulation of capital also has a contradictory effect on the amount of employment and on the trend of wages. To the extent that machines replace men, the reserve army grows. But to the extent that surplus-value is accumulated, that capital enlarges its spheres of operation, that new enterprises continually arise and existing ones are expanded, the reserve army is reduced and capital sets out to find fresh labour to exploit.†

Taking all these factors into consideration, one can explain the main trends in the evolution of wages since the beginning of capitalism. Two main epochs must be distinguished where the countries of Western Europe are concerned: the epoch that runs from the sixteenth century to the middle of the nineteenth, during which wages fell further and further to the level of the mere *sitos*; and then the epoch that runs from the middle of the nineteenth century to our own day, during which wages first rose, then became stable or declined, then rose once again. The *opsonion* and the extras have increased in quantity and become immensely varied, but have in some instances declined in quality, which is also true of the *sitos*.

The epoch of the primitive accumulation of industrial capital was an epoch of fall in real wages, caused principally by the over-abundance of labour, by the continual increase in the industrial reserve army, and by the lack of effective organisation of the working class resulting from this. Capital increased the production of absolute surplus value by reducing wages to the point at which, in order to meet his need of bread in one year the British worker had to work, in 1495, 10 weeks; in 1533, 14 or 15 weeks; in 1564, 20 weeks; in 1593, 40 weeks; in 1653, 43 weeks; in 1684, 48 weeks, and in 1726, 52 weeks. With the help of the price revolution all "idleness" had been successfully overcome.[45] Recently, E. H. Phelps Brown and Sheila V. Hopkins have fully confirmed these classic data of J. E. Thorold Rogers. They have found that the real wages of British masons fell from index 110–115 in 1475–1480 to 56 in 1528, 45 in 1600, 38 in 1610–1620, 55 in

---

* "Two centuries ago not one person in a thousand wore stockings; one century ago not one person in five hundred wore them; now not one person in a thousand is without them," triumphantly proclaimed in 1831 the pamphlet "The Results of Machinery", published by the Society for the Diffusion of Useful Knowledge.[44]

† In a country which is already highly industrialised, a sudden large-scale demand for labour can be met only by incorporating millions of housewives, youngsters and retired people in the proletariat, after full employment has been attained. This is what happened during the Second World War, in the United States, in Germany, in Britain, etc. Thereafter, the only thing to do is to import or attract foreign labour.

1700, 65–70 in 1740–1750, 53 in 1765–1770, 47 in 1772 and 38 in 1800. Only around 1880 did the figure again rise above index 100![46]

Nor were matters different in France. The Vicomte d'Avenel has calculated that betwen 1376 and 1525 a carpenter had to work, on the average, 5 days in order to earn the equivalent of a hectolitre of wheat; his daily pay was worth 3 kilogrammes of meat. In 1650 he had to work 16 days to obtain the same equivalent of wheat, and his daily pay was worth no more than 1·8 kilogrammes of meat.[47]

From the middle of the nineteenth century, however, real wages began to rise. In Britain and France they practically doubled between 1850 and 1914.[48] The capitalists succeeded during an entire period (abolition of the Corn Laws in Britain; increasing exports from overseas countries) in bringing about a considerable decline in agricultural prices. The capitalist mode of production experienced a remarkable expansion, conquering enormous international markets. In this way it has to some extent absorbed the industrial reserve army in the countries of Western Europe, only to reproduce it, to "re-export" it on a larger scale, in India, China, Latin America, Africa and the Near East. The mass emigration from Europe to overseas white-settlement countries reduced still further the supply of labour on the European labour market. All these factors, closely interlinked and characteristic of a certain structure of the world market, created conditions favouring the reinforcement of trade-union strength and the rise of real wages in Western Europe.

Competition from female and child labour was for a long time one of the chief means of reducing average wages.*

Another means to the same end from the Middle Ages onward was the *truck system*: payment of wages in kind, i.e. in products of which the employer arbitrarily determined the price or reduced the quality. Opposition by the workers eliminated this form of super-exploitation despite strong resistance from the employers.[50] It continues, however, in a special form, in the institution of shops which belong to industrial concerns, shops in which the workers have to buy the goods they

* Down to 1816, several London parishes were in the habit of "selling" hundreds of poor children to textile mills in Lancashire and Yorkshire, some two hundred miles from London! These children were sent "by wagon loads" and the philanthropist Sir Samuel Romilly declared that they were lost to their parents for ever, no less than if they had been sent to the West Indies. The same writer quotes this particularly frank, cynical and odious passage from a speech made in 1811 in the House of Commons by a Mr. Wortley:

"Mr. Wortley, who spoke on the same side, insisted that, although in the higher ranks of society it was true that to cultivate the affections of children for their family was the source of every virtue, yet it was not so among the lower orders, and that it was a benefit to the children to take them away from their miserable and depraved parents. He said too that it would be highly injurious to the public to put a stop to the binding of so many apprentices to the cotton manufacturers, as it must necessarily raise the price of labour . . ."[49]

need and to which they fall into debt, thus finding themselves tied for life to the same employer (this is one of the forms still prevalent today of *peonage* in the southern states of the U.S.A., e.g. in the turpentine industry).

Leaving aside wages paid in kind, the two most common forms of wages are *time wages* and *piece wages*. Time wages have fewer disadvantages from the standpoint of the interests of the working class. Piece wages, on the other hand, which urge the worker to constant increase in output, to speed-up the pace of production and ceaseless intensification of work, are the ideal tool for the employers to use to increase production of relative surplus value.

A concealed form of piece wages is the *bonus* system, which appeared in the American metal industry about 1870. There are now several different methods of calculating bonus: the Rowan, Halsey, Bedaux, Emerson, Refa and other systems. All these methods have in common that the worker's output increases faster than his wages. Of the mass of value created by the worker, a *smaller and smaller* fraction returns to him, and the relative surplus value increases proportionately. Thus, under the Rowan system, if output increases by 50 per cent, wages rise by 33 per cent; if output increases by 100 per cent, wages rise by 50 per cent; if output rises by 200 per cent, wages rise by 66 per cent, etc.

As for the Bedaux system, it has been estimated in the U.S.A. that it has generally led to an increase in production by 50 per cent, against an increase of 20 per cent in wages.[51]

Writers who are frankly in favour of the bonus system, like Dr. A Perren, admit the advantages that the employers derive from these various systems.[52] The same result is achieved by the various systems of *profit sharing* by which the workers are induced to increase not only their individual output but also that of the entire enterprise.

Additional note on the theory of absolute impoverishment

The "theory of absolute impoverishment" is not to be found in the works of Marx. It was ascribed to him by political opponents, especially what was called the "revisionist" trend in the German Social-Democratic Party. It is to say the least paradoxical that a whole school claiming to be orthodox Marxist has thought it necessary to adopt this "theory of impoverishment" and defend it with persistence and bad faith, bringing discredit on Marxist theory.*

---

* We will restrict ourselves to two examples:

In the *Textbook of Political Economy* published in August 1954 in the U.S.S.R., it was stated that: "Absolute impoverishment is expressed in the fall in real wages . . . In the twentieth century the real wages of the workers in Britain, the U.S.A., France, Italy and other capitalist countries are lower than in the middle [!] of the nineteenth century."[53] "In the United States . . . real

The idea that the real wages of the workers tend to decline more and more is totally alien to Marx's writings; it was formulated by Malthus and taken up most notably by Lassalle, who wrote of an "iron law" of wages. Marx waged a lifelong fight against this "iron law", a fight which one cannot really dismiss as due to a mere misunderstanding, as John Strachey does.[58] Actually, as we have shown above, he always insisted on the fact that wages are determined by complex laws and that denunciation of the capitalist order must be independent of the relative level of wages.*

What one finds in Marx is an idea of the absolute impoverishment not of the workers, the wage-earners, but of that section of the proletariat which the capitalist system *throws out* of the production process: unemployed, old people, disabled persons, cripples, the sick, etc., *die Lazarusschicht des Proletariats* as he calls it, the poorest stratum "bearing the stigmata of wage labour". This analysis retains its full value, even under the "welfare" capitalism of today.

In the United States poverty has certainly not disappeared, despite the considerable increase in real wages.[61] It is enough to look at the frightful slums that fill entire districts of New York, Chicago, Detroit, San Francisco, New Orleans, and other southern towns, to realise that these victims of an inhuman society, brutalised and dehumanised by this same society, continue to constitute a terrible reproach to the

wages had fallen by 1938 to 74 per cent of what they were in 1900. In France, Italy and Japan . . . real wages fell during the nineteenth and twentieth centuries even more than in the U.S.A."[54] "In France and Italy, real wages amounted in 1952 to less than half of pre-war."[55] "In the U.S.A. 72·2 per cent [!] of all American families had in 1949 incomes which were lower than the excessively modest official subsistence level,"[56] etc.

In the Soviet newspaper *Trud*, Academician A. Leontiev published in July 1955 a series of articles in which the following appeared: "Absolute impoverishment is expressed above all in the fall in the real wages of the bulk of the workers . . . The average real wage of an American worker . . . was in 1947–51 15 per cent less than in 1938–40; in 1951, the real wage of an American worker was 23 per cent less than in 1946 and 21 per cent less than before the war. With their wages the American workers could buy 59 per cent as much food, clothing and other consumer goods [!]."[57]

For amusement's sake one may put these two statements together. Wages in 1951 are 21 per cent less than wages in 1938 which are 74 per cent of wages in 1900. Consequently, from 1900 to 1951 American real wages must have fallen from 100 to 58·5. But in 1900 they were already below the level of the middle of the nineteenth century. One would have to assume then, according to these "statistics", that between 1850 and 1950 American real wages declined by over a half. Is there a single economist capable of really believing such nonsense?

* Roman Rosdolsky[59] has collected all the passages in Marx's economic writings which relate to the theory of wages and has found only one passage that might be found confusing, as to the possibility of an upward trend of real wages when there is a marked increase in productivity. See also Steindl, in his important work *Maturity and Stagnation in American Capitalism.*[60]

richest capitalism in the world.* To this permanent absolute impoverishment of the "infra-proletariat" there must be added the *periodical* absolute impoverishment of the workers hit by conjectural unemployment, the fall in wages during crises, etc.

A more subtle variant of the "absolute impoverishment" school tries to prove that this expression can apply even when real wages are rising. Discussion then gets lost in a semantic maze. Arzumanian declares that "absolute impoverishment" is expressed in intensification of labour, increase in accidents at work, the increase [!] in the value of labour-power and the fact that (rising) real wages fall further and further behind this value.[63] An "absolute impoverishment" which is expressed in an *increase* in the value of labour-power and an *increase* in real wages does violence to logic—formal logic no less than dialectical logic. It seems obvious to us that all these formulations imply a *relative* impoverishment, i.e. an impoverishment *not* in terms of absolute data (in these there is an improvement in status) but *relatively* to social wealth as a whole, to surplus value, to the productive effort contributed by the proletariat, etc.

In fact, the phenomenon of *relative impoverishment* is most typical of the capitalist mode of production. Increase in the rate of surplus value is at once the essential tool of capital for achieving accumulation of capital and also its chief weapon for countering the tendency to a fall in the average rate of profit. It is in this increase in the rate of surplus-value that the exploiting character of capitalist economy is expressed.

Empirical data broadly confirm this tendency to a decline in the relative place of *wages*† in the net product created by labour. John Strachey, though a stern (and unjust) critic of Marx's economic system, states: "In Britain . . . it [the share of wages in the total national income] appears to have been around 50 per cent in Marx's day: to have declined to about 40 per cent in the early years of the twentieth century; to have stayed about there till 1939, and then (including, as you must, the pay of the Forces) to have gone back to around 50 per cent by the end of the Second World War."[64]

By deducting the pay of the Forces, who after all are not producers, we arrive at a percentage of 47 in 1949 and a decline by several points

* Allison Davis has observed that people of this class are so used to living on the brink of disaster and hunger that they do not know what ambition is, or the desire to acquire higher knowledge. "In a sense," he writes, "ambition and the drive to attain the higher skills are a kind of luxury. They require a minimum *physical* security; only when one knows where his next week's or next month's food and shelter will come from can he and his children afford to go in for long-term education and training . . ."[62]

† We shall deal in the next chapter with the question of the extent to which office-workers can be regarded as producing surplus value and whether they are paid out of the surplus value produced by the workers.

after 1951.[65] This slight tendency to decline (or, if preferred, this remarkable stability of labour's share in the national income), has not resulted from the normal functioning of the system, but from a determined struggle by the wage-earners to increase their share. Is it possible now to deny that capitalism shows an inherent tendency to relative impoverishment, to a reduction in labour's share in the net product of industry? "No," replies Mr. Strachey.[66]

These calculations are not completely exact, moreover, since they leave out of account the numerical increase (both absolute and relative) of the proletariat as compared with Marx's time, with the beginning of the twentieth century, or even with the period before the Second World War. Even if "labour's share" in the national income had remained the same as a percentage, it would still have declined from the moment that this 50 per cent of the national income was being shared no longer among 60 per cent but among 80 or even 90 per cent of the population. The most exact mode of calculation would compare income per wage-earner with income per head of population, and study the fluctuations in the relation between these two magnitudes. There is little doubt that the former has declined in relation to the latter as compared with the middle of the nineteenth century, with the beginning of the twentieth century, and with the 1930s, in all the main capitalist countries.

In the United States the tendency is very clear. Here is the share of wages in the net product ("value added") of manufacturing industry:

	%
1880	48·1
1890	45·0
1899	40·7
1909	39·3
1919	40·5
1929	35·5
1939	36·7
1949	38·5
1952	35·0[67]

Still more to the point, here is the evolution of the gross real product per hour of work and gross real time wages, in decade averages:

	Real product per hour, in indices	Real time wage, in indices
1891–1900	100	100
1901–1910	122·8	102
1911–1920	146·0	109·1
1921–1930	196·4	137·2
1931–1940	233·5	158 [68]
1941–1950	281·3	209

Periodical absolute impoverishment of the unemployed and other victims of the capitalist production process; more or less general relative impoverishment of the proletariat (i.e. increase in real wages which over a long period is less than the growth in social wealth and the average productivity of labour): these are the laws of development for the working class under the capitalist system.

Dual function of labour-power

In the age of petty commodity production the essential instruments of labour—looms, forges, etc.—were acquired once for all and passed down from generation to generation. Like the peasant's land they did not constitute means of production subject to depreciation out of current production, but merely the conditions, the instruments, of men's livelihood. The clothier sold raw material to the small clothing worker and bought from him his finished product. The difference between these two prices merely represented, in fact, the craftsman's wage. When the entrepreneur took to organising weaving on his own account, his costs of production were confined essentially to costs of raw material and wages. The function of the labour-force whose labour-power he bought was exclusively that of adding to the value of the raw material a newly created value, one part of which (corresponding to wages) increased the entrepreneur's costs of production, while the other part (in exchange for which the workers got nothing) represented surplus-labour, surplus value appropriated by the capitalist.*

Things change with the flowering of industrial capital, of the capitalist mode of production. *The purchase of machines* now becomes the preliminary condition for production intended for a market which is governed by competition. In order to buy these machines, a substantial amount of capital has to be advanced. The machines will not be passed down from generation to generation, nor even used throughout the lifetime of the entrepreneur. They will be used so intensively that after a certain time they will be *physically worn-out*. And not much time will pass before competitors have built more modern machines, producing more cheaply, which will have to be bought if one is not to be overcome in the battle of competition. Thus, the old machines undergo a *moral depreciation* before their physical depreciation properly so called. The capitalist entrepreneur, unlike the petty commodity producer, does not look on them as a mere means of livelihood, but as *capital enabling him to accumulate surplus value*.

The capital advanced for the purchase of machines will thus have

* It was therefore logical that the first classical writers of political economy, especially Adam Smith, reduced the value of commodities to the incomes of the producers and the owners, forgetting the part of this value which reproduced a fraction of the instruments of labour.

to be depreciated within a definite period of time, or else the capitalist will not be in a position to keep up with technical progress and acquire more modern machinery. In the United States it is at present estimated that a machine-tool is physically worn-out after ten years; however, it is morally worn-out after only seven years, and must be replaced by something more up-to-date.[69] Thus, after seven years the capitalist will have to have depreciated the value of his machines, the capital he laid out on their purchase. This "depreciation" can be accomplished in one way only—by transferring to each commodity produced a fraction of the value of the means of production with which it was produced.

In this way labour-power fulfils a dual function from the capitalist's point of view: it conserves the value of the means of production which are used in production; and it creates new value. As part of this new value represents the equivalent of wages, capital advanced by the capitalist, it can be said that labour power *conserves all the value of existing capital and creates all the new value* appropriated by the capitalist.

Every industrialist understands this quite well. He tries to reduce to the utmost possible extent the time during which his machinery, etc., is out of use. Each day, each hour that a machine is not being used to produce is a day, an hour during which it is wearing out physically, and still more morally without a corresponding fraction of its value being conserved by labour power. This is what leads, in many enterprises, to continuous shift work, 24 hours a day.

The capitalist who starts up an industrial enterprise has to divide his capital into two different parts. One part is for acquiring machinery, buildings, raw material, auxiliary products, etc. This part of capital has its value *conserved* in the course of the production process by being incorporated in the value of the finished product. For this reason it is called *constant capital*. The other part of capital goes on the purchase of labour-power. This is the capital that is increased by the surplus-value which the workers produce. For this reason it is called *variable capital*. The ratio between constant and variable capital is called the *organic composition of capital*. The more advanced an enterprise, a branch of industry or a country is, the higher is the organic composition of capital, i.e. the bigger is the share of total capital which is spent on buying machinery and raw material.

The product newly created by labour-power is divided between employers and workers in accordance with the ratio between surplus value and wages. This ratio is called the *rate of surplus-value*: it shows the degree to which the working class is exploited. The higher it is the bigger is the share of the new value created by labour power which is taken by the capitalist. This rate is therefore of the greatest interest to the workers themselves.

But it is of no interest to the employer. *He* is interested in concealing this exact ratio of exploitation, which is hidden behind the exchange of labour-power for wages. What interests the capitalist is the ratio between the mass of surplus value that his business brings him in and the total amount of capital he has advanced: for did he not invest all this capital in order to make a profit on it?

The purchase of machinery is "productive expenditure" for the capitalist only to the extent that the capital laid out for this purpose brings profit, exactly as with the capital laid out for the purchase of labour-power. If it did not, he would not buy a single machine. He therefore looks on the mass of surplus-value produced by his enterprise as a return on his capital as a whole. This ratio is called the *rate of profit*.

If we represent constant capital by *c*, variable capital by *v*, and surplus-value by *s*, we thus obtain the following formulae:

$$\text{Organic composition of capital}: \frac{c}{v}$$

$$\text{Rate of surplus value}: \frac{s}{v}$$

$$\text{Rate of profit}: \frac{s}{c+v}$$

The equalisation of the rate of profit in pre-capitalist society

Under petty commodity production, two kinds of commodities are put on the market: a mass of articles of primary necessity, belonging to producers who work with their own means of production (craftsmen and peasants) and who are thus outside the sphere of operation of capital; and a series of luxury articles and exotic products brought in by merchant capital. In normal times, the articles of primary necessity are sold at their exchange value (determined by the amount of labour socially necessary to produce them); the luxury articles are sold at monopoly prices; i.e. above their value, the merchants accomplishing to their own advantage a transfer of value at the expense of both producers and customers.*

---

* In mediaeval Europe the price of food was usually fixed in the towns and did not allow big profit margins, except when purchase prices were below value, as was long the case with purchases made by the Hanse towns. In the Islamic Empire, where this fixing of prices was not usual and where the corn trade was more highly capitalised, the alternation of good and bad harvests caused violent fluctuations of prices (and profits). Here are the prices of wheat in Baghdad, in French (Germinal) gold francs per metric quintal and in annual averages: in 960, 29·04 F.; in 970, 12·10 F.; in 993, 163·20 F.; in 1025, 96·81 F.; in 1083, 4·84 F.[70]

For these two commodity circuits to remain separated from each other two conditions were needed. On the one hand, it was necessary that for economic reasons (stability and normal satisfaction of outlets) and also social ones (legislation, defining the conditions of entry into a craft industry) capital should have no access to the sphere of production. On the other, it was necessary that the comparative scarcity of capital and comparative abundance of outlets should make possible the· establishing of a series of *parallel monopolies* in the sphere of trade in luxury products. The first condition remained in force right to the end of the Middle Ages. From the sixteenth century, manufacture and domestic industry entered into increasing competition with the crafts, but only with the triumph of the big factory did capitalist industrial enterprise come to produce the bulk of articles of current consumption and so to determine their value.

It was otherwise with the second of these conditions. From the beginning of the fourteenth century, capital engaged in international trade in Western Europe began to outgrow the limits of the outlets to hand. While the big monopoly profits of former days were still to be found in adventurous and distant enterprises (overland trade with India and China), in what Robert Lopez calls "the inner circle" of the international trade of that time, which embraced the whole of Europe and the Near East, fierce competition led on the one hand to increasing costs of purchase at the source, and on the other to considerable reductions in selling prices, and so of profits.[71]

Whereas the Byzantines, at the start, and then the Venetians, had formerly enjoyed real monopolies in the sale of silk and of certain spices, the Genoese, the Catalans, and later the French and Germans, now participated in this trade on an equal footing. Whereas the Flemish master-clothiers had monopolised the trade in cloth, from the fourteenth century the Italians, Brabanters, English, French and Germans broke this monopoly. Whereas the German Hanse had monopolised the trade in herrings, timber and wheat from the Baltic, English, Flemish and especially Dutch merchants were soon to crack open these monopolies.[72]

The fourteenth and fifteenth centuries were thus characterised by a vast ebb and flow of merchant capital, breaking down the monopolist compartments of earlier centuries. This flow of capital made its way towards the sectors in which prices and profits were highest. In this way an *equalisation of the rate of commercial profit* came about, the formation of an average rate of profit which Lopez evaluates at 7 to 12 per cent. Though the sudden increase in profits which accompanied the commercial revolution of the sixteenth century continued for at least a century, commercial competition soon smashed the Spanish and Portuguese monopolies, and the equalisation of prices and profits of luxury articles continued, on a much vaster scale, in the great *entrepôts* and trading centres of the modern world: Antwerp, Amsterdam, London, Venice, Hamburg, Bordeaux, etc.*

The equalisation of the rate of profit in the capitalist mode of production

A similar phenomenon occurred after the advent of the capitalist mode of production. When a new sector of production opens up, capital at first risks itself in this new sector only with circumspection. The first builders of mechanical looms became textile manufacturers and often continued to make their own machines. Capital begins to flow into a branch of industry only from the moment when high profits can be got from it. Thus, during 1820–1830, when the demand for textile machinery was constantly growing, big independent works for making machines were set up in Britain.[74]

In the same way, when, after the Napoleonic Wars, the price of coffee rose steeply in a Europe freed from the Continental blockade, whereas the price of cane sugar declined in face of the competition of beet sugar, many planters in Java, Cuba, Haiti and San Domingo set themselves to replace their plantations of sugar-cane with plantations of coffee. After 1823 a collapse of prices and profits occurred, and the rates of profit on coffee and cane sugar became equal.[75]

The first technician of Portland cement in Germany, M. Bleibtreu, was for ten years the only person to carry on this branch of industry. It needed the boom of 1862–1864 and a profit of 25 per cent per ton to attract other capital, which in turn brought prices down.[76]

The equalisation of the rate of profit in the capitalist mode of production thus results from the ebb and flow of capital, which flows into the sectors where profits are higher than the average and out of the sectors where profits are lowest. The ebbing of capital reduces production, creates a shortage of goods in the given branch, and so leads to an increase in prices and profits. The influx of capital, on the contrary, causes intensified competition in the sectors affected, resulting in a fall of prices and profits. Thus an *average rate of profit* is attained in all the sectors, through competition in capital and commodities.

Under petty commodity production, the producers sell their goods, as a rule, at their actual value (labour time socially necessary to produce them). Under capitalist production, the goods still possess an actual value. It breaks down into value *conserved* by labour-power, the value of the constant capital expended for the production of these

* The Augsburg house of Welser participated in financing the Portuguese expedition to India in 1505, financed another expedition (half-commercial, half-military) to Venezuela in 1527, engaged in the spice trade between Lisbon, Antwerp and South Germany, was a partner in exploiting the silver and copper mines of the Tirol and Hungary, and possessed trading establishments in the chief towns of Germany, Italy and Switzerland.[73] In short, its capital penetrated into every sphere where a high profit was to be obtained.

goods, and value *newly created* by labour-power (variable capital + surplus-value). The value of each capitalist commodity can be represented schematically by the formula $c + v + s$.

Let us imagine three enterprises in different branches of industry: A, B and C. A, let us say, is a *pasta*-making factory, where comparatively few machines are used and a lot of labour; B is a textile mill, where more machinery is used; and C is an engineering works, where even more machinery is used than in A and B. We shall thus have a higher organic composition in B than in A, and in C than in A and B.

Let us now suppose that an average level of productivity and intensity of labour exists and that the rate of surplus-value is the same in the three factories, namely 100 per cent. The value of the production of these three factories could then be expressed like this (each unit representing, say, 1,000 francs).

A: $3,000 \ c + 1,000 \ v + 1,000 \ s = 5,000$

$$\frac{s}{v} = 100\% \quad \frac{s}{c+v} = \frac{1,000}{4,000} = 25\%$$

B: $4,000 \ c + 1,000 \ v + 1,000 \ s = 6,000$

$$\frac{s}{v} = 100\% \quad \frac{s}{c+v} = \frac{1,000}{5,000} = 20\%$$

C: $5,000 \ c + 1,000 \ v + 1,000 \ s = 7,000$

$$\frac{s}{v} = 100\% \quad \frac{s}{c+v} = \frac{1,000}{6,000} = 16.6\%*$$

The rate of profit is thus lowest in the sector with the highest organic composition of capital. This is understandable, since only variable capital produces surplus-value. But the capitalists, as we have seen, are interested only in the rate of profit returned on the whole of their capital. Capital will thus flow towards the sectors with the lowest organic composition of capital, where the rate of profit is highest. And influx of capital means intensified competition, increased use of machinery and rationalisation of work. But these changes lead precisely to an increase in the organic composition of capital. And increase in the organic composition of capital means fall in the rate of profit. The ebb and flow of capital thus tends to equalise the rate of profit in the different branches of production by changing, through competition, the organic composition of their capital.

* This table, like that on page 160, is directly inspired by those used by Marx in *Capital*. Technically speaking, these tables are not quite correct, since they calculate the rate of profit on the basis of the *flow* (in percentage of current production), whereas the capitalists calculate on the basis of the *stock* of capital invested. This distinction between "flow" and "stock" has become current in the contemporary macro-economic techniques: to overlook it would lead to serious mistakes. Nevertheless, it is sufficient to imagine an enterprise which has to renew all its invested capital each year for these examples to become technically correct.

Price of production and value of commodities

Does this mean that a levelling of the organic composition of capital in different branches of industry must actually *precede* the equalisation of the rate of profit? Not at all. Let us look again at our three factories A, B and C, each characteristic of a different branch of industry. The differences in organic composition of capital between these factories broadly correspond to differences in productivity of labour, which we can regard as more or less proportionate to the organic composition of capital.

Let us say that factory B, with its organic composition of capital $\frac{4,000\ c}{1,000\ v}$ represents exactly the average of the productivity of labour at the given period in the given country. If this is so, then factory A, with a productivity of labour which is lower than B's, is working below the *average* conditions of productivity. From the standpoint of society, *it is wasting labour* (just as a weaver who is too slow wastes labour under petty commodity production). On the other hand, factory C, with a productivity of labour higher than B's, is *saving human labour from the standpoint of society*.

Now, it is the amount of labour *socially* necessary—i.e necessary under *average* conditions of productivity—that determines the social value of a commodity. The social value of A's production will thus be lower than the amount of labour actually expended on producing these commodities, lower than its individual value; the social value of C's production will be higher than the amount of labour actually expended on producing these commodities. Through the competition of capital and commodities a transfer of value and surplus-value thus takes place, from sectors where productivity is low to sectors where productivity is high.

But only what exists can be transferred. The total value of all the commodities cannot exceed the total value conserved and newly created in their production. It is in the redistribution of surplus value between the different sectors that this transfer of value is effected, through the equalisation of the rate of profit. In the example we have taken, the total amount of surplus value produced was 3,000. The total amount of capital advanced $(4,000 + 5,000 + 6,000)$ was 15,000. The average rate of social profit works out thus at $\frac{3,000}{15,000}$, or 20 per cent. The prices that the commodities A, B and C will fetch on the market will be:

$$A: 3,000\ c + 1,000\ v +\ \ \ 800\ s = 4,800\ \frac{s}{c+v} = \frac{800}{4,000} = 20\%$$

$$B: 4,000\ c + 1,000\ v + 1,000\ s = 6,000\ \frac{s}{c+v} = \frac{1,000}{5,000} = 20\%$$

$$C: 5,000\ c + 1,000\ v + 1,000\ s = 7,200\ \frac{s}{c+v} = \frac{1,200}{10,000} = 20\%$$

These prices fetched by the commodities on the capitalist market, consisting of the capital advanced for producing them together with this capital multiplied by the average rate of profit, are called their *prices of production.* The formation of these prices under normal conditions of competition means that each unit of capital appropriates a fraction of the total surplus-values produced by society, a fraction equal to the fraction of social capital represented by the unit of capital in question.

Though the formation of prices of production may cause these to vary considerably from the *individual value* of commodities, this in no way means an impairment of the law of value. It is merely the particular application of this law to a society governed by profit, producing under conditions of competition, with levels of productivity constantly changing. It is precisely through competition that it is discovered whether the amount of labour embodied in a commodity constitutes a *socially necessary* amount *or not.* The fact that, through the competition of capital and the equalisation of rates or profit, a part of the surplus-value produced in branches of industry with a low organic composition of capital is drained off towards the branches with high organic composition corresponds to the waste of social labour that occurs in the former branches. A part of the human labour expended there was expended uselessly, from the standpoint of society, and therefore will not be given equivalent recompense in the process of exchange.*

The operation of the well-known "law of supply and demand" is nothing but an illustration of the same law of value. When the supply of a certain commodity exceeds the demand for it, that means that more human labour has been spent altogether on producing this commodity than was socially necessary at the given period. The market price of these commodities then falls below the price of production.

When, however, supply is less than demand, that means that less human labour has been expended on producing the commodity in question than was socially necessary: the market price will then rise above the price of production.

When market prices fall, profits fall; the capitalists adapt themselves to the situation by improving the average productivity of labour (reducing costs of production), which eliminates enterprises where productivity is too low and brings supply down to the level of demand (which may then rise, when market prices fall to a serious extent). When market prices rise, capital is attracted into the branch concerned,

---

* Numberless writers, from Böhm-Bawerk to Pareto, have claimed that Marx, after setting out the labour theory of value in Volume I of *Capital,* had to tacitly revise this theory when he tried, later on, in Volume III, to analyse the working of capitalist economy as a whole. It is now known, since the publication of the *Grundrisse,* that Marx had worked out the theory of prices of production not later than 1858, i.e. before he had ever written Volume I![77]

by the high profits obtainable, and production increases until supply exceeds demand and prices start to fall. The working of competition, the variation of market prices around the values (around the prices of production) of commodities, is the only mechanism whereby, in an anarchic society which produces for a blind market, the capitalists can tune in to social needs. But the working of the "law of supply and demand" explains only the *variations* of prices; it does not at all determine the *axis* around which these variations occur, and which remains determined by the labour expended in the production of commodities.

The equalisation of the rate of profit and the distribution of capital and resources between the different branches of the economy in accordance with the needs revealed on the market can take place in classic fashion only if conditions of perfect competition exist at all levels, among buyers, among sellers, and between buyers and sellers.* Such perfect competition has never existed; this is why in the initial period of capitalism there was only an *approximation* to an equalisation of this kind, taking into account the monopoly and semi-monopoly sectors which then survived as vestiges of earlier epochs. Later, when the capitalist mode of production itself reached the stage of monopoly, the equalisation of the rate of profit assumed a new and special form.†

Centralisation and concentration of capital

The equalisation of the rate of profit favours those capitalist enterprises which have the highest degree of productivity. It works against those enterprises that operate with costs of production above the average prices of production. Now, reducing costs of production and increasing the productivity of labour means, first and foremost, improving and adding to the means of production, replacing living labour (labour-force) by dead labour (instruments of labour which are nothing but the crystallisation of unpaid labour). It is therefore the best equipped enterprises, those with the highest organic composition of capital, that come out on top in capitalist competition.

"The industrial employer . . . found himself urged on to new conquests by the pressure of the machine itself. He had to be abreast of his competitors in reducing prices; and this was a perpetual incentive to

* This last condition is *institutionally* put out of the question by the capitalist mode of production so far as the owners of labour-power are concerned.

† The whole problem of the transformation of value into price was examined in great detail, with meticulous calculation, by Natalie Moszkowska: *Das Marxsche System: ein Beitrag zu dessen Aufbau*, a book which appeared in 1929 and which attracted little comment outside Germany. In the next edition of this *Traité* we shall discuss, in a spirit of appreciation and criticism, this contribution of Natalie Moszkowska's to the development of Marxist economic theory.

him both to increase his scale of production and to avail himself of the improved machines that were constantly being produced. There was doubtless . . . an optimum size for any given business beyond which it is could not grow without loss of productive efficiency. But as the optimum was growing larger with very great rapidity, the great majority of businesses were probably well below it and racing to catch up."[78]

The further machine production advances, the higher becomes the organic composition of capital needed for an entrepreneur to secure the average profit. The average capital needed in order to start a new enterprise capable of bringing in this average profit increases in the same proportion. It follows that the average size of enterprises likewise increases in every branch of industry. Those enterprises will be the most likely to succeed in competition which have an organic composition of capital which is above average, which possess the largest reserves and funds for most rapidly advancing along the road of technical progress. Here, as one example among hundreds, is a table showing the increasing size of investments, and so of technical progress, in proportion to the size of enterprises, in West Germany:

Investments in percentages of turnover in 1955.[79]

Enterprises with:	Chemical industry	Engineering	Electrical industry	Textile industry
1 to 49 employees	3·4	1·5	—	—
50 to 199 employees	3·8	5·5	5·7	4·2
200 to 999 employees	4·7	6·0	6·1	4·3
Over 1,000 employees	13·6	8·2	7·1	4·8

The evolution of the capitalist mode of production thus inevitably entails a *centralisation* and *concentration* of capital. The average size of enterprises increases uninterruptedly; a large number of small enterprises are beaten in the competitive struggle by a small number of big enterprises which command an increasing share of capital, labour, funds and production in entire branches of industry. A few large enterprises centralise means of production and a number of employees such as were not to be found previously except in dozens or even hundreds of manufactories added together.

In competitive struggle the large enterprises defeat the small ones. These latter produce at prices which are too high, they are unable to continue to dispose of their products at a profit, and they go bankrupt. In periods of crisis and economic depression, failure like this is the fate of hundreds and thousands of small enterprises. Thus, capitalist competition continues that *process of expropriation* with which the capitalist mode of production began. Instead of independent producers as the chief victims, however, it is now the capitalists themselves who have become the object of this process. *The history of capital is the* *history of the destruction of the property of the majority for the benefit of the property of an ever smaller minority.**

What happens to the capitalist entrepreneurs who are crushed by competition? They lose their capital, either directly by bankruptcy or else by the taking over of their property, completely or partially, by the big capitalists. At best, the capitalists who are dispossessed in this way remain as managers, mere employees, of their enterprises. Otherwise, they become under-managers or technicians. If their enterprise was too small, and their connections with the business world were quickly destroyed, they may even become mere workers, in factory or office. This is the *proletarianisation*† of the middle classes, their transformation from owners of capital into mere owners of labour-power. This evolution is evidenced by the following table, which relates to the United States and West Germany:

EVOLUTION OF THE CLASS STRUCTURE‡ IN THE UNITED STATES, IN PERCENTAGES OF THE OCCUPIED POPULATION[80]

	1880	1890	1900	1910	1920
Employees of all kinds	62	65	67·9	71·9	73·9
Entrepreneurs of all kinds	36·9	33·8	30·8	26·3	23·5

	1930	1939	1950	1960	March 1965
Employees of all kinds	76	78·2	79·8	84·2	86·3
Entrepreneurs of all kinds	20·3	18·8	17·1	14·0	12·4

EVOLUTION OF THE CLASS STRUCTURE IN GERMANY, IN PERCENTAGES OF THE OCCUPIED POPULATION[81]

	All Germany				
	1882	1895	1907	1925	1933
Independent (incl. assistants belonging to the family)	48·2	39·1	35	31·2	20·0
Employees	57·2	60·9	65	68·8	70·1

		Territory of Federal Republic only	
	1939	1950	1956
Independent (incl. assistants belonging to the family)	28·6	26·4	24·8
Employees	71·4	73·6	75·2

* See figures in Chapters 7 and 12.

† This is the scientific meaning of this term, which does not necessarily imply impoverishment in the sense of a lowering of the standard of living.

‡ Strictly speaking, this formulation is not quite correct, as the category of "employees" includes a certain number of managers, engineers, higher executives, etc., who, regardless of their *mode of employment*, belong rather to the bourgeoisie by their way of life, their exact social function, etc.

In France, similarly, employees made up 47 per cent of the occupied population in 1906, 54·3 per cent in 1921, 57·6 per cent in 1931, and 65 per cent in 1953.

When the destruction of medium and small enterprises, especially those of the craft type, is not accompanied by an all-round industrial advance which creates new needs for labour-power, the former owners of means of production, dispossessed through competition, are not transformed into employees but simply thrown out of the production process. They are no longer proletarianised but are completely pauperised. This is what happened at the dawn of industrial capitalism in Western Europe, and later in the backward countries into which capitalist commodities penetrated. A phenomenon of this sort is constantly being repeated on a small scale.

In the United States, the silk industry underwent a remarkable boom during and after the First World War, centred on the small town of Paterson. When overproduction and then the appearance of rayon (synthetic silk) dealt a heavy blow to the silk industry, many workers put out of employment, who had been able to accumulate savings thanks to the high wages they had received in the preceding period, bought second-hand looms and became small entrepreneurs. From 1927 to 1940, however, more than 50 per cent of those enterprises worked continually at a loss. Incomes of six or seven dollars a week were not unusual for these "entrepreneurs".[82] As with peasants owning tiny plots of land, we see here a concealed impoverishment in which the "possession" of means of production conceals the fact that the income obtained is lower even than that of unemployed industrial workers. The "productivity" of this work is so low that this is a phenomenon of *under-employment*, of concealed unemployment.

However, the process of centralisation and concentration of capital is not accompanied by a proportionate disappearance of the middle classes. Many small and medium capitalists withdraw voluntarily from a branch of production when the competition of big enterprises becomes too dangerous, and endeavour to open up new branches. On the other hand, industrial concentration itself gives rise to new activities which are described as "independent". Giant factories surround themselves with numerous repair-shops. They pass on many orders for separate articles or specialised work to small enterprises which can handle this sort of work more profitably.

Finally, the tremendous growth of constant capital engenders a *new hierarchy* in the enterprise, inserted between the old foreman and the general manager: technicians, engineers, chief engineers, production managers, planners, sales chiefs and publicity chiefs, market research staffs, heads of research laboratories, and so on. These are the *new middle classes*, which come into being in this way and whose standard of living broadly corresponds to that of the old middle classes. These new middle classes are distinguished, however, from the old middle bourgeoisie by the *fact that they are no longer owners of their means of production*, but mere employees who are separated from the proletariat in the social sense only by the level of their wages, their traditions, way of life and prejudices.

The tendency of the average rate of profit to fall

The equalisation of the average rate of profit modifies the sharing-out of surplus-value among the enterprises, in favour of the enterprises with the highest organic composition of capital. But if the average organic composition of capital increases for *all* enterprises, the average rate of profit falls, all other things being equal. If, for example, between one decade and the next, the value of annual production grows from 300 million c + 100 million v + 100 million s = £500 million, to 400 million c + 100 million v + 100 million s = 600 million, the increase in the organic composition of capital from 3 to 4 entails a fall in the rate of profit from $\frac{100}{400}$ = 25% to $\frac{100}{500}$ = 20%. "As a system accumulates more and more productive plant and equipment, the rate of return on new and existing capital becomes depressed."[83]

And increasing organic composition of capital, increase in dead labour as compared with living labour, is the basic tendency of the capitalist mode of production. *The tendency of the average rate of profit to fall* is thus a law of development of the capitalist mode of production.

Here are the rates of profit of American manufacturing industry for successive years.*

| | Constant capital | | Wages and | | Rate of |
	Fixed	Circulating	salaries	Profits	profit %
1889	350	5,160	1,891	1,869	26·6
1899	512	6,386	2,259	1,876	20·5
1909	997	11,783	4,106	3,056	18.1
1919	2,990	36,229	12,374	8,371	16·2†[84]

Seindl gives the following figures showing the tendency for the pace of capital accumulation to slow down under classical capitalism:[85]

Formation of new business capital in percentages of existing business capital, during a decade:

		%			%
1869–1878	=	3·75	1909–1918	=	2·76
1879–1888	=	4·65	1919–1928	=	2·18
1889–1898	=	4·30	1929–1938	=	0·38
1899–1908	=	3·75			

* Calculated as follows: Value of product-value added = circulating constant capital. Depreciation = fixed constant capital. Value added − (wages + salaries + depreciation) = profit.

† For the evolution of the rate of profit in the epoch of monopoly, see Chapters 12 and 14.

We know that labour power both conserves value and creates new value. When we say that the rate of profit falls we mean that an increasing fraction of the annual product consists merely of the *maintenance* of the value of the existing stock of capital, while a decreasing fraction increases the value of this stock. This fact, established theoretically, is to be found empirically in the following statistics, given by Kuznets, of the annual percentage of American production of equipment which is not destined to replace to existing equipment but to *extend* it:

	%		%
1879–1888 =	57·2	1909–1918 =	43·1
1889–1898 =	57·9	1919–1928 =	36·6
1899–1908 =	54·1		

Kuznets also gives the following figures of the cost of depreciation of existing fixed capital, as a percentage of the gross formation of capital:

	%		%
1879–1888 =	39·7	1919–1928 =	62·4
1889–1898 =	43·0	1929–1938 =	86·7
1899–1908 =	46·5	1939–1948 =	67·8[86]
1909–1918 =	50·1		

However, the tendency of the rate of profit to fall does not work uniformly, from year to year or from decade to decade. Its operation is restricted by a series of factors which work in the opposite direction. *(a) Increase in the rate of surplus-value* = growth in the organic composition of capital means growth in the productivity of labour, which may mean increase in relative surplus-value, and so increase in the rate of surplus-value. If from one decade to another the total value of production grows from: 300 million c + 100 million v + 100 million s = 500 million, to 400 million c + 100 million v + 125 million s = 625 million, the rate of surplus value $\frac{s}{v}$ has grown from 100 to 125 per cent, and in spite of the increase in the organic composition of capital from 3 to 4 the rate of profit has remained the same: $\frac{100}{400} = 25\%$, $\frac{125}{500} = 25\%$.

An *equivalent* increase of the rate of surplus value and of the organic composition of capital is in the long run, however, impossible to achieve, because with the increase in the productivity of labour there often comes an extension of workers' needs and a corresponding increase in the value of labour-power, which in turn encourages the development of the labour movement, thus restricting the growth in the rate of surplus value. We must further mention that the increase in the rate of surplus value comes up against *absolute* limits (the impossibility of reducing necessary labour to zero), whereas there is no limit to the increase in the organic composition of capital.

The breakdown theory (*Zusammenbruchstheorie*) is based ultimately on this incapacity to overcome, in the long run, the tendency of the rate of profit to fall, by way of increasing the rate of surplus value. This incapacity has become a burningly topical question in connection with automation. The inevitability of periodical crises, explained in Chapter 11, also contributes to it.

(b) Reduction in the price of constant capital: The organic composition of capital expresses not the ratio between the *material bulk* of the instruments of labour and the number of workers, but the ratio between the *value* of the means of production and the *price* of the labour power hired. If the over-all productivity of labour increases, the value of each individual commodity declines. This law applies to all commodities, including machinery and other means of production. The growth in the organic composition of capital also works in the direction of a lowering of the prices of machines, and so of the value of constant capital in relation to variable capital, and thus opposes the tendency of the rate of profit to fall.

If, however, all progress in productivity undoubtedly reduces the value of each unit of constant capital, this progress implies at the same time a considerable increase in the number of these units. The value of a machine falls, but the number of machines increases in a bigger proportion, and the value of the total mass of machines thus increases instead of remaining stationary. For example, in the United States the values of producer durables in relation to the national wealth increased from 7·4 per cent in 1900 to 8·3 per cent in 1910, 10 per cent in 1920, 9 per cent in 1930, 8·7 per cent in 1940, 10·9 per cent in 1950 and 11·9 per cent in 1955[87]

(c) The extension of the basis of capitalist production: Through foreign trade, capital brings in raw material and articles of primary necessity at cheaper cost, which reduces both the value of constant capital and that of labour-power, and increases both the rate of surplus-value and the rate of profit. The introducing of the capitalist mode of production into new branches or new countries, where at first a lower organic composition of capital prevails, also counters the fall in the rate of profit.

Nevertheless, the widening of the basis of capitalist production inevitably means an extension of exchange. In exchange for the commodities which the industrial countries import from the backward ones they export thither manufactured goods and capital which end by destroying the indigenous mode of production and introducing the capitalist mode of production. The capitalist mode of production, as it extends and becomes world-wide, reduces the sectors in which a higher rate of profit can be obtained. Though this expansion played a big part throughout a long period in checking or halting the tendency of the rate of profit to fall, its efficacy decreases more and more and it may even produce the opposite effect when the backward countries, industrialised in their turn, compel the advanced countries to undertake a substantial increase in the organic composition of capital in order to stand up to their competition.

(d) *Increasing the mass of surplus-value:* The steady expansion in the sphere of operation of capitalism, the accumulation of capital, the growth in the number of wage-earners, imply a constant increase in the *mass* of surplus-value. When the fall in the average rate of profit is comparatively modest, this absolute increase is such as to "reconcile" the capitalist to the system. Indeed, the capitalist is not upset by the prospect of making "only" 10 per cent on a billion, instead of 12 per cent on 200 millions. The increase in the mass of profit from 24 to 100 million makes up for the slight fall in the rate of profit. The reduction in the time taken for circulating capital to circulate contributes to a special extent to the growth in the mass of surplus-value.

The value of a commodity under the capitalist mode of production takes the form $c + v + s$. The laws of development of the capitalist mode of production may be represented in the form of relations between the constituent terms of this formula:

(a) The growth of $\frac{c}{v}$ means growth in the organic composition of capital.

(b) The growth of $\frac{s}{c}$ means the growth in the rate of surplus value.

(c) The reduction of $\frac{s}{c + v}$ means fall in the average rate of profit.

But these three tendencies of development appear differently according to whether one considers them from the standpoint of their general historical significance in relation to the development of the productive forces, or else in relation to the *specific form* they assume under the capitalist mode of production.

The increase in the mass of instruments of labour set in motion by living labour in the process of production; the reduction in the part of the working day devoted to the production of mere means of subsistence (production of the necessary product); the reduction of the wealth produced each year as compared with the wealth gradually accumulated by society—these are the general indices of the progress of civilisation, of a high development of the productive forces, in any society at all, including a socialist society.

The specific form in which these tendencies appear under the capitalist order is the *antagonistic form.* The increase in the social surplus product in relation to the necessary product does not lead to a tremendous increase in well-being and comfort for society as a whole, but to an increase *in the surplus labour appropriated by the possessing classes*, in a growth in the degree of exploitation of the working class. The decrease in the ratio between the new wealth created each year and accumulated social wealth does not mean that mankind can live more and more exclusively on this accumulated wealth, it does not mean a constant increase in leisure, but becomes, on the contrary, a periodical source of convulsions, crises and unemployment. The growth in the mass of dead labour in relation to living labour does not mean an ever-greater saving of human labour, but the creation of a vast industrial reserve army, under the pressure of which consumption by the producers remains restricted to the necessary product, and their physical effort is lengthened or intensified. This antagonistic form which is taken by the tendencies of development of the capitalist system is what makes its destruction inevitable.

The supreme contradiction of the capitalist system

All the contradictions of the capitalist mode of production can be summed up in one general and fundamental contradiction, that between *the effective socialisation of production* and the *private, capitalist form of appropriation.*

The socialisation of production under the capitalist system is the most important and most progressive effect of the generalisation of the capitalist mode of production. In place of the fragmentation of patriarchal, slave-owning or feudal society into thousands of little cells of production and consumption, each one independent of every other, with only rudimentary links (particularly exchange links) between them, there has come *the world-wide relationship between men.* The division of labour has become general and advanced not only in a single country but on a world scale. Nobody any longer produces first and foremost the use-values he needs for his own consumption. The work of each is indispensable to the survival of all, so that each can survive only thanks to the work of thousands and thousands of other men. Individual labour survives only as a tiny part of social labour. It is the objectively co-operative labour of all men that makes production under modern capitalism function, or keeps it going. This production is thus objectively socialised, drawing the whole of mankind into its orbit.

The socialisation of production under the capitalist order makes possible an immense development of the productive forces. The growth of constant capital, especially of the mass of machinery and equipment in industry and transport, has been possible only through an extreme development of the division of labour. This prodigious expansion of the productive forces is implicitly contained in the growth of the organic composition of capital, in the concentration of capital, in the increasing extension of the basis of the capitalist mode of production, which tends towards conquest of the entire world. It implies a no less immense development of human needs, a first awareness of the possibility of an all-round development of every man.

But this socialisation of production which transforms the labour of all mankind into objectively co-operative labour is not regulated, directed, managed according to any conscious plan. It is governed by blind forces, the "laws of the market", in fact by the variations in the rate of profit and the working of the equalisation of the rate of profit, the particular form that the law of value takes in the capitalist system. This is why the totality of production, though objectively socialised, develops independently of the human needs it has itself aroused, and is urged onward only by the capitalists' thirst for profit.

The private form of appropriation makes profit the only aim and driving force of production. It causes the development of the productive forces to be uneven and spasmodic. Production develops by leaps and bounds, not in the sectors where the most urgent real needs are to be found, but rather in those where the highest profits can be achieved. The production of alcoholic drinks, of "comic books" and of drugs takes precedence over the struggle against air-pollution, the preservation of natural resources, and even the building of schools and hospitals.[88] In Britain today more money is spent on gambling than on the fight against cancer, poliomyelitis and arteriosclerosis . . . The private form of appropriation of the social surplus product, of surplus value, determines the *anarchy* of capitalist production. Underproduction in one branch regularly coincides with overproduction in another, until general overproduction and crisis bring periodical punishment for the misdeeds of this anarchy. Disequilibrium and disproportion between the different branches of production are the inevitable elements of this anarchy. The distribution of human labour between the different branches of production never corresponds exactly to the distribution of purchasing power for the products of these branches. When this disproportion becomes too extreme, it is resolved by a crisis, which leads to a new equilibrium, itself temporary and ephemeral.

The contradiction between the *de facto* socialisation of capitalist production and the private form of appropriation finds expression as a contradiction between the tendency to unlimited development of the productive forces and the narrow limits in which consumption remains confined. The capitalist mode of production is thus the first one in which production appears to be completely detached from consumption, in which production seems to have become an end in itself. But the periodic crises remind it harshly that production cannot, in the long run, be divorced completely from society's possibilities of effective consumption.

Free labour and alienated labour

The producer in a primitive society does not usually separate his productive activity, "labour", from his other human activities. Thus, this high degree of integration of his whole life is more an expression of the poverty of society and the extreme narrowness of his needs than a conscious effort towards the all-round development of all human potentialities. The tyranny to which he is subjected is that of the forces of nature. It implies a poor knowledge of the natural setting, a degrading subjection to magic, a primitive development of thought. But the effect of this degradation is greatly mitigated by the high level of social solidarity and co-operation. The integration of the individual with society is achieved in a comparatively harmonious way. When the natural setting is not too hostile, labour is combined with pleasure of body and mind. It satisfies needs both physical and social, aesthetic and moral.*

As the productive forces increase, mankind frees itself more and more completely from the tyranny of the forces of nature. It gets to know its natural setting and learns to change this in accordance with its own ends. It subjects these forces to which formerly it was itself doomed to be more or less passively subject. So begins the triumphal march of science and scientific techniques, which will make man the master of nature and the universe.

But mankind pays a heavy price for this emancipating progress. The transition from a society of absolute poverty to a society of relative scarcity is at the same time transition from a society harmoniously united to a society divided into classes. With the appearance of individual leisure for a minority of society there also appears the alienated time, the time devoted to slave labour, the unpaid labour provided for others by the majority of society. As man frees himself from the tyranny of natural forces he falls more and more under the tyranny of blind social forces, the tyranny of other men (slavery, serfdom) or the tyranny of his own products (petty commodity production and capitalist production).

The alienated nature of slave labour does not need to be explained. The slave and the serf are no longer masters of their lives and of the bulk of their time. Not only the free development of their personality but any development at all is closed to them by their social condition. But labour in capitalist society is also alienated labour, it too implies human alienation to an extreme degree.

This alienation appears primarily as a radical separation between labour and all non-"economic" human activities. The overwhelming majority of the citizens of a capitalist society work not because they like their trade, because they fulfil themselves in their work, because

* See, for example, the description of the *dókpwê*, communal labour in Dahomey.[89]

they regard it as a necessary and adequate condition for the development of their physical, intellectual and moral capacities. They work, on the contrary, *from necessity, in order to satisfy their human needs other than labour.* At the beginning of the capitalist system—as still today in a large part of the "third world"— these needs were reduced, moreover, to the almost animal level of subsistence and physical reproduction. As these needs grow bigger and as the duration of working time grows less, the contrast between "time lost" and "time regained" becomes all the more striking and acute.

Alienation is then expressed in the worker's total loss of control over his conditions of labour, over his instruments of labour, over the product of his labour. This loss of control becomes more marked precisely in proportion as the increase of relative surplus-value replaces the increase of absolute surplus-value, as the working day is shortened, but at the cost of a more and more inhuman intensification and mechanisation of this labour.

Shift work, which deprives the workers of the normal rhythm of the succession of day and night, the conveyor belt and semi-automation, the break-up of old skills, the generalisation of detail-work, are so many stages in this process of alienation. At the end of this process the worker is nothing but an insignificant link in two monstrous mechanisms, the machine in the literal sense, i.e. the instruments of labour that crush him,* and the social machine which crushes him no less with its orders, its hierarchy, its commands, its fines and its organised insecurity. With the crushing of the individual is associated the boredom caused by his mechanised work, a boredom which ends by sapping the vitality of the worker at the bench, and to which the office-workers too will be subject in proportion as office work becomes mechanised as well.†

Alienation is, finally, expressed by the all-round commercialisation and atomisation of capitalist society. Everything is bought and sold. The struggle of all against all implies the negation of the most fundamental and most characteristic of human motives: the protection of the weak, of the old and of children; group solidarity; the desire for co-operation and mutual help; love of one's neighbour. All the qualities, aspirations, potentialities of humanity are no longer realisable

---

* In both the literal (enormous increase in accidents at work) and the metaphorical sense of the word.

† "A hard-working semi-skilled operative learns, after twenty-five years on the job, that the 17-year-old kid next to him, who just quit high school to go to work, is making, within a few pennies, the same hourly wage as he is. And the repetitious arm movement he makes hour after hour is excruciatingly boring. His father, he recalls, was poor, but a craftsman who was proud of the barrels he made. Here the machine has all the brains, all the reasons for pride. Perhaps the rules also forbid him to talk to workers nearby, or to get a drink of water except at the break period."[90]

except by way of acquiring things or services on the market; an acquisition process which capitalism commercialises more and more, thereby levelling and mechanising it. Thus, the shortening of working time is accompanied much less by a growth in humanised and humanising individual leisure than by leisure which is increasingly commercialised and dehumanised.

Recently some Protestant clergymen in West Germany, following the example of the Catholic worker-priests, worked for several months in large factories. On the basis of this experience they have sketched in striking fashion the alienated nature of labour under capitalism:

"The attitude (of the workers) towards labour is usually negative, except for some craftsmen, for whom the skill they have acquired and the experience they are constantly obtaining still play a certain part. As for the rest, they regard work in the factory as a *necessary evil*. His job is the worker's 'enemy', to which he *has to submit* every day for a long stretch, with all that that implies: machines that he must serve; the hierarchy of the enterprise, from the foreman to the management, to which he has been *handed over*, without any possibility of discussion (joint management, i.e. the works council, plays practically no part in our enterprises); but also his fellow-workers, in so far as they themselves are only integral parts of that world which one joins *reluctantly* at the beginning of one's stint and which one leaves *as though escaping* at the end of it . . .

"The time spent in the factory is regarded as a waste of one's life.

". . . The mode and form of labour (whether exhausting physical work or merely the watching of mechanical processes) is not so important as its social status, which is likewise expressed, in the workplaces we have come to know, by *the placing of the worker under authority, as the mere object of decisions taken concerning him* . . .

"The worker is undoubtedly, in spite of the trade unions and the works councils, the weakest feature of our economic system: business fluctuations, temporary stoppages and crises find in him their first victim, threatening his job, whereas they can be absorbed without great human damage by the other factors in the production process. *The feeling of insecurity of livelihood* and of *total dependence on an arbitrary process* of evolution of our entrepreneurial economy is nowhere so high as in this social stratum . . . Without any doubt the urgently desirable change in the social consciousness of the workers is conceivable only in conjunction with a real change in their social situation."[91]* [Emphasis ours.]

The class struggle

Never since the division of society into classes has existed have men

* See the analyses, similar in all respects, of the position of the workers in France, in A. Andrieux and J. Lignon: *L'Ouvrier d'aujourd'hui.*

resigned themselves to the reign of social injustice under the pretext that this could be regarded as an inevitable stage in social progress. The producers have never accepted as normal or natural that the surplus product of their labour should be seized by the possessing classes, who thus obtain a monopoly of leisure and culture. Always and unceasingly they have revolted against this order of things. And unceasingly the most generous spirits among the possessing classes have themselves felt compelled to condemn social inequality and join the struggle of the exploited against exploitation. The history of mankind is nothing but a long succession of class struggles.

The dawn of class society was marked by slave revolts. Only the revolt led by Spartacus and the slave revolts in Sicily under Verres are widely known. About the same time, however, there was the revolt of 40,000 slaves working in the mines of Spain, the revolt of the slaves of Macedonia and Delos, and, a half-century later, the great revolt of the miners of Laurium, in Greece.[92] From the third century A.D. a vast uprising of slaves and impoverished peasants spread over the whole western part of the Roman Empire (the movement of the Bagaudae) and North Africa (the Donatist movement). The importance of the part played by these revolts in the collapse of the Roman Empire has usually been underestimated.[93] The spirit that animated them was clearly grasped by the Arab chronicler Abu Zakaria, who wrote as follows about the Donatists:

"They hate the masters and the rich, and when they meet a master riding in his chariot and surrounded by his slaves, they make him get down, put the slaves in the chariot, and oblige the master to run on foot. They boast that they have come to re-establish equality on earth, and they summon the slaves to liberty."[94]

The invasions of the Visigoths in the Byzantine Empire were likewise accompanied by slave revolts, notably those of the miners in Thrace.[95] Later (820–823) a new and terrible revolt broke out in the Byzantine Empire, helped by the poor, which the Emperor Michael II could only crush after three years of fighting.

In the same period, an army of black slaves used by the Arabs to drain the Shatt-el-Arab rose in revolt (868) and held out for fifteen years against the imperial armies. Again, when commercial and manufacturing capital revived slavery overseas in its most abject forms, there were many insurrections, such as that led by Soerapati, in Java (1690–1710), those of the Indians in Bolivia (1686, 1695, 1704, 1742, and 1767) and that of the Black Jacobins of Haiti.[96]

The peasants, crushed by labour-services or land-rent, themselves endeavoured many times to shake off the yoke of exploitation. The entire history of Antiquity—of Egypt, Judaea, Athens and Rome—is filled with peasant revolts against usury, indebtedness and the concentration of property. In the Persian Empire of the Sassanids the fifth and sixth centuries A.D. show the movement of the Mazdakites, who demanded community of goods, abolition of all privileges and prohibition of the killing of any living thing. This is no doubt why historians in the service of the possessing classes call them "barbarians" and "degenerates".

Throughout Chinese history the reigning dynasties were overthrown by revolts of the oppressed peasants. The dynasties of Han and Ming were themselves dynasties established by peasant leaders, who at first strove to combat not only landed property but even usurer's and merchant capital as well.[97] The fourteenth century in Western Europe was marked by "jacqueries" in nearly every country: France, Britain, Flanders, Bohemia, Spain, etc. The sixteenth century saw the development of the great German peasants' war, with comparable social tendencies in the towns, where the boldest revolutionary ideas appeared with Thomas Münzer and the Anabaptists. The history of Japan in the seventeenth and eighteenth centuries was punctuated by a long series of peasant risings against the increased exploitation to which the peasants were subjected as a result of the generalisation of money economy. No less than 1,100 insurrections occurred between 1603 and 1853.[98]

Finally, the small craftsmen, their journeymen and their hirelings, the ancestors of the modern proletariat, rose up against both the lack of political rights in the great towns and their exploitation by merchant capital.* It was not only the craftsmen of the Flemish and Italian cities of the Middle Ages who waged such struggles, but also the craftsmen of the cities of the Islamic Empire, among whom the powerful international movement of the Carmathians had in the ninth century A.D. welded together all the progressive ideas of the age, and which was continued in insurrections by town guilds in Anatolia and Istanbul right down to the seventeenth century.[100] This movement even succeeded in establishing a communist state in Bahrein and the Yemen which survived for over a hundred years (from the eleventh to the twelfth century).

Why did all these movements fail in their attempt to abolish social inequality; either being defeated or else, if victorious, themselves reproducing social conditions similar to those against which they revolted? † Because material conditions were not yet ripe for abolishing social exploitation and inequality.

---

* The first workers' strike recorded by history was that of Egyptian workers who were working, about 1165 B.C., under Rameses III, at Dehr-el-Medina, on the west bank of the Nile, near Thebes.[99]

† One may quote in this connection the evolution of the Catholic monasteries in which community of goods was at first established, and that of the Czech city of Tabor. When this city was first set up, people had to give up all their possessions, depositing them in "public graves"; but petty commodity production reappeared a few years later.[101]

The absence of classes in man's pre-history is explained by the fact that the social product was there broadly equivalent to the necessary product. The division of society into classes corresponds to a development of the productive forces which already allows of the constitution of a certain surplus, but not yet enough to ensure for the whole of society the leisure needed to exercise functions of social accumulation. On the basis of this inadequate development of the productive forces, the reappearance of social inequality, of the division of society into classes, even where this division had been for a moment abolished, could not in the long run be avoided.

It is the capitalist mode of production that, by the extraordinary advance of the productive forces which it makes possible, creates for the first time in history the economic conditions needed for the abolition of class society altogether. The social surplus product would suffice to reduce extensively the working time of all men, which would ensure an advance of culture that would enable functions of accumulation (and of management) to be exercised by the whole of society. The conscious organisation of labour, already objectively socialised by capitalism, becomes an indispensable condition for a new all-round development of the productive forces.

The development of the capitalist mode of production does not create only the *economic* conditions for the abolition of class society. It likewise creates the *social* conditions. It produces a class which acquires a major interest in abolishing every form of private owner- ship of the means of production because it possesses none. This class at the same time gathers in its hands all the productive functions of modern society. Through its concentration in big factories it acquires by instinct and experience the conviction that it can defend its lot only by assembling its forces, by exercising its great qualities of *organisation, co-operation* and *solidarity*. To begin with, it uses these qualities to take from the employers a larger share of the new value it creates. It fights for a shorter working day and for higher wages. But soon it learns that this struggle can prove effective in the long run only on condition that the entire domination of Capital and its State is challenged.*

---

* In *The Town Labourer*, J. L. and B. Hammond describe graphically how in the nineteenth century the State was wholly at the service of Capital. In the areas of Caerphilly and Merthyr Tydfil the only magistrates were two iron- masters who had continually to sit in judgment [!] on their own workers. These same magistrates were responsible for applying the laws which forbade [!] them to employ the truck system. The same writers describe the movements of troops in industrial areas which "came to resemble a country under military occupation . . . ; soldiers were moved about in accordance with fluctuations in wages or employment."[102]

REFERENCES

1. Capt. Elias Joannes: *Staatkundig-godgeleerd onderzoekschrift over de slaverij, als niet strijdig tegen de Christelijke vrijheid*, Leyden, 1742, quoted in R. P. Rinchon: *La traite et l'esclavage des Congolais par les Européens*, p. 139.

2. Jean Yernaux: *Contrats de travail liégeois du XVIIe siècle*, p. 42.

3. R. H. Tawney: *Religion and the Rise of Capitalism*, p. 220.

4. G. Espinas: *Les Origines du capitalisme*, Vol. II, p. 125.

5. Ferdinand Tremel: *Der Frühkapitalismus in Innerösterreich*, pp. 58-59.

6. Espinas: op. cit., Vol. I, pp. 218-19.

7. G. Glotz: *Le Travail dans la Grèce antique*, pp. 104, 223-51.

8. Espinas: op. cit., Vol. IV, p. 263.

9. W. Sombart: *Der moderne Kapitalismus*, Vol. I, p. 37.

10. Otto Hue: *Die Bergarbeiter*, Vol. I, pp. 262-9.

11. Sombart: op. cit., Vol. I, 802-8.

12. J. Dorfman: *The Economic Mind in American Civilization*, Vol. I, pp. 45, 117.

13. Tawney: op. cit., p. 209.

14. Alfred Bonné: *State and Economics in the Middle East*, pp. 155-8.

15. Audrey I. Richards: *Land, Labour and Diet in Northern Rhodesia*, p. 3.

16. J. Kulischer: *Allgemeine Wirtschaftsgeschichte*, Vol. II, p. 186.

17. Ibid., p. 464.

18. E. Levasseur: *Histoire des classes ouvrières de l'industrie en France*, Vol. I, p. 370.

19. A. P. Usher: *An Introduction to the Industrial History of England*, p. 310.

20. 13th Annual Report, U.S.A. Commissioner of Labour, Vol. I, pp. 24 et seq.

21. G. Friedmann: *Où va le travail humain?*, pp. 64-65.

22. Daniel Bell: *Work and Its Discontents*, p. 7.

23. Ibid., pp. 2-3.

24. J. Gouin: in *Revue française du Travail*, January-February 1951.

25. G. Friedmann: *The Anatomy of Work*.

26. Bell: op. cit., p. 17.

27. Friedmann: op. cit., p. 80.

28. P. Sargant-Florence: *The Logic of British and American Industry*, pp. 149-50.

29. Vance Packard: *The Status-Seekers*.

30. R. B. Tennant: *The American Cigarette Industry*, pp. 15-17.

31. W. IJzerman: *De Geboorte van et moderne kapitalisme*, pp. 85-86.

32. G. Jacquemyns: *Histoire de la crise économique en Flandre*, p. 48.

33. A. D. Gayer, W. W. Rostow and A. J. Schwartz: *The Growth and Fluctuation of the British Economy*, p. 239.

34. E. P. Cheyney: *An Introduction to the Industrial and Social History of England*, revised edition, p. 189.

35. Gouin: op. cit.

36. G. Friedmann: *Où va le travail humain?*, pp. 151-3.

37. G. M. Trevelyan: *English Social History*.

38. Espinas: op. cit., Vol. I, p. 165.

39. Jacques Lacour-Gayet: *Le roi Bilalama*, p. 4.

40. F. Heichelheim: *Wirtschaftliche Schwankungen der Zeit von Alexander bis Augustus*, pp. 98-99.

41. International Metal Workers' Federation: *Les plus grandes sociétés sidérurgiques du monde libre*, a study with a preface written for the steel conference held at Vienna between 19th and 21st March, 1959.

42. K. Polanyi: et al., *Trade and Market in the Early Empires*, p. 269.

43. Joan Robinson: *The Accumulation of Capital*, pp. 49, 73.

44. J. L. and Barbara Hammond: *The Rise of Modern Industry*, p. 210.

45. Thorold Rogers: *Six Centuries of Work and Wages*.

46. E. H. Phelps Brown and Sheila V. Hopkins: "Seven Centuries of Prices of Consumables, compared with Builders' Wage-Rates", in *Economica*, New Series, Vol. XXIII, 92, November 1956, pp. 311-14.

47. *Palgrave's Dictionary of Political Economy*, Vol. III, p. 193.

48. J. Kuczynski: *Die Theorie der Lage der Arbeiter*, p. 256.

49. J. L. and Barbara Hammond: op. cit., pp. 199-200.

50. J. L. and Barbara Hammond: *The Town Labourer*, p. 65.

51. M. Dobb: *Wages*, p. 71.

52. A. Perren: *Les primes sur salaires dans les entreprises industrielles*, pp. 38, 43, 73.

53. *Textbook of Political Economy*, German translation of the 1st edition, p. 167

54. Ibid., p. 153.

55. Ibid., p. 330.

56. Ibid., p. 331.

57. *Trud*, 8th July, 1955.

58. John Strachey: *Contemporary Capitalism*, pp. 104-6, *et al.*

59. Roman Rosdolsky: *Der esoterische und der exoterische Marx*, in *Arbeit und Wirtschaft*, November and December 1957 and January 1958.

60. J. Steindl: *Maturity and Stagnation in American Capitalism*, pp. 229-336.

61. J. K. Galbraith: *The Affluent Society*, p. 333.

62. Vance Packard: *The Status Seekers*.

63. Arzumanyan: "*Questions de théorie marxiste-léniniste sur la paupérisation*", in *Economie et Politique*, October 1956, especially pp. 8, 9, 11, 12-13.

64. John Strachey: op. cit., p. 133.

65. Ibid., pp. 144, 146.

66. Ibid., pp. 149-51.

67. U.S. Department of Commerce: *Historical Statistics of the U.S.A., 1789-1939*; *U.S. Statistical Abstract*, 1958.

68. Real product per hour: Frederick C. Mill: *Productivity and Economic Progress*, Occasional Paper 38 of the National Bureau of Economic Research, p. 2. Wages per hour: series published by the *Bureau of Labor Statistics*. Cost of living: series published by Paul Douglas: *Real Wages*, by *Historical Statistics of the U.S.A.*, and by *U.S. Statistical Abstract*, 1958.

69. J. G. Glover and W. B. Cornell: *The Development of American Industries*, p. 659.

70. Aly Mazahéri: *La Vie quotidienne des Musulmans au moyen âge*, p. 213.

71. R. S. Lopez: "The Trade of Medieval Europe: The South", *Cambridge Economic History of Europe*, Vol. II, p. 334.

72. M. M. Postan, "The Trade of Medieval Europe: The North", *Cambridge Economic History of Europe*, Vol. II, pp. 249-55.

73. Tawney: op. cit., p. 70.

74. Clapham: op. cit., Vol. I, p. 152.

75. Hans Roth: *Die Uebererzeugung in der Welthandelsware Kaffee*, p. 23.

76. Kurt Ehrke: *Die Uebererzeugung in der Zementindustrie*, pp. 16-40.

77. Karl Marx: *Grundrisse der Kritik der politischen Oekonomie*, pp. 338-9, et al.

78. G. D. H. Cole: in *Encyclopaedia of Social Sciences*, Vol. VIII, p. 20.

79. *Deutsche Zeitung und Wirtschaftszeitung*, 2nd October, 1957.

80. Figures for 1880–1939, Spurgeon Bell: *Productivity, Wages and National Income*; figures for 1950, *U.S. Statistical Abstract*, 1958. Figures for 1960 and 1965, *U.S. Statistical Abstract*, 1965.

81. *Statistisches Jahrbuch für das Deutsche Reich 1934. Statistik der Bundesrepublik Deutschland*, Vol. XXXVI, section 3, pp. 28 et seq.

82. E. B. Alderer and H. E. Mitchell: *Economics of American Industry*, pp. 431-4.

83. Lawrence R. Klein: *The Keynesian Revolution*, p. 68.

84. U.S. Department of Commerce: *Historical Statistics of U.S.A.*

85. J. Steindl: op. cit., p. 167.

86. Sumner H. Slichter quotes the first figures in *What's Ahead for American Business?*, p. 83. The second series is from S. Kuznets: "International differences in capital formation", in *Capital Formation and Economic Growth*, p. 62.

87. *U.S. Statistical Abstract*, 1958.

88. Galbraith: op. cit., pp. 257-8 et al.

89. Melville J. Herskovits: *Dahomey*, Vol. I, p. 64. See the similar description of communal work at Nupe, in Nigeria, in S. F. Nadel: *A Black Byzantium*, pp. 248-9.

90. Vance Packard: *The Status Seekers*.

91. Horst Krockert: in *Die Mitarbeit*, No. 7, 1958.

92. Heichelheim: *Wirtschaftsgeschichte des Altertums*, Vol. I, pp. 630, 642.

93. Robert Latouche: *Les grandes invasions et la crise de l'Occident au V⁰ siecle*, p. 48.

94. Quoted in E. F. Gautier: *Le passé de l'Afrique du Nord*, p. 259.

95. M. V. Levtchenko: *Byzance, des origines à 1453*, pp. 28-29.

96. Rutgers: *Indonesië*, p. 57; *Handbook of American Indians*, p. 512; C. L. R. James: *The Black Jacobins*, etc.

97. See in *An Outline History of China* the long list of peasant revolts, pp. 44-46, 66-67, 101-3, 122-5, 141-4, 158-60, 166-7, 182-3, etc.

98. Hugh Barton: *Peasant Uprisings in Japan of the Tokugawa Period*, p. 1.

99. Article *"Grèves"* in *Dictionnaire de la civilisation égyptienne*.

100. Louis Massignon: "Islamic Guilds", in *Encyclopedia of the Social Sciences*, Vol. VII, p. 216.

101. Joseph Macek: *Le mouvement hussite en Bohème*, pp. 40-41 and 55-59.

102. J. L. and Barbara Hammond: *The Town Labourer*, pp. 65, 85.

CHAPTER SIX

TRADE

Trade, outcome of uneven economic development

IN a society based mainly on production of use-values, merchants' profit arises from buying commodities below their value and selling them above their value. Consequently, at the beginning, trade could not develop between peoples living at a more or less identical level of economic development. In such a case, the approximate amount of labour-time needed to produce the commodities being exchanged is known in both countries. Neither buyers nor sellers would let themselves be drawn into making exchanges which would be extremely unfavourable to them.* Only exceptional circumstances, with the occurrence of sudden shortages of currently needed consumer goods or indispensable raw materials, enable substantial profits to be made through trade under these conditions.

Trade, however, with peoples who are at a lower economic level of development offers ideal conditions for the making of such profits. Raw materials or provisions (metals, timber, wheat, fish, wine) can be bought from them cheap, and finished craft products (pottery, metal utensils, ornaments, textile goods) can be sold them for more than their value. In the uneven economic development between peoples is to be found the origin of the expansion of trade starting with the period marked by the metallurgical revolution and the beginnings of civilisation: *

". . . Inequality and diversity of resources between different societies which are neighbours or which can communicate with each other, the permanent conditions for all exchange, . . . are to be found everywhere on the world's surface, however far back prehistorians go in studying and learning about our ancestors."[1]

Empirically-observed data fully confirm this view. In the first place, they confirm that trade appears in every primitive society in the form of the *foreign trader* come from a more advanced society. The first traders mentioned in the Egyptian sources are foreigners.[2] In ancient Greece, in the archaic period, foreign merchants were the first to appear in the young cities.[3] In the most ancient texts of the *Avesta*, the holy book of Iran, the merchants are foreigners who bring luxury goods

* See Chapters 2 and 3.

182

for the king and the nobles.[4] In the *Rig-Veda*, the oldest written document of Hindu civilisation, the merchants are foreigners (*pani*) travelling in caravans.[5] Hellenised foreigners were the first traders in Rome.[6] In Byzantium, large-scale trade was at first in the hands of Syrians, Jews and Orientals.[7] In the Islamic empire, the first traders were Christians, Jews and Zoroastrians.[8] Jews and Syrians were likewise the first traders in the Western European Middle Ages,[9] while in the same period the Koreans were the first to introduce trade into Japan.[10] In China, from the Tang to the Ming dynasty, foreigners, principally Indians and Moslems, controlled all foreign trade. The predominance of German traders in Scandinavia, Jewish traders in Poland, Hungary and Rumania, Armenian traders in the Turkish empire in Asia, Arab traders in East Africa, Chinese traders in South-East Asia, continued for centuries this initial phase of large scale trade.

On the other hand, empirically-observed data underline how this same law of uneven economic development implies rapid reversals of the currents of trade as soon as a people acquires the comparatively simple craft technique of petty commodity society, in circumstances where the absence of expensive industrial installations makes it easy to transfer both techniques and technicians. The *metoikoi* from Asia Minor were the first traders in mainland Greece, but soon the Greek colonies came to monopolise trade in Asia Minor, down to the time when, in the Hellenistic epoch, Asia Minor again took its revenge on Greece. Jews, Christians and Persians were the first traders in the Islamic empire; but, soon, Arab traders were playing the chief part in trade in Europe, the Middle East and Persia. In the fifth century A.D. Indian merchants dominated trade in the Arabian Sea; a few centuries later, Arab traders were dominating trade in India;[11] then, under the Mogul Empire, in the seventeenth century, Indian and Persian traders again pushed back the Arab merchants. Jews and Syrians from Byzantium monopolised Italy's large-scale trade in the early Middle Ages; from the eleventh century onward, Venetians and Genoese conquered the dominant place in trade in Byzantium itself.

The history of the Roman empire consists entirely of sharp swings like this. In the second and first centuries B.C., the Roman conquest and the trade which followed in its wake had destroyed the economic preponderance of Asia Minor which had been established since the age of Alexander. But from the first century A.D., Roman trade surrendered the East to the new stratum of Syrian merchants, and withdrew towards Gaul—which, from the second century, pushed back Roman trade in its turn, and shared with the Syrians economic predominance throughout the Empire.[12]

Production and realisation of surplus-value

In the pre-capitalist modes of production, merchant capital is the predominant form of capital. It embodies money economy coming to birth in the midst of an economy essentially based on the production of use values. It makes its appearance in the risky dual form of large scale international trade and local peddling. The more petty commodity production develops, the more producers themselves sell their goods on the market, and no room is left for professional trade except outside this normal circulation of goods.

But the union of production and trade presents technical problems that can be solved only within a restricted framework. The craftsman who himself takes his products to the market has to stop producing while he is travelling; this is why, in a petty commodity society, markets are usually held on holidays. Discussing with Malay fishermen, Raymond Firth noted that as a rule they do not engage in trade on a working day. It is only when not going fishing, for one reason or another, that "one buys fish to sell".[13] To facilitate the petty producer-merchants' journeys to the markets, the Chorti Indians have adopted "the custom of providing food, a bed, and pine torches to anyone, even strangers, who may request them. The giver does not expect to be paid but in turn may request the same hospitality in the future when he needs it . . ."[14] All these customs are effective only if the distance between the place of production and the market is not too big. When the distance increases, the producer finds it too much of a burden to carry his products to the market himself. The craftsmen of Nuremburg in the Middle Ages brought their goods as far as the Frankfurt Fair; but for more distant centres they handed over their products to professional traders.[15]

Professional trade thus appears as the result of a division of labour which spares the producers the losses they would have suffered by interrupting production in order to sell their products directly.[16] Professor Jacquemyns has worked out these losses in the case of the Flemish linen-weavers of the first half of the nineteenth century, who had to go and buy raw material for themselves, in small quantities, in the neighbouring markets, and then to sell their fabric, piece by piece, in these same markets. He estimates them at one-fifth of their small incomes.[17]

Professor Ashton arrives at even more definite conclusions when he studies the situation in the British textile industry in the eighteenth century:

"Generally the [textile] worker had to do his own fetching and carrying [of the products he needed] . . . On the roads of the North large numbers of weavers were to be seen bearing yarn in packs on their backs, or heavy rolls of cloth under their arms. The distances covered were often as great as most men would care to traverse in a day . . . It is said that in the hosiery trade of the east Midlands as much as two and a half days a week might be taken up in getting orders and material, returning finished work, and collecting wages."[18]

Observing a community based on petty commodity production, Professor Sol Tax notes that the producers calculate, in the literal meaning of the expression, the *labour-cost* of the direct selling of their goods to possible customers, and prefer to sell to traders only when the *saving in labour-time* is a real one (when the production which could be carried out during this time lost in selling is worth more than the trader's profit):

"In Panajachel, where merchants come to the farm and bargain for beds of onions even before they are harvested, the farmer calculates his chances of getting more by harvesting the onions, taking them to market, and so selling them at wholesale or retail. In doing so he calculates the value of his time . . ."[19]

The problem arises in the same way when industrial capital takes the place of the independent petty producer, and commercial capital replaces the old merchant. When the production of commodities is completed, the industrial capitalist already possesses the surplus-value produced by his workers. But this surplus-value exists in a particular form; it is still crystallised in commodities, just as the capital advanced by the industrialist is, too. The capitalist can neither reconstitute this capital nor appropriate the surplus-value so long as they retain this form of existence. He must transform them into money. To realise the surplus-value he must sell the commodities produced. But the industrialist does not work for definite customers (except when he carries out orders for the "ultimate consumer"); he works for an anonymous market.

Every time that a production cycle is completed, he would thus have to stop work at the factory, sell his commodities in order to recover his outlay, and only then resume production. By buying what the industrialist produces, the traders relieve him of the trouble of going himself to look for the consumer. They save him the losses and charges involved in interrupting production until the commodities have reached their destination. They, so to speak, advance him the money-capital that allows him to carry on producing without any interruption.

But the traders, who advance to the industrialists the funds they need to reconstitute their capital and realise their surplus-value, must in their turn quickly sell the goods thus bought, so as to begin the operation anew as soon as possible. As the capitalist mode of production spread and commodity production became general, towns and villages were covered with an ever denser network of wholesale and retail shops. Just as the expansion of the luxury trade in the Middle Ages was characterised by the transformation of travelling merchants into sedentary merchants,[20] in the same way the expansion of trade in products of primary necessity, at the dawn of industrial capitalism, was marked by the transformation of the little itinerant hawker into a retailer permanently stationed in the village.[21]*

In the Middle Ages, wholesale and retail trade were not separated so far as products intended for the local market were concerned, and wholesale trade was often completely absent. Specialised retailers begin only with the *mercers*; there were 70 in the whole of France in 1292, 200 in 1570 and 2,800 in 1642.[23] It was after the commercial revolution that the separation of wholesale from retail trade took place as regards luxury products, the big colonial companies keeping only the wholesale trade for themselves.

The industrial capitalist does not only want to *realise* his surplus-value. He further wishes to *capitalise* it, to transform into machines, raw material and wages all that part of it which he does not consume unproductively to meet his own needs. The capitalisation of surplus-value thus itself implies a circulation of commodities in which the industrialist, instead of being a seller, appears as a buyer. In this capacity he is also interested in reducing to the utmost the period of circulation of machinery and raw materials, the waiting period between orders and deliveries. Commercial capital thus does him the twofold service of reducing the circulation-time of his own commodities and also that of the commodities he wishes to buy.

Annual amount of surplus-value and annual rate of profit

The small craftsman who avoids the expenses of waiting and not producing to which he is exposed if he sells the products of his labour himself, thus realises a gain a part of which it is to his interest to hand over to the merchant. The industrial capitalist knows no other gains than the surplus-value produced by his labour-force. Does the reduction in the circulation-periods of the goods he sells and those that he buys increase the amount of surplus-value produced by the workers?

From the standpoint of its circulation, industrial capital comprises two parts. One part of this capital, called *fixed capital*, consists of buildings and machinery which are not replaced until after the lapse of a fairly long period, after a number of production cycles. The value

---

* In Eastern Europe, in the Balkans and in Russia, these travelling retailers were still to be met right down to the beginning of the twentieth century, together with travelling craftsmen who themselves sold the products of their labour. In the under-developed countries they may still be encountered today, and even in the advanced countries they have not completely disappeared. The *White Book* (1953) of the Belgian Ministry of Economic Affairs shows that the number of travelling merchants who sell from door to door is quite high in the Flemish areas, where the peasants live scattered about the countryside.[22]

of this capital, advanced all at one go by the industrialist, is reconstituted—amortised, or depreciated—little by little. At the end of each production cycle, when the goods produced have been sold, a mere fraction of this fixed capital has been reconstituted. The period needed for reconstituting the whole of this fixed capital, called the rotation period of fixed capital, thus comprises a number of production cycles.

It is otherwise with *circulating capital*, that is, the part of constant capital which consists of raw material and auxiliary products, together with variable capital, the wages advanced by the capitalist. Circulating capital has to be advanced at the beginning of each production cycle. But as soon as the goods produced during this cycle have been sold, the capitalist is back in possession of this circulating capital, and can recommence a fresh production cycle. The rotation period of circulating capital thus breaks down into a production cycle of commodities and a circulation period of these same commodities. Substantially reducing the circulation period of commodities means reducing the rotation period of circulating capital and thus enabling a larger number of production cycles to be accomplished in a given period of time—say, a year.

Let us suppose that in a cotton mill each rotation period of circulating capital comprises two months; one month to produce a given amount of cotton cloth and one month to sell it and buy a fresh stock of raw material. There will thus be six production cycles in a year. By reducing from a month to a week the period needed for selling the cotton goods and buying fresh raw material, the rotation period of circulating capital is reduced to 5·3 weeks, and there will then be ten cycles a year instead of six.

Now, each production cycle brings in the same amount of surplus-value, provided that the capital and the rate of surplus-value remain the same. Increasing the number of production cycles accomplished in one year means increasing the total amount of surplus-value produced in that year. Reducing the circulation time of commodities is thus not only a way of realising surplus-value *more quickly*, it is also a way of *increasing the amount*.

"The quicker the rotation of money-capital in the enterprise the higher is its profitability (its annual rate of profit)."[24]

From the standpoint of the value of the commodities there is no change resulting from the reduction in the rotation period of circulating capital. So long as the production cycle of commodities is not changed, the value of the commodities remains the same. But it is otherwise with the rate of profit on the capital. This rate is not calculated in relation to the production cycle but to the fiscal year. Suppose that the capitalist has installations valued at 1,000 million francs, one per cent of which is depreciated in each production cycle. Further, suppose that in each cycle he has to advance 20 millions, 10 millions to buy raw materials and 10 millions to pay his workers' wages. The value of the production in each cycle will thus emerge as follows, the rate of surplus-value being 100 per cent:

$$20 \text{ millions } c + 10 \text{ millions } v + 10 \text{ millions } s = 40 \text{ millions.}$$

The value of a year's production, after six production cycles, will thus be 240 millions. But when he calculates his annual rate of profit the capitalist does not compare his profit with his *turnover* but rather with his *capital actually expended*: 6 per cent of his fixed capital, i.e. 60 millions, plus his circulating capital of 20 millions, making a total of 80 millions. And as each cycle has brought him 10 millions in profit, his annual rate of profit will be $\frac{60}{80}$, or 75 per cent. If now the number of production cycles in a year is increased from 6 to 10, the capital expended every year increases to ten times 10 million of fixed capital, i.e. 100 millions, plus 20 millions of circulating capital, making 120 millions. The profit will rise to ten times 10 millions, or 100 millions. The annual rate of profit will thus increase to $\frac{100}{120}$, or 83·3 per cent as compared with the previous 75 per cent.

Reducing the circulation period of commodities thus makes it possible to increase the annual rate of profit. Uninterrupted production is an important form of capitalist *rationalisation*; it effectively counters the tendency of the average rate of profit to fall. Japanese manufacturing industry has accomplished a significant rationalisation of this kind since the defeat of 1945 and the American occupation, in order to make up for the loss of the Chinese and Korean markets and the increase in labour-costs (the fall in the rate of surplus-value). The number of rotation periods in a half-year for the whole of the capital invested in Japanese industry (except mining and transport) has increased from 0·66 in the first half of 1936 to 1·54 in the first half of 1950 and 1·84 in the second half of 1951. Whereas, twenty-five years ago, 40 weeks had to pass before the industrial capitalists as a whole had recovered the capital they had advanced, today only 14 weeks are needed.[25]

In order to reduce to the utmost the circulation-time of commodities, this network of shops and businesses is complemented by a dense network of roads, canals and railways. Capital is not merely athirst for surplus-value; it is, further, obsessed with the need to reduce to the utmost the rotation period of circulating capital. This reduction makes it possible *continually to transform circulating capital into fixed capital*, reducing the former in comparison with the latter. This is the very essence of what is called the industrial revolution.[26]

Commercial capital and commercial profit

It is very much to the interest of the industrial entrepreneur that the circulation period of commodities should be reduced as much as possible. This is why he hands over the greater part of all the operations in the distributive sphere (transport, storage, selling and buying at the source, advertisement, etc.) to a specialised branch of capital, commercial capital. For this specialisation to occur, however, it is necessary that capital invested in the sphere of distribution should bring the same rate of profit as the total capital invested in industry. Since commercial businesses need much smaller initial outlay than large-scale industrial concerns, there is much quicker fluctuation as regards entries into and and exits from the sphere of distribution than is the case with that of production. A commercial rate of profit higher than the rate of profit in industry would lead to a flow of capital into trade, a flow which would lower the rate of profit, owing to the increased competition. A rate of profit in trade lower than the industrial rate would lead to an ebbing of capital from the distributive into the productive sphere, an intensification of industrial competition and a corresponding fall in the industrial rate of profit.

Commercial capital thus participates in the general share-out of surplus-value, but without itself producing any part of it. The total amount of surplus-value produced always results exclusively from *production* of commodities, only from the incorporation of unpaid labour in these commodities while they are being produced. Though itself not producing surplus-value, commercial capital shares in the division of the total surplus-value, on an equal footing with industrial capital, because by reducing the circulation-time of commodities it helps the industrialists to increase the total amount and the annual rate of surplus-value. This applies to each branch of commercial capital: wholesale, semi-wholesale, and retail. Commercial profit is thus proportional to the capital invested in trade, on the same basis as industrial profit. Owing to the equalisation of the rate of profit, it constitutes a fraction of the total amount of surplus-value in proportion to that fraction of total social capital constituted by the capital which brings it in.

Suppose that a country's total production is worth 900 billion francs, of which 800 billion represent capital (constant and variable) conserved by labour-power and 100 billion represent surplus-value produced by it. Suppose that commercial capital in this country amounts to 200 billion francs, made up of 100 billion in wholesale trade, 40 billion in semi-wholesale trade and 60 billion in retail trade. The average rate of profit will be $\frac{100}{1,000}$, or 10 per cent. The industrialists will sell the commodities produced to the wholesalers for 880 billion francs, making the average rate of profit, 10 per cent. The wholesalers will sell these commodities to the semi-wholesale traders for 890 billion, so making

10 billion profit, or 10 per cent on their capital of 100 billion. The semi-wholesale traders will re-sell them to the retailers for 894 billion, making a profit of 4 billion, i.e. 10 per cent on their capital of 40 billion. Finally, the retailers will sell the goods to the consumers for 900 billion, making a profit of 6 billion—10 per cent on their capital of 60 billion. At the conclusion of these successive sales, the goods are sold at their exact value: 900 billion francs. No new value has been created in the course of their circulation. Each unit of capital has realised the same average profit, 10 per cent.

It could be claimed that, if commercial capital had not intervened, industrial capial would have made a higher profit, namely, 12·5 per cent. But this would mean forgetting that the total amount of surplus-value, 100 billion, would have been less without the reduction in the circulation-time of commodities which commercial capital ensured, or, what comes to the same thing, that industrial capital would have had to operate with a larger quantity of money-capital, thrown into the production process as the latter went forward continuously, before the commodities of the preceding cycle had been sold to the consumers. In the last analysis, nobody has suffered in the total operation carried out.

In practice, such an *absolute* identity of rates of profit in the different branches of trade and between trade and industry is naturally not found to exist. The variations in commercial profit are many, depending largely on the actual stage of the industrial cycle. In the phases of economic recovery and boom, when prices are rising quickly, stocks can be realised and disposed of with ease, demand exceeds supply, and traders make super-profits in comparison with industry. At such moments, the number of traders rapidly increases. As trade necessitates very much smaller advances of constant capital than industry, many small capitalists can appear, to try their luck in a period of general euphoria. A phenomenon like this was seen in Western Europe after 1945, and in West Germany after the currency reform of summer 1948. But, generally speaking, the rate of commercial profit cannot vary for long from the average rate of profit; otherwise, the industrialists would themselves start to expand their own organisations for direct sale to the public.

Contrariwise, on the eve of and during periods of crisis and depression, the traders are the first to be hit by the fall in sales. Possessing smaller reserves than the big industrialists, and obtaining bank credit less easily, they will be forced to get rid of their stocks at any price, that is, to sell at a loss. The commercial rate of profit then falls below the industrial rate of profit. Through these conjunctural variations the equilisation of the rate of profit in trade and in industry becomes effective.

These conjunctural contractions and expansions in trade can be illustrated by the following figures: in 1929, a year of prosperity, the turnover of the retail shops in the U.S.A. represented 61·3 per cent of the total expenditure of the consumers. In 1933, a year of crisis, it represented no more than 49 per cent. In 1939 it rose to 62·9 per cent, and reached 72·9 per cent in 1945, a boom year.[27]

Commercial capital and labour-power engaged in distribution

At first sight it would seem that commercial capital passes through the same metamorphoses as industrial capital. The large-scale trader launches his enterprise by investing initially a certain amount of money-capital in the form of *fixed capital* (buildings for shops, depots, warehouses) and *circulating capital* (stocks of goods and wages for labour). It would even be possible to talk of the "organic composition" of his capital, since, just as with the industrialist, his fixed and circulating capital have very different rotation-periods.

But there the apparent parallel ends. In reality, the "variable capital" of the trader—the capital needed for the purchase of the labour-power employed in distribution—is not variable at all, since it produces no new value, no surplus-value. The labour-power bought by the commercial capitalist merely enables him to participate in the general share-out of the surplus-value produced by the productive workers.

The concepts of productive and unproductive labour from the standpoint of *production of new value* must not be confused with the concepts of productive and unproductive labour from the standpoint of the general interests of society. When they produce dum-dum bullets, opium or pornographic novels, workers create new value, since these commodities, finding as they do buyers on the market, possess a use-value which enables them to realise their exchange-value. But from the standpoint of the general interests of human society, these workers have done work which is absolutely useless, and even harmful. By recording the arrival and departure of goods in a big shop, or by enabling consumers to choose between different examples of a given commodity, workers employed in the sphere of trade do work which is useful and productive from the standpoint of society's general interests—without, for all that, creating any new value.

Nevertheless, the line separating labour which produces new value and labour which does not is hard to draw. In general, one can say that all labour which creates, modifies or conserves use-values or which is *technically indispensable* for realising them is productive labour, that is, it increases their exchange-value. In this category belong not only the labour of industrial production properly so called, but also the labour of storing, handling and transport without which the use-values cannot be consumed.*

It goes without saying that this does not apply to the storing of goods in the traders' depots, which results from speculation, non-sale, competition, or the trader's mistakes in his estimation of the market. In this case, not only does the commodity not increase in value, it even loses value, because the storage period usually implies a degree of deterioration (real or moral). Similarly the commercial packing of most commodities adds nothing to their value; it represents overhead costs of distribution, included in the outlay of commercial capital on which the latter expects to realise its average profit. But this does not apply to the containers for liquids (milk, syrup, preserved fruit, jam of all kinds) without which these commodities would not reach their consumers. Here it is again a matter of costs which are indispensable for realising the use-value of a commodity, and which therefore add to the value, the price of production, of the latter. Often, these costs actually make up the largest element in the price.

From the trader's point of view, all these outlays, whether used for buying goods or for hiring labour or for renting premises, represent capital on which he has to realise the average profit. The industrialist's position is not the same. He regards as indispensable only those outlays by the traders which make it possible to realise the value of his goods in advance. All the rest constitutes, in his view, extra and useless expense, an increase in distribution charges of which he complains, since it increases the amount of capital which will participate in the share-out of the surplus-value created by his workers. Under the influence of industrial capital, political economy distinguishes the trader's "capital", needed for the purchase of goods, from his "overheads", needed for buying labour, renting shops, etc., "overheads" which are not very flexible and which "uselessly" enhance the price of goods.

It must be added that the "organic composition of capital" is much lower in trade than in industry, and that funds for fixed investments are often lacking. In the United States, insurance companies and building societies often buy sites, build shops on them and then let these to retailers.[29]

The concentration of commercial capital

Like industrial capital, commercial capital is subject to the fundamental tendency towards concentration. In periods of crisis and intensified competition, the big shops which have better reserves and substantial credit resist the blows of bad luck better than the small shop-

---

* It is interesting to observe that, six centuries before Marx, St. Thomas Aquinas laid down essentially the same distinction between these two forms of "commercial" labour—the one productive and the other not.[28]

keepers who are really working for a modest wage. Similarly, in periods of boom, large-scale traders are able to invest larger amounts, buy bigger stocks of goods and profit to a larger extent from the possibility of realising super-profits. The big shops can sell cheaper because they buy as wholesalers, and are in a position to cut down to a considerable extent the retail profit margin which is added to the wholesale price of commodities where the small shopkeepers are concerned.

"Brokers' fees, wholesalers' commissions, salesmen's salaries, advertising expenditures—all are partially chargeable to the efforts of sellers and manufacturers to find retail outlets for their goods . . . This is the key to much, if not most, of the advantage which the grocery chains have over the independent retailer-wholesaler system. When the function of wholesaling is integrated with that of retailing, it is no longer necessary to 'sell' the retail store."[30]

Other advantages consist in the possibility of using more modern and effective equipment, and of profiting immediately from the creation of new needs for expensive products, in being able to site shops more conveniently, to specialise the staff, standardise goods, rationalise services, and so on.[31] The big shops also received enormous free subsidies for advertisement purposes from the big industrial concerns. For the year 1934 the American "Atlantic and Pacific" chain stores received 6 million dollars for "advertising charges" and 2 million dollars for "advertising commissions", despite the fact that their actual advertising costs did not exceed 6 million dollars![32]

The concentration of capital resulting from commercial competition has taken a variety of forms:

(a) *The department stores* which first developed in Paris, through the extension of what were called "novelty" shops (1826: foundation of *La Belle Jardinière*), and then spread in the second half of the nineteenth century throughout all the capitalist countries. In 1852, foundation of the *Bon Marché* in Paris; about 1860, foundation of Whiteley's and Peter Robinson's, then of Selfridge's and Harrods, in Britain; about the same time, foundation of R. J. Macy's in New York (1858), of Marshall Fields in Chicago and of Wanamaker in Philadelphia (1861), in the U.S.A.; in 1881, foundation of Karstadt, and in 1882, of Tietz, in Germany; and so on. Department stores profit especially from an increase in turnover proportionally greater than the increase in capital outlay.[33]

(b) *The one-price stores* began in the United States, where Woolworth's was established in 1879. About 1910 a branch of Woolworth's was opened in Britain, about 1925 these one-price stores spread in France and Germany, and in the following decade they spread all over Europe. These stores reduce to the utmost their overheads—less packing, no specialised staff for paying invoices, no delivery to customers' homes, etc.—are able to turn over their capital much more rapidly

(8·4 times a year, compared with 3 or 4 times a year in the French department stores in 1938), and thus realise a higher annual rate of profit.[34]

(c) *The chain stores* are the most characteristic form of concentration of commercial capital. They enable the range of operations to be extended considerably without any increase in the amount of capital tied up in fixed installations. The increase in the rate of profit results in their case mainly from buying cheaper, because on a large scale, and from saving in administration charges.[35]*

The chain stores, which have developed strongly from the end of the last century onwards, have succeeded in absorbing a considerable share of all trade.

In France in 1906 there were 22, with 1,792 branches, in the food sector. In 1936 there were already 120, with over 22,000 branches, or 16 per cent of all the food shops in France.

In Britain the number of chain store firms and the number of their branches has steadily increased since the last quarter of the nineteenth century:

	Number of firms with more than ten branches	Number of branches
1875	29	978
1880	48	1,564
1885	88	2,787
1890	135	4,671
1895	201	7,807
1900	257	11,654
1905	322	15,242
1910	395	19,852
1915	433	22,755
1920	471	24,713
1925	552	29,628
1930	633	35,894
1935	668	40,087
1939	680	44,487
1950	638	44,800[37]

Since then, these firms have themselves undergone the process of concentration: their number has declined while the number of branches has gone on increasing.†

* Galbraith, Holton and others point out that in Puerto Rico the turnover per employee increases from 254 dollars a month to 466; 724; 1,061; 1,485 and 1,901 as one proceeds from shops with a monthly turnover of less than 500 dollars to those with one of 500 to 1,000, 1,000 to 2,000, 2,000 to 4,000, 4,000 to 10,000 and 10,000 to 40,000.[36]

† In 1880 there was only one firm which had more than 200 branches; in 1900 there were already 11, in 1920 there were 21, and in 1950 there were 40. The first firm with more than 500 branches had appeared by 1890. In 1910 there were two firms with over 1,000 branches, and in 1950 five firms with over 1,000 (9,695 branches altogether).[38]

In all, the share of chain stores in British retail trade rose from 3 to 4·5 per cent in 1900 and 7 to 10 per cent in 1920, to 14 to 17 per cent in 1935, and 18 to 20·5 per cent in 1950. For certain products, however, this proportion is very much bigger, notably for clothes and footwear, in which it rose from 3·5 to 5 per cent in 1900, to 11·5 to 14 per cent in 1925 and 27 to 30·5 per cent in 1950.[39]

In the United States the chain stores, the most powerful of which is the Atlantic and Pacific Tea Company trust, founded in 1859, accounted in 1929 for 20·8 per cent of the total turnover of retail trade; this percentage rose to 22·7 per cent in 1939 and 30·7 per cent in 1954.[40] The number of branches increased from 8,000 in 1914 to 105,000 in 1950.

We also find in the commercial sector the classical indices of concentration of capital. The number of wage-earners employed in the big shops has increased as compared with the number employed in the small shops. In France the number of wage-earners employed in trading establishments with a staff of more than ten increased from 268,187 in 1906 to 765,293 in 1931, whereas the number of establishments with not more than ten only increased from 517,650 to 631,796. Small and medium shops accounted in 1906 for 66 per cent of all commercial wage-earners, but in 1931 for only 45 per cent.[41] In 1958, 23 per cent of commercial employees were working in enterprises with more than 100 employees—that is, in 0·33 per cent of the total number of shops!

In Germany, commercial enterprises employing more than 50 wage-earners embraced in 1882 2·5 per cent of the total number of commercial employees, in 1895 3·2 per cent, in 1907 8·9 per cent, and in 1925 14·5 per cent.

The turnover of a small number of big stores is equal to that of a very large number of small shops. The census of distribution carried out in England in 1950 showed that in the food sector the 255 largest concerns had a joint turnover of £40 million a year, which was the same as that of 27,000 small shops; 75 per cent of the enterprises accounted for only 35 per cent of the total turnover.[42]

In West Germany, taking retail trade as a whole, 76·7 per cent of small shops (those with an annual turnover less than 100,000 DM) accounted in 1956 for only 22 per cent of the total trade turnover. The 4,447 large or medium-sized firms, 0·85 per cent of the total number of retailers, were responsible for 35 per cent of the total turnover.[43] The tendency towards concentration has been rapid since 1950. It is estimated that in Hanover the share of the big stores in the food trade has risen from 16·2 per cent in 1951 to 19·4 per cent in 1952, 23·6 per cent in 1953, 27·1 per cent in 1954 and 28·6 per cent in 1955.[44]

In the United States in 1954, 65 per cent of the retail shops accounted for only 17·5 per cent of the turnover. One per cent of the retailers (with an annual turnover exceeding a million dollars) accounted for 26 per cent of the total turnover. Among the food shops, 6 per cent of the total, the supermarkets, accounted in 1955 for 60 per cent of the turnover, while the 80 per cent of small shops had only 13·9 per cent of it.[45]

Finally, in Britain, the share of the small retailers in the total amount of retail trade has steadily fallen: from 86·5 to 90 per cent in 1900 to 81·5 to 85·5 per cent in 1910, 77 to 82·5 per cent in 1920, 76 to 80 per cent in 1925, 71 to 76 per cent in 1930, 63·5 to 67·5 per cent in 1939, and 61·5 to 67·5 per cent in 1950.[46]

Though commercial concentration has made enormous progress, especially in this century, the obstacles to such concentration, and especially to complete domination by the big stores, are much greater than in the sphere of production. We have already noted that the small amount of money needed to start a small trading business makes possible the appearance from time to time of new shops, opened by former peasants, craftsmen, or even skilled workers, especially in periods of boom. Sometimes this small-scale trade can be carried on with a tiny return that does not even cover the wages of a worker; the wife, or the pensioned relatives, of a worker seek a modest extra source of income in this field.

Confronted with this tiny profit, the competition of the big store loses its effectiveness, since the use of machines cannot spread in this branch of the economy as it can in industry, to replace human labour-power:

"The highly competitive conditions which prevail in these industries [i.e. the wholesale and retail trades] and the small amount of money which suffices to set up a store result in a rapid influx of new enterprises who just as rapidly drop out again but who have meanwhile operated at a loss, have conducted an inefficient business, and thus contributed toward keeping down the level of productivity in the industry as a whole . . . Some of the persons absorbed must . . . be regarded as having assumed a status of disguised unemployment, judging from the higher rates of mortality of establishments engaged in retail trade and the incomes of large sections of the small business-men."[47]

The comparative ease of entry into this "capitalist" branch is obviously linked with a frightful mortality rate among the enterprises concerned. Between 1944 and 1945, 21·7 per cent of all the retail shops, 28·9 per cent of all the cinemas and other places of entertainment, 37·2 per cent of all the cafés, bars and restaurants, and 39·2 per cent of all the petrol stations either disappeared or changed ownership, in the U.S.A.[48] About 320,000 enterprises were involved in these two years.

The concentration of capital is accompanied, in trade as in industry, by an increase in fixed costs and, consequently, a tendency for the rate of profit to fall. But whereas in industry this tendency to fall is partly offset by the appearance of *monopoly profit*,* this kind of profit is much harder to realise in the sphere of distribution, where monopolies are rare or non-existent. Thus, the net profits are, in "normal" times, much lower in trade than in monopolised industry. The Harvard Business School estimates them for 1955 at 2·6 per cent in the big stores, 5·1 per cent in the drug-stores, 4·6 per cent in the drapers' shops, 2·5 per cent in the hardware business, and so on.[49] It follows that the expansion of commercial businesses comes up against a profitability barrier, beyond which the concentration of capital leads to a reduction in profit margins. The increase in fixed and overhead costs already obliged the big stores in France to increase their share in selling prices from 25 to 30 per cent towards the end of the nineteenth century to 35 to 40 per cent around 1939.[50] In the U.S.A. this share increased from 27·1 per cent in 1944 to 31·2 per cent in 1948 and 35·2 per cent in 1954.[51] Thereby, the big stores became a factor in relatively raising prices instead of lowering them, and their power to compete with the small shops suffered accordingly.†

On the other hand, the increase in industrial concentration and the appearance of monopolistic trusts in the sphere of production leads to a substantial intervention by these trusts in the sphere of distribution. This intervention takes place not so much by way of establishing big stores as through founding a large number of small dependent businesses (cafés subsidised by the wine, beer and aperitif trusts; petrol stations subsidised by the petrol trusts; motor-car shops, garages and repair shops dependent on the motor-car trusts, etc.). The "heads" of these businesses are really managers appointed by the trusts. But their profit margins are sufficiently small to hinder the concentration of capital. The most striking example is that of the motor-car industry in the U.S.A., where three trusts concentrate over 85 per cent of production, whereas the trade in cars is dispersed among 40,000 enterprises whose profits come, to the extent of 97 per cent from the sale of single items, and 25 per cent of which, on the average, closed down every year before the Second World War.[53] Alderer and Mitchell add judiciously: "The distribution of automobiles is organised so that the burden of competition falls upon the dealers rather than upon the manufacturers."[54]

The ties of dependence which increasingly subject the retailers to

* See Chapter 12.
† This evolution has given rise to a reaction, the appearance of the "supermarkets", which endeavour to reduce their margins by restricting to the minimum the numbers they employ. Nevertheless, these margins remain around 18-20 per cent, and tend to get larger.[52]

the big trusts are also expressed in the spread of resale price maintenance. In Britain, it was estimated in 1938 that 31 per cent of retail sales
were made at a price fixed by the manufacturer. In 1955 the percentage
was estimated at 55 per cent! [55] In West Germany some trusts impose
commercial profit-margins so low as 10–15 per cent.[56]

Capital invested in transport

Improvement in the means of transport makes possible a considerable reduction in the circulation period of commodities and at the
same time a reduction in their value, as the indispensable costs of
transport are embodied in their exchange value. At the beginning of
the Middle Ages, bringing back luxury products from the East was
a complicated problem and a dangerous business. Transport costs
were enormous. Only trade in goods very small in weight and very
high in value was profitable.[57] In the sixteenth and seventeenth centuries both sea and land travel was a matter of much time and great
risk. This was one of the major obstacles to the development of trade
in goods which were both heavy and cheap.

The building of railways and steamships completely changed this situation. Henceforth, every part of the world was more closely linked with
the big manufacturing centres than the towns of a single country had
formerly been linked together. The establishment of a real international
division of labour and a real world market would have been impossible
without the prodigious development of means of transport and communication in the nineteenth century.

From the days of itinerant traders, commercial profit and "transport costs" were mixed up together, the latter constituting in fact only
a small part of the former and including the subsistence of the merchant himself, his agents and his beasts of burden. Boats, carts, bags
were cheap, and their value was replaced in a single expedition. This
was no longer so, once the means of transport had undergone their
enormous extension, in our own epoch. Railways, vessels that can
cross the Atlantic, transport aircraft, all demand substantial outlay.
The replacement of this outlay takes effect over a fairly long period.
Transport costs thus become fixed charges which are embodied in the
prices of commodities, regardless of the stage of the industrial cycle.
This compels commercial capital to seek cheaper transport routes for
non-perishable goods, even at the cost of considerably prolonging the
time these goods spend in transit. In 1933 the cost of transporting
grain, per ton-kilometre, varied between 5·50 francs for sea transport to 126 francs for land transport. For coal the figures were respectively, 3·5 francs and 107 francs, and for petrol 4 francs and 210
francs.[58] Commercial competition thus leads capital not to reduce but
to extend the circulation period of heavy goods.

Furthermore, the immense investment of capital in the transport sector has given the latter a special dual function in the history of capitalist industry. In the first place, the buiding of means of transport has played a key role in determining the growth of heavy industry; first, railways, and then motor-cars and aircraft soon after, have been its best customers. Consequently, the concentration of capital has been much more radically and rapidly accomplished in the transport sector than in the other sectors of industry. The struggle against the high costs of transport waged by other branches of capital, has generally concluded either with the absorption of the transport sector by monopolistic trusts, whether industrial or financial, or else by the nationalisation of this sector. In the end, the State alone has been shown to be capable of gathering sufficient capital to lower transport costs in the general interest of the capitalist class. Only through the appearance of road haulage on a large scale has medium and even small-scale private capital recently re-entered the transport sector.

International trade

Pre-capitalist large-scale trade was exclusively foreign trade. It drew its strength from the unevenness of economic development as between different parts of the world. With the rise of the capitalist mode of production, international trade attained a volume without precedent. But the nature of this trade changed at the same time as it became general. In former times essentially a trade in luxuries, it now became above all a trade in goods of current consumption, raw materials and means of production. The creation of a unified *world* market cut out, right from the start, fraud and trickery as essential sources of commercial profits. The majority of goods were now sold throughout the world at their actual prices of production. Commercial profits were henceforth deducted from the total amount of surplus-value produced by the workers.

This, however, does not mean that the unevenness of economic development, which continues, and is indeed intensified and worsened by the world development of the capitalist mode of production, has ceased to constitute a source of additional profits, and transfers of wealth from one country to another. The capitalist mode of production, the export of industrial commodities produced by the first great industrial countries, has indeed unified the *world market*. But it is far from having unified *world production*, its technical and social conditions, its average degree of productivity of labour.

On the contrary, the unification of the world market effected by capitalism is a unification of antagonistic and contradictory elements. The gap between the average productivity of labour of an Indian peasant and that of an American or British worker exceeds by far the gap between the productivity of labour in the largest Roman slave enterprise and that of the poorest peasant on the borders of the Empire.

This unevenness of development has become, under the capitalist mode of production, a special source of *super-profits*.

The value of a commodity is the amount of labour socially necessary to produce it. This amount of socially necessary labour depends in turn on the average level of productivity of labour. From the moment that marked differences exist between the average levels of productivity of a number of countries, the value (the price of production) of a commodity may differ markedly as between these countries.

Now, the formation of a world market implies the formation of world prices. As the modern textile industry has not covered from the start, and, in fact, still to this day does not cover, *all* the clothing needs of all the world's inhabitants, part of the human labour expended on making clothes with hand-looms, or by other archaic methods, still constitutes socially-necessary labour on the world market. The value of imported industrial cotton goods will thus be fixed in the backward countries at a higher level than in their countries of origin.

But only *a part*, and a continually shrinking part, of the total human labour expended on making clothes by old-fashioned methods is not socially-wasted labour, that is, actually finds purchasers for its products. This is why the value of cotton goods in the backward countries is fixed well below their local price of production (before the introduction of the most modern production methods).

When they export their goods to backward countries and import from them raw materials, foodstuffs, etc., the industrially advanced countries thus sell goods above their value and buy goods below their value. Behind a seemingly equal exchange "at world market prices", trade between an economically advanced country, possessing an advanced degree of productivity or even a monopoly in the given field, and an economically underdeveloped country, thus represents the exchange of less labour for more labour, or, what comes to the same thing, a transfer of value from the backward country to the advanced country: *

"It has often been said that the European peoples became rich by the impoverishment of other parts of the world, and there is truth in the charge."[60]

International trade is not only a source of super-profits for the advanced capitalist countries. It is also the indispensable safety-valve for the development of capitalist industry. Industrial production expands at a much faster rate than the market in the home countries;

---

* This explains the enormous profits made by British capital at the beginning of modern capitalism thanks to the notorious "triangular trade"; selling cotton goods in West Africa, where slaves were purchased who were then sold from the same ships in the West Indies, from which in turn these ships fetched sugar and rum to be sold in England itself.[59]

indeed, the contradiction between the tendency to unlimited development of production and the tendency to constant limitation of popular
consumption, is one of the essential ways in which the basic contradiction of the capitalist mode of production shows itself. The prodigious development of capitalist industry, above all of British industry,
in the first half of the nineteenth century, was possible only because,
over and above the national market there was an international market
to be conquered which seemed limitless. Exports of British cotton
goods expanded with the capitalist mode of production, growing from
£300,000 in 1781 to £30 million in 1825.[61] Trade with India grew from
250 million francs in 1820 to over 3 billion in 1880. And the total
value of world trade grew from 10 to 30 billion francs between 1830
and 1850.[62]

Costs of distribution

All the expenses of distribution—trade, advertisement, telecom-
munications, etc.—are undertaken by commercial capital, which shares
in the general division of surplus value. So long as this capital is above
all ensuring the *increase* in the amount of profit, and the annual rate
of profit, by reducing the circulation period of commodities and the
rotation period of circulating capital, it contributes, as a whole, to
the all-round lowering of prices which is characteristic of the capitalist
epoch. The annual amount of surplus value thus increased is in fact
transformed into ever more up-to-date industrial plant.

But this role undergoes a profound alteration as the capitalist
régime evolves. As the productive forces expand prodigiously, and at
more and more frequent intervals come up against the limits of the
capitalist market, the essential role of distribution becomes less that
of increasing the amount of surplus value than that of *ensuring its
realisation*.

This realisation becomes a more and more complicated matter for
the total mass of capitalist commodities. It requires longer and longer
periods of time. The most frenzied competition dominates it. Stocks
of commodities begin to pile up as a regular thing, at all levels, from
the manufacturer to the small retailer. They accumulate not just for
weeks but for months, and in the case of certain products, for years.*

To the *costs of distribution* which are technically necessary must
thus be added the *selling costs* which are determined by the nature
of the system, costs which grow unceasingly, making bigger and bigger
the price the ultimate consumer has to pay for commodities.†

* Note, however, that these stocks fulfil, *to some extent,* the necessary function
of social reserve funds, thanks to which society can face up to a sudden increase
in demand, or to the effects of social or natural catastrophes.

† E. H. Chamberlin and Steindl have revealed this difference between distribution costs properly so called and socially determined selling costs.[63]

This increase in distribution costs is expressed first and foremost in the considerable increase in the number of persons employed in the distributive sphere. In the United States trade employed the following percentage of gainfully-occupied persons: in 1880, 10·7 per cent; in 1900, 16·4 per cent; in 1910, 18·9 per cent; in 1920, 21·2 per cent; in 1930, 23·9 per cent; in 1939, 24·4 per cent; in 1950, 24·7 per cent; in 1960, 27·6 per cent.[64]

Harold Barger estimates that 6·1 per cent of the total active population of the United States was engaged in distribution in 1870, 9·9 per cent in 1920, and 16·4 per cent in 1950.[65]

In Germany the proportions engaged in trade were, in 1861 one German in 83, in 1875, one in 65; in 1882 one in 54; in 1895, one in 39; in 1907, one in 30; in 1925, one in 19; in 1939, one in 17·5.[66]

This increase is then manifested in an increase, in the strict sense of the word, in the trade margins in the ultimate selling price. The growth in the general costs and fixed charges of trade is not accompanied by a rationalisation movement such as that which, in industry, accompanies the growth of fixed capital in relation to circulating capital. It is estimated as generally true that distribution costs make up 35 to 40 per cent of the average prices of commodities sold retail in the large capitalist countries.* At the same time, a more and more substantial part of the total available capital is tied up in the various spheres of distribution and in the form of stocks accumulated in the industry itself.

There is no more striking proof of the more and more *parasitic* character that the capitalist mode of production is beginning to assume as it approaches its maximum extension than the more and more limited place occupied by the *producers*, in the strict sense, in certain important branches of industry.

Thus, on 1st July, 1948, there were 2 million wage-earners in the petroleum industry in the United States, of whom only 400,000 were employed in exploration, production, refining and other productive activities; whereas 125,000 were employed in administration and scientific research, 225,000, in transport, 120,000 in supplies and services—in all, about 24 per cent in the spheres intermediate between production and trade. In all forms of distribution and sales, over 1·1 million people were employed, or 55 per cent of all the wage-earners in this branch of industry.[68] Similarly, in the motor-car industry, in the

---

* For the year 1939 the *Journal of Marketing* estimated at over 50 per cent of the total value added in national production the "value added" by distribution and transport. A recent study carried out in West Germany fixed at 44 per cent (including turnover tax) or 37 per cent (excluding this tax), the element of distribution costs in the prices of all products other than food. For bananas the distribution and transport costs have been estimated in the U.S.A. at 75 per cent [!] of the selling price, the distribution costs alone making up 55 per cent.[67]

same year, there were 978,00 wage-earners in the production sphere, as against 1·5 million in the sale and distribution of cars.[69]

The shift of capital into the struggle not for producing but for realising surplus value becomes a real obsession when capitalism has reached maturity and is entering its declining phase. "The American citizen lives in a state of siege from dawn till bed-time," writes the magazine *Fortune*. "Nearly everything he sees, hears, touches, tastes and smells is an attempt to sell him something . . . To break through his protective shell, the advertisers must continually shock, tease, tickle or irritate him, or wear him down by the drip-drip-drip or Chinese water-torture method of endless repetition."[70]

And a mission from the Belgian Department for Increasing Productivity, made up entirely of executives of capitalist firms, which visited the United States in 1953, summed up admirably the absurd blind-alley of present-day capitalism:

"Production is becoming easier and easier, and perhaps gives cause for alarm [!] by this very ease; it tends to run ahead of effective [!] consumption. Technological unemployment can be avoided only by a continuous extension of consumption, and it is the task of distribution to foster to utmost this increasingly rapid evolution. It is distribution that decides what production will be useful if the consumer buys. 'Why produce if you cannot sell?' It is the last three feet of the course followed by the product on its way to the consumer that decides the success or the failure of the entire production-consumption cycle.

"The great danger at present threatening [!] the economy in several sectors is overproduction. As regards both agricultural and industrial products, the capacity for production is much bigger than needed . . .

". . . The wheels of production nowadays turn at such a rate that the slightest hesitation to buy on the part of the consumer [!] may make the entire economic edifice shake."[71]

Specialists in new techniques, from market study to public relations, including experts in advertising, marketing and motivational research, accordingly strive to avoid or forestall these "hesitations". In 1955 more than 9 billion dollars were assigned to advertising expenses.* This conditioning of the consumer (which makes ridiculous the apology for capitalism as a system which guarantees the freedom of the consumer!) leads to an extreme form of human alienation: the large-scale employment of means of persuasion which mobilise the unconscious, instinctive forces in men so as to cause them to buy, to "choose" and to "act" independently of their own will and their own consciousness! In *The Hidden Persuaders*, Vance Packard has drawn a frightening picture of this conditioning of the masses. He

---

* In general it is the consumer himself who pays the bill, for advertising costs are included when the cost of production of many products is calculated!

quotes a specialist who declares frankly in *The Public Relations Journal:*

"One of the fundamental considerations involved here is the right to manipulate human personality."[72]

We thus find the contradictions of capitalism pushed to the point of absurdity. Instead of freely distributing the wealth created by the rise in the productivity of labour; instead of making it the foundation for a free development of the human being, capitalism, wishing to keep profit and the market economy under conditions of semi-abundance, is forced to outrage and mutilate people more and more, at the same time the possibilities for their free development are increasing from day to day! The artificial organisation of want amid plenty; the artificial unleashing of passions when the age of reason could be coming to triumph; the dishonest creation of a feeling of dissatisfaction, when all needs could be satisfied; the ever more marked enslavement of man to things (things, moreover, of mediocre quality and dubious value), when man could become the absolute master of matter; this is what the capitalist mode of production has come to, in its most benign, prosperous and ideal form . . .

The Tertiary Sector

Taking up a remark by Sir William Petty, dating from before the industrial revolution, the economist Colin Clark has developed a theory according to which the "tertiary sector" (trade, transport, public services, public administration, insurance, banking, the professions, etc.) is more "productive" than the "secondary", meaning industrial production. According to this theory, the larger the proportion of the active population that is engaged in the "tertiary" sector the higher is the national income.[73] Far from merely serving to realise surplus value, and expressing the increasing difficulties of realising it, the rise in the "tertiary" sector marks an important economic advance by mankind.

We must observe first of all that the definition of this sector (a definition which has been adopted, amplified and modified by the French economist Jean Fourastié, in *Le Grand Espoir du XX* Siècle*, where he writes of the "services" sector) is extremely confused. Colin Clark here lumps together productive activities (transport, public services such as production and distribution of water, gas and electricity) and unproductive ones; useful activities (teaching, health, public administration and accountancy) and others of a much more qualified, or even doubtful, utility (advertising, the armed forces, the police). The militarisation of Nazi Germany, which caused the "tertiary" sector to grow at the expense of the "secondary", was certainly not a sign of economic progress.

The concept of "productivity" is used by Colin Clark in the most vulgar sense, that of "bringing a return". But from the fact that *in a certain social and political context* an expert in motivational research, an admiral of the fleet or a prima ballerina earn more money than an engineer, a miner or a foundry worker it would be mistaken to draw the conclusion that a nation would become richer if all the latter were replaced by the former . . .

Finally, Colin Clark's theory is contradicted by his own statistics. These show that before the Second World War, 34 per cent of the active population were engaged in the "tertiary" sector in Japan, compared with 30·4 per cent of them in Sweden and 33·2 per cent in Switzerland. Yet nobody would deny that Sweden and Switzerland were (and are) more prosperous than Japan. In China 20 per cent of the active population worked in the tertiary sector compared with 16·8 per cent in Bulgaria and 15 per cent in Yugoslavia; yet, despite their backwardness, the latter two countries were nevertheless a lot less poor than China. Egypt and Italy had the same percentage of people employed in the tertiary sector, though an abyss of poverty separated the former from the latter, etc.[74]

Colin Clark's mistake consists precisely in the confusion in his definition of the "tertiary" sector. At least five different phenomena need to be distinguished here, which are moreover *contradictory* in their relation to the economic progress and the average level of productivity of a nation:

1. The *survival* of a mass of small "retailers" and "middlemen" which is merely the manifestation of a degree of under-employment, of disguised unemployment, the absorption of which into manufacturing industry would constitute an enormous step forward economically. This phenomenon explains the inflation of "employment" in the "tertiary" sector in under-developed countries like old China and Egypt.

2. The *specialisation* of certain nations in transport activity (especially maritime) which are in reality productive activities that should be classed in the "secondary" sector. This phenomenon explains the inflation of employment in the "tertiary" sector in countries like Norway, and to some extent Japan.

3. The *backwardness* as regards mechanisation and rationalisation of certain distributive activities and personal services (such as retail trade, insurance and banking, footwear and clothing repairs, hairdressing, beauty parlours, etc.), compared with the mechanisation of industrial production,* which causes employment in the "tertiary" sector

---

* It is interesting that Alfred Marshall notices the same phenomenon, when he writes of activities in which the use of machinery plays little part,[75] or, still more, when he refers to activities in which the progress of invention has contributed too little to the saving of effort in the attempt to meet a growing demand.[76]

to become inflated as a result of the growth in *industrial* productivity. This inflation of employment, far from expressing the higher productivity of the "services" expresses, rather, their backwardness. But this is, of course, only a *temporary* backwardness; the mechanisation of office work, the appearance of supermarkets, the use of "disposable" napkins and plates, and other phenomena of the same order, make it possible to look forward to a quite different line of development. Further, it must be mentioned, in this connection, that Colin Clark *reverses* the relationship of cause and effect. It is true that the richer a *capitalist* country is, the bigger is the proportion of surplus-value that can be devoted to the purchase of services, the more diversified are the needs of the better-paid workers, and the larger is the proportion of their wages that goes on the purchase of services. It is thus not the development of the services sector that is the *cause* of social enrichment, but social enrichment that is the cause of the development of services.

4. The excessive inflation of the "services" connected with distribution, owing to the increasing difficulty of realising surplus-value in the period of the decline of capitalism. This is an irreversible tendency, but only within the framework of present-day *capitalism*, not that of present-day technique.

5. Finally, the development of creative occupations not linked with the direct production of commodities: pure and applied science, the arts, medicine and public health, education, physical culture, and all the "non-productive" activities connected with leisure. This is the only one of the five phenomena that seems to be definitely and irreversibly linked with economic progress and the rise in the productivity of labour. It means that a larger and larger section of mankind are freed from the obligation of carrying on uncreative work. Here we have not a survival from a dreary past but the harbinger of a wonderful future. When automatic machines will do all the work needed to produce goods for current use, men will all become engineers, scholars, artists, athletes, teachers or doctors. In this sense, but in this sense only, the future is indeed with the "tertiary sector".*

* See Chapter 17.

REFERENCES

1. *Histoire du Commerce*, Vol. III, p. 129.
2. Herman Kees: *Kulturgeschichte des Alten Orients*, Vol. I, *Aegypten*, p. 103.
3. G. Glotz: *Le Travail dans la Grèce antique*, p. 17.
4. F. Heichelheim: *Wirtschaftsgeschichtedes Altertums*, Vol. I, p. 227.
5. S. K. Das: *Economic History of Ancient India*, p. 422.

6. *Histoire du Commerce*, Vol. I, p. 151.

7. G. I. Bratianu; *Etudes byzantines d'histoire économique et sociale*, pp. 137-8.

8. P. K. Hitti: *History of the Arabs*, p. 343.

9. H. Pirenne: *Histoire économique et sociale de l'Occident médiéval*, p. 127.

10. Yoshitomi: *Etudes sur l'histoire économique de l'ancien Japon*, p. 212.

11. N. K. Sinha and A. Ch. Banerjee: *History of India*, p. 193.

12. Rostovtzeff: *Social and Economic History of the Roman Empire*, p. 158.

13. Raymond Firth: *Malay Fishermen*, p. 188.

14. Charles Wisdom: *The Chorti Indians of Guatemala*, p. 25.

15. Alexander Dietz: quoted in J. C. van Dillen: *Het economisch karakter der middeleeuwse stad*, p. 98.

16. J. Kulischer: *Allgemeine Wirtschaftsgeschichte*, Vol. II, p. 113.

17. G. Jacquemyns: *Histoire de la crise économique des Flandres, 1845–50*, pp. 198-200.

18. T. S. Ashton: *An Economic History of England—The 18th Century*, p. 102.

19. Sol Tax: *Penny Capitalism*, pp. 14-15.

20. H. Pirenne: *Périodes d'histoire sociale du capitalisme*, p. 18.

21. J. H. Clapham: *An Economic History of Modern Britain*, Vol. I, p. 220.

22. *L'Economie belge en 1953*.

23. *Histoire du Commerce*, Vol. I, p. 254.

24. W. Steffen: *Die Geldumlaufgeschwindigkeit in der Unternehmung*, p. 42.

25. Japanese Government Economic Stabilization Board: *Economic Survey of Japan, 1951–52*, p. 133.

26. Ashton: op. cit., p. 112.

27. *U.S. Statistical Abstract: Historical Statistics*.

28. Selma Hagenauer: *Das iustum pretium bei Thomas von Aquino*, pp. 28-29; Karl Marx: *Das Kapital*, Vol. III, pt. 1, p. 250.

29. James B. Jefferys: *Retail trading in Britain, 1850–1950*, p. 117.

30. A. C. Hoffmann: Temporary National Economic Committee Monograph No. 35, *Large-Scale Organization in the Food Industry*, p. 67.

31. Jefferys: op. cit., pp. 27-31.

32. Geoffrey M. Lebhar: *Chain Stores in America, 1859–1950*, p. 206.

33. *Histoire du Commerce*, Vol. I, pp. 308-9; J. G. Clover and W. B. Cornell: *The Development of American Industries*, p. 1020.

34. *Histoire du Commerce*, Vol. I, pp. 312-14.

35. Jefferys: op. cit., p. 27.

36. J. K. Galbraith, Holton: et al., *Marketing Efficiency in Puerto Rico*, p. 17.

37. *Histoire du Commerce*, Vol. I, pp. 316-17; Jefferys: op. cit., pp. 22, 61.

38. Jefferys: op. cit., p. 65.

39. Ibid., p. 72.

40. *U.S. Statistical Abstract*, 1958.

41. J. Saint-Germès: *Les Ententes et la concentration de la production industrielle et agricole*, pp. 80-81.

42. *Wörterbuch der Volkswirtschaft*, 1932, Vol. II, p. 285; *The Wholesale Grocer*, September 1954.

43. *Deutsche Zeitung und Wirtschaftszeitung*, 16th April, 1958.

44. Ibid., 30th May, 1956.

45. *U.S. Statistical Abstract*, 1958; S. May and G. Plaza: *The United Fruit Company in Latin America*, p. 63.

46. Jefferys: op. cit., p. 73.

47. Weintraub and Magdoff: in *Econometrica*, October 1940, p. 297.

48. *Survey of Current Business*, December 1945.

49. M. Moreuil: in *Documents de l'Association Française pour l'Accroissement de la Productivité*, No. 109, 15th February, 1957.

50. *Histoire du Commerce*, Vol. I, p. 310.

51. Cornell and Clover: op. cit., p. 1026; Moreuil: art. cit.

52. Moreuil: art. cit.; Mellerowicz: in *Deutsche Zeitung und Wirtschaftszeitung*, 14th December, 1957.

53. E. B. Alderer and H. E. Mitchell: *Economics of American Industry*, p. 157.

54. Ibid., p. 158.

55. Margaret Hall: in *The Listener*, 25th March, 1955.

56. *Deutsche Zeitung und Wirtschaftszeitung*, 14th December, 1957.

57. H. Pirenne: *Le Mouvement économique et social au moyen âge*, p. 38.

58. *Histoire du Commerce*, Vol. I, p. 55.

59. Ibid., p. 55.

60. J. B. Condliffe: *The Commerce of Nations*, p. 204.

61. J. Schumpeter: *Business Cycles*, Vol. I, p. 271.

62. B. Nogaro and W. Oualid: *L'Evolution du Commerce, du Crédit et du Transport depuis 150 ans*, pp. 273, 283.

63. E. H. Chamberlin: *The Theory of Monopolistic Competition*, pp. 117 et seq.; J. Steindl: *Maturity and Stagnation in American Capitalism*, pp. 56 et seq.

64. S. Bell: *Productivity, Wages and National Income: U.S. Statistical Abstract*, 1954, 1962.

65. Harold Barger: *Distribution's Place in the American Economy since 1869*, p. 61.

66. *Wörterbuch der Volkswirtschaft*, article *"Handel"*: *W.W.I. Mitteilungen*, 1952, No. 1.

67. *Journal of Marketing*, April 1946; *Bulletin d'Information de l'Institut d'Etude Economique et Sociale des Classes Moyennes de Bruxelles*, August 1959; May and Plaza: op. cit., pp. 40-67.

68. Cornell and Glover: op. cit., p. 265.

69. Ibid., p. 801.

70. Quoted by Daniel Bell in "The Erosion of Work", in *The New Leader*, 13th September, 1954.

71. Report of the Belgian Mission to the U.S.A., 14th October to 26th November, 1953: *Techniques de Vente*, pp. 15-16.

72. Vance Packard: *The Hidden Persuaders*, p. 259.

73. Colin Clark: *The Conditions of Economic Progress*, pp. 397-401.
74. Ibid., pp. 398-9.
75. Alfred Marshall: *Principles of Economics*, p. 276.
76. Alfred Marshall: *Economics of Industry*, p. 155.

CHAPTER SEVEN

CREDIT

Mutual aid and credit

TRADE was born of the uneven development of production in different communities; credit was born of the uneven development of production among different producers within the same community. When cattle breeding or cultivation are carried on as private activities, the differences of aptitude between individuals, the differences of fertility between animals or soils, innumerable accidents of human life or the cycle of nature, bring about this uneven development of production as between different producers. In this way there appear, side by side, farms which accumulate several yearly surpluses and farms which are working at a net deficit, that is, producing less than is needed for current consumption and for seed.

The uneven development of production as between different producers within the same nation does not *automatically* lead to the development of credit. This is not a natural institution but a product of certain social relationships. The private mode of exploitation of flocks and herds, or of the soil, develops within primitive communities which are slowly breaking up. During a long transition period it is combined with labour co-operation. A society based on co-operation does not know credit, but only mutual aid. The better-off members of the community usually come to the help of the less well-off, without expecting to get any material advantages in return for this help. This is still true among several primitive peoples.

Among the Dakotas, a North American Indian tribe, food and hunting equipment are freely lent.[1] In the Indonesian *desa* interest on advances of seed or fruit for planting or loans of cattle, etc., is unknown.[2] The Malay fishermen receive free loans of rice and money from their friends or relations during the monsoon periods, when they cannot go to sea.[3]

When primitive society has been disintegrated to the point where exchange relations and division of labour have become general, the concept of equivalence of values, based on the economy of labour time, replaces the concept of unstinted mutual aid among members of the same community. The more that production of mere use values is ousted by production of exchange-values, the more does the loan charged for replace the free advance made in the spirit of mutual aid.

Among the natives of the New Hebrides it was the custom to advance *food* to members of the same clan without any idea of getting payment in return for such advances. But advances *in the form of shell-money*, or the loan of a canoe to carry on trade with, had to be paid for by gifts.[4] Alonzo de Zurita and Mariano Veytia, two sixteenth-century writers who have left us interesting accounts of the life of the natives of pre-Columbian Mexico, record in the same way that among the Aztecs advances were usually made without any profit being sought. In certain parts of Mexico, however, the custom had developed of obtaining a payment in return for advances in *money* (chocolate-nuts, gold dust, copper discs, jade, etc.). Credit thus separates off from mutual aid at the *periphery* of primitive economic life, in those spheres of activity not directly linked with subsistence in the strict sense.

The ancient custom of mutual aid to ensure the subsistence of all the members of the community was kept up in agricultural societies long after the village community had begun to break up. Lending of wheat without interest went on in China right down to the time of the Chou dynasty.[5] Prohibition of taking interest on loans of corn or cattle is found in the earliest collections of laws: Vedic, Jewish, Persian, Aztec, Moslem.[6] At Susa, in ancient Iran, in the epoch called that of the High Commissaries, interest-free loans continued around 2000 B.C. alongside loans at interest.[7] In the Middle Ages the monasteries gave loans without charging interest.[8] Even in the fully-developed society of petty commodity production in Babylonia which we know from the Code of Hammurabi, "free loans" (mutual aid) for the poor, the sick, peasants hit by harvest-failure, are common alongside business loans at interest.[9]

Today still, "in many indigenous communities (in Latin America) there is a strong tradition of mutual help among independent small landholders and tenants in the granting of small loans without interest."[10] Bauer and Yamey note, similarly, that mutual aid is widespread wherever the "large family system still flourishes, as in India."[11]

The separation of credit from mutual aid thus takes place in the sphere of relations with foreigners sooner than in that of relations within a community. In the Old Testament and in the Koran, this distinction is clearly expressed. The principle of collective payment of taxes by a village, which has survived in all societies where the village community and petty commodity production exist together, represents a special form of mutual aid, preserving the poorest peasants from complete ruin.[12]

The origin of banking
The development of petty commodity production causes the circulation of commodities to be accompanied by circulation of money,

and the development of a money economy in the pores of a society based on the production of use values only. This explains the grip secured by *usury* on the producers at this stage of social development. But in a money economy money is not merely the *instrument* of exchange, it also becomes an *object* of exchange. The trade in money separates off from trade in the narrow sense just as the latter previously separated off from the crafts.

At the beginning of money economy, the precious metals were rare and their circulation was limited. They constituted primarily a reserve and security fund for society, and they were hoarded rather than put into circulation. Now, in those disorderly epochs, keeping one's treasure at home meant an excessive risk, especially of confiscation, robbery or destruction. So the custom grew up of entrusting them to the most respected institution of the time, namely, the *temples*. Had not the precious metals, like all objects regarded as precious, had originally a magico-ritual function, which made temples the obvious depositories for important hoards? This concentration of precious metals in the hands of the temples transformed the latter into the *first institutions of occasional credit*, from the first rise of a money economy.

This happened in Mesopotamia, from the first great temple-bank of Uruk (3400 to 3200 B.C.) to the age of Hammurabi (2000 B.C.), when the average rate of interest was fixed by the temple of Samas.[13] In ancient Iran the temples were the first moneylenders,[14] and this was still true in the days of the Sassanids.[15] In Israel, the Temple remained, right to the time of its destruction the chief place for storing movable wealth.[16] In ancient Greece, the temples of Olympia, Delphi, Delos, Miletus, Ephesus, Cos, all the temples of Sicily, functioned as storeplaces for money and as banks.[17] This position remained the same in the Hellenistic epoch.[18] In Rome the Pantheon was the centre of banking.

In the Byzantine Empire the monasteries were, from the fifth century onward, the chief owners of hoards; it took the Iconoclasm of the eighth century to bring these hoards into circulation as money.[19] Something similar happened in China, under the Tang dynasty. The Buddhist temple-banks increasingly monopolised both the stock of monetisable metals and credit operations; the State attacked them, secularised several thousands of temples and monasteries, and had all statues made of precious metal melted down in 843.[20]*

In Japan "the religious establishments . . . were the only places of safety during the Middle Ages, a period marked by civil disturbances . . . People carried on business under the protection of shrines

---

* Yang Lien-sheng notes that the practice of granting loans on security began, in China and in Japan, in the Buddhist temples. The expression "pawnshops" (*ch'ang-shing k'u*) originally meant "monastery treasuries".[21]

and temples. Some entrusted their precious documents and treasures to these sacred places in order to protect them from the destruction and pillage of warfare. Shrines and temples also acted as financial organs and made loans; organised co-operative credit facilities known by the names of *mujin* and *tanomoshi*; and utilised bills of exchange."[22]

In the period of the Lower Empire, the Buddhist temples were the only banks in the eastern part of Central Asia, where natural economy still prevailed.[23] Finally, in the early Middle Ages in Europe the monasteries likewise appeared as the only credit institutions giving loans à *mort-gage*.[24]* At the beginning of the twelfth century the religious order of the Templars became the first international bank of deposit, clearing and mortgage credit.[25]†

When large-scale trade developed, the precious metals began circulating to a greater extent. Now, as we have seen, large-scale trade was, at the start, above all international trade. This trade thus pre-supposed the simultaneous appearance of a large number of minted coins of different origins and amounts, which had to be exchanged one for another in accordance with their true value. This inevitably led to the appearance of a new technique with money itself as object, the technique of the money-changers. Offering in their turn reliable guarantees to the owners of precious metals who wanted to deposit them somewhere safe, these money-changers and traders in precious metals thus became the first lay guardians of hoards, and then the first *professional bankers*. The word "bank" comes from Italian *banco*, the table on which the money-changers carried out all their operations. Similarly, in ancient Greece, the word for a banker, *trapezites*, comes from *trapeza*, a money-changer's table.

In the ancient world the money-changers were the first professional bankers.[26] This was so in India, too,[27] and in China, where the diversity of coins was not the result of international trade but of the diversity of regional currencies.[28]‡ The money changers became real bankers in Japan in the age of the Tokugawas.[29]

In the Islamic empire of the Abbasids the introduction of a gold standard alongside a silver standard made the money-changers, or

* A loan à *mort-gage* is one where the lender receives as security a piece of land, a house, a mill, etc., from which he draws the revenue until the loan is repaid. This was the chief form of mortgage credit in the Middle Ages, down to the twelfth century, when it was forbidden by a bull of Pope Alexander III, being replaced by the sale of bonds (see Chapter 4). The expression gave rise to the English term "mortgage". It was contrasted with the loan à *vif gage*, in which the revenue from the security (land, or whatever it might be) was set against the debt, gradually reducing it.

† The Templars accumulated their starting capital from the ransoms they extorted from Moslem prisoners.

‡ See Chapter 3.

jahbadh, economically indispensable persons; soon they were fulfilling all the functions of bankers.[30] Kulischer[31] lists the chaotic conditions which determined the appearance of the money-changers in the Middle Ages and favoured their transformation into bankers:

"In the thirteenth and fourteenth centuries there were circulating in France, alongside coins of royal origin, or struck by the great vassals, also Arab, Sicilian, Byzantine and Florentine coins; in southern France, Milanese *libri* and Venetian ducats, in Champagne Spanish *reals*, Burgundian and English *nobili* and crowns from the Low Countries. People everywhere accepted coins minted at Lübeck and Cologne, English *sterling* and French *tournois*. The *grossi* and *ducats* of Venice and the *fiorini* of Florence were the most widespread coins."

The origin of the mediaeval banks has been thus described by R. De Roover:

"The Genoese money-changers specialised first in exchange by hand, but they soon extended their field of action by accepting deposits repayable on demand, carrying out settlements of accounts by transfer in accordance with their clients' instructions, and, finally, advancing loans to their clients on current account. The tables or offices of the money-changers thus gradually became banks of deposit and clearing. In Genoa the evolution was complete before the end of the twelfth century."[32]

The famous Bank of Amsterdam, founded in 1609, owed its formation likewise to the monetary confusion prevailing in those days in the young republic of the United Provinces.[33]

Credit in pre-capitalist society

The first banking operations, money-changing by hand, receiving and guarding hoards, and giving loans on security of land (mortgage loans) were not operations in the "money trade" in the strict sense. Indeed, in the age of the *depositum regolare*, the deposit to be looked after and returned on the mere demand of the depositor, the trustee, far from paying interest to his client, claimed a fee for his services as guardian of the wealth deposited with him.[34] This was still the case with the Bank of Amsterdam in the seventeenth century.[35]*

These operations involved essentially classes of society which were outside the production and circulation of commodities, or only on their periphery. With the development of a money economy, these classes became the classic victims of usury, either large-scale or petty. In the Middle Ages the big international commercial and banking societies practised the loan on security at the expense of kings and

---

* The practice of charging a small safeguarding rate on hoards deposited reappeared in the second half of the nineteenth century, in the system of safe deposits inaugurated in 1861 by the Safe Deposit Company of New York.

princes, while the more modest Lombards looked after the feudal small fry and the commoners.[36] This was, basically, a form of *consumer's credit*.[37]

The real "trade in money" appeared only in connection with the classes engaged in the circulation of commodities and capital, that is, the young bourgeoisie, usurers and merchants. The development of international trade itself created an inherent need for credit. The separation in time of purchase from delivery;* the separation in space of buyer from seller; the need to transfer substantial sums of money over considerable distances, while the coins concerned were subject to continual fluctuations in value[39] all this gave rise to the need for commercial credit or *circulation credit*. Every society with a developed international trade creates the essential instruments of this credit: bills of exchange and letters of credit. "The negotiation of bills of exchange has its roots in international trade."[40]

We see them appear in 2000 B.C. at Ur in Babylonia, under the Chou dynasty in China (1134–256 B.C.) and at the beginning of the Buddhist epoch in India.[41] In ancient Greece they were in wide use from the fourth century B.C. and subsequently spread throughout the Hellenistic world.[42] From there they passed to Byzantium and the Islamic world from which they made their way back into Europe in the Middle Ages.[43]

The circulation credit provided by these first non-negotiable merchants' bills did not widen the sphere of operation of capital. It only made possible a more rapid turnover and a larger return; when investment credit appeared, that is, the advancing of funds for a business which would bring in surplus value, the sphere of activity of capital was extended; "sterile" money, hoarded money, was transformed into capital and participated in the production of surplus value.

The oldest form of this entrepreneur's credit was the *maritime loan*, the association of a lender with an adventurous captain to carry out an enterprise of maritime trade, a loan which was itself derived from the practices of groups of pirates, as was shown especially in the stipulations regarding the division of profits.[44] From ancient Greece and the Hellenistic world this "loan for a great venture" was passed to the Byzantine and Islamic empires, to reappear from the ninth century in Byzantine Italy and spread from there throughout Europe in the form of *the commenda contract*.[45]

At first, this sort of trading association was confined to a single venture. Later, however, with the transition from itinerant trade to

---

* "In so far as the Genoese buy wool, paying for it before it is supplied to them, they take care to lower the price they pay . . . They are themselves ready to raise the price by one or two *reals* for each unit of weight, on condition that they pay for it only when they receive the wool, and especially if, for at least half of the bill, there is a further three-months period of grace."[38]

sedentary trade, the *commenda* gave place to *multi-partnership companies* formed for a certain number of years. From the thirteenth century onward, all the big Italian companies (Peruzzi, Bardi, Medici, etc.), were associations of this sort. The Bardi, for instance, were working in 1331 with a capital made up of 58 shares, belonging to 11 partners.[46]

Finally, when international trade became regular and lost its adventurous character, at least in a certain sphere, it attracted a large share of idle capital. This was deposited with the big merchant-banking concerns as *depositum irregolare*, the merchants being authorised to operate with it as they chose, the money not being repayable at short notice, and *fixed interest* being paid on it by the merchants, as a share of the merchants' profit they realised.[47]

The bankers thus became, with petty commodity production, "middlemen between the suppliers of money-capital and the demand for it."[48] Now, at this time, it was not private individuals but the State (kings, princes, communes, etc.) that mainly had need of money. The *public debt* thus developed parallel with circulation credit and investment credit, taking precedence over them.

The oldest known example of public credit is that recorded by the pseudo-Aristotle in the Second Book of the *Economics*: the Ionian colony of Klazomenae, in Asia Minor, lent leaders of mercenaries the means of settling their men's arrears of pay, and covered this loan by a forced loan from its rich citizens, who were obliged to accept iron money in exchange for their gold and silver coins. The annals of Hanchow record that in 154 B.C. a Chinese usurer named Wu Yen-chih had lent 1,000 catties of gold (about 530 lb. or a little under one million gold francs) to the government to enable it to wage war against the "rebellion of the seven kingdoms". He was paid 1,000 per cent interest, or 10 million gold francs.[49]

Public credit soon assumed its classical form by being provided with the *future revenues of the State* as security. In most societies based on petty commodity production, operations of public credit remained rare and risky, and normally ended in the bankrupty of the lenders.

But from the sixteenth century onward, *negotiable bonds based on the public debt** effected a revolution in the history of credit and made it possible to extend considerably the field of operation of capital, by transforming into capital masses of non-capitalised money. Encouraged by the expeditions of the Kings of France into Italy and by the

---

* "Francis I spent on an enormous scale. In order to have funds, he found himself obliged to resort to a new technique. Turning to the municipality of Paris, he assigned to it 20,000 *livres* of revenue which he collected in the Paris area. The town gave him 200,000 *livres* which it received from its citizens in return for a regular payment of 8 per cent (the twelfth *denier*): these payments were the famous *rentes sur l'Hotel de Ville*."[50]

scattered disposition of the states ruled over by Charles V, public credit became international.

"Credit, after being a mere means of settling accounts, became a value in itself, a negotiable and transmissible object of exchange."[51]

On the Antwerp stock-exchange the obligations of the King of Castile, the letters of credit of the government of the Low Countries and of the Kings of England and Portugal, bonds issued by the great cities of Europe, all were fully negotiable. During the currency upheavals and the disorder of public finances during the sixteenth century, all the old banking houses failed. From this circumstance arose the *modern public banks* which combine the guarantee of the security of deposits which is indispensable for the bourgeois public with the promise to the State that it will be the chief, if not the only beneficiary of these deposits. The *Bank of the Rialto* of Venice, founded in 1587, corresponded above all to the first purpose; the *Bank of Amsterdam*, founded in 1609, added to it the need to regulate the circulation of money. The *Bank of Hamburg*, founded in 1619, united with these functions that of lending to the State. The same applied to the *Bank of Sweden*, founded in 1656, whereas for the *Bank of England*, founded in 1696, it was the last-mentioned function that became predominant.[52]

The remarkable development of international trade after the commercial revolution of the sixteenth century led to a fresh extension of commercial credit. Following the example of the public debt bonds, merchants' bills became negotiable in their turn from the sixteenth century onward, following the practice of endorsement and discounting.[53] At the same time, the development of the colonial joint-stock companies widened the sphere of activity of investment credit. But it was necessary to wait for the development of the capitalist mode of production for credit to pass from the sphere of trade, properly so called, to that of production.

Supply and demand of money capital in the epoch of commercial capital

Thus, with the rise of commercial capital, credit became, from having been an exceptional phenomenon, a regular institution of economic life. The discounting of merchants' bills spread widely from the seventeenth century onward in England, and from the eighteenth century in France and in the big centres of international trade, first for foreign trade purposes, then for internal trade as well.[54] The geographical extension of trade, the long time taken by trading operations with America and the Far East, the concentration of the chief trading concerns in a few big international centres, all favoured this use of trade bills to mobilise capital.

Whereas the bill of exchange had hitherto been only a means of speculating on variations in exchange-rates,[55] it now became a regular means of supplying circulation credit to trade, and also means of short-term investment of "sterile" money capital. In this way a *market for money capital* was developed.

The chief representative of demand on this market was the State, which continued to be, in the epoch of commercial capital, the great, insatiable borrower. Clapham observes that down to the Industrial Revolution the Bank of England carried out the bulk of its credit operations with the King's government.[56] It was the same with the Caisse d'Escompte, founded in 1776, not to mention the ill-starred bank set up by Law, which was sunk by its operations in the sphere of public credit.[57]

Alongside the State, however, other borrowers began to appear. These were, in the first place, the big joint-stock trading companies, whose need for money was enormous for those days and which often had to apply to credit institutions for cover for their needs until a fleet returned to port.

Thus, the Dutch East India Company borrowed money from the Bank of Amsterdam, while, along with the State, the English East India Company was the chief debtor of the Bank of England throughout the eighteenth century.[58]

Next came holders of public bonds (rentiers, nobles, traders and bankers) and the bills of merchants who, needing ready money, discounted this paper. At first the discounting of public bonds predominated, but in the closing decades of the eighteenth century the discounting of private bills began to be more important.

Finally, as in the epoch of petty commodity production, there was demand for money—consumer's credit—on the part of the nobility and the high officials of the State, and this was met by loans on security, the latter taking the form of precious metals, jewellery, deeds, etc.

The supply of money capital came from persons holding liquid capital, principally the large landowners, together with traders who accumulated more money than they could invest in their own businesses. The bankers on the Continent were engaged exclusively in exchange and deposit operations in the seventeenth century and the first part of the eighteenth century, and gave no credit. In England, however, from the seventeenth century onward there appeared the trader who occasionally advanced money to his customers.

With the growth in the circulation of money, the enrichment of society, the parallel development of this demand and this supply of money capital, local private banks began to be formed, about the middle of the eighteenth century, in England first of all, with the function of acting as middlemen between those who were looking for capital and those who were looking for opportunities of transforming into capital their reserves of ready money. These local banks, which normally developed from prosperous trading houses, accepted deposits, issued bank notes and discounted trade bills: this was the birth of the modern banking system.[59]

The Industrial Revolution rapidly expanded this initial network of banks. Whereas in 1750 there were only a dozen local banks, the number had risen to over 200 by the end of the century (even to 350, according to some writers).[60]* The organic way in which these banks developed in the midst of the mode of production of that time is indicated by the example of the house of Gurney, at Norwich, as described in a circular sent by this house itself to bankers on 5th October, 1838:

"The collecting of yarns from . . . manufacturers of the East of England and holding them in stock to supply those who are employed in weaving . . . was a very lucrative business, and we deliberately question whether the Gurneys did not at one time derive from it an annual income greater than is obtained by any bank in the Island of Great Britain . . . In the course of dealing with the worsted spinners for their yarn, this family began to supply them with cash to pay the wages of labour and enable them to carry on their operations in business. Out of these circumstances arose the great banking operations of this family . . ."[62]

This rapid development is explained above all by the uneven development of the different regions of England. The banks in the regions that remained agricultural usually had deposits for which they sought a field of investment,† whereas the banks in the industrial areas were under pressure to furnish credit and were constantly looking for funds. The London money market was born of this situation; it acted as intermediary between the banks with too much in the way of liquid funds and those with too little.

Supply and demand of money capital in the epoch of industrial capitalism

With the Industrial Revolution, however, the market for money capital was greatly enlarged and changed. Alongside supply and demand coming from the pre-capitalist strata of society (landowners,

---

* On the basis of a study of the records of the private bankers of London at the end of the seventeenth century and during the eighteenth, D. M. Joslin observes that these banks did not as a rule advance funds to traders or entrepreneurs. It was only when, around 1770, some banks were established which included indistrialists among their founders that the first credit operations directed toward industry began.[61]

† Down to the beginning of the nineteenth century rural banks paid commissions to London brokers so that the latter would procure them merchants' bills to discount.[63] This shows how scarce and sought-after were fields for the short-term investment of capital!

traders, craftsmen, civil servants, rentiers, etc.) appeared supply and demand arising from the mechanism of capitalist production itself.

Money capital is the starting point and the finishing point of the rotation of capital. But it does not appear only at the beginning and the end of this process of rotation. Constantly, during the production process itself, money capital is eliminated from the process and turned into money which is "unproductive" from the capitalist's point of view. And, also constantly, a demand for *additional* money capital arises from the entrepreneurs, to enable them to achieve the investment of their own capital in the most profitable way.

The money capital needed to renew the fixed capital of an enterprise is not accumulated until several years and several rotation cycles of circulating capital have passed. This *depreciation fund*, unless it be used meanwhile for other purposes, will lie "unproductive" during this period. The *wages fund* of a big enterprise, advanced at the beginning of each production-cycle, would remain unproductive to the extent that this production-cycle was longer than a month (for employees paid monthly) or even a week (for those paid weekly). The share of the annual profit put aside by the capitalist for his own consumer needs (*unproductive consumption fund*) is expended only during the course of an entire year, so that a large part of it will remain unproductive for a large part of the year. The *accumulation fund* of the enterprise, the share of the profits which is reinvested in the business, is not used in its entirety right from the start of a fresh production-cycle. The capitalist will await the favourable moment, for instance, a good market conjuncture, before investing these profits. There we have four sources of money capital temporarily excluded from the production process and so made unproductive.

On the other hand, the renewal of fixed capital does not take place exactly at the moment when the necessary depreciation funds have been accumulated. Necessitating as it does the involvement of substantial amounts of capital, and entailing very large risks, this renewal will be effected, for preference, at particular moments of the economic cycle, when the capitalists expect a significant expansion of the market.[64] If a certain capitalist has not yet accumulated the depreciation (and accumulation) fund by this precise moment, he will have to try and borrow the capital he needs, so as not to let slip this opportune occasion. The capitalist who has at his disposal a technical invention which would enable him to expand his market at the expense of his competitors is in a similar situation if he lacks the capital needed to exploit this invention.[65]

At certain moments of the economic cycle, the industrialist knows that any increase of production whatsoever can be absorbed by the market. That is the moment when he needs to get his capital together and invest his profits. If he has not yet realised his profits, he will have to borrow so as to be able to invest them in advance.

Finally, the recovery of production, after the close of a production cycle, should in theory begin as soon as the circulation cycle of commodities has concluded. But, as we have seen, the amount and annual rate of profit depend on the number of annual production-cycles, and so on the industrialist's capacity to resume production *before* his circulating capital, invested in commodities which have been produced but not yet sold, has come back to him. For this purpose, too, he will seek to borrow additional money capital, which he will be able to repay as soon as he has received the money from the sale of his goods.

The function of credit institutions under capitalism is to fulfil the same role of intermediary between those who hold unproductive sums of money and those who are looking for opportunities to increase their own capital with the aid of borrowed capital. The pre-capitalist relationship between bank capital and the other forms of capital is thus reversed; in the capitalist mode of production, bank capital begins as a subordinate servant of industrial capital. But whereas the separation of the modern capitalist trader from the capitalist industrialist is only a question of functional division of labour, the separation of the capitalist banker from the capitalist industrialist or trader is inevitable from the very first appearance of the capitalist mode of production.

Contrary to the industrialist and the trader, the banker has in fact to play a social role *directly*. He is useful to the capitalist mode of production only to the extent that he can overcome the fragmentation of social capital into a multitude of individual properties. It is in this function of *mobiliser and centraliser of social capital* that his whole importance to society consists. This function goes beyond the class limits of the bourgeoisie in the strict sense and embraces the centralisation of the funds saved by landowners, rich and middle peasants, craftsmen, civil servants, technicians, and even skilled workers in prosperous periods.

"[By about 1875] the organisation by which all free British capital was sucked into the London money market was functioning almost perfectly. Compared with other national organisations, or lacks of organisation, it had been highly efficient even twenty years earlier. In the interval, Scottish and provincial branch banking had drawn in almost the last of those rustic hoards which country folk had kept 'in their desks and cupboards'; and a smooth open channel had been cut, down which the northern surpluses flowed South. The channels from East Anglia, the South-West, and rural England generally, had been cut long before . . . From Town, what was not used there ran out into the industrial districts, by way of the discount or re-discount of manufacturers and merchants' bills. These were the greatest days of the London bill-brokers, the Lombard Street houses."[66]

At the same time the market for money capital became more and more specialised, and two distinct markets came into being:

(1) The money market, the supply and demand of *short-term credit*, dominated by the banks, except in England, where the bill brokers have long played a predominant part, and (2) The finance market, the supply and demand of *long-term credit*, at first dominated by the banks and the stock-exchange, joined in the twentieth century by the insurance companies, the savings banks, the building societies and other organisations of institutional saving (pension funds, health insurance funds, semi-public institutions, etc.), which seek to transform into capital (often without any profit to the owner)* all money income not immediately spent. The centralisation of money capital thus attains its highest, perfected phase; the banks "allow no sum of money to remain unproductive".

Interest and rate of interest

Like the profit on usurer's capital with which it is identified in its beginnings, interest is at the time of its first appearance in the economy only a *displacement* of value from debtor to creditor. When a peasant has to borrow X amount of wheat in order to survive till the next harvest, and when he then has to deduct from this harvest X + Y amount of wheat in order to repay his creditor, the total amount of wheat in the possession of these two people will not have increased owing to the loan. An amount Y will merely have been transferred from the debtor to the creditor. This form of usury, which is far from having disappeared, permanently impoverishes its victims and enslaves them to their creditors:

"In Cochin-China the farmer, or *ta dien*, borrows from his landowner the means of feeding himself and his family until the harvest; when the harvest is in it is usually not big enough to release him from his debt, and the *ta dien* remains tied to the land by his debt no less surely than a mediaeval serf was tied by custom."[67]

This is no longer true with circulation and investment credit in capitalist society. The advancing of funds no longer has for its aim the survival of the debtor, but is intended to *enable him to realise a profit*:

"Business will pay a positive interest if a present sum can be so used in commerce and industry as to yield a greater sum in future" [i.e. the sum borrowed, plus a surplus value, a profit.][68]

"It is a well-recognised principle . . . that in the last analysis the

---

* This is in particular the case with the funds of the savings banks and the social insurance funds, which are used to finance the State's expenditure. See Chapter 13, section "War Economy".

money rate of interest depends upon the supply of and demand for *real capital* . . . that the rate of interest is regulated by the profits from the employment of capital itself . . ."[69]

Circulation credit is intended to realise in advance the value of commodities already produced: investment credit has for its purpose to increase the capital of an enterprise. In both cases the amount of surplus value increases, either by reduction in the rotation-time or by growth in the amount of capital. The interest is thus nothing but *a fraction of the extra surplus-value obtained through the borrowing of capital.* It is lower than the profit,* because if it were equal to the latter there would normally be no advantage in borrowing, since the capital borrowed is expected itself to bring in the average profit. The creditor is satisfied, because before he lent his capital it was "lying idle" and bringing no return. And the debtor is also satisfied because, though he has to surrender interest to the creditor, he still makes more than if he had borrowed nothing.

The interest paid by a capitalist entrepreneur for the borrowing of capital is a fraction of the total surplus value produced by his workers, a fraction surrendered by the entrepreneur because the loan has enabled him to increase this total surplus-value by an amount greater than the interest due. But with the generalisation of the capitalist mode of production every entrepreneur is on the look-out for additional capital. At the same time, the socially-centralising function of the banks enables *every* sum of money to be transformed into additional money-capital. Thus, by the working of supply and demand in relation to money capital the *average rate of interest* is constituted, the "normal return" on every sum of money which is not "lying idle". This, needless to say, has nothing to do with the "intrinsic qualities" of the money, but represents the outcome of definite relations of production, which enable this sum of money to be *capitalised,* so that it may appropriate a fraction of the surplus value produced by the totality of workers in the given society. From this basis the habit spreads in bourgeois society of regarding all income as the income on an imaginary capital, capitalised at the average rate of interest: †
"With the growth of capitalist mentality an obviously useful habit has developed, the beginnings of which are in Germany, for instance, observable since the fourteenth century, of expressing any returns,

---

* Except in the backward countries, where the rate of interest also includes part of the ground rent. It thus exceeds the rate of profit on merchant capital, which is what explains the predominance of usurer's capital in these countries. The *New York Times* reported in 1955 the case of a laundryman of Karachi (Pakistan) who paid 3,925 rupees in interest on a loan of 100 rupees, at the rate of 25 per cent a month, or 300 per cent a year, for 13 years and one month.[70]

† An income of £500, when the average rate of interest is 5 per cent, would be regarded as the return on an assumed capital of £10,000.

except returns to personal services, as a percentage of a capital value."[71]

This habit has led bourgeois economists to the idea of similarly separating, in the case of a capitalist entrepreneur who operates with his own capital only, the interest on his capital and the entrepreneur's profit (called "a sort of rent" by some writers, such as Marshall) which is left when this interest is deducted from the total profit. This is obviously an "ideological" operation, that is, a fictitious one, since any entrepreneur expects to obtain on his capital not the average rate of interest but the average rate of profit. This practice is all the more useful for bourgeois economists in that it enables them to dodge the problem of profit, that is, of exploitation, and replace in their systems all theory of profit by a simple theory of interest.*

The credit organisations do not fulfil their function, as intermediaries between those who have money capital to offer and those who want it, out of pure altruism. They, too, operate with a capital of their own which must bring in the average rate of profit. Their profit appears in the form of *banker's profit*, which consists mainly in the difference between the rate of interest paid by these institutions for money entrusted to them on deposit and the rate of interest they exact from those to whom they grant credit. To this must be added other income derived from, e.g. commission and brokerage for making investments, carrying out exchange transactions, etc.

As credit institutions, the banks especially, pay interest (even though very little) on every sum of money deposited with them, even for a few days (current accounts), it is to their advantage to lend out in their turn all the money at their disposal, so that these transactions may end in a profitable balance for them. Thus there appears on the money market, alongside circulation credit in the strict sense, *day-to-day credit* ("call money"). It began in England in 1830, when, on the eve of the quarterly payments of interest on government stock, large sums of money accumulated in the Treasury's accounts in the Bank of England, which caused a shortage of money on the money market. To offset this shortage, and so as not to let these sums remain "unproductive", they were advanced for a period of a few weeks, or even a few days, to clients desirous of this sort of credit, especially to the discount houses, which used them to increase the volume of their rediscounting operations. These advances made on security of deeds and bonds deposited could be recalled merely on demand. The deposit banks, too, adopted the practice of lending available funds from day to day.[72]

In this way a whole scale of rates of interest has been established,

---

* With Keynes the bourgeois economists rediscovered that interest relates only to the demand for *liquid* capital, that is, money capital, and so cannot determine the profit brought in by productive capital.

rising higher and higher, from the rate paid on long-term deposits and demanded for investment loans. At each level there is a difference between the rates paid by the banks and credit institutions and the rates they in turn demand from their clients.

The difference between these different rates arises in the first place from the degree in which the credits contribute to increasing directly the amount of surplus value produced by society. Clearly the rate of long-term interest, that which governs investment credit, which means especially the purchase on credit of means of production, is the highest, closest to the average rate of profit, and governs *ultimately* all the variations in the different rates of interest. The rate of short-term interest, which mainly governs circulation credit, is lower than the rate of long-term interest to the extent that circulation credit, by reducing the rotation-period of capital, makes *possible* but does not ensure the increase in the amount of surplus value. The short-term rate of interest may, however, sometimes exceed the long-term rate, for instance when there is a shortage of money on the money market which threatens not merely to extend the rotation period of capital but to destroy capital itself (danger of bankruptcy).

Also to be taken into account is an insurance and risk premium which is contained in interest and which varies according to the duration of the loan and the particular moment in the industrial cycle and also according to the particular conditions of supply and demand of money capital at the various levels, which (given a free market) subject the different rates of interest to daily fluctuations.* But these fluctuations occur around an average figure determined in the last resort by the level of the average rate of profit.

This is why, apart from the regular fluctuations resulting from the phases of the industrial cycle, it is hard to establish laws of long-term evolution applicable to the rate of interest. The latter depends in the last analysis on the *relative* shortage or plenty of money capital, in relation to the relative level of the rate of profit.

Thus, the rate of interest goes down in a society of petty commodity economy which has unified a vast international market within which the unevenness of economic development between different regions is increasingly reduced. This is what happened in Antiquity from the time of Caesar,† and in mediaeval Europe (Western and Southern Europe) from the second half of the fourteenth century.[73] The rate of interest goes down also when money economy becomes general in an agricultural country, and when in consequence the agricultural

---

* For the reciprocal effect of variations in long and short-term interest during the industrial cycle, see Chapter 11.

† At this moment it becomes more profitable to make *loans in kind* to the peasants, loans which continue to bring in very high interest. These loans in kind became the main form of usury in the Roman Empire.

classes free themselves a little from the oppression of usurer's capital; interest then no longer includes as heretofore a part of the ground rent.

On the eve of the great imperialist expansion of the last quarter of the nineteenth century, the industrialised countries all experienced a marked lowering of the average rate of interest, owing to the lack of fresh fields of investment for capital. On the morrow of the Second World War, in the United States and in Switzerland, the plentiful supply of capital and the lack of fields for investment offering the average profit severely reduced the rate of interest, whereas it was rising in the other capitalist countries, where a shortage of capital prevailed as a result of war damage and general impoverishment (Germany, France, Italy).

Circulation credit

All credit granted so as to make possible the realisation in advance (i.e. before actual sale) of the *value of commodities* is a circulation credit.[74] This is a short-term credit, rarely for longer than three months, which is granted by banks, both specialised and other.

With the generalisation of the capitalist mode of production, production becomes increasingly separated from the market, and the realisation of the value of commodities and surplus-value becomes more and more complicated, with risk of prolonging the rotation period of capital, even taking into account the intervention of commercial capital. But it is precisely at this epoch that, in order to react against the tendency of the rate of profit to fall which results from the immobilisation of an ever-growing fraction of capital as fixed capital, the capitalist seeks to *shorten* the rotation time of circulating capital. This is the essential function of circulation credit, which makes it possible to cut down to the minimum the entrepreneur's own circulating capital.

"The Bullion Report, referring to the increased operations of brokers in the four or five years before 1810, pointed out that the improved discount facilities available in London had tended to increase the business of the country manufacturer, by enabling him to turn over his capital more quickly."[75]

Macrae estimates that 30–40 per cent of the circulating capital of the whole of British industry is provided by credit.[76]

In the nineteenth century, circulation credit functioned mainly in the form of *discounting merchants' bills*. The producer of cotton goods does not pay his supplier in cash, but gives him a draft or promissory note. The supplier goes to a banker who takes over this merchant's bill, paying him the sum due, less an interest called discount. When the promissory note falls due to be paid, the cotton manufacturer pays the amount stated on it to the banker. The latter has thus in reality lent this sum for three months to the supplier of raw cotton, so enabling him to reduce by three months the rotation time of his capital (and also that of the cotton manufacturer, who receives credit from his supplier only because the latter in his turn receives credit from his banker).

Since the Middle Ages, however, another form of circulation credit has existed.[77]* Each capitalist has a current account with the local banker which enables him to make payments and receive sums of money by way of mere written orders (transfers from one account to another). All the payments in and out thus pass through the hands of the banker, who becomes a sort of central book-keeper. At a given moment a manufacturer has in his bank only a current account of one million francs to his credit. To continue production, however, he needs immediately two million francs, so as to be able to pay wages. The banker knows that, a few weeks later, the manufacturer will make large payments-in of money arising from the sale of his commodities. He therefore allows him to draw out of his account more money than he possesses (to have an overdraft); in fact, he advances him one million francs. Naturally, the manufacturer will pay interest for such an "advance on current account", normally not less than 5 per cent, except when very large firms are involved.†

From the last quarter of the nineteenth century, the advance on current account has more and more taken the place of the discounting of merchants' bills as the main form of circulation credit.[79] The concentration of capital leads to the formation of enterprises so big that they possess sufficient credit with their banks to obtain by way of advances on current account all the short-term credit they need. Small enterprises, however, are more and more embarrassed by the need to settle the discounted merchants' bill at *a fixed date*, and fear the discredit attached to the non-payment (protesting) of drafts when this becomes known. Finally, the integration of big enterprises with their suppliers of raw material and their selling organisations in trusts, financial groups, etc., abolishes the classical partnerships that made use of merchants' bills.[80] Thus, in Great Britain, the volume of ordinary merchants' bills discounted fell from £250 million in 1913 to £100 million in 1937, whereas advances on current account to industry reached £850 million in 1929 and £1 billion in 1938.[81]

Nevertheless, since the great crisis of 1929, especially in the United States, advances on current account to large-scale industry have begun to decline in their turn, owing to the accumulation of huge reserves of ready money by monopoly capital,‡ the relative decline of the

* Polanyi declares that a system of advances on current account was already practised by the bankers of ancient Assyria.[78]

† On the *monetary* consequences of this form of credit, see Chapter 8.

‡ See Chapter 14, section "Overcapitalisation".

industries especially dependent on bank credit, the extension of cash payments in retail trade, and the development of specialised credit institutions. It is above all the small and medium entrepreneurs who are responsible for the bulk of requests for advances on current account.[82] Along with this, in the last few years there has been a growth in the amount of discounting in some European countries, such as Switzerland, France and Belgium, as a result of an attractive policy of rediscounting on the part of the currency authorities, who expect to be able to influence more directly the fluctuations in the volume of money if circulation credit takes the form of discounting rather than of credit on current account.[83]

Investment credit and the finance market

All credit given in order to increase the *amount of capital* of an industrial or commercial entrepreneur is an investment credit. It is a *long-term credit* involving comparatively substantial sums, and is given, from the creditor's point of view, with the purpose of bringing in *a lasting income*.

The immediate origins of this form of credit are to be found in the purchase of ground-rent in the Middle Ages, in the constitution of the mediaeval trading companies, in the depositing of sums of money at fixed interest with the great trading associations of the fourteenth century, and in the long-term loans granted to kings, princes and cities by merchants and usurers in the Middle Ages.* It did not assume its modern character until the sixteenth century, with the appearance of the stock-exchange and negotiable instruments. From then onwards there was a social class which sought to dedicate its wealth—its capital —to investment in long-term credit operations, so as to increase this capital by the product of these investments. These people furnished the *supply* of capital on the embryonic finance market. The *demand* for capital was provided above all by the State, and then, to an ever-increasing extent, by the joint-stock companies. The predominance of government stock on the finance markets of Western Europe continued throughout the whole epoch of commercial capital, that is, in the majority of countries, down to the beginning or even the middle of the nineteenth century.

The public debt quickly took on the form of *fixed-income* stock payable from the future receipts of the State;† private stock was and remained above all *variable-income stock*, the actual return depending

---

* See Chapter 4, where also described are the origins of the stock-exchange, the public debt and joint-stock companies.

† Governments unable to pay the interest on their public debts experienced the seizure by foreign powers of their customs administration, this being the principal source of their income! This happened to China in the nineteenth century and to Venezuela in the twentieth.

on the yearly (or half-yearly, etc.) profits of the companies issuing the stock. In both cases the purchase of a share represented for the capitalist the purchase of a *claim to income*, a right to participate in the future share-out of society's surplus-value. The social nature of investment credit became more and more marked as stock-exchange operations widened their scope and numerous bourgeois built up portfolios containing shares in a growing number of companies, together with stock issued by many States, provinces, communes and other public entities.

The risk run in lending substantial sums to an enterprise for a lengthy period of time logically implies that additional guarantees are sought: the right to supervise the management of the money lent and the general administration of the business. This is why direct share-holding in the enterprises being aided, that is, the formation of multiple-partnership companies, has always been the most usual form of investment credit.

The old companies of the Ancient World, of China, of the Middle Ages, of the Arab and Byzantine civilisations, and so on, were all companies of *unlimited liability*: the partners were liable for the company's debts to the full extent of their possessions, whether these were invested in the company or not. This brought about the rapid collapse of all the mediaeval banks which granted investment credit. In Venice, of the 103 banks set up in the fourteenth century, 96 went bankrupt.[84] The development of the capitalist mode of production ended by *depersonalising* credit, a process which reached its stage of perfection in the joint-stock company and limited liability company of modern times. The purchase of shares and debentures in a business has become the normal way of giving investment credit.

Though the joint-stock company began to appear in the sixteenth century, it was not until the nineteenth century that it finally became dominant. Two shattering bankruptcies which occurred at the opening of the eighteenth century, that of the South Sea Company in Britain and that of the Mississippi Company in France, had developed in the bourgeoisie a holy terror of the risk implicit in this form of credit.[85] Actually, the manufacturing epoch was not yet propitious to such an extension of credit as the later rise of industrial capitalism demanded.

Thus, the investment credit given to private businesses increased little between the sixteenth century and the end of the eighteenth. While joint-stock companies developed but slowly, the deposit banks, remembering the lessons of the end of the Middle Ages,[86] turned away from investment operations, which, moreover, were forbidden them if they were chartered as public banks. The banks confined their long-term operations to the State and a few rare privileged customers.

Only when the British merchant bankers and the Continental *"haute banque"* establishments appeared, towards the end of the eighteenth century, did bankers begin afresh to interest themselves in private business, commercial and industrial. In 1822 the *Société Générale de Belgique* was the first business bank in the true sense, which, by at first granting short-term advances to industrial enterprises, soon found itself suffering from excessive tying-up of capital and was thus led to acquire shares and to take the initiative in founding joint-stock companies.[87]

The example of the *Société Générale* was followed in France, but the resounding downfall of the Pereira brothers' *Crédit Mobilier* set back the expansion of business banking in most European countries until after 1872.[88] Several countries then saw the rise of mixed banks, that is, banks which accept deposits and which also give investment credit.

In the twentieth century the finance market has become transformed under the influence of the development of insurance companies, savings banks, social insurance funds, etc., which, while assembling huge amounts of capital, cannot use them to buy securities with variable income. Several countries have passed laws defining these limitations or even extending them to the deposit banks. As a result, government stock has assumed the preponderant place on the contemporary finance market in most countries, just as used to be the case before the nineteenth century.[89] This phenomenon has accompanied that of *self-financing* of big concerns.*

It would be wrong to regard the sums deposited in the social security funds, the savings banks, etc., as an *accumulation of money-capital* more or less equivalent to the accumulation of capitalist funds in the banks. In reality, workers' savings constitute a *deferred consumption fund* which will be mostly spent during the depositor's own lifetime. In a global figure of the incomes of *the class of wage and salary earners*, there must be set off against these workers' savings the debts of sick, disabled and pensioned workers, the aid they have to seek from public assistance, or from family or other private sources, the reductions in level of consumption by these sections falling below the subsistence minimum, etc. The overall balance, which these figures confirm, shows that one generation of workers accumulates practically nothing in the way of transferable securities in the course of its lifetime taken as a whole.

The Stock Exchange

The capitalists and credit institutions who invest their available money capital in the form of shares and debentures in joint-stock

---

* See Chapter 14, section "Self-financing".

companies expect to obtain for these loans the *average rate of interest*. With debentures and fixed-income shares this is guaranteed them in advance. With the mass of shares in the proper sense of the word, the interest obtained fluctuates with the profit realised; it is called the *dividend*.

But shares, debentures and other transferable securities, as claims to income, become negotiable and are bought and sold on the stock-exchange. Their price is then simply *the capitalisation of the annual dividend (income) at the average rate of interest*. This price is the share's quotation on the stock-exchange.* Since the dividend paid by a company varies from year to year, and as estimates of probable dividend likewise vary throughout the year, these quotations may fluctuate violently. Real speculation on a rise or a fall is organised, often causing artificial changes in quotations; false rumours are circulated, or imminent sharp changes affecting the profitability of the business are concealed.

In some countries this speculation is carried on to a large extent on credit; thus, in New York, credits to speculators on Wall Street constitute the chief operations of the money market.[90]

Holders of shares and debentures receive the *average interest*; joint-stock companies in industry, trade and finance realise the *average profit*. Where does the difference go? In so far as it is not reinvested in the business and transformed into reserves, it is *capitalised in advance* in the form of *founder's profit*: additional shares, special preference shares, etc., are assigned to the founders of the company.

Let us suppose that an industrial enterprise has a capital of 100 million francs, and it wishes to obtain a further 200 million francs from the public to expand its business. Let us suppose that the average rate of profit is 10 per cent and the average rate of interest 5 per cent. If shares were issued for the sum of 300 million francs, they would be expected to bring in every year, on the average, 15 million francs in dividends. But the founders of the joint-stock company anticipate an annual profit of 30 million francs. The difference between the average interest and the average profit, or 15 million francs, will be capitalised at the average rate of interest of 5 per cent thus forming an additional capital of 300 million francs, which the founders take for themselves. The founder's profit thus materialises in the fact that the total capital for which shares have been issued will be 600 million francs, whereas only 300 million francs will have actually been paid in. The 300 million francs of additional shares will constitute merely *claims to income*, enabling their holders—the founders of the busi-

---

* This is not absolutely true. Also to be taken into account is possible reimbursement in the event of the winding-up of the company. This factor does not enter into calculations, however, except when such winding-up is in actual prospect.

ness—to take every year the difference between the average profit and the interest (the dividend), or entrepreneur's profit. Thus, when the great British chemical trust, Imperial Chemical Industries, was formed in 1926, its nominal capital was £56,803,000, whereas the aggregate of enterprises merged together to form it had capital totalling only £39 million.[91]

The capitalisation of founder's profit explains the remarkably rapid enrichment of "captains of industry" in the great periods of foundation of joint-stock companies (*Gründerjahre*). But in fact it capitalises *in advance* the *future* difference between the average profit and the interest, and so includes a large speculative element. Many joint-stock companies, overcapitalised in this way, prove unable to pay for long dividends equivalent to the average interest, precisely as a result of this overcapitalisation, while others even go bankrupt.

Another way of appropriating founder's profit is to boost the quotations of shares on the stock-exchange. Take a company founded with a capital of 10 million francs, divided into 1,000 shares each of 10,000 frances. This company is expected to earn an annual profit determined by the average rate of profit, say, 15 per cent, or an annual profit of 1·5 million francs, or 1,500 francs per share. Now, the average interest being 5 per cent, a sum of money lent is not expected to bring in more than 5 per cent, and 1,500 francs is regarded as the normal annual income on 30,000 francs. The founders will therefore succeed in selling their shares on the stock exchange for 30,000 francs each instead of 10,000 francs, and thus appropriate the difference, which is again the capitalisation of a difference between *future* average profit and the present average interest. When Dunlop, the British rubber trust, was refloated in 1896, shares issued at £3 million were sold six weeks after issue for £5 million.[92]

A good example of a combination of these two forms of founder's profit is provided by Harrods, the large British department store, established as a joint-stock company in 1889. The company had a capital of £1 million, of which £1,400 was preference shares for the founders, who assured themselves a large and increasing participation in the profits. Despite the fact that Harrods' ordinary shares paid annual dividends of 10 per cent at first, and later 20 per cent, on the average, during over 20 years, the founders' shares were immediately capitalised at £140,000 and were worth on the stock-exchange in 1911 not less than £1,470,000, ten times their nominal capital and 1,000 times the capital actually paid in . . .[93]

While shares and debentures continue their independent circulation on the stock-exchange, among brokers, the real values they represent may have long since disappeared. The warships built with capital borrowed by a government may long since have gone to the bottom of the sea, just as the machines bought with the money raised by the sale of shares may have been transformed into so much old iron. The divorce between real capital and the mass of negotiable claims, already marked as a result of the overcapitalisation of many joint-stock companies, thenceforth becomes complete. The mass of claims no longer represents anything but a *fictitious capital* which, under the appearance of a fraction of the total capital of society, hides its true nature, that of a mere claim to income, which confers a right to participate in the share-out of society's surplus-value.

Joint-stock companies and the evolution of capitalism

For a long time some people have wanted to see in the development of joint-stock companies a proof that capital, far from becoming concentrated, is "democratising" itself. Are there not millions of shareholders in some countries, for instance, in the United States? Is it not possible for any skilled worker to use his savings to buy shares in big industrial companies?

This notion is based on a twofold confusion. First, not everybody is a capitalist who claims an income from the sharing-out of society's surplus-value; if that were so, every disabled ex-Serviceman would be a "capitalist". Only those shareholders who, thanks to the income on their capital, can live without selling their labour-power, and live at a standard which corresponds at least to that of a small industrialist, can be classed in this category.

Investigations carried out by the Brookings Institute in the U.S.A. in 1952 showed that out of more than 30 million American workers only 2 per cent held shares. Out of a total of 6·5 million shareholders, 4·5 million held fewer than 100 shares each and received from them an *annual* income of less than 200 dollars, or less than the *monthly* wage of an average worker. It would therefore be absurd to regard them as being "capitalists".

Consequently, though the joint-stock companies appear formally as institutions which *diffuse* ownership of the means of production, in reality they constitute an important stage in the *concentration* of capital. It is a mere legal fiction to regard a small shareholder as being "co-proprietor" of a giant trust like General Motors, for instance. In return for this title he has in practice handed over his savings to the big industrialists and bankers to do what they like with them. The joint-stock company is therefore rather a disguised form of *expropriation* of small savers, not for the benefit of a nameless force but for that of the *big capitalists*, who thus succeed in getting control of a mass of capital which greatly exceeds their own property.

"In effect, when an individual invests capital in the large corporation, he grants to the corporate management all power to use that capital to create, produce and develop, and he abandons all control over the product. He keeps a modified right to receive a portion of the profits, usually in the form of money, and a highly enhanced right to sell his participation for cash. He is an almost completely inactive recipient."[94]

It is interesting to note that the decision of a British court has confirmed this view. Lord Evershed declared in 1949: "Shareholders are not, in the eye of the law, part owners of the undertaking. The undertaking is something different from the totality of shareholdings." And the *Economist* adds: "In other words, an ordinary stockholder does not own an aliquot part of the company's assets. He is entitled to an aliquot part of the profits that the directors recommend for distribution . . ."[95]

Before the rise of the joint-stock company one had to own the greater part of the capital of a business in order to control it effectively. Gardiner C. Means has shown how, thanks to the development of these companies and the dispersal of their shares among small shareholders, a few big shareholders can be sure of controlling the trusts with shareholdings which give them only a minor part of the capital.[96] In the American Telegraph and Telephone Company, for instance, 43 big shareholders held in 1935 more shares than 242,500 small shareholders. In one of the chief American cigarette trusts, the Reynolds Tobacco Company, there were in 1939 66,357 shareholders; but 20 of these held 59·7 per cent of the "A" ordinary shares and 22·5 per cent of the "B" ordinary shares.[97] The British Bowaters trust had 42,866 shareholders on 1st June, 1959; but the 26,000 smallest shareholders held altogether £2·8 million ordinary shares, compared with £4·3 million in the hands of 151 big shareholders—63 of whom held £3·4 million worth!

The Brookings Institute investigation already mentioned showed that 2 per cent of the total number of shareholders, or less than 0·1 per cent of the American people, or 130,000 persons, each one holding 1,000 shares or more, together account for 56 per cent of the stock-exchange value of all American shares, and so control the bulk of American capital.

Professor Sargant Florence has examined in detail the distribution of shares among the small and large shareholders of the chief joint-stock companies of Britain and the U.S.A. The result is significant. In 1,429 American companies 98·7 per cent of the shareholders— the mass of small shareholders—hold only 38·9 per cent of the shares, whereas 0·3 per cent of the shareholders—those who each hold more than 5,000 shares—concentrate 46·7 per cent of the shares in their hands. If we take only the big companies with a capital exceeding 100 million dollars, these percentages remain practically the same. (These figures relate to the situation in the years 1935–37.)

In Britain, in the case of the 30 largest companies, 96·4 per cent of the shareholders—the small ones—hold 40·1 per cent of the shares, while 0·5 per cent of the shareholders—the big ones—hold 35·9 per cent of the shares.

Of the 126 largest joint-stock companies in the U.S.A., the 20 principal shareholders hold over half the shares in one quarter, from 30 to 50 per cent in another quarter, and from 20 to 30 per cent in a fifth. In Great Britain, out of the 82 largest joint-stock companies, the 20 principal shareholders hold over half the shares in 40 per cent, from 30 to 50 per cent of the shares in 17 per cent, and from 20 to 30 per cent of the shares in 21 per cent.

Finally, analysing the way all these companies are run, one finds that 58 per cent of the British and American companies are clearly dominated by the principal shareholders, while 33 per cent of the British and 15 per cent of the American companies are "marginal" cases.

And Professor Sargant Florence concludes: "Proceeding thus from the known to the unknown there is certainly evidence for believing that the managerial revolution has not proceeded as far as is sometimes thought (or stated without thought) and that leadership and the ultimate decision on top policy may remain in many companies or corporations with the larger capitalist shareholders."[98]

Norman Macrae estimates that in Britain 2 per cent of the population holds over 90 per cent of all the shares, and that between 100,000 and 150,000 people (0·2 to 0·3 per cent of the population) hold more than 50 per cent of these.[99]

It is the same in India, where the shares of some of the biggest companies are distributed like this: [100]

Category holding	Advance Mill		Tata Mills		Tata Hydro-Electric	
	share-holders %	shares %	share-holders %	shares %	share-holders %	shares %
From 1 to 25 shares	93·6	40·0	79·0	14·1	82·0	24·2
Over 150 shares	0·9	36·5	2·4	64·0	2·2	48·33

In each case, a small number of large shareholders hold as many shares as or more shares than the great mass of small shareholders and thereby control the joint-stock companies. In reality, a still narrower group wields a preponderant influence on the joint-stock companies: *

"The company form favours the creation of a real aristocracy or oligarchy. It gives rise to professional administrators whose role consists exclusively of undertaking the administration of the big capitalist companies . . . By multiplying the links which connect them with numerous companies they form among themselves a sort of personal dynasty. An entire system of interlocking relationships comes into being, to which a great variety of names are given: 'communities of interest', 'inter-directorates' . . . this dual fact of personal freedom from

* See Chapter 12.

responsibility and possession of administrative authority favours the making of alliances and agreements (i.e. monopoly)."[101]

The generalisation of joint-stock companies (limited liability companies, corporations, etc.), constitutes an important stage in the *de facto* socialisation of credit and of the economy as a whole. When the bank lends an industrialist the money that a small rentier has deposited with it, the industrialist remains the owner of most of the capital with which he operates. With the formation of joint-stock companies we see a more and more marked separation of the entrepreneur from the *rentier*-owner. The entrepreneur's capital becomes a means of control over capital many times larger than his own.

Consumer's credit

Circulation credit and investment credit essentially remain within the circle of the bourgeoisie, big and small. But the capitalist epoch also sees the reappearance of consumer's credit, whether provided by way of usury or otherwise. Falling into debt in the shops where they have to buy goods of primary necessity, the workers, office-workers, unemployed, and declassed people may soon find themselves chained for life to a pitiless creditor who seizes a large part of their meagre incomes as interest on a debt which they will never be able to shake off. This form of usury is particularly hateful when it is practised by shops which belong to the very enterprise to which the worker sells his labour-power.

With the mass production of what are called consumer *durables* (cookers, sewing-machines, refrigerators, washing-machines, radios and television sets, motor-cycles and cars, etc.) there appeared, around 1915, another modern form of consumer's credit.[102] Usually, the wages of workers and office-workers, even skilled ones, are inadequate for them to buy such goods for cash. The payment of a fraction of their weekly or monthly wage enables them, however, to acquire the goods as their own property, after a certain time. Industrialists and traders are interested in fostering this *hire-purchase* method of selling because it constitutes the only way to expand the market for these consumer durables, and because as a rule they receive considerable interest on this credit (difference between the cash price and the hire purchase price).* Also the traders' overheads (storage and handling) are substantially reduced, since the purchasers take responsibility for these charges. But even apart from the exploitation which is implicit —return to the company of articles on which an instalment has not been paid—the excessive development of the hire-purchase system is a factor of instability in the capitalist system, especially

---

* This interest is often usurious, since it continues to be calculated on the total price of the article, even after 50 per cent or 75 per cent of the price has already been paid.

towards the end of the boom and on the eve of the slump in each economic cycle.[103]

The close link between this modern consumer's credit and the mass production of consumer durables is clear from the fact that, almost non-existent before 1914, these credits developed in the U.S.A. after the First World War—6·3 billion dollars in 1929, 25 billion in 1952— and in Great Britain, West Germany, Belgium, Sweden, France, etc., after the Second World War, at the very moment when the motor car, motor-cycle, refrigerator and T.V. industries were expanding in these countries.[104]

Credit and the contradictions of capitalism

Credit has thus deeply marked the history and development of capital. It has mightily extended the field of operations of capital, by making possible the capitalisation of every available reserve of money. It has facilitated, accelerated, generalised the circulation of commodities. It has stimulated capitalist production, competition, the concentration of capital, in short, all the developmental tendencies of capitalism. Credit appears as an instrument no less indispensable to the capitalist mode of production than trade, making possible a substantial reaction against the tendency of the average rate of profit to fall.

Credit has likewise transformed the bourgeois class itself. The separation of interest from profit, of a class of rentiers from the mass of the bourgeoisie, marks at the same time both the logical culmination of capitalist development and the first definite sign of its decay. Here, indeed, is a fraction of the bourgeoisie who live merely on their *ownership* of capital, and who, by doing this, are placed completely outside the production process, without any direct contact with the machines or the workers. The *private* character of capitalist appropriation, which remains personal and tangible in the capitalist enterprise which is family property, becomes more and more objective, abstract, in the joint-stock company. The rule of capital assumes its most general and anonymous form. Apparently it is no longer men of flesh and blood who embody exploitation, but "companies", synonyms of objective, blind economic forces.

Like trade, credit makes possible a considerable reduction in the rotation-time of capital, *an ever greater mobility of circulating capital, in contrast to the tying-up of a growing share of capital* in gigantic fixed installations.* It thus mitigates for the immediate future the

---

* At the beginning of the crisis, credit even makes it possible to absorb the first shock of a sudden fall in prices. In so far as the entrepreneur is operating with borrowed capital, he can sell *below the price of production*. The price obtained need only be sufficient to pay the interest, which is less than the average profit.

contradictions resulting from the evolution of capitalism. At the same time, however, it intensifies these contradictions in the long run. At the beginning of industrial capitalism, each capitalist was able to check very quickly whether the labour-time expended to produce his commodities was socially-necessary labour-time or not. It was enough to go to the market-place and there look for buyers of these goods at their price of production. When trade and credit insert themselves between the industrialist and the consumer, the former begins by realising automatically the value of his commodities. But thereafter he is unaware whether or not they will find a real outlet, whether they will find an "ultimate consumer". Long after he has already spent the money representing the value of the commodities produced, it may turn out that the latter are unsaleable, not really representing *socially necessary* labour-time. The slump is then unavoidable. Credit tends to postpone the slump while making it the more violent when at last it comes.

By making possible an expansion of production without any direct relation to the absorption capacity of the market, by concealing for a whole period the real relationships between the production potential and the possibilities of effective consumption; by stimulating the circulation and consumption of commodities over and beyond the real purchasing power available, credit puts off the date of the periodical crises, aggravates the factors of disequilibrium, and thereby makes the crisis the more violent when it breaks. Credit merely develops the basic divorce between the two essential functions of money—means of circulation and means of payment—and between the circulation of commodities and the circulation of the money which realises their exchange value, contradictions which are the primary and general sources of capitalist crises.

REFERENCES

1. Ruth Bunzel: *The Economic Organization of Primitive Peoples*, p. 346.
2. J. H. Boeke: *De Theorie der Indische Economie*, p. 49.
3. Raymond Firth: *Malay Fishermen*, p. 162.
4. H. Cunow: *Allgemeine Wirtschaftsgeschichte*, Vol. I, p. 241.
5. Kin Wei-Shan: *Democracy and Finance in China*, p. 66.
6. Cunow: op. cit., Vol. I, p. 240; R. Thurwald: article *"Wirtschaft"* in *Reallexicon der Vorgeschichte*, Vol. XIV, p. 408.
7. C. Huart and L. Delaporte: *L'Iran antique*, pp. 138-9.
8. H. Pirenne: *Le Mouvement économique et social au moyen âge*, p. 17.
9. E. Cuq: *Les Nouveaux fragments du Code de Hammourabi sur le prêt à intérêt*, pp. 21-28; W. Eilers: *Die Gesetzgebung Hammurabis*, p. 23.
10. International Labour Office: *Les populations aborigènes*, p. 407.
11. P. T. Bauer and B. S. Yamey: *The Economics of Under-developed Countries*, p. 65.

12. For Byzantium, G. Ostrogorsky: *Geschichte des byzantinischen Staates*, pp. 88, 217; for India, *Cambridge History of India*, Vol. IV, pp. 451-4; for China, K. A. Wittfogel: *Wirtschaft and Gesellschaft Chinas*, pp. 349-50; for Japan, M. Takizawa: *The Penetration of Money Economy in Japan*, pp. 21-22, etc.

13. A. Dauphin-Meunier: *Histoire de la Banque*, p. 5; E. Cuq: op. cit., pp. 26-32.

14. Huart and Delaporte: op. cit., p. 141.

15. A. Christensen: *L'Iran sous les Sassanides*, pp. 166-7.

16. A. Dauphin-Meunier: *La Banque à Travers les âges*, Vol. I, pp. 30-31.

17. F. Heichelheim: *Wirtschaftsgeschichte des Altertums*, pp. 351-2.

18. M. Rostovtzeff: *Social and Economic History of the Hellenistic World*, pp. 1278-80.

19. Steven Runciman: *La Civilisation byzantine*, p. 90-92.

20. Jacques Gernet: *Les Aspects économiques du bouddhisme dans la société chinoise du Ve au Xe siècle*, pp. 167-8, 20, *et al.*

21. Lien-sheng Yang: "Buddhist Monasteries and Four Money-Raising Institutions", in *Harvard Journal of Asiatic Studies*, Vol. XIII, June, 1950, Nos. 1-2, pp. 174-6.

22. Eijiro Honjo: *The Social and Economic History of Japan*, pp. 72-73.

23. Aly Mazahéri: *La Vie quotidienne des Musulmans au moyen âge*, p. 302.

24. G. Génestat: *Le Rôle des monastères comme établissements de crédit*, p. 19, for Normandy; Karl Lamprecht: *Deutsches Wirtschaftsleben in Mittelalter*, Vol. I, p. 1446, for Germany; G. G. Coulton: *The Mediaeval Village*, pp. 284-6, for Italy; Mackinnon: *Social and Industrial History of Scotland*, p. 74, for Scotland; H. van Werveke: in *Annales*, Vol. IV, pp. 459-60, for the Netherlands, etc.

25. A. Dauphin-Meunier: op. cit., Vol. I, pp. 86-89.

26. Heichelheim: op. cit., Vol. I, p. 342.

27. G. B. Jathar and S. G. Beri: *Indian Economics*, Vol. II, p. 329.

28. Ki Fein-Shen: *Essai sur l'origine et l'évolution des banques en Chine*, pp. 4-5.

29. Paul E. Eckel: *The Far East since 1500*, p. 105.

30. Walter J. Fischel: *Jews in the Economic and Political Life of Mediaeval Islam*, pp. 3, 7, 13-14, 26-28.

31. J. Kulischer: *Allgemeine Wirtschaftsgeschichte*, Vol. I, p. 330.

32. R. De Roover: *L'Evolution de la lettre de change, xive-xviiie siècle*, p. 24.

33. J. C. Van Dillen: *History of the Principal Public Banks*, pp. 81-84.

34. R. G. Rodkey: article *"Deposits"* in *Encyclopaedia of Social Sciences*, Vol. II, p. 416.

35. A. E. Sayous: *Les Banques de dépôt, les banques de crédit et les sociétés financières*, p. 12.

36. G. Bigwood: *Le Régime juridique et économique du commerce de l'argent dans la Belgique du moyen âge*, pp. 362-7 et passim; R. De Roover; *Money, Banking and Credit in Mediaeval Bruges*, pp. 117-20.

37. J. Schumpeter: *Business Cycles*, Vol. II, p. 614.

38. R. P. L. Molina: *De Iustitia et Iure*, Vol. II, 1597-359: 15.

39. R. De Roover: *L'Evolution de la lettre de change*, Vol. II, p. 26.

40. Ibid., p. 23.
41. Dauphin-Meunier: op. cit., Vol. I, p. 9; Ki Fein-Shen: op. cit., pp. 144-5; *Cambridge History of India*, Vol. I, pp. 218-19.
42. G. Glotz: *Le Travail dans la Grèce antique*, p. 73.
43. Boissonnadex: *Le Travail dans l'Europe chrétienne du moyen âge*, pp. 65-66; Fischel: *Jews in the Economic and Political Life of Medieval Islam*, pp. 17-24; N. S. B. Gras: article "Bill of Exchange" in *Encyclopedia of Social Sciences*, II, p. 450.
44. G. Glotz: op. cit., p. 73.
45. Glotz: op. cit., p. 142; R. S. Lopez: "Trade in Mediaeval Europe: The South", in *Cambridge Economic History of Europe*, Vol. II, p. 267.
46. A. Sapori: *La Crisi delle compagnie*, p. 249.
47. R. De Roover: *Money, Banking and Credit in Mediaeval Bruges*, p. 40.
48. Fischel: op. cit., pp. 28-29.
49. Nancy Lee Swann: *Food and Money in Ancient China*, p. 393.
50. Robert Bigo: *Les Bases historiques de la finance moderne*, p. 100.
51. H. Hauser and A. Renaudet: *Les Débuts de l'âge moderne (Peuples et Civilisations, Vol. VIII)*, p. 346.
52. Van Dillen: op. cit., passim.
53. R. De Roover: *L'Evolution de la lettre de change*, Vol. I, p. 350, Vol. II, p. 83.
54. W. T. C. King: *History of the London Discount Market*, p. 5; R. Bigo: *La Caisse d'Escompte et les origines de la Banque de France*, p. 16; J. H. Clapham: *The Bank of England*, pp. 6, 18, 27, 123.
55. R. De Roover: *L'Evolution de la lettre de change*, Vol. I, p. 119.
56. Clapham: op. cit., p. 153.
57. Bigo: *La Caisse d'Escompte . . .*, passim.
58. Clapham: op. cit., p. 118.
59. Schumpeter: op. cit., Vol. I, p. 292.
60. King: op. cit., pp. 7-8.
61. D. K. Joslin: "London private bankers, 1720–1785", in *Economic History Review*, Vol. VIII, No. 2, 1954, pp. 171-2, 182.
62. King: op. cit., p. 18.
63. Ibid., p. 11.
64. G. Von Haberler: *Prospérité et Dépression*, Vol. II, p. 333.
65. Schumpeter: op. cit., Vol. I, p. 124.
66. J. H. Clapham: *An Economic History of Modern Britain*, Vol. II, pp. 352-3.
67. René Dumont: *Le Problème agricole français*, p. 334.
68. Schumpeter: op. cit., Vol. I, p. 124.
69. J. G. K. Wicksell: *Lectures on Political Economy*, Vol. II, p. 190.
70. *New York Times*, 17th January, 1955.
71. Schumpeter: op. cit., Vol. II, p. 608.
72. King: op. cit., pp. 83, 270-1.
73. Heichelheim: op. cit., Vol. I, p. 687; Lopez: art. cit., pp. 309-10; De Roover; *L'Evolution de la lettre de change*, Vol. II, p. 35.
74. S. Schweizer: in *Evolution récente du rôle des banques*, p. 79.

75. King: op. cit., p. 16.

76. Norman Macrae: *The London Capital Market*, p. 130.

77. R. De Roover: *Money, Banking and Credit in Medieval Bruges*, pp. 294-7.

78. K. Polanyi: et al., *Trade and Market in the Early Empires*, p. 14.

79. Clapham: *An Economic History of Modern Britain*, Vol. II, p. 336.

80. Fernand Baudhuin: *Crédit et Banque*, pp. 47-49.

81. M. Compton and E. H. Bott: *British Industry*, pp. 170, 178.

82. R. S. Sayers: *Modern Banking*, p. 44.

83. S. Schweizer: in *Evolution récente du rôle des banques*, p. 95.

84. J. Kulischer: *Allgemeine Wirtschaftsgeschichte*, Vol. I, p. 343.

85. J. B. Condliffe: *The Commerce of Nations*, p. 96.

86. R. De Roover: *L'Evolution de la lettre de change*, Vol. I, p. 16.

87. F. Baudhuin, op. cit., p. 188; Paul H. Emden: *Money Powers of Europe*, passim.

88. Clapham: *An Economic History of Modern Britain*, Vol. II, p. 355.

89. Macrae: op. cit., pp. 88, 177.

90. Sayers: op. cit., p. 65.

91. Patrick Fitzgerald: *Industrial Combination in England*, p. 101.

92. Clapham: *An Economic History of Modern Britain*, Vol. III, p. 234.

93. Ibid., p. 242.

94. A. A. Berle: *The XXth Century Capitalist Revolution*, p. 30.

95. *The Economist*, 14th February, 1959, p. 613.

96. Gardiner C. Means: *The Structure of American Economy*, p. 153.

97. Richard B. Tennant: *The American Cigarette Industry*, p. 101; *Manchester Guardian*, 5th June, 1959.

98. Sargant Florence: *The Logic of British and American Industry*, pp. 183, 189, 203, 193.

99. Macrae: op. cit., pp. 386-9, 104.

100. A. Mehta: *Democratic Socialism*, p. 105.

101. Oualid: *Répétitions écrites de législation industrielle*, pp. 184-5.

102. Seligman: *Instalment Credit*, Vol. I, pp. 13 et seq.

103. F. Baudhuin, op. cit., pp. 16-17.

104. Schweizer: op. cit., pp. 92-93.

CHAPTER EIGHT

MONEY

The two functions of money

MONEY, the universal equivalent, is above all a commodity in the value of which all other commodities express their own exchange value.[1] The equation: 25 sacks of wheat are worth 1 pound of gold expresses an equivalence in exchange value, that is, in socially-necessary labour-time. As a common measure of value money possesses no mysterious quality. It can fulfil this function because it is itself a product of human labour and itself possesses a definite value.

When exchanges are simple, and buying and selling are gradually replacing barter, this basic quality of money is obvious. At the beginning of petty commodity economy there are usually two or three universal equivalents, which are used together as measures of value: wheat and gold or copper in Egypt and Mesopotamia; wheat, rice and silver in China, etc. Under these circumstances, nobody could regard money as being merely a conventional instrument of exchange.

The social division of labour is still relatively simple and transparent. When 25 sacks of wheat, 5 cows and a pound of silver are exchanged, the respective labour of the cultivator, the cattle-breeder and the miner appear reduced to a common measure, a common fraction of the total labour-time available to the given society based on accounting in labour-time.

But when exchanges become numerous and more and more common, this simple and quite transparent relation vanishes. Money is no longer merely the common measure of values, it has also become the means of exchange.[2] A large number of commodities come together on the market, in the possession of their respective owners. These commodities will pass from hand to hand until they reach those purchasers who wish to realise their use value. The latter take them finally off the market. Money facilitates these successive exchanges and makes them possible in the conditions of a unified market.[3] For it to carry out this function, however, its own intrinsic value is only of secondary importance. If the value of 25 sacks of wheat is equal to that 5 cows, it matters little to the cultivators and the cattle breeders that they have exchanged these two commodities after having first received and then paid one pound of fine silver, or ten pounds of crude-alloy silver. Because the entire circulation of commodities looks like a succession of exchange transactions in which money plays only the part of an *intermediary*, the illusion may arise that the value of the universal equivalent itself is of no importance for the proper functioning of the economy.

This is indeed an illusion. In so far as the circulation of commodities develops into a circulation of commodities and a circulation of money, money itself develops simultaneously into a means of circulation and a *means of deferred payment*. In a society which is essentially commodity-producing, a mass of commodities is in circulation thanks to credit. The money equivalent of these commodities will not be received until later.[4] Every fluctuation in the intrinsic value of money, the universal equivalent, immediately gives rise to disturbances in the relations between debtors and creditors, harming the former when the value of money rises (as happened with copper in the days of the Roman Republic) and ruining the latter when the value of money collapses.

The value of metallic money and price movements

Since the moment when the precious metals were more or less universally adopted as universal equivalents, fluctuations in their intrinsic value have always caused great upheavals in commodity prices, that is, in the expression of the value of these commodities in money terms. A rise in the value of metallic money causes a fall in prices expressed in this money, whereas a fall in the value of metallic money causes prices to rise.

The first great revolution in the value of money occurred when, as a result of the use of iron tools, the conditions of production of silver were much improved, and this led to a fall in the value of the metal, about 900 B.C. This decline in value caused a marked rise in prices expressed in silver: the price of a "qur" of wheat rose from two silver shekels under Hammurabi (2,000 B.C.) to 15 shekels about 950 B.C.[5] Six centuries later, Alexander the Great seized huge amounts of precious metals accumulated in the Persian imperial treasury, and this loot had the same effect as very cheap production—it led to a fall of about 50 per cent in the value of gold and silver, and a corresponding rise in prices.[6]

From the second century A.D. the reverse process occurred. The increase in the price of slaves, the decline in their output, the closing of numerous mines, the ebbing of the plundered treasure back towards India, increased the value of gold and silver, and caused a fall in prices expressed in precious metal (though this was obscured by the debasement of the coinage by successive Emperors).[7] This movement reached its culmination about the eighth and ninth centuries A.D. Then the trend was again reversed. From the fourteenth and fifteenth centuries onward, a real technical revolution in silver mining brought about a fall in the value of this metal and an all-round rise in prices. This became general in the second half of the sixteenth century, following the opening up of the silver mines of Potosi in Bolivia, and those of Mexico, by means of slave labour, which greatly reduced the costs of production and led to the closing of many mines in Europe.

When comparing the fluctuations in value of metallic money with the fluctuations in prices, one must not lose sight of the fact that the same technical upheavals that, by increasing productivity, cause a fall in the value of the metal, may likewise bring about a fall in the value of *all* commodities. In these circumstances, a fall in the value of gold and silver may be accompanied by stability or even decline in the prices of commodities. Thus, the same revolutionary technique of the iron age which lowered the value of silver in the tenth century B.C. made possible a considerable extension of agricultural production at lower costs, and led to a collapse of agricultural prices between the tenth and seventh centuries B.C. (the price of wheat, for instance, fell from 15 shekels to half a shekel per "qur").[8]

So long as the world market was fragmented into thousands of regional markets whose mutual relations were infrequent and slight, the coexistence of numerous universal equivalents in the world was not felt as any special difficulty in the way of exchanges. When the Portuguese, and later the Dutch, began trading in Indonesia, they found there various currency standards in force side by side. Gold and silver money has been able to coexist with shell money in aboriginal communities.[9] Only when industrial capitalism has effectively unified the world market, when nothing but exchange values are being produced, does the need for a universal equivalent for all countries make itself felt. The attempt made by several countries to base the universal equivalent simultaneously on gold and on silver (bimetallism) was doomed to defeat. These two metals having each their own exchange-value, which is subject to many variations in the capitalist epoch, constant disturbances were inevitable in the expression of the price of one metal in terms of the other and in the expression of the prices of commodities in either of them.[10] Finally, towards the end of the nineteenth century, nearly all countries were obliged to come round to accepting the gold standard; gold became the universal measure of gold for all countries. Resistance was prolonged, however, in the Far East, where, from the sixteenth century, silver had been used as the universal equivalent, first in China and later in India and Japan.

The circulation of metallic money

The precious metals serve as instruments of exchange by themselves representing a definite exchange-value. Equal values exchanging for equal values, it seems obvious that with the use of metallic money a precise ratio is established between the total price of all the commodities in circulation and the amount of currency needed for the exchange value of these commodities to be realised. To determine this ratio, account has to be taken of the fact that one unit of currency can effect several successive exchanges.

A peasant has brought a coin to market in order to buy some cloth. With the same coin the cloth merchant buys a supply of flour from the miller. The miller in his turn buys some wheat from a peasant, still using the same coin. The latter will thus have effected in one day three exchange transactions, each being equal to the value of the coin itself. If we represent by v this velocity of circulation of the currency—the number of exchange transactions carried out by one coin in a certain period of time—by Q the number of commodities in circulation, and by p the average index of prices, we get the following formula which defines the amount of currency in circulation, M:

$$M \times v = Q \times p^{11}$$

The total amount of currency in circulation, multiplied by the velocity of circulation of the currency, must be equal to the total amount of commodities in circulation multiplied by the average index of prices. From this we get the following formula for the amount of currency needed for exchanging all the commodities in circulation:

$$M = \frac{Q \times p}{v}$$

Finally, by replacing $Q \times v$ by P, the total sum of the prices of all the commodities in circulation, we get the following formula:

$$M = \frac{P}{v}$$

The total amount of currency in circulation must be equal to *the sum of the prices of all the commodities exchanged*, divided by the velocity of circulation of the currency.

This formula must not be regarded as reversible. Nor must it be considered as an algebraic formula in which the knowledge of three factors enables one automatically to deduce the fourth.[12] It is P that must be seen as being normally the *only independent variable* of the formula. The prices of production of the commodities may fluctuate with their value; technical progress may cause a more or less radical fall in prices. In that case, some of the metallic money may be withdrawn from circulation, and perhaps hoarded. If the quantity of commodities in circulation increases markedly, without any corresponding increase in productivity (i.e. a corresponding decrease in the value of each commodity), an extra amount of metallic money will be needed to make exchanges possible. There will therefore be a drive to increase by all possible means the production of precious metals (reopening of closed mines, search for new mines, etc.). This is what happened from the end of the fourteenth century down to the sixteenth. But the velocity of circulation of currency is not an autonomous factor. "The velocity with which currency circulates tends to vary with production itself, and, in this sense, variations in currency circulation do not affect prices."[18]

Origins of private fiduciary currency

From the rise of petty commodity economy, however, the use of metallic money alone could put a brake on the rapid settlement of exchanges. A sharp expansion in international trade could cause a shortage of coin and so hinder economic growth. This happened not only in Western Europe in the fourteenth and fifteenth centuries but also in the Islamic Empire in the days of the Abbasids,[14] in Egypt in the Hellenistic epoch,[15] in ancient Greece before the discovery of the mines of Laurium,[16] in China in the ninth century A.D.[17] Periods of shortage of currency are usually characterised by an ever more rapid circulation of coins, which wear out more quickly and so deteriorate in weight and value.

Moreover, the use of metallic money alone entails a number of difficulties in the setting of fully developed petty commodity production. The departure of maritime expeditions and caravans which have to carry their means of exchange for a long period may cause sudden shortages of currency. R. de Roover quotes a fifteenth-century treatise on trade,[18] written by Uzzano, which shows that in Venice, every year, in the months of June and July, there was a shortage of currency owing to the departure of the galleys for Constantinople. This "tension" on the mediaeval "money market" regularly continued until after the departure of the galleys for Alexandria at the beginning of September, and was repeated between 15th December and 15th January, after the departure of the galleys sent to fetch cotton. On the other hand, in October and November there was plenty of currency around, because at that time the German merchants who had come to buy spices brought a lot of money to Venice.[19]

The simple need to transport often substantial amounts of coin in order to make payments shows that the use of metallic money could become very cumbersome.

"[Under Louis XVI] the transport of coin undertaken by the stage-coach service was very burdensome . . . On the 10th, 20th and 30th of every month, Mercier tells us in his *Tableau de Paris*, between ten o'clock and mid-day one encountered porters lugging bags full of money, and bending under their weight, running as though an enemy army was about to surprise the town . . ."[20]

These transport difficulties were found particularly troublesome in countries like China, where the metals used for coinage were baser than gold and silver, namely, copper and even iron.

To this must be added the great monetary insecurity that usually prevailed in those days, as a result of the simultaneous circulation of a wide variety of coins,* and also of fraudulent operations such as clipping, etc., especially on the part of the royal exchequers. In the sixteenth and seventeenth centuries this phenomenon existed on so large a scale in England that in 1695 50 per cent of the value of the country's tax receipts was lost through the inadequate weight of the coins paid in.[21]

All these reasons explain why, at a certain stage of development of petty commodity production, the growth of trade leads merchants to invent *tokens for money* by means of which exchanges can be accelerated and their settlement simplified. The two classical forms of these tokens, which appear more or less generally in every society with a developed merchant capital, are bills of exchange and transfers of bank deposits (bank money).

We have seen how the bill of exchange was born of the separation in time between purchase and delivery and in space between the buyer and the seller.* In mediaeval Europe these bills were, at first, exchange contracts and credit instruments. In other societies, they were mere credit instruments, like the "rice bonds" of Japan,[22] or cheques payable in metallic money or in specific commodities, like the "tea bonds" in China under the Sung dynasty.[23] What is characteristic of these documents, leaving aside the part they play as credit instruments, is that when their use has become general it is possible for them to serve as tokens for money. All that is needed is that they be capable of circulating, that is, be accepted by persons other than those named on the given document. In Western Europe this circulation was ensured though the practice of *endorsement of bills of exchange* which became widespread there in the sixteenth century.[24] At the beginning of the nineteenth century, in Scotland and Lancashire, bills of exchange still circulated as means of exchange, each being covered with many signatures.[25]

The technique of transfers of bank deposits by writing was more extensively used to make up for the inadequacy of metallic money, at least in Western Europe from the Middle Ages onward. The majority of merchants opened accounts with the big merchant banker houses. When they bought goods they instructed their banker to enter in his books the sum to be paid, on the debit side of their account and on the credit side of their supplier's account. Similarly, when they sold products, they had entered on the credit side of their account the sum due

* See Chapter 7.

to them, while the same sum was entered on the debit side of their customer's. At certain intervals, the net balances of the debit and credit accounts of each merchant were settled by means of deposits which they placed with the bankers, and possible extra payments of cash which had become necessary. This clearing system, which developed mainly through the fairs of the thirteenth century, enabled mediaeval society to make a tremendous saving in currency.

"These great fairs, where the trade in the spices of the Levant and the cloth of the West was centralised, were familiar with payments by setting-off one deal against another. Very little money was actually handled at Troyes or Provins; what was exchanged was chiefly bills, and at the end of the fair the money-changers' shops became a real clearing-house. The unpaid bills could, moreover, on payment of a commission, be carried forward from one fair to another."[26]

De Roover found in Bruges thousands and thousands of clearing entries in the books of the Bruges bankers of the fourteenth and fifteenth centuries; he estimates that, at that time, bank deposits had become a real currency.[27] Bank clearings used as means of exchange and payment are called bank money because the transfer of funds is carried by mere written entries in the bankers' books.

Bills of exchange, like bank money, can be used instead of metallic money to carry out a series of money transactions. But these money-tokens constitute a fiduciary currency, because they are accepted in payment only to the extent that the people concerned have confidence in the issuer, or in the banker who carries out the clearing. This is a *private fiduciary currency*, because it is issued by private persons.

Tokens for metallic money can serve as means of exchange and payment of commodities only provided they are *ultimately convertible into metallic money*, the universal equivalent. The circulation of private fiduciary currency always implies an ultimate settlement in public currency which is universally acceptable. Each merchant is naturally alone responsible for the convertibility of his own bills. If these are ultimately not paid, the merchant goes bankrupt, and those who are left holding his bills have lost the money they advanced. Private fiduciary currency is thus, by definition, a form of credit, a *credit currency* the solidity of which—the degree of its equivalence with the metallic money of nominally the same value—depends on the solvency of those who issue it.

Origins of public fiduciary currency

There is, however, something odd in the *private* effort to make up for the inadequacy of metallic currency. Money, the universal equivalent, is by definition a *social* instrument which has to neutralise precisely that which is purely private in commodities so as to make possible a development of exchange with the minimum of restrictions in time and space. Currency tokens the use of which depends on the solvency of individual bourgeois cannot in the long run fulfil such a social function. This is why the development of merchant capital demands the creation of *public currency tokens*, that is, the creation of a public fiduciary currency. Historically, public fiduciary currency derives from a third form of private fiduciary currency, deposit receipts functioning as bank notes. This originated in China.

The merchant's bill was known there from the time of the Chou dynasty (1134–256 B.C.).[28] In the ninth century A.D., which was marked by a severe shortage of metallic currency, the merchants arriving in provincial capitals adopted the habit of depositing their precious metals with private persons and circulating the *deposit receipts* they obtained from them.[29] This private fiduciary currency was called *fei-ch'ien*, or "flying money". The central government forbade this practice because it feared that the precious metals might disappear from circulation. As, however, the shortage of currency was genuine, the State was obliged, in the year 812, to open deposit offices itself, in the capital. With the receipts given them by the central government, the owners of these deposits could have metal coins paid to them in any of the provincial branches of the imperial offices. Later, in the tenth century, a "Bank for Easy Currency" was set up to regulate the system as a whole.

The deposit receipts issued by this bank were still made out to named individuals. But at the beginning of the eleventh century the metal coins of Szechwan province, made of iron, were hindering the circulation of commodities by their excessive weight. The merchants then decided to stop the circulation of coins completely. Sixteen rich merchant houses assembled all their metal coins and issued letters of credit, no longer by name, but *to the bearer*, covered by this stock, and replacing all the metal currency in circulation. The issue of these notes was undertaken rashly and the merchants were ruined. But the central government now intervened again and set up, in 1021, a Bank in Szechwan for the issue of *public bank-notes*. Two years later, these notes began to circulate throughout the Empire. A special bank was then set up to issue and convert this paper money. In 1161 the latter was already circulating to the value of 41,470,000 *kwan*, whereas there were only 700,000 *kwan* of metal coins. Under the following dynasties of Yang (the Tatars) and Ming, paper money remained preponderant, with many phases of depreciation and inflation. The fall of the Ming dynasty was partly due to a galloping inflation of paper money.* After this disaster, the Manchu dynasty, in the seventeenth century, abolished paper money, which was not re-established in China until the middle of the nineteenth century.

Public fiduciary currency was born in Europe in exactly the same

* See later in this Chapter, page 254.

fashion. From the fifteenth century onward, private banks in Venice and Barcelona had adopted the custom of giving deposit receipts to their depositors. When they crashed, towards the end of the sixteenth century, the *Banco di Rialto*, later the Bank of Venice, both public institutions, issued deposit certificates "to bearer", which circulated as paper money, but which soon became depreciated. The Bank of Amsterdam, founded in 1609, issued only certificates of equivalent of the metal coins deposited with it to the currency of the United Provinces. These notes remained remarkably stable down to the end of the eighteenth century. The first issues of bank notes in the strict sense were made by the Bank of Sweden in 1661.[30]

Creation of public fiduciary currency. First source: discounting

It was in Britain that public fiduciary currency, the bank note, received its classical form. In this country, too, it originated from private fiduciary currency, the *goldsmith notes*. The English merchants at first deposited their jewels and private hoards with the King. But in 1640, Charles I, struggling with ever more serious financial difficulties, confiscated their wealth. Thereafter the merchants adopted the custom of depositing their riches with goldsmiths who, in exchange, issued deposit receipts called "goldsmith notes", and then, when the goldsmiths began calling themselves bankers, "banker's notes".[31]

At first, these notes were issued for the total amount of the deposit; if the depositor withdrew part of this deposit, the note was given an additional inscription recording this withdrawal. Later, the bills were drawn up in fixed sums, and a depositor received a number of notes, the total value of which was equal to that of his deposit. Private bankers in Scotland, and the Bank of England, founded in 1697, issued notes which likewise went through these two successive stages.[32]

Now, from a certain moment onward, the Scottish bankers and the goldsmiths began lending to third parties the stock of metal currency which did not belong to them. In exchange for these loans they were given acknowledgements of debt. From that time, the fiduciary currency circulating among the public was covered not only by a stock of metal coins but also by acknowledgements of debt from third parties (one of these covering another). When the Bank of England was founded, in 1697, it issued notes covered by its stock of metal coins and by a State debt owed to it.[33]

Experience taught the bankers that bank-notes covered by third parties' acknowledgements of debt can be issued up to a definite limit (for example, three or four times the value of the stock of metal currency), because the public never all try at once to convert their bank notes into metal coins. Slowly, during the course of the eighteenth century, the Bank of England established a procedure by which the issue of bank notes was regulated both by the stock of metal currency in its possession, and by the discounting, first, of government bonds only, and later also of merchants' bills.[34] The discounting, and later above all the re-discounting, of merchants' bills, was during the nineteenth century the chief source of the creation of bank notes, of public fiduciary currency, not only in Britain but in all the capitalist countries.

When the bank of issue discounts (or re-discounts) a merchant's bill, it pays the owner of the bill (or his bank) the face value less the interest; it thus puts into circulation bank notes for a value equal to this amount. When the time comes for the bill to be paid, it receives this sum back; the same amount in bank notes is withdrawn from circulation. The fluctuations in the volume of its collection of bills will thus determine the amount of paper money in circulation. As the volume of merchants' bills presented for discounting increases in periods of good conjuncture and declines in periods of crisis and depression, the issue of paper money covered by the discounted bills constitute a very flexible currency instrument, which makes it possible to adapt the stock of currency to the economy's need of means of exchange.[35]

Creation of public fiduciary currency. Second source: advances on current account (overdrafts)

So long as the discounting of merchants' bills was the chief form of circulation credit, the bulk of the fiduciary currency in circulation originated from the discounting and re-discounting transactions of the central banks of issue. But from the moment that advances on current account (overdrafts) replaced discounting as the main form of short-term credit—from the end of the nineteenth century in Britain, at the beginning of the twentieth century in the rest of the capitalist world, it was the circulation of bank deposits (of bank money) that became the principal element in currency circulation.

The capitalists do not in fact keep more than a small part of their circulating capital in the form of ready money. Most of it is deposited in the banks. The bankers function as their cashiers, paying out the amounts they owe and taking in the sums paid to them. All these payments are effected by cheques* or by clearing, and are thus completed without cash playing any part, through mere comparison of entries.

* The word cheque comes from the English "to check", i.e. to compare, to verify, and relates to the practice of tearing bills payable to order in such a way as to make an irregular edge which can be compared with the corresponding edge of the other half.[36] In Antiquity the same method was used with potsherds. The first paper cheques were used in Barcelona and Venice in the fourteenth century, but they were then forbidden.[37] The custom of tearing bills payable to order in such a way as to make an irregular edge was kept up in the Middle Ages for recognizances of debt, such as those which Des Marez discovered at Ypres.[38] The first English cheque that has been preserved dates from 1675.

One might suppose that this bank money originates from payments in of cash by the depositors, but this is only partly true. A large share of bank deposits do not originate from payments in actually made by the bank's clients but from advances on current account (overdrafts) granted by the bank to capitalists. These are the "loans that make deposits":

"The bulk of the deposits arise out of the action of the banks themselves; for by granting loans, allowing money to be drawn on overdraft, or purchasing securities, a bank creates a credit in its books which is equivalent to a deposit."[39]

The bank deposits thus created—or at least the current accounts—really represent *currency*, since they can be used for any transaction of purchase or payment within the country. They represent a *fiduciary currency*, because in the last resort their circulation depends on the good management and solvency of the banks, and not on the intrinsic value of the universal equivalent. And they represent a *public fiduciary currency*, because in all the advanced countries all the important deposit banks are linked to the central bank of issue by a special system which ensures that the bank money is covered by the bank notes of the central bank.

The credits given by the banks to the capitalists and which are at the origin of many current accounts, are intended for use. The banks create deposits so that these may circulate. If a bank, by granting a loan on current account to Mr. X, increases his deposit from 4 to 6 million francs, Mr. X will use these 6 millions to pay a debt to Mr. Y or buy goods from Mr. Z. These other capitalists also have bank accounts. If their accounts are with the same bank, all these transactions will take place by comparison of entries and will not require any transfer of bank notes. The deposit of 6 millions will merely be transferred from the account of Mr. X to that of Mr. Z. If their accounts are with other banks, the transfers in question will require a transfer of cash only to the extent that these other banks do not have to transfer an equal amount to Mr. X's bank. Actually, clearing houses specially set up for this purpose reduce to the absolute minimum any transfer of cash from one bank to another.*

Banks, finally, are able to increase their loans on current account

---

* The cashiers of the London banks, who had the task of transporting the amounts of money needed for settlements between these banks, adopted the custom, in the second half of the eighteenth century, of meeting together over drinks in order to compare their accounts and hand over only the difference between the amounts due and the amounts to be received, and vice versa. Starting in 1775 the bankers themselves imitated their example, which gave rise to the Clearing House. Clearing houses have developed in all the big cities of the world. Their transactions involve huge sums. In 1945, for instance, the Federal Reserve Banks carried out in the U.S.A. clearing operations for a total of 688 billion dollars.[40]

and thus create bank money, to the extent that other banks grant them credit or the central bank allows them to increase their debit accounts with it.[41] Experience has shown bankers that in normal times the public does not withdraw its cash from the banks in excess of a relatively small fraction of the total amount deposited.* It is thus sufficient that these deposits should not exceed a definite relationship with the liquid assets, called the cash ratio, or liquidity ratio (i.e. minimum cash in hand, expressed as a percentage of the total assets) for the banks to be able in normal circumstances to give loans on current account and create bank money. At exceptional moments the central bank has to step in to prevent the collapse of this credit system from entailing the collapse of the entire currency system. In order to avoid rashness, the majority of advanced countries lay down a "cover ratio" fixed by the government.†

In Britain this has been 8 per cent since 1946.[43] In the U.S.A. it is 24 per cent for current accounts in the big banks, in Belgium 4 per cent for short-term deposits, in Sweden and Italy 25 per cent, etc. Furthermore, in Belgium 65 per cent of the total of current accounts have to be covered by public bonds.[44]

It is thus apparent that bank money makes up a large share of the stock of currency, that is, of the totality of means of exchange and payment circulating in a particular country. In 1952, bank money constituted 78·6 per cent of this stock in the U.S.A., 74 per cent of it in Britain, 65 per cent in Australia, 51 per cent in Italy, etc.[45] To this must be added that bank money usually circulates more rapidly than bank notes.[46]

Creation of public fiduciary currency. Third source: public expenditure

The public fiduciary currency created by discounting or by overdrafts corresponds to needs—for credit, exchange, payment—inherent in the economic system. The fact that the State regulates the creation of this fiduciary currency corresponds to the social character of money, which becomes more and more marked as exchange-relations become increasingly interlocked and complex in modern capitalism. But this regulation, which is indispensable for the proper functioning of the economy, can at the same time give rise to many disturbances.

The State which regulates the issue of paper money and ultimately determines the volume of the stock of currency as a whole is actually itself both buyer and seller, and so needs means of exchange

---

* These withdrawals are mainly made in order to pay wages and salaries or to meet the needs for unproductive consumption of the capitalists and other savers.

† Distinction is made between the *cash ratio* (ratio between cash in hand and total deposits) and the *liquidity ratio* (ratio between holdings of cash, money at call or short notice, and bills discounted on the one hand, and total assets on the other).[42]

and payment. From the beginnings of public fiduciary currency, the governments which regulate its issue have been subjected to the temptation to use it at the same time to meet their own needs. The first experiments in issuing paper money have invariably led to inflationary disasters. This happened with China's paper money which, under the Tatar emperor Kublai Khan, attained the circulation, fantastic for those days, of 249,652,290 *kwan* issued.[47] It was the same with the first experiments in others continents, such as the "card money" in the British and French colonies in America in the seventeenth century, the "Continental money" issued during the American War of Independence, the *assignats* issued during the French Revolution, etc.[48]

Even in a bourgeois state conducted according to principles of strictest monetary orthodoxy, it is inevitable that a certain seasonal and cyclic movement of increased need for disposable funds (e.g. on the eve of the dates for payment of civil servants' salaries) should lead the Treasury to increase its debts to the central bank which in turn will increase the stock of currency. This extra mass of currency is usually re-absorbed in time. But when the State increases the circulation of currency in order to finance its long-term expenses or, still worse, its budgetary deficit, risks of loss of value of the currency arise in so far as no extra mass of commodities corresponds to this extra mass of currency in circulation.[49]

Socially-necessary stock of currency

The whole pyramid of bank money is thus built up on a basis of paper money. It is the same with private fiduciary currency, as we have already shown. All credit money needs, as means of final settlement, a definite amount of currency. In reality, it is a question of a mass of bills which, after clearing, have to be honoured financially. The mass of currency thrown into circulation in a capitalist society thus has to fulfil a dual role, that of constituting the equivalent of the *commodities* which enter into this circulation (money acting as means of circulation), and that of representing the value of the *bills* which fall due, taking into account those which neutralise each other (money acting as means of payment). Here we meet again the two functions of money already described.

Money as means of payment, effecting the payment of bills, like money as means of circulation, has a definite velocity of circulation: the same sum of money may, passing from hand to hand and from firm to firm, effect a successive series of payments in a given period of time. We thus obtain the following formula for the amount of currency needed to settle all payments due (e.g. during one month):

$$\frac{\textit{Total of payments due, minus total of payments which cancel each other out}}{\textit{Velocity of circulation of means of payment}}$$

By adding the stock of currency needed for the circulation of commodities and the stock needed for the payment of bills, one can determine the total stock of currency which is essential for the proper functioning of the capitalist economy. It must be remembered that the same bank note may be used successively to purchase a commodity, and then to enable the seller of this commodity to pay a bill. The stock of currency needed by the economy for a certain period of time must therefore be equal to:

$$\frac{\textit{The sum of the prices of the commodities in circulation}}{\textit{The velocity of circulation of money as means of circulation}}$$

$$+ \quad \frac{\textit{The sum of payments due, minus the sum of mutually-cancelling payments}}{\textit{The velocity of circulation of money as means of payment}}$$

The sum functioning successively as means of circulation and means of payment.

It follows directly from this formula that the *stock of currency necessary* for the proper working of the economy is a very elastic quantity, which varies uninterruptedly during the course of a month. On the eve and at the moment of the first day of each month, for instance, very much more currency, as means of payment, is needed than eight days later. The stock of currency necessary likewise fluctuates in accordance with the ups and downs of the conjuncture. It also follows that a currency instrument of a *very flexible* kind is needed in order that it may be rapidly adapted to the constantly changing needs of the economy.

In the nineteenth century a series of credit crises were caused in Britain by the fact that the Bank of England was obliged by the Peel Act to keep within a rigid maximum in its issuing of banknotes. This act had to be suspended on each occasion.[50]

In the twentieth century bank money has proved a currency instrument even more flexible than paper money. When the mass of bank notes and current accounts remains stationary, while the demand for circulation credit and means of payment is increasing, the increase in the *velocity of circulation of bank money*—that is, the use of the same deposit for the increased number of transfers in a given period of time—offers a solution to the difficulty. This is what happened in Belgium in 1950 and at the start of 1951, when this velocity of circulation increased by 20 per cent.[51]

The circulation of inconvertible paper money

Bank money is based on public paper money. So long as the latter is convertible and remains based on the stock of metal currency in the bank of issue, the use of token currency does not present any problems regarding the nature of currency. The latter is continuing to serve as universal equivalent by virtue of its own intrinsic value. The fact that only a fraction of the banknotes are covered by the metal in hand (just as only part of the bank money is covered by banknotes) merely represents a social saving in circulation devices, a saving made possible by the laws of behaviour on the part of the public which have been discovered empirically.

These laws reflect in their turn *the increasing socialisation of the capitalist economy, the more and more objective nature of money.* In order that the working of the currency mechanism be not hindered it is sufficient to keep the use of convertible fiduciary currency within the limits of the socially necessary stock of currency. Any issue which went substantially beyond this would cause an outflow of precious metals and a stoppage of convertibility which would doom the currency to devaluation.

By starting from this more and more objective nature of modern capitalist money it is possible to grasp the problem of the circulation of inconvertible paper money. This does not necessarily entail a fall in purchasing power, an obvious depreciation. Experience showed this already in the nineteenth century. The French franc was made inconvertible between 1870 and 1877, but it lost hardly 1·5 per cent of its value in relation to gold and to convertible currency.

In fact it is enough to restrict severely the issue of inconvertible paper money (and the creation of bank money) to the currency stock which is socially necessary, in order to avoid in the main any manifestation of fall in the value of money. All the currency thrown into circulation being absorbed by current economic transactions—exchanges and payments—an inconvertible paper currency of this kind circulates representing only the same amount as a convertible paper currency would have represented in its place, and *within the limits of the national market* no disturbance can occur.

Some writers have seen in this phenomenon proof that money has never been a commodity with its own value, but has always had a "rate" determined by the public authorities.[52] However, nineteenth century experience, especially in countries with bimetallic currency, showed that currency fluctuations were caused by fluctuations in the intrinsic value of gold and silver: "After the great gold discoveries in California and Australia [in the 1850s], silver was an expensive metal and hard to keep in circulation . . . Soon, however, an abrupt reversal took place. From 1842 on, metallurgical processes were discovered which improved the recovery of silver from lead ones. These were widely used after what are now the Rocky Mountain States were taken over by the United States from Mexico in 1848 and 1853. A flood of silver cheapened the metal in relation to gold, and silver was progressively demonetised."[53]

In reality, the transition from the money based on the gold (or silver) standard of the nineteenth century to *partly inconvertible* money after the First World War corresponded to two quite different phenomena. On the one hand, a real currency depreciation caused by the huge expenditure on arms and war, together with the burden of a constantly growing public debt. This currency depreciation even hit the U.S.A., the country possessing a big share of all the world's gold reserves, since in purchasing power a dollar in 1958 was worth less than 50 cents before the war (of 1939). On the other hand, the increasing intervention of the State in economic life, the growing organisation of certain sectors of the economy by the State in the interests of the bourgeois class as a whole, and thereby the elimination of the "pure" conditions of a market economy, an elimination also achieved through the intervention of other "organising" and "conscious" forces, the cartels, trusts, holding companies and monopolistic groupings in general.* A currency with an intrinsic value is essential to a pure market economy based on exchange. The more elements of "economic organisation" are introduced into the economy, the more completely can an "abstract" currency, a money of account, be substituted for this currency of intrinsic value.[54]

But the elements of organisation that capitalism introduces into the economy during its period of decline are disparate and contradictory. They abolish the anarchy and automatic working of the market at one level, only to reproduce them at higher level. In the days of currencies based on the gold standard, many of the payments made, not only on the national market but also on the international market, were carried out without the use of precious metals. In the days of inconvertible or only partly convertible national currencies, international settlements are more complicated; gold (or currency convertible into gold) is insisted on more than before for payments on the international market.

Consequently, even under the régime of inconvertible paper money, the precious metals, commodities with intrinsic value, remain ultimately the only universal equivalent on the world market. A "managed" world currency, the only one which would finally sever the instrument of circulation from its metallic base, cannot be created in a capitalist economy. It can result only from a world-wide planning of the economy, the outcome of the world-wide victory of socialism.

This is why modern currencies are not in reality completely severed from a metallic base, even when the law lays down that no quantity of gold may be obtained in exchange for a banknote (become paper money).† Through foreign trade and the movement of international

---

* See Chapters 12 and 14.

† It is interesting to observe that this duality has been given curious applications in the courts. French law normally recognises only the "nominal" franc in all disputes that arise between persons resident in France. But as soon as it

payments, every national currency is linked at once to gold and to other national currencies, and the fluctuations in its relative purchasing power, the fluctuations in its rate on the free or black market, are indices of the extent to which it is or is not depreciated. This depreciation results from a property which is peculiar to public fiduciary currency alone: *the solidarity, the collective equivalence, of all the banknotes printed by the State.*

Metallic currency, a product of human labour, possesses an intrinsic value. The increase in its circulation, over and above the stock of currency socially necessary, does not lead to its becoming depreciated but to its being hoarded. It is the same with convertible banknotes, the excessive issue of which may furthermore lead to a flight of gold. *Private* fiduciary currency, issued by insolvent capitalists, brings about its own complete depreciation along with the bankruptcy of the issuer, but does not automatically depreciate the private fiduciary currency issued by other private persons.

Public inconvertible paper money, on the contrary, is subject to depreciation as soon as an excess issue takes place, not accompanied by an equivalent increase in the commodities in circulation. All the banknotes being depreciated together, the increase in the currency in circulation, far from leading to their being hoarded, causes, on the contrary, their de-hoarding. Their value thenceforth depends on their declining purchasing power. The quantity theory of money here applies with a certain amount of validity.*

As this currency is now depreciated, people try to get rid of it and instead to hoard precious metals, metallic money or other, non-depreciated paper money.† Private hoarding of gold between 1946 and 1951 was estimated at an annual average of 250 million dollars. In this way Gresham's Law made itself felt: "bad" money (more or less depreciated) drove good money out of circulation.

The automatic rise of prices as a result of the depreciation of paper money occurs only in a country where price-formation is more or less "free", i.e. determined by economic forces alone. The inconvertible

is a question of international disputes, only the gold value counts, whether this be to the advantage of the French parties to the dispute (dispute about Serbian and Brazilian loans before the Hague Court in 1929, and about the Norwegian loans in 1957) or to their disadvantage (loan issued by the *Messageries Maritimes*).[55]

* On the quantity theory of money, see Chapter 18.

† The depreciation of paper money is a very relative notion. Between 1938 and the end of 1946 the bank notes in circulation in the U.S.A. increased by 400 per cent, whereas industrial production barely doubled. The dollar lost nearly 40 per cent of its purchasing power. This was an obvious case of depreciation. Nevertheless it was not so serious as the depreciation of other paper currencies, such as the French franc and the lira, so that dollar bills were hoarded in France and Italy.

banknotes can be imposed on a country for a certain time, along with strict regulation of the exchanges, which makes it possible to limit to the minimum the increase of prices, in spite of a substantial issue of paper money, shown only on the free currency market abroad and the "parallel", illegal markets in the country itself. This was the case in Nazi Germany.[56] However, a system like this of "deferred inflation" implies other contradictions which need to be studied separately, within the framework of the "managed" economy and the economy of rearmament and war.

The balance of payments

Even when a paper currency is "solid", i.e. when it has not been issued in excess of the socially *necessary stock of currency*, and when it possesses a gold cover traditionally regarded as adequate, it may lose its convertibility into gold. This happened to the pound sterling after 1931. The cause of this inconvertibility lies in the *dual function of gold*, at once cover for paper money and also sole international means of payment. Just as private fiduciary currency circulates within a country only to the extent of the private issuer's solvency (i.e. his capacity to pay a bill when it falls due), public fiduciary currency circulates internationally only to the extent that the issuing country is solvent, that it has the capacity to settle in gold (or in currency convertible into gold) its debts to other countries.

This does not mean that every purchase made abroad entails a transfer of gold to the selling country. On the international plane as on the national and local plane a clearing system operates which implies the transfer of the *net balances* only between the amounts due to the foreign country and the amounts due from it to the country in question. These net amounts appear in the balance of payments, which is mainly made up of the following entries:

(*a*) The trade balance, i.e. the difference between exports to a given country and imports from it. If exports exceed imports in value, there is a credit entry in the balance of payments, if the opposite, there is a debit entry.

(*b*) The movement of capital, i.e. the difference between the outflow and inflow of capital. Into the first of these categories go the purchase of shares, factories and bonds abroad, and foreign landed property, together with the placing of capital in foreign banks, and the sending abroad of dividends, interest, assurance premiums or insurance for foreigners who own property in the country in question. Into the second go the purchase of shares, bonds, factories, land in the country in question by foreigners who bring in their capital, the placing of foreign capital in national banks, the repatriation of dividends, interest, assurance premiums, etc., by residents of the country, and the sending of gifts, public and private, from abroad to the country in question. If the import of capital exceeds the export, this will mean a credit entry in the balance of payments; if the reverse, a debit entry.

(c) Maritime traffic. Ships of the given nation which carry goods abroad are paid for the freight in foreign currency which they bring into the country. Contrariwise, foreign ships which bring goods into the country are paid in currency which they take out of the country. If the first total is greater than the second, there will be a credit entry in the balance sheet; if the other way round, a debit entry.

(d) Tourist traffic. If the tourists of the country in question spend more money abroad than foreign tourists spend when they visit this country, the entry will be on the debit side. If the opposite is true, it will be on the credit side.

(e) The movement of immigration and emigration. If immigrants bring more funds with them than emigrants take out, the entry will be on the credit side; if the contrary, there will be a debit entry. Etc.

So long as a country has normally a credit balance of payments, the convertibility of its paper currency is secured by a relatively modest stock of metal. But as soon as the balance of payments begins to become regularly a debit balance, only a substantial stock of metal can, as a rule, maintain the convertibility of the paper currency. Otherwise, the outflow of gold risks causing speculation and panic.[57] Finally, if the majority of the commercially important countries abandon the gold standard, as happened during the 1930s, the other countries are compelled to follow suit, since otherwise their national currencies become the object of international speculation and are systematically withdrawn from circulation.

The balance of payments affects the volume of money in circulation, and thereby, when the paper currency is partly or totally inconvertible, the purchasing power of money. A permanent deficit in the balance of payments is the product of inflationary tendencies, a surplus is the product of deflationary tendencies.* However, in the short run, when the Central Bank pays exporters the equivalent of the currency surplus it accumulates, a surplus in the balance of payments may provoke an inflationary tendency, because this extra purchasing power finds no counterpart on the market.[58] To avoid these effects, the surplus in the balance of payments would have to be neutralised by an increase in domestic saving.[59]

---

* A credit balance of payments over a long period corresponds in fact to a *sterilisation of purchasing power*; the gold which is accumulating in the vaults of the central bank could have been used to import various goods, that is, to create extra income. In the same way, a persistently deficitary balance of payments expresses the fact that *surplus purchasing power*—inflation!—has been created in the country, in exchange for which more and more goods and services have to be imported from abroad.

Central banks and bank credit

So long as a currency is based on the gold standard, the role of the issuing institution consists in safe-guarding first and foremost the convertibility of the currency. The restriction of credit that it can bring about by raising the discount rate is conceived in the first place as a means of restricting the fiduciary circulation, and only indirectly as a means of correcting the excesses of a boom. In the age of inconvertible paper money, however, the tasks of the central bank extend to become a function of supervising the entire economy. It has in fact to regulate the credit policy of the commercial banks, which, in their turn, influence the whole progress of the economy.[60]

The central banks of the nineteenth century had as cover the banknotes which they issued, their supply of gold (or silver), and the bills they discounted. They influenced the volume of credit by means of the discount rate.

The economic and financial instability characteristic of the epoch of decline of capitalism, after the First World War, compelled the central banks to resort to extra cover and to different methods of influencing credit. On the one hand the large private banks possess considerable reserves which render them largely independent of the discounting policy of the central bank. On the other, in a period of marked depression, the mere lowering of the discount rate is no longer an adequate stimulus to increase the volume of credit, exchanges and circulation of money. In these conditions, the central bank resorts to an old technique, which was already in extensive use by the public banks of the seventeenth and eighteenth centuries: the policy called that of the "open market".

This policy had always been permitted in the U.S.A. but was practised on a large scale particularly after 1933. It was authorised by a special act in Britain in 1931, and in France and Belgium in 1936. It provides that the central bank may buy and sell government stock (loans, treasury bonds, etc.) on the open market. When the government wants to effect a contraction in the volume of money in circulation (credit), it can sell government stock, which results in an ingathering (and so a sterilisation) of banknotes, or, what comes to the same thing, a reduction in the current credit accounts of the private banks with the central bank, and a reduction in the amount of bank money that these banks can henceforth create.[61] Contrariwise, when the government wants to enlarge the volume of money in circulation (credit) it must buy up government stock, which results in an issue of new banknotes or an increase in the credit accounts of the private banks with the central bank. The open market system can, however, easily degenerate into a means of covering state expenditure due to a budget deficit.[62]

It is in the U.S.A., where the depreciation of the currency has nevertheless gone less far than in Europe, that government stock today represents the chief corresponding value to the bank money of the private banks, and a far more important entry in the assets of the central bank than the private obligations:

"Until 1933, the principal way in which money came into existence was through short-term borrowing by business concerns. In 1929, the loans of commercial banks accounted for nearly two-thirds of the country's supply of money . . . At the end of 1950, they accounted for less than one-third . . . The largest single source of money supply is borrowing by the government. The holdings of government obligations by commercial banks are half again as large as their short-term loans."[63]

However, the supervisory function that the central bank can exercise in its capacity as ultimate source of cash is not absolute. It can either rigidly determine the amount of currency or else rigidly determine the cost of money-capital (cash), that is, the rate of interest. The first path was followed in the nineteenth century, the second is being followed now.[64] But to regulate simultaneously and rigidly *both* the amount of currency *and* the rate of interest is impossible in a capitalist economy.

Currency manipulations

The dual function of gold, that of serving as metallic basis to paper money and that of acting as international means of payment, makes this precious metal an instrument of economic and commercial policy. When the national currencies are freely convertible into gold, their respective value is determined directly either by the metal content of the coinage or else by the gold cover of the banknotes, which are mere tokens for the precious metals. When the convertibility of paper currencies is more or less abolished, these currencies acquire a *forced rate* in relation to foreign currencies. This rate is usually determined by international conventions, but it can be modified unilaterally. If it corresponds to the actual relationship between the purchasing power of the two currencies, it will usually be respected and will undergo only slight ups and downs, caused by temporary fluctuations in the balance of payments between two countries, in the reciprocal supply and demand of their respective currencies.[65]

If this rate is, on the contrary, an artificial one, a "parallel", "free" or "black" market will appear, on which the currency thus officially over-valued will be depreciated in exchange for other currencies.

A government may attempt to bring about internationally such a depreciation, with the aim of favouring its exports, either in order to improve the balance of payments or to help the general state of business. As the rate of exchange of an inconvertible currency is a forced rate, the government can lower it by mere decree. It can

announce arbitrarily that henceforth there will correspond to the
unit of currency a gold equivalent devalued, say, by 20 per cent,
and that consequently, foreign currencies will henceforth be quoted
at a rate 25 per cent higher than before. A depreciation of the currency
effected like this, called devaluation, causes the prices of a country's
products in foreign markets to fall.

American and British cars are competing on the Australian market.
Let us suppose that the current selling price of the American car
most frequently sold in Australia is 3,000 dollars, which is worth
£A750, at the rate of £A1 = 4 dollars. The British cars, which cost
£600 sterling will be sold at £A750 too, if £1 sterling is worth £A1·25.
But if the pound sterling is devalued by 20 per cent, this same
car will be sold at £A600, without any reduction in the cost of production or the manufacturers' profit.

The use of devaluation as a weapon in competition comes up
against two obstacles, however:

(a) It risks starting a snowball, with all countries trying to improve
their trade balance in the same way. This is what happened after the
devaluation of the pound sterling in 1931, which entailed the devaluation of 34 other national currencies between 1931 and 1935. The same
phenomenon recurred after the devaluation of sterling in 1949.

(b) Every country has not only to export but to import as well.
If devaluation reduces export prices, it increases the prices of imports.
It thus favours the industries working for the export trade using home-
produced raw materials, as against the industries working for the home
market using imported raw material, and so leads to a redistribution
of the national income. These effects can be mitigated if substantial
stocks of foreign raw material have been accumulated before devaluation, or if a fall in the price of these goods is expected, a favourable
change in the "terms of trade".* In the end, the elasticity of the
foreign demand for the products exported by the country devaluing its
currency will prove decisive.[66]

A currency policy opposite to devaluation can likewise tend to bring
about an increase in exports. Without modifying the backing of the
country's paper money in gold or currency, it is possible to cause a
fall in prices on the home market by restricting credit and the amount
of money in circulation, lowering nominal wages, etc. This fall will
then react on export prices. As a rule, however, this policy of *deflation*
increases the stagnation of business and the degree of unemployment
within the country,[67] so destroying all the advantages to be expected
from an increase in exports, which, moreover, are neutralised, as with
devaluation, by international chain reactions:

"If pressure on money wage rates improves a country's balance

* The expression "terms of trade" is used to mean the relationship between
the price index of exported goods and the price index of imported goods.

[of payments], it becomes possible for home producers to gain advantages at the expense of foreign producers, and thus to shift the incidence of unemployment on to other countries. These other countries who find their exports declining and their imports rising will react to the resulting unemployment by putting pressure on their own wages. If, however, wage cuts in country A are followed or outpaced by wage cuts in country B the former does not obtain a net advantage."[68]

In fact, after the outbreak of the economic crisis of 1929, there followed one after the other two international chain reactions, first a deflationary one, then one of devaluation.

The manipulations of paper currency by governments who try to use it as a weapon against the trade cycle have created illusions as to the possibility of correcting serious excesses in the conjuncture by means of a "managed currency". By increasing the amount of fiduciary money in circulation and lowering the rate of interest, the banks of issue can in fact encourage an expansion of credit by the commercial banks, which is expected to favour economic recovery when there is depression.

However, the influence of the rate of interest on economic conjuncture should not be exaggerated. An investigation undertaken in the U.S.A. shows that the interest paid by the entrepreneur represents there a very small element in the cost of production: 0·4 per cent of the cost of production of manufactured goods: 0·2 per cent of the cost of production in the building trade; 0·8 per cent of that of mineral products; and 0·2 per cent of distribution costs.[69]

It is an illusion to suppose that the banks can ensure on their own (with the aid of the central bank) an expansion of credit and of the stock of currency. They can at most grant loans more easily and at lower cost. But for the stock of currency to increase effectively by way of credits on current account, it is further necessary that the entrepreneurs should *effectively use* the facilities thus provided. It is the entrepreneurs and not the banks who are really the initiators of the expansion of bank money at the start of recovery.[70] Now: "In a [deep] depression things look so gloomy that no conceivable drop in the rate of interest is likely to induce [a businessman] to embark upon any but the most blatantly desirable adventures."[71]

It is then, in the last analysis, the factors that determine the economic conjuncture as a whole that explain the transition from a depression to an economic recovery—and among these factors the manipulation of the stock of currency and the rate of interest play only a subordinate role.*

Three forms of inflation

Depreciation of the currency is as old as public currency itself. It is

* See Chapter 11.

engendered by the needs of the State which mints the coins or issues the notes. Its oldest form is the falsification of the alloy, base metals being substituted for precious ones. Owing to the sharp oscillations in prices to which it gives rise, it disorganises the economy of any society based on petty commodity economy. The Czech chronicler Cosmas, who died about 1125, called it "worse than the plague, more disastrous than an enemy invasion, than famine or other calamities."[72]

Paper money, which seems to free itself from its metallic basis, offers by its very nature a strong temptation to depreciation, either intermittent or continuous.

Accordingly, in the imperialist epoch, this depreciation or inflation has become a quasi-universal phenomenon. Several degrees of gravity need, however, to be distinguished.

Moderate inflation corresponds to an issue of fiduciary currency (or an increase in the stock of currency by other means) without any immediate equivalent increase in goods or services, but in circumstances in which the volume of employment and production increases. For this to happen a certain amount of unemployment and a reserve of unemployed means of production are needed, among other things.[73]* When the State uses the increased stock of currency to buy goods and labour-power which serve to make means of destruction—i.e. goods which do not come back into the reproduction process—it can, by imposing a strict control of prices, *conceal* the inflation for the time being, until the disproportion between the amount of money in circulation and the actual circulation of commodities breaks the ephemeral equilibrium. The balancing equivalent to this price-control has in these conditions to be the sterilisation of a part of the public's income in the form of forced saving.[74] In this case, *concealed* or "deferred" *inflation* represents a promise to increase the circulation of goods some time in the future through an increase in home production converted back to normal uses, or else by the plundering of foreign countries. If this reabsorption of purchasing power without any counterpart does not take place, the inflation effected will eventually bring about a rise in prices.

When a substantial issue of inflationary paper money is accompanied by a stagnation or a diminution in the circulation of purchasable commodities over a prolonged period—notably, when full employment has already been achieved, or in the setting of a war economy—the rise in prices takes place at once, and starts a vicious circle. *Inflation feeds on itself.* Depreciation of the currency leads to a rise in prices, this increases the budget deficit, which in turn is covered by a fresh inflationary issue of paper money, and that entails a new

---

* See Chapter 10, section "War Economy", and Chapter 14, section "A crisis-free capitalism?"

wave of price increases. The depreciated fiduciary currency does not go out of circulation any more. Everybody who can tries to get rid as soon as possible of this depreciated currency and hoards *real values*: gold, foreign currency, jewels, works of art, industrial shares, property in land and buildings, etc. The wage-earning classes are hardest hit.[75]

When the State's expenditure begins to exceed its income by a big margin, as the result of a lost war, occupation costs, reparations to be paid, etc., what appears is *galloping inflation*. The depreciation of the currency goes from bad to worse every day, if not every hour. Banknotes are issued with astronomical face-values, and depreciate faster than they can be printed. Exchanges by means of money grow fewer and fewer, and people go back to barter. Industry risks being unable to reconstitute its capital and no longer realising surplus-value if it exchanges commodities for such depreciated currency. Its products are therefore withdrawn from the market and stored, which brings about a stoppage in the economy and the complete collapse of the currency. These phenomena occurred in Germany in 1922–23 and in 1945–48, in China in 1945–49, in Rumania and Hungary in 1945–47, etc.*

Purchasing power, circulation of currency, and rate of interest

When interest is seen as "the rent for money" and it is thought to depend on the supply and demand of *cash*, there is a temptation to seek some ratio between the amount of currency in circulation and the rate of interest. But this is to forget that the rate depends on the supply and demand of *liquid money capital* and that definite *social* conditions are needed if the currency in circulation is to be transformed into *capital*. In fact, this mass of currency is divided socially into two major categories:

(a) The amount corresponding to the wages and salaries of workers and other employees, together with that part of the capitalists' funds earmarked for their expenditure as private consumers.

(b) The amount corresponding to the circulating capital of enterprises, profits not yet reinvested, depreciation funds of fixed capital not yet used, and "savings" from all sources.

The first category does not represent in any way a supply of liquid money-capital, but is instead a *demand for consumer goods*. The second category may represent both a *demand for means of production* and a *supply of liquid money-capital*.[76] It is only through the quantity of this second category of currency in circulation that the rate of interest may effectively influence the proportion of money-capital that will be hoarded, the proportion that will be lent to banks or to industrial and commercial firms, and the proportion that will be directly used by the owner for buying means of production. But this

* On the inflationary tendencies inherent in declining capitalism, see Chapter 14.

allocation of the mass of money-capital between different destinations will not depend exclusively, or even primarily, on the rate of interest but on the general state of business (the exact stage in the industrial cycle, the rate of profit, the ratio between rate of profit and rate of interest, etc.). "It cannot be asserted that an increase in the stock of money causes the rate of interest to fall and a diminution of the stock of money causes it to rise. Whether the one or the other consequence occurs always depends on whether the new distribution of property is more or less favourable to the accumulation of capital."

"There is no direct connection between the rate of interest and the amount of money held by the individuals who participate in the transactions of the market; there is only an indirect connection operating in a roundabout way through the displacements in the social distribution of income and wealth which occur as a consequence of variations in the objective exchange value of money."[77]

This does not mean that expansion of the volume of currency plays only a secondary role in the evolution of capitalism. On the contrary, its expansion is an essential condition for this evolution, for two reasons.

On the one hand, the tremendous increase in production and productivity which is characteristic of capitalism would have been impossible without a corresponding increase in the stock of currency, independently of the ups and downs of the exploitation of mines of precious metals.[78]

On the other hand, given the influence it exercises on the level of prices, the expansion of the stock of fiduciary and bank money determines the particular form taken by the redistribution of the national income, i.e. the *increase in the rate of profit* which occurs at the beginning of every economic recovery and without which this recovery would not be possible in a capitalist economy.

Economists such as Von Mises and Schumpeter have sufficiently described the phenomenon they call *forced saving*.[79] Forced saving, i.e. the reduction in the purchasing power of wages through depreciation of the currency, is indicated by Von Mises as a source of the formation of capital. And in this indirect way these writers, who reject any theory of surplus-value based on exploitation, recognise that capital is not the product of the thrift and self-sacrifice of the capitalists, but of the forced saving and sacrifices *imposed on the wage-earners by the way capitalism works*:

"One class has, for a time, robbed another class of part of their incomes; and has saved the plunder. When the robbery comes to an end, it is clear that the victims cannot possibly consume the capital which is now well out of their reach. If they are wage-earners, who have all the time consumed every penny of their income, they have no wherewithal to expand consumption. And if they are capitalists, who have not shared in the plunder, they may indeed be induced to consume now a part of their capital by the fall in the rate of interest; but not more so than if the rate had been lowered by the 'voluntary savings' of other people."[80]

In other words, and paradoxically, only a fall in the rate of interest *accompanied by a rise in the rate of profit* at the expense of the wage-earners (i.e. of their purchasing power) constitutes a real stimulus to capitalist production.

REFERENCES

1. B. Nogaro: *Cours d'économie politique*, Vol. I, p. 323.
2. R. P. Kent: *Money and Banking*, pp. 6-7.
3. B. Nogaro: *La Monnaie et les systèmes monétaires*, p. 6.
4. R. P. Kent: op. cit., p. 9.
5. F. Heichelheim: *Wirtschaftsgeschichte des Altertums*, pp. 202-4.
6. Ibid., pp. 421, 428.
7. Ibid., pp. 684-6.
8. Ibid., p. 204.
9. P. Bakker: *Eenige Beschouwingen over het Geldwezen in de inheemsche Samenleving van Nederlandsch-Indië*, pp. 1-3.
10. B. Nogaro: *La Monnaie et les systèmes monétaires*, pp. 87-88.
11. Irving Fisher: *Purchasing Power of Money*, (1911), p. 24.
12. B. Nogaro: *Cours d'économie politique*, Vol. I, pp. 391-2.
13. B. Nogaro: *La Monnaie et les systèmes monétaires*, p. 218.
14. F. Løkkegaard: *Islamic Taxation in the Classic Period*, p. 94.
15. Heichelheim: op. cit.
16. G. Glotz: *Le Travail dans la Grèce antique*, p. 278.
17. Chen Huan-Chang: *The Economic Principles of Confucius and His School*, Vol. II, p. 432.
18. *Pratica della Mercatura*, pp. 152-5.
19. R. De Roover: *L'Evolution de la lettre de change*, Vol. II, p. 52.
20. R. Bigo: *La Caisse d'Escompte et les origines de la Banque de France*, p. 19.
21. J. Kulischer: *Allgemeine Wirtschaftsgeschichte*, Vol. II, p. 346.
22. *Histoire du Commerce*, Vol. III, p. 445.
23. Ibid., Vol. III, p. 303.
24. R. De Roover: op. cit., Vol. II., p. 83.
25. R. Bigo: *Les Bases historiques de la finance moderne*, p. 22.
26. H. Hauser: *Les Débuts du capitalisme*, pp. 21-22.
27. R. De Roover: op. cit., Vol. I, p. 115; id., *Money, Banking and Credit in Mediaeval Bruges*, p. 283.
28. Ki Fein-chen: *Essai sur l'origine et l'evolution des banques en Chine*, pp. 144-5.
29. Chen Huan-Chang: op. cit., Vol. II, p. 433.
30. J. C. Van Dillen: *History of the Principal Public Banks*, pp. 40-41, 81-82 et seq., 336, *et al*.

31. Kulischer, op. cit., Vol. II, p. 346.

32. Ibid., p. 348.

33. A. Dauphin-Meunier: *La Banque à travers les âges*, Vol. I, p. 318.

34. J. H. Clapham: *History of the Bank of England*, pp. 122-31.

35. Kent: op. cit., pp. 104-6; Jean Marchal: quoted by L. Camu in *Evolution récente du rôle des banques*, p. 23.

36. R. Eisler: *Das Geld*, p. 204.

37. A. P. Usher: *The Early History of Deposit Banking in Mediterranean Europe*, pp. 21-22.

38. Kulischer: op. cit., Vol. I, p. 332.

39. MacMillan Report, quoted in John Strachey, *A Programme for Progress*, p. 106.

40. Kent: op. cit., p. 125.

41. B. Nogaro: *La Monnaie et les systèmes monétaires*, p. 23.

42. N. Macrae: *The London Capital Market*, p. 239.

43. R. S. Sayers: *Modern Banking*, pp. 35-36.

44. L. Camu: in *Evolution récente du rôle des banques*, pp. 29-31.

45. Ibid., pp. 21-22.

46. Macrae: op. cit., p. 195.

47. H. J. Laurence Laughlin: *A New Exposition of Money, Credit and Prices*, Vol. II, p. 35.

48. Nogaro and Oualid: *Evolution du Commerce, du Crédit et des Transports depuis 150 ans*, pp. 59-60, 143-50.

49. *Palgrave's Dictionary of Political Economy*, Vol. II, p. 792.

50. F. Baudhuin: *Crédit et Banque*, p. 112.

51. *Problèmes Economiques*, 21st August, 1951.

52. Mossé: *La Monnaie*, pp. 30-37.

53. J. B. Condliffe: *The Commerce of Nations*, pp. 186-9.

54. J. Strachey: op. cit., pp. 120-2.

55. L. A. Rabinovitch: in *Le Monde*, 19th-20th May, 1957.

56. B. Nogaro: *La Monnaie et les systèmes monétaires*, pp. 68-70.

57. Baudhuin: op. cit., pp. 152-3.

58. Sayers: op. cit., p. 179.

59. Ibid., p. 83.

60. G. D. H. Cole: *Money, its Present and Future*, pp. 40-41.

61. Baudhuin: op. cit., p. 58.

62. Ibid., p. 58.

63. Sumner H. Slichter: *What's Ahead for American Business?*, pp. 6-7.

64. Sayers: op. cit., p. 131.

65. B. Nogaro: *La Monnaie et les systèmes monétaires*, pp. 48-59; *Rapport de la Banque Internationale des Payements*, 1952, pp. 145-6.

66. T. Balogh: in *The Economics of Full Employment*, p. 142.

67. Ibid., p. 136.

68. F. A. Burchardt: in *The Economics of Full Employment*, pp. 9-10.

69. H. G. Moulton: *Controlling Factors in Economic Development*, p. 306.

70. Strachey: op. cit., p. 112.

71. Sayers: op. cit., p. 196; Balogh: op. cit., p. 129.
72. Eisler: op. cit., p. 178.
73. J. M. Keynes: *General Theory*, pp. 311 et seq.; Hawtrey: in *La Monnaie*, p. 18; F. A. Burchardt: in *The Economics of Full Employment*, p. 21.
74. J. M. Keynes: *How to Pay For The War*.
75. R. Lewinsohn: *Histoire de l'inflation*, pp. 27-29.
76. B. Nogaro: *La Monnaie et les systèmes monétaires*, pp. 215-16.
77. L. von Mises: *Theory of Money and Credit*, pp. 346-8.
78. Strachey, op. cit., pp. 108-9.
79. J. Schumpeter: *Sozialprodukt und Rechenpfennige*.
80. Piero Sraffa: in *Economic Journal*, March 1932, p. 48.

CHAPTER NINE

AGRICULTURE

Agriculture and commodity production

THE development of agriculture lays the foundation for a real division of labour, the separation of town from country, and for generalising exchange-relations.* But agriculture long remains outside the mode of production which it has engendered. Long after petty commodity production has appeared in large towns, centres of international trade, production of use-values continues to predominate in the countryside, only a few leagues from these metropolises. Only the surplus of the production of a few farms is sent to market.

When the Roman Empire undertook to ensure the feeding of the Roman proletariat, together with its numerous Legions, the trade in wheat, oil, wine and olives experienced a great expansion. The oscillations in the trade in these commodities have even been regarded by some authors as the decisive index of the decline of the Empire.[1] But this was actually a matter of providing supplies not for an anonymous market but for the State,[2] and, furthermore, supplies which were unpaid for or paid for at a very low price,[3] and thus a direct or concealed form of taxation. It was only in the centralising and transport of these masses of agricultural produce that merchant capital played a big part. The State in its turn distributed this produce free to the population of big centres such as Rome and Byzantium and to the Legions. In this way the entire cycle of supply remained outside the realm of commodity production. The latter appeared, so far as agricultural produce was concerned, only in the sale on the local markets of the surpluses of the peasants and nobles, and in the sale to the State of the produce of the slave plantations in Sicily. It was, generally speaking, the same in all pre-capitalist societies.

When, from the sixteenth century onward, money economy became general in Western Europe, commodity production extended more and more in the countryside. At the same time, the development of capital gave rise to a new social class, the farmers. These men did not want land as a means of obtaining their subsistence; they wanted it as a basis for producing agricultural *commodities*, the sale of which would bring in a *profit*.

Domestic industry and rural crafts, heavily attacked by the products

* See Chapter 1.

of large-scale factory industry from the eighteenth century onward, began to fade away. This evolution was fully completed in Western Europe only during the nineteenth century. In Eastern Europe and other economically backward parts of the world, the corresponding evolution took place only at the end of the nineteenth and the beginning of the twentieth centuries. It is today far from complete in all countries. Nowhere, moreover, has the production of agricultural commodities completely done away with the production of use-values, since even in highly-industrialized countries like the U.S.A., Germany and Belgium, subsistence farmers still exist to this day—i.e. peasants who sell on the market only the surplus of their production (their numbers were estimated, in the U.S.A., at 1,250,000 families in 1939).[4]

Pre-capitalist rent and capitalist ground-rent

In civilised pre-capitalist society agriculture constitutes man's chief economic activity. Ground rent is therefore the essential form of society's surplus-product. It is produced by agricultural producers who, in practice, dispose of their own means of production and possess at least a customary right to their land, in exchange for which they surrender part of their labour-time (labour-service) or of their production (rent in kind) to the property-owning classes. This division of the peasant's product into necessary product and surplus-product (ground rent) takes place wholly outside the market, in the sphere of the production of use-values.

In pre-capitalist society, the transformation of ground-rent from rent in kind into money rent is already in itself a sign of social decomposition. It presupposes an extensive development of the production and circulation of commodities, and also of the circulation of money. It is by selling part of their production that the peasants obtain the money they need to pay this new form of rent that they owe to their feudal lords. Although, however, commodity production is necessary for money rent to appear, the latter remains quantitatively independent of market conditions. What is typical of it, and situates it at the end of the evolution of *pre-capitalist rent*, which always has this characteristic, in all its previous forms, is that it is *fixed*, and, thereby, independent of the movement of prices and of the total money income of the producer.[5]* It was precisely to the extent that rent remained fixed that the peasants were the great beneficiaries of every period which saw a marked rise in agricultural prices (notably the period between the beginning of the thirteenth and the middle of the fourteenth centuries).[6]

Moreover, in the epoch of pre-capitalist rent, the land itself is only

---

* This naturally does not mean that pre-capitalist rent remains fixed during entire centuries. But it does not fluctuate from one harvest to another.

by way of exception regarded as an investment for money-capital
which is expected to bring in an income proportional to this capital:
"In the barbarian period and the first part of the feudal period, only a
small part of the land was freely negotiable: immense areas, left as
forest and grassland, were royal domain; other huge areas were the
inalienable property of the Church and the monasteries; and even the
secular possessions were mostly tied up with a whole hierarchy of
relations between those who granted land and those to whom it was
granted, whereby their alienation, though not completely impossible,
was nevertheless hindered in a thousand ways. No less fixed were the
relations between owners and cultivators. As regards the latter, the tie
of custom took the place of the bond of contract, reducing the great
majority of the workers on the land to the condition of *coloni* tied to
the soil, who could not freely leave the land and yet could not be
evicted from it, either."[7]

Capitalist ground rent is quite different from this. It appears in a
society in which the land itself and its main products have become
commodities. It results from the investment in agriculture of capital
which has to bring in the average profit. Like capitalist industry it
thus presupposes a separation of the producers from their means of
production. It further implies a separation between the basic means of
production and the farmer-entrepreneur, between the owner of the
land and the owner of capital. It is in this circumstance that it is distinguished and is separated from capitalist profit.

Origins of capitalist ground-rent

The origin of a *market for agricultural produce* in Europe is intimately linked with the development of the towns in the Middle Ages.
An initial development of trade disorganised the manorial supply
system, and favoured the appearance of these first local territorial
markets:

"The lord's manorial marketing system was giving way to the
organisation of a local territorial market slowly being worked out.
It was found unprofitable to cart corn long distances to a home manor
for consumption, or to a market centre within the manorial group,
when good market places had to be passed on the way, and when, perhaps, the corn was finally deposited in a district of a large surplus,
and therefore low price. In other words, the territorial market gradually cut in upon the manorial corn supply system, and ultimately
supplanted it."[8]

This evolution was a slow one, however; it was only in the second
half of the fifteenth century that real local markets became predominant in Britain.[9] Moreover, the formation of territorial markets was
hindered by the supply policy of the towns, which endeavoured by all
means to prevent an increase in the price of foodstuffs.[10] In these

conditions the unification of the national market was not possible, and in each country a series of regional markets were established with markedly different price-levels, reflecting the particular regional conditions of comparative plenty or want. In mediaeval England the region with the highest price for wheat and that with the lowest were only 50 miles apart; in April 1308 there was a difference of 40 per cent in the price of wheat between the towns of Oxford and Cuxham, separated by only 12 miles! [11]

It is in the evolution, from the sixteenth century onward, of these local markets supplied essentially out of the surpluses of producers of use-values, into great metropolitan markets, that we must look for the origin of agricultural capitalism. The prodigious development of urban centres like London, Paris, Antwerp, Amsterdam, Hamburg, etc., upset the relations of supply and demand as regards agricultural produce.[12] These great cities concentrated within their boundaries a considerable proportion of the national population—in the case of London, 10 per cent of the British population from the end of the seventeenth century and 20 per cent by the nineteenth century. The supply of foodstuffs to these populations depended no longer merely on the neighbouring agricultural areas, but on a large proportion of the entire agricultural production of the whole country.[13] This tended to level out agricultural prices on the national scale, and this in the sense that the prices paid in the metropolitan area became the basis for the national price of wheat.

Thereby, contrariwise to what happened in the local markets of the Middle Ages, the areas with big wheat surpluses which were near the capital could sell their wheat dearer than remote areas where there was a shortage (allowing for transport costs).[14] After the metropolitan market the next stage, achieved in a single century, was the *world grain market*: London attracted not only the wheat needed for its own feeding but also all the wheat intended for export, for maximum valorisation on the markets of the world.[15]

The appearance of vast metropolitan markets from the sixteenth and seventeenth centuries onward was accompanied by a complete reversal of the food-supply policy of the big towns. For these it was no longer a question, as in the Middle Ages, of restricting the price of foodstuffs by every means. On the contrary, it was a question of ensuring by every means an adequate supply of foodstuffs for the town *at any price*.[16] It was in this sense that the metropolises played the part of an apparently unlimited market, thus fostering the introduction of capitalism in agriculture. No longer were only the surpluses of rural production sent to the town; the maximum possible amount of wheat was sent, so that often the country people were reduced to subsistence level.[17]

The movement for the enclosure of common land was stimulated not only by attractive prospects for sheep-raising but also by very high prices of wheat. The appearance of the metropolitan market and the ending, for the agricultural producers, of free use of the soil (i.e., the introduction of capitalism in agriculture), were intimately linked together.[18] The importance of this stimulus can be judged if one considers that, from 1500 to 1800, the price of wheat in Britain rose from index 100 to index 275, and in France from index 100 to index 572, whereas the prices of metals and textiles rose by only 30 per cent during the same period.[19]

In the same epoch, the rationalisation of agriculture, the transition from the three-field system to the planting of crops which restore the soil's fertility, and the growing use of chemical fertilisers, increased, first in Flanders, Holland and some parts of Germany, then later in Britain and France, the minimum funds needed by a farmer if he were to take advantage of this miraculous manna of rising agricultural prices. From the end of the eighteenth century one needed, in England, to dispose of a minimum capital of £5 an acre in order to exploit an arable farm, £8 an acre for a mixed farm, and £20 an acre for a cattle or sheep farm.[20] The ownership of *capital* thus became the condition for any viable agricultural enterprise, however modest. In this way all the conditions for the penetration of capital into agriculture were realised.

Now, as it penetrated into agriculture in the old countries of Western and Central Europe, this capital was confronted by two circumstances which were utterly different from those existing in industry and trade. Whereas in industry all the material factors of production—machinery, raw materials, labour—could be produced and reproduced by capitalism itself, and produced at a price relatively or absolutely lower and lower (in the case of labour, thanks to the industrial reserve army!), in agriculture, the basic material element of production, the land, is given, in *limited* quantity, once for all. It constitutes a natural monopoly, marked for ever with the stamp of shortage.[21] Whereas capital could freely enter and leave every sphere of industry, it could not freely enter agriculture. There, the ownership of the land had been seized by a class of *landowners* who forbade access to it unless a rent was paid.

The land thus constituted a twofold monopoly at the beginning of the capitalist mode of production: a natural monopoly and a property monopoly. So long as agricultural productivity lags behind the increase of the population and the productivity of industry, a dual differentiation of prices will exist. Since the whole of agricultural production is absorbed by the market, the selling price of wheat will be determined by the conditions of production prevailing on the plots of land which are *least profitable* (through their degree of fertility, the way they are cultivated or their geographical position), so that this price will greatly exceed the price of production on the more profitable farms, which will thus realise a *super-profit*. Since, furthermore, agriculture does not participate in the general equalisation of the rate of profit, owing to the existence of the monopolies mentioned, even the wheat produced under the least profitable conditions is not sold at its price of production but at its *value*, which is higher than the price of production just because of the technical backwardness of agriculture as compared with industry, the lower organic composition of capital in the agricultural sphere. *Capitalist ground rent originates in this dual differentiation, and exists only to the extent that this differentiation exists.*

Differential ground-rent

In industry, superprofits are realised when the productivity of an enterprise is higher than the average. Even if this higher productivity makes it possible to sell commodities above their price of production, it leads to a *lowering* in the average market prices. In agriculture too, big differences in productivity enable certain enterprises and the owners of certain pieces of land to realise a surplus profit. But this profit does not coincide with a reduction but with an *increase* in the market price. So long as, through increase in population and a lag in agricultural productivity, the demand for agricultural produce exceeds the supply, this price will remain determined by the value of the agricultural commodities produced under the worst conditions of profitability. If all the human labour expended for the production of foodstuffs is socially necessary labour—so long as all the products of agriculture find purchasers!—even those agricultural commodities which are produced under the least profitable conditions will find an equivalent for their value; it will thus be this value that will determine the average selling price of wheat. The difference between this price and the price of production of the wheat produced on land with a higher productivity represents a *differential* rent which is taken by the landowner.

This differential rent may arise in two different ways: from the difference in natural fertility, or geographical situation, between different plots of land, or from the investment of different amounts of capital. We call these two cases differential rent of the first type and differential rent of the second type.

Take three plots of land of the same area, on which three farmers are working, each with capital identical in amount and organic composition. This capital, for one million francs expended in a year, produces 80 quintals of wheat from plot A, 100 from plot B, and 120 from plot C. If the average rate of profit is 20 per cent, the selling price of the wheat will be $\frac{1,200,000}{80}$ francs, or 15,000 francs per quintal, the price of production of the wheat on the least fertile of the plots.

Plot A will thus bring in no differential rent. The product of plot B will be worth 1·5 millions; if this plot be let, the owner will receive a differential rent of 300,000 francs; the farmer who actually cultivates it will have to be content with the average profit of 200,000 francs. The product of plot C will be worth 1·8 millions; if this plot be let, the owner will receive a differential rent of 600,000 francs, the farmer who actually cultivates it having, once more, to be content with the average profit of 200,000 francs.

As transport charges are incorporated in the selling prices of agricultural products, the plots nearest to a metropolitan centre will bring in a substantial differential rent. Here is an example taken from the United States:

Distance from Louisville (Kentucky) in miles	Rent of land per acre dollars	Price of land per acre dollars
8 or less	11·85	312
9 to 11	5·59	110
12 to 14	5·37	106
15 or over	4·66	95[22]*

From 0 to 5 miles from an urban centre: dairying zone: average rent, 15 dollars.

From 5 to 17 miles from an urban centre: maize zone: average rent, 8 dollars.

From 17 to 27 miles from an urban centre: wheat zone: average rent, 5 dollars.

From 27 to 50 miles from an urban centre: ranching zone: average rent, 2 dollars.

So long as agricultural prices tend to rise, the capitalists are interested in investing in agriculture, so as to extend cultivation to uncultivated land or to get higher production from land already under cultivation. In the first case, it is not necessarily a matter of less fertile land: it may involve land which is less accessible, more remote, land which needs considerable drainage or irrigation if it is to produce more than land already under cultivation. But these investments of capital have to be depreciated over a certain period; during that period they therefore increase the cost of production, and, thereby, the price of production.

The same is true when production is increased on land already cultivated, through the use of additional quantities of fertiliser, a better

* Though all these plots are not suitable for the same crops, their relative distance from the urban markets determines to a large extent the profitability of the different kinds of agriculture, taking into account the costs and the relative speed of transport, the perishable nature of the produce, etc. Ely and Wehrwein[23] give the following table of average rent per acre in the United States:

selection of seed, the introduction of agricultural machinery, the employment of agronomists—in short, through further investment of capital.

Experiments in the U.S.A. have shown that in the fifties an average of 12·33 bushels of wheat per acre could be got there when wheat is grown without a break and without using fertiliser; 23·58 bushels when a certain optimum amount of fertiliser is used, but without any break in the growing of wheat; and 32 bushels when an optimum quantity of fertiliser is used and a four-year rotation system followed.[24]

Let us go back to our example of the three plots of land, A, B and C. Assume that an extra investment of one million francs in plot C results in an increase in production from 120 to 220 quintals. On the two million francs thus invested, the capitalist has to realise an average profit of 20 per cent, or 400,000 francs. But the 220 quintals will be sold for 3·3 million francs, if the selling price continues to be determined by the price of production of wheat on the least fertile plot, or 15,000 francs per quintal. Of these 1·3 million francs of surplus value, 400,000 francs will go to the capitalist as average profit, 600,000 francs will go to the landowner, as differential rent of the first type; and 300,000 francs represent the differential rent of the second type which the farmer will endeavour to keep but which the landowner will try to get included in the rent, when the lease is renewed.* Unlike differential rent of the first type, rent of the second type is less obvious and therefore less directly seizable by the landowner.

Absolute ground-rent

Up to now we have encountered rent, super-profit, only on land where, through better fertility or geographical position, or through additional investment of capital, the price of production is lower than it is on less profitable land, so long as the latter price determines the price at which agricultural products are sold. What will happen, though, to land of this latter category? Where the cultivator and the owner are the same person, there is no problem, since the capitalist will, in principle, be content with the average profit alone. It will not be the same, however, where the owners of these plots of land do not cultivate them themselves. In this case, the payment of a rent to these landowners remains a pre-condition for the plots concerned to be opened to cultivation. So long as the selling price of wheat is less than or equal to the price of production of wheat on these plots, they will

---

* This is not grasped by a number of critics of Marx, who, like Arthur Wauters, reproach him with mixing up interest and differential rent of the second type. Interest goes to the owner of *capital*; differential rent goes to the owner of the *land*, even if he has not invested a single centime in his land. At least, it goes to him after the renewal of a tenancy. It must be noted that Marx himself answered this criticism, when it was levelled at Ricardo.[25]

remain uncultivated, because farmers would not be able to pay the rent without encroaching on their own average profit. Why should they, when, by transferring their capital to industry and trade, they can realise this average profit? But from the moment that the selling price rises sufficiently to bring in a rent even on these least fertile plots of land, their exploitation will be undertaken.* And throughout the first period of the capitalist mode of production, the lagging behind of agricultural productivity, as compared with industrial productivity and the increase of population, actually did create such a situation.

Where does this rent come from which appears on the least fertile land? Its source lies in the fact that the wheat produced under these conditions is not sold at its price of production but at its value, and that the latter exceeds the price of production because the organic composition of capital is lower in agriculture than in industry, whereas the monopoly of landed property prevents the free flow of capital in and out of agriculture, so that agricultural capital is thus prevented from "sharing" in the social equalisation of the rate of profit, giving up part of the surplus-value created in "its" sphere to the general share-out of this surplus-value.

Suppose that the annual production of industry amounts to: 400 billion c + 100 billion v + 100 billion s = 600 billion.

Agricultural production might be determined somewhat like this: †
20 billion c + 100 billion v + 105 billion s = 405 billion.

The average rate of profit in industry would be $\frac{100}{500}$ = 20 per cent.

In agriculture, the products will not be sold at their price of production, embodying a profit of 25 per cent (i.e. at 375 billion),‡ but at their value, or 405 billion, i.e. with 30 billion super-profit. This will be the *absolute ground rent* which appears by way of this super-profit. The rate of profit in agriculture will be $\frac{105}{300}$, or 35 per cent.

Let us now go back to the three plots of land, A, B and C, which we quoted as examples in connection with differential rent of the first type:

Plot	Capital	Production	Selling price per quintal	Total received	Average profit
A	1 million	80 q.	16,875	1,350,000	200,000
B	1 million	100 q.	16,875	1,687,500	200,000
C	1 million	120 q.	16,875	2,025,000	200,000

* This does not mean that these plots are necessarily the last to be cultivated. The spread of cultivation to more fertile land may cause cultivation to be given up on less fertile land, if the selling price of wheat goes down.

† The rate of surplus-value is usually higher in agriculture than in industry because agricultural wages, as is well-known, are lower than wages in industry.

‡ Total social surplus-value of 205 billion gives an average rate of profit of 25,625 per cent on a social capital of 800 billion.

	Absolute rent	*Differential rent*
A:	150,000	—
B:	150,000	337,500
C:	150,000	675,000

The selling price is equal to the *value* of a quintal of wheat produced on the least profitable of the plots, A, that is, to the capital invested, 12,500 francs, plus 35 per cent profit, 4,375 francs, or, altogether, 16,875 francs. The absolute rent arises from this difference between the value of a quintal of wheat produced on plot A and its price of production, 15,000 francs (12,500 francs + 20 per cent average profit).

Ground rent, needless to say, is not "produced" by the land. A piece of waste land does not "produce" an atom of rent. Ground rent is produced by labour-power engaged in cultivation. It is thus surplus-value, unpaid labour, exactly like industrial profit. But it is a special kind of surplus-value, *which does not participate in the general equalisation of the rate of profit,* owing to private property in land, and which thus provides a super-profit as a result of the lower organic composition of capital in agriculture as compared with industry (absolute rent). This super-profit is further increased by a super-profit which arises from the fact that all the labour engaged in agriculture is socially necessary, even if it is engaged under conditions of productivity lower than in industry.

Ground-rent and the capitalist mode of production

Ground rent thus represents a *twofold loss* for the bourgeoisie as a whole. On the one hand, a certain amount of surplus-value does not participate in the equalisation of the rate of profit, and as this amount is produced by capital with an organic composition lower than in industry it could have increased the average rate of profit. On the other hand, the prices of agricultural products are increased, since they are sold according to the value of the products coming from the least profitable plots. This makes necessary a minimum level for wages which is higher than would be the case if rent were abolished, and thus means to some extent a transfer of value from industry to agriculture.

This is why the most logical representatives of the liberal industrial bourgeoisie, notably Ricardo and John Stuart Mill, fought for the abolition of private ownership of land. In newly settled countries like the United States, Australia or Canada, where enormous expanses of virgin land were at the disposal of the settlers, absolute rent could disappear completely: the land was distributed free, on payment of a purely nominal tax due to the state. In the U.S.A., under the Homestead Act of 1862, it was possible to become the owner of 160 acres of uncultivated land after five years of effective occupation. In Canada,

90 per cent of the 58 million acres occupied by the settlers were distributed in the same way.[26] The source of absolute ground rent, namely, the private monopoly of ownership of land, was thus proved, by a negative experiment. Where this monopoly is not found, neither does absolute rent exist.

The existence of ground rent is not only an obstacle to the optimum development of the capitalist mode of production in general. It especially hinders the development of capitalist relations in the countryside. The rent taken by the non-cultivating landowners is withdrawn from agriculture and not reinvested. It reduces the investment fund available and slows down the accumulation of capital in agriculture. Thus, in Switzerland, between the eve of the First World War and the eve of the Second, the farmer's total capital increased from 1,160 to 1,673 Swiss francs per hectare, whereas the landowner's capital increased from 4,280 to 6,167. Only a small fraction of this latter increase, 52 Swiss francs to be exact, came from improvements in the land![27] The rate of accumulation of capital in agriculture is thus lower than in industry. This determines a productivity of labour in agriculture which is much lower than in industry, as may be seen from the following table:

Occupational distribution of the population, and contribution of industry and agriculture respectively to the formation of the national product, in percentages, in 1950-51:

Country	Industry		Agriculture	
	Pop.	Gross national product	Pop.	Gross national product
Italy	23	34	49	29
France	29	40	36	29
Denmark	32	36	28	22
Netherlands	32	39	19	12
Norway	32	46	31	15
West Germany	44	55	22	12[28]

For 1956 the "Report on the Economic Situation in the Countries of the Community" of the Common Market Commission shows that the agricultural product per head of active population amounts to no more than 76 per cent of non-agricultural income in the Netherlands, 58 per cent in Belgium, 57 per cent in France, 56 per cent in West Germany and 38 per cent in Italy.[29]

The fact that a great part of farmers' capital is tied up in the renting or purchase of land* entails a period of *rotation of capital* which is longer in agriculture and building than in industry: a rotation cycle takes 4 to 5 years, on the average, in agriculture, and 8 to 10 years in the building trade in the towns in the United States.[31]

* "Nearly two-thirds of investment in agriculture is accounted for by investment in (the price of) land."[30]

But the appropriation of differential ground rent by the landowner presents above all a major obstacle to *land improvement*. Farmers have little interest in working to achieve an improvement which will inevitably cause the landowners to increase the leasehold charge they have to pay! Landowners try to make tenancies renewable as frequently as possible (annually, if they can), so as to ensure a correspondingly regular increase in differential rent. Farmers, for their part, are interested in securing long leases, so as to be able to benefit by the improvements due to their capital (or their labour, in the case of small farms).

Nineteenth-century Ireland offers the classic example of the injustice resulting from the appropriation of differential rent by the landowner:

"In the year 1870 there were 682,237 farms in Ireland, of which 135,392 were leasehold and 526,628 belonged to the class of yearly tenancies. A yearly tenancy was terminable at six months' notice without compensation. Only in the case of about twenty estates were the buildings and standing farm equipment provided by the landlords . . . In all other cases the tenant had to supply the fixed capital as well as every other form of capital required on his farm. The termination of the tenancy thus enabled the landlord to confiscate the capital invested by the tenant. Between 1849 and 1880 nearly 70,000 families were evicted and dispossessed. The alternative to eviction was willingness and ability to pay a higher rent, and this in fact enabled the landlord to confiscate by another method the capital as well as the industry of an industrious tenant."[32]

Such an unjust system inevitably leads to a defensive reflex by the farmer which is detrimental to land improvement:

"Even with [a lease of] nine years . . . the farmer had too often to spend the first three-year rotation reconstituting the fertility impaired by his predecessor; he cultivated the land normally during the second three-year period, and then spent the last three years exhausting the land in one way or another. A friend of mine who is familiar with agricultural problems estimates at 20 per cent the resulting underproduction."[33]

Certain crops, such as orchards, which require constant attention over many years, are incompatible with leasehold and the separation of landownership from the actual cultivation of the land.[34]

The price of land and the evolution of ground rent

With the world-wide extension of the capitalist mode of production, all income is conventionally regarded as being a return on capital, real or imaginary, invested at the average rate of interest.* Ground rent is a real economic category, with its source in the surplus value produced by all the workers on the land. But the "value of land" is

* See Chapter 7.

an expression which in itself is meaningless. Land has no value, any more than air, light, or the wind that moves a sailing-ship. It is a "factor of production" provided by nature, not a commodity produced by human labour.* Where the monopoly of private ownership of land has not been established, land has neither "value" nor price. So recently as the present century, the white settlers in Rhodesia obtained their land for the token price of a penny an acre!

Only where private appropriation of land has transformed it into monopoly property does land acquire a *price*. This price is nothing but *ground rent capitalised* at the average rate of interest:

"The price of land is determined by the price of the products [of the soil] and not the reverse."[35]

Buying a piece of land is not buying a "value" but a *claim to income*, future income being calculated on the basis of present income: [36]

"The buyer of land is actually buying the right to receive a series of annual incomes, and the most tangible basis for judging what these annual incomes will be in the future is what they have been in the immediate past. Studies show that income received from land for a seven-year or ten-year period preceding sale is a most effective gauge of the price the purchaser will agree to pay."[37]

This origin of the price of land is confirmed by the way this price has evolved since the end of the eighteenth century. The price of land does not vary around a "real value", but follows the oscillations, often sharp and violent, of the agricultural conjuncture.

The increase of population, the bringing under cultivation of less fertile land which required considerable investment of capital if it was to be cultivated, brought about a marked rise in agricultural prices in the second half of the eighteenth century, followed immediately by a corresponding rise in rents. Between 1750 and 1800 the price of wheat increased on the average by 60 per cent in England, 65 per cent in France, 60 per cent in North Italy, and 40 per cent in Germany. In the same period d'Avenel estimates that average rent per hectare rose in France by 50 per cent. In England and Germany an even bigger increase in rent was observed, owing to a marked fall in the rate of interest.[38] The rise in agricultural prices on the Continent between 1820 and 1870 was likewise accompanied by a notable rise in rents.

The average value of all agricultural land in the U.S.A. has for a century followed the movement of agricultural prices: from 1860 to 1890, a rise of 16·32 dollars per acre, to 21·31 dollars; from 1890 to 1900, a decline to 19·81; from 1910 to 1920 [war boom!], a rise of 39·60, to 69·38; between 1920 and 1935, decline [the great crisis!] to 31·16, etc.[39]

* This does not apply to land which, like the *polders* of Flanders and Holland, has been literally "produced" by human labour, which has reclaimed it from the sea.

For differential ground rent to appear, the selling price of agricultural products must ensure the average profit even on capital invested in the least profitable land. For absolute ground rent to appear, this same selling price must ensure the sale of wheat produced under the worst conditions of productivity, not at its price of production but at its value. When the prices of agricultural products fall, these conditions, or one of them, may be eliminated, temporarily or for good. At that moment rent vanishes from certain plots of land. They cease to be cultivated unless they are exploited directly by their owners. If they are, the owners have to be satisfied with an income lower than the average profit, perhaps merely equivalent to a wage.

This phenomenon, which occurred already during all the pre-capitalist crises of agriculture,* made itself vigorously felt in the last quarter of the nineteenth century. At that time, vast expanses of prairies and pampas were beginning to be brought under cultivation in overseas countries, with the aid of mechanical methods, which reduced the cost of production by 50 per cent.[40] At the same time, the improvement in means of transport made possible a reduction in freight charges, which, for wheat despatched from New York to Liverpool, fell from 0·60 gold francs per bushel in 1860 to 0·25 in 1866 and 0·05 in 1910.[41] These two developments together brought to Europe quantities of agricultural produce from overseas, often without any ground-rent entering into their prices, and thus caused a collapse of agricultural prices.

This collapse led both to a fall in the price of land and to the abandonment of all cultivation on the less profitable plots of land. In France between 1875 and 1900 the "value" of rural property was reduced by 35 per cent, on the average.[42] The area of land under the plough shrank from 25 million hectares in the middle of the nineteenth century to 18 million in the middle of the twentieth.[43] Clapham notes that after the fall in agricultural prices at the end of the nineteenth century the fate of some land was to " 'tumble-down' to third-rate pasture, as on the Essex 'three-horse' clays."[44]

True, the agriculturists of Europe strove by various reactions to reverse this current. In some countries, such as France, Italy and Germany, there was an attempt, by means of *protective tariffs*, artificially to maintain high agricultural prices. These prices thus ensured the difference between the average price on the world market and the price on the least profitable plots of "national" land—that is, precisely, the differential rent of the best-endowed landowners! * In

* In France "the purchase price of wheat is calculated on the basis of the cost of production on the most old-fashioned farms of Ariège and Rouergue ... The big capitalist agriculturists of the Paris basin, whose real costs of production are almost 60 per cent lower than those of these small peasants, pocket the difference!"[45]

* See Chapter 11.

other countries, such as Denmark, Holland, Belgium, etc., attempts were made to consolidate ground rent and the price of land by a considerable investment of capital, large-scale use of fertilisers—per hectare-year, 30 kilogrammes of nitrogenised fertiliser were used in 1938 (49 kilogrammes in 1956) in Belgium, as against 6·7 (9·7 in 1956) in France; 35 kilogrammes of phosphates (51 in 1956) in Belgium, as against 13 in France (18 in 1956); 46 kilogrammes of potash in Holland (68 in 1956; 76 in this same year in Belgium) as against 8·7 in France (14·5 in 1956)[46]—and above all by transforming cultivated land into meadows, the animal products of which (meat, butter, milk, etc.) serve as basis for a more stable rent, because a substantial section of the population of the big towns prefers to consume fresh animal products, even at a higher price.[47]

In the 1920s this new equilibrium of Europe's agriculture was upset by a violent shock: the world agricultural crisis which went on down to the Second World War, and reasserted itself from 1949 onward. The expansion of agriculture in overseas countries creates a permanent "surplus" of agricultural produce, despite the state of chronic undernourishment in which hundreds of millions of human beings live in China, in India, in the rest of Asia, and in most of Africa and Latin America.[48]

It has now been shown that, within the setting of the capitalist mode of production, the relative stability (inelasticity) of the demand for agricultural produce, once a certain degree of industrialisation has been attained* (the same inelasticity which has been the source of agricultural super-profit through several centuries), may become a source of permanent crisis as soon as agriculture experiences, belatedly, upheavals in productivity comparable to those in industry.[51]† In the

* This stability is only relative. For the U.S.A., Renne declares: "If all consumers in the United States were to have diets considered adequate by nutritional experts, vegetable consumption would probably be increased at least 50 per cent, and consumption of dairy products at least 15 or 25 per cent."[49] Statistics show, moreover, that in 1939 the industrial workers in England and Germany consumed, per head, half the amount of milk consumed in Sweden and Switzerland, a third of the amount of butter consumed in Canada, Germany and Holland, half of the amount of sugar and meat consumed in Australia, etc.[50]

† Here is a striking summary of the advance in the productivity of agricultural labour:[52]

To reap and bind one hectare of wheat in one hour, there were needed in France:

About 1750, using sickles, 40 to 50 men	Productivity
About 1830, using scythes, 25 to 30 men	increased
About 1870, using reaping machines, 8 to 10 men	by 500 per cent
About 1905, using reapers and binders, 1 to 2 men	Productivity
In 1950, using reaper-binder-threshers, less than one man—and the harvest is threshed at the same time.	increased by over 1,000 per cent

period 1930–1955 agricultural productivity increased by over 100 per cent in the U.S.A. As regards the cultivation of grain, productivity has *trebled* in 30 years![53]

Between 1930 and 1950, the increase in productivity in American agriculture was almost equal to that in industry. The same increase took place in Great Britain.* In its turn, the U.S.A. experienced the shrinkage of the area sown to wheat and the transformation of cultivated fields into meadows, if not the disappearance of all agricultural use of the least fertile land.

Thus, between 1919 and 1929, cultivation was abandoned on 20 per cent of the land in the South and West of the U.S.A., where, in spite of mechanisation, the cost of production of a bushel of wheat did not fall below one dollar, whereas in the plains of Montana, Kansas, Nebraska, etc., it fell to 60 cents.[56] As for the old countries of Europe, rent could vanish or become insignificant for a large part of the least fertile land, as happened in France on the eve of the Second World War.[57] Recently Baron Snoy, secretary-general of the Belgian Ministry of Economic Affairs, has stated that the abandonment of the policy of agricultural protection in Western Europe would make it possible to reforest very large areas where agriculture had been given up.

Landed property and the capitalist mode of production

Private property in land, far from being a condition for the penetration of the capitalist mode of production *into agriculture*, is a hindrance and brake upon it. The private appropriation of *all cultivable land*, which prevents free settlement of new peasants on the land, nevertheless remains an absolutely indispensable condition for the rise of *industrial capitalism*. So long as there are vast expanses of land available, urban labour-power has a refuge from the factory prison, there is practically no industrial reserve army, and wages may well rise in consequence of competition between industrial and agricultural employment. The high wages which existed in the U.S.A. before the disappearance of the Western "frontier", which definitely established a

---

* In Great Britain, since 1950, 40 per cent of the farms of 5 to 10 hectares, 60 per cent of those between 10 and 20 hectares, and practically all the larger farms have possessed at least a tractor. Between 1944 and 1952 the number of tractors per 100 farms increased from 10·4 to 28 in Sweden. It grew from 8·9 to 23·7 between May 1949 and April 1952 in West Germany. It doubled between 1949 and 1951 in Denmark, and between 1949 and 1952 in Austria and Belgium. In 14 countries of Western Europe (including Great Britain) there were about a million tractors in 1951 and their number was increasing by 15 per cent per year.[54] What is typical of the countries with the most highly mechanised agriculture, namely, Britain, West Germany and Sweden, is that the increase in the number of tractors concerns more and more the middle-sized and small farms, the big ones having already been mechanised nearly 100 per cent.[55]

wage scale higher than any in Europe, are to be explained to a large extent by this factor.

From the middle of the eighteenth century, American politicians frankly recognised this fact and demanded, like Benjamin Pale, of Connecticut, that migration westward be stopped. And Samuel Blodget, one of the first American economists, observed in 1806 that cheap land makes labour dear.

"No freeman will work for another if he can buy good land sufficiently cheap to provide him comfortable subsistence with two days' labour a week."[58]

Private appropriation, by robbery and legal or illegal violence, of the greater part of the virgin land in the countries with reserves of land accompanied the entire progress of the capitalist mode of production outside Western Europe, where, moreover, a similar phenomenon occurred in the form of the private appropriation of the common lands. The idea of private ownership of land has become to such an extent a fundamental idea of bourgeois society that the courts even recognised as a transfer of property the gift of a 600-acre forest by the State of Pennsylvania to God, and subsequently "expropriated" this "owner" for non-payment of tax![59]

From the end of the eighteenth century the East India Company transformed into landlords of entire provinces the *zamindari* or tax-farmers of the Mogul Empire.[60] In the Argentine, between 1875 and 1900, 30 million hectares of land were sold for insignificant sums: most of it has been left waste to this very day, but the whole of the public domain was alienated in this way. In Canada nearly a third of the entire public domain was taken over by the railway companies.[61] In the U.S.A., while 96 million acres were distributed under the Homestead Act and other laws of the same kind (a considerable part of this land, moreover, going to capitalist companies, for whom farmer applicants acted as men of straw), 183 million acres were left to the railway companies.[62]

In North Africa, French colonisation led to large-scale alienation of native land: 3 million hectares appropriated by the French settlers in Algeria, under specific laws;[63] 1·4 million hectares in Tunisia, or half of all the arable land in that country;[64] 1 million hectares appropriated in Morocco by 4,700 European settlers, while 8 million Moroccans have to subsist on 3·8 million hectares of less fertile land.[65]

Also in Africa the British settlers seized 50 million acres in Southern Rhodesia, on which live 100,000 whites, while 1·6 million Africans have only 29 million acres to live on. The settlers have taken 12,750 square kilometres in Kenya, which are at the disposal of 29,000 Europeans, leaving 43,500 square miles for 5 million Africans!

Thanks to this system, the "native reserves" as they are cynically called by the whites, furnish abundant labour-power both to the settlers and to the European mining and industrial companies. Many forms of serfdom, forced labour either open or concealed,* ground rent paid in the form of labour service, are imposed on the wretched Africans who have been brutally torn from the land, that is, from their customary means of existence.[67] This system has been carried to an extreme in South Africa, where 2 million whites have appropriated 88 per cent of the land, leaving 12 per cent, much of it useless, for the subsistence of 8 million Africans, herded into "reserves" and ferociously exploited: the total annual wages of the 400,000 Africans working in the South African gold mines amount to £30 million, if one estimates very generously the value of the meagre food-rations given these workers, whereas the annual profits of the gold-mining companies amount to £50 million.[68]

Striking the balance of the agrarian laws introduced by Britain in Ceylon, an official Ceylon Government commission remarks that they served to deprive the villages of their common forests and meadows, together with some of their land used for secondary crops, and this exclusively in the interests of capitalists coming, in the first place, directly from Europe, and later, from the coastal provinces of the island.[69]

Production-relations and property-relations in the countryside

The special relations which, by the creation of the industrial reserve army and by the economic role of ground rent, link agriculture with industry in the capitalist epoch, gave rise to the special forms of development in agriculture itself. The introduction of slavery in the American colonies between the sixteenth and nineteenth centuries, the introduction of forced labour in the African and Oceanian colonies at the end of the nineteenth and in the twentieth century† were, in the special conditions of the countries in question, necessary conditions for creating *capitalist property-relations* in these countries. They none the less hindered for a long time the penetration of capitalist *production-relations* in the country.

A similar and still more important phenomenon appeared in Eastern Europe, and in the Middle East and Far East at the end of the nineteenth century and in the first part of the twentieth. The penetration of capitalist products into these countries, their inclusion in the world market, brought about the destruction of the age-old equilibrium of village economy, based on the combination of crafts with agriculture.[70] The land itself not being capable of supporting the whole of the non-

* See the chapters dealing with the Belgian, British, French and Portuguese colonies in the publication of the United Nations International Labour Office, "Report of the *Ad Hoc* Committee on Forced Labour".[66]

† The sugar industry of Queensland was based exclusively on the semi-slave labour of the Kanakas from 1860 until about 1900.

urban population, and no substantial increase in employment being forthcoming in the towns, *chronic overpopulation of the countryside* made its appearance—a mere concealed form of chronic unemployment.*

This overpopulation of the countryside gives rise to a fierce competitive struggle among the peasants for the tenancy of little plots of land, not so much as means of acquiring the average profit as mere means of livelihood. It is to the interest of the landowner to let out his land in small lots rather than to exploit it as a large-scale capitalist enterprise. *The bourgeois property-relations prove an obstacle to the introduction of the capitalist mode of production in agriculture.* The extreme fragmentation of units of production which results from this is especially marked in India, where the average area of a farm is 4·5 acres, while in the highly-populated state of West Bengal, one-third of the farms are less than 2 acres in size. The same phenomenon leads to a formidable increase in ground-rent and to *overcapitalisation* of the land.[71] The peasants impoverished in this way eventually lose their little holdings and become proletarianised, either obviously or in some disguised way. The small farmers, clinging desperately to their little plot of land, pay a *usurious rent* which expresses their super-exploitation, their income often being less than that of an agricultural worker. When they have not even the minimum capital and have to exploit the land they have leased in the form of share-cropping,† they transform themselves into real proletarians, working for a wretched wage:

"In Arabic, share-cropper is *mraba*, that is, one who has a quarter share. This is, in fact, the usual arrangement. In grain-growing villages the landowner provides the fellah with a house, land, seed and the means of ploughing. The latter is pretty sketchy: two oxen—sometimes only two cows—and the sort of plough used in the region. The share-cropper, it will be seen, contributes nothing but his labour, together, of course, with that of his whole family. Having nothing that belongs to him, except his wife and children [this is the literal translation of 'proletarian'! E. M.] . . . he is wholly dependent on the landlord, who can, in theory, evict him at the end of each agricultural year. As reward for this year of labour, he receives a quarter of the harvest . . ."[72]

The extreme forms that this usurious rent can take was shown by the example of pre-war Korea. H. K. Lee observed there in 1936 that rent amounted in such extreme cases to 90 per cent of the harvest.[73]

And as share-croppers reduced to such a level of poverty invariably

* See Chapter 13, "Imperialism", section "The economic structure of the underdeveloped countries."

† Share-cropping is a transitional form between pre-capitalist and capitalist rent.

end by falling into debt, the usurer being most often the landlord himself (or the big farmer standing between the share-croppers and the landlord), they easily pass from the status of proletarian to that of serf: "In Iraq (there is) . . . a law which forbids the sharecropper to leave the land as long as he is indebted to his landlord, which is generally the case."[74]

Alfred Bonné has further shown that this system, like the similar system introduced in Eastern Europe in the sixteenth century, represents the landlord's response to a dangerous shortage of labour-power when this makes itself felt on his broad estates.[75]

Concentration and centralisation of capital in agriculture

Because in agriculture, in contrast to industry, bourgeois property relations and capitalist production relations do not necessarily coincide,* the problem of the concentration of capital presents itself in a special way. The law of the concentration of capital is a law which springs from the *capitalist mode of production*; it is not a universal law springing from the mere existence of private ownership of the land.

Where the capitalist mode of production is merely *beginning* to penetrate agriculture, where we are still confronted with old semi-feudal estates in process of disintegration, it would be as absurd to look for agricultural concentration as it would be to study industry as it was at the end of the eighteenth century from the stand-point of the concentration of capital. *It is only when agriculture as a whole has been subjected to the technical upheavals inherent in the capitalist mode of production that the problem of concentration can arise.* Such phenomena as the remarkable concentration of landed property in Eastern Europe before the Second World War, in Spain, or in most of the countries of Latin America, have nothing to do with this category: in these cases it is a matter either of survivals of pre-capitalist property or else of investment of capital in land owing to the lack of industrial outlets for it (in Chile, for example, 2,300 landowners possessed in 1952 31 per cent of the cultivable land and 60 per cent of all the land in the country, whereas 150,000 small enterprises covered only 16·5 per cent of the cultivable land and 6 per cent of the total).[77]

Once given the capitalist mode of production in agriculture, two

* For this same reason, present-day agriculture conserves in one way or another all possible forms of pre-capitalist society. Thus, there are parts of South Africa, especially in the Transvaal and Natal, where the black farmers have to pay their rent in the form of 90 to 180 days of labour-service (unpaid work) on the white landowner's farm. These forms of mediaeval exploitation can also be found in a number of countries of Latin America: "This form of tenancy is often met with in Bolivia, Chile, Colombia, Ecuador, Peru and Venezuela, among the agricultural workers of the plantations, to whom the landowner assigns a small plot of land, in return for which they have to work without payment a certain number of days every week."[76]

factors hinder the manifestation in it of the concentration and centralisation of capital. We know that ground rent arises from the fact that the least profitable enterprise determines the price of production of agricultural products. But the concentration of capital operates precisely through the elimination of the least profitable enterprises! So long as the latter have a guaranteed market in spite of their technical backwardness, the centralisation of capital cannot show itself in agriculture. Concentration will nevertheless show itself by way of the enormous difference which emerges between the price of the least profitable land and that of the most profitable, that is, by way of the capitalisation of a huge differential rent.

Similarly, plots of land which are below the threshold of profitability can nevertheless be exploited, not to produce the average profit but to provide a mere subsistence-basis for a small farmer who in this way sacrifices his standard of living in order to cling to "his" farm.[78]* Working with little or no capital, doing without rent and profit, he remains notwithstanding at the mercy of bad harvests and conjuncture fluctuations. This is what accounts for the very high mortality of these small agricultural enterprises. In the U.S.A. in 1935, 25 per cent of all the heads of agricultural enterprises had been in occupation of their farm for only one year or less; 47 per cent of all the farmers and 57 per cent of all the sharecroppers had been in occupation for less than two years.[80] It is estimated that 100,000 family farms have vanished each year during the decade beginning in 1950.[81]

When this guaranteed market disappears, in practice from the last quarter of the nineteenth century, small enterprises can continue to compete with big ones by going over to *intensive cultivation*,† which makes possible an output higher than that given by the extensive cultivation of the big estates.

For this reason, even though the amount of capital invested has increased enormously‡—an indirect form of concentration of

---

* Thus, in Belgium it has been calculated in the 'fifties that the income per hour of the small farmers is only 14·5 francs in the case of farms of 5 hectares, whereas the minimum hourly wage in industry was 25 francs. In West Germany several inquiries have led to the finding that on small farms the monthly income per worker can be as low as 150 DM, far below the lowest wages paid in industry.[79]

† The difference between extensive and intensive cultivation relates to *output per unit of area*. In 1935–39, Denmark, Holland and Belgium produced, respectively, 45, 45 and 40 quintals of wheat per hectare, as against 10 in the U.S.A. and 12 in Canada, Argentine and U.S.S.R.[82] Intensive cultivation is the result either of a higher investment of capital per hectare, as in the above-mentioned countries, or of a tremendous extra expenditure of highly-skilled labour, as in the cases of Japan, China, Thailand, etc.

‡ In the U.S.A. in 1940 the investment needed for a profitable farm was estimated at 29,000 dollars for maize-growing, 25,000 dollars for sheep-raising, and 17,000 dollars for wheat-growing. By 1958 these figures had risen to 97,000, 84,000 and 81,000 respectively.[83]

capital—enterprises of intensive agriculture have not been able to increase in area, and there have been no obvious manifestations of centralisation.

Wherever these two restrictive factors have not operated, and where, in fact, capitalist agriculture in the strict sense has been able to develop in the pure state, the tendency towards concentration and centralisation of capital has, however, clearly shown itself in agriculture. This is especially true of the U.S.A., and to a smaller extent of Germany.

Agricultural concentration in the United States[84]

Type of farm	1920	1925	1930	1935	1940	1945	1954	1959
1. Less than 50 acres:								
% of total number	35·7	37·9	36·5	39·5	37·5	38·4	36·5	28·4
% of total area	6·0	6·1	5·7	5·6	4·7	4·1	2·9	2·0
2. Between 50 and 500 acres:								
% of total number	61·0	58·8	58·7	56·7	58·2	56·8	57·8	62·5
% of total area	60·4	59·0	55·3	54·2	50·4	45·2	39·8	36·5
3. Between 500 and 1,000 acres:								
% of total number	2·3	2·3	2·5	2·5	2·7	3·0	4·0	5·4
% of total area	10·6	10·5	11·0	10·8	10·8	10·6	11·4	12·3
4. Over 1,000 acres:								
% of total number	1·0	1·0	1·3	1·3	1·6	1·9	2·7	3·7
% of total area	23·1	24·3	28·0	29·4	34·3	40·3	45·9	49·2

In other words, the largest farms (categories 3 and 4), which in 1920 occupied only a *third* of American agricultural land (33·7 per cent), by 1959 already occupied more than *three fifths* of it (61·5 per cent). This growth was moreover nearly entirely accomplished by the largest farms, those exceeding 1,000 acres.

In Italy, where the penetration of capitalism into the countryside has been going on at a rapid rate for over a century, comparative statistics are not available, but the result is extremely eloquent. Here is the division of landed property and income from land among private persons in 1948, as given in publications of the I.N.E.A. (National Institute of Agrarian Economy):

Type of property	Percentage of total number	Percentage of total area
Up to 0·5 hectares	53·9	4·1
From 0·5 to 2 hectares	29·4	13·3
From 2 to 5 hectares	10·1	13·6
From 5 to 25 hectares	5·5	24·2
From 25 to 50 hectares	0·6	9·7
Over 50 hectares	0·5	35·1

This means that the 0·5 per cent of large landowners possess more land than the 95 per cent of small landowners. 502 very large landowners, owning more than 1,000 hectares each, possess more land than 5,135,851 small landowners, each of whose properties is no larger than 0·5 hectares.

Bracket of taxable income	Percentage of No. of taxpayers	Percentage of total taxable income
Up to 100 lire	49·1	2·2
From 100 to 400 lire	27·8	8·5
From 400 to 1,000 lire	12·5	11·3
From 1,000 to 5,000 lire	8·5	25·1
From 5,000 to 10,000 lire	1·1	11·0
Over 10,000 lire	1·0	41·9

We find here an income structure fully corresponding to the structure of property. One per cent of the landed taxpayers have a total income which is *double* the income obtained by 30 per cent of the land-owners; 3,531 very large landowners who declare more than 100,000 lire of taxable income possess the same share of the total income declared for taxation as 7,030,397 small landowners who declare less than 400 lire each.*

The wretched lot of the agricultural worker
It is the constant pressure brought to bear on the wages of the agricultural workers by the thousands of small peasants clinging to their little bit of land and ruthlessly sacrificing their own standard of living and that of their family, that basically explains the poverty of these workers, and their pay which is much lower than that of the workers in industry and trade. Country life, the absence of the new needs created by urban existence, the payment of wages partly, or even wholly, in kind, are factors which still further bring down the wages of the agricultural worker. The latter is often a seasonal worker, or even a migrant; if he has another job during the dead season he may be able just to reach subsistence level. If, however, this second job is not to be had, especially in the under-developed countries, he sinks to the lowest depths of human misery.

In the long run, however, the evolution of the agricultural worker's lot depends less on the special conditions of agriculture than on the general rate of expansion of industry. When this rate is such that it results in reducing the industrial reserve army, the exodus from the countryside will become bigger and bigger. An all-round shortage of agricultural labour will appear in the countryside, entailing a rise

* In Mexico, thirty years after the agrarian reform of 1910 which distributed part of the old semi-feudal estates among the landless peasantry, for cultivation in the form of agrarian communities, or *ejidos*, 63·87 per cent of the peasants had been again reduced to the lot of landless agricultural workers, 26·42 per cent of the peasants lived in the *ejidos*, and 4·25 per cent of the peasants, the landowners, had acquired the best land and the rich farms. Since 1946 this tendency has become still more marked.[85]

in agricultural wages, though these will not reach the same level as wages in industry.

When the long-term tendency is, on the contrary, for the industrial reserve army to grow, the agricultural workers, competing fiercely among themselves in order to find some work for a few months of the year at least, put up with the lowest possible wage, often a mere pittance. Their ranks are swollen, moreover, by the mass of small landowners and small farmers whose incomes from their "enterprises" are insufficient for them to make ends meet. Under these conditions there can be no question of a long-term rise in agricultural wages:

"When there is a surplus of agricultural labour and, consequently, unemployment and under-employment exist, each worker is probably more concerned with finding work than with getting a high wage . . ." writes the official report of the United Nations Organisation on *Problems of Agrarian Reform*.[86] It should be added that the big farmers in many countries endeavour to create artificially this plentiful supply of agricultural labour by organising large-scale *immigration of seasonal workers*. This was notoriously the case in Germany before the Second World War (Polish workers). It remains so in the U.S.A., where nearly half a million *braceros* (Mexican seasonal workers, often recruited on a more or less compulsory basis), working for wages as low as 16 to 25 cents an hour, bring about a fall in the wages of agricultural workers, which are as a rule *less than half* the average wages paid in non-agricultural employment.[87]

From the theories of Malthus to agricultural Malthusianism

In 1798 the British clergyman Robert Malthus published anonymously a pamphlet entitled: *Essay on the Principle of Population*, in which he sounded the alarm for mankind by outlining an extremely gloomy prospect: observing that the increase in population was taking place in geometrical progression (2, 4, 8, 16, 32, 64, etc.) whereas, so he claimed, agricultural production could increase only in arithmetical progression (2, 4, 6, 8, 10, 12, etc.), he concluded that mankind was threatened with overpopulation unless it managed to restrict its own procreation. One should therefore applaud the efforts of industrialists to keep workers' wages down to the minimum, as this would set a natural limit to procreation by the workers. As, however, the risk of overproduction of goods might arise in this way, it was necessary to increase the share of the national product which served unproductive consumption by landowners, that is, ground rent. Malthus thus appeared as the defender of the landowners, in face of the agitation for the abolition of ground rent.

The experience of the nineteenth century has shown that Malthus was wrong on two counts. On the one hand, the increase in population fell off with the subsequent progress of technique and culture in the advanced countries.* On the other, the mechanical revolution, belatedly taking hold of agriculture, has increased production in this sphere to a degree much greater than "arithmetical progression". As a result, since the last quarter of the nineteenth century, it has no longer been overpopulation but *overproduction of agricultural products* that has seemed to threaten society.[89] Instead of restricting births, it is agricultural production that men have tried to restrict by all possible means: agricultural Malthusianism had appeared.

In the same period, however, serious scientists, notably the German Liebig, had drawn attention to a really disturbing phenomenon, the increased exhaustion of the soil, the *Raubbau*, resulting from greedy capitalist methods of exploitation aimed at getting the highest profit in the shortest time. Whereas agricultural societies like China, Japan, ancient Egypt, etc., had known a rational method of carrying on agriculture which conserved and even increased the fertility of the soil over several thousand years, the capitalist *Raubbau* had been able, in certain parts of the world, to exhaust the fertile layer of soil, the humus, in half a century, and thereby to cause erosion on a large scale, with all its harmful consequences.

These warnings were not listened to. The great agricultural crisis at the end of the nineteenth century attracted attention more and more to the problem of overproduction. The agricultural crisis which prevailed between 1925 and 1934 created a permanent psychosis of agricultural overproduction in the bourgeois world. Agricultural Malthusianism triumphed. Huge bonuses were given to peasants for them *not* to cultivate their land or grow certain crops. Eight million head of cattle were slaughtered in the U.S.A. in 1934. The area planted with cotton was reduced by nearly a half in that country—from 17·3 million hectares, on the average, between 1923 and 1929, to 9·8 million in 1938. In Brazil, 20 million bags of coffee were burnt between 1932 and 1936, or an amount sufficient to meet *the whole world's needs for eighteen months*. Nobody was then worrying about a threatened over-population of the world.

The Second World War, the great setback to agricultural produc-tion which it caused in some countries, the beginning of the industrial-isation of backward countries, accompanied by a great increase in population, the rise of the revolutionary movement in the Far East, driven forward by the waves of famine which swept over that region, made the ideas of Malthus topical again. An old British writer, a precursor of Utopian socialism, Robert Wallace (1679–1771), had

---

* Defending a bold thesis, Joshua De Castro declares that, in our age, it is not overpopulation that causes famine, but famine (or, more precisely, chronic undernourishment) that causes overpopulation. He endeavours to prove this thesis by examining the influence of undernourishment (especially in animal protein) on the index of human fertility.[88]

already maintained, in his work *Various Prospects,* that, though socialism was good in itself, it would nevertheless lead to a great mis-
fortune, namely, the overpopulation of the world and the danger of
mankind's extinction. Prophets of doom who have appeared since the
Second World War have tried to show that it is much more urgent
to combat the increase of population than to raise the standard of
living of the colonial masses, which would entail the risk of causing
still greater over-population.

Two important works especially, *The Road to Survival,* by William
Vogt, and *Our Plundered Planet,* by Fairfield Osborne, have seemed
to reach these conclusions. Both of them describe a real evil: the
irrational methods of agriculture inherent in the frenzied search for
profit have exposed a large part of Asia, Africa, and both Americas,
to a rapid erosion of the soil. There has followed from this a chain
reaction which increasingly restricts the extent of land normally cultivable. To check this evil it is above all necessary to check the erosion
process, through a vigorous intervention by the public anthorities.
Beyond this first conclusion, which he himself regards as cautious,
Osborne sees no long-term solution of the problem. Indeed, he declares that there is no such solution. Vogt suggests vigorous measures
to restrict the growth of the population, and welcomes disasters such
as wars, epidemics, etc., because they operate radically in this direction.

Though the danger indicated by Vogt and Osborne is a real one,
it is from the very start wrongly defined. Several of their assertions,
such as that it is impossible to reconstitute the layer of humus which
gives the soil its fertility, do not correspond to reality. Again, it is
wrong to calculate the possibilities of feeding mankind on the basis
of the land surface *at present cultivated.* U.N.O. statistics estimate
at 440 million hectares the world's reserves of cultivable land, an amount
equivalent to all the land under cultivation in the U.S.A., India,
China, France, Australia and Canada, or an area capable of feeding
1·5 billion people, given a rational system of agriculture.* Over and
above these immediate reserves, it is possible to improve a huge
area of land which is regarded by Vogt and Osborne as finally lost
to agriculture.

* "According to Kellogg (*Food, Soil and People*) it may be assumed that at
least 20 per cent of the unused tropical soils of the Americas, Africa and the
great islands, such as New Guinea, Madagascar and Borneo, are cultivable;
this would add one billion additional acres to the 300–400 million acres [of
reserves] in the temperate zones. This area of 1300–1400 million additional
acres would indeed be a tremendous reserve for increasing food production. To
translate this potential into reality will mean a complex and difficult job which
is bound to employ humanity for years. It will require careful planning and
in particular simultaneous development of transportation and secondary
industries."[90]

New chemical products such as *krilium** or liquid ammonia fertiliser, make possible a considerable increase in the fertility of the soil. The transition to intensive agriculture in countries like the U.S.A., Canada, Australia, the Argentine, and the improvement of agricultural technique in the backward countries would make it easily possible to double the output per hectare and greatly increase the world's production of agricultural produce. If modern agricultural science were used throughout the world, it would be possible to produce sufficient foodstuffs to feed four billion people, so claimed the Finnish Professor Arturi I. Virtanen, recipient of the Nobel Prize for chemistry, at the 12th international conference of pure and applied chemistry, held in New York between 10th and 13th September, 1951.[91]

Outside agriculture in the strict sense of the word, the first experiments in food production otherwise than from the soil have already proved satisfactory. In Jamaica a factory is at work producing food from yeast; the cultivation of algae offers unlimited prospects of food supply; and cultivation without land (hydroponics) would make possible a purely "industrial" solution of the food problem.

It is true than an effective struggle against erosion, a rational organisation of agriculture, a transition to intensive cultivation in overseas countries, a development of food production otherwise than from the soil "would bring with them a social revolution of such magnitude that the whole structure of human society would be torn apart."[92]

But when mankind is confronted with the choice between perishing and reorganising society on a more rational basis, it is not possible to doubt which decision is dictated by both reason and feeling. This is all the more so because at the very moment when erosion threatens to destroy the material foundation of all agriculture, and when hundreds of millions of human beings are terribly undernourished —the daily intake of calories in India was 1700 in 1952, or *half* the normal level! —agricultural Malthusianism is manifesting itself again in the most scandalous way, foodstuffs (including 3·5 billion bushels of grain) to the value of 10 billion dollars (4,500,000,000,000 French francs!) being put in store in the U.S.A. and vast destructive operations being carried out on crops of maize, potatoes, and vines,† etc. At the end of 1957 the United States authorities boasted that they had "saved" a billion dollars by . . . *preventing* the cultivation

---

* *Krilium* increases the growth of plants and prevents the soil from being carried off by water or wind, through increasing its capacity for retaining water and air. It is considered that *krilium* is between 100 and 1,000 times more effective than humus, natural fertilisers or compost.

† *Le Monde*[94] reported that 17 million hectolitres of wine were "denatured" in France in 1951–53 and that an unsaleable surplus of more than 15 million hectolitres was expected at the end of August 1953.

of some nine million hectares! [93] More than ever is it obvious that the problem does not lie in the absolute increase in population but in the capitalist condition of production and distribution which creates a situation of plenty and poverty side by side.

Ground-rent and the marginal theory of value

The theory of ground rent worked out by Ricardo and perfected by Marx was the point of departure of the marginal theories of value which, in the second half of the nineteenth century, challenged the labour theory of value.* According to Marx's theory of ground rent, it is in fact the *demand for agricultural products* which in the last resort determines the price of these products. This price is based on the value of the unit produced on the plot of land with the worst conditions of productivity (marginal price) where products find a buyer. According to the fluctuations of demand it either will or will not embody the absolute ground rent (in those countries where there is no more unoccupied land, i.e. where the monopoly of landowner-ship is complete) and it either will or will not embody a differential rent (depending on whether the less profitable plots of land are culti-vated or given up).

The transformation of this theory of ground rent into a general theory of value is based on two mistakes of analysis. In the first place, it leaves out the *special conditions of property in land* which give rise to ground rent. Further, it leaves out the different institutional conditions that govern ownership of land, ownership of capital and "ownership of labour-power", respectively, under the capitalist system.

Ground rent does not arise because the land is a fundamental factor in the process of production. It arises only because there inserts himself between the land and this production process a land-owner who *arbitrarily demands* his share of the amount of income created in this production process. To proceed from the way in which this share is obtained in order to construct from it a general theory of the division of *income created in the production process* creates a serious error of logic. In a "pure" capitalist society from which ground rent was banished, for example, by nationalisation of the land (and the economy of certain overseas countries in the second half of the nineteenth century was somewhat like that), it would be difficult to proceed from . . . nothing to explain the whole mechanism of the division of income and the production of value within the capitalist mode of production!

A generalisation from the special case of ground rent would be justified, theoretically, only in a society in which the "capitalist" entrepreneurs were faced simultaneously with landowners, slave-

* Other aspects of these theories, their subjectivist nature, etc., will be dealt with in Chapter 18.

owners and owners of machines. The laws determining the share taken by these three categories of owner from the current income created by "capitalist" production would doubtless be similar to those which determine the appearance and fluctuations of ground rent. But we have been careful to put the word "capitalist" between inverted commas because such a society, in which there existed neither monopoly of the means of production by the bourgeois class nor free labour (free from serfdom or slavery), would, of course, not be a capitalist society.

For ground rent to appear it is necessary not only that ownership of land be a monopoly* which the bourgeoisie has not managed to break, so that the landowners are able to prevent the capital invested in agriculture from participating in the general equalisation of the rate of profit, and thus to collect their share of the value created in agriculture; it is further necessary that the production of agricultural commodities be carried on under special conditions which escape from control by capital.

According to the supporters of the marginal theory of value, three kinds of "owner" appear on the market, in order to "exchange" on an equal footing, three different "commodities", the prices of which will thus be determined, in complete equity, by the "marginal product, or income", that is, by the last, that is the least profitable, unit sold— owners of land, owners of capital, and owners of labour-power.

Now, there is a fundamental qualitative difference—through the very functioning of the capitalist mode of production—between these three categories of "owner". In the classical capitalism of the nineteenth century in Western Europe (the very capitalism in which ground rent appears in its complete and classical form!) there is *an absolute shortage of land*; total potential agricultural production hardly covers society's need for food. It is for this reason, and for this reason alone—because capital cannot extend at will the area of cultivable land, at least in Western Europe—that ground rent can appear and continue for a long period. As Marx observes, the importation of food plays only a regulatory role, preventing the prices of agricultural products from exceeding even their value, and the landowners from securing for themselves part of the surplus value *produced in industry.*†

Capital, for its part, comes on to the market in conditions of *relative shortage.* By its very logic it prevents an abundance of capital from undermining the profitability of capital: this is the objective

---

* We shall see later on (Chapter 12) that a mechanism comparable to that of ground rent regulates *monopoly profit* in the present phase of capitalism (cartel rent, etc.).

† Comparable conditions exist today in countries like India, where a "secular shortage" of foodstuffs prevails.

function of the cyclical crises.* But the "owners of labour-power" are weakened in advance by the conditions of *relative abundance* in which they have to offer their commodity on the market. This abundance (industrial reserve army) is not only the result of the historical conditions in which capitalism was born. It is also a result of the mechanism of capitalist production itself, which continually replaces men by machines and periodically "releases" masses of unemployed from the production process.

It will now be seen that there can be no question of negotiation on the market "on an equal footing" between these three classes. The dice are loaded. The rules of the game are such that one class lays down conditions dictatorially (the class of owners of land) whereas another class *has to accept* what is offered it (the proletariat).

These rules of the game operate all the more in a sense which reduces to absurdity the idea of an exchange of "marginal products", as the capitalist class does not "work" for subsistence but in order to accumulate capital. Its subsistence is guaranteed. When the wages demanded by the workers seem to it to be too high, it may prefer to close the gates of its factories rather than "work" for an insufficient profit, or at a loss.

In their turn, the landowners may prefer to leave some of their land to lie waste rather than let it at a price such that the total rent they draw is too low. By withdrawing this land from cultivation they contribute, moreover, to reducing agricultural production and so to reconstituting their rent at a later stage.

In contrast to this, the proletariat is in a special situation: that of not possessing any reserves beyond its two hands, which it *must* hire out if it is not to die of hunger. Not being in a position to "await a more propitious moment of the conjuncture", it is thus compelled to accept a wage which is not determined by the "marginal productivity of labour" but merely by the average subsistence needs in the given country and period. Once again, the dice are loaded.

To resume our imaginary description of a society in which this "negotiation on an equal footing" might be established, it would be necessary that, on the one hand, the bourgeois should possess reserves of foodstuffs, say, for several years (or that there should be large tracts of land without an owner), and that, on the other hand, the workers should likewise possess reserves of foodstuffs, or money, that would enable them to supply their needs and those of their families, for several years. In such conditions as these, "negotiations" between landowners, capitalists and producers would be placed on a relatively equal footing, and the division of income that would result would be quite different from that which governs the capitalist mode of production. But it is obvious that in a society like this there would neither

* See Chapter 11.

exist a monopoly of capital in the hands of the bourgeoisie nor a proletariat as a class, so that it would not be capitalist society.

A critic of Marx whom recently there have been mistaken efforts to rehabilitate, L. von Bortkiewicz,* does not grasp why the owners of land are able to *compel* the capitalist farmers to pay absolute ground rent, even on the least profitable land.[96] He approaches this question logically instead of historically.† Seen in this way the answer is simple: they can compel the farmers to pay absolute rent, and avoid the giving-up of the least fertile land, so long as there is a permanent shortage of foodstuffs, that is, so long as, owing to the delay in revolutionary technical changes in agriculture, the whole of a country's agricultural production is hardly adequate to meet its needs.

When this condition disappears, especially as the result of the opening up of the vast uncultivated lands of the two Americas and Australia, absolute rent may indeed tend to disappear, over large areas, as Marx foresaw. In fact it would already have vanished over a large part of Western Europe, but for the protectionist policy by which it is artificially maintained (or re-established). Under these conditions, it is only through exceptional circumstances of shortage (notably during world wars) that prices suddenly flare up, re-establishing absolute ground rent in its former grandeur.

* This is attempted by Sweezy in *The Theory of Capitalist Development.*[95]

† Von Bortkiewicz shows a similar lack of historical sense when, following Lexis, Böhm-Bawerk, Sombart, Stolzmann, Cornélissen and others, he declares that the transformation of value into price of production does not reflect any real historical process[97] Today it has become almost commonplace to stress that this transformation reflects the transition from petty commodity production (based on *stable* technological conditions) to capitalist society, based on technological conditions which are in *perpetual revolution*.

REFERENCES

1. F. Heichelheim: *Wirtschaftsgeschichte des Altertums*, pp. 691-2, 704.
2. M. Rostovtzeff: *Social and Economic History of the Roman Empire*, pp. 148-9.
3. G. I. Bratianu: *Etudes byzantines d'histoire économique et sociale*, p. 139.
4. E. O. Heady: *Economics of Agricultural Production*, p. 418.
5. Diehl: in *Schmollers Jahrbuch*, Sonderheft, 1932, p. 28.
6. W. Abel: *Agrarkrisen und Agrarkonjunktur in Mitteleuropa*, pp. 15-16.
7. Gino Luzzato: *Storia Economica d'Italia*, Vol. I, p. 211.
8. N. S. B. Gras: *The Evolution of the English Corn Market*, p. 28.
9. Ibid., p. 45.
10. Luzzato: op. cit., Vol. I, pp. 246-7.
11. Gras: op. cit., pp. 47-56.
12. Abel: op. cit., p. 54.

13. Gras: op. cit., p. 123; F. J. Fisher: "The Development of the London Food Market", in *Economic History Review*, Vol. V, No. 2, p. 50; A. P. Usher: *History of the Grain Trade in France*, pp. 61-62, 56.

14. Gras: op. cit., p. 218.

15. Ibid., pp. 123, 144-9, 220.

16. Ibid., pp. 76-77; Usher: op. cit., p. 60.

17. Usher: op. cit, pp. 6-8, *et al.*; Fisher: art. cit., p. 64.

18. Gras: op. cit., p. 218.

19. Abel: op. cit., p. 61.

20. N. S. B. Gras: *A History of Agriculture*, p. 218.

21. R. T. Ely and G. S. Wehrwein: *Land Economics*, p. 119; article *"Grundrente"* in Conrad's *Handwörterbuch der Staatswissenschaften*, Vol. V, p. 167.

22. Ely and Wehrwein: op. cit., p. 137.

23. Ibid., pp. 134-5.

24. I.B.R.D Mission Report: *The Economic Development of Iraq*, p. 235.

25. A. Wauters: *"Les sources doctrinales du marxisme"*, in *Revue des sciences économiques*, A. L. D. Lg., 33rd year, No. 116, December, 1958, p. 232; Karl Marx: *Das Kapital*, 1st edition, Vol. III, pt. 2, pp. 278-9.

26. N. S. B. Gras: *A History of Agriculture*, p. 274.

27. F. Baudhuin: *Economique agraire*, p. 89.

28. *Bank of International Settlements*, 22nd annual report, 1952, p. 41.

29. *Rapport sur la situation économique dans les pays de la Communauté*, September 1958, p. 35.

30. U.S. Dept. of Agriculture, *Changing Technology*, p. 37.

31. R. R. Renne: *Land Economics*, p. 421.

32. J. Johnston: *Irish Agriculture in Transition*, p. 5.

33. René Dumont: *Le Problème agricole français*, p. 329.

34. N. S. B. Gras: *A History of Agriculture*, p. 148.

35. Ely and Wehrwein: op. cit., p. 121.

36. Ibid., p. 120

37. Renne: op. cit., p. 215.

38. Abel: op. cit., pp. 103, 118-22.

39. Ely and Wehrwein: op. cit., p. 172.

40. F. A. Shannon: *The Farmer's Last Frontier*, pp. 126-7.

41. Nogaro and Oualid: *Evolution du Commerce, du Crédit et du Transport depuis 150 ans*, p. 194.

42. A. Garigou-Lagrange: *Production agricole et économie rurale*, p. 66.

43. René Dumont: op. cit., preface.

44. J. H. Clapham: *An Economic History of Modern Britain*, Vol. III, pp. 83-84. See also Conrad's *Handwörterbuch der Staatswissenschaften*, Vol. I, article *"Agrargeschichte"*, p. 218.

45. Serge Mallet: in *France-Observateur*, 10th December, 1959.

46. René Dumont: op. cit., p. 317, and *Rapport sur la situation économique dans les pays de la Communauté*, September 1958, p. 35.

47. Baudhuin: op. cit., p. 91.

48. J. de Castro: *Géopolitique de la faim*, passim.

49. Renne: op. cit., p. 268.
50. G. D. H. Cole: *World in Transition*, p. 89.
51. Heady: op. cit., p. 701.
52. Henri Brousse: in *Revue économique*, September 1953.
53. Gilbert Burck: in *Fortune*, June 1955.
54. Food and Agriculture Organisation: *Annuaire de Statistiques*, 1952.
55. *Bulletin du Comité National belge de la FAO*, Vol. VIII, No. 3, 1954.
56. J. Schumpeter: *Business Cycles*, p. 739.
57. René Dumont: op. cit., pp. 324-5.
58. J. Dorfman: *The Economic Mind in American Civilization*, pp. 118, 338.
59. Ely and Wehrwein: op. cit., p. 76.
60. Palme Dutt: *India Today*, pp. 243-8, German edition, 1951.
61. Ely and Wehrwein: op. cit., p. 97.
62. Shannon: op. cit., p. 64.
63. *Cahiers algériens*, No. 3, pp. 17-18.
64. *La Question tunisienne*, No. 2, p. 25.
65. *Morocco*, pp. 73-74.
66. *Report of the Ad Hoc Committee on Forced Labour, U.N.O.*, p. 621.
67. George Padmore: *Britain's Third Empire*, pp. 38-40, 50, 59-60.
68. Ibid., pp. 17-18, 28.
69. *Kandyan Peasantry Report*, pp. 71-73.
70. Condliffe: *The Commerce of Nations*, p. 316.
71. For Egypt, Hans Briner: in *Basler Nationalzeitung*, 8th May, 1953.
72. Weulersse: *Le Pays des Alaouites*, p. 225.
73. H. K. Lee: *Land Utilisation and Rural Economy in Korea*, p. 163.
74. I.B.R.D. Report, *The Economic Development of Iraq*, p. 6.
75. Alfred Bonné: *State and Economics in the Middle East*, p. 132.
76. *La Réforme agraire*, U.N. publication, 1951, p. 18.
77. *Panorama Economico*, 1953, No. 1, p. 34.
78. Fleddérus and Van Kleeck: *Technology and Livelihood*, p. 92.
79. Institut d'Economie Agricole de Gand: *Berichte über Landwirtschaft*, 1, p. 43, Hamburg
80. Ely and Wehrwein: op. cit., p. 207.
81. *Socialist Call*, April-May 1957.
82. G. D. H. Cole: *World in Transition*, pp. 26-27.
83. *La Libre Belgique*, 12th December, 1959.
84. *U.S. Statistical Abstract, 1958 and 1965* and *Historical Statistics*.
85. Jacques Séverin: *"Démocratie mexicaine"*, in *Esprit*, May 1952, p. 791.
86. *Progrès de la Réforme agraire*, published in 1954 by the U.N., p. 181.
87. *New York Times*, 10th September, 1959, and *Socialist Call*, April-May 1957.
88. J. de Castro: *Géopolitique de la faim*, pp. 47, 90-93.
89. Nogaro and Oualid: *Evolution du Commerce, du Crédit et du Transport depuis 150 ans*, p. 165.
90. Alfred Bonné: *Studies in Economic Development*, p. 146.

91. *Facts on File*, September 1951.
92. Fairfield Osborn: *Our Plundered Planet*, pp. 74-75; *New York Times*, 20th February, 1959.
93. *New York Times*, 27th December, 1959.
94. *Le Monde*, 24th July, 1953.
95. Paul M. Sweezy: *The Theory of Capitalist Development*, pp. 115-25, *et al.*
96. L. Von Bortkiewicz: *Die Rodbertus'sche Grundrententheorie und die Marx'sche Lehre von der absoluten Grundrente*, in *Archiv für die Geschichte des Sozialismus und der Arbeiterbewegung*, by Karl Grünberg, Vol. I, 1911, pp. 426-9.
97. Ibid., pp. 423-4.

CHAPTER TEN

REPRODUCTION AND GROWTH OF THE NATIONAL INCOME

New value, new income and tranferred income

IN a society where there was no economic activity other than the capitalist production of commodities there would be no income other than that created by this production. Labour-power, as we know, has the dual function of conserving the value of constant capital (the stock of machinery, raw materials, buildings) by transferring part of this value to currently produced commodities*, and of producing all the new value available to society. The first-mentioned property of labour-power makes it possible to conserve the accumulated stock of social wealth and instruments of labour, which determines the average level of the productivity of labour and the material civilisation of the given society. The second makes it possible to create an income—a "value added"—which in capitalist society is divided between income of labour (wages) and income of capital (surplus-value).

In practice, however, bourgeois society—the only form of society which makes the production of commodities universal—does include other economic activities and other sources of income besides this capitalist commodity production. One can in fact distinguish:

(a) The sector of petty commodity production which survives in capitalist society (craftsmen and small peasants working for the market without employment wage-labour);

(b) The sphere of distribution and that of transport which is *not* indispensable for the consumption of commodities. The wages paid in this sphere come out of society's capital; the capitalists obtain part of the surplus-value of society.†

(c) The sector of private services, the enterprises in which capitalist entrepreneurs and wage-earners provide specialised labour services to the consumers;

(d) The sector of public services, in which the employees are paid by the State (and subordinate public authorities), and which sell

---

* "The raw material is considered as receiving an increment of cost . . . from the machine; the machine gives off, so to speak, a part of its value, which becomes embodied in the finished product."[1] But the machine cannot "give off" any part of its value unless it be used, set in motion, by living labour. Without the application of the latter it purely and simply depreciates.

† See Chapter 6, sections "Commercial capital and commercial profit", and "Commercial capital and labour-power engaged in distribution".

services to the consumers (the sale of piped water, gas and electricity by public enterprises must be included in the commodity production branch, since here it is material goods that are being sold, not specialised labour);

(e) The public services provided free by the State or by public enterprises (free primary education, etc.);

(f) The production of use-values which do not appear on the market: production by subsistence farms, household production, "do-it-yourself", etc.

Of these six sectors which are outside the realms of capitalist commodity production in the strict sense, the first four retain the outward form of buying and selling. Except in the first case, that of the production of value which is not accompanied by production of surplus-value,* what is involved is the buying and selling not of material goods but of labour-time, specialised labour, etc. As for the last two sectors, they are outside commodity production as such.

The circulation of commodities in capitalist society results in their consumption, whether productive or unproductive; the intermediate phases that these commodities pass through before being consumed do not create new value. The enterprises which have charge of them during these phases cannot make profit from them except by appropriating part of the surplus-value already produced during the production-process. But distributive activity creates *new incomes*—the incomes of the wage and salary earners who work in the distributive sector. *These incomes do not constitute a part of the surplus-value currently produced by the productive workers, but a part of the social capital invested in this sector.*

Do these incomes tend to reduce the wages of the industrial workers? This view can be maintained only on the basis of the theory of the "wages fund", which regards the total amount of wages paid out during a given period as pre-determined. In reality, that would be so only if all the social capital available were wholly invested—if, in other words, every sum not invested in trade, or in the service sector, were automatically invested in industry, and if the organic composition of capital were rigid and stable.

* In so far as the peasants and craftsmen produce commodities *in competition* with the capitalist sector, three cases may present themselves. Either the productivity of their labour is equal to the average, in which case their products are sold at their exact value; or their productivity is lower than the average (this is the usual situation), in which case part of the value they have created is transferred to certain capitalist sectors; or else their productivity is, by way of exception, higher than the average (or, what comes to the same thing, the total production of a craft sector is not adequate to meet the effective demand), in which case, the petty commodity producers appropriate a small quantity of the surplus value produced in the capitalist sector of the economy. This last case occurs especially in periods of sudden shortage, during or just after wars, etc.

Actually this does not happen. The division of social capital between the different branches of the economy; the division of income between surplus-value (potential new capital) and wages, and of capitalised surplus-value between new constant capital and new wages (variable capital); the division of savings (new potential capital) between investment and hoarding—all depend on a number of different relations and many different mechanisms, which are much more complicated than is supposed by the supporters of the "wages fund" theory.*

The production of commodities and the allocation of available social capital thus create essentially the incomes of the workers (both productive and unproductive) and those of the capitalists (in the different spheres of capital investment). But the *circulation* of incomes complicates the picture; when these incomes buy a commodity they merely realise their value and create no new incomes, but when they buy services,† they create the illusion of giving rise to new incomes. Actually, they are only transferred.

It is not easy to draw the line between new and transferred incomes. This must be done, however, if we are to estimate economic growth adequately and make comparisons of national income, in time and space. The problem may be regarded as a purely conventional one when it is a matter of calculating this income in one country during a very short period; but it becomes vital when this calculation is extended over a long period and international comparisons are brought in.

If we neglect the distinction between new value, social income newly created, and incomes which are merely transferred, we inevitably land ourselves in obvious contradictions, for instance, *Pigou's paradox.* If we add to the national income of a nation the wages of its domestic servants, we come to the conclusion that the national income declines, the nation becomes poorer, when bachelors marry their housekeepers, who thenceforth no longer receive wages for doing the same work as they were doing before they married.[3] The transformation of a million beggars into producers (e.g. agricultural producers, as a result of

---

* Jean Marchal and Jacques Lecaillon[2] have undertaken a somewhat Byzantine exegesis of the writings of present-day Marxists in order to show that, according to Marx, the payment of the unproductive wage-earners takes place at the expense of the productive ones. True, they do quote other writings which maintain a different point of view. The whole of their study is fundamentally mistaken, however, because it does not proceed from *the real conditions in which the accumulation of capital takes place.* In a period in which there is a lack of fields for investment where more than the average profit can be obtained, when it is more and more difficult to realise surplus value, the development of the unproductive sectors tends notably to limit the scope of chronic unemployment, and thereby to make possible a greater stability (or even growth) of real wages.

† A service is the useful effect of a use-value—essentially of a contribution of skilled labour—the production and consumption of which coincide, because it is not embodied in a material product.

internal colonisation) would in no way increase the national wealth, if the money incomes of these peasants did not exceed the money incomes they received when they were beggars.*

The attitude of academic economics is contradictory in this respect. It eliminates from the calculation of the national income a whole series of paid activities, or incomes regarded as transferred incomes (notably the payments made to unemployed persons, policemen, firemen, etc.).[5]† But it includes most of these activities as soon as they become private instead of public. It eliminates from the national income every addition to prices which results from indirect taxes, but on the other hand it includes increases—usually quite arbitrary ones—in the case of services, which nevertheless do not create any new value but merely increase the incomes *transferred* from other sectors to the services sector.

Of course, the two series of additions each serve different purposes. The total amount of *incomes of all the households, private enterprises and public organisations* provides the data needed for various analyses, for example, in order to determine at what total of money incomes danger of inflation will arise, given a certain productive capacity. The total amount of net value newly *produced* in society is, however, the essential concept for measuring the possibilities and successive staging-points of economic growth. The way national income is nowadays calculated by official Western economics is a hybrid compromise between these two principles, and leads to serious mistakes in both directions.

Certain writers implicitly accept the soundness of this view. In *The Organisation Man*,[6] William H. Whyte, Jnr., correctly observes, for example: "The great majority of small business firms cannot be placed on any continuum with the corporation. For one thing, they are rarely engaged in primary industry; for the most part they are the laundries, the insurance agencies, the restaurants, the drugstores, the bottling plants, the lumber yards, the automobile dealers. They are vital, to be sure, but essentially they service an economy; they do not create new money within their area and they are dependent ultimately on the business and agriculture that does."‡

* Bauer and Yamey point out that in a number of under-developed countries the incomes of the beggars are not at all inconsiderable.[4]

† On the grounds that these activities are paid for out of the product of indirect taxation.

‡ See in Chapter 18 a surprising application of this idea. This quotation has all the greater value in that it relates to the most advanced capitalist country in the world. Some writers, such as J. Markovitch,[7] have declared that while the purchase of services may properly be regarded as transfer expenditure in backward countries, this is not so in advanced countries. Above all, the *exchange of services for services* ought not to be overlooked. All the same, even according to the present academic method, the purchase of a service by an unemployed person must be left out of account. Transfers at the third stage do not modify the problem at all.

Carl Shoup writes, from his standpoint: "National income analysis is interested in production, and it reserves the term 'investment' for the kinds of things that imply production, either current or past. The purchase of a share of stock, even if it is newly issued stock, is not an act of investment, in national income terminology."[8]*

Again, Simon Kuznets argues in favour of the exclusion from the national income of what he calls the "negative consequences of large-scale urbanisation" in the case of *international* comparisons between national incomes (but why include them, then, in estimates on the national scale?):

"A clear case is the transportation of employees to and from work —an activity that can hardly be said to constitute direct welfare to ultimate consumers and is merely an offset to the inconvenience that large-scale industrial production imposes upon the active participants in it . . . Payments to banks, employment agencies, unions, brokerage houses, etc., including such matters as technical education, are payments not for final goods flowing to ultimate consumers, but libations of oil on the machinery of industrial society—activities intended to eliminate friction in the productive system, not net contributions to ultimate consumption."[10]

Nevertheless, these fragmentary opinions have not yet made it possible to re-examine objectively, using precise scientific criteria, the way of calculating the national income, which, consequently, is overestimated by some 20 to 30 per cent, according to Kuznets.[11]

In order to determine the *value of (gross) production* in a country during one year, it is not enough merely to add up the values of all the commodities that issue from any enterprise in the course of this year. Otherwise one would inevitably include duplicated entries, since some of the finished products of one enterprise reappear in the form of raw material in the ultimate value of the products of another. It is necessary either to set aside altogether all the unfinished products, and add to the value of the finished products manufactured during

---

* The same writer nevertheless falls immediately into the error of mixing up productive and unproductive labour, when he goes on: "In a country where household services have come to be performed largely outside the home, or inside the home for pay, and the housewives use the time thus freed to work in paid occupations, the national income as at present computed will be larger than in a country where most of these services are performed by the family itself. The production of the former country is not actually as much greater as the difference in national income figures would indicate."[9]

The author forgets that during "the time thus freed", the housewives, having become working-women, produce new commodities and create new value, something which, for once, is faithfully reflected in the calculations of national income. And even from the standpoint of national accounting in hours of work, the saving accomplished by the carrying out of domestic work in specialised enterprises is enormous.

the year merely the fluctuation in the stocks of raw materials, or else to add up merely the value added in each enterprise.[12]

No different method should be employed when the *new social income* of a country during the same period is to be established. Just as one cannot merely add up the value of all the commodities, one cannot merely add up all the individual incomes. It is necessary to determine exactly which incomes—created by *production*—represent a net addition to the national income, and which are merely the result of transfers, whether private or public. Otherwise, the total amount of income will contain duplicated entries, exactly as would happen with the total amount of the prices of all the commodities.

The State, surplus-value and social income

Up to now we have brought into our model of a "pure" society of commodity producers only persons engaged in distributive activities, together with persons selling personal services to the consumers. We must now add the totality of the economic relationships characteristic of the activities of what are called the "public authorities", in the widest sense of the expression.

In so far as the State is itself a commodity producer, the incomes created by this production are naturally added to the income of the entire community under consideration. It is of little significance, in this case, that the "profit" (or the "loss"), that is, the surplus value created, is annexed not by a group of capitalists but by the State budget. Similarly, it makes little difference that the producers are public employees.

But in all the capitalist countries the bulk of the State's income, and of the income it distributes, does not originate in the production and sale of commodities by the State itself. This income originates in four main ways:

(a) Direct Taxes: these represent part of the income created by commodity production, and so part of the wages and the surplus value produced during the period under consideration.

(b) Public Loans: these transfer part of the accumulated wealth of the nation from individuals to the State. To this can be added a small part of the wages of the most highly skilled workers, which is used for the purchase of bonds. The income thus obtained by the State comes, accordingly, from the surplus value actually or potentially accumulated, and from the saved income of the middle classes, which is thus transformed into capital. In exchange, the State transfers to subscribers to public loans a part of its own current income.

(c) Indirect taxes: turnover tax, customs duties, excise, purchase tax, etc. What is involved here is not a share of already created income which is thereby redistributed, but *a general addition to the selling price of commodities*, which, through an all-round increase in prices,

brings about a reduction in the real income of all consumers. This reduction is not proportional to *total* income but only to income spent on goods subject to these taxes. In fact, almost the whole of wages is spent on these goods, whereas the bourgeois classes do not need to spend a considerable share of their income in this way. Indirect taxation thus affects the workers much more severely than the capitalists, and is the fiscal device preferred by every reactionary capitalist government, to the extent at least that goods in current consumption are not systematically relieved of tax-burdens and the latter shifted on to luxury goods.

(d) Inflationary issue of bank notes: this, provided it remains within certain limits, is a source of real income for the State, since it enables the State to purchase commodities and pay salaries with these depreciated notes. It has the same effect as an increase in indirect taxes: an all-round increase in prices which hits the wage-earners and lower income-groups much harder than the well-to-do classes, who can transform a substantial part of their income into "stable values" (gold, foreign currency, real estate, industrial shares, works of art, etc.).

These four kinds of public income thus constitute only an appropriation by the State—whether directly, or indirectly in the form of the reduction of real income resulting from the rise in prices—of income created by the production of commodities, or subsequently redistributed by the circulation of income and commodities. They cannot be taken into account when it is a question of determining the growth (or the reduction) of the newly-created value, that is, the net social income, of a community. In calculating this income one can start from the gross income of the wage-earners and the gross surplus value, or one can start from net incomes, adding to these the total of direct taxation and deducting the consequences of currency inflation, using stable price indices.[13]

If the State merely annexes incomes which result from production, in so far as it is not itself a producer, the way in which it makes use of this income may have decisive effects on the volume of net social income, that is, on the level of production itself. Its expenditure consists, in fact, of purchases of commodities, investments, wage and salary payments and gifts of various kinds, together with the payment of interest on the public debt. When the State budget absorbs a substantial share of social income, the allocation of this expenditure between the different sectors mentioned above can modify the "spontaneous" allocation of demand as between different commodities, and thus influence the general progress of business, or even modify the way the industrial cycle evolves.*

* These problems are dealt with in more detail in the last section of this chapter, and also in the following chapter and in Chapter 14, section "A crisis-free capitalism?"

The sharing-out of surplus-value

An official Japanese publication shows, for the year 1951, the following share-out of "value added", i.e. newly-created value, in Japanese industry as a whole:

	billion yen
Wages and salaries	706·8
Interest	111·8
Taxes	317·2
Dividends	40·3
Undistributed profits	150·9
	1,327·0[14]

The apparent rate of surplus value (without taking into account the surplus-value appropriated by the capitalists operating outside the sphere of production) is thus around 100 per cent. Actually, the category of *wages and salaries* includes the income of all the higher managerial personnel (managers and business executives) who belong sociologically to the bourgeois class rather than to the working class. Their incomes should be regarded as taken from surplus-value: "But although part of the salaries and other emoluments, of managers and executives should, by the economist, be included in wages, another part is a rough contractual equivalent for, or share in profits in our sense" states Schumpeter.[15]

And Woytinsky[16] justifiably criticises the official statistics which include in "income of labour" "the fees of directors of limited companies, the salaries of higher civil servants and many other officials ... The statistics of national income almost always tend to over-estimate the income of labour, while underestimating other forms of income."

To go back to our Japanese table: the total of wages in the strict sense will thus be lower than 700 billion yen, and probably lower even than 663·5 billion yen, that is, half of the "value added" in industry. Let us, however, stick to the hypothesis of an amount of wages exactly equal to half of this "value added" of 1,327 billion, i.e. 663·5 billion yen. In this case, the apparent surplus-value also amounts to 663·5 billion yen, shared out as follows:

	billion yen
Factory managers, company directors, etc.	43·3
Banks, rentiers and landowners	111·8
Shareholders	40·3
Undistributed profits (accumulation funds of businesses)	150·9
The State (taxes)	317·2
	663·5

In the case of Japan, as with most large industrialised countries, the State takes a substantial share of the "value added" (the surplus value which arises in industry). It is not without point, however, to make clear that this means, very largely, a *redistribution of surplus value* among the various sectors of the bourgeoisie. The latter, in fact, profits from the national debt, State contracts and the salaries of the high dignitaries and officials of the State, the Army, the Church, the Judiciary, etc.

The total *surplus-value* produced *exceeds*, moreover, the figure which results from the above sum. The Japanese statisticians, in calculating the value "added", i.e. "newly created" by labour-power, went no further than the factory gates. But, as we know, *commercial profits*, which are not included in these figures, together with the share of these profits which, in their turn, the traders have to surrender to the banks, the landowners, the State, etc., likewise make up part of the total surplus value produced by the worker-producers. Re-examining the share-out of this surplus value from a functional standpoint, we can define the following categories of income:

(i) entrepreneur's and founder's profit, partly represented by the salaries of directors and executives, partly by dividends (on preference shares, founders' shares, etc.), and partly by undistributed profits, which are *available* to the entrepreneurs even if they do not use them as income in the strict sense of the word;

(ii) commercial profit, represented by the incomes of large and medium-scale traders, the dividends and undistributed profits of commercial joint-stock companies;

(iii) interest (income of individuals, companies and institutions advancing money-capital);

(iv) bank profits, which appear partly as interest and partly as undistributed profits or dividends of the banks;

(v) ground rent, the income of landowners (or of building societies), likewise deducted from the total amount of social surplus-value.

In so far as there is no longer a landlord class separate from the bourgeoisie, at least in the chief capitalist countries, the total of these incomes can be regarded as *income of the bourgeoisie*, the sharing-out of which involves only a struggle (competitive, in one way or another) between different sectors of this one class.

The ultimate origin of all the incomes distributed in capitalist society is shown more clearly still in the following table of national income in the United States in 1947[17] (in millions of dollars):

Wages and salaries	121,913
Social security payments	5,588
Income of unincorporated enterprises	45,997

Net Interest	4,293
Dividends	6,880
Undistributed profits	11,195
Corporate profits taxes	11,709

The only entry in this table that presents any problem is that of the profits of individual (unincorporated) enterprises. This includes the income of peasant producers, craftsmen, etc., which cannot, as a whole, be regarded as surplus-value. But, allowing for this qualification, the total amount of surplus value is determined by the total amount of all the entries except wages and social security payments.

The entry "wages", in the strict sense (which moreover includes the income of wage-earners in trade, banking, transport, etc.) constitutes only a part, often remarkably small, of the entry "wages and salaries". Thus, in Great Britain in 1951, out of a total of £8·4 billion shown as "income of labour", only £5 billion or 60 per cent was wages. Salaries—defined by the British blue book as the income of non-manual personnel, namely, managers, supervisors, foremen, technicians, office-workers, researchers, etc.—came to £2·5 billion. Employers' contributions to the national insurance fund amounted to £500 million, the pay of the armed forces to £300 million, etc.[18]

Social product and social income

The value of all the finished commodities produced by a society (a country) during a certain period (a year, for instance) represents the value of the *gross social (or national) product*.[19]

The value of this gross product is made up of newly-created value and conserved value. If we regard the raw material *additionally* produced during the year as finished products, the conserved value contained in that of the gross (national) product is that of the fixed capital used up (machinery, industrial plant and buildings, etc.) together with that of the stock of raw materials. The newly created value, called the *net (national) product* is equal to the value of all the commodities produced, less the value of the constant capital conserved. Or, put another way: the value of the net annual product is equal to the value of all the consumer goods produced together with that of all the *new* means of production.[20] We here find again the distinction between the *value of the annual product* $(c + v + s)$ and the value newly-created each year $(v + s)$. This new value can be rediscovered more easily by simply adding the new value (the value added) created in all the enterprises.

Assuming that all the commodities produced in the year have been effectively sold, the production of these commodities has created the following incomes: v, the total wages of all the workers; and s, the total surplus-value of the entire bourgeoisie (broken down as shown above). When the calculation is made on the basis of prices, the indirect taxes added to the selling prices of the commodities, and absorbed by the State, must be added,[21] while taking into account the fact that among the commodities produced (and the incomes distributed) we must also include those produced by the State. *The (national) income is thus equal to the net (national) product,* at market prices, less the indirect taxes, or rather, to the total value of all the finished products, less the conserved value of the constant capital (indirect taxes being regarded as an arbitrary addition to the value).*

Ruggles[22] offers the following table (in millions of dollars) of the *gross national product* of the United States in 1947, which enables us to rediscover with ease our fundamental categories: †

Category	Item	Value			
Fixed constant capital used up	Capital consumption allowances (Depreciation charges)	13,299			Gross national product at market prices
Variable capital	Wages and salaries	121,913		Net national product at market prices	
	Social insurance contributions	5,588	National income at factor prices		
Surplus-value‡	Income of unincorporated enterprises	45,997			
	Net interest	4,293			
	Dividends	6,880			
	Corporate profits taxes	11,709			
	Undistributed profits	11,195			
Arbitrary addition to commodity prices	Indirect taxes	18,488			

In the equation between *incomes* and *values of commodities produced,* the word "income" is used, however, in a quite special sense.

* The following problem could be discussed *ad infinitum*—should indirect taxes be regarded as an integral part of the surplus-value produced, and the national income be evaluated at market prices? Or should the national income be estimated on the basis of factor prices, re-evaluating the constituents and deducting the share taken by the State in indirect taxes? The result is practically the same.

† The price of circulating constant capital renewed during the year, the stock of raw materials reproduced, has been similarly broken down in this table into its constituent elements: c (fixed) $+ v + s +$ indirect taxes. From the Marxist standpoint this operation is valid, in so far as the value of this stock has been conserved. For, while the raw material embodied in the production of finished products does not represent a new value but only a conserved value, nevertheless the *production* of this raw material obviously gives rise to new value.

‡ Except for part of the income of the independent petty commodity producing producers.

It simply means *potential purchasing power*. Let us study these incomes more closely.

The incomes of the workers, wages, are usually spent, being quickly exchanged for commodities. The working class cannot go on living without realising its wages in commodities. The incomes of the capitalists, however, are divided into two parts:

(i) a part which is *consumed unproductively*, being usually transformed into consumer goods in order to keep the bourgeois class alive, and

(ii) a part which is *saved*, that is, not transformed into consumer goods. This part of bourgeois income is further divided into a part which is *invested* (serving to buy additional means of production, including fresh supplies of raw materials, goods or values, which bring in an income etc.) and a part which is *hoarded*, i.e. kept for a longer or shorter time in the form of money capital.[23]

For all the commodities produced in a given period to be effectively bought, the incomes distributed in the course of this same period must all be effectively spent. If some of the bourgeoisie's income (surplus-value) is hoarded, some of the commodities produced will not immediately find buyers. In the calculation of the national product, as it is normally carried out, the entry "stocks" will become larger for a time. If, however, this process goes on to the point where a crisis of overproduction occurs, the reduction in prices following the slump will reduce the absolute value of this entry, and of the gross product, bringing it down to the level of the value of the raw material, etc., effectively replaced as a result of production.

The above is, of course, only a crude approximation. To find a more exact formula one would have to take a large number of other factors into account. The sale of a commodity does not merely produce income: it also brings in the counter-value of the constant capital used up (sums serving to renew the stock of raw material and depreciate the fixed capital). And this counter-value can for a moment serve as additional purchasing power for commodities which are unrelated to this renewal of constant capital. In this case, the sale of all the commodities currently produced can disguise the reduction of the social capital available in the country concerned.

The stocks of raw material may fluctuate in both directions. If they increase, it has been possible to use part of their counter-value to buy other commodities, which again means that, despite the hoarding of part of the surplus-value, all the commodities produced during this period will have been effectively sold.

Also needing to be taken into account is the movement of prices. If, between the moment when commodities are produced and that when they are sold, prices fall, then the incomes distributed at the time of production will be capable of buying all the commodities produced, even if some of them have been hoarded.

Finally, there is the effect of relations with other countries. A net export of capital has, in principle, the same effect as the hoarding of a part of surplus-value, while a net import of capital, on the other hand, creates an additional demand for the commodities produced in the country. Similarly, a balance of trade surplus reduces, in principle, the amount of commodities available in relation to the incomes created by producing them. A trade balance deficit however, increases the amount of commodities circulating in the country, in relation to the incomes created by national production.

Despite all these qualifications, and many others, the establishment of a comparatively simple relation between national income (distributed during a year) and the value of the commodities produced during this same period makes it possible to determine the primary origin of the cyclical movement of capitalist production and of crises: the separation in time between the *production* of commodities—and the distribution of incomes which it implies—and the *realisation* of their value by their owners. It is as a result of this lack of an automatic coincidence between purchasing power distributed and commodities produced that the problem of realisation of surplus value can arise for the capitalist owners of commodities.

Distribution of income and realisation of commodities

The relation between incomes distributed in the course of production and commodities produced and offered on the market as counter-value to these incomes is further expressed in qualitative terms:

"Most commodities and services are purchased by two classes of users: consumers and business firms . . . Consumers buy goods to satisfy some physical or psychological need. Businessmen buy goods in order to increase the profits of their companies. The second are aptly called investment goods, the first, consumer goods."[24]

We shall retain, from this definition, first of all this division of the mass of commodities into two broad categories: consumer goods, which are "bought in order to satisfy physical or psychological needs", and investment goods (capital goods), bought in order to enable capitalists to increase their profits. Businessmen are also consumers, and as such they buy consumer goods in order to meet their own needs and those of their families. They devote to this purpose the part of surplus value which is not accumulated. The workers, however, are consumers only, they are not purchasers of investment goods, since their wages are usually inadequate to meet all their "physical and psychological" needs. The total of commodities produced and incomes (purchasing power) distributed, thus corresponds to the following diagram:

	Supply		Demand
Consumer goods	$\left\{\vphantom{\begin{array}{c}a\\a\\a\\a\end{array}}\right.$	Wages.	
		Unaccumulated surplus value.	
		Surplus value accumulated in order to hire more workers.	
Investment goods	$\left\{\vphantom{\begin{array}{c}a\\a\end{array}}\right.$	Depreciated constant capital.	
		Accumulated surplus value.	

The dynamics of capitalist production depend essentially on the relations of equilibrium (or disequilibrium) between these different categories.

The value of the consumer goods offered on the market—produced during a certain period of time, say a year—can be broken down into its constituent elements: $c + v + s$. The income created by the production (and sale) of these commodities is obviously inadequate to create the purchasing power needed to constitute their counter-value.

In fact, only the wages (v) of the workers who have participated in producing them, and the part of the profits not accumulated in c (s minus s in c) represent purchasing power relevant to consumer goods. The *conserved* value comprised in the value of these consumer goods, along with the part of surplus value accumulated in constant capital, represent purchasing power for capital goods (machinery, raw materials, etc.). If, in the course of a given year, all production consisted of consumer goods, there would be an inevitable disequilibrium, a supply of consumer goods equal to $c + v + s$, but a demand equal only to $v + $ (s minus s accumulated in c). The *phenomenon of overproduction*, that is, of a quantity of commodities not finding on the market any counter-value in purchasing-power to realise their value, and thus remaining unsaleable or having to be sold off at a loss, would make its appearance.

Alongside consumer goods, however, capital goods are also produced in the course of each year. *And the production of capital goods gives rise to purchasing power for consumer goods.* The workers who work in factories where machines are made receive wages with which they buy, not machines, but consumer goods. The capitalists who own these factories likewise devote part of their surplus value to buying consumer goods. It is thus the total purchasing power created by the production of the two categories of commodities that must be studied in order to determine whether or not there is overproduction of consumer goods.

Furthermore, we have already seen that the production of consumer goods, in its turn, gives rise to purchasing power for capital goods, needed to replace the constant capital used up in production and perhaps to make possible the purchase of additional constant capital with the aid of the accumulated part of surplus value.

If we represent the value of capital goods by $Ic + Iv + Is$ and that of the consumer goods by $IIc + IIv + IIs$, we can thus reconstruct as follows the overall diagram of supply and demand on the capitalist market.

Supply	*Demand*
Consumer goods: $IIc + IIv + IIs$	$Iv + I$ (s minus s accumulated in c): demand for consumer goods on the part of workers and capitalists in the capital goods sector. $IIv + II$ (s minus s accumulated in c): demand for consumer goods on the part of the workers and capitalists in the consumer goods sector.
Capital goods: $Ic + Iv + Is$	$Ic + Is$ accumulated in c: demand for capital goods on the part of the capitalists working in this sector. $IIc + IIs$ accumulated in c: demand for capital goods by the capitalists working in the other sector.

For the system to be in equilibrium, both equations must be effective, supply and demand must balance for the two categories of commodity:

$$Ic + Iv + Is = Ic + Is \text{ acc. in } c + IIc + IIs \text{ acc. in } c.$$
$$IIc + IIv + IIs = Iv + I (s \text{ minus } s \text{ acc. in } c) + IIv + II (s - s \text{ acc. in } c).$$

By eliminating in the two equations the terms common to both sides we twice obtain *the same equation, the conditions for general equilibrium of capitalist production:*

$$Iv + I (s \text{ minus } s \text{ acc. in } c) = IIc + IIs \text{ acc. in } c.$$

This equation of equilibrium of the capitalist market does not represent a fiction. $Iv + I$ (s minus s acc. in c), i.e. the wages paid and the part of surplus value not accumulated in constant capital in the capital goods sector, *is the total demand for consumer goods created by the production of capital goods.* $IIc + IIs$ acc. in c, i.e. the constant capital to be replaced and the constant capital to be accumulated in the sector of consumer goods, is the *total demand for capital goods created by the production of consumer goods.* The equation between these two magnitudes, as the equation of equilibrium of the capitalist market, signifies simply this: *capitalist economy is in equilibrium when the production of capital goods gives rise to a demand for consumer goods equal to the demand for capital goods to which the production of consumer goods gives rise.* Or, in other words, the capitalist market is in equilibrium when reciprocal supply and demand is equal as between the two sectors of capitalist production.

Production and reproduction

The equation of equilibrium establishes a relation between the value of the commodities produced and the purchasing power which serves as counter-value to these commodities from a *static* point of view, in the setting of a specific, well-defined period. But the reality of capitalist production is that of a process which unfolds in time, one cycle of production succeeding another. The question of the *continuity* of capitalist production presents problems of both a social and an economic character which can be called problems of reproduction.

For capitalist production to be continuous in time, it must reproduce, first and foremost, the fundamental conditions of the capitalist mode of production: the monopoly of the means of production (of capital) in the hands of one class of society; and the existence of another social class which is obliged to sell its labour-power in order to get the money it needs to acquire the means of life. It is thus necessary, first, that wages be "obviously determined and distributed so as to enable those who receive them merely to keep themselves alive, so as to be able to go on working in the service of whoever pays them and keeps them alive for his own personal and exclusive profit, but not so as to enrich them to the extent that they may gradually free themselves from their former masters, attain equality with them and enter into competition with them."[25]

St. Thomas Aquinas had already described the condition of the wage-earners as that of persons unable to accumulate any wealth: "Because they are poor they become wage-earners, and because they are wage-earners they are poor."[26]

Statistics of savings show quite plainly that the overwhelming majority of the working population of the capitalist countries consume in the course of their lives everything that they have earned, and thus cannot accumulate any capital. Their savings are only *deferred consumption*, in the literal meaning of the term: their "accumulations" relate only to consumer durables—or, at most, to houses.

Thus, in the period 1946–1950, 62·4 per cent of the British population possessed only 3 per cent [!] of British capital, or a "capital" per head of some £44.[27] In Belgium, during the same period, 27·5 per cent of the families possessed only 2·2 per cent of the privately owned *wealth* (less than 50,000 francs per family) and 48·8 per cent of the families possessed 20 per cent of it (less than 250,000 francs per family, or the value of a small working-class house). In the United States, in 1935–36, 90 [!] per cent of the households possessed only 19 per cent of the savings; in 1947–48 90 per cent of the households still had only 22·5 per cent of the savings. It should be stressed that, in these same years, 40 to 50 per cent of households had no savings at all! [28]

It is further necessary that the sale of the commodities produced should enable the capitalists to reconstitute the capital they have expended in production, and to acquire newly-produced means of production. The analysis of the capitalist mode of production has shown us that it fulfils these two conditions.

This was not so in the societies which preceded capitalism. Herkovits relates the following about the Chuckchee tribe, who live as reindeer-herdsmen in the north-east of Siberia:

"Some Chuckchee families are so poor . . . that they own almost no herds at all, and such people enter the service of the more wealthy for extended periods. For the hard work they do, they receive supplies of meat and skins, though they must furnish their own pack-animals, when they move from one camp to another. A family working under this arrangement receive about ten fawns annually in addition to the subsistence return mentioned, if their employer is pleased with their work. In the course of five favourable years these animals and their increase give such a family a herd of some hundred reindeer, sufficient to permit them to attain independence."[29]

Similarly, the journeymen of the Middle Ages normally became master-craftsmen, or could at least nurse a legitimate hope of becoming such. Capitalist society is, on the contrary, characterised by this special feature that it constantly reproduces a proletarian class.

The continuity of capitalist production further demands a certain qualitative breakdown of the commodities produced. For it to exist, the capital used up in production must, in the course of a series of production cycles, at least be reconstituted. It is necessary therefore that it be possible at least to reproduce the machinery and raw material used up in the course of successive production processes and to produce at least sufficient consumer goods to reconstitute the labour-power needed.

We know that every society is in the last analysis based on an economy of labour-time. A certain proportion of the social labour-time totally available has to be devoted to the maintenance, repair and reproduction of the instruments of labour and to the upkeep of the fields and buildings, or otherwise, after a certain time, production can no longer be resumed on the same scale as before: society will be impoverished in the absolute sense of the word.

What in societies which produce use-values is a simple problem of allocating the social labour-time totally available is complicated in capitalist society by the fact that it is a mode of producing *commodities*. For the continuity of capitalist production to be guaranteed, it is necessary that during a series of production cycles:

1. The capital goods needed to replace those used up in the course of production, and the consumer goods needed to reconstitute labour-power, be materially produced;

2. Purchasing power capable of realising the value of these capital goods and consumer goods be created and actually spent; and

3. This purchasing power be distributed in such a way that supply and demand balance as regards both capital goods and consumer goods.

The study of the economic problems of reproduction in capitalist society is essentially the study of the questions raised by these three conditions, without which the continuity of capitalist production is broken.

Simple reproduction

Simple reproduction appears as a succession of production cycles which makes possible the *maintenance* of social wealth but not its increase. In a society which produces use values, simple reproduction means that the annual amount of products is sufficient to support a stable population and to replace the instruments of labour used up during this year. In a society which produces commodities, simple reproduction means that the value of the annual product (gross national product) suffices exactly to reproduce labour-power, the instruments of labour and the stock of raw material used up during the year, and to support the possessing classes. In a capitalist society simple reproduction means that the annual surplus value is wholly consumed unproductively by the bourgeois class and that there is no accumulation of capital.*

While the pre-capitalist modes of production passed through long periods of simple reproduction, they mostly ended by attaining at a certain moment in their evolution a stage of *expanded reproduction*, that is, a certain development of the instruments of labour, a certain accumulation of social wealth in the form of stocks of products and above all of stocks of additional tools. The mere accumulation of food reserves was already a primitive form of expanded reproduction.

As for the capitalist mode of production, it is distinguished from all previous modes of production precisely by the fact that it is not unproductive consumption but productive consumption, the capitalisation of the social surplus product, that represents the driving force of action and exploitation on the part of the possessing classes. In this case, expanded reproduction is the normal form of reproduction under

---

* Since she starts from the assumption that the capitalists use no part of their profits for their own unproductive consumption, Joan Robinson has described simple reproduction in its state of bliss, when "all labour is . . . employed on producing consumption goods and maintaining capital . . ."[30]

the capitalist régime, simple reproduction being possible only at exceptional moments in the capitalist production cycle.

How will the three conditions for the continuity of capitalist production present themselves in the setting of simple reproduction? Let us assume, for instance, that the total value of the annual production of all the commodities is 9,000 (millions of currency units). For continuity of production to be ensured, one part of these commodities must represent capital goods—machinery, raw materials, industrial buildings, auxiliary products, power, etc.—and the other must represent consumer goods. Let us suppose that, in value, two-thirds of production, or 6,000, represent capital goods, while the remaining third, or 3,000, represent consumer goods. Annual social production can then be defined as follows, assuming the rate of surplus value and the rate of profit to be the same in the two broad sectors of production:

$$\text{I}: \ 4,000 \ c + 1,000 \ v + 1,000 \ s = 6,000 \text{ capital goods}$$
$$\text{II}: \ 2,000 \ c + 500 \ v + 500 \ s = 3,000 \text{ consumer goods.}$$

In the course of production, capital goods to a total value of 6,000 have been used up (4,000 in the sector I and 2,000 in sector II). These goods can be replaced, since in the same period capital goods to the value of 6,000 have been produced. The social labour power needed requires consumer goods to the value of 1,500 in order to reconstitute itself. This can be done, because consumer goods to the value of 3,000 have been produced.

The sale of all the commodities brings the capitalists 9,000. Of this 9,000, 6,000 is needed to reconstitute constant capital (capital goods) and 1,500 to reconstitute variable capital (money capital with which labour power will be bought in the following year). The remaining 1,500 represents profit, the year's surplus-value. As, by definition, surplus value is wholly consumed unproductively in a case of simple reproduction, this 1,500 will be used to buy consumer goods. These consumer goods will actually be available, since they have been produced to the value of 3,000, and 1,500 have sufficed to reproduce the labour-power used up during the year.

Finally, supply and demand balance in the two sectors, since we have:

CAPITAL GOODS

Supply: 6,000, total production.   *Demand:* $\begin{cases} 4,000 \text{ capitalists I} \\ 2,000 \text{ capitalists II} \end{cases}$

CONSUMER GOODS

Supply: 3,000, total production.   *Demand:* $\begin{cases} 1,000 \text{ workers I} \\ 500 \text{ workers II} \\ 1,000 \text{ capitalists I} \\ 500 \text{ capitalists II} \end{cases}$

The purchasing power created by production has been distributed in such a way as to make possible the purchasing of all the commodities produced. These have thus vanished from the market, and we begin a new annual production cycle with a constant capital of 4,000 in sector I and 2,000 in sector II; money-capital, available as variable capital, to the value of 1,000 in sector I and 500 in sector II; a labour force of the same size as at the beginning of the previous cycle, and completely reconstituted. In other words: the new cycle starts from exactly the same level of production as the previous one. Simple reproduction has been achieved.

Expanded reproduction

Expanded reproduction takes the form of a succession of production cycles which makes possible an increase in social wealth. In a society which produces use values, expanded reproduction means that the yearly amount of products is greater than is needed for the support of the whole population and the conservation of the stock of instruments of labour. Social wealth grows in the form of an increased stock of instruments of labour, increased reserves of food, etc. Such an expanded reproduction is the indispensable condition for a more or less sustained increase in population.

In a commodity-producing society, expanded reproduction means that the value of the annual product (gross national product) is greater than the value of the labour-power, the instruments of labour, and the stock of raw material used up during the year, together with the goods needed for the upkeep of the possessing classes.

In a capitalist society, expanded reproduction means that surplus value is divided into two parts: one part consumed unproductively by the capitalists, their families and their hangers-on, and another consumed productively, i.e. accumulated and invested, capitalised in the form of machinery, raw materials, *additional* wages, which make it possible to start a new production cycle with a larger capital—capital of a greater value—than in the previous cycle.

How will the three conditions for the continuity of capitalist production appear in the setting of expanded reproduction? In the case of simple reproduction, the value of all the capital goods produced in a single cycle must be equal to the value of the constant capital used up in the course of this production cycle. In the case of expanded reproduction this will not do, for the capital goods needed to start the next cycle with an increased constant capital will be lacking. The first condition for expanded reproduction is thus the production of an *additional amount* of capital goods, over and above what have been used up in the previous production cycle (an additional amount does not mean a *larger number* but a higher *value*). The equivalent of this additional amount of capital goods is precisely the part of surplus value destined to be accumulated as additional constant capital.

Similarly, the production of an additional amount of consumer goods, over and above those bought during the previous cycle by the workers and the capitalists, is necessary, since these consumer goods are to provide the counter-value of the additional variable capital (wages) which part of the accumulated surplus value represents, and which is destined to purchase an additional quantity of labour power.

Let us assume that the total gross product of a year has a value of 11,400 (million currency units), divided between 7,000 worth of capital goods and 4,400 worth of consumer goods. The value of the gross product may, let us imagine, be analysed like this, if we assume an equal rate of surplus value in the two sectors but a higher rate of profit in sector II, where the organic composition of capital is lower:

$$\text{1st cycle} \left\{ \begin{array}{l} \text{1: } 4,000\ c + 1,500\ v + 1,500\ s = 7,000 \\ \quad \text{capital goods} \\ \text{II: } 2,000\ c + 1,200\ v + 1,200\ s = 4,400 \\ \quad \text{consumer goods} \end{array} \right\} \quad 11,400$$

Let us assume, again, that the capitalists in sector I allocate their surplus-value like this: 500 consumed unproductively and 1,000 accumulated, of which 700 as constant capital and 300 as variable capital. As for the capitalists in sector II, they allocate their surplus-value, let us suppose, like this: 700 consumed unproductively, 500 accumulated, of which 300 as constant capital and 200 as variable capital.

During the previous production cycle 6,000 had been used up as constant capital in the two sectors together. Total production of capital goods exceeds this 6,000—it amounts to 7,000. The 1,000 additional capital goods enable the capitalists of sector I to accumulate constant capital to the value of 70 and the capitalists in sector II to do the same to the value of 300. During the same previous cycle 3,900 consumer goods had been used up (2,700 for the workers in both sectors, 500 for the capitalists of sector I, and 700 for the capitalists of sector II). But the production of consumer goods attains a value of 4,400. These 500 extra consumer goods will enable the extra workers hired under expanded reproduction to find the counter-value of their wages, the surplus value accumulated as variable capital, namely, 300 in sector I and 200 in sector II.

Thus, both the commodities and the purchasing power needed for expanded reproduction have been supplied by the previous cycle. The continuity of production is assured because the allocation of this purchasing power makes it possible to balance supply and demand in the two sectors:

CAPITAL GOODS

Supply: 7,000, total production.

Demand: $\begin{cases} 4{,}000\text{, capitalists I: reconstitution of } c. \\ 2{,}000\text{, capitalists II: reconstitution of } c. \\ 700\text{, capitalists I: accumulation of } c. \\ 300\text{, capitalists II: accumulation of } c. \end{cases}$

CONSUMER GOODS

Supply: 4,400, total production.

Demand: $\begin{cases} 1{,}500\text{, workers I.} \\ 1{,}200\text{, workers II.} \\ 500\text{, capitalists I.} \\ 700\text{, capitalists II.} \\ 300\text{, counter-value of accumulation of } v \text{ by} \\ \quad\text{capitalists I.} \\ 200\text{, counter-value of accumulation of } v \text{ by} \\ \quad\text{capitalists II.} \end{cases}$

The new production cycle will thus begin with the following capital:

$$\text{I: } (4{,}000 + 700)\ c + (1{,}500 + 300)\ v.$$
$$\text{II: } (2{,}000 + 300)\ c + (1{,}200 + 200)\ v.$$

Still assuming a rate of surplus value stable at 100 per cent, production in this second cycle of enlarged reproduction will have the following value:

2nd cycle $\left\{\begin{array}{l} \text{I: } 4{,}700\ c + 1{,}800\ v + 1{,}800\ s = 8{,}300 \\ \quad \text{capital goods} \\ \text{II: } 2{,}300\ c + 1{,}400\ v + 1{,}400\ s = 5{,}100 \\ \quad \text{consumer goods} \end{array}\right\}$ 13,400

Assuming that the surplus-value of capitalists I is allocated like this: 600 consumed unproductively and 1,200 accumulated, of which 800 as c and 400 as v; that the surplus value of capitalists II is allocated like this: 700 consumed unproductively and 700 accumulated, of which 500 as c and 20 as v, we can, as indicated above, deduce a third cycle of expanded reproduction, production in which will have the following value:

3rd cycle $\left\{\begin{array}{l} \text{I: } 5{,}500\ c + 2{,}200\ v + 2{,}200\ s = 9{,}900 \\ \text{II: } 2{,}800\ c + 1{,}600\ v + 1{,}600\ s = 6{,}000 \\ \quad \text{consumer goods} \end{array}\right\}$ 15,900

and so forth . . .

It will be seen that expanded reproduction is expressed in the increase, between one cycle and the next, in the total value of the commodities in each sector, as also in the increase of surplus-value in each sector. Under simple reproduction these values remain stable from one cycle to another.

Expanded reproduction and the laws of development of capitalism

In the diagrams of expanded reproduction set out above, each sector realised the whole of the surplus-value produced by the workers in that sector. This is in contradiction to the actual development of the capitalist mode of production, in which an equalisation of the rate of profit occurs whereby the sectors with a higher organic composition of capital—sector I—annex a share of the surplus value produced by the workers of the other sectors. The diagram can easily be corrected, however, by calculating the average rate of profit on the whole of capital, then transforming the value of commodities I and II into their prices of production.* In this way the following succession of cycles of expanded reproduction would be obtained:

1st cycle

I: $4,000 c + 1,500 v + 1,705$ profit $= 7,205$ capital goods
II: $2,000 c + 1,200 v + 995$ profit $= 4,195$ consumer goods $\Big\}$ 11,400

2nd cycle

I: $4,905 c + 1,800 v + 2,060$ profit $= 8,765$ capital goods
II: $2,300 c + 1,400 v + 1,140$ profit $= 4,840$ consumer goods $\Big\}$ 13,605

3rd cycle

I: $6,005 c + 2,160 v + 2,450$ profit $= 10,615$ capital goods
II: $2,760 c + 1,600 v + 1,310$ profit $= 5,670$ consumer goods $\Big\}$ 16,285

etc.

At the same time we also observe in these diagrams the tendency of the rate of profit to fall, with 31 per cent in the first cycle, 30·75 per cent in the second and 30 per cent in the third.†

---

* In the first cycle, $1,500 s + 1,200 s$ give a total surplus value of 2,700, or 31 per cent of profit on a total capital of 8,700. The price of production of I and II is calculated by adding 31 per cent of profit to the respective capitals. In the second cycle, $1,800 s + 1,400 s$ give a total surplus value of 3,200, or 30·75 per cent profit on a total capital of 10,405. In the third cycle, $2,160 s + 1,600 s$ give a total surplus value of 3,760 on a total capital of 12,525, or 30 per cent profit. We assume an unproductive consumption of profit of 500 in I and 495 in II during the first cycle, and of 600 in I and 480 in II during the second.

† Some writers[31] declare that calculation carried out in this way must inevitably lead to mistakes and contradictions because the value of c and v in each cycle is not itself transformed into price of production. This view is unfounded. The price of production of c results from the equalisation of the rate of profit *during the previous cycle*. It is a constant because, independently of the gains or losses of a capitalist in competition with others, he has paid (or owes) a *previously determined price* for the machines, raw material, etc., he has bought. As for the transformation of values into prices of production, as applied to the diagrams of simple reproduction, this is indeed incorrect, but not for the reason alleged by the writers mentioned above. This transformation results from *capitalist competition*, which is just what is missing in the

Nevertheless, one must be careful not to ascribe to these formulae a significance they do not possess. By arbitrarily choosing one's starting figures, or the initial relations between the different terms in the formula, one may succeed in "discovering" laws of capitalist reproduction, including its "inevitable collapse" (as the Marxist economist Henryk Grossman has done), after a certain number of cycles. This is a perfectly useless and sterile game.

In reality, reproduction formulae merely indicate the conditions of continuity of *capitalist production as a whole,* leaving aside all the *concrete conditions* under which the capitalist mode of production progresses: birth in a non-capitalist setting; transfers of capital from one sector to another; role played by credit; fluctuation of money prices, etc. In so far as capitalist production is production for the market, a production of commodities and not a conscious allocation of society's resources between different branches of production, it is these *concrete conditions* in which the capitalist mode of production operates that determine both the laws of development of capital—without the whip of competition, for instance, the increase in the organic composition of capital and the tendency of the rate of profit to fall which is implicit in it would be inexplicable—and the cyclical form taken by economic life under capitalism.

The reproduction formulae which leave out all these concrete conditions therefore cannot and should not be expected to "reveal" these laws of development, or the causes of this cyclical movement. They can at most indicate how, *despite* the operation of thousands of individual capitalists fiercely competing one with another and thereby determining the actual progress of the capitalist mode of production, the continuity of production is maintained *in the long run,* notwithstanding frequent periodical interruptions. The usefulness of these formulae is appreciated when one asks this question: how can it happen that the continuity of production is maintained, when the value and the proportions of this production seem to result from individual decisions by thousands of businessmen who hide their intentions from each other? The reproduction formulae show the conditions that must be fulfilled if this continuity is to be safeguarded.

In the real life of capitalism, these conditions of continuity are achieved *through the breaks in continuity. Capitalist economy is seen as a unity of continuity and discontinuity in its economic activities.* "Progress . . . not only proceeds by jerks and rushes but also by one-sided rushes productive of consequences other than those which

diagram of simple reproduction and in an economy based on petty commodity production such as this formula reflects. It is to be observed, incidentally, that these writers confuse price of production and market prices expressed in money terms, since they bring the conditions of the gold-producing industry into their argument.

would ensue in the case of co-ordinated rushes . . . The history of capitalism is studded with violent bursts and catastrophes . . . Evolution is a disturbance of existing structures and more like a series of explosions than a gentle, though incessant transformation."[32]

In this sense, the formulae represent, so to speak, *averages* over a *decade* or over a cycle, reciprocal proportions between the different elements in capitalist production. They imply precisely the *elimination* from the abstract formula of all the factors which determine the cyclical progress of production. They cannot therefore explain concretely either capitalist expansion or the reason why crises break out.

Expanded reproduction, economic growth and social accounting

The analysis of the different conditions of expanded reproduction is at the same time the analysis of the factors which ultimately determine the economic growth of the capitalist mode of production.

In any society, the two conditions which are necessary and sufficient for economic growth are:

(1) that *per capita* production be greater than the necessary product, that is, that the society produce more than it consumes (including in consumption the wearing out of its instruments of labour);

(2) that this net surplus assume, at least in part, the form of extra instruments of labour, that is, that it be consumed productively. A borderline case is that in which this net surplus is used to support a larger number of *producers*, and in which it makes possible, thanks to better feeding of these producers, an immediate increase in their output. In this case, however, one merely puts off for a stage the need to see a net product of additional instruments of labour appear as a necessary condition for economic growth.

In capitalist society, these two conditions appear precisely as the conditions for expanded reproduction:

1. There is a surplus value which is not wholly consumed by the capitalists.

2. Its unconsumed residue is partly invested in fresh constant capital.

Generally speaking, three proportions are thus fundamental in determining the rate of growth of a capitalist society:

(a) The absolute amount of profit (s) and its ratio to the gross national product;

(b) The absolute amount of profit not consumed unproductively (s minus s cons.) and its ratio to the gross national product (and the total quantity of surplus value);

(c) The absolute amount of these accumulated profits which is invested in capital goods (s minus s cons. minus s acc. in v minus s hoarded) and its ratio to the gross national product and to the total quantity of surplus value.

Because these three proportions are intertwined, it is not possible to isolate a single one of them in order to determine the source of the relative slowness (or the speed) of economic growth.

Thus, a country may have a very low rate of productive investment not because the amount (or the rate) of profit or of surplus value is low, but because a very high proportion of this surplus value is consumed unproductively or accumulated in ways other than productive investment (for instance, speculation in land, hoarding of precious metals, export of capital for non-productive purposes, etc.). This is particularly the case in a number of under-developed countries.*

It would similarly be quite wrong to assume that a considerable rise in real wages, bringing about a fall in the rate of profit, must automatically slow down economic growth. This hypothesis is correct only if, during the previous phase, nearly all the surplus value was invested productively. Given any other conditions, such a rise in wages may, on the contrary, stimulate economic growth, by compelling the possessing classes to reduce their unproductive consumption and their accumulation outside productive spheres, so as to neutralise the monetary fall in the rate of surplus value by an increase in relative surplus value (an increase in the productivity of labour).

Calculations of the national accounts which are based on the hybrid, and purely descriptive, criteria of the theory of income cannot enable us to distinguish the *potential sources of accumulation of productive capital*, or in other words the total amount of surplus value or of social surplus product. They do not distinguish between the productive consumption of workers' households, the unproductive consumption of the possessing classes, the easily reducible consumption of luxuries, and pure waste. In the same way the building of houses for the people, which corresponds to a pressing need, is included in the same entry with the building of luxurious banking and office premises which are often ways of evading taxation and not "productive investments" in any sense. In the category of public investments, productive investments are mixed up with the purchase of military equipment, a typical form of unproductive expenditure!

It is thus urgent to modify the way of calculating the national accounts, in accordance with the social structure, so that abstract (or purely monetary) concepts of saving may be replaced by the concept of total surplus value and of the available potential accumulation fund.†

In the foregoing we have assumed that the existing enterprises and labour force were already fully employed. This assumption does not correspond to a permanent reality. Consequently, economic growth

* See Chapter 13.

† In Chapter 16 we endeavour to show that the *maximum* rate of accumulation *never gives* the highest rate of growth, is never the *optimum* rate.

may result not only from an additional creation of means of production, but from a better (more rational, uninterrupted, etc.) use of those which already exist. It is not so much the increase in productive investment as the better use of the existing productive forces (human and mechanical) that matters in this case. Nevertheless, though such a possibility is very important in the short run (especially in crises!) it constitutes only an intermediate phase in longer term views. As soon as full employment of the existing means of production has been attained, economic growth is again identified with their expansion.

Contracted reproduction

Contracted reproduction occurs as a succession of production cycles which no longer allow social wealth to maintain itself but instead cause it to shrink. In a society producing use-values, contracted reproduction means that the annual amount produced is not sufficient to support the whole population or to maintain the existing stock of tools of labour, or both. In a commodity-producing society, contracted reproduction means that the value of the gross annual product is less than the total amount received in payment by the working classes, the value of the instruments of labour and raw materials used up in the course of production, and the value of the commodities serving to support the ruling classes. In capitalist society contracted reproduction means that for various reasons the capitalists are unable to renew the constant capital used up and that the wages paid out do not enable the producers completely to reconstitute their labour-power.

In pre-capitalist societies, contracted reproduction might result from two different combinations of circumstances. First, a *sudden decline in production*, owing to natural or social calamities, drought, floods, earthquakes, invasions, epidemics, wars, civil wars, etc.

Let us suppose that the total needs of an agricultural community amount to 1,000 tons of wheat a year, of which 750 are for consumption and 250 for seed and for use in exchange for other articles of prime necessity. If during several consecutive years the harvest declines to 500 tons and no external help is received, there will be contracted reproduction all along the line. The amount of seed will be inadequate; some of the land will remain uncultivated; part of the population will perish; the number of producers (the labour force) will shrink. Even when a good harvest does come, a smaller number of producers working on a smaller sown area will produce less wheat than before.

Contracted reproduction could also result from a *change in the distribution of available social resources*. For production to ensure the continuity of economic life at a certain level, it must in fact produce use values which are such as to *reconstitute the material elements of production*: labour power and instruments of labour. However, it is possible to use these elements *for purpses which are sterile as far as reproduction is concerned,* i.e. for producing goods which do not make possible renewal either of the labour force or of the instruments of labour used up during the given period of production. In this case there will inevitably be contracted reproduction, since part of the productive resources used will not have been reconstituted and work will therefore be continuing with smaller resources.

Thus, during the reign of the Mongol emperors in China, says the historian Eberhard, a large number of poor peasants subject to labour service were concentrated for the purpose of building luxurious imperial establishments.[33] These peasants were obliged to abandon their fields while they were carrying out this work; these fields therefore remained uncultivated. A series of cycles of contracted reproduction was thus started, the distribution of the labour-power totally available to society having been carried out in such a way that production in the basic sector, that of agriculture, had to be contracted.

In the capitalist mode of production we encounter both of these forms of contracted reproduction. First, that which is caused by a sudden fall in production, by an economic crisis. Contrary to what happened in pre-capitalist society, it is not the decline in the *amount* produced but in its *value* that brings about the break in continuity, the economic crisis. But the cumulative effect of the shrinking of economic life remains no less characteristic in the case of capitalist economic crises. A fall in the value of production leads to the closing of factories and dismissing of workers. This then causes a sudden fall in the total purchasing power, which further accentuates the piling up of unsold goods, the fall in prices and the closing of businesses. From one month to the next—and during prolonged crises, from one year to the next—less and less is produced, with less capital and fewer workers; the basis of production shrinks.

Similarly, capitalism can experience contracted reproduction due to a change in the distribution of available productive resources. If part of constant capital and labour power is used to produce commodities the use value of which does not make possible either the reconstitution of this constant capital or the reconstitution of this labour-power, at the end of a certain time contracted reproduction will prevail, that is, production carried on with a reduced amount of constant capital and labour-power.

War economy

War economy is the typical example of contracted reproduction under capitalism. War economy implies that part of the productive resources of constant capital and labour-power are devoted to the making of *means of destruction*, the use-value of which does not make possible either the reconstruction of machinery, or of stocks of raw material, or of the labour force, but tends, on the contrary, to bring about the destruction of these resources. For this reason, war economy can reach a point at which either the maintenance (depreciation from the financial standpoint, replacement from the physical) of the constant capital is no longer guaranteed,* or the labour force is not completely reconstituted, because consumption by the workers falls to too low a level, and the productivity of labour declines, to which may be further added the effect of an absolute reduction in the number of workers.

Thus, the British national income during the last war assumed this form, compared with peacetime (in millions of £):

	1938	1943
	(figures in 1938 pounds)	
Government expenditure	837	3,840
Private consumption	4,138	3,270
Private investment at home	305	−95
Foreign investment	−55	−485[35]
National income:	5,225	6,530

It will be seen that a war economy can be accompanied by an *increase* in real national income and the value of the gross national product, as it is at present calculated: ". . . an increase in any one type of product must be accompanied either by a decrease in other kinds of product or an increase in total production. If the goods and services that government uses in time of war are counted as a final product, as is the custom in current computations, the record might be expected to show some increase in total output, but also a decrease in non-war products, during the war period."[36]

The production of tanks, aircraft and shells, sold by the capitalists engaged in the sector of means of destruction, is a production of commodities the value of which is realised on the market. But as these commodities do not enter into the process of *reproduction*, this increase in national income is accompanied by an absolute reduction in the amount of existing constant capital and a very big reduction in the productivity of labour.

The British example during the last war was, moreover, a relatively benign one. In Japan, the textile industry had, in the same world war,

* This point of *contracted reproduction* was actually reached in the United States during the Second World War. The production of new fixed capital (durable equipment) declined from 7·3 billion dollars in 1929 and 6·9 billion in 1940 to 5·1 billion in 1942, 3·1 million in 1943 and 4 billion in 1944, while the annual wearing-out of existing fixed capital was estimated at 8 billion dollars during the same period. The net formation of new capital declined to less than 1 per cent of the national income in 1943. During the same period, war expenditure absorbed in 1942 32 per cent, in 1943 43 per cent and in 1944 43 per cent of the gross national product of the United States.[34]

to transform into scrap-iron two-thirds of all the cotton spindles.[37] The fixed capital of sector II became circulating capital for sector I. In Germany and elsewhere the average productivity of labour fell to a point at which it was again possible to use forced labour on a large scale.

This contracted reproduction can be presented diagramatically by introducing a third sector into a reproduction formula, that of destruction goods:

1st cycle

$$\left. \begin{array}{l} \text{I:} \quad 4,000\,c + 1,500\,v + 1,500\,s = 7,000 \text{ capital goods} \\ \text{II:} \quad 2,000\,c + 1,200\,v + 1,200\,s = 4,400 \text{ consumer goods} \end{array} \right\} \quad 11,400$$

2nd cycle

$$\left. \begin{array}{l} \text{I:} \quad 4,000\,c + 1,500\,v + 1,500\,s = 7,000 \text{ capital goods} \\ \text{II:} \quad 2,000\,c + 1,200\,v + 1,200\,s = 4,400 \text{ consumer goods} \\ \text{III:} \quad 1,000\,c + 500\,v + 500\,s = 2,000 \text{ destruction goods} \end{array} \right\} \quad 13,400$$

3rd cycle

$$\left. \begin{array}{l} \text{I:} \quad 3,900\,c + 1,200\,v + 1,100\,s = 6,200 \text{ capital goods} \\ \text{II:} \quad 1,800\,c + 900\,v + 800\,s = 3,500 \text{ consumer goods} \\ \text{III:} \quad 1,300\,c + 600\,v + 500\,s = 2,400 \text{ destruction goods} \end{array} \right\} \quad 12,100$$

This diagram is based on the assumption that, after the first cycle, the capitalists of categories I and II invest all their surplus value in the arms industry. As a result, production in these two sectors does not increase in the second cycle. It would, of course, be possible to introduce several intermediate cycles during which a decreasing fraction of the accumulated surplus value would continue to be invested in sectors I and II.

The 7,000 capital goods produced during the second cycle are to be divided in the third cycle between categories I, II and III, which means a reduction in the capital goods available for sectors I and II, where the phenomenon of contracted reproduction starts to appear. Part of the surplus value of capitalists I and II can no longer be invested in these sectors, for lack of any counter-value on the market; it is transformed into means of financing the third sector, or else is hoarded (forced loan, company reserves, etc.). The value of the consumer goods available to the workers similarly contracts, which causes a fall in output and a shrinkage in the rate of surplus value.*

---

* During the Second World War the U.S.A. reached approximately this second cycle of contracted reproduction, at least so far as stagnation of the sector of capital goods was concerned. Towards the end of the war, Great Britain, Germany and, still more, Japan, experienced the third cycle, with reduction of production in I and II. Professor Jacquemyns was able to analyse the state of health of some 500 Belgian miners and metal-workers in May— June 1941, after a year of rationing which had reduced by 25 per cent the normal consumption of bread, by 60 per cent that of fats, meat and potatoes,

The contracted reproduction of consumer goods and of certain capital goods, under the influence of the production of destruction goods, in the setting of a war economy, is revealed very clearly in the following table: [89]

Value of the production of the different branches of industry in percentage of the value of Germany's total industrial production

	1936	1939	1944
Raw material industries;	34·4	31·4	33·3
of which, coal and other mines	7·5	7·4	6·3
Industries producing capital goods;	39·5	34·9	41·4
of which, metal-work, incl. production of destruction goods	15·3	21·8	25·5
Consumer goods industries;	30·5	27·6	19·0
of which, textiles	7·5	5·0	3·7
of which, foodstuffs	11·4	11·9	7·0

Redistribution of the national income by the State

The rise of the labour movement and the increasing popular antipathy to the inequality of income characteristic of modern capitalism have led to defensive reactions on the part of the possessing classes. Since income tax was introduced in Great Britain, and above all since the New Deal experiences in the U.S.A., many economists have stressed the fact that, through its budget, the State—especially in the Western countries of bourgeois democracy—redistributes a large proportion of the national income at the expense of the possessing classes and for the benefit of the working classes.

Progressive income tax and death duties, they say, reduce the inequality of incomes and wealth. The services which the State places freely at the disposal of all its citizens—compulsory education, upkeep of roads, public health, with free medicine in Great Britain, etc.—are above all advantageous to the poorest classes of the population, and tend to equalise citizens' incomes still further. The evolution of present-day capitalism is said to be not towards a concentration but, on the contrary, a dispersion, an ever-greater levelling of incomes.

So far as wealth and property are concerned, especially the ownership of industry and property in capitalists' savings, these allegations are a crude untruth: all the facts we have point to an increasing concentration of this ownership.* But as regards income it is usually accepted that the action of the public authorities has served effectively to reduce the inequality of income. Is this really so, and, if it is, what

and by 75 per cent that of eggs and fish. The result was a loss of weight of at least 4 kilogrammes—and in some cases as much as 15 kilogrammes—below the normal in the case of 64 per cent of the workers, leading to decline in arterial tension, permanent fatigue and a rapid falling-off in output.[38]

* See Chapter 7, section dealing with the "scattering" of shares, and Chapter 12.

place must be given to this phenomenon in the recent evolution of the capitalist mode of production?

The State's income, as we have already said, normally comes from two different sources—direct taxes on income, and indirect taxes, increasing the selling prices of goods (the issue of paper money by the State having the same effect as indirect taxation). If progressive income taxation hits the well-to-do classes harder than the poorer ones, this is not at all true of indirect taxes.

"In general, taxation of consumption will fall more heavily upon the lower income brackets than upon the higher, and accordingly it will to a certain extent make up for the income-levelling effects of the taxation of income."[40]

In fact we observe that in France the wage-earners paid in 1949 450·5 milliard francs in indirect taxes, as against 271·5 milliard paid by businessmen and professional men. In Great Britain the total taxation of all kinds paid by the poorest class of taxpayers (those earning less than £500 a year) increased from £499 million in 1937 to £1,791 million in 1949, because indirect taxes increased five-fold in this period. In Denmark, indirect taxes reduced the income of the poorer classes of taxpayers by 11·2 per cent, whereas their incidence on the incomes of the middle classes is only 9·1 per cent.[41]

It is true that in the U.S.A. indirect taxes are responsible for only a small part of public revenue. But in that country it is necessary to take into account the effect of direct taxation on wages and salaries, a factor which is indeed playing an even greater role in other capitalist countries. Actually, in France the wage-earners pay more in direct taxes than the businessmen and professional men! In Belgium the wage-earners, who receive barely 50 per cent of the national income, paid, in 1959, 57·5 per cent of the income tax.[42*]

If we draw up the overall balance-sheet of the taxes paid by the working people and the benefits they receive from social security, etc., we usually reach the conclusion that the redistribution of income in their favour is slight or even non-existent. Thus, for France, Rottier and Albert remark:

"Limiting ourselves . . . to the group of non-agricultural wage and salary earners, we have not been able to obtain precise results on the vertical redistribution of income within this group. However, it is probably not very large . . . [The] relative increase in the share of the social wage has not been accompanied by a growth in the total share of wages and salaries in the national income. There has thus been a marked decrease in the share of this income which a wage or salary earner can spend as he likes."[43]

* In West Germany indirect taxation brought in 27·5 billion DM in 1960, as against 3·8 billion RM in 1928–29 for the entire Weimar Republic. In the same period, wages and salaries increased by 150 per cent only.

And for Great Britain F. Weaver reaches similar conclusions: "A primary feature of the increase in post-war redistribution in the United Kingdom is that it occurs mainly within different income classes on the basis of consumption habits rather than between classes . . . Most of the post-war increase in personal taxes has been levied indirectly on consumption and has fallen on those who smoke and drink or consume non-utility clothing and household goods. The incidence of regressive taxes is mainly on the working class who are also the chief recipients of the benefits of redistributive governmental expenditures. Generally, the low income group pays for its benefits . . ."[44]

It may be objected that this purely monetary calculation does not take into account such free material benefits as the general improvement on the level of health and education, the lengthening of life which has resulted, a certain change in the structure of consumption, an increase in what workers spend on culture and leisure in the industrially advanced countries, etc. This is a pertinent argument.

But, as the Danish economists Lemberg, Ussing and Leuthen observe, the "services" rendered to the workers by the State in this way are to be explained less by a desire to redistribute income than by a desire to "qualify the recipients as fully as possible for productive work."[45] In the same way, the lengthening of the average expectation of life also means the lengthening of the workers' productive life; instead of producing surplus value for 25 years for the capitalists, the worker now produces for 40 or 45 years. In so far as the price of labour power includes a relative element,* namely the average needs determined by the average level of civilisation in a country at a certain epoch, the State, by guaranteeing to the wage-earners certain services which they do not have to purchase with their money wage, *merely guarantees, on behalf of the bourgeoisie as a whole, the payment of an integral part of wages*. The State does not transform surplus value into wages; it merely plays the role of central cashier for the bourgeoisie, *paying part of wages in a collective form, so as to socialise certain needs*.

There are situations in which the redistribution of the national income benefits the working class on a larger scale. But this is not, paradoxically, the case with "social capitalism"; rather does it apply in the case of society's great penances.

When a capitalist country is hit by the cataclysm of a serious economic crisis, or a lost war, the redistribution of the national income does indeed take place in favour of the poorest strata—the unemployed, in the first instance, the victims of war in the second. These sections of the population must be included in the proletariat; they constitute precisely that "Lazarus stratum" of which Karl Marx speaks,

* See Chapter 5.

In Western Germany, where there are millions of cripples and badly wounded war-victims, together with victims of fascist and racial repressions, war veterans and people who are sick as a result of wartime privations, this "Lazarus stratum" receives nearly 10 per cent of the national income, by way of redistribution through the State. It will be agreed, however, that the workers cannot derive much satisfaction from the conclusion that they do not "profit" from the redistribution of national income except in so far as they become unemployed or war-cripples.

It is obvious that what we have here is a measure with political and social aims, a lubrication of the social mechanism intended to avoid an explosion, and not an *economic* evolution which in some way or other contradicts the relative impoverishment of the proletariat.

A study by Simon Kuznets[46] which appeared in 1953 tried to work out in figures the effects of the redistribution of national income in the U.S.A. He came to the conclusion that the net share taken by the rich (after paying direct taxes)—and by the rich he meant the richest one per cent of the taxpayers—of the national income had been reduced to a striking extent, from 14·3 per cent, on the average, in 1919–38 to 7·9 per cent in 1948.

This study suffers, however, from grave methodological weaknesses. In the first place, it is based exclusively on the taxpayers' own declarations, which in the case of self-employed people, and especially of the rich, are notoriously underestimates aimed at dodging taxation.*

It takes account of direct taxation but not of the rise in the cost of living, which is particularly unfavourable to the lower income groups. It employs arbitrary categories ("the one per cent richest taxpayers", "the seven per cent richest taxpayers," etc.) and not *concrete social* categories.

If we re-examine the official statistics, without even taking into account undeclared income, we observe nevertheless that the share of the lower income group has not increased at all, as may be seen from these figures:

	Percentage of households	Percentage of personal family income received
In 1910	50	26·8
In 1918	50	26·6
In 1929	50	22·0
In 1937	50	21·2
In 1944	51·9	24·9
In 1956	51·7	25·2

* Dr. Selma Goldsmith, of the National Bureau of Economic Research, estimates that in the U.S.A. 24 per cent of dividends, 29 per cent of businessmen's income and 63 per cent of interest payments were not declared in 1946.[47]

It is hard to interpret these figures in the sense of an historical improvement on the part of the lower income groups, especially if we note that 51·7 per cent of families quoted for 1956 earned less than 5,000 dollars a year; that the 51·9 per cent of families quoted for 1944 earned less than 3,000 dollars a year; and that between 1944 and 1956 the purchasing power of the dollar fell by 40 per cent, so that the 5,000 dollars of 1956 were exactly equivalent to the 3,000 dollars of 1944.[48]

According to Kuznets, in 1929 the 7 per cent of the taxpayers with the highest incomes received 30·3 per cent of personal income; in 1956 the 10 per cent highest-paid taxpayers received 31 per cent of personal income. The "redistribution" consisted merely of a certain *enlargement of the upper middle classes,* a phenomenon characteristic of every period of boom (and "exaggerated" in these figures owing to tax-dodging). This impression is further reinforced when one observes that the 3·8 per cent of all families who receive more than 15,000 dollars a year received in 1956 altogether 17·3 per cent of family income, whereas in 1929 the same percentage was received by some 2 per cent of the families.* The share of the "rich" has not changed at all; they have merely become somewhat more numerous.†

But if we know that 40 per cent of the taxpayers together receive less than this 3·8 per cent of the population (their share was reduced from 20 per cent in 1916 to some 13 per cent in 1950!) it is impossible to find in these figures any pointer to a reversal of the classical tendencies to concentration of capital and income in the capitalist mode of production.[51]

---

* The German official statistics show that in 1928 88·84 per cent of the taxpayers received 61·1 per cent of the private incomes; in 1950, 86·05 per cent of West German taxpayers received 59·7 per cent of the private incomes. At the other end of the pyramid, in 1928 0·45 per cent of the taxpayers received 11·1 per cent of private incomes; in 1950 1·24 per cent of the taxpayers received 10 per cent of private incomes. In 1928 the share of the 4·3 per cent most prosperous was 24·7 per cent; in 1950 the share of the 4·4 per cent most prosperous was 23 per cent.[49]

† "Despite the laments about high taxes, the number of American families with a net worth of a half-million dollars has doubled since 1945. Most of the very rich manage, one way or another, to hold on to the bulk of their new incomes each year. Meanwhile, corporate lawyers have applied their ingenuity to find non-taxable benefits for key executives. These range from deferred payments in the form of high incomes for declining years and free medical check-ups at mountain spas, to hidden hunting lodges, corporate yachts, payment of country-club dues (according to one survey, three-quarters of all companies sampled did this), and lush expense accounts."[50]

REFERENCES

1. Carl Shoup: *Principles of National Income Analysis*, p. 27.
2. Jean Marchal and Jacques Lecaillon: *La Répartition du revenu national*, Vol. III, pp. 141-53.
3. Carl Shoup: op. cit., p. 85.
4. P. T. Bauer and B. S. Yamey: *The Economics of Underdeveloped Countries*, p. 20.
5. Simon Kuznets: *Government Product and National Income* in *Income and Wealth Series*, Vol. I, pp. 193-4.
6. William H. Whyte, Jnr.: *The Organization Man*, p. 19.
7. F. J. Markovitch: *Le problème des services et le revenu national, Bulletin S.E.D.E.I.S.*, No. 699, 1st June, 1958, pp. 44 et seq.
8. Carl Shoup: op. cit., p. 24.
9. Ibid., p. 85.
10. Simon Kuznets: *Economic Change*, pp. 161-2.
11. Ibid., p. 196.
12. *National Income Statistics, Sources and Methods*, published by the (British) Central Statistical Office, pp. 3, 10, 31-32.
13. Alvin Hansen: *Business Cycles and National Income*, p. 96.
14. *Economic Stabilisation Board of Japan: Economic Survey of Japan 1951–1952*, p. 272.
15. J. Schumpeter: *Business Cycles*, Vol. II., p. 566.
16. W. Woytinsky: *Les conséquences sociales de la crise*, publication of the International Labour Office, pp. 139-40.
17. R. Ruggles: *An Introduction to National Income and Income Analysis*, p. 68.
18. *National Income Statistics, Sources and Methods*, p. 72.
19. Hansen: op. cit., p. 94.
20. Ibid., p. 96.
21. Ibid., p. 96.
22. Ruggles: op. cit., p. 68.
23. Rudolf Eckert: *Les théories modernes de l'expansion économique*, p. 42.
24. M. Abramovitz: *Inventories and Business Cycles*, p. 329.
25. G. Espinas: *Les Origines du capitalisme*, Vol. I, p. 165.
26. Quoted in Pitirim A. Sorokin: *Society, Culture and Personality*, p. 274.
27. A. Carr-Saunders, D. Caradog Jones and C. A. Moser: *A Survey of Social Conditions in England and Wales*, p. 176.
28. Shoup: op. cit., p. 326; Kuznets: *Shares of Upper Income Groups in Income and Savings*, p. 216; Shoup: op. cit., pp. 326-30; *Federal Reserve Board and Michigan Survey Research Centre: 1950, Survey of Consumer Finances*.
29. M. Herskovits: *Economic Life of Primitive Peoples*, p. 93.
30. Joan Robinson: *The Accumulation of Capital*, pp. 82-83.
31. L. Von Bortkiewicz: *Zur Berechtigung der Grundlagen der theoretischen Konstruktion von Marx in 3. Band des Kapitals*, in *Jahrbücher für Nat. Oekonomie und Statistik*, July 1907; Paul Sweezy: *The Theory of Capitalist Development*, pp. 114-28,

32. Schumpeter: op. cit., Vol. I, p. 102.
33. Wolfram Eberhard: *Chinas Geschichte*, p. 264.
34. Shoup: op. cit., pp. 179, 194, 216.
35. *Economist*, 6th May, 1944.
36. Shoup: op. cit., p. 214.
37. F. Barrett: *Evolution du capitalisme japonais*, Vol. III, p. 345.
38. G. Jacquemyns: *La Société belge sous l'occupation allemande 1940–1944*, Vol. I, pp. 123, 132-3, 138.
39. Bruno Gleitze: in *W.W.I. Mitteilungen,* March 1955, p. 55.
40. Leinberg, Ussing and Zeuthen: in *Income Redistribution and Social Policy*, ed. by Alan T. Peacock, p. 69.
41. Ibid., pp. 114, 156-7, 144–5, 81.
42. Rottier and J. F. Albert: in ibid., p. 114; *Rapport au congrès du P.S.B.*, 12-13 December 1959, p. 51.
43. Rottier and J. F. Albert: in *Income Redistribution and Social Policy*, pp. 135-6.
44. F. Weaver: "Taxation and Redistribution in the United Kingdom", in *Review of Economics and Statistics*, August 1950, p. 206.
45. Leinberg: etc., op. cit., p. 63.
46. Kuznets: *Shares of Upper Income Groups . . .*, passim and pp. 36-39.
47. *Studies in Income and Wealth*, published by N.B.E.R., Vol. CXXXII, p. 302, New York 1951.
48. *U.S. Statistical Abstract*, 1958.
49. *W.W.I. Mitteilungen*, October-November 1950.
50. Vance Packard: *The Status Seekers*.
51. Kuznets: *Shares of Upper Income Groups . . .*, p. 216, and *U.S. Statistical Abstract*, 1958.

CHAPTER ELEVEN

PERIODICAL CRISES

Pre-capitalist and capitalist crises
AN economic crisis is an interruption in the normal reproduction
process. The human and material basis of reproduction, the mass of
productive labour power and of instruments of labour effectively
employed is reduced. There follows a decline in both human consumption and productive consumption, that is, a reduction in the
amount of labour both living and dead available for production during
the next cycle. In this way a crisis reproduces itself spirally, the break
in the normal production process causing a shrinkage in the starting-
basis of this process.

In pre-capitalist societies crises took the form of *material destruction* of the elements of reproduction, whether simple or expanded, as
a result of natural or social catastrophes: "Before and even during the
eighteenth century, crops, wars, plagues, and so on were absolutely
and relatively very much more important [than business fluctu-
ations]."[1]

Wars, plagues and other epidemics, floods, draught, earthquakes,
all destroy society's productive forces, the producers and the means
of production. Depopulation and faminine condition one another and
bring about an overall reduction in both current production and social
reserves. As agriculture is the basis of all expanded reproduction, it
is above all a reduction in agricultural production, in the output of
agricultural labour, that lies at the root of pre-capitalist crisis. This
reduction is usually caused by non-economic factors.[2] Causes inherent
in the mode of production—increasing exhaustion of the soil, without
any possibility of extending cultivation to fresh land, and flight of the
producers from increasing exploitation—may, however in certain circumstances take the place of non-economic disasters as causes of
crisis.

Crises occur in a different way in capitalist society. In this society
the material destruction of the elements of production occurs not as
the cause but as the result of crisis. It is not because there are fewer
workers engaged in production that a crisis happens, it is because a
crisis breaks out that there are fewer workers engaged in production.
It is not because hunger reigns in people's homes that the output of
labour declines and crisis breaks out, but the other way round.

Pre-capitalist crisis is a crisis of *under-production of use-values*. It is due to inadequate development of production, or to inadequacy of exchange and of transport facilities. A crisis like this, in a particular province or country, may coincide with normal conditions of reproduction in a neighbouring province or country. A capitalist crisis, however, is a crisis of *overproduction of exchange-values*. It is due to inadequacy not of production or physical capacity to consume, but of *monetarily effective demand*. A relative abundance of commodities finds no equivalent on the market, cannot realise its exchange value, remains unsaleable, and drags its owners down to ruin.

Unlike a pre-capitalist crisis, a crisis in the capitalist epoch thus presupposes the universalisation of commodity production. Whereas pre-capitalist crisis is by definition local and limited in space, capitalist crisis is by definition general, and involves most of the countries united in the capitalist system of production and exchange of commodities: *

"Whereas the crises of the Ancien Régime were phenomena of shortage suddenly experienced, and for thousands of years the very idea of crisis was linked with under-production and famine . . . crises since the Revolution are always, except during wars, phenomena of overabundance of an explosive nature, which also lead to deep-going social changes."[3]

General possibility of capitalist crisis

This new type of crisis, called a crisis of over-production, seems to result from the very characteristics of the commodity, and of the general development of commodity production. The intrinsic contradiction of the commodity, the contradiction between use-value and exchange-value, leads in fact to the *splitting of the commodity into the commodity itself and money*. This splitting is what creates the general possibility of capitalist crises.

So long as society essentially produces use-values, a situation of "poverty amid plenty", of masses of use-values being destroyed while masses of people are condemned to poverty, cannot occur. The direct appropriation of use-values by the consumers prevents any such paradoxical coincidence. As soon, however, as commodity production becomes general, this direct appropriation ceases to be possible. Henceforth, in order to consume a commodity, it is necessary to possess the equivalent of its exchange-value. To appropriate use-values one has to be able to *buy* them.

From this time forward crises of overproduction are theoretically possible. For them to occur, all that is needed is for the owners of

---

* This does not mean, of course, that all the crises of the capitalist epoch necessarily have to affect *all* countries. The universality of capitalist crisis is a matter of a predominant feature, not an absolute and mechanical rule.

commodities to find themselves unable, for whatever reason, to encounter customers who possess sufficient money-capital to realise the exchange-value of their commodities. The system of trade and credit tends to bridge over temporarily the separation between the commodity and its equivalent in money. The longer this bridge becomes, however, both in time and space, the more closely trade and credit bind all countries together in a single system, the more the contradiction inherent in the commodity and its divided condition is intensified.

If during the circulation of commodities *their price of production changes*, as a result, say, of the introduction of new methods of work, the intensifying of competition, or of a fall in the average rate of profit, a large number of commodities no longer find their equivalent on the market, and a large number of debts cannot be met. It is enough for an income not to be spent today but only tomorrow for it to be incapable of buying the same number of commodities, if their prices have risen in the meantime.[4] The contradiction between the commodity and the money equivalent which it has to find on the market thus develops into a contradiction between money as medium of circulation and money as medium of payment, a contradiction which in turn leads to the contradiction between the whole process of commodity circulation and the process of reproduction.

The law of markets

Vulgar political economy set up against this analysis of the theoretical possibilities of overproduction the idea that the value of commodities is by definition equal to the total incomes of the various classes of society which in one way or another take part in the production of these commodities. Deduced from this was the conclusion that all production of commodities is at the same time production of the incomes needed to absorb these commodities. Hence arose the well-known "law of markets" which is unjustly called "Say's law", since it was discovered not by the French economist J. B. Say but by the British economist James Mill, father of John Stuart Mill. This "law of markets" leaves no room for general overproduction; at most it allows of the existence of partial overproduction, overproduction in some sectors accompanied by underproduction in others, due to faulty distribution of the "factors of production" among the different sectors of the economy.

The mistake in the law of markets arises from the fact that it neglects the *time-factor*, that is, it assumes a static and immobile system instead of the dynamic capitalist system.* We know already that during the period between production and sale the prices of commodities can vary, in either direction, so creating either a surplus of

---

* This is admitted by Guitton.[5]

incomes or a surplus of commodities without counter-value in money on the market.*

On the other hand, the incomes distributed during a certain period of time will not necessarily be used to buy commodities during this same period; only the incomes of wage-earners, intended for the purchase of perishable consumer goods, will be so spent. This is not true of capitalist incomes, which *tend to be accumulated*, nor of that part of the value of commodities which represents not an income but the counter-value of used-up constant capital. The capitalists are under no obligation to invest these sums *immediately*, that is, to use them at once as purchasing power to acquire a certain category of goods. When the capitalists expect not a rise but rather a fall in their profits they may well put off such expenditure. The hoarding of incomes, non-productive saving, may thus give rise to a surplus of income which will correspond to an overproduction of certain commodities.[7] This brings about an initial reduction in employment which may entail overproduction spreading throughout all parts of the economy, which will cause a further decline in employment, and so forth.

In fact, the "law of markets" is valid only:
(a) if all problems of investment are eliminated,
(b) together with all problems of credit; and
(c) if the immediate sale, for cash, of all the commodities produced assumed, together with
(d) complete stability in the value of these goods and
(e) no difference of productivity between different enterprises.

These assumptions boil down to an assumption that production is not capitalist production, stimulated by thirst for profit and by competition, but petty commodity production.

Even in that case, monetary phenomena can upset the perfect equilibrium between incomes and commodity values. The law of markets is thus truly valid only for natural economy.[8] In this way we come again to the argument set forth at the beginning of this chapter, that a society which produces use-values cannot experience "overproduction".

The cyclical progress of capitalist economy

Increase in the organic composition of capital and a downward tendency of the average rate of profit, conditioned by this, are the general laws of development of the capitalist mode of production. By bringing about a periodical modification in the price of production of commodities they create the theoretical possibility of general crises of

* Marx notes that there is no automatic, immediate unity between production and realisation of value under capitalism. This unity results only from a process and is connected with a series of conditions.[6]

overproduction, if an interval between the production and sale of commodities is assumed. The capitalist mode of production thus acquires its characteristic rhythm of development—*uneven, unsteady,* proceeding by leaps which are followed by periods of stagnation and retreat.

The introduction of new machines and new production methods does not change the price of production in an imperceptible, gradual way. It changes it through sudden jerks, at more or less regular intervals, when society becomes aware *after the event* that too much social labour has been expended in producing certain commodities. This results, leaving all other factors out of account, from the rotation cycle of fixed capital, which embraces a whole succession of production cycles and rotation cycles of circulating capital. Keynes says:

"There are reasons, given firstly by the length of life of durable assets in relation to the normal growth in a given epoch, and secondly by the carrying-costs of surplus stocks, why the duration of the downward movement should have an order of magnitude which is not fortuitous, which does not fluctuate between, say, one year this time and ten years next time, but which shows some regularity of habit between, let us say, three and five years."[9]

A number of other writers express the same view, e.g., Aftalion, Pigou, Schumpeter, etc.[10] The "interval" factor operates in agricultural affairs too. There is a gap between the moment when, on the basis of favourable prices, a decision is taken to increase the cultivation of a certain product, or the raising of certain animal stock, and the moment when this decision actually results in an increase in production.[11]*

On the other hand, a certain period has to elapse before the market can react to the introduction of new production methods, that is, before it can be established whether these methods will continue to bring super-profits to their initiators or if they will lead, on the contrary, to an all-round lowering of prices of production. This period is precisely that during which the splitting of the commodity into the commodity itself and money is *stretched* to the utmost, which leads to the inevitable slump.

Capitalist production is production for profit. The variations in the average rate of profit are the decisive criteria of the actual condition of capitalist economy.†

* This leads to a phenomenon of inevitable cyclical fluctuations known as the "cobweb theorem".

† A large number of writers accept this view as self-evident, e.g. Aftalion, W. C. Mitchell, Keynes, Schumpeter, Hansen and Guitton.[12] Haberler, however, in his work on economic cycles, which is otherwise so clear, is guilty of the following enormity in order to remain faithful to the terminology of the marginalist school: "Variations in profits (or losses) are often regarded as the barometer of economic cycles. It does not, however, seem justified to put

The long-term tendency of the average rate of profit is a downward one. But this does not show itself in straight-line fashion. It becomes effective only through periodical adjustments and increases, in a cyclical movement the primary origin of which has just been shown. This cyclical movement can be briefly characterised in its main phases by the change in the average rate of profit:

(a) *Economic recovery*. Part of production capacity not having been used any more for a certain period, the stocks previously accumulated have been got rid of, and the demand for goods now exceeds the new supply. Prices and profits start to rise again. Some of the factories which have been closed now reopen, for the same reason, which encourages the capitalists to increase their investments—because when demand exceeds supply it means that *less* social labour is crystallised in the commodities present on the market than is socially necessary. This implies that the total value of these goods easily finds it equivalent on the market. The factories working at a level of productivity higher than the average will realise a substantial super-profit: the less productive enterprises still surviving after the crisis will realise the average profit. The circulation period of commodities is reduced, most enterprises undertaking production to order. The gap between the moment of purchase and the moment of payment for goods is very short.*

(b) *Boom and prosperity*. All available capital flows into production and trade, in order to take advantage of the increase in the average rate of profit.† Investments rapidly increase. During a whole period the establishment of new enterprises and the modernisation of existing

this factor on the same footing with the three fundamental criteria above-mentioned. The term 'profit' is vague and ambiguous [!] ... It is a combination of interest, rent, monopoly profits, etc. Profits in the doctrinal sense are part of the national income and are included under that head in 'real income'. The absence of profit (or loss) in the strict sense of the word is the very essence of the perfect equilibrium [!] of the economic system."[13] We are ready to lay odds that any business-man would explain to Mr. von Haberler that his "doctrine" is in conflict with reality ... It is to be observed, furthermore, that Gayer, Rostow and Schwartz[14] have confirmed empirically that the cyclical movement of the textile industry coincides in the first part of the nineteenth century with cyclical fluctuations in the rate of profit.

* We leave aside for the moment many factors which enter into the cyclical movement and which we shall deal with later. It is above all necessary to grasp the *fundamental* mechanism of the rate of profit, which underlies the cyclical movement.

† It is thus not wrong to speak, as do Aftalion and Pigou, about "mistakes by too optimistic entrepreneurs". But it must be grasped that these are "mistakes" (of over-investment) from the *social* standpoint; because, from the point of view of the *private* entrepreneur, it is logical to try to increase production and sales to the maximum *at the moment when profit is highest*. Each one hopes he will survive the ensuing slump, that this will affect only the other man. And in fact, are not the most modern new plants those that stand up best to crises? "The trouble seems to be not so much that business men mistake their interests ... as that their actual interests lie in doing the things

enterprises is the essential source of the general expansion of economic activity: "industry is industry's best customer". The newly-launched enterprises raise the average level of productivity well above the former average, but so long as supply is exceeded by demand prices continue to rise and the average rate of profit remains at a high level. The most modern enterprises realise substantial super-profits, which stimulates fresh investments and develops credit, speculation, etc.

(c) *Overproduction and slump.* As the newly-made investments increase more and more the total production of society, and thereby the quanity of commodities hurled on to the market, the relations between supply and demand change, at first imperceptibly, then more and more obviously. It is now seen that some of the commodities produced in the least favourabe conditions of productivity actually contain labour-time which is *wasted*, from the social standpoint. These goods have become unsaleable at their prices of production. For a certain period the factories where these unfavourable conditions exist nevertheless go on producing—*that is, wasting social labour-time*—thanks to the expansion of the credit system, and this is reflected in the accumulation of stocks, the lengthening of the circulation time of commodities, the widening of the gap between supply and demand, etc. At a certain moment it becomes impossible to bridge this gap with credit. Prices and profits collapse. Many capitalists are ruined; the enterprises which work at too low a level of productivity[17] have to close down.

(d) *Crisis and depression.* The fall in prices means that production is henceforth profitable only for the enterprises that work under the most favourable conditions of productivity. The firms that were realising super-profits now have to be satisfied with the average profit. In fact, a new level of average profit is thus established, corresponding to the new organic composition of capital. At the same time, however, the crisis, through the bankruptcy and closure of many factories, means the destruction of a mass of machinery, of fixed capital. By the fall in prices, capital, as exchange value, is also lowered in value, and the total value of society's capital is reduced. The smaller amount of capital which is left as a result of this destruction can more easily be utilised. It will be invested easily under conditions making possible, at the moment of economic recovery, a new rise in the average rate of profit.

which bring on the cycle, so long as they are acting as individual business men or representatives of individual business interests."[15]

Natalia Moszkowska does not understand the periodical coincidences of these "errors of judgment". Why does everybody make the same sort of mistake?[16] Perhaps because every entrepreneur is forced by competition to try for the highest profits? Is this not a vivid illustration of the contradiction between the *social* character of production and the *private* character of appropriation (the hunt for private profit) under capitalism?

The cyclical movement of capital is thus nothing but the mechanism through which the tendency of the average rate of profit to fall is realised. At the same time, it is the system's reaction to this fall, through the lowering of the value of capital during crises. Crises make possible the periodical adaptation of the amount of labour actually expended in the production of commodities to the amount of labour which is *socially necessary*, the individual value of commodities to their socially-determined value, the surplus-value contained in these commodities to the average rate of profit. Because capitalist production is not consciously planned and organised production, these adjustments take place not *a priori* but *a posteriori*. For this reason they necessitate violent shocks, the destruction of thousands of lives and enormous quantities of values and created wealth.

The internal logic of the capitalist cycle
The contradiction between use-value and exchange value, the contradiction between the commodity and its money equivalent, provide only the *general possibility* of capitalist crises of overproduction. They do not yet explain why, or in what specific conditions, these crises periodically follow one another. The variations in the rate of profit reveal the inner mechanism of the economic cycle. They explain the general significance of it as a periodical readjustment of the conditions of equilibrium of capitalist reproduction. But they do not reveal the "concrete causes" of crises. These factors can be distinguished from the causes of crises in the strict sense by contrasting, in the tradition of Aristotle's logic, and as the economist G. von Haberler does, the causes *sine qua non*—without which there would not be any crises—with the causes *per quam*—which explain the immediate reasons why crises break out. To analyse the latter requires a concrete analysis of all the elements of capitalist production.

For expanded reproduction to take place without interruption, the *conditions of equilibrium*, indicated in Chapter 10, must be constantly reproduced. The purchases of consumer-goods by all the workers and the capitalists engaged in producing capital goods must be equivalent to the purchases of capital goods by the capitalists engaged in producing consumer goods (including in both categories the purchases needed in order to expand production). The constant reproduction of these conditions of equilibrium thus requires a *proportional development* of the two sectors of production. The periodical occurrence of crises is to be explained only by a periodical break in this proportionality or, in other words, by an *uneven development* of these two sectors.

Up to now, however, we have not left the province of definition, that is, of tautology. To say that periodical crises occur because of disproportion between the two sectors of production is like saying that opium puts you to sleep because it has sleep-inducing properties. The crisis is the *expression* of the disproportion. But if we are to regard it as being *inherent* in the process of capitalist development, we have to show why this process gives rise *periodically and necessarily* to such a disproportion.

Capitalist production is production for profit. The periodical disproportion between the development of the capital goods sector and that of the consumer goods sector must be linked with periodical differences between the rates of profit in the two spheres. The causes of these periodical differences are to be observed in the different ways in which the basic contradictions of capitalism show themselves in the two sectors. We get the following picture, for the successive phases of the economic cycle:

(*a*) *The depression.* Stocks having accumulated during a whole period, their disposal takes time, since the incomes available for buying consumer goods have been severely reduced as a result of unemployment. All investment activity slows down considerably after the outbreak of crisis.[18] As, at the same time, many enterprises have had to use for other purposes the funds available to them for renewing fixed capital, the activity of the enterprises in the capital goods sector is much reduced.[19] The production of consumer goods likewise declines to a considerable extent, but not so much.[20] Even the unemployed do not stop eating, and the purchase of perishable goods cannot be put off till tomorrow; moreover, though the workers' wages have grown less, this reduction has often been less than the fall in prices since the onset of the crisis.[21] As for purchases of semi-durable consumer goods, they decrease less than purchases of durable consumer goods. The latter, the sale of which seriously declines, nevertheless sell more easily than capital goods.[22] During the period of depression we thus see the beginning, in the sphere of production, of the disproportion between the two sectors which, from the start of economic recovery, will spread to the sphere of prices and profits.

(*b*) *The turn to economic recovery.* While the economic depression lasts, industrial activity remains at an abnormally low level. When the rate of profit is very low, no reduction in the rate of interest can cause a revival of investment.[23] But the very logic of this stagnation creates the elements of a recovery. As stocks are disposed of, thanks to the lowering of production, the consumer-goods sectors whose sales have not been much reduced are able slightly to increase their activity; prices of these goods stop falling, though without at once rising. It is enough, however, for them to remain stable for a certain period, for the enterprises in these sectors to start thinking about re-equipment.[24]

Everything encourages this. The prices of raw materials and means of equipment are unusually low; re-equipment at this moment is therefore a profitable undertaking. Wages continue to remain low, under the pressure of unemployment, even after prices have been stabilised. These low wages likewise encourage expansion of production, since they give a promise of higher profits.[25]

The stoppage or reduction in investment activity during an entire period has made it possible to accumulate the funds needed for depreciating fixed capital. These funds, at first hoarded, start to make their way back to the banks, there to bring in interest which is still moderate but not, in a period of depression, negligible.[26]* The absence of any investment activity markedly reduces the demand for money capital, so that the average rate of interest falls in a period of depression: [29] another reason for the capitalists in the consumer goods sector to undertake investments on credit towards the end of this period. Finally, the still low rate of profit encourages them to seek out and to introduce new methods of production which have accumulated since the end of the boom without any possibility of being applied. (See Keynes and Hansen, as well as Aftalion, Pigou, Schumpeter, and a large number of others writers.)[30]

The resulting reduction in costs of production makes it possible to increase the rate of profit with the existing market prices. In this way, investment activity starts again in the consumer goods sector, which brings about economic recovery.†

(c) *Economic recovery.* The orders for equipment for the consumer goods sector which arise from the inner logic of the depression itself in their turn make possible the recovery of production in several sectors making capital goods. This recovery reduces unemployment, increases available purchasing power, and develops sales of consumer goods, which in its turn stimulates a new wave of investment. The *multiplier principle* comes into play.[32]

This explains that an initial investment increases the total final in-

---

* Woytinsky[27] notes that the total amount deposited in savings banks increased by 1932, as compared with the level at 31st December, 1929, to: 129 in the U.K., 137 in Germany, 140 in Holland, 140 in the U.S.A., 142 in Italy, 143 in Japan, 148 in Switzerland, 166 in Sweden, 193 in France, 192 in Belgium, etc. To these sums, and to those in bank deposits, must be added the considerable sums which were *hoarded.*[28]

† Supporters of the theory of pure underconsumption, like Natalia Moszkowska and Léon Sartre,[31] regard this way of describing the progress of economic recovery as question-begging. In assuming that the majority of enterprises renew their fixed capital at the same time, instead of supposing that this renewal is spread equally over each year, they say, we are already *presupposing* the existence of the cycle, that is, we are starting from what we have subsequently to prove. To this objection we answer: (a) it is enough to start from a *first cycle*—determined, e.g. by the initial introduction on a large scale of steam-driven machinery into the English textile industry—to see that this objection is historically invalid; and (b) we do not see in this renewal of fixed capital the "cause" of the cycle but only a convenient point of departure for our exposition.

come by a sum which exceeds the value of this investment; it explains likewise that one independent investment can give rise to one or more waves of investment stimulated in this way.[33] Statisticians have tried to work out the value of the multiplier in the industrially advanced countries for 1919–1939 and have evaluated it at between 2 and 3 (calculations by Kalecki and Kuznets).[34] These statistics are, however, to be handled cautiously. In any case, they do not apply to an entire historical epoch.[35]

Let us now see what happens with the rate of profit. The production of capital goods is much less elastic than that of consumer goods. To supply cotton mills with the spindles they require it is necessary to delve into the stock of steel and coal, increase the production of these raw materials when the stocks have been exhausted, put to full use the machines that build machines, or else build these first of all, when there are no more reserves of productive capacity. As soon as recovery is well under way an interval thus appears between the order for additional constant capital and its delivery. During this interval *competition* rages between the enterprises, all striving to acquire the equipment and raw materials already on the market. The prices of these goods will thus rise more than the prices of consumer goods, and this difference produces an equivalent difference between the rate of profit in the two sectors.[36] The disproportion between the two sectors is thus shifted from the sphere of production to that of prices and profit.

Moreover, the rate of profit recovers all round. Whereas prices start to rise as soon as excess stocks are dispersed, wages do not rise at all, or rise very little, at the beginning of recovery, owing to the pressure exercised by unemployment on the labour market. At the same time, the factories which were not working at full pressure during the depression start to re-engage workers without at first changing their plant. The organic composition of their capital thus declines momentarily, thereby raising the rate of profit. The reduction in the circulation time of commodities increases the number of production cycles in a year and works in the same direction.

The expansion of production being slow at first, the demand for capital remains at a level lower than the supply, which implies that the rate of interest remains very low. The coincidence of a low rate of interest with a rising rate of profit determines a growing rate of entrepreneur's profit, which likewise explains a general tendency on the part of entrepreneurs to renew their fixed capital and invest an increasing proportion of their profits at this moment of the cycle: *

* Keynes and other writers speak of the rise in the "value of capital in relation to its cost". This means that the income anticipated from the purchase of capital goods exceeds the cost of purchasing (or replacing) these capital goods. The more this difference exceeds the interest, the more favourable are conditions for investment.[37] The whole of this reasoning leads to the same conclusions that we have just been setting forth.

"Investment in new plant could not, of its nature, be undertaken in small increments. Assuming a constant rate of increase in output, an individual firm could not alter its fixed plant at a parallel constant rate, and if our data are at all reliable it would appear that [in the first half of the nineteenth century in Britain] increases in capacity capable of dealing with the secularly increasing volume of output tended to occur largely in a few years of each decade."[38]

(d) *Boom, prosperity.* The disequilibrium between prices and rates of profit in the two sectors, which appears from the start of economic recovery, is now transformed into disproportion between the rate of increase of their production, a disproportion opposite to that which occurred during the depression. At first, the available capital will flow for preference towards the capital goods sector, the rate of profit in this sector being the higher. Furthermore, the *accelerator principle* starts to operate.[39] We know that a very limited proportion of fixed capital is used up and renewed during each production cycle. This proportion is determined by the relative longevity of fixed capital.

Let us suppose that its average age is ten years. That means that the value of the total production of a one-year cycle contains only 10 per cent of the value of all the fixed capital available to society. If we assume that the value of the annual product is 1,500 (million), of which 500 represents the value of fixed capital used up, a stock of fixed capital to the value of 5,000 is implied. If all the fixed capital in existence is already fully employed in ensuring an annual production of 1,500, an increase of this production from 1,500 to 1,800 (or an increase in overall demand in the same proportion) requires the installation of fresh fixed capital to the value not of 100 but of 1,000, 10 per cent of which, or 100, will be embodied in the value of the extra production of 300. The increasing of production by 20 per cent thus requires that the current production of fixed capital be *tripled*. The manufacture of new industrial plant, the capital goods sector, then experiences a burst of frenzied activity. Production in this sector increases more markedly than in the consumer goods sector.[40]

This feverish development of the capital goods sector again sets going the multiplier principle and makes it possible to absorb the bulk of the unemployed labour. It again increases the purchasing power available for consumer goods, and even causes a temporary shortage of these goods, which once more stimulates investment and the purchase of fixed capital in this sector. Full employment comes about. Wages start to rise, though not so fast as prices, and for this reason the rate of surplus value continues to rise, and in fact real wages decline or stagnate at the beginning of the boom.[41]

Given that in both sectors supply is less than demand, the firms with the highest level of productivity realise lush superprofits. In general, the high level of the rate of profit favours vigorous activity in the fields of investment, speculation and credit. The capital hoarded during the depression is progressively absorbed into economic activity, and consequently the rate of interest starts to recover. But the banks give circulation credit all the more readily because many firms are working on orders, that is, with guaranteed outlets. The discount rate thus remains comparatively low.

The more enterprises producing capital goods finish re-equipping themselves and begin to fulfil the orders that have piled up, the more equipment (and consequently production) increases in the consumer goods sector. At a certain profit it becomes sufficient to meet the increased demand caused by full employment. At this moment, one might suppose that these enterprises would start progressively reducing their orders for capital goods. But the orders for these goods placed earlier have only just been fulfilled. The *delay* between the moment when an order is placed and the moment when it is fulfilled thus plays an important role in the preparation of the crisis (see Aftalion, Tinbergen, Frisch on the cycle of shipbuilding, Kalecki, Hansen, etc.).

The cycle thus reaches here its first critical point. The industries producing consumer goods ought now to halt all expansion of production, and even begin to reduce it. Such a "rational" attitude on their part is impossible, however, and not only because of the anarchy of production, which means that each enterprise waits for its competitor to give ground, and hopes that it will itself attain a maximum of profit with a maximum of sales and production. This rationality is also ruled out by the dictation of production for profit. These enterprises have just re-equipped themselves. A restriction of production would increase depreciation charges on current production. It would reduce the rate of profit. Wages have been rising since full employment has been attained. There is therefore a risk that the rate of surplus-value and the rate of profit will fall, a risk that the capitalists try to offset by rationalisation, more intensive use of the productive apparatus, and intensification of effort on the part of the producers, all of which implies an increase in production.[42] The gradual recovery of the rate of interest likewise reduces the rate of entrepreneur's profit. The increase in the amount of profit needed to offset the lowering of this rate again implies increased production.[43]

Finally, it must not be forgotten that it is very difficult for the capitalists of the consumer goods sector to know at what moment exactly the point of equilibrium between the supply of their products and the demand for them has been reached.

"When this point comes, few men are aware of the fact, because the volume of commodities offered for sale does not indicate either the large volume in the making or the invisible supply in the hands of speculators . . . On account of the time it takes to produce commodities and get them into the shops, the markets do not feel the full effects of maximum productivity until months after that stage has been reached. Production, therefore, continues at a high rate; and the volume of commodities coming upon the market, as a result of loans previously made, continues to increase ... As there is a limit, however, to the expansion of bank credit, the time comes when there is a decrease in the amount of money advanced by banks to producers, that reaches consumers' hands."[44]

When the total amount of purchasing power available for consumer goods has already ceased to increase, a considerable part of current production still goes on being sold: the shopkeepers and the firms in the intermediate stages of production have to replenish their stocks, exhausted at the end of the depression and throughout the recovery and the boom.* The increase in their sales encourages industrialists to undertake a fresh increase in production, which may thus coincide with a stagnation or even a slight shrinkage of ultimate consumption, at any rate during an initial period.

(e) *The slump, the turn towards depression.* The disequilibrium between the capital goods sector and the consumer goods sector, which first shows itself in the sphere of prices and the rate of profit, thus spreads more and more into the sphere of production and then into that of demand, sales and markets. Full employment having been attained, the total amount of purchasing power for consumer goods does not increase any further, or at best, very little.† On the other hand, the production of these same goods continues to increase throughout an entire period, for the reasons indicated above. "There is a suggestion here that the accumulated financial difficulties are accompanied (perhaps in part produced) by a slower growth of distribution [or, more correctly, sales. E.M.] to consumers, at the same time that

---

* Often, at the start of a boom, and before the accelerator principle has begun to operate thoroughly, enterprises and shops begin to replenish their stocks, and when this movement remains unaccompanied by a corresponding increase in sales to the public, they may be led to dispose quickly of these stocks and in the meantime restrict their own purchases. This explains the occurrence of minor recessions in the middle of the economic cycle, first elucidated by the economist Kitchin,[45] and also known as *inventory* recessions (Metzler and Abramovitz).[46]

† This is to be understood in real and not monetary terms. Currency inflation may of course increase nominal wages at the end of a boom, but this rise is largely skimmed off by the rise in the cost of living. It is true that at this moment any fresh increase in production leads to an increase in real wages (overtime, etc.) which reduces the rate of profit. At the same time, at the top of the boom, the rate of surplus value tends to decline, average output per wage-earner tending to fall, particularly as a result of the employment of inexperienced workers and also of the following phenomena: "It cannot be denied that, in many establishments, the output of labour has declined since full employment has been exceeded, owing to the fluidity of the labour-force, absenteeism, and lack of conscientiousness."[47]

physical output is growing faster."[48] Stocks thus begin to grow, first at the final stage (retail trade), then at the intermediate stages, finally in the industrial enterprises themselves.

As this increase in stocks develops, the industrialists and traders to whom it is happening resist any immediate lowering of prices which would mean for them a reduction in the value of their stock, that is, a serious loss. They therefore increasingly apply to the banks, to get circulation credit. The banks themselves, which have already extended substantial credit to the enterprises in this sector, put off as long as possible any refusal of credit, which would risk bringing about the bankruptcy of these enterprises and so the loss of the capital already lent. A regular credit inflation thus occurs, a dangerous tension of the whole system, linked with many phenomena of speculation and pure and simple swindling, which flourish in the boom atmosphere. This tension on the money market and the finance market comes just before the reversal of the conjuncture, and is marked by a sharp rise in the rate of interest.[49]

The entrepreneurs are now obliged to put off, further and further, the carrying-out of their current investment projects. They have to use as circulating capital a part of the money capital intended for these investments. Their orders for capital goods thus fall off more and more, while production stagnates or starts to decline in the consumer goods sector. Thus, the production of consumer goods reaches its climax, stagnates, or even starts to fall off, before the same phenomenon occurs in the capital goods sector.[50]

We have now reached the second critical point in the cycle. The enterprises in the capital goods sector re-equipped themselves at the beginning of the cycle, so as to be able to meet orders for *increased* fixed capital coming from the consumer goods sector. It is enough for this increase to come to a halt for phenomena of over-production to start appearing in the capital goods sector, for the industries of this sector to begin working below their new maximum production capacity. Furthermore, a *slowing-down in the rate of increase* in investments leads to the same result:

"The rhythm of production in the industries producing equipment is governed by the *expansion* of production in the industries making consumer goods. If the latter stop expanding, the former lose part of their markets and are forced to cut down their activity, even supposing they can obtain the funds they need in order to keep their production up to the former level."[51]

The enterprises in this sector, too, have recently made substantial investments; they thus have substantial amounts of capital to depreciate. They work much more with borrowed capital than do the enterprises in the other sector, since it is into them that available money capital has mainly flowed, attracted by a higher rate of profit.

The rise in the rate of interest resulting from the increasing shortage which becomes apparent on the capital market* will thus hit them harder than the enterprises in the consumer goods sector. This will be felt all the more severely because about the same time the rate of profit will likewise tend to decline, owing to the rise in overheads, the rise in wages (overtime, etc.), the increase in wastage, etc.[52]

In view of the emptying of their order-books, these enterprises find themselves compelled, in turn, to restrict production, dismiss some of their employees, and adopt other economy measures. But all this means that the volume of purchasing power distributed by this sector tends to decline. There results from this, so far as consumer goods are concerned, a real decline in demand, a fresh increase in stocks, a further shrinkage in production, a new fall in profits.

At a certain point in this cumulative process of shrinkage, disequilibrium necessarily extends to the last phase, that of credit. Demand for circulation credit is accumulating on every side. The supply of money capital, however, declines, because the difference between the rate of profit and the rate of interest disappears. In the face of the increase in stocks and the stagnation in sales, the enterprises are, moreover, continually short of ready money, they draw out their bank deposits, and they sell off their property and securities, etc.[53]

Finally, all the reserves accumulated during the previous period of stagnation have been absorbed in the feverish activity of the boom. It is thus inevitable that during such a process the disequilibrium between supply of and demand for money capital should to a certain extent cause a stoppage in the expansion of the credit system. The banks start to refuse new requests for circulation credit, except at more and more exorbitant rates. Rates of interest and discount rates both increase rapidly.† Bankruptcies occur in increasing numbers, debtors dragging down creditors. Soon an avalanche sets in. Hundreds of enterprises shut their doors and dismiss their workers. In order to find the ready money which has suddenly become the only thing capable of keeping the worst disasters at bay, enterprises are forced to sell off their stocks at any price. Prices collapse, profits vanish, a new wave of bankruptcy spreads. Prices, profits, production, incomes, employment, fall to an abnormally low level.‡

* This shortage need not necessarily result from an actual shortage of capital. Often, the owners of this capital refuse to lend it at this moment, because the fall in the rate of profit implies a growing risk of instability on the part of the borrowers.

† It must not be forgotten that the rise in the rate of interest in relation to credits for production has only a minor effect nowadays in the advanced capitalist countries, where self-financing by enterprises plays a dominant role.[54] This is not true, however, of circulation credit.

‡ Kaldor[55] gives four reasons for the cessation of the boom: an increasing rate of interest, which halts investment; a fall in the rate of profit caused by

The extension of the basis of capitalist production

Our analysis of the cyclical progress of capitalist economy is based on the typical behaviour of capitalist enterprises, who at any moment of the cycle are seeking the maximum profit, under the whip of competition, without troubling themselves about the system or the market as a whole. But how does it happen that the periodical occurrence of crises does not induce enterprises to be more prudent, that is, to restrict their investments when recovery comes, so as to avoid overproduction at the end of the boom? How, in other words, does it come about that booms are every time as feverish and exaggerated as before, leading every time to an especially disagreeable collapse?

This question is all the more justified because the sectors especially subject to fluctuations in demand during the cycle do learn to adapt themselves to these fluctuations:

"Producers becoming familiar with the recurrent shift of demand in the course of the cyclical phases, learn to provide . . . for the peak demand of prosperity. Industries more subject than others to such fluctuations, . . . which we shall call cyclical industries, are particularly likely to do this. They will set up productive capacity which is intended to be fully used only in times of prosperity."[56]

It is not as though such foresight on the part of the capitalists could *prevent* the cyclical development of the economy. We have seen that the mere fact of the periodical renewal of fixed capital, determined by its expectation of life, is enough to account for this cyclical pattern. But the question that arises is this: why do we not simply see the renewal of fixed capital at the start of each recovery phase, accompanied by investment which broadly corresponds to the increase in population during the cycle? Why do we see, instead, a substantial expansion in production capacity proceeding by leaps, which, through the working of the accelerator principle, causes booms in the strict sense of the word?

Historically, there is only one reply to this question. The cyclical development of capitalist economy becomes particularly feverish through the *extension of the basis* of this economy at the beginning of each recovery, and this happens through the sudden appearance of *new markets* for important sectors of industry, which thus stimulates the activity of the capital goods industry.

These new markets may result either from the geographical extension of capitalist production[57] (penetration into a non-capitalist milieu),

---

this rise in the rate of interest; the inadequacy of the expansion of demand for consumer goods; the appearance of excess capacity, owing to the shortage of labour. We have commented on the operation of three of these four factors, even if not in the same order as Kaldor's. The fourth is quite exceptional. The influence of full employment is felt above all on the rate of profit.

from the appearance of new sectors of production (technological progress) or from sudden leaps in relations between competitors (disappearance of a powerful competitor as a result of war, of technological backwardness, etc.). To this must be added, in the twentieth century, the role of replacement markets played essentially by the armaments orders of the State*

Each successive boom in the history of capitalism can be explained in this way by such an extension of the basis of production:

(a) 1816–25 cycle. British industry conquers the markets of Latin America; building of gas-works and canals in Britain; beginning of Belgium's industrialisation.

(b) 1825–36 cycle. Rise in British exports to Latin America and U.S.A.; industrial expansion in Belgium, France, and the Rhineland; beginning of railway construction.

(c) 1836–47 cycle. Rise in British exports to Asia, especially to India and China (after the Opium War). Railway construction at a feverish pace throughout Western Europe.

(d) 1847–57 cycle. Expansion of the American market after the discovery of gold deposits in California. Railway building in the U.S.A. and throughout Europe. Establishment of new industries in the U.S.A., in Germany and in France. First expansion of joint stock companies.

(e) 1857–66 cycle. Expansion of the market in India and Egypt, especially through the development of cotton plantations, to replace the American cotton missing because of the American Civil War.

(f) 1866–73 cycle. Development of the iron and steel industry in Germany, Austria-Hungary, the U.S.A., especially stimulated by the wars of 1866 and 1870–71. Great railway building boom in the U.S.A.

(g) 1873–82 cycle. Feverish railway building in the U.S.A. and in Central Europe. Increase in naval construction. Expansion of markets in South America, Canada and Australia, due to their mechanised agricultural production.

(h) 1882–91 cycle. Last big expansion in railway building in the U.S.A., in Russia and in Latin America (especially in Argentina). Export of British and French capital. Development of the African market.

(i) 1891–1900 cycle. Building of tramways throughout the world; building of railways in Russia, Africa, Asia and Latin America; export of British, French and German capital. Development of the oil and electrical power industries.

(j) 1900–07 cycle. Expansion of the iron and steel industries (arms

* See Chapter 14.

race), of naval construction, of tramways, of electric power stations and telephone networks. Development of the Turkish, North African and Middle-Eastern markets. First development of heavy industry in Italy. Last wave of railway building in Africa and Asia.*

(k) 1907–13 cycle. Rise in iron and steel production, armaments and naval construction. End of the tramway-building boom. Development of the Middle-East market.

(l) 1913–21 cycle. In the U.S.A. and Japan, feverish industrial construction, boom in iron and steel, naval construction, armaments industries, boom in the chemical industry in these countries, as also in Germany and Britain; first expansion of the motor-car industry.

(m) 1921–29 cycle. World-wide expansion of the motor-car, rubber, oil, machine-tool, electrical-apparatus and chemical industries. Boom in American exports of capital, especially to Germany.

(n) 1929–37 cycle. Rise in the armaments industry, especially in Germany and Japan. Development of the Chinese and Latin-American markets. First expansion of the aircraft industry.

(o) 1937–49 cycle. Expansion of the armaments industry in the U.S.A., Canada, Australia, Germany (until 1944) and Britain. New division of world markets, especially in Western and Eastern Europe, Africa, Latin America and the Far East. Expansion of the aircraft, electronics and chemical industries. Beginnings of the atomic power industry. Industrialisation of the under-developed countries.

(p) 1949–53 cycle. Expansion of the armaments and aircraft industries. Development of the Atomic power industry. Renewed expansion of Germany heavy industry, focused on reconstruction needs. Development of the African market. Continued industrialisation of the underdeveloped countries.

(q) 1953–58 cycle. Expansion of the electronics, chemical (plastics) and engineering (industrial equipment of all kinds) industries. Capital construction for the armaments race and the industrialisation of the underdeveloped countries. Boom in building development, expansion of consumer-durable sectors in Europe; first large-scale development of automation.

---

* In Europe, apart from Russia, railway building reached its climax in the decade 1870–80, when there was an average annual increase in railway lines of 5,000 kilometres. In the U.S.A. this climax was reached in the decade 1880–90, with an average annual increase of 11,800 kilometres. From the decade 1890–1900 onward the annual construction in the rest of the world exceeded the total of railway construction in Europe and the U.S.A., reaching its climax between 1900 and 1908, with an annual average of 12,031 kilometres.[58]

Under-consumption theories

In the history of economic thought, two great schools of explanation of the capitalist economic cycle are to be distinguished: the underconsumption school and the disproportionality school. Each puts its finger on a fundamental contradiction of the capitalist mode of production, but goes astray in isolating this contradiction from the other features of the system.

In order to explain the periodical crises, the supporters of underconsumption theories start from the contradiction between the tendency to unlimited development of production and the tendency to limitation in consumption by the broad masses, a contradiction which is indeed characteristic of the capitalist mode of production. The periodical crises thus *appear as crises of the realisation of surplus-value*. The inadequacy of the purchasing power of the masses prevents them from buying all the goods manufactured during a particular period. The surplus value has been produced all right, but it remains crystallised in unsaleable commodities.

Among the representatives of this school may be listed pre-Marxist socialists such as Owen, Sismondi and Rodbertus, the Russian Populists, and a series of Marx's own disciples: Kautsky, Rosa Luxemburg, Lucien Laurat, Fritz Sternberg, Otto Bauer (in his last work), Natalia Moszkowska, Paul M. Sweezy, etc. Among non-Marxist representatives of this school may be mentioned Major Douglas, Professor Lederer, Foster and Catchings, Hobson, and Keynes, along with some of the latter's followers, such as Professor Hamberg.

The crudest defenders of this idea find the origin of crises in the fact that the workers receive as wages the equivalent of only *part* of the new value they produce. They forget that the other part of this value corresponds to the purchasing power of the bourgeois class (capitalist families and firms). Even a writer with such claims to scholarship as Fred Oelssner writes in his work *Die Wirtschaftskrisen*: [59]

"It follows from this contradiction between the worker's role as producer of surplus value and his role as consumer or buyer on the market that the development of the market can never [!] correspond to the extension of production. Demand always [!] develops more slowly than supply under capitalist conditions [of production]."

An idea like this does not explain why crises have to occur—it would rather serve to explain the *permanence* of overproduction, the impossibility of capitalism.

The workers are not at all expected to buy all the commodities produced. On the contrary, the capitalist mode of production implies that a part of these commodities, namely, capital goods, is *never* bought by the workers, but always by the capitalists. In order to uphold the theory of underconsumption one would have to show that under the capitalist mode of production the ratio between wages and the part of surplus value not transformed into constant capital, on the one hand, and the national income, on the other, is *necessarily and periodically less* than the ratio between the value of consumer goods and the value of production as a whole. This has never been shown in a convincing way.

Rosa Luxemburg,[60] though she starts from similar considerations, raises the discussion to a level more worthy of interest by inquiring into the origins of accumulation, of expanded reproduction. Expanded reproduction means, in fact, that the capitalists withdraw from commodity circulation, at the end of a rotation cycle of capital, more value than they have introduced into production. This surplus is nothing else but realised surplus value!

Now, Rosa Luxemburg goes on, both the workers' wages (variable capital) and the replacement value of the machinery and raw material used up in production (constant capital) were *advanced* by the capitalists. As for the capitalists' unproductive consumption (the unaccumulated part of surplus value) this is also paid for by the capitalists themselves. If, then, the whole of production were bought by the workers and the capitalists, that would simply mean that the capitalists recovered funds they had themselves put into circulation, and bought their own surpluses from each other.

This would make sense if one were to look on each capitalist enterprise as an isolated unit. But for the capitalist order taken as a whole the conclusion seems absurd. This capitalist order presents a picture of increase in wealth, in the value accumulated by the capitalist class, an increase which cannot be the result of exchange between capitalists. Rosa Luxemburg concludes, therefore, that the realisation of surplus value is possible only to the extent that non-capitalist markets are open to the capitalist mode of production. She sees these markets above all in the purchasing power of the non-capitalist classes (peasants) within the capitalist countries and in the external trade of the latter with non-capitalist countries.*

It is certain that, historically, the capitalist régime was born and developed within a non-capitalist setting. It is no less certain that the extension of its basis received a particularly dynamic stimulus from the

---

* Bukharin replied to this argument that in trade with non-capitalist classes or countries there is also exchange of commodities, and therefore no new outlets. He did not grasp that this trade can take the form not of an exchange of commodities but of an exchange of *non-capitalist incomes* (e.g. semi-feudal ground rent) arising from non-capitalist modes of production, against capitalist commodities. There are therefore, indeed, new outlets and transfers of value in favour of the bourgeoisie. Sternberg adds that if one starts from the hypothesis that only a residue of consumer goods is unsaleable in a "pure" capitalist society, these consumer goods could be exchanged against capital goods (raw materials) imported from non-capitalist countries, so favouring both the realisation of surplus value and the accumulation of capital.[61]

conquest of fresh space. But from that it does *not* follow that if a non-capitalist setting is absent then surplus value cannot be realised.

Rosa Luxemburg's mistake lies in treating the world capitalist class as a whole, i.e. in *leaving out competition*. It is true that Marx, in his calculations of the average rate of profit in Volume III of *Capital*, also starts from the capitalist class as a whole, and Rosa quotes this reference triumphantly, to confirm her view.[62] But she seems to be unaware that in his overall plan for *Capital* Marx stressed that *crises fall outside the sphere of "capital taken as a whole"; they result precisely from the phenomena which he calls those of "different capitals", i.e. competition*. It is competition that determines the whole dynamic, all the laws of development, of capitalism.

Now, competition implies exchange of commodities with other capitalists. This shift of value within the capitalist class may very well be at the basis of the "realisation of surplus value". Within the setting of these exchanges between capitalists, the "totality" of the capitalist class may see its total profits increase, realised *successively* by the circulation of one and the same sum of money.*

It is the unevenness of the rate of development[63] *as between different countries, different sectors and different enterprises that is the driving force of the expansion of capitalist markets*, without non-capitalist classes necessarily having to be brought in. This is what explains how expanded reproduction can go on even without any non-capitalist setting, how under these conditions the realisation of surplus value takes place through a market accentuation of the *concentration of capital*. In practice, exchanges with non-capitalist surroundings are only one aspect of the uneven development of capitalism.

Critique of models of "underconsumption"

Several writers have tried to give a more subtle form, supported by figures, to the theory of "underconsumption", that is, of the impossibility of realising surplus value as the ultimate cause of periodical crises. Otto Bauer (in his last work), Léon Sartre, Paul M. Sweezy and Fritz Sternberg provide the most interesting examples. Nevertheless, these various "models", arithmetical or algebraic, of underconsumption all suffer from a common weakness. They always *beg the question* by regarding as already shown, in their exposition of the problem, the solution which they wish to offer.†

---

* See Marx's very interesting observation in the *Grundrisse*: "Surplus value created at one point demands the creation of surplus value at another point, so that this may be exchanged for that."

† The same observation applies, incidentally, to most of the "models" of econometry used to demonstrate one theory or another of the cycle. See the more detailed comment given in Chapter 18, section on "The econometricians."

Thus, Paul M. Sweezy[64] sets up his model by starting from the assumption that a certain increase in the value of the production of capital goods is necessarily accompanied by a *proportionately increased* production capacity of consumer goods. In other words: the ratio $\dfrac{\text{value I}}{\text{value II}}$ remains stable, while the ratio

$$\frac{\text{surplus value accumulated in c}}{\text{wages + surplus value not accumulated in c}}$$

increases more and more, and along with it, the ratio

$$\frac{\text{purchasing power of I}}{\text{purchasing power of II}}$$

If one starts from this assumption, the "necessity" of the overproduction of consumer goods is, of course, proved, since it is already contained in the assumption.

Otto Bauer[65] follows a similar line of reasoning. He deduces the inevitability of the crisis from the fact that constant capital accumulates more rapidly than the need of constant capital for the production of the extra consumer goods bought by the extra workers taken on in the course of expanded reproduction. This follows logically from the employment of an increasing rate of surplus value. But Otto Bauer's model presumes that society absorbs new constant capital only *in the same proportion* as it increases its ultimate consumption. It thus presupposes a *stable proportion* between the value of production in the two sectors—which is just what has to be proved.

It should be observed that Otto Bauer is the first Marxist writer to introduce the idea of *stock of existing fixed capital* (total production capacity) and *rate of technical progress* into his model. These two ideas have been extensively used by the neo-Keynesian and econometric school, notably by Harrod, Domar, Pilvin and Hamberg.*

Léon Sartre[67] starts from the assumption that the ratio between the constant capital in the two main sectors of industrial production remains the same. He deduces this asumption from a basic hypothesis about the identity of the rate of surplus value and the rate of accumulation in the two sectors. But he supposes at the same time that the demand for capital goods increases more quickly than the demand for consumer goods. If $\dfrac{\text{value I}}{\text{value II}}$ remains stable while $\dfrac{\text{demand I}}{\text{demand II}}$ increases,

---

* Hamberg[66] shows that there is a stable proportion between the increase in the stock of existing fixed capital and the increase in production which results from the full employment of this stock. But he is careful not to claim that a stable proportion exists between the increase in the *total* stock of the fixed capital and the production capacity of *consumer goods* alone. He thus avoids the mistake common to all the supporters of the underconsumption theory.

crisis is obviously inevitable, and takes the form of a crisis of over-production of consumer goods.

Here we have not only question-begging but also an error of reasoning. Sartre, like Sternberg, deduces from capitalist competition the maintenance of a constant proportion between the productive forces engaged in the two sectors. This is a mechanistic, "idyllic" idea of competition. The latter does not at all lead to equalisation of the organic composition of capital in all sectors. On the contrary, it leads to an *overall increase in the organic composition of capital*, and thereby to a relative redistribution of the productive forces, in favour of the capital goods sector. This is one of the fundamental hypotheses of Marxism, which is moreover confirmed by statistical data.* But if one incorporates this assumption in a "model" of the cycle, all notion of a constant proportion between the value of production in the two sectors collapses, and therewith all "mathematical demonstration" of the inevitable overproduction of consumer goods through under-consumption.

Sternberg's theoretical model is the most interesting one. He proceeds from a twofold basis—on the one hand, the mathematical formulae illustrating expanded reproduction in Volume II of *Capital*, and on the other, the very nature of competition.

When she studied the formulae of expanded reproduction used by Marx in Volume II of *Capital*, Rosa Luxemburg had already insisted on the fact that equilibrium of exchange between the two sectors was made possible only by the fact that the rate of accumulation, which was 50 per cent of the surplus value in Sector I, fell during the same cycle to 20 per cent of the surplus value in Sector II. Sternberg[69] takes up this critique and carries it further. He declares that this inequality between the two rates of accumulation is indispensable for the achievement of equilibrium between the two sectors, with increasing organic composition of capital in both sectors.†

* In the U.S.A., according to Shaw,[68] the production of capital goods increased from 296 million dollars in 1869 to 6,033 million in 1919; the production of consumer goods increased in the same period from 2,428 million dollars to 28,445 dollars. Sector I thus increased its production more than 20-fold, Sector II only 12-fold (and the production of this sector is over-valued, since it contains in the category of "durable consumer goods", products which are actually capital goods). For the period between 1919 and our time we have no exact calculations of the same kind. But the figures of the *Statistical Abstract* relating to different categories of commodity are revealing. Between 1919 and 1952 the production of durable goods (mostly belonging to Sector I) increased 5-fold (growing from index 72 to index 340) whereas that of non-durables only trebled (growing from index 62 to index 190).

† An interesting variant: Kalecki[70] emphasises that it is the allocation of expenditure by the capitalists, that is, the rate of accumulation of surplus value, that underlies the cycle. According to him, this rate is a function of the gap between the *rate of profit expected* and the *present* rate of profit, a gap which shrinks as production capacity rises at the end of the cycle.

Sternberg goes on to say that there is no reason to suppose that the rate of accumulation of capital would be different in the two sectors; this rate would be equalised through capitalist competition. In his formula the disequilibrium results, however, not from an equal rate of accumulation in the two sectors but from the *opposition* between an equal rate of accumulation and a different organic composition of capital in I and II.

Now, both theory and empirically-established data confirm to us that this organic composition of capital must actually be different in these two sectors. It is enough, under these conditions, to follow the working of competition to understand that the rate of accumulation *must* also be lower in Sector II. The capitalists of sector I in fact annex part of the surplus value produced by the workers of sector II, because they exploit the fact that they are technologically ahead of light industry. This conclusion, which fits the facts, leaves Sternberg's argument without a leg to stand on.

Theories of disproportionality

The other school of economics sees the fundamental cause of crisis in the *anarchy of production*, which periodically upsets the conditions of equilibrium between the two main sectors, that of consumer goods and that of capital goods, conditions which we have explained in Chapter 10. In this category can be placed those disciples of Marx such as the Russian "Legal Marxists" Tugan-Baranovsky and Bulgakov, the Austrians Hilferding and Otto Bauer (in his youthful writings), the Pole Henryk Grossman, the Soviet theoretician Bukharin, etc. Among the non-Marxist economists of this school special mention must be made of Aftalion, Schumpeter and Spiethoff.

All these theoreticians see the origin of crises in the fact that each entrepreneur endeavours to increase his own profits to the utmost, without taking into account, in his investments, the tendencies of the market as a whole. It follows logically from this idea that if the capitalists were capable of investing "rationally", i.e. so as to maintain proportions of equilibrium between the two main sectors of production, crises could be avoided. Some theoreticians have even claimed that the production of capital goods could be separated completely from the ultimate consumption of consumer goods and that it would be quite possible to imagine a system in which the whole of economic activity consisted exclusively in the making of machines to make machines, without the consumption of consumer goods coming into the system, so to speak.

The American economist Myron W. Watkins writes: "It may be asked, 'Is there no economic limit to the deferment of consumption?' The answer is that there is none, save . . . the continuance of such consumption as is essential to the proper sustenance of life. In economic theory, the indefinite [!] extension of the roundabout process [of production] is a logical aim [!] A society is conceivable in which men may for several generations (which means indefinitely) be content [!] to get along with salt, bread, milk and a loin cloth the while they are industriously and profitably [!] engaged in the production of machines and equipment of every sort."[71]

What we have here is obviously an absurd idea. No maker of textile machinery is going to double his production capacity, if analysis of the market shows him that no expansion of sales of textile products is expected, since stocks are already fully adequate: "The ultimate aim of accumulation of capital is of course to increase the production of consumer goods."[72] The production of capital goods may separate itself for a whole period from this initial basis and undergo a big expansion without *for the moment* worrying about the increase in ultimate consumption. But it is precisely this *momentary* separation that has to be paid for in the form of a crisis.

It is, moreover, false to suppose that "rational organisation" of investment in a capitalist society, i.e. the "regulation" of competition, could fully do away with economic fluctuations. Experience, notably that of German and Japanese war economy, has given striking proof of this.* No reasoning will lead all the capitalists to restrict their production voluntarily when demand exceeds supply. No logic will induce them to maintain their investments at an average level, at the moment when their current production is no longer being absorbed by the market. To eliminate crises completely, the entire cyclical development of production must be abolished, i.e. every element of uneven development, i.e. all competition, all endeavour to increase the rate of profit and of surplus value, i.e. everything that is capitalist in production . . .

The anarchy of capitalist production therefore cannot be regarded as a cause in itself, independent of all the other characteristics of this mode of production, independent in particular of the contradiction between production and consumption which is a distinctive feature of capitalism.

The supporters of the disproportionality theory forget, moreover, that a *certain* proportion between production and consumption (not a *stable* proportion, as the supporters of the underconsumption theory suppose), between the production capacity of the entire productive apparatus, the production capacity of consumer goods and the purchasing power available for these same goods, is inherent in the conditions of proportionality necessary for avoiding a crisis, and that these conditions can never be realised for a long period under capitalism.

It is to be observed that some supporters of the underconsumption

* See Chapter 14.

theory, carried away by the symmetrical beauty of their "numerical" models, have arrived at conclusions very close to those of Tugan-Baranovsky and Co. This in particular is what has happened to Léon Sartre, who writes:

"One may wonder what would become of capitalism if a well-informed economic dictatorship were to insist that an increasing share of the accumulated surplus value at the disposal of the consumer-goods industries be invested in the capital-goods industries, to the same extent as purchasing power shifted in that direction. If this happened, Tugan-Baranovsky rightly says, basing himself on the diagram, equilibrium would be maintained. The result would be a perfectly viable [?] economy in which the production of means of production would increase faster and faster and that of consumer goods would grow only very slowly . . . But a capitalism like this, producing means of production only so as to produce more means of production, remains in the world of theory, being impracticable under a competitive system."[73]

N. Bukharin also upheld the view that a *state capitalism* would know no more periodical crises of overproduction.[74]

Such "solutions" would be impracticable not only because of the impossibility of establishing a "universal trust" embracing all enterprises but also because of the *technological ratio* that exists between a certain production capacity and a production capacity of consumer goods. They would be impracticable because it is impossible, as we have shown above, completely to separate production from consumption, which remains its ultimate purpose. They would be impracticable because no "logic" would induce the capitalists to buy more and more machinery at a time when the production capacity of their machinery already exceeds the market's capacity to absorb consumer goods.

Outline of a synthesis

An attempt at synthesising underconsumption theories and theories of disproportionality has been undertaken by a whole school, which bases itself on the accelerator principle: Aftalion and Bounatian in France, Harrod in Britain, J. M. Clark and S. Kuznets in the U.S.A., etc. This attempt has been continued by synthesising the multiplier principle with the accelerator principle, as is done by the neo-Keynesian econometry school, notably Samuelson, Goodwin, Hicks, Kalecki, Harrod and Joan Robinson. These syntheses, excessively simplified, succeed merely in showing the basic instability of the capitalist system.

They are only distant approaches to the real cycle, to the understanding of which they nevertheless make important contributions.

To show how this synthesis should be undertaken in Marxist terms, we must briefly reformulate the incorrect views about the ultimate causes of crises, which are, let us repeat, crises of *an economy which aims at profit realised by selling commodities*:

(1) The vulgar supporters of the under-consumption theory declare that crisis could be avoided by increasing the workers' purchasing power during the last phase of the boom. These theoreticians forget that the capitalists do not work simply in order to sell, but to *sell at a profit*. And when wages are raised at a moment when the rate of profit is already declining, the latter risks collapsing altogether—far from prolonging the boom, this additional increase in wages would strangle it.

(2) The vulgar supporters of disproportionality theories, and especially the supporters of what is called the "under-accumulation" school (von Hayek, von Mises, Pigou, Hawtrey, etc.),* declare that a crisis could be prevented if one were to resist any fall in the rate of profit during the last phase of the boom (for example, by freezing wages, reducing excessively high rates of interest, attempting to prevent any distortion of prices, etc.). But these theoreticians forget that if the rate of profit rises *at the same time as markets are shrinking*, this will not stop investment from slowing down. What interests the entrepreneur, indeed, is not the *theoretical* profit he can deduce from a certain rate of wages, a certain rate of interest and certain costs of production, but the *real* profit he expects to realise when he compares costs of production with the *selling possibilities* of his goods:

"High income and profit levels may be a necessary condition of investment, but they cannot be considered a sufficient one. It is questionable whether business firms have so little acumen as to expand capacity on the basis of currently high profits alone. Unless they have been operating at full capacity, with order backlogs piling up, and have been unable or unwilling to expand in the absence of more equity funds, or unless they anticipate further *growth* in sales, induced investment is likely to contract [at the peak of a boom] even in the face of high profits."[76]

And Moulton[77] opportunely recalls an example from history relevant to this subject:

"The increasing concentration of income in the higher brackets and also the rising level of urban incomes generally were serving more or less automatically [between 1919 and 1929] to increase the proportion of the aggregate national income set aside as money savings. That is, although the current income into trade and service channels continued to expand, it expanded less rapidly than the flow of funds into investment channels. While an abundance of funds was thus available with which to construct new plant and equipment, it was evidently clear to business enterprisers that prospective consumptive demands were

* In 1927 Pigou confidently asserted that draconic [!] wage-cuts could avoid a crisis. Von Hayek proclaimed the same "truth" in 1932 [!] in the midst of huge masses of unsaleable consumer goods.[75]

not sufficiently large to warrant as much expansion as the available funds made possible.''

There are, then, *two simultaneously-needed conditions* for economic recovery and the beginning of a boom: *an increasing rate of profit and expanding real markets*. At the start of the economic cycle, these two conditions may coincide for a certain number of reasons: reduction in the organic composition of capital (a larger number of workers with the same amount of equipment), comparatively low wages; increase in the rate of surplus-value, acceleration of the velocity of rotation of capital, on the one hand; and the other, increase in the overall purchasing power of the wage-earners as a whole (through the return of the unemployed to employment), investment of funds saved during the crisis and the depression (notably depreciation funds), and increasing profits quickly realised.

But the same forces that bring about the coincidence of these two factors at the start of the cycle undermine their existence more and more as the cycle progresses, and bring about their collapse towards the end of the cycle. We have already examined, above, the conditions which determine a fall in the rate of profit towards the end of the boom: increase in the organic composition of capital; fall in the rate of surplus value; slowing-down of the velocity of rotation of capital; credit becoming more expensive; increased overhead charges; rising wages, etc. We must now look at what happens as regards markets.

Demand for consumer goods rises very little after full employment has been more or less attained. As for capital goods, when the renewal of fixed capital has been completed, industry is re-equipped with a production capacity exceeding the possibilities of absorption by the market. New investment becomes increasingly improbable. Shrinkage of markets thus takes place in both sectors. The coincidence of the fall in the rate of profit with the shrinkage of markets brings about the crisis.

Is there general overproduction at the moment of the crisis? Undoubtedly there is. It follows necessarily from the two basic aspects of the boom.

Economic recovery, by causing a rise in the rate of surplus value and a rise in the rate of profit, changes the allocation of the national income among the classes, to the advantage of the bourgeoisie and at the expense of the wage-earners. Many writers confirm this opinion (Haberler, Schumpeter, Lederer, Foster and Catchings, Hobson, Moszkowska, Hicks, etc.)[78]* Sombart expresses the idea like this:

* Professor Guitton gives the following picture of the average cyclical variations in France during the nineteenth century: prices rise by 17 per cent in boom and fall by 16 per cent in depression; wages rise by 12 per cent in boom and fall by 3 per cent in depression; profits rise by 40 to 200 per cent [!] in boom and fall by 14 to 38 per cent in depression.[79]

"It is the conjuncture of expansion itself . . . which, in periods of recovery, has the effect that wages do not rise to the same extent as surplus value, owing to the rise in prices; this also, by regular movements of contraction, by expelling workers (from the production process), is what fills up the labour market to the desired degree, so creating the industrial reserve army which prevents an excessive rise in wages."[80]

But at the same time as the wage-earners' share of the national income relatively falls, the production capacity of the industries producing consumer goods is constantly growing. The moment has to come at which the increase in this production capacity exceeds the level of demand.

Furthermore, the increase in the production capacity of the sector producing capital goods corresponds to the need for renewing a substantial part of the fixed capital of all industry. When this renewal has been achieved, sector I will be able to avoid overproduction only on condition that investment *continues at the same pace*, which is obviously not possible.[81]

Society's greatly increased production capacity cannot be used to a more or less complete extent until after a preliminary destruction of value, adaptation of the value of the commodities to the new amount of labour socially-necessary to produce them, a smaller amount than that which determined the previous level of value of these commodities. *The collapse of the boom is thus the collapse of the attempt to maintain the former level of values, prices and rates of profit with an increased quantity of capital*. It is the conflict between the conditions for the accumulation of capital and for its realisation, which is merely the unfolding of all the contradictions inherent in capitalism, *all* of which enter into this explanation of crises: contradictions between the great development of production capacity and the not-so-great development of the consumption-capacity of the broad masses; contradictions arising from the anarchy of production resulting from competition, the increase in the organic composition of capital and the fall in the rate of profit; contradictions between the increasing socialisation of production and the private form of appropriation.*

The conditions of capitalist expansion

The historical conditions which ensure the expansion of the capitalist mode of production, have already been explained above. They arise essentially from the *uneven development* of different sectors, branches and countries drawn into the capitalist market. The creation of the world market, which precedes the great advance of the capitalist mode

---

* On crises in the epoch of declining capitalism, and the role of public expenditure in the economy, see Chapter 14, section on "A crisis-free capitalism?"

of production, establishes the general setting for this uneven development. The latter shows itself in:

(a) Unevenness of development as between industry and agriculture. As industry develops, its commodities drive out the products of the domestic and craft labour of the peasantry, ruining a section of the country people, who become proletarians and form a mass of labour available to expanding industry. The value of industrial production increases as compared with that of agricultural production; the industrial labour force increases as compared with the number of persons occupied in agriculture. The peasants buy more means of production (which previously they made for themselves) from large scale industry, which buys raw material from the peasants, though in smaller proportions.

(b) Unevenness of development as between the countries first to be industrialised and the colonial and semi-colonial countries. The industry of the first-industrialised countries destroys the craft and domestic production of the colonial and semi-colonial countries, which are transformed into markets of the advanced countries. The labour-power "released" as a result of this destruction of the age-old equilibrium between agriculture and industry cannot find occupation in an expanding national industry, because it is the expansion of industry in the *metropolitan* country that has made it possible to conquer this market. In consequence there appear the related phenomena of chronic under-employment and pressure of over-population on the land. "The results come quickly: in 1813 Calcutta exported £2 million worth of cotton goods; in 1830 it imported cotton goods to the same value. The import of cotton goods into India as a whole rose from £8 million in 1859 to £16 million in 1877 and £20 million in 1901, that of silks from £1·4 million to £7 million and £16 million, and that of cotton thread from £1·7 million to £2·8 million."

At the same time India became more and more agricultural, and in the same period 1850–1877 the export of raw cotton increased from £4 million to £13 million, that of jute from £0·9 million to £3 million, that of tea from £0·15 million to £2·6 million, and that of oil from £2·5 million to £5·4 million. [82]

A combination of four obstacles to the capitalist industrialisation of the colonial and semi-colonial countries resulted: competition from commodities produced in the metropolitan country; competition between the very cheap local labour-power and modern machinery; shortage of capital owing to investment of the accumulated income of the ruling class in landed property; and lack of adequate internal markets such as would make possible a rapid development of some industrial sectors.*

(c) Unevenness of development as between different branches of

* See Chapters 6, 9 and 13.

industry, especially between declining ones and those which are on the upgrade owing to successive technological revolutions. The declining branches see their markets, their turnover, the numbers employed in them, getting smaller and smaller, at first relatively, then absolutely. After trying to defend themselves by increasing the organic composition of capital and reducing prices (relatively or absolutely), they submit, and henceforth renew only part of their fixed capital. A share of the surplus value and the depreciation funds of these sectors spills on to the capital market, attracted by the sectors which are expanding rapidly. The latter carve themselves a place in the market by tearing resources (fixed capital, raw material, purchasing power) from the existing sectors, either by slowing down the growth of some of them or else by causing absolute setbacks to others.

(d) Unevenness of development as between different parts of a single country. This phenomenon, usually underestimated in Marxist economic writing, is in reality one of the essential keys to the understanding of expanded reproduction. *By creating depressed areas within the capitalist nations, the capitalist mode of production itself creates its own "complementary" markets, as well as its permanent reserves of labour-power.* This happened with Scotland and Wales in Britain, the Southern States in the U.S.A., the eastern and southern parts of Germany, Flanders in Belgium, Slovakia in Czechoslovakia, the South in Italy, the South and the North in the Netherlands, France south of the Loire, and so on. What is characteristic of the spasmodic, unequal, contradictory development of the capitalist mode of production is that it cannot industrialise systematically and harmoniously the whole of a large country. The gradual abolition of old depressed areas is itself accompanied by the appearance of new depressed areas: New England in the U.S.A., the Borinage and the la Louvière region in Belgium: Lancashire in Britain; Haute-Loire in France; Genoa in Italy, etc. The irony of history is such that often these new depressed areas were formerly the cradles of capitalist industry in these countries.

No growth without fluctuations?

Since the great crisis of 1929 the idea of a harmonious and balanced development of the capitalist order has finally fallen into discredit. The most fashionable bourgeois writers, such as Schumpeter, have, like Marx, put stress on the basic instability of the capitalist mode of production. For Schumpeter this instability results from the fact that "innovation", i.e. the application of technical discoveries to industry, cannot be spread evenly over the whole duration of the economic cycle, but tends to be concentrated in certain spaced-out periods.[83] For the econometricians the basic instability of the mode of production results from the fact that the conditions needed for unbroken growth are unrealisable in practice, owing to the special nature of investment under capitalism: * "The system will not remain in progressive equilibrium unless it is *completely adjusted* to it . . . A system is unlikely to be completely adjusted in a progressive equilibrium until it has been in approximate equilibrium for a long time. It is not sufficient that the capital stock should be adjusted to current output; it is also necessary that it should fall due for replacement at the right dates. The induced investment of the future which is already preconditioned (to a considerable extent) by past changes in output, the effects of which are embodied in existing equipment, must be such as to be consistent with steady development."[85]

Joan Robinson makes the same point: "An economy which existed in a state of tranquillity, lucidity and harmony would be devoted to the production and consumption of wealth in a rational manner. It is only necessary to describe these conditions to see how remote they are from the states in which actual economies dwell. Capitalism, in particular, could never have come into existence in such conditions, for the divorce between work and property, which makes large-scale enterprise possible, entails conflict; and the rules of the game have been developed precisely to make accumulation and technical progress possible in conditions of uncertainty and imperfect knowledge."[86]

And, further: "For each individual entrepreneur the future is uncertain even when the economy as a whole is developing smoothly, and the actions of each entrepreneur affect the situation for the rest. For this reason there is an inherent instability, under the capitalist rules of the game, which generates fluctuations, so to say, from within the economy, quite apart from any change in external circumstances. The typical entrepreneur, as soon as he finds his existing capacity operating at what seems to him a reasonable rate of profit, wants to operate more capacity. Unless investment just hits off the golden-age rate, at which demand grows with capacity (or unless it is effectively controlled), it will always be oscillating, for whenever it happens to rise it generates a seller's market, and so stimulates a further rise."[87]

Writers who conscientiously try to emphasise the advantages of the capitalist mode of production as the most progressive mode of production, like Arthur F. Burns and David McCorde Wright, have taken a step further and declared that it is *impossible* to conceive of an economy open to the benefits of technological progress or possessing a substantial stock of fixed capital which would not be subject to fluctuations. According to them, the choice is not between progress with or without fluctuations but rather between progress with fluctuations and complete stagnation.

Thus, David McCorde Wright writes: "The *fundamental* cause of the business cycle is the failure of changes in taste and technique to occur at rates which smoothly offset one another. It is *durability* of

* Including fluctuations in stocks: see Metzler, Abramovitz, Eckert.[84]

equipment plus asymmetrical *changeability* of wants plus inevitable frictions plus *consumer sovereignty* [!] which produces the business cycle . . . Any growing society which wants to meet the pattern of consumer spending will inevitably suffer certain [!] instabilities and insecurities."[88]

Let us first of all throw Noah's garment over the most absurd aspect of this apologia, namely, the allegation that the innovations which bring the big waves of investment result from "changes in taste on the part of the consumer". It was not, after all, the "need to have a car" that created the motor-car industry; it was this industry that created the need to have a car. It is the investment of enormous amounts of capital in new sectors of industry (and, to a subsidiary extent, publicity for their products) that changes the taste of consumers, and not the changing taste of consumers that brings about the flow of enormous amounts of capital into certain sectors, or, even less, technical inventions.

But would these innovations not occur in an irregular way in a planned economy, a socialist economy?*

Would not the durability of industrial equipment bring about equally in such an economy the phenomenon of "overproduction", through the need to meet *sudden demands* (e.g. the introduction of colour television; or the effect of a sudden increase in the population on the building industry, etc.)?

According to McCorde Wright,[90] *any* economic system has *a choice only between two evils*: either to keep up the planned pace of growth, of production, in these sectors, and so provoke prolonged irritation on the part of the consumers (reflected in a rise in prices, etc.), or else to increase rapidly the rate of progress of production by exceptional investments, and so expose oneself to over-equipment (the appearance of excess capacity) from the moment when the exceptional demand has been satisfied (e.g. when all the extra population has been provided with housing, and the demand for renewal declines owing to a changed age-structure of this same population).

Arthur F. Burns had already set forth the same view in his article *Long Cycles in Construction*, published in 1935 and reproduced in his collection *Frontiers of Economic Knowledge* (1954). He there explains the instability of the demand for housing in a "collectivist society", and strives to show that such a society would experience marked cyclical fluctuations in the building trade.[91] But his entire argument is based on a simplistic assumption, namely, that what is available to each family must remain *fixed* and that house building fluctuates exclusively in accordance with fluctuations in the population (and the more-or-less correct forecasting of this).

From the moment when we abandon this assumption and accept, on

* Schumpeter and Cassel[89] emphasise the same idea.

the contrary, that planned economy has a *twofold* aim—first and foremost, to provide each family with the indispensable "housing unit", constituting the minimum standard of comfort, but then, after that, to bring the minimum standard of housing up to the *optimum* standard (from the standpoint of comfort, town-planning, hygiene, upbringing of children, etc.)—the whole of Burns' theory collapses. As soon as a surplus of capacity, in relation to immediate needs, makes its appearance, this capacity can be used to bring about an improvement in the living conditions of part of the population. And as one may reasonably assume that this *optimum* itself has a tendency to rise, as a result of scientific and technical progress, no "excess capacity" is conceivable for a long period of time.

McCorde Wright's mistake is exactly the same. In order to demonstrate the "fluctuations" inevitable in a planned economy he imagines an economy which has abolished only one aspect of capitalism (private ownership of the means of production), while retaining all its other aspects. Thus, when a backlog of demand has been satisfied, he sees no other result than "overproduction" or "excess capacity"; it does not occur to him that it would be possible to make an additional and new range of consumer goods available to society.* When the productive apparatus is "hypertrophied", he does not realise that one can "adapt it to need" by reducing the producers' working time. When he brings in an "absolute excess capacity" without the possibility of making "new products", he does not realise that the putting into reserve of part of this machinery would be accompanied by no reduction of consumption or "income" for society, and so by no *economic* fluctuation, since this withdrawal of machinery would have been *caused* precisely by the fact that the *real needs* (and not merely effective monetary demand) of society had been *previously and completely satisfied*.

The fluctuations of production which entail fluctuations in income and consumption, through overproduction of commodities, and which thus imply periodical unemployment and poverty, are peculiar to capitalism. They did not exist before capitalism, and they will not survive it.†

* Hamberg[92] emphasises what a ceaselessly expanding range of products can be manufactured with the same modern equipment.
† See Chapter 17.

REFERENCES

1. J. Schumpeter: *Business Cycles*, Vol. I, p. 225.
2. W. Abel: *Agrarkrisen und Agrarkonjunktur in Mittelalter*, p. 158.
3. Jean Fourastié: *Le Grand espoir du XXᵉ siècle*, p. 141.
4. J. M. Keynes: *General Theory*.

5. H. Guitton: *Les fluctuations économiques* (9th volume of Gaëtan Pirou's *Traité d'économie politique*), pp. 174-5.

6. Karl Marx: *Grundrisse*, Vol. I, p. 310.

7. L. R. Klein: *The Keynesian Revolution*, p. 8.

8. F. A. Von Hayek: *Geldtheorie and Konjunkturtheorie*, pp. 51, 103.

9. J. M. Keynes: op. cit., p. 317.

10. G. Von Haberler: *Prospérité et Dépression*, pp. 154-5.

11. Alvin H. Hansen: *Business Cycles and National Income*, p. 50; Hans Roth: *Die Uebererzeugung in der Welthandelsware Kaffee*, pp. 104-5; Richard B. Tennant: *The American Cigarette Industry*, pp. 192-4, etc.

12. A. Aftalion: *Crises périodiques*, Vol. I, pp. 359-64; W. C. Mitchell: *Business Cycles and Employment*, pp. 10-11; Keynes: op. cit–Schumpeter: op. cit., Vol. I, pp. 4, 123; Hansen: op. cit., p. 564; Guitton: op. cit., p. 321.

13. Von Haberler: op. cit., p. 298.

14. A. D. Gayer, W. W. Rostow and A. J. Schwartz: *Growth and Fluctuation of the British Economy*, p. 557.

15. J. M. Clark: quoted in Hansen, op. cit.

16. Natalya Moszkowska: *Zur Kritik Moderner Krisentheorien*, p. 62.

17. Schumpeter: op. cit., Vol. I, p. 148.

18. Von Haberler: op. cit., p. 414.

19. Keynes: op. cit.

20. Von Haberler: op. cit., pp. 32, 154-5; Abramovitz: *Inventories and Business Cycles*, pp. 360-9.

21. Schumpeter: op. cit., Vol. II, pp. 576-7.

22. W. C. Mitchell: *What Happens During Business Cycles?*, pp. 106, 116-17.

23. Von Haberler: op. cit., p. 429.

24. Ibid., p. 378.

25. Spiethoff: in von Haberler: op. cit., p. 90.

26. Keynes: op. cit.; von Haberler: op. cit., p. 442.

27. W. Woytinsky: *Conséquences sociales de la crise*, pp. 72-73.

28. Jan Tinbergen: *Les Cycles économiques aux Etats-Unis*, p. 105.

29. Schumpeter: op. cit., Vol. II, p. 637.

30. Hansen: op. cit., p. 60; Keynes: op. cit.

31. Moszkowska: op. cit., p. 62; L. Sartre: *Esquisse d'une théorie marxiste des crises périodiques*, p. 101.

32. Hansen: op. cit., p. 145.

33. Ibid., p. 173.

34. R. Eckert: *Les Théories modernes de l'expansion économique*, p. 35.

35. J. R. Hicks: *A Contribution to the Theory of the Trade Cycle*, p. 108.

36. Schumpeter: op. cit., Vol. II, p. 400.

37. Hansen: op. cit., pp. 123-4.

38. Hayer, Rostow and Schwartz: op. cit., p. 554.

39. Hansen: op. cit., pp. 182-3.

40. Hansen: op. cit., p. 60; G. von Haberler: op. cit., pp. 316-17.

41. Schumpeter: op. cit., Vol. II, pp. 576-7.

42. Hansen: op. cit., p. 125.
43. Von Haberler: op. cit., p. 404.
44. W. T. Foster and W. Catchings: *Money*, p. 274.
45. Eckert: op. cit., p. 12.
46. Abramovitz: op. cit., p. 498; Metzler: "Business Cycles and the Modern Theory of Employment", in *American Economic Review*, June 1946.
47. *Die Welt*, 22nd October, 1960.
48. W. C. Mitchell: *What Happens During Business Cycles?*, pp. 302-3 (see also pp. 32, 40, 73); Hansen: op. cit., pp. 82-83.
49. W. C. Mitchell: *What Happens During Business Cycles?*, pp. 161 *et al.*
50. Ibid., pp. 32, 34, 41.
51. Von Haberler: op. cit., p. 416.
52. Ibid., p. 120; W. C. Mitchell: *What Happens . . .*, pp. 132-3.
53. Von Haberler: op. cit., pp. 375-80.
54. Harold G. Moulton: *Controlling Factors in Economic Development*, p. 306.
55. N. Kaldor: *Stability and Full Employment*, reprinted in A. Hansen and R. V. Clemence, *Readings in Business Cycles and National Income*, pp. 499-500.
56. J. Schumpeter: *Business Cycles*, Vol. I, p. 158.
57. Gayer, Rostow and Schwartz: op. cit., p. 544; Schumpeter: op. cit., 499.
58. K. Kautsky: *"Finanzkapital und Krisen"*, in *Neue Zeit*, Vol. XXIX, No. 1, pp. 843-4 (1911).
59. Fred Oelssner: *Die Wirtschaftskrisen*, Vol. I, p. 38.
60. Rosa Luxemburg: *Die Akkumulation des Kapitals*, passim.
61. N. Bukharin: *Der Imperialismus und die Akkumulation des Kapitals*, pp. 95-108.
62. Luxemburg: op. cit., p. 407.
63. Karl Marx: *Theorien über den Mehrwert*, Vol. II, pt. 2, p. 315.
64. Paul M. Sweezy: *The Theory of Capitalist Development*, pp. 180-4.
65. Otto Bauer: *Zwischen zwei Weltkriegen?*, pp. 51-53, 351-5.
66. Hamberg: *Economic Growth and Instability*, pp. 55-56 *et al.*
67. Sartre: op. cit., pp. 62-66.
68. Shaw's estimates in *Historical Statistics of the U.S.A.*
69. Fritz Sternberg: *Der Imperialismus*, pp. 20 et seq.; *Der Imperialismus und seine Kritiker*, pp. 163 et seq.
70. Kalecki: "A Theory of the Business Cycle", in *Review of Economic Studies*, Vol. IV, 1936–7, pp. 77.
71. Myron W. Watkins: "Commercial Banking and Capital Formation", in *Journal of Political Economy*, Vol. XXVII, July 1919, pp. 584-5.
72. Von Haberler: op. cit., pp. 43-44.
73. Sartre: op. cit., p. 61.
74. Bukharin: op. cit., pp. 88-89.
75. In Hansen: op. cit., p. 518; Von Hayek: in *Weltwirtschaftliches Archiv*, July 1932, Vol. I, pp. 90, et seq.
76. Hamberg: op. cit., p. 323.
77. Moulton: op. cit., p. 70.

78. Von Haberler: op. cit., p. 324; Schumpeter: op. cit., pp. 155, 561; Moszkowska: op. cit., p. 26; Hicks: op. cit., pp. 126-7, etc.

79. Guitton: op. cit., p. 94.

80. Werner Sombart: *Der moderne Kapitalismus*, Vol. II, p. 586.

81. Hamberg: op. cit., p. 55; Hansen: op. cit., pp. 495-6.

82. André Philip: *L'Inde moderne*, p. 87.

83. Schumpeter: op. cit., Vol. II, p. 1033.

84. Eckert: op. cit., pp. 59-64.

85. Hicks: op. cit., pp. 63-64.

86. Joan Robinson: *The Accumulation of Capital*, p. 60.

87. Ibid., p. 209.

88. David McCord Wright: *Capitalism*, pp. 147, 153, 154.

89. Schumpeter: op. cit., Vol. II, p. 803; Cassel: in *Readings in Business Cycles and National Income*, p. 124.

90. Wright: op. cit., pp. 144-6.

91. Burns: op. cit., pp. 314-34.

92. Hamberg: op. cit., pp. 223-4.

FOUNDATIONS
—OF—
RADICAL
POLITICAL
ECONOMY

FOUNDATIONS
—OF—
RADICAL POLITICAL ECONOMY

HOWARD J. SHERMAN

M. E. Sharpe, Inc.
Armonk, New York
London, England

Copyright © 1987 by M. E. Sharpe, Inc.
80 Business Park Drive, Armonk, New York 10504

All rights reserved. No part of this book may be reproduced in any
form without written permission from the publisher, M. E. Sharpe, Inc.

Available in the United Kingdom and Europe from M. E. Sharpe,
Publishers, 3 Henrietta Street, London WC2E 8LU.

Library of Congress Cataloging in Publication Data

Sherman, Howard J.
    Foundations of radical political economy.

    Bibliography: p.
    1. Marxian economics. 2. Capitalism. 3. State, The. 4. Socialism.
I. Title.

HB97.5.S5117   1987   330.1   86–33849
ISBN 0-87332-416-1
ISBN 0-87332-431-5 (pbk.)

Printed in the United States of America

This book is presented, with love,
to Barbara Sinclair

It is also presented, with respect for his
leadership in radical political economy,
to Paul Sweezy

CONTENTS

PREFACE

This book is brand new from beginning to end. It is similar to my old book, *Radical Political Economy*, only in that it covers most of the same issues and reaches the same overall conclusion in favor of democracy and socialism. Many of my analyses and conclusions on particular subjects, however, have changed because of the flood of new literature in every area of radical political economy and because the world has changed.

The most important issue is the prevention of nuclear war. As a child I was shocked by the millions of people killed in the Second World War and then was horrified by the effects of the atomic bombs dropped on Hiroshima and Nagasaki. I believe that the roots of war lie in imperialism and the unjust social systems that give rise to imperialism. Only by changing the present dominant social systems can we abolish the threat of a nuclear war disaster.

As a child in the Second World War I was also deeply affected by the evidence that fascism had killed six million Jews. The fact that fascism treated women like slaves penetrated deep into my consciousness. As a result, I grew to despise all types of racial, religious, and sexual prejudice and discrimination. Radical political economy focuses on the social conditions under which all people will be treated equally.

I have observed the effects of undemocratic dictatorships in fascist Germany, in racist countries like South Africa, and in the Stalinist repression in the Soviet Union. Thus, I believe that an understanding of the causes of dictatorship and the ways to achieve democracy constitutes one major task of radical political economy.

Not only political democracy, but economic democracy is necessary. My deepest feelings revolve around the fact that every day millions of men, women, and children go to bed hungry in this world. Millions live in poverty even in the rich United States. Yet we have the technology to create a better world in which no one will lack food, clothing, and shelter. The problem is that many live in poverty and are exploited for the benefit of the wealthy few. Growing up in Chicago, I witnessed workers striking for a decent living and being beaten up by the police, who always acted on behalf of the wealthy. We need a world with democracy in the economic sphere (socialism if you wish to label it) so that no one is exploited and no one lives in poverty.

Finally, I live in Southern California and frequently witness the unpleasant effects of air pollution, a dirty yellow cloud in which one can hardly breathe. These are some of the issues that caused me to write this book about political economy.

Before discussing the exciting questions of political economy itself, it is necessary to understand the sociological, historical, and philosophical framework of these issues. That is the task of part I.

In part II, the evolution and problems of capitalism are discussed. Why are some people rich and others poor? Why are some nations developed and some underdeveloped? What are the causes of exploitation and oppression by race, sex, and class? What causes wars? Pollution? Unemployment? Part III looks at similar problems in the Soviet Union and other statist systems. In addition, it asks, what is the relation of democracy to capitalism, statism, and socialism? What are the relative strengths and weaknesses of central planning and the use of the market? Part IV discusses how we might build a better society.

Acknowledgments

I thank the Research Committee of the University of California, Riverside, for an intramural grant that has been very helpful. I thank the *International Review of Applied Economics* for permission to use some of the material from my article, ''The Business Cycle of Capitalism,'' in the *International Review of Applied Economics* 1 (1987), pp. 72–85.

I am very grateful to a number of coauthors of previous books and articles, who have helped me to understand certain areas in depth. Those coauthors were Andrew Zimbalist, James Wood, Barbara Sinclair, E. K. Hunt, and Robin Hahnel; each of them will recognize some points in this book where I benefited from lengthy discussions with them.

I wish to thank Shirlee Pigeon and Mary Lou Shields for an excellent job of typing as well as some editorial corrections.

Finally, I wish to thank the following people for criticisms and constructive comments on this book: Samuel Bowles, Paul Diesing, Peter Dorman, Howard Engelskirchen, John B. Foster, David Gleicher, Mark Gottdeiner, Robin Hahnel, Rajani Kanth, Victor Lippit, Warren Samuels, Barbara Sinclair, and Howard Wachtel. I owe a special debt of gratitude to Lynn Turgeon, who read the whole manuscript and made many helpful comments. Many other people have influenced the book over many years, including a good number of graduate students who criticized parts of it in some detail, readers of various articles from which it evolved, and friends and colleagues who read and commented on earlier draft manuscripts that were eventually replaced by this one.

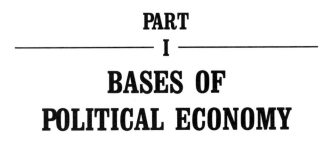

PART
I
BASES OF
POLITICAL ECONOMY

— 1 —
PHILOSOPHICAL BASES OF POLITICAL ECONOMY

Thomas Kuhn (1962) created a major stir in all of the sciences, including economics, when he wrote his book on scientific revolutions. He argued that science does not proceed smoothly, but has periods of slow, incremental progress, followed by revolutions. He used the term "paradigm" to describe the hardcore of a science during the long periods of incremental progress; a paradigm means an approach, a general theory, and some important conclusions all taken for granted by 99 percent of the scientists in a field. This is a useful concept, though—as will be seen below—there is a vast literature expanding, criticizing, and modifying Kuhn's concept of a paradigm.

In economics, Kuhn's concepts must be modified considerably, but they are a fruitful starting point. When economics has a scientific revolution, it is never accepted by everybody, so the old paradigm lingers on in competition with the new one. Thus, economics at present has several paradigms, each believed by many economists. In the United States, the dominant paradigm is called neoclassical economics (which now includes a conservative variant of Keynesian economics). In his presidential address to the American Economic Association in 1972, the institutionalist John Kenneth Galbraith emphasized that "Within the last half-dozen years what before was simply called economics in the nonsocialist world has come to be designated neoclassical economics with appropriate overtures to the Keynesian and post-Keynesian development. From being a general and accepted theory of economic behavior this has become a special and debatable interpretation of such behavior" (1973: 1).

In the Soviet Union, the dominant paradigm is called "Marxism," and it constitutes an official religion. The official Marxism of the Soviet Union and other Communist countries is a hardened dogma: it states the *truth*, and only the boss of the country can suddenly alter the *truth*; it is very unhealthy for a Soviet social scientist to alter the *truth* without official sanction. Only a few of all U.S. political economists consider themselves purely orthodox Marxists, and they are usually called "fundamentalists."

In opposition to both of these dominant paradigms is the paradigm of radical political economy. Modern radical political economy includes three or four older traditions. First, there is the classical tradition, with emphasis on David Ricardo and the neo-Ricardian tradition, especially in the work of Piero Sraffa. Second, there is the Marxist tradition, taken as a set of powerful hypotheses, but not as an eternal truth. Third, there is the left Keynesian tradition and the post-Keynesian writers, such as Joan Robinson. Fourth, the radical paradigm has been strongly affected by the institutionalist economics of Thorstein Veblen. All of these traditions have merged to some extent in modern radical political economy, in different proportions in different writers.

At most points this book refers only to the three overall paradigms: the neoclassical-Keynesian (often shortened to just neoclassical), the official Marxist, and the radical (or independent Marxist, post-Keynesian, neo-Ricardian, institutionalist). Of course, for many purposes one should differentiate these traditions somewhat further. For example, there are liberal as well as conservative neoclassical economists. Also, there are considerable differences between the official Marxists of the Soviet Union (not to speak of other countries) and what are called here the fundamentalists in the United States. Both are alike in accepting Marxism as an unchallenged dogma, but they are extremely different in many of their interpretations of that dogma. They differ on many vital points, from their views of monopoly to their views of the Soviet Union—so when fundamentalists are criticized, this is not necessarily a criticism of Soviet Marxists, and vice versa.

Although official and fundamentalist Marxists are often criticized in this book, this book is not an attack on Marx. On the contrary, most of this author's "radical" paradigm is seen as evolving from the insights and inspirations of Marx—and from his indignation against oppression. This book could be considered as an unorthodox, independent, nondogmatic view of Marx. (In my opinion, the official and fundamentalist Marxists differ in a basic way from Marx himself, who was unorthodox, independent, and willing to consider changing his views.) But the radical paradigm rejects the notion that Marx or anyone else has the last word; every radical must think things through for herself or himself. Moreover, important parts of the radical tradition do come from the neo-Ricardian, post-Keynesian, and institutionalist views mentioned above. Therefore, this author does not label any radical as a "Marxist" or "non-Marxist," because such labels are not helpful to a scientific understanding of society and are misleading in the sense that radicals make use of many other theorists besides Marx (and do have various disagreements with Marx).

Some neoclassicals have denied that radicals have a fully developed paradigm, but this book is intended to present such a radical paradigm. Of course, since radicals are all heretics by nature, they seldom agree with each other, and there is nothing in the institutional arrangements to force such agreement. Therefore, I shall report in full some of the disagreements among radical economists within that paradigm (just as there are many disagreements within the neoclassical paradigm). Where no disagreements among radicals are indicated, the radical view given is my own.

Radical versus Neoclassical Paradigm

To clarify the difference between the two paradigms, the main lines of disagreement between radicals and neoclassical economists should be noted. Each of these points will later be discussed in detail with documentation.

1. Neoclassical economics is equilibrium-oriented, whereas radical economics is dynamic, considers conflicts, and is evolutionary (discussed in this chapter and chapter 2).

2. Neoclassical economics considers only incremental change within one set of institutional relations, whereas radical economics considers both incremental change and the complete change between one system and a new one (see this chapter and chapter 2).

3. Neoclassical economics views economics as a technical subject, isolated from social and political issues and conflicts. Radical economics contends that one cannot understand the economy except as a set of human relations, interacting with the human relations in the government, the family, and so forth. Thus, for example, radicals see sexism and racism as part of the entire political economy. Neoclassicals for decades had nothing to say about race and sex, then—when they began

to examine the subjects—still saw them as isolated from the class relationships of the whole political economy (see chapter 5).

4. Neoclassical economics has no theory of exploitation but sees the economy as purely harmonious, concentrating on equilibrium as its main analytic tool. The concept of power by one group over another is missing from neoclassical economics. Radicals view the economy as an arena of conflict and exploitation of one group by another, more powerful group (see chapter 4).

5. In examining race and sex, the narrow neoclassical approach finds that capitalist competition automatically ends all discrimination, while radicals see capitalist attempts to maximize profits (by divide and rule) as a major cause of sexism and racism (see chapter 5).

6. Neoclassicals join the crudest pluralists in political science by conceptualizing government as the sum of decisions by different interest groups, voting with numbers of voters as consumers vote with dollars. Radicals see government as an arena of conflict, with the dominant economic class usually dominant in the governmental sphere (see chapter 8).

7. Neoclassical Keynesians have no theory of cyclical crises but rather see each crisis as a deviation from automatic full employment caused by incorrect government policies. Monetarism merely takes this tendency to its reductio ad absurdum. Radicals see crises as inherent in the capitalist system of relationships (see chapter 6).

8. Neoclassicals see monopoly as a minor deviation from pure and perfect competition. Most radicals see monopoly as a new stage of capitalism, in which the giant corporation is dominant and many economic laws have changed (see chapter 7).

9. Neoclassicals see environmental destruction as a minor deviation from the best of all worlds (given by competition) as predicted by Adam Smith. Radicals see external diseconomies (environmental harm not accounted for by private profit-making calculation) as being pervasive in the economy (see chapter 5).

10. Neoclassical economics always starts out from the viewpoint of the individual, so every problem (such as racism) comes down to individual preferences. Radicals explain individual preferences in terms of the structure of society, so phenomena such as racism result from the nature of capitalist society (see chapter 5).

11. Neoclassical economics sees the competitive market as the solution to all problems; it conditions its students so that any collective plan, such as free health care, is automatically seen as an evil reduction of efficiency and individual welfare. Radical economics recognizes the

disadvantages as well as the advantages of the market. Collective decisions on subjects such as education and health care are both necessary and rational; we need cooperation and planning to replace the market and greed in some areas (see chapters 17 and 18).

Official Marxism versus
Radical Political Economy

Official Marxism is just as rigid and just as apologetic as neoclassical economics, though each apologizes for different types of societies. Radicals are critical of both societies and both ideological defenses. Differences between radicals and official Marxists include the following.

1. For official Marxists, dialectics is a set of universal laws of movement, stating how everything changes, interacts, and evolves. For radicals, a dialectic approach merely is a method according to which one asks certain questions about changes in society and about conflicts in society, while seeing society as a totality (see this chapter).

2. For official Marxists, historical materialism means that the economy determines the rest of society, and ideas are merely reflections of the economy. Radicals see a never-ending interaction between ideas and the economy. Moreover, the economy itself is seen as a site of conflict and human relationships, not merely technological forces (see chapter 2).

3. Official and fundamentalist Marxists view the labor theory of value as a set of laws of commodity exchange, including the exchange of labor-power; it is a sacred cow, not to be further investigated, but only accepted. Radicals see much that can be improved in Marx's statement of the labor theory of value, and they see the theory as mainly stating a set of human relations, not a purely technical economic relation among commodities (see chapter 4).

4. Official Marxists view race and sex as purely secondary complications to the basic class theory. Radicals see class as the most important analytic tool, but they view race and sex as equally or more important in some situations. The official theory concludes that racism and sexism will automatically die away in socialism, while radicals conclude that socialism sets a better framework for fighting those evils, but that a continuing fight will be needed (see chapters 5 and 16).

5. The official Marxist theory of the state says that government merely is the tool of the ruling class, so the government represents the capitalists in the United States and the workers in the Soviet Union.

Since Soviet workers control their state, this is the highest form of democracy. Radicals believe, on the contrary, that the U.S. situation is one of conflicting classes in the governmental area, though with the capitalist class usually dominant (but frequently divided into warring factions). Not only class structure, but political mechanisms of democracy are important. Lacking those political mechanisms of democracy, the Soviet Union can only be a dictatorship over the people—or over the working class, if you prefer (see chapters 8 and 13).

6. Official Marxism forces all contemporary major societies into the tight boxes of either capitalism or socialism. Radicals find that Soviet-type societies are something else, which I call statism (see chapter 10).

7. Orthodox, fundamentalist Marxists appear to think that the labor theory of value solves all problems, and they refuse to clutter their social theory with other real problems of the world. So they dismiss monopoly and stick to a world of competition about as much as the neoclassicals. Most radicals see monopoly as pervasive in the U.S. economy (see chapter 7).

8. Similarly, both fundamentalist Marxists and neoclassicals accept Say's law, which argues that there cannot be deficiency of aggregate demand, so it cannot cause cyclical unemployment. Fundamentalist Marxists stick to a rigid notion of an absolute law that the rate of profit keeps falling (how far below zero will it go?) to explain all macroeconomic problems. Radicals recognize problems of producing profits, but they also recognize problems of realization of profits due to lack of demand (see chapter 6).

9. Official Marxists assume that socialism means central planning. Radicals believe that central planning must be used along with the market, in the context of worker control of enterprises (see chapters 14 and 15).

10. Official and fundamentalist Marxists think that Marx said correctly everything that could ever be said, so they solve arguments by quoting Marx. Radicals do not venerate any authority but always think through every problem anew on the basis of their own knowledge of the world (see this chapter).

Philosophical Approaches

With this brief outline of the different paradigms, it is time to examine systematically their contrasting philosophical approaches. Briefly, the neoclassical paradigm includes the views that economics begins with individual human psychology, not interconnected social relations; that economics focuses on equilibrium and harmony, not conflict or power; that economics is mainly ahistorical and uses comparative statics, not evolutionary theory; and that economics is an objective science, with no need for an ethical position. The radical paradigm is diametrically opposed on each of these issues (and is also opposed to the official Marxist paradigm on most issues). The different points of controversy between paradigms may be considered under the headings of dialectics, determinism, humanism, and materialism.

Dialectics

The term "dialectic" was made popular by G.W.F. Hegel in the nineteenth century. Hegel saw the universe as a dynamic system that was an interconnected totality, changing through conflict. The strength of Hegel's dialectic view is its emphasis on change and movement. The weakness is his concentration on the realm of abstract ideas, though these ideas are always moving and evolving. An idea cannot stay the same; it goes somewhere and in the process discloses its own inadequacy, so it makes way for another idea. Thus, Hegel attempts to disclose the inherent laws of movement of ideas and of the whole universe. The system is very impressive and thought-provoking, but it still appears to be purely speculative and therefore nonscientific in the last analysis.

Marx's dialectic is very different. Marx's dialectic is not a complete and closed system; it is not an ontology or dogma of any sort. It is a flexible tool of analysis. Marx's dialectic is a nondogmatic method of approach to problems of science or politics or everyday life. Even Lenin, who was heavily influenced by Hegel, stresses that "anyone who reads the definition and dialectic method given . . . by Engels . . . or by Marx . . . will see that the Hegelian triads are not even mentioned, and that it all amounts to regarding social evolution as a natural-historical process of development of social-economic formations. . . . What Marx and Engels called the dialectic method . . . is nothing more or less than the scientific method in sociology, which consists in regarding society as a living organism in a constant state of development (Lenin, in Selsam and Martel, 1963: 110–11).

Official Marxism: Dialectics as a System

Unfortunately, many Marxists in official positions in various countries and parties do not see dialectics as a rational part of scientific method. They prefer to see it as an omniscient system of the whole universe, just as Hegel did. True, they no longer talk about disembodied ideas as that which is developing, but they do see dialectics as a systematic statement of the most general laws of the universe. They admit in theory that dialectics is not a system or dogma but a method; in practice, they apply it as a finished product.

Official Marxists—especially in the USSR under Stalin—stated three "dialectic" laws of the universe. The first is the Unity of Opposites. This "law" states that everywhere in the natural and social universe, "opposites" interpenetrate each other. The term "opposite" is undefined or is given many different meanings. Common examples are the two poles of a magnet, or the relations of production versus forces of production, or slave versus slaveowner. Opposites are said to be unified at any given time, but in the long run their strife produces change.

The second "law" is that quantitative change becomes qualitative change, that is, small marginal changes eventually produce major jumps or leaps in any process. Common examples from nature are the increases in heat in water that eventually lead to boiling steam, the increases in tension in a volcano that eventually lead to an eruption, or the slow growth of an embryo that eventually leads to birth. In society, examples are the centuries of slow socioeconomic change that finally led to the French Revolution, or the many years of accumulating misery that led to the black riots in U.S. cities in the 1960s.

The third "law" has the mysterious title of the Negation of the Negation. It states that a new stage of any developmental process repeats many features of the previous stage, but at a "higher" level, as in an ascending spiral. A commonly given natural example is a plant that produces many seeds which produce many new plants. In human history, there is the development from the classless society of the primitive economy to the class societies of slavery, feudalism, and capitalism back to the classless society of socialism or communism. This law is sometimes stated as the clash of a thesis (the first stage) with an antithesis (its opposite) to produce a synthesis (a higher stage).

Just as Hegel's mystic writing on the dialectic stirs our imagination, so too do these official Marxist statements of universal laws convey certain important insights. The trouble is that they claim too much; it is absurd to claim that anyone has a comprehensive and omniscient knowledge of all of the past and future history of the universe. Social science is finished if we already know all about social development without any research. "In Soviet Marxism, the dialectic has been transformed from a mode of critical thought into a universal 'world outlook' . . . and this transformation destroys the dialectic" (Marcuse, 1961: 122).

The official Marxist view of the dialectic is not scientific because, first, it originates not from scientific research but from philosophic contemplation. Second, the official dialectic covers all times and places without any of the constraints and conditions of scientific laws. Third, the official dialectic is ambiguous and not precise enough to be made operational, tested, or used in a specific manner.

Official Marxism: Dialectics as a Logic

Some official Marxists offer a second version of dialectics, either as a substitute for the first or as an addition to it; they see dialectics as a "logic." They reject all of the academic writing on logic from Aristotle to the present, calling it "formal logic" and claiming that it deals only with static forms.

The official view—that of a dynamic dialectic logic encompassing a more limited, static, formal logic—has been endorsed by a Maoist Chinese philosopher as follows: "The laws of the movement, change, and development of things, reflected in men's consciousness, constitute the dialectical laws of thought; the laws of fixity, inactivity, and stability within the process of movement, change, and development, reflected in men's consciousness, constitute the laws of thought of formal logic" (Shen, 1969: 30). Thus formal logic is relegated to a small subset of "lower stage" of dialectic logic.

Seen as a logic, the three laws of dialectics are sometimes restated to contrast with those of formal logic:

Formal logic

1. Identity: Any true proposition is true.
2. Noncontradiction: No proposition can be both true and false.
3. Excluded middle: Every proposition is either true or false.

Dialectic "logic"

1. Unity of opposites: Because each thing is interconnected with and changing into its opposite, every proposition is both true and false.

2. Quantity and quality: Because everything is changing, sometimes slowly and sometimes by a leap, every true proposition is slowly or rapidly becoming false, and vice versa.

3. Negation of negation: Because every stage is negated, every true proposition eventually becomes false, but it returns to truth at a higher level.

The formal logic presented above discusses consistent ways of dealing with propositions. In the "logic" presented by official Marxists, there is a confusion between statements about propositions and about the world. "Logic" means all sorts of things these days. If we think of logic as a deductive process that insures consistency, dialectics is not logic. Dialectics is a method. It is not a way of deducing anything, but a way of looking for something.

Here, I use the term "logic" in the narrow sense that logic is the set of rules for *consistent* thinking or, more precisely, the consistent use of propositions. It does not deal with the truth or falsity of the factual content of a proposition; in this view, logic only deals with the forms of propositions and their relations. Statements in logic (or mathematics) are statements with blank spaces (called variables) in them. The statements are such that any particular content may be inserted in the blank spaces, so long as it is the same content throughout, and the statement will necessarily hold true. For example, we may say that "One thing plus another of the same thing always equals two of that thing." This statement is true of any thing on the basis of the definitions of "one," "two," "plus," and "equal." In the syllogism and other forms, logic also connects whole sentences "in such a way that the resulting combination is true independently of the truth of the individual sentences" (Reichenbach, 1951: 3).

The official Marxist philosophers refuse to consider logic in this strict definition because they are not primarily concerned about the rules of consistent thinking, but only about the theory or "logic" of a world in constant change. Therefore, a Maoist Chinese philosopher attacks this view of logic, saying, "the position that in reasoning we only ask whether the syllogism is valid or not, and do not ask whether the statements are true or false is an expression of . . . idealist logic

. . . also called imperialist logic'' (Shen, 1969: 28–29). On this basis he treats all academic or formal logic as a continuation of the medieval view of a static world, while he claims that all dynamic propositions must be in a broader dialectic ''logic.'' As mentioned earlier, this confuses two different categories of statements: statements about change in the world and statements about the formal connections of propositions.

Radical (or independent Marxist) philosophers have stated that the rules of logic, including noncontradiction and other rules of consistent thinking, can and must be applied to all statements, including statements about change and conflict or contradiction in the world. Radicals (and independent Marxists) must ''talk about the dialectic contradiction . . . in a logically noncontradictory way. Otherwise, all judgments would be equally valid and all principles and laws would lose all sense and meaning'' (Schaff, 1960: 250). In other words, any consistent thinking must involve the laws of noncontradiction. Otherwise, one can prove anything.

Richard Norman points out that the usual usage of the term ''contradiction'' by Marxists refers to very important conflicts but notes that this has nothing to do with logical contradiction, so he questions whether this confusing term should continue to be used: ''Anyone who is at all impressed by Marxist social theory must, I think, accept (a) that society is the arena of fundamental and irreconcilable conflicts (despite constant ideological affirmations of 'national unity' and 'the national interest'), and (b) that such conflict . . . is the generator of all historical progress. But . . . by what right are such conflicts referred to by the logical term 'contradiction'?'' (Norman and Sayers, 1980: 57). In this book, the picturesque but confusing term ''contradiction'' will be avoided (unless it refers to a logical contradiction).

Dialectics as a Method

When dialectics is treated as a method of political economy, the usual criticisms of it do not apply. A method is not falsifiable by confrontation with any facts; it is not ''testable'' in the usual scientific way because it does not assert any facts. A method is either useful or not useful; a method is either appropriate or not appropriate to the subject under investigation; a method is ''tested'' by seeing whether it is useful or not in practice. It grows out of our empirical knowledge of the way that social scientists behave. But it does not consist of statements about their behavior; that is the job of the history of the sciences. It rather tries to tell political economists—or anyone else—the best ways to approach any social problems.

The test of a method is not whether it corresponds to any facts, but whether it is useful or not. In other words, is it fruitful? Does it produce anything in practice? If it is useful for radical social scientists, the method is a good one; if it is not useful, it should be discarded.

Exactly what is meant by a "useful" method? A method is most useful if it directs us to choose the most important problems, to select the facts that are most relevant to solving those problems, and helps provide a framework for interpreting the facts so as to solve the problems, formulate new theories, and lead to better social practice. A method does not explain or predict anything, but it may be judged on its success in leading to theories that do explain and predict.

From the concrete experience of radical political economists, a few rules can be stated very tentatively. They are labeled here as rules about interconnection, change, unity and conflicts, and quantity and quality.

Interconnection

The approach to problems of political economy should be relational; never try to treat a problem in isolation. Radical political economists always ask: what are the interconnections of this problem to all of society? Never assume that a particular social phenomenon, such as drug-pushing or suicide or unemployment, is accidental or isolated; ask how it is related to the entire social-political-economic environment surrounding it. Although one may analytically separate a single phenomenon from the whole for study, no valid policy conclusions can be drawn until the possible relations to the rest of the social system are also studied. As an example, always ask how ideologies are related, not only to each other and their own internal past development, but also to the class relations of production, and vice versa.

On the contrary, the neoclassical paradigm does not begin with human relations, but with individual things and individual people. It begins with a mass of commodities with different prices. The neoclassicals make a fetish of each commodity, speaking as if it has an inherent value aside from the particular social relations involved in its production and consumption. Michael Reagan criticizes this isolation or reification of economic concepts, pointing out that "property" is not a tangible thing but a socially defined bundle of rights, based on human relationships: "The hired managers of property . . . exercised rights of use and disposition that in fact affected not just the property holders, but also the employees, the consuming public, and the community in which the firm was located" (1963: 55).

The neoclassical analysis begins with the relation of things to things, such as the price of tea to the price of coffee. It presents only the relation of things to individuals, such as the price of tea to consumer demand. The psychology of the individual consumer is taken to be not only fundamental but also given, that is, its explanation is not considered by the economist. The neoclassical economist assumes that individual consumer preferences come from someplace—from God or innate instincts perhaps—but never considers how society shapes those preferences. It is merely assumed that the highest goal of a well-functioning economy is to follow consumer preferences, not to question their origin. The neoclassical economist then proceeds to show how consumer preferences in a capitalist economy do indeed determine the prices and amounts produced of all things (given pure and perfect competition and at least sixteen other assumptions, see Graff, 1967). Thus neoclassical theory makes individual psychology the ultimate source of the value of commodities, whereas radical (or independent Marxist) theory sees the value of a commodity as a function of the human relationships involved in producing it.

The relational aspect of the dialectic method emphasizes the need to look at humans in their group relations rather than as isolated individuals. Karl Popper has criticized this Marxist view; he attacks the relational theory that

> the social sciences study the behavior of social wholes, such as groups, nations, classes, societies, civilizations, etc. . . . . This view must be rejected as naive. It overlooks the fact that these so-called social wholes are very largely postulates of popular social theories rather than empirical objects; and that while there are, admittedly, such empirical objects as the crowd of people here assembled, it is quite untrue that names like "the middle class" stand for any such empirical groups. . . . Accordingly, the belief in the empirical existence of social wholes or collectives . . . has to be replaced by the demand that social phenomena, including collectives, should be analyzed in terms of individuals and their actions and relations. (1958: 281)

Popper does a service in criticizing glib or mystic accounts of social wholes greater than their individual parts (such as Hitler's Fatherland or Hegel's State). In this quote, however, he is mistaken in rejecting any concepts of social wholes. Obviously, a class does not exist beyond its "individuals and their actions and relations." But that does not mean that we should reject such concepts as "class" or "nation" when carefully used for analytic purposes. For example, serfs and feudal lords are identical human individuals in biological terms (such as brain capacity), but a social analysis of a feudal society without this distinction would be useless; these concepts of social wholes are methodologically both necessary and fruitful.

These relations of individual to class have been discussed by Elster (1985) and other members of the so-called rational choice Marxists (see Carling, 1986). They assert that collective entities, such as classes, do not exist prior to individuals. Second, they contend that collective entities, such as classes, must be understood and explained in terms of individual motives and desires. They do not, however, deny the usefulness of collective concepts, such as classes, the way Popper does—provided that actions and motivations of classes are always interpreted in the light of the actions and motivations of the individuals who constitute those classes.

Not only are social statistics about groups meaningful, they also result in valid predictions. How is that possible if each individual psyche is so unique? The answer is that the individuals in the group we study, such as all industrial workers or all black voters, have the same objective relationship to society in some one aspect. The fact that the relation is the same produces a meaningful statistical average; otherwise, all statistics would be useless. For example, on an issue of rent control, we can predict the majority response of all landlords and the majority response of all tenants. There will obviously be many exceptions, with some exceptional landlords advocating the tenant side and vice versa. These exceptional responses usually exist because other relationships are more important for these individuals than the one under study. Thus, the landlord-tenant relation may be overshadowed for some individuals by differences in family background, education, geography, and so forth. Literally everything in the environment goes into shaping our psychologies, so each individual is unique. Yet on any social issue, the average attitude of all people with the same relevant relation to society will be predictable.

Concentration on human relations, rather than just individuals, is important because "explanations" in the social sciences do not merely describe isolated "facts," as the empiricists or positivists assert. Rather, a social analysis must link this phenomenon to other related and already known phenomena; good social analysis expands our knowledge of interconnections or patterns. Social "understanding or interpretation is a matter of the ordering of . . . facts; that is, determination of their relations" (Dewey, 1939: 511). From an understanding of these interrelations, one can then predict or deduce other social phenomena.

The contrary individualist approach results in sterile discussions of the economics or sociology of isolated individuals like Robinson Crusoe and Friday. Those who view society as an amorphous collection of such isolated individuals overlook the fact that "Society does not consist of individuals; it expresses the sum of connections and relationships in which individuals find themselves. It is as though one were to say: from the standpoint of society there are neither slaves or citizens: both are men. Rather they are so *outside* society. To be a slave or to be a citizen are social determinations, the relationships of Man A and Man B. Man A is not a slave as such. He is a slave within society and because of it" (Marx, 1973: 77).

To speak of the psychology of a slave, without examining his or her relation to the class of slaves and to the class of slaveowners, is not to understand anything, including the slave's psychology. Can anyone believe that a Roman slave or a Southern sharecropper, if snatched from the cradle and brought up as an emperor or a Rockefeller, would have the same psychological characteristics in his or her adult make-up? Thus, individuals may be understood only in relation to their group in society, and groups can be understood only in relation to each other and to the social structure. Of course, the actions and motivations of classes or other groups must also be understood in terms of the actions and motivations of the individuals in the group. There is not a one-way causation, but an interaction between individual and group.

Change

Dynamic changes in reality cannot be assumed to be impossible; there is no reason in general to be content with a static picture. The radical political economist should ask (not assume): Is the social system changing? Specifically, what changes are going on in its ideas, institutions, productive relations, or productive forces? What are the specific historical features of this historical period? What kind of society preceded this one, and how did this one evolve from it? What kind of structural changes have occurred in the political economy between the previous stage and this stage?

Resistance to consideration of change is a pillar of the neoclassical paradigm. Whether they look at a primitive New Guinea society or at the modern U.S. economy, neoclassicals see only the possibilities of optimal efficiency through achieving equilibrium in the market. There will always be a market! Since the alternative is chaos, only small incremental changes may be made. The motto of the father of neoclassical economics, Alfred Marshall, was "Nature makes no leaps"— and, he believed, neither should society.

The modern neoclassical George Stigler boasts that economic training brainwashes all young economists into conservatism: "He is drilled in the problems of all economic systems and in the methods by which a price system solves these problems. . . . He cannot believe that a change in the form of social organization will eliminate basic economic problems" (quoted in Lekachman, 1973: 300). Thus, even if a neoclassical economist has liberal sympathies in favor of a welfare program, such as national health care, his or her training (and one graduates only if one is saturated in it) makes him or her uncomfortable and suspicious of such a wild leap to an inefficient (by assumption) nonmarket form. Neoclassical economics is certainly the most elegant and elaborate of the conservative paradigms in the social sciences. "The only trouble is that it amounts to an ideology inherently hostile to significant change and implicitly friendly to all handy status quos" (Lekachman, 1973: 307).

Let us look at some examples of ahistorical, functionalist (functioning to create efficiency) approaches by neoclassicals. First, Gordon Tullock (1971) argues that legal rights should not be decided by ethics, but by efficiency; therefore, to speed up the functioning of the legal process, he would end many of the procedural safeguards the poor need so badly against the police and prosecutors. Second, conservatives in international economics know all about money and commodity exchange ratios, but have never heard of unequal imperialist power relationships between countries. Third, for a century and a half most conservative economists have accepted Say's Law, which "proves" that general unemployment is impossible because any level of supply generates its own demand; a competitive economy automatically returns to equilibrium; workers are unemployed because they are lazy and "prefer" unemployment compensation and less work. Fourth, if we ask why so few blacks and women are employed in high-wage positions, conservatives such as Gary Becker (1957) tell us this merely reflects the preferences of employers for white males, or the preferences of blacks and women for less demanding jobs, or the "fact" that blacks and women are less qualified. Milton Friedman (1962) goes further: If an employer does not choose the most qualified people because of his irrational preferences, then he will lose money, and competition will put him out of business. Therefore, capitalism automatically eliminates discrimination and produces the best of all possible worlds.

Unity and Conflict

Always ask: what are the opposing forces in this political-economic process? How are they related? What kinds of conflicts exist, and in what direction are they moving? The radical political economist should ask (not assume): What are the opposing interests of different classes? What holds the opposing classes together in the relative unity of the present system? Which classes are growing in power and which declining? What tensions and disharmonies exist between the present evolution of ideologies, institutions, class relations, and productive forces?

In a period of apparent prosperity, what disproportions are accumulating between demand and supply, revenues and costs, consumption and production, savings and investment, and so forth? One may examine dialectic interactions between culture and the economy, between harmonious class relations and class conflict, between frozen socioeconomic institutions and rapidly changing technology, and between incremental change in the present situation and drastic changes in the whole institutional set-up.

On the contrary, a major conservative feature of neoclassical economics is its emphasis on the harmonious and optimal outcome of market competition for all individuals, ruling out any class conflict. The center of neoclassical analysis is the mechanism by which the market functions to reach a goal of optimal equilibrium. This is similar to functionalism in sociology (although the economists' equilibrium approach came earlier), a theory that emphasizes those institutions that function to maintain the stability of the status quo. One liberal discussing functionalism in economics says: "Functional theory commonly predisposes analysis to those equilibrating forces which make for cooperation and harmony. . . . The stress of functional theories on goal-maintenance markedly reduces their capacity for dealing with conflict-ridden systems'' (Krupp, 1965: 65, 78). In other words, neoclassicals see nothing but a Panglossian world of harmony and equilibrium and totally ignore the social conflicts, such as racism, sexism, or exploitation.

An example of this outlook may be seen in the marginal productivity theory of income distribution, first promoted by John Bates Clark (1899). In Clark's version, still repeated in many current textbooks, each factor of production (providers of land, labor, and capital) is paid according to that factor's marginal product, and this constitutes its fair share. It was shown long ago, most delightfully by George Bernard Shaw, that the ideological conclusion does not follow from the technical theory. Even if a piece of capital receives only ''its'' marginal product, a piece of capital is not the same as a capitalist. Again, neoclassical economics substitutes relations between things for relations between people. On the technical side, the marginal productivity theory has been shown to be either false or meaningless in the vast flood of literature called the ''capital controversy'' (see Hunt and Schwartz, 1972).

The basic neoclassical paradigm also leaves no room for power or conflict in its picture of the functioning of the political economy. According to the neoclassical view, the economy is not run by the monopoly corporations; on the contrary, the pattern of production is forced on the firm through the market which reflects the preferences of consumers who vote via their monetary demands (never mind that one person may have a thousand times the vote of another). The state is not ruled by the economic power of the capitalist class; on the contrary, decisions are made by the votes of the citizens (and never mind that one citizen may spend millions of dollars to influence a campaign directly and through ownership of the media). Galbraith points out that this flaw in neoclassical or neo-Keynesian theory is fatal. Because it lacks knowledge of power or conflict, it ''offers no useful handle for grasping the economic problems that now beset the modern society. . . . Rather in eliding power—in making economics a nonpolitical subject— neoclassical theory . . . destroys its relation with the real world'' (1973: 2). Indeed, realistic political economy died when neoclassical theory became ''economics'' and left ''politics'' for political scientists, while neither ''science'' is concerned with the economic basis of political conflicts.

One last example of the prohibition on discussion of conflict in economics is the sad state of so-called welfare economics. In the nineteenth century and up to the 1920s, liberal economists, even such famous neoclassicals as A. C. Pigou, argued that an additional dollar to a millionaire is worth less than an additional dollar to an unemployed worker, so more equal distribution of income may increase total social utility or happiness. This subversive view was eliminated by the modern argument that no two people have the same psychology. In welfare economics, "interpersonal comparisons are verboten" (Lekachman, 1973: 307). Today, even if we could take ten dollars from a Rockefeller and give ten dollars to a starving child, the neoclassical economist would say there is no "scientific" way to tell whether total utility or happiness is increased. Since there is no way to compare different income distributions, so-called welfare economics takes it as given, and concentrates its sole energy on the goal of "efficiency." This amounts to exactly the same goal as the functionalist goal of making the present system run better or smoother or more stably. Class interests and the possibility of change cannot be considered.

Qualitative and Incremental Changes

When a political-economic process shows a discontinuity or qualitative jump, ask what continuous, incremental evolution led it to that point. When a process shows only continuous, incremental change for a long period, ask what discontinuities or qualitative leaps may occur in the future. The radical political economist should ask (not assume): What are the present, slowly evolving trends in ideologies, institutions, classes, and productive forces? Will these trends eventually create a sufficient level of class conflict to cause a revolutionary change? In what direction is that change likely to be? Will it be good or bad from the viewpoint of the oppressed class or classes? For example, is there increasing economic concentration, and has it brought qualitative changes in the operation of the economy? Is there increasing government economic activity, and has it brought qualitative changes in the operation of the economy?

    Neoclassical economics, on the contrary, limits its analysis of change to quantitative analysis of incremental changes. For example, it may calculate changes in the degree of monopoly. It cannot, however, recognize an evolution in the structure of economic relations from the earlier small competitive firms to a stage of monopoly capitalism. Neoclassical economics measures changes of size or amount in a variable, but it does not see institutional changes that mean a qualitative change from one set of relationships to another. Thus, the founder of institutionalism, Thorstein Veblen, makes a striking point against the neoclassical paradigm when he points out that it "confines its interests to the definition and classification of a mechanically limited range of phenomena. Like other taxonomic sciences, hedonistic economics does not, and cannot, deal with phenomena of growth except so far as growth is taken in the quantitative sense of a variation in magnitude, bulk, mass, number, frequency" (Veblen, in Hunt and Schwartz, 1972: 178).

One curious symptom of the neoclassical propensity to see only smooth, incremental change is in the argument by Stigler and Kindahl (1970). They argue that their findings of smooth price changes are more likely to be correct than the findings of sticky prices with infrequent jumps—shown by the usual BLS price indexes—because nature usually progresses smoothly.

Gardiner Means comments that "the authors cite Alfred Marshall's famous dictum that *natura non facit saltum* [nature does not make jumps] in support of their contention. . . . In this day of worldwide knowledge of earthquakes, quantum mechanics and biological mutations, it is somewhat quaint to offer the view that 'nature does not like jumps.' It is hardly a reason for not facing up to the implications of the price jumps in the actual data or the challenge to classical theory which they present" (1972: 305). Clearly, neoclassical economics has a strong resistance to the notion of any kind of change except slow, continuous, incremental change.

Even when neoclassicals examine the economic history of the nineteenth-century United States, they apply the same econometric analysis of incremental, quantitatively measured changes with an assumption as to the stability of the basic economic relations. This prevents them from analyzing the qualitative changes that occurred in U.S. economic development from a backward colony to a developed capitalist country—and prevents similar analysis of needed changes in Third World countries. Similarly, what neoclassical economists (or anthropologists afflicted by the neoclassical economics disease) see among the stone-age peoples of the Kalahari desert or the activities of a Chinese manager in Canton is simply good entrepreneurial effort maximizing profits. The notion that one should examine the qualitatively different relationships resulting from totally different institutions does not occur to them.

In his beautiful, sarcastic style, Veblen speaks of the basic categories of the timeless, ahistorical neoclassical paradigm. He writes:

They are hedonistically "natural" categories of such taxonomic force that their elemental lines of cleavage run through the facts of any given economic situation, regardless of use and want, even where the situation does not permit these lines of cleavage to be seen by men and recognized by use and want; so that, for example, a gang of Aleutian Islanders slushing about in the wrack and surf with rakes and magical incantations for the capture of shell-fish are held, in point of taxonomic reality, to be engaged on a feat of hedonistic equilibration in rent, wages and interest. And that is all there is to it. Indeed, for economic theory of this kind, that is all there is in any economic situation. (in Hunt and Schwartz, 1972: 178-79)

Since neoclassicals do not recognize the importance of institutions, they never focus on the evolution from one set of institutional relations to another. Neoclassical economists tend to focus on incremental changes within one structure that can be expressed quantitatively—so there is a tendency to equate any mathematical formulation with science. "Uncritical enthusiasm for mathematical formulation tends often to conceal the ephemeral substantive content of the argument behind the formidable front of algebraic signs" (Nobel laureate Wassily Leontief in Marr and Raj, 1983: 322).

The institutionalists do focus on qualitative analysis of institutional change, though their attention is on evolutionary rather than revolutionary changes. The Marxist concentration on major, discontinuous, revolutionary changes (as well as the quantitative analysis of long, slow incremental changes leading to a revolutionary situation) is unique among economists.

The suggestions of the dialectic method are all grounded in past empirical research and scientific practice. Yet they do not presume to make statements of any sort, but only direct the political economist to ask certain questions. Therefore, criticisms of them as to their truth or even their indefiniteness are inappropriate. The only test of this method is whether it leads social analysts in fruitful or useful directions.

The Evolution of Methodological Rules

As Einstein pointed out, the development of methodological rules is a never-ending process in which we learn from practice, formulate a set of rules to guide practice, then eventually learn more from practice to develop better rules. To explain and use the rules, we create particular scientific concepts and categories in which to express them. As more is learned from practice, the rules change and so do the categories—though we treat them as fixed at any one time.

Hegel turned this process upside down. He saw certain categories, such as Being and Nothing, or Quantity and Quality, as absolute ideas, which develop from their own inner movements and conflicts. The natural and social worlds of human beings merely reflect this ideal development of categories. Marx, on the other hand, saw the categories of method as reflections of the process of development of human knowledge, which in turn reflects the processes of natural and social development.

A flexible, dialectic approach to categories can help resolve some of the sterile disputes of those who see rigid dichotomies between categories. For example, "facts" are opposed to "theory" as if one must choose between narrow empiricism or pure speculation. The notion of "free will" is opposed to a completely predetermined "fatalism," without considering that humans may make their own history, but under certain determining conditions. "Ethical values" are said to be opposed to "value-free science," as if one cannot be both ethical and scientific. If social science is viewed as an ongoing process in which each of these are aspects, the mystery disappears.

Determinism

Concerning determinism and free will in social processes, many economists incorrectly conclude that there are only two logically possible positions. One view is rigid determinism: Everything is predetermined, people are puppets, and the political result is fatalism. The second view is free will, which says that humans are at liberty to do whatever they will, and the political result is voluntarism. My own opinion (which happens to be my interpretation of Marx) is that both of these views are inaccurate and one-sided. A truly scientific determinism includes human behavior based on human choice.

Predeterminism and Fatalism

Hegel spoke of the "world spirit" requiring (or predetermining) a particular development, such as the rise of Napoleon. Some historians explain the rise of American imperialism by the notion of "manifest destiny." Fox example, "These great changes seem to have come about with a certain inevitableness, there seems to have been an independent trend of events, some inexorable necessity controlling the progress of human affairs. . . . History . . . has not been the result of voluntary efforts on the part of individuals or groups of individuals, much less chance; but has been subject to law'' (Cheney, 1927: 7). The fatalism expressed here must be distinguished from a scientific view of determinism. The law to which the writer refers may be quite compatible with scientific determinism, but if it means inexorable necessities—or forces beyond human control—then he lapses into fatalism.

This distinction has been clarified as follows:

> *Fatalism* is the view that everything is predetermined, that what happens is not affected by what we do. . . . Everything . . . just happens to us, for nothing is the result of our own decisions. *Determinism* is the view that everything occurs lawfully. That is, for any event there is a set of laws or regularities connecting it with other events. With respect to human conduct, this implies, first, that there are circumstances—in our constitutions, background, environment, and character—that are jointly sufficient conditions for our behavior, including the choices we make. It implies, second, that these choices have causal consequences. . . . In contrast to fatalism, it follows that our choices sometimes make a difference. (Brodbeck, 1968: 671)

Determinism means explaining events in the matrix of relationships and regularities of human behavior. But, unlike the fatalists, a social scientist includes human beings and their decisions among the factors causing any social event, even though our behavior is conditioned by our social and biological inheritances and environments.

Many dogmatic ''Marxists,'' particularly Joseph Stalin and his followers, have interpreted Marx in terms of an inevitable march of history. This type of fatalism or predeterminism ''insists that there are comprehensive laws of the social process that are wholly independent of actions of individuals. Men's choices do not and cannot affect these large-scale, collective historical developments. . . . Predeterminism is not only different from scientific determinism, it is inconsistent with it'' (Brodbeck, 1968: 671). Whereas the predeterminism of theologians and Hegelians refers to the inevitable movements of general ideas, the predeterminism of dogmatic (or mechanistic or official) Marxists refers to general historical or economic forces—so it is often called ''economism.'' Somehow, economic forces are considered to operate regardless of human psychologies or actions.

Some official Marxists declared that "history" had in some fashion determined—independently of human decisions—that socialism is inevitable because of the march of economic forces. This view makes very nice propaganda because everyone likes to be on the side of the inevitable winning cause. In addition to being incorrect, however, the drawback of this view is that fatalism leads to neglect of political struggle. If the revolution is "inevitable," why do we have to work for it?

Indeterminacy, Free Will, and Voluntarism

There are those who deny any determinism in history. They point out that men and women make decisions, that they have the "free will" to do what they will in many cases. One can choose to vote for candidate X or candidate Y. They therefore conclude that human actions are not determined in any way, that each of us has the free will to do as he or she pleases. The political consequence of this thinking is "voluntarism," the notion that "we" merely have to decide something, and it will be done. Tomorrow, if all Americans should consider which alternative economic system they desire and decide in favor of socialism, then the country will be socialist. If most Americans decide that all goods and services shall be free, and that people shall work simply for the good of society without wages, then that shall be so. The neoclassical economics notion that everything is a matter of individual choice and individual preference completely obscures the functioning of the socioeconomic institutions and environment within which we live.

Scientific Determinism

Neither the dogmatic views of predeterminism (leading to fatalism) nor the equally dogmatic views of free will (leading to voluntarism) are defensible. A scientific determinism must oppose both, while recognizing the grain of truth in each. Predeterminism claims that man is a puppet of fate, God, economic forces, or whatever, which leads to the position of fatalism, which cannot be defended. The free will position claims that history is accidental, there are no historical laws, humans can do anything. This position leads to voluntarism in politics, religious mysticism, or opium dreams, and it also cannot be defended. A scientific determinist position simply asserts that everything—not only natural but also social events—is explainable on the basis of observed relationships, *including the existing psychology and behavior of humans*. In this view, humans make their own history; that is, humans can make their own decisions on the basis of their own ideas and psychologies, but under given natural and social constraints. Human beings make history, but history shapes human beings. "Scientific determinism is the view that every event occurs in some system of laws . . . *if* we knew [all] these laws and the state of the universe at any time, then we could explain the past and predict the future. This frame of references includes, as it consistently must, human actions which, therefore, can be the object of scientific study" (Brodbeck, 1968: 669).

Of course, we can never know all of the laws of the universe, nor the complete state of the universe at a particular time, so our explanations and predictions must always be partial, although we may hope that they will improve as we learn more laws. Furthermore, "laws" are not absolutes given forever by God or Darwin, but merely our best description of certain regularities as known at present. The future will take place in some particular way, but our knowledge of social "laws" and our predictions based upon them are always limited. We are constrained at any given time by (1) the extent of known facts; (2) the analytic theories available (including restricted mathematical knowledge); (3) our imperfect reasoning power; (4) the time available to research a problem; and (5) the fact that we are part of the social process and, therefore, have "limited" or biased views of it. Economists may know something about social laws at any given time, but not everything.

Human beings are free to make (or not make) a revolution, but our actions are predictable by a knowledge of present and previous conditions, *including our psychologies*, and the laws or regularities of human behavior under these conditions. "To say that the revolution is inevitable is simply (in Marx's scheme) to say that it will occur. And it will occur . . . not in spite of any choices we might make, but because of choices we will make" (Addis, 1968: 335). The prediction of socialist revolution, however, must be expressed as a probability rather than a certainty because of our limited knowledge of the conditions and the laws.

Humanism

In the medieval period, science and theology were all mixed together. In economics, the normal price was not just average, it was "good" according to Aquinas. This odd mixture was critiqued by Hume, who argued the logical point that no accumulation of facts can lead to an ethical judgment and no ethical judgment tells us anything about actual relationships. Therefore, science and theology are logically separate—a view that was enormously important in the foundation of modern science.

This logical distinction, however, has been extended to an apologetic defense of mainstream economics as pure and free of ethical values or biases. Milton Friedman (1968) says that economists should base theories only on "objective" facts, leaving aside partisan ethical judgments. George Stigler says that "economics as a positive science is ethically—and therefore politically—neutral" (1959: 520).

Yet everyone knows that all economists, such as Ronald Reagan's advisers, are ethically and politically partisan. This is especially obvious in the case of Friedman and Stigler, who have never written anything that was not vehemently partisan in favor of conservative, status quo positions. How can we resolve this confusion? It is true that facts and ethical values are logically distinct. It is not true that the practice of economists is unaffected by their values and biases. In practice, any economist must make decisions at every step of research involving ethical judgments. Thus (1) economists must choose what problem to study; (2) some facts must be selected, while many other of the infinitely available facts must be ignored; (3) there are many ways to define factual categories and many different methods to collect facts; and (4) facts do not speak for themselves, but must be interpreted according to the researcher's viewpoint. Adam Smith, Marx, Marshall, and Keynes all advanced economics as a science, but they all had ethical values and all advocated policies.

It is their ethical values (reflecting ruling class interests) that lead Stigler and Friedman to find corroboration of conservative theories whenever they look at the "facts." For example, Friedman (1962) discovers the "facts" that capitalism is mostly competitive and that competition under capitalism has automatically ended almost all racial and sexual discrimination in wage payments. Neoclassical theory says that each factor (labor, capital, and land) receives its marginal product; the founder of the marginal productivity theory, J. B. Clark, stated explicitly that this means that each class gets what it deserves. Likewise, neoclassical economists preach that the capitalist economy is ruled by consumer preferences, and not by the giant corporations. Galbraith (1973) observed, in his presidential address to the American

Economic Association, that neoclassical economics "tells the young and susceptible and the old and vulnerable that economic life has no content of power and politics because the firm is safely subordinate to the market and to the state and for this reason it is safely at the command of the consumer and citizen. Such an economics is not neutral."

Some radicals are so outraged by the pseudo-objectivity of mainstream social scientists that they return to the medieval view that ethics must rule supreme; they espouse the view that there is no objective truth at all in the social sciences. Thus, historian Howard Zinn gives many examples of how historians twist the facts to suit their conservative preconceptions. He concludes: "I can choose by the way I tell the story, to make World War I seem a glorious battle between good and evil, or I can make it seem a senseless massacre. There is no inherently true story of World War I . . . there is only the question of which version is true to which present purpose" (1970: 275). Zinn instructs historians not to worry about objective research, but to be biased in favor of the oppressed.

Zinn is wrong. The fact that social scientists are biased does not prove that there is no true scientific content in their research. Atomic scientists have often expressed many ethical judgments about their research (especially their horror at contributing to atomic destruction), but the atomic bomb does work. Some of the results of social scientists and historians may be correct and useful even though their observation and interpretation is colored by their values and biases.

Most radicals conclude that one must attempt to do objective research, even though one's viewpoint is always governed by one's ethical values. But what ethical values should one have in the social sciences?

A Radical Ethical View

Some Marxists argue that Marx himself was a pure scientist, with no set of ethics and no ethical biases expressed in his work. It is silly, however, to say that all mainstream social scientists are biased, but that Marx and the Marxists are unbiased. We all live in this world and are shaped by it; Marx was affected by his knowledge of the suffering of the workers during the industrial revolution in England.

Part of the confusion lies in the identification of ethics with the supernatural. Most ethical systems have been part of religions; God commands people to behave this way and it is ethical to follow God's commands. But Marx does not believe in superstitions or in the supernatural. Marx's ethics are based on his belief in humanity, as indicated by his frequent indignation at oppression or exploitation of any human beings and by his motto (adopted from Terence) that "Nothing human is alien to me." If one believes that there is no supernatural power above humanity, and if one has an empathy for other human beings, then our ethics must be humanist, the good of humanity.

Within humanism, radicals and independent Marxists do recognize class conflict. Under slavery, the interests of slaves and slaveowners are opposed. Abolition of slavery is good for slaves but takes away the property of slaveowners. In analyzing slavery from the viewpoint of the slaves, radical political economists will favor the abolition of slavery. Thus, economic theories are affected by ethical values, which reflect class interests, either of the ruling class (or a part of it) or of an oppressed class. Robert Heilbroner (in Marr and Raj, 1983: 34) points out that, since economics directly affects people's living standards and material interests (including those of economists), such interests must affect economics. Economics may or may not be honest, but it is never neutral. The position of radical political economy is that we should always do honest and careful analysis from the viewpoint of humanity, particularly from the viewpoint of that majority of humans who suffer discrimination, exploitation, or other oppression.

Materialism

In the middle ages, it was common to believe that all truth comes from authorities, such as Aristotle or Aquinas, or from direct revelations from God. In early capitalism, the need for scientific understanding of the world led to the overthrow of argument by authority or revelation and the beginnings of scientific method. The empiricist (or positivist) approach specifies that all scientific research must begin with the facts from patient observation and experimentation.

Eventually, some empiricists took the extreme position that no theoretical generalization is possible or necessary till all the facts are known. The opposite extreme view, called rationalism (also a reaction against the medieval approach), claims that one must first have a clear conceptual and theoretical framework before the facts have any meaning, so pure thinking must come before any empirical research. In practice, most mainstream economists spend 99 percent of their time as data grubbers, but they sometimes construct unreal models without any worry about empirical assumptions. When nondialectical economists see an absolute dichotomy between empiricist and rationalist approaches, it forces them toward an eclectic practice. Now let us examine in detail the empiricist view, the rationalist view, and Marx's materialism.

A few extreme philosophers (and most mainstream economists in practice) take the view that one must do nothing but empirical research, that is, fact gathering; all else is useless speculation. Once all the facts are collected, then one can formulate a generalization to fit the facts; that resulting generalization is a theory. But no economist or other social scientist can do any factual research without definitions, concepts, and a whole theoretical baggage. First, one must decide what problem is worth studying; that is not a factual question, but is prior to fact gathering. For example, should one study the best ways to speed up workers or should one study the causes and amount of unemployment in the United States?

Second, if an economist has chosen a problem, how does she or he decide which of the infinite number of available facts should be collected? For example, if an economist studies unemployment, should she or he stand on a corner and ask people if they are employed or not—or should the economist study the historical record from 1800 to the present—or what?

Third, once an economist has chosen a problem and has decided which facts to gather, how should these facts be interpreted? Facts do not speak for themselves. For example, suppose we found that unemployment rose to 11 percent in the Reagan administration. Does that show his policies were bad because they led to such high unemployment? Or does that show his policies were good because otherwise unemployment would have been higher (and because he held down inflation)? Only with a theoretical framework can the facts answer such questions.

A few political economists, who have rejected the empiricist view for the above reasons, have gone to the opposite extreme. A brilliant critique of empiricism by E. K. Hunt leads him to the view that one must begin with true concepts, definitions, and theories before doing any empirical research: "The rationalist tradition in science (in contrast to the empiricist or positivist position) is built on the belief that . . . a definition . . . may . . . be true or false. . . . If a definition includes all of the essential qualities or features of a thing, it is a true definition'' (1983: 332). While sympathizing with his criticism of empiricism, one must nevertheless reject this antiscientific rationalist view.

Definitions, concepts, and theories can only reflect our knowledge of the world; how can one know the ''essential qualities'' of anything, such as a social process, before investigating it? Our definitions must always be limited because our knowledge is limited; we never reach a perfectly true definition. Definitions must change over time as knowledge improves and must also change when addressing different problems. For example, what is the true definition of the rate of profit? The most useful definition depends on what question is asked. For example, what is the best place to invest? Or how efficient is the enterprise? Or what expectations cause a cyclical decline? Another important controversy over a definition is in the literature that asks: How do we define the mode of production of the Soviet Union? That question depends on detailed empirical investigation of the Soviet Union, not on any rational thought process.

It appears that political economists (as Marx's materialism emphasizes) must know the facts before they can formulate any theories or definitions, yet they cannot investigate the facts until they have some theory and definitions. How can one get out of this dilemma? Official Marxist dialectics and official Marxist materialism has always answered that the two categories (facts and theories) must form a unity of opposites, so one begins with a synthesis of theory-and-fact. But that only puts a name on the problem.

The way to remove the dilemma is to approach scientific research as a process, not a static either-or situation (which comes first, the chicken or the egg?). Thomas Kuhn's work (1962) on the history of science, and the enormous literature discussing it, points to a concrete process of changing fact-and-theory. Most of what scientists (including political economists) do is called ''normal science,'' that is, the everyday working out of incremental research, assuming the big picture set by dominant theories is true. Sometimes, however, a few scientists challenge the dominant view (called a ''paradigm'') and conduct a successful revolution. The dominant paradigm will then be changed and a new normal science emerges. In some sciences, however, two paradigms struggle for a long time, so scientists do normal science differently under each of them.

In political economy, we are in a period of methodological strife between two paradigms. On the one side, there is the traditional neoclassical economics, including mild Keynesian or monetarist theories. On the other side, there is radical political economy, built on the insights of Karl Marx, Thorstein Veblen, Piero Sraffa, and the post-Keynesian interpretation of J. M. Keynes and Michal Kalecki. No end to this conflict is in sight.

The conflict between paradigms in economics will not be easily resolved because each paradigm is related (in very complex ways discussed in chapter 2) to class viewpoints and class interests. A full history of the evolution of these paradigms in the context of their class bases is in Hunt (1979) (also see Kanth [1985] on the crucial shift to the neoclassical paradigm). Since the conflict between paradigms includes different basic assumptions, different methods and approaches, and different statements of the main "facts," there are no single experiments that could settle the conflict. Moreover, it is usually impossible to conduct controlled experiments in the social sciences. The observed facts, however, can easily be made to fit either paradigm because of the differences in method and definition.

Normal Science

Thomas Kuhn (1962) describes the usual textbook view of the history of science (before he wrote) as a smooth, linear growth. "One by one, in a process often compared to the addition of bricks to a building, scientists have added another fact, concept, law, or theory to the body of information supplied in the contemporary science text" (p. 139). This purely incremental, quantitative picture of growth does fit the activities of most scientists (including most economists) most of the time; it is the normal picture and is called "normal science."

Normally, the researcher takes for granted a given set of dominant theories (or paradigm, defined below). Working within that paradigm, the scientist finds some gap or unresolved puzzle and sets out to improve the theory in this respect. The unquestioned paradigm may be astrology or alchemy or the latest neoclassical approach to econometrics. For example, an economist formulates a new hypothesis suggested by the paradigm, which would be an amplification or slight modification of the accepted paradigm. Then the economist gathers the facts suggested by the paradigm (a natural scientist may do a controlled experiment to gather facts). On the basis of the new facts, the economist then amplifies or modifies the paradigm.

"In so far as he [or she] is engaged in normal science, the research worker is a solver of puzzles, not a tester of paradigms'' (p. 2). Normal science should not be defended or condemned for its limitations; it is not only usual, but is a necessary part of progress. People like Marx or Marshall or Veblen or Keynes made scientific revolutions in economics, but their work was pioneering and rough-edged in some respects. Their followers have spent decades polishing their work and amplifying it and making it more useful for the goals set by the pioneers in each paradigm. Einstein created a revolutionary paradigm, but others applied it to a whole host of problems, resulting in technological progress.

Revolutions in Scientific Paradigms

Contrary to the pre-Kuhnian textbook, there are at times conflicts within science, leading to discontinuities and revolutions in which an old paradigm is junked and a new one conquers the field in spite of resistance. Kuhn defines a paradigm to be a set of ''universally recognized scientific achievements that for a time provide model problems and solutions to a community of practitioners'' (p. *x*). Kuhn describes a long process of progress by normal science, followed by a conflict over paradigms, followed by renewed normal science progress under the new paradigm.

Kuhn's interesting idea has been critiqued from many points of view. Lakatos (1970) says it is more accurate to say that scientists follow an accepted research program rather than merely a single model or paradigm; I prefer the word ''paradigm'' because it gives a better feel for the differences in economics. Some historians have argued that scientific revolutions are not as discontinuous as painted by Kuhn. It is true that each revolution differs in the degree of continuity. All revolutions, however, have in common a long period of quantitative progress with increasing problems, followed by some kind of qualitative jump (persuasively described by Kuhn).

A more serious criticism is the fact that in economics or political economy (and several other sciences) there is no one ''universally recognized'' paradigm, but a continuous conflict between paradigms. The neoclassical-Keynesian paradigm is certainly dominant, but Marxist and institutionalist and post-Keynesian paradigms (or partial paradigms) challenge it—and this conflict has continued ever since the dissolution of the classical paradigm in the 1840s. Thus, conflict of paradigms is more usual in economics than one universally recognized paradigm, but most economists and political economists continue to do normal science within one of the paradigms.

Kuhn's description of a scientific revolution is compelling. He shows that a revolution is necessary because a major new finding is not merely the addition of one factual brick to a house of a particular theory. "Scientific fact and theory are not categorically separable, except perhaps within a single tradition of normal-science practice. That is why the . . . scientist's world is qualitatively transformed as well as quantitatively enriched by fundamental novelties of either fact or theory" (p. 7). The neoclassical economics paradigm combines a hard core of methods, facts, and theory, so change to another paradigm would be a revolutionary leap for any neoclassical economist. To put it dramatically, "after a revolution, scientists work in a different world" (p. 134).

Kuhn emphasizes that the qualitative change in paradigm does not occur without lengthy preparation and follow-up; it is not all done at one blow by one genius apart from the whole process of scientific development. The assimilation of a new paradigm is "an intrinsically revolutionary process that is seldom completed by a single man and never overnight. No wonder historians have difficulty in dating precisely this extended process that their vocabulary impels them to view as an isolated event" (p. 7). Kuhn criticizes those historians of thought who see only quantitative advances and deny revolutionary leaps.

Yet, Kuhn's description also destroys the view that sees only sudden qualitative leaps and denies the lengthy quantitative process of development leading up to and through them. In this respect, Kuhn speaks of the parallelism between scientific and political revolutions:

> Political revolutions are inaugurated by a growing sense, often restricted to a segment of the political community, that existing institutions have ceased adequately to meet the problems posed by an environment that they have in part created. In much the same way, scientific revolutions are inaugurated by a growing sense, again often restricted to a narrow subdivision of the scientific community, that an existing paradigm has ceased to function adequately in the exploration of an aspect of nature to which that paradigm itself had previously led the way. (p. 91)

Thus, the revolution (and the revolutionaries) are only slowly shaped by a growing objective tension and a growing subjective sense of that tension.

Kuhn paints the revolutionary conflict in the period just before a qualitative jump in science. He shows that the new interpretation is usually first voiced by a few individuals who have concentrated on those problems most difficult to answer under the old paradigm. In economics, radical political economy emerged first in neglected areas such as poverty, discrimination, and environmental destruction. "Usually, in addition, they are men so young or so new to the crisis-ridden field that practice has committed them less deeply than most of their contemporaries to the world view and rules determined by the old paradigm" (p. 143).

Furthermore, Kuhn rightly points out that, whereas science normally proceeds with little attention to methodology, a prerevolutionary or revolutionary period is usually marked by deep conflicts over the rules of the game—this follows from the fact that theories and methods are so closely tied together in the ruling paradigm. It is partly because of the ingrained strength of the old paradigm among scientists (and their immense intellectual investments in it) that a new paradigm is always preceded by conflict and crisis and is often first enunciated by "amateur" outsiders and first accepted by the younger scientists. Obviously, all of these features characterize the scene in the social sciences today.

Although Kuhn does a magnificent job of pointing out the inner dialectics of a scientific revolution, Sweezy (1961) has shown that he overlooks the external relations linking it to the rest of society (Kuhn acknowledges this lack in his preface, but does not return to it). These links obviously exist in all of the social sciences (as shown above) but are also present in the history of the natural sciences. Thus, Galileo had to contend not merely against a preceding paradigm (and scientists committed to it), but against the overwhelming power of the Church. And the Church fought against his subversive notions about the real shape and movements of the earth, not merely because of intellectual commitment to a theological dogma, but because that dogma was considered important to protect the Church's earthly power and vested interests. Moreover, the new paradigm did not emerge at that time by accident (or merely due to a puzzle), but because the growth of commerce demanded better ships and better navigation, which in turn depended on a better knowledge of physics and astronomy. Furthermore, the new paradigm did not triumph merely because Galileo gave better answers to "puzzles," but because of the whole Renaissance and Reformation, including the rising power of the bourgeoisie, as well as their concrete needs for better scientific knowledge. Thus, the external conditions giving rise to paradigm changes include (1) changing technological and economic conditions, and (2) the changing power of various classes with differing interests. (The relations of paradigms to other conditions are discussed in detail in chapter 2.)

Revolutions and Relativity

Kuhn's description of scientific revolutions as discontinuous brought some disagreement. But the storm of criticism came from his implication that differences between paradigms could not be settled by empirical tests, only by conflict and revolution. Kuhn says that the choice between competing paradigms "is not and cannot be determined merely by the evaluative procedures characteristic of normal science, for these depend in part upon a particular paradigm, and that paradigm is at issue. When paradigms enter, as they must, into a debate about paradigm choice, their role is necessarily circular" (1962: 93).

Kuhn's description certainly applies to the current struggle in economics and its impossibility of resolution (even aside from the competition of vested interests). Kuhn also sounds like he is describing economics when he says: "To the extent . . . that two scientific schools disagree about what is a problem and a solution, they will inevitably talk through each other when debating the relative merits of their respective paradigms" (p. 108). If one accepts these descriptions by Kuhn, then simplistic empiricism is dead forever. Normal science may settle an argument within a paradigm by empirical tests, but struggles between paradigms cannot be settled by any number of empirical tests.

Nevertheless, Kuhn is not a pure relativist; though he sometimes exaggerates rhetorically, he does not hold the silly position that any paradigm is as good as any other. He recognizes—and stresses in his later works, not discussed here—that chemistry has triumphed over alchemy because of its objectively better performance. He seems to recognize that the most "viable" (useful, fruitful) paradigm will survive, and that survival of the fittest is "progress."

A similar view is spelled out with great elegance in Lakatos. "Progress is measured by the degree to which a problem shift is progressive, by the degree to which the series of theories [a new paradigm] leads us to the discovery of novel facts" (1970: 118). He is not tossing out empirical testing, but he is changing the standard for empirical testing and falsification. "Our empirical criterion for a series of theories [a paradigm] is that it should produce new facts. The idea of growth and the concept of the empirical character are soldered into one. . . . There is no falsification before the emergence of a better theory" (p. 118).

Lakatos describes the evolution of scientific honesty and scientific standards. First, there was the view called *justificationism*, that is, a thesis must be proven. The critics argued, however, it is impossible to prove cause and effect. This criticism brought a second view called *neojustificationism*, that is, a thesis must at least be probable. Statistical tests, however, can only disprove or falsify; they cannot prove or accept a hypothesis. Third, there was *naive falsificationism*, that is, a scientific hypothesis must be testable and falsifiable. Even this standard fails, however, because a set of interconnected theories, a paradigm, cannot be falsified. So there is a fourth view, *sophisticated falsificationism*, that is, choose the paradigm that explains more facts and leads to more discoveries. More precisely:

> Justificationist honesty demanded the acceptance of only what was proven and the rejection of everything unproven. Neojustificationist honesty demanded the specification of the probability of any hypothesis in the light of the available empirical evidence. The honesty of naive falsification demanded the testing of the falsifiable and the rejection of the unfalsifiable and the falsified. Finally, the honesty of sophisticated falsificationism demanded that one should try to look at things from different points of view, to put forward new theories which anticipate novel facts, and to reject theories which have been superseded by more powerful ones. (p. 122)

Lakatos's notion that one should be open-minded, that a new paradigm should explain new facts, and that a new paradigm should be more useful and fruitful for further research is obviously commonsensical. But it does not solve the problems easily and it needs some important qualifications. In normal science within a single paradigm, scientists will continue to use testing and falsification as their usual procedure. Between paradigms, there is still the problem of what is a new fact. There is also the problem of vested interests, so deciding on which paradigm (or research program) works better or is more useful will be neither swift nor easy.

Usually, results can be seen more swiftly in the natural sciences than in political economy. When Trofim Lysenko's theories led to disaster in Soviet agriculture, his dominance was soon ended. Although neoclassical-Keynesian economics has led to many economic disasters (for example, the depression of 1982, the continuing crisis in farming, the budget and trade deficits, increasing poverty, high levels of unemployment, and so forth), it may take many more decades for U.S. economists to recognize an alternative and switch to it. The reason is that political-economic paradigms are fiercely supported, not only because of intellectual investment in them, but because changes threaten the interests and position of the political-economic ruling class.

Suggested Readings

For Marx and Engels, the best book in this area is probably *The German Ideology*. One of the most offbeat and interesting Marxist views of method (mixing dogma and highly independent thinking) is Christopher Caudwell (1971). A good modern work is Diesing (1982), particularly his outstanding chapter on "Science and Morality." Of course, one should read Kuhn (1962) and the lively critique of Kuhn in Lakatos and Musgrave (1970). For an orthodox and dull neoclassical view by neoclassical economists, see Latsis (1976).

For a very orthodox, but well-written, Marxist view of philosophy, read Gollobin (1986). Sweezy's (1961) brief article is excellent. The best journal in this area is *Radical Philosophy*. An interesting debate about dialectics between an orthodox and an independent Marxist is in Norman and Sayers (1980). A good mainstream book on the philosophy of science is Kaplan (1964).

The institutionalist view of evolutionary change is stated very persuasively in Hamilton (1970) and in Wilbur and Jameson (1983). There is a very well-written liberal statement on the utilitarian ethic in economics by Yunker (1986) and an excellent Marxist statement on ethics by Elliott (1986b). There is a Marxist critique of methodological individualism in Hodgson (1986).

A good statement of the post-Keynesian paradigm is in Arestis and Skouras (1985). For an excellent comparison of the Marxist and Freudian paradigms, see Richard Lichtman (1982). The best book on the history of paradigms in economics is E. K. Hunt (1979). Excellent books on paradigms in other social sciences include ones on political science by Lustig (1982), on sociology by Schwendiger (1974), and on anthropology by Harris (1968). Three very interesting and somewhat different views of the philosophy of science are Habermas (1984), Foucault (1972), and Bhaskar (1978, 1979).

— 2 —

HISTORICAL AND SOCIOLOGICAL BASES
OF POLITICAL ECONOMY

All society may be divided into two parts, following Marx. One part may be called the economic structure (otherwise known as the mode of production), which includes all economic activity and economic relations. The other part of society may be called the social structure, which includes ideas as well as social and political institutions. Thus, by definition:

$$\text{society} = \text{economic structure} + \text{social structure} \qquad (1)$$

These two categories are also called by some Marxists the economic foundation and the social superstructure. But this analogy with a building suggests that the economic structure is in some sense more important than the social structure, which is a misleading concept, as is shown below.

The Economic Structure

The economic structure, in turn, may be divided into the relations of production and forces of production. Thus, by definition:

$$\text{economic structure} = \text{relations} + \text{forces} \qquad (2)$$

The *forces* of production are the factors operating in the productive process. The forces are human labor, plant and equipment, land and natural resources, and—last but not least—technology. The amount of labor available depends on population, on laws, and on sociological attitudes toward work participation by age and by gender. The amount of plant and equipment depends on what was produced in the past as well as the rate of wear and tear and obsolescence. The availability of land and resources is reduced by use and erosion but is expanded by new geological discoveries. Technology is determined by education and science.

"*Technology* can be defined quite narrowly as tools, less narrowly as the material arts, and much more broadly as knowledge about how to do things" (Samuels, 1977). The broadest definition is used here. Technological improvements in turn affect the education and training levels of labor, the quality of plant and equipment, and the usefulness of natural resources (for example, coal was once just dirty, useless black lumps). Neoclassical economics tends to think of the forces as the only component of the economic structure. It views the forces of production as a set of inputs combining together in a social vacuum, with little or no discussion of institutions and relationships and no discussion of specific historical setting.

Marx, on the contrary, emphasized the *relations of production* as the heart of the political economic structure. The relations of production are the interconnections between groups of human beings in the process of creating goods and services. In all of recorded history, Marxists find in each society a major exploiting class (which also rules politically) and a major exploited class (which is also subordinate politically). There may be—and always have been—numerous other small classes, either remnants from previous economic systems or new groups beginning to arise and foreshadowing a new economic system. In the long period before recorded history, which constitutes 99 percent of human existence, there were no classes, and all productive relations were cooperative. In the future, it is expected that society will soon again be classless, so the period of class division will be viewed as a brief, deviant period.

In all class-divided societies the productive relations describe the interconnections of *classes* of humans in the production process. Classes are defined by their own relation to the productive process. Note that the concern here is with actual economic relations, not their legal reflections, which are part of the social structure. The productive relations may be summed up in the answer to two questions. First, which class does the work of society? For example, all labor was done in slavery by slaves, was done in feudalism by serfs, and is done in capitalism by workers.

Second, which class owns or controls the means of production and the product? In slavery, the slaveowners own the land, own the slaves, and own the product of the slaves' labor. In feudalism, the church, nobility or monarch possess the land and the product of the land, except what is produced on the small plots worked by the serfs on their own time. In feudalism, the serf is not owned directly but is bound to the land. Most serfs also own some instruments of production and have the right to possess and use some land for themselves. The serfs also have the duty to work on the lord's land for some days (often two hundred or more) per year. Under capitalism, the capitalist class owns the means of production and the entire product. The worker under capitalism is not bound to one job but may look elsewhere, is free to take a job at any wage, and is free to be fired and starve.

Only two classes have been discussed so far in each society, but Marx found more than two classes in every society he investigated. In slavery, Marx found patricians and plebians as well as slaves and masters. In feudalism, he found guildmasters and journeymen as well as serfs and lords. In capitalism, he depicts beggars and farmers and artisans as well as workers and capitalists (see Amin, 1985). Every actual society is a mixture of several different economic and social structures; pure models may help clarify our thinking but are not true to reality. Thus, radicals speak of each actual existing society as a "social formation," which includes several different modes of production in reality, not just one type. The U.S. economy is mainly capitalist but has other modes as well.

The Social Structure

Since everything not in the economic structure is defined to be in the social structure, it is an extremely broad concept. The social structure includes both ideas and social and political institutions.

Ideas in the social structure include all ideologies, such as racism, sexism, or patriotism. The social structure also includes all viewpoints in the social sciences, such as neoclassical economics, Marxist economics, or sociobiology. Furthermore, it should be stressed that individual psychology is not given at birth, but arises from our interactions with other human beings and is part of social structure. Margaret Mead's work (1971) in anthropology demonstrated that the typical psychology or character of men and women (such as passivity or macho behavior) is a purely cultural phenomenon.

The social structure also includes many types of institutions and structures. Most obvious is the political system, including the legislature, executive, political parties, courts, prisons, armies, and police. The education system tries to institutionalize our thinking. The news media—including television, radio, and newspapers—further attempt to shape our thinking. In the medieval period, religious institutions were the most important spreaders of ideology. The family is a vital institution shaping young minds to certain views and behaviors. Each of these institutions, as well as the ideologies spawned by them, changes drastically in each historical period.

The full framework of social analysis outlined here is illustrated in figure 2.1. The dichotomy between social structure and economic structure is exhaustive, but it is not meant to be either rigid or unchanging. The framework is designed as a useful tool and the tool may be changed when the task is changed. Where a particular aspect of society belongs is often not clear and may change with the problem. For example, Marxists had a lengthy controversy over whether language is part of social structure or part of technology; it depends on the problem. Knowledge of biology might normally be considered part of technology, but Arthur Jensen's racist genetics are clearly an ideology as was most of Trofim Lysenko's so-called agronomy. No framework can consider in advance the place of every aspect of society; the only issue is whether this framework is clear enough and spotlights important enough distinctions to be a useful (albeit changing) tool of social analysis.

How Economic Structure and Social Structure Interact

There are three views of the way that the economic structure and the social structure interact. One view is that the ideas and political-social institutions of the social structure fully determine the economic structure, and that the economic structure has little or no effect on the social structure. This view may be called *cultural determinism*. For example, laws of private property determine a capitalist system. It may be pictured as: social structure → economic structure. In its extreme form, some of its advocates see ideas alone determining everything else, so they may be called *psychological determinists*. For example, innate

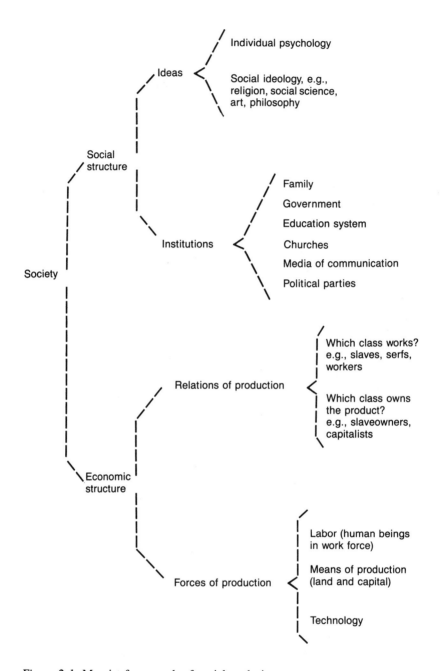

Figure 2.1. Marxist framework of social analysis

aggressive instincts cause wars; innate greedy instincts cause competition.

The second view maintains that the economic structure determines the social structure, and that the cultural ideas and institutions have little or no effect on the economic structure. This view may be called *economic determinism* or economism. For example, money rules politics through bribery and corruption. It may be pictured as: economic structure → social structure. In its extreme form, some of its advocates see technology alone determining everything, so they may be called *technological determinists*. For example, atomic power inevitably leads to nuclear war.

The third view—which is that of Marx—is called *historical materialism*. It maintains that there is a reciprocal, dialectic, two-way relation between the economic structure and the social structure. Economic forces and relations do help determine cultural ideas, values, and social and political institutions. But it is equally true that cultural ideas, values, and institutions help determine economic forces and relations. It may be pictured as: social structure ↔ economic structure. For example, capitalist competition leads to greedy attitudes and private property laws, while these attitudes and laws support capitalist competition. The following sections examine each of these three views in detail.

Cultural and Psychological Determinism

Some nineteenth-century writers argued that ideas determine society. Thus, the ideas of Liberty, Equality, and Fraternity characterize and determine the French Revolution.

Many writers have argued that American values of individualism, competition, and material greed have determined our society. It is claimed that such values have prevented the spread of Marxism and socialism because socialists give priority to group relations, cooperation, and group needs.

Some pluralist political scientists believe that the political system governs the economic system. They contend that the political system produces our laws, the laws determine property relations, and these relations set the framework for the forces and relations of production.

Neoclassical economics is cultural determinist in a profound sense. It always begins its arguments with the assumption of a given psychology attributed to consumers, workers, and capitalists. Thus, individual preferences determine the allocation of resources and the prices of products.

Freudian psychology stresses the primacy of biologically given instincts in the determination of social behavior. An extreme example is the view of Lewis Feuer (1969) that attributes most modern social conflicts to the innate instinct of youth and student movements to rebel and destroy their fathers. Feuer finds that student movements were responsible for (1) World War I, because a student assassinated Archduke Ferdinand; (2) Hitlerism, because a student assassinated a right-wing dramatist in 1819 which led to a repression and a heritage "transmitted to the Nazis"; (3) the Bolshevik Revolution, because a student assassinated liberal Tsar Alexander II when he "was about to give a constitution"; (4) Stalinism, because students assassinated Stalin's friend Kirov in 1934; (5) World War II, because student pacifism in the 1930s reduced resistance to Hitler; (6) the Chinese Communist revolution, because "Mao's conflict with his father and its primacy as a motivation for his political ideas were typical of the Chinese students who emerged with him"; (7) the Cuban Revolution, because for the student Fidel Castro "the United States became a surrogate father to be blamed"; and (8) espionage and treason in America, because alleged spies Ethel and Julius Rosenberg had a "reason-blinding passion of generational hatred [which] begot a corrupted idealism which led to treason."

Feuer claims that students rebel because they have "intense, unresolved Oedipal feelings, a tremendous attachment to their fathers." The radical historian Howard Zinn comments: "The value of Feuer's book is that, by carrying to absurdity what other social scientists do with more sophistication, it may awaken us to their methodological inanity" (1970: 164–65). Notice that any event can be explained by some alleged psychological instinct of human nature, that the theory buries all class conflicts, and that it allows no way to change anything.

All cultural and psychological determinist theories are one-sided and do not explain the origins of the ideas themselves. Their only explanation for ideas is that people are born that way, but this unchanging biology cannot explain how social change ever occurs.

There is a tendency by most cultural and psychological determinists to use their theory to support a right-wing political ideology. If all society is determined by ideas, and if those ideas are determined by biological instincts (or by an eternal human nature or by God), then it is impossible to change social institutions. Any basic political-economic change would be rejected by people's instincts or nature. Thus, according to psychological determinism, all reformers and revolutionaries are building dream castles in the sand that cannot stand up to reality.

Economic and Technological Determinism

The official Marxism of the Soviet Union argues for a type of economic determinism. According to this view, the economic foundation of capitalism determines a capitalist social superstructure, with the appropriate laws and attitudes. So capitalists are completely dominant in all social and political institutions. Thus, democracy under capitalism is a fraud. On the contrary, the Soviet Union has a socialist economic base, so its superstructure is a socialist democracy of all the people, and it is, therefore, the most democratic state ever seen. Furthermore, given changes in the forces of production, capitalism inevitably leads to socialism, regardless of people's opinions. These simplistic views are also one-sided; everything else is based on the development of the forces of production; but the theory cannot account for the evolution of the forces of production.

The official Soviet Marxists frequently use the metaphor of base (or foundation) and superstructure when referring to the relations between the economic structure and the social structure. This metaphor is misleading because it implies (1) that the economic structure determines the social structure, but not vice versa, so (2) it is only necessary to understand the economic structure and to change the economic structure. Thus, it concludes that revolutionaries—and political economists—may, for all practical purposes, ignore the social structure (including political and social institutions as well as ideologies, prejudices, and psychological attitudes).

G. A. Cohen (1978) has written a very sophisticated defense of economic determinism. He claims that the forces of production dominate the class relations of production. He emphasizes that there is a tendency for the forces of production to continue to advance, regardless of human institutions and class relationships. He claims this is so because the environment is one of scarcity of goods and services, because people are rational by human nature, and because people therefore keep trying to improve their standard of living. Secondly, he argues that the class relations of production must conform to the changes in the productive forces. His most substantive argument is that specific productive forces allow only a specific, limited range of the productive relations; for example, a low technology limits people to primitive, communal relations.

Cohen claims that the class relations of production in turn fully determine class consciousness and the rest of the social structure, but not in any simple, mechanical way. He argues that "class" should be defined by economic structure in an objective way, even though a person may or may not be consciously aware of his or her class position. Thus classes—such as slaves and slaveowners or workers and capitalists—exist in a purely objective manner, regardless of an individual's conscious notion of his or her class position.

Technological determinism has also received a very thorough and sophisticated defense by Marvin Harris (1985). In theory, he sees all of society determined by technological changes and neglects all feedback. Thus, in explaining why cows are not eaten in India, he dismisses religion and shows how it is profitable to the peasants. He is so extreme that he considers Marx a cultural determinist because Marx concentrates attention on the human relations of production. Yet Harris's own application of his theory to concrete social processes is often wonderfully perceptive and delightful to read; in my opinion, many of his own applications do not stick within the narrow confines of his strict theory.

Harris defines an infrastructure, structure, and superstructure. The infrastructure includes the mode of production (defined mainly as technology) and the mode of reproduction (including demography, sexual habits, etc.). The infrastructure of society determines the structure of society. Harris defines the social structure to be the family and the political economic structure, including class relations, caste, government, political parties, the military organization, corporations, etc. The structure determines the social superstructure. The superstructure includes ideology, art, dance, science, sports, religion, and so forth. He says that his approach may be called "infrastructural determinism." The infrastructure ultimately determines everything else because it is the interface with nature, so it is based on the laws of chemistry, physics, and biology, which cannot be changed by the social structure or superstructure.

Institutionalist Views of
Technology and Institutions

Warren Samuels, a leading institutionalist, writes: "The received doctrine of the Veblen-Ayres tradition of institutionalism maintains, first, that progressive technology may be juxtaposed to passive and inhibitive institutions . . . , and, second, that technology is the primary . . . force in economic and social evolution'' (1977: 873). In a similar vein, Marx wrote:

> In the social production which men carry on they enter into definite relations that are independent of their free will; these relations of production correspond to a definite stage of development of their material powers of production. The totality of these relations of production constitutes the economic structure of society—the real foundation on which legal and political superstructures arise and to which definite forms of social consciousness correspond. The mode of production of material life determines the general character of the social, political and spiritual processes of life. It is not the consciousness of men that determines their being, but, on the contrary, their social being determines their consciousness. (1904: 11–12)

Samuels, however, goes on to state that the more sophisticated versions of the institutionalist doctrine totally reject technological determinism as ''untenable,'' ''narrow,'' and ''inflexible,'' as a ''narrow mechanism . . . [involving] reification, . . . misplaced concreteness'' (p. 877). Instead of a rigid technological determinism, Samuels substitutes an interaction and tension between technology and institutions, showing that each is a function of the other. He writes: ''that institutions are a function of technology, and technology is a function of institutions, technological change creates opportunities and necessities for new property and other rights'' (p. 884).

Most radicals would strongly agree with Samuels's formulation as a statement of the sophisticated radical view, although there might be some differences in terminology. As noted above, the most famous school of technological determinists is not Marxist, but is a school of non-Marxist anthropologists. It is not Marxists but neoclassical economists who are enamored of the idea that technological changes cause necessary adjustments in property rights, ideas, and institutions.

In my view (and, I believe, in Marx's), the radical or independent Marxist position is that (1) the social structure (including ideas and institutions) is a function of the economic structure (including productive relations and forces) and (2) the economic structure is a function of the social structure. In the language of Samuels, institutions are a function of technology, but technology is also a function of institutions. Obviously, both functional relations are possible at the same time like a set of simultaneous equations in mathematics.

Historical Materialism

There are practically as many interpretations of historical materialism as there are writers. Marx himself never spelled it out in detail. Official Soviet interpretations make it sound very similar to economic determinism. Some of the Frankfurt school of Marxists, such as Herbert Marcuse, make it sound very similar to psychological determinism. The following view, although called historical materialism, is the sole responsibility of this author—though it is inspired by and builds upon Marx and many other social scientists (particularly Veblen).

The ideas of human beings clearly affect, shape, and influence the mode of production. For example, ideas result in laws, which determine property ownership. Moreover, human ideas result in technological innovation. Thus, it may be said that the economic structure is a function of the social structure (including ideas and political-social institutions). Hence:

$$\text{economic structure} = \text{function of (social structure)} \qquad (3)$$

Yet it is also the case that the economic structure (including human relations in production as well as forces of production) affects, shapes, and influences the social structure. For example, the birth control pill (a technological innovation) has profoundly changed human sexual views and behavior. Some technological advances, such as the use of fire or of writing, affected practically every aspect of human social structure. One's position in the relations of production, such as whether one is a slave or a slaveowner, shapes a person's way of thinking as well as one's style of life. In the United States today, there is an enormous difference between the viewpoint of a frequently unemployed worker and that of a millionaire corporate executive. Thus:

$$\text{social structure} = \text{function of (economic structure)} \qquad (4)$$

Now the reader may ask: how is it possible for A to be a function of B while B is a function of A? In mathematics, such simultaneous equations are used all the time. In physics the earth influences the moon, but the moon also influences the earth (witness tides). In economics, the aggregate wage bill is greatly influenced by the amount of goods and services demanded by consumers. Yet, as Keynes and Marx both emphasized, consumer demand is certainly influenced by the amount of wage income. Thus, it is perfectly possible for the economic structure to be a function of the social structure, while the social structure is also a function of the economic structure—though, of course, the two functional relationships are quite different, operating in very different ways.

Our social structure is partly a function of the economic structure, but it is also a function of its own previous evolution. For example, a novelist is influenced by her socioeconomic environment, but she is also influenced by the whole past history of literary technique. Similarly, the forms in which lawyers and judges speak are mostly determined by previous legal cases, yet changes in the economic structure obviously influence the content of legal developments. Thus, social structure is determined in part by the evolution of the economic structure, but in part by its own previous evolution. If t is a time period, then:

$$\text{social structure } [t]$$
$$= f \text{ (economic structure } [t-1...t-n], \text{ social structure } [t-1...t-n]) \text{ (5)}$$

At the same time, the economic structure is a function of both the social structure and its own previous evolution. For example, the inventing and building of the atomic bomb resulted partly from previous technological advances, but partly from the political-military pressures of the Second World War. Thus:

$$\text{economic structure } [t] = \text{function of}$$
$$\text{(social structure } [t-1...t-n], \text{ economic structure } [t-1...t-n]) \quad \text{(6)}$$

To understand the internal evolution of the economic structure, we must also clarify the relationship between the relations of production and the forces of production. Technology changes partly because of previous scientific advance and partly because of the relations of production. For example, slavery holds back the use of complex tools because the slaves will damage them or use them as weapons. Slavery also holds back invention because all work and all practical use of technology is considered a fit occupation only for slaves.

Likewise, the ideas and institutions within the social structure interact. An artist's work will be influenced in part by the past history of painting, but also by political events, such as wars, or by changes in his or her family relationships. So our ideas are influenced by the past history of ideas, but also by changes in political-social institutions and the whole environment.

To sum up, each element in society is influenced by the other elements and by its own history. Thus, a comprehensive sociology of ideas would say that ideas are influenced by (1) the evolution of social-political institutions, (2) the evolution of the relations of production, and (3) the evolution of the forces of production, but also (4) the previous evolution of ideas. In equation form:

$$\text{Ideas } [t] = \text{function of (institutions } [t-1...t-n], \text{ relations} \\ [t-1...t-n], \text{ forces } [t-1...t-n], \text{ ideas } [t-1...t-n]) \quad (7)$$

Similar equations could be written for the determination of social-political institutions, relations of production, and forces of production. But such general formulas are not very enlightening, so let us turn to the concrete analysis of each area.

Sociology of Knowledge: The Evolution of Ideas

As one example of the functions stated in equation (7), let us examine the origins of Keynesian economics. It is no coincidence that Keynes's major book, *The General Theory*, was written in the midst of the Great Depression and appeared in 1936. In 1929 the forces of production had evolved the potential to produce a vast flood of goods and services. But the relations of production (for example, limitations on working class income) were such as to present a barrier to the further advance of production. The result was the Great Depression.

It would be a mild understatement to say that the depression brought some economic institutions, such as the banking system, to collapse, while threatening political institutions with revolutionary unrest. No one would dispute that drastic steps had to be taken by the capitalist ruling class to save capitalism. But this conclusion of economic determinism, while correct to an extent, is terribly inadequate. Why was capitalism saved in one way by Adolph Hitler and in quite a different way by Franklin Roosevelt? To answer that question, one must go beyond the general analysis of economic relations to consider the different shape of the specific political and economic problems in each country, as well as the different political institutions, the different strength of opposing classes, and the differing political traditions.

Germany under Hitler's fascism and America under Roosevelt's New Deal each required ideologies to justify their policies. It is wrong to think of either movement as creating totally new ideologies. Rather, each selected ideas from the many that are always in circulation in addition to the current dominant one. Fascism selected ideas to justify repression and aggression; the New Deal selected ideas to justify liberal reform. Moreover, New Deal reforms, such as the National Labor Relations Act, were not merely shaped by ruling class ideas on how to save capitalism; the reforms were also shaped by the upsurge of the labor movement and its intellectual allies.

Within this context, Keynes and many others searched for ways to end the depression within the limits of the capitalist economic structure. Keynes's ideas were taken over by some New Deal economists to justify welfare spending. His ideas came too late to have more than a minor impact in the 1930s, but they had become the standard rhetoric of most U.S. economists by the 1950s and 1960s. Of course, Keynes did not merely present ideological propaganda; he also offered a core of useful analysis leading to policy steps for capitalist administrators.

Keynes's analysis and policy suggestions were "revolutionary" only in one sense: they meant a drastic change in economic analysis to acknowledge the fact that capitalism does not automatically reach full employment, implying an equally drastic new intervention by the capitalist state to restore full employment. Because this drastic change in analysis and policy exposes a weakness of capitalism, capitalist ideology only reluctantly abandoned its old laissez-faire religion. If Keynes had published his book ten years earlier, before the great political and economic crisis forced new policies on the ruling class, it would not have caused a "revolution" in economic thought. It would not have been selected for entrance into the dominant viewpoint; it would have been neglected as several similar earlier writers (such as John Hobson) were neglected.

Once Keynesianism was accepted into the ruling pantheon and taught to every college student, it had an immense impact upon government institutions, class relations, and the development of the forces of production. Once an ideology comes into being and grasps the minds of women and men, it is vital to the system, either as an apology or as a critique. No system can survive without its own ideological apology being dominant. No revolution can occur unless a new ideology becomes accepted by millions. Keynesianism has served as an important apologia for capitalism, admitting that it has problems but that they can be cured and reformed within the system.

The analysis to this point is still an inadequate approximation because it has so far neglected the important fact of the previous evolution of ideas. Keynes did not write on a clean slate in economics; neither did he completely negate or disregard all previous economic thought. He himself had previously worked in the development of orthodox monetary theory. In addition, Keynes draws some of his terminology and concepts from the neoclassicals, plus a little (but perhaps more than he is aware) indirectly from Marx and from other heterodox economists. Without all this previous theory, Keynes's work would have a very different form.

On the individual level, it is necessary to examine Keynes's personal biography to understand why it was he, and no other orthodox economist, who brought forth a new—or partially new—viewpoint. One would have to examine his education (British universities), work experience (the civil service), social connections (the fascinating Bloomsbury group of artists and intellectuals), and so forth. Originally, he saw himself solving routine puzzles—contradictions between fact and theory—in the old viewpoint, from which he admits it was a hard struggle to tear himself loose. Most academicians just follow the prevailing viewpoint without ever thinking about it. Keynes broke free mostly because of the drastic new experience of the Great Depression, the same circumstance that guaranteed the widespread acceptance of his new work.

The conclusion is that the forms (including terminology and concepts) of Keynes's work were largely determined by the knowledge and forms of debate under the old theory. The direction of the new content and its impact and influence were mainly determined by the larger social situation, including the status of class relations and the way these relations held back the forces of production in the depression. There is, so to speak, an internal dynamic of ideas within each discipline constraining the forms of discussion. Yet, that internal dynamic does not operate in isolation, but always within the context of the problems and issues defined by the external world. Even individual "inspirations" are influenced by the surrounding world, which then selects and reinforces some ideas over others. Ideas battle through human protagonists among themselves, but not in some impartial arena with the best winning out. Ideologies are not at all the same as class relations, but they are used as weapons by a class if they aid its survival. If not, they often remain insignificant.

The predominant ideas will be those that, ultimately, are most useful to the ruling class. There is a confused notion that Marxism means that each class simply learns from its own work conditions and always votes in its own interest. On the contrary, "Marx did not say that everyone's beliefs and attitudes flow from his class position. Marx said that the ruling ideas of an epoch are the ideas of the ruling class. If other sectors of the population had ideas corresponding to their class positions and interests, then they would change the social order to their own benefit, which is . . . why the ruling . . . ideas have to conform to the . . . needs of the ruling class" (Horowitz, 1971: 9).

As long as there is not a revolutionary situation, the working class does not have a clear consciousness of its own position and interests, but has a "false consciousness" given it by the ideology of the ruling class. The ruling ideology is not imposed by any magical means, but through the control of the media, schools, churches, government, and jobs. Workers are taught an ideology of harmony to cover the facts of oppression. The ideologies of racism and sexism similarly justify and help continue types of oppression. Male and female are socialized by the family and all the other institutions of society to fit certain stereotypes. It is therefore no surprise that most do fit the stereotype. For the few women who might try to break the stereotype to get into "male" (read: high-paying) professions, there have always been both laws and informal discrimination to keep women in their "place." As late as 1874, the U.S. Supreme Court ruled that a state could prevent women from becoming (unladylike and high-paid) lawyers. To protect their purity, women until recently could not become high-paid bartenders, but could become low-paid barmaids.

All of the stereotypes of racism, sexism, and the lazy, ignorant worker are useful to maintaining the power and high profits of the ruling class. These stereotypes are propagated, as noted above, by all the social institutions controlled by the ruling class. Thus, the attitudes of the working class are manipulated by propaganda, advertising, religion, and so forth. In Herbert Marcuse's *One Dimensional Man* (1964), he seems to think that this manipulation can be 100 percent perfect, with the pessimistic conclusion that revolutionary change is almost impossible. That conclusion does not follow because drastic, new experiences can shake people loose from false attitudes and the spell of the ruling ideology. Blacks in the early 1960s came alive to their situation and to the possibilities of change and acted accordingly through legal actions and through demonstrations. In the last half of the

1960s, students and youth protested the Vietnam War in enormous demonstrations that did have some effect eventually. In the late 1960s and early 1970s, women became more conscious of their true situation—many through experience in the civil rights and antiwar movements—and were able to wrest many reforms from the ruling class.

In a similar way, in most periods most social scientists are conditioned by society to follow the dominant conservative paradigm without much thought about it. Social scientists do pursue new theoretical analysis for many individual reasons, including the pure love of theoretical games and puzzles, the desire for more money and prestige or job security at a university, and—for a few, such as Keynes—the desire to change or to preserve society. Mostly, this results in routine work, expanding and making more elegant the dominant viewpoint. Only in a very unstable period, such as the 1930s, will it result in a major reform of the dominant theory. Only in a period of social revolution, such as the French or the Russian, will it result in an overthrow of the old dominant theory.

Class Conflict

Class in a Marxist sense may be defined as a ''relationship of exploitation'' between groups in a social structure, where each class is defined by its relationship to the conditions of production and to other classes (see Ste. Croix, 1985: 27-28). This is an objective relationship; it may be reflected in the subjective consciousness of a class, but it may not. In the capitalist world, class position affects income level, so it is usually correlated with income, but not always—and class is not defined by income.

Wolff and Resnick (1986) have written a very useful clarification of the concept of class. They find three different meanings of ''class'' in Marxist writings: (1) some writers define class in relation to ownership of types of property or nonownership; (2) some writers define class in relation to the holding of power; and (3) some writers define it in relation to the extraction or exploitation of a surplus from one group to another.

On the first meaning of class (ownership), one can speak of a capitalist as someone who owns the means of production. But this definition is inadequate because it leaves out the relation of the capitalist to workers, which is the core of class analysis of capitalism. Also, if the question is only ownership of the means of production, then the dominant Soviet group is not a class by definition because the government—rather than any individual—owns the means of production.

On the second meaning of class (power), the fact that government officials hold formal political power does not help one to understand why capitalists as a class may be called a "ruling" class. Capitalists as a class have certain political power because of their economic relations, so power by itself is not a helpful place to begin. Similarly, in the Soviet Union, it is easy to identify a group that rules and has power, but the question is whether they exploit labor or not. Again, it is that economic relation of the Soviet ruling group that defines them as a class and aids our understanding of their behavior.

Thus, Wolff and Resnick (like myself and many others) find that it is the existence of relationships of economic exploitation between groups that provides the most useful definition of classes. It is the key relation that is reflected in property ownership and in political and social power.

They also point out that it is incorrect to speak of class as a "more important" relation than others because there are interactions between all social processes, but it is the most useful starting point in exploring the social problems that Marx investigated. "The point was not to claim that class was any more important a part of society than power or individual preferences or race or sex. Rather Marx emphasized class by making it his entry point into social analyses for a specific, concrete purpose: to remedy the ignorance and under-estimation of class which, in his view, undercut the revolutionary projects which he supported" (p. 38).

For some purposes one may wish to concentrate on just two classes in a given situation, but it is very clear that the fabric of society is woven by the interaction of several classes. Although Marx is often accused of seeing only two classes, he wrote that "the actual composition of society . . . by no means consists only of two classes, workers and industrial capitalists" (1968: 493).

Since class relations are based on exploitation, class conflict is an objective aspect of the social structure. Of course, people are not always aware of conflict, are seldom actively engaged in it, and often display cooperative and harmonious aspects of the relationship.

Class conflict is not something that Marx desires; what he wishes is an end to conflict. Nor is class conflict a product of Marx's philosophical speculations; rather, the fact of conflict in many societies (but not all) is Marx's generalization from a very lengthy empirical research. It is not a rigid statement about all societies at all times, but rather a methodological approach for investigating and understanding past and present recorded societies. Marx did not find class conflict in prehistoric, primitive societies; nor does he expect conflict in a future classless socialism.

Conflict Between Forces and Relations

The most fundamental conflict observed by Marx is that between the rapidly advancing potential of new productive forces and the relatively frozen human relations of production. For example, the relations of feudalism in late medieval France held back productive progress until those relations were swept away by the French revolution; the resulting capitalist economic structure made far more rapid economic progress than feudal France. The slave relations in the U.S. South before the Civil War held the South to a stagnant plantation economic structure and impeded progress in the rest of the country by its strength in the U.S. government; rapid industrialization in the United States commenced only after the Civil War. Tsarist Russia was very backward economically because of the stranglehold of the court and the semifeudal aristocracy and the oppression of the workers and the peasantry. After the revolution changed the relationships, the Soviet Union was transformed from a mostly illiterate, mostly agricultural, mostly rural country to an educated, mostly urban, industrialized country in a remarkably short time.

Aside from revolutionary situations, the tension between obsolete relations and changing productive forces also shows itself in economic crises of all sorts. For example, in the Great Depression in the United States, farmers destroyed crops, factories were half used, businesses went bankrupt, and workers were unemployed—so the economic structure declined rather than made progress. Why? The reasons are complex, but they are all inherent in the structure of capitalism. One problem was that class relations limited the wage income of consumers, so many kinds of goods and services could not be sold. Capitalists produce only for private profit in this social structure, but in the 1930s they expected only losses, so they reduced production. Such tensions surface in every recession or depression; other tensions lead to inflation or reduced productivity. Eventually, the tensions between improving productive forces and frozen human relations lead to class conflicts.

Conflict Between Classes in the Economic Structure

In the ancient slave economic structure, slaveowners made their income from the labor of the slaves. Slaves produced a product that was far larger than the subsistence bundle of commodities they were given. The surplus went to the masters. The conflict was reflected in the slaves' attempts to slow the work pace, in the resistance of slaves to the commands of the slave drivers, and even in actual revolts (such as the revolt of Spartacus against Rome).

In the feudal economic structure, feudal lords made their income from the labor of serfs. Serfs worked without direct compensation for 150 to 200 days a year on the lord's land. Serfs' indirect compensation was that they were allowed to work the rest of the year on a plot of land from which they could keep the produce. The serfs often argued with the lords over their traditional economic rights and duties.

Under capitalism, capitalists make their income from the labor of workers. Workers are paid a particular wage for which they are expected to work a particular number of hours. The product may be—and usually is—much larger than the workers' wage. There are conflicts over the wage rate. There are conflicts over the intensity of labor. There are conflicts over the conditions of labor. There are sometimes strikes; the history of U.S. labor is a dramatic story of strikes, police brutality, and workers' heroism in the face of violence.

U.S. workers tend to be alienated from their work and from the boss. Most have a low opinion of the boss and view him or her as an enemy—though a few identify with the boss. Most see their work as boring, tedious, and unpleasant, so they slow the pace and often produce low quality, but a few still see their work as a craft and try to do their best. Those few who do their best are likely to be in very skilled or semi-professional jobs. Both alienation and exploitation are major disadvantages of capitalism.

Part II of this book includes a detailed discussion of the determination of wages, prices, and profits, as well as the degree of exploitation under capitalism. Part III examines the class relations and degree of exploitation under Soviet statism.

Social-Political Class Conflicts

The class conflict at the level of production is mirrored in and affected by the class conflict within all social and political institutions. Briefly, the interests of capitalists, workers, and other classes clash within the news media, the churches, the education system, the legal system and the courts, and the legislative and executive branches of government. Although capitalist interests usually dominate (else it would not be capitalism), there is always pressure from workers and other classes, and sometimes successful reforms in their interests.

One good example of class conflict in the U.S. political sphere is the ongoing argument over the tax system. To satisfy the legitimate desires of the working class, the federal income tax is progressive in form, with higher rates for higher income levels. But capitalists have gotten so many concessions in the tax code that the effective rate is lower for many high-income receivers than for middle-income workers. In 1984, fifty of the top five hundred corporations—with good profits in a prosperity year—paid no taxes at all. There is much talk of tax reform because the system is scandalous, but every reform hurts some group, so class conflict makes any but a cosmetic reform very difficult.

There are innumerable ways in which the economic power of big business is translated into political power. First, and least important, is the large amount of money spent on lobbyists and bribery (the most money is spent by military contractors). Second, somewhat more important, immense sums of money are given to probusiness candidates and parties to give them overwhelming superiority in campaign spending.

Third, and very important, is the general milieu created by big business influence and control of most of the channels of communication from the media to the churches to the universities. In spite of our formal guarantees of free speech, over 95 percent of American cities have only one newspaper or two newspapers owned by the same corporation. Thus, wealth is a major factor in shaping our ideological views.

Fourth, and equally important, the behavior of the political system is constrained by the economic structure. Assume a working-class-oriented candidate is chosen by a party (in spite of business spending), is elected (in spite of the media and spending of probusiness candidates), and refuses to be corrupted. In an issue such as subsidies or tax breaks for a corporation providing jobs in their own district, a proworker congressperson will usually feel forced to vote for (and even push strongly) the subsidy or tax break.

The relationship of democracy to class power under capitalism is discussed in detail in part II; the relation of class power to democracy under statism is discussed in part III.

Ideological Class Conflict

Class conflict is reflected in and affected by ideological conflict. There are very real conflicts between ideologies, such as between those defending our environment (e.g., the Green party in Germany) and the growth-at-any-cost school. Each ideology develops with more and more sophistication and elegance. The path of development of each opposing idea is partly determined by the battle with its opposite. Yet these internal developments of ideologies are not independent of class relations but are both highly influenced by and highly influential on the course of class relations. For example, class relations in South Africa tend to produce an ideology of racism as their reflection, but that ideology also supports the system of class and racial relations existing in South Africa. The fact that U.S. capitalists might lose some profits if they had to take measures to prevent pollution tends to get them to support an ideology opposing pollution prevention, while the spread of that ideology helps defeat measures to prevent pollution.

A Model of Historical Change

Four kinds of conflicts have been discussed: (1) tension between productive relations and productive forces, (2) ruling class versus exploited class over the degree of exploitation in the economic structure, (3) rulers versus exploited over who holds political power, and (4) ideological conflicts between rulers and exploited (or between ruling factions).

The presentation here mirrored the usual course of social change. First, the way in which the structural tension between frozen class relations and expanding productive forces leads to class conflicts was described. Second, purely economic conflicts among classes were examined. Third, it was shown how economic struggles lead to political conflicts among classes. Fourth, the way in which economic and political strife is reflected in ideological conflicts among classes was examined. When the dominant ideology is challenged and a new ideology spreads, the ground is prepared for extreme political conflicts, leading to a political revolution. Thus, one can point to the ideological change as the final link (or proximate cause) leading to the revolution.

The revolution puts a new class in power and allows the emergence of a new set of class relations in production. These new relations are harmonious with the latest productive forces and allow a more rapid expansion. Soon the new productive relations are frozen in place, protected by the (new) political and legal structure, and supported by the (new) dominant ideology. Eventually, however, the productive relations are inadequate for the growing forces and the whole process repeats itself.

Many Marxist historians have explored in these terms the classic case of the transition from feudalism to capitalism. Very briefly, for example, in feudal France, a class system of lords and serfs continued for many centuries in harmony with an apparently static productive system of relatively isolated agricultural estates using simple technology with little change from year to year. Yet over many centuries the productive forces did change, better methods led to agricultural surpluses, to more trade, the creation of towns, and small crafts and early manufacturing processes in the towns. The many petty regulations on finance (e.g., prohibition of usury) and trade and manufacturing, designed in the interests of the dominant landlord class, came to be seen as fetters on progress by the bourgeoisie. The bourgeoisie engaged in an expanding net of finance, trade, and manufacturing. This economic conflict brought about political struggles over the power to change such regulations. The political fight was reflected in the great ideological onslaught of writers such as Voltaire and Rousseau (or Locke in England or Tom Paine in America).

These conflicts culminated in the French Revolution of 1789, as well as the similar British Revolution of 1688 and the similar U.S. Revolution of 1776. The bourgeois revolution in France, fought with the aid of workers and peasants who also faced oppression by obsolete feudal regulations, brought the capitalist class to power. The new regime ended feudal relations and restrictions and released the power of capitalism. The capitalist system made fantastic productive advances in all of Western Europe and the United States.

Social Evolution

The official or dogmatic view interprets Marx to mean that human society must "inevitably" pass through certain preordained stages: primitive communism, slavery, feudalism, capitalism, socialism, and communism. Thus, the Soviet "Marxism" of Stalin insisted on a simple unilinear view of rigidly similar evolution in all societies: "All peoples travel what is basically the same path. . . . The development of society proceeds through the consecutive replacement, according to definite laws, of one socioeconomic formation by another" (Keiusinen, 1961: 153).

Strictly economic definitions of the various stages of society are given by official Marxism: "Primitive communism" means collective ownership and use of all goods at a very low technological level. "Slavery" means private ownership by individuals of land and human beings. "Feudalism" means control, but not ownership, of land and workers; so the serfs are bound to the land and the king may transfer control of the land from one landlord to another, but the feudal landlord does not own the serf and may not sell the serf (nor can the feudal lord sell the land). Under "capitalism" capitalists buy and sell land, buy and sell factories and equipment (which become much more important than land), and buy workers' power to labor (but may not buy and sell workers, as was the case in slavery). Of course, slaveowners and capitalists own all the products produced under their direction and may sell them for a profit in the market; feudal lords owned the product produced on their own land, but not that produced on the serf's land (though some of it might be owed to the landlord as rent in some forms of feudalism).

"Socialism" is defined by the Soviets to mean government ownership of the means of production, with continued differences in wages according to work done, and purchase of consumer goods for private use. "Communism" is said to mean government ownership plus sharing of goods according to "need" (no wages or prices).

Many areas of the world, however, have not followed this exact progression. Moreover, the models are never met in pure form, and real societies always contain elements of other systems. The official or dogmatic version of Marxism not only turns out to be wrong on methodological and factual grounds, but more recently published manuscripts of Marx show that his view was quite opposite and was at an entirely different level of sophistication. A very careful summary of Marx's manuscripts finds that "the general theory of historical materialism requires only that there should be a succession of modes of production, though not necessarily any particular modes, and perhaps not in any particular predetermined order" (Hobsbawm, 1964b: 19).

A concrete Marxist study of the socioeconomic stages in humanity's early history concludes from a lengthy examination of the archaeological and anthropological facts that "it is not in the least surprising that the development of societies observed in different parts of the Old World, to say nothing of the New, should exhibit divergence rather than parallelism. This conclusion does not invalidate the use of the term 'evolution' to describe social development" (Childe, 1951: 166). In fact, one can still use the analogy between social and organic evolution because "organic evolution is never represented pictorially by a bundle of parallel lines, but by a tree with branches all up the trunk and each branch bristling with twigs" (ibid.: 166). The evidence shows not only divergence and differences, but also convergence and broad similarities. Of course, there are a great many differences in detail between the processes of cultural evolution and organic evolution. "But to admit this is not to deny cultural evolution, to deny that cultural change is an orderly and rational process that can be understood by the human intellect without invoking any necessarily incalculable factors and miracles. On the contrary, it can be described in general intelligible formulae . . . there is no need to assume supernatural interpositions" (ibid.: 175–79).

Independent Marxists emphasize that there are many alternative evolutionary roads followed by human societies. Some very specific qualifications to any general schema must be stressed. First, even similar stages of evolution will be found at different times in different places. Second, there are cases of regression from a "later" to an earlier stage. Moreover, many times in history a nation that has been a leader becomes frozen in its ways, so it suffers a relative decline and is replaced by younger, more vibrant societies. England was the leading power of the nineteenth century, but it was overtaken by the United States and Germany in the twentieth century. The United States was totally dominant in the 1950s, but it now faces stiff competition from some countries, such as Japan, that suffered great destruction in the Second World War and were very poor in the 1950s. Thus development is never linear but is very uneven, with major shifts in which country is relatively backward and which is relatively advanced.

Third, older modes of production may persist for centuries next to newer, "more advanced" modes both within the same society and in neighboring societies. Thus, although large slave plantations came to dominate ancient Roman agricultural structure, large numbers of small peasant farms continued to fight for existence.

Fourth, many of the political-economic transformations in human history did not take place through the internal evolution of one society, but through diffusion from a more advanced society. Diffusion has come in many guises, including conquest, colonialism, trade, and religious and political missionary work. Obviously, diffusion opens the possibility for jumps over the stages of history. Thus, primitive as well as feudal societies have jumped to statism. Perhaps even the recorded jumps from primitive to feudal societies (as in the case of the German barbarian tribes) were all caused by diffusion. Moreover, diffusion may be "regressive" as well as "progressive." In later chapters it will be seen that the diffusion of capitalism by conquest in the last four centuries has not always resulted in advance, but often has led to deformed socioeconomic structures and stagnation in many of the conquered areas (such as India, Ghana, Cuba, and Vietnam).

Most independent Marxists begin an analysis with the internal evolution of a society. For example, to understand the decline of the Roman Empire, one must examine the internal tensions caused by slavery. On the other hand, the external environment frequently shapes a country's development, given a certain internal evolution. It is a fact that the Roman Empire was eventually destroyed by barbarian invasions—but earlier invasions of the same magnitude did not destroy the Empire because it was still internally strong. Similarly, many countries were devastated by the First World War, but only Russia (and for a brief time Hungary) had a major social revolution; the reason was that internal social tensions had prepared Russia, so any external shock could trigger a revolution. The lesson is that one cannot merely assume internal evolution as the cause of changes, nor can one assume that external shocks and impacts are the main cause of change. One must examine each case concretely.

With all these qualifications, one can still speak of an evolutionary social process. The analogy of Marx with Darwin might even be extended to speak of the survival of the fittest society. That society will survive whose socioeconomic institutions (or class "relations of production") are best adapted to the fullest development of the means of production—which sometimes means the fullest development of human potential.

It might be said that such a framework, with all of its qualifications, is a truism to any rational social scientist. Yet one set of institutional pressures and ideological commitments has led official Marxists to speak of universal, unilinear evolution. A different set of institutional pressures and ideological commitments has led some conservative Western social scientists to deny any validity to the concept of social evolution (see, e.g., Nash, 1967: 3–4). The liberal Anthony Giddens (1981) says that some of the most abstract elements of historical materialism are "indispensable contributions to social theory," but he is completely opposed to any theory of evolution (which he seems to confuse with nineteenth-century normative notions of inevitable "progress" to better and better societies). Only radicals have conceptualized a complex form of evolution with all of the qualifications suggested above.

Suggested Readings

An interesting history of European Marxist and radical thought in the 1970s and early 1980s on historical materialism is in Perry Anderson (1983). There is a fine study of class in England by Westergaard and Resler (1975). There is a useful discussion of difficult problems in Marxist views of social change in John Elliott (1986a). Theda Skocpol (1984) has an excellent collection of views on historical sociology and has produced her own model work of historical sociology (Skocpol, 1979). Class categories are discussed in Meiksins (1986). By far the best discussion of class is in Wolff and Resnick (1986).

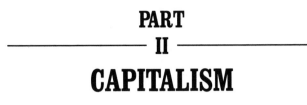

PART
II
CAPITALISM

— 3 —

ORIGINS OF CAPITALISM

How did our present economic system come into being? To answer the question fully, the investigation must begin in the mists of prehistory to examine the evolution that produced capitalism. As discussed in chapter 2, the evolution was not in a smooth, straight line, but proceeded with many dead ends, backward steps, uneven development in different areas, diffusion from one area to another, and jumps over stages in some areas. Yet there is an evolutionary process at work, as may be seen in the following brief account.

Primitive Societies

Engels did the earliest systematic Marxist work on primitive societies (1884). Naturally he built his general analysis on the known anthropology of his day, mostly Morgan's work, now completely outdated. In Stalin's era Soviet Marxists raised the detailed structure of Engels' classifications to a divinely given "truth." They held that every society begins with the stage of primitive communism, which is always subdivided into the stages of (1) the primitive herd, (2) the primitive community, (3) matriarchal clan society, (4) patriarchal clan society, and (5) breakup of tribal society (Thompson, 1961). Now even Soviet Marxists have recognized that no such detailed universal stages can be read into the evidence. They have reverted to the more neutral, open-ended, non-Marxist classifications such as Old Stone Age and New Stone Age (Bordaz, 1959).

What is important in Engels is not his now obsolete classifications of primitive societies, but his fundamental point that such societies were very different from ours in basic ways. Not only were family structures different, but in the most primitive societies there is little or no evidence of class division and class repression. One British archaeologist with a Marxist approach lists the characteristics of most areas of human settlement in our first half million years or so as follows: (1) very small communities, (2) isolated, self-sufficient communities with little or no trade, (3) no full-time specialists, (4) no writing, (5) a homogeneous group of people, (6) the economic unit is the family or extended family of kinsmen, (7) relationships are personal and status hereditary rather than economic, and (8) few political institutions (Childe, 1951).

Many non-Marxist anthropologists have given us detailed studies showing the validity of this view in at least some areas. Even Nash (1967), who criticizes Engels' detailed stages of evolution, reports one contemporary primitive community where even today "there is no private property in productive goods, and whatever the hunting band manages to kill is shared out among the members of the group." In general, the most primitive societies have no market exchange, no money, and no economic competition in the modern sense (Dalton, 1964). It is true that even the most primitive peoples known to anthropologists usually own their weapons, tools, and ornaments as individual private property; but the basic "means of production" at this stage are the hunting grounds, and these are owned collectively.

The point cannot be overstressed that in primitive societies men and women are not hired for jobs, they are not paid money, and purely economic relations do not prevail in any area (nor is force used in most cases). Rather, "men work together because they are related to each other, or have social obligations to one another" (Forde and Douglas, 1967: 17). Furthermore, work is done collectively and the results shared collectively. Or, as another non-Marxist anthropologist writes, "with qualifications such as the special shares locally awarded for special contributions to the group endeavor—the principle remains . . . 'goods collectively produced are distributed through the collectivity'" (Sahlins, 1965).

Official Marxists have referred to societies with these characteristics as "primitive communism." This term is misleading, however, partly because societies reveal such a wide range of structures that it is wrong to force them all into any one box. More important, the term implies that this was a golden age of innocence with a consciously chosen collective ideology. On the contrary, the "communist" features observed in some primitive societies are imposed by dire necessity for bare survival (and it is hardly much "communism" to find cooperation within a family group of perhaps ten to fifteen members). Collective activity is necessary because life is very insecure and on the margin of subsistence, so each person knows that his or her own life depends on his or her neighbors' cooperation and "generosity." Moreover, the results of a hunt may come in all at once, and there is no way to preserve perishable goods in the primitive situation. Furthermore, any person who is not "generous" and who does not fulfill the traditional "voluntary" social obligations would eventually be exiled from the tribe, to face almost certain death through inability to cope with the world alone.

Slave, Asiatic, and Alternative Modes of Production

Evidence on transformation from "primitive communism" to the classic type of slavery is mostly limited to Egypt; elsewhere evolution took different paths. Even Greek and Roman slavery seems obviously to be explained in part by diffusion from the neighboring areas. Going farther afield, an independent evolution may be assumed for the Inca, Maya, and Aztec areas of America. Information on these areas, however, is very limited; and even that limited information shows great differences from the Middle Eastern pattern, in both institutional and technological developments.

Furthermore, in India and China and in Mesopotamia itself, although slavery does appear at some time after the agricultural revolution, it is not the predominant system in most of these areas. In Mesopotamia, it is true that "at the bottom of the social hierarchy were slaves, individuals who could be bought and sold" (Adams, 1965: 102). Still, the rest of the social hierarchy was very complex, including free craftsmen as well as priests, warriors, and several ranks of a nobility that might well be called feudal. To complicate matters, it was the priesthood that was mainly in control in early times, only later giving way to a degree to the warriors. The complex interaction of church and government in most or all of these early societies is another feature usually overlooked in the official Marxist model.

In India, a Marxist analysis by Kosambi (1965) still seems to find primitive communist hunters and gatherers in the earliest remains. In the period following the neolithic agricultural revolution, however, he discovers only a small amount of slavery. Not only was the percentage in the total population very low, but almost all the slaves were either domestic servants or held by the royal family. India from that time until well into the twentieth century was mainly characterized by the caste system. In this system each person's rank and occupation in society was fixed by birth to be the same as that of the parents. Yet there was no slave caste; even the lowest caste was theoretically free (though with many restrictions) and was paid some pittance for its product or services. In the countryside during most of Indian history, farmers were "free," owning their own product except for taxes, rents, and tributes, which left very little. Actually, it was usually the village commune that owned or possessed the land rather than the individual farmer. Finally, above the village commune there was imposed by a conquest a ruling hierarchy, which extracted tribute from the village.

In China, even an official Chinese Communist history states that slavery existed only as a small part of the whole economy, and only from the Shang to the Qin dynasties (*Outline History of China*, 1958). The main economic basis for society in these dynasties was the peasant commune, which possessed its land in return for the payment of a tribute to the noble landowners. After the Qin dynasty, a very small amount of slavery continued up to the Yuan dynasty. The official history terms the dominant system after the Qin dynasty "feudalism" in view of the decentralized power of many provincial warlords (most Marxists place the beginning of "feudalism" in the Zhou dynasty, just before the Qin). Nevertheless, the peasant commune and its tribute remained the economic base for a very long time. Even through the nineteenth century the important role of the Chinese extended family is reported by all observers.

In light of the new facts on precapitalist societies revealed by archaeologists, anthropologists, and economic historians—and because of the mind-freeing renaissance of Marxist thought since the 1960s—a heated debate has taken place concerning the classification of societies into the Marxist stages of history. Although the discussion continues, some new and less dogmatic views have already been accepted, even in the Soviet Union.

One of the new trends is the revival of interest in what Marx called the Asiatic mode of production (sometimes referring to its Oriental form and sometimes to its Slavonic form). Since it has existed in many places other than Asia, it would be better to call it by the descriptive name "tributary mode of production." Marx defined it as based in large part on the continued existence of communal property, with the entire tribe (or kin group) owing tribute in the form of goods or services to various ruling classes. Logically, it might be viewed "merely" as a transitional form from primitive communism to slavery (or at least to feudalism). Yet the facts show, as Marx argued, that this is a surprisingly stable economic mode, lasting in some areas for thousands of years.

Stalin, however, did not like the concept of the tributary (or Asiatic) stage because it complicated his simple unilinear picture and because it implied no compulsion to "progress" (toward Stalinist socialism) in some societies. For propaganda and diplomatic reasons, these features were unattractive to Stalin. Therefore, he prohibited all Soviet Marxists from making use of the concept of the tributary mode of production. Only recently have many Marxist writers come to use this term as the best description of ancient India, China, and Mesopotamia, perhaps the Inca Empire of Peru, and much of Oceania and Africa, though with many unique features in each case. They argue that the institution of the tributary mode may have been a major reason for the comparative stagnation of many of these economies for centuries.

In a striking turn away from dogmatism, several Marxist scholars have emphasized that many economies *never* went through a slave phase. Soviet theory has specifically rejected the dogma of a universal stage of slavery. Moreover, in addition to the tributary alternative to slavery, it appears that for Marx himself "feudalism seems to be an *alternative* evolution out of primitive communalism" (Hobsbawm, 1964a: 28).

The Transition to Class Society

When "civilization" became established in the Middle East in the Bronze and Iron Ages, it was marked by (1) large-size communities, (2) taxes, (3) public works, (4) writing, (5) use of mathematics and astronomy, (6) internal and foreign trade, (7) full-time specialists such as farmers and metallurgists, (8) political organization beyond family or kinship, (9) a privileged ruling class, and (10) an exploited class of workers, whether slaves or feudal serfs or peasants paying tribute (Childe, 1950). The key revolution, however, is the earlier transformation from hunting and gathering to animal herding and agriculture (Redfield, 1953). Once this initial agricultural revolution has taken place, it may be argued that the coming of "civilization" (and class rule) depends merely on further quantitative increases in community size and productivity.

How did the agricultural revolution occur, and how did it end the primitive classless societies of these areas (and bring about class rule)? We know there was a slow expansion of knowledge and improvement of tools over hundreds of thousands of years. Then, in a few particularly fertile areas—perhaps more or less independently in China, Mesopotamia, Egypt, Mexico, and Peru—men and women discovered how to tame and breed animals and how to grow desired plants. This "revolution" did not occur in a momentary flash of insight to some individual. Rather, it seems to have been a very gradual process over thousands of years.

A detailed picture of this process has been based on the available evidence for Mesopotamia and the Aztec areas of Mexico (see Adams, 1965: 39-43). First, communities became more permanently settled, intensively collected food, and hunted in a smaller area than previously. Second, the New Stone Age saw better tools being produced, including improved bows, drills, digging tools, and even boats and nets. Third, some crop, wheat for example, that was already growing in the area might be moved to different areas as desired, protected by such means as removing weeds, and eventually selected so as to obtain the desired food characteristics. Similarly, hunters of goats or cows might begin to follow one particular herd, protect it against its other enemies, and finally feed and shelter it at times. All these changes could take thousands of years.

Once the pastoral-agricultural revolution is well under way, several important changes occur as a direct result. Obviously, the level of productivity per worker increases. The first consequence of this fact is a much higher population density. Hunting and gathering require several square miles per person, whereas herding and agriculture can support many people per square mile. At the same time, agriculture means that the population must settle in one place rather than move here and there around the country. Such large, settled agglomerations mean the founding of permanent villages and, eventually, towns and cities in the most favored places.

There is enough economic surplus over immediate needs that the economy may support various specialists, such as carpenters, shoemakers, and the like. Specialization, in turn, calls for exchange of products between individuals and between groups. When exchange becomes too complex for barter to be convenient, money, the medium of exchange, rears its ugly head. Moreover, the higher productivity makes available hoards of "money" (whether cattle or gold) as well as consumer durables. Then, the specialization and exchange slowly destroy the collective use and possession of the hoards and the durables, so some individuals come to own more wealth than others.

With this increase of private property and the larger, more permanently located groups of people, there is a need for broader and stronger political structure to replace the family unit. At first, both in possession of private property and in control of political power, the families or clans retain the semblance of unity and direction. But just as individuals slowly accumulate private property, as there is more of it and as specialists demand more, so too do individuals slowly accumulate more political power as politics grows more complex.

A war chief may be elected from time to time in small tribal conflicts; the post is likely to become lifetime or even hereditary as larger armies come into being. The area and intensity of wars are increased at this time because advanced agricultural societies use wars for economic motives to acquire cattle or slaves. Most large-scale introductions of slavery seem to follow as the effect of a war of conquest. Yet such wars are in turn the effect of a new technology, high enough so that it is profitable to keep a slave (because the slave can produce a surplus). Slavery and wars of conquest are thus intertwined as cause and effect at a certain level of economic evolution.

A similar increase of power may accrue to those in charge of public works. A director of irrigation for a small tribe may be appointed for a short time in one season; a director of irrigation for a large agricultural area along the Nile must be given more power for a lengthy period of time. Thus, in Egypt, the government separates from and rises above family or clan for two different reasons: to carry through public projects, including irrigation and warfare, and to guard private property, including slaves (and to prevent slave revolt).

The main question of this section must still be faced more directly and analytically. How and why were so many primitive economies transformed into slave economies (and other kinds of class societies, such as feudal or tributary modes) in the ages following the agricultural revolution? The official Marxist answer was that better technology led to a higher product per worker. The higher product, in turn, meant that a society could for the first time "afford" to have some nonworking individuals (such as slaveowners, landlords, priests, full-time warriors). Conversely, until product per worker passed the point where one worker could just keep himself or herself alive, there could have been no surplus left for the ruling classes. Before that point, slavery or serfdom could not pay—hence prisoners were simply killed or eaten. Even some otherwise anti-Marxist writers agree that "among hunters and fishers the requirements of a nomadic existence render slavery rather unproductive; out of eighty-three hunting and fishing tribes examined by one student, in sixty-five there were no slaves. On the other hand, among agricultural tribes slavery tends to be productive and therefore more widely used" (Dahl and Lindblom, 1953).

Nevertheless, this simplistic argument of direct economic determination, with a one-to-one relation of productivity and institutional change, must be considerably modified. In the first place, there were a few exceptionally well-off societies with some specialists and some slaves even before the agricultural revolution. Moreover, in the period immediately after the agricultural revolution, most of the earliest farming communities were mainly nonstratified, nonclass, nonslave societies. While a surplus product above some very minimum point of subsistence may be a necessary condition, it is clearly not a sufficient condition to ensure the emergence of full-time specialists and a class-divided civilization.

Furthermore, where the earlier Marxists speak of a "surplus" as an easily recognizable phenomenon, its amount rather turns out to be itself conditioned by ideology and sociopolitical institutions. Even in terms of food alone, the number of calories required to sustain life varies not only according to geographical facts, such as temperature, but also according to the type of activity undertaken (Orans, 1966). The necessary calorie consumption not only depends on the type of economic work done, but also on activities considered necessary for recreation or religion: for example, the great amount of dancing done by primitive peoples. Finally, while the potential surplus over subsistence depends merely on technology and labor available (in a given geographical environment), the actual surplus gathered depends on class relationships in the economic and political spheres as well.

The appearance of class rule coincides with the beginnings of formal governmental structure in many societies. Both class rule and government, however, usually come with very long and varied lags after the agricultural revolution (and both usually arise with the conquest of one community by another). Nevertheless, it is only these basic institutional changes to class rule and government that provide a stable base for further progress. After these changes, there appears a comparatively rapid technological advance (and increased potential surplus) and rapid population increase.

Independent Marxists agree that in the very long run the agricultural revolution "leads to" economic surplus, which "leads to" the possibility of a profitable slavery; but the process involves long, constant, and complex interactions between economic developments and ideological-social-political changes. The concept of a "surplus" over basic needs is certainly not a figment of imagination. Even a hundred years ago, agriculture still required 60 or 70 percent of the U.S. population; whereas in the 1980s there is "overproduction" of farm commodities with only 3 or 4 percent of the population working in agriculture. Yet when the effective surplus in a primitive community can be drastically modified by changes in religion, not to speak of government, it is well to realize that it is anything but a simple technological concept. Moreover, the greater agricultural surplus affects organization (such as class relationships) slowly over a long period, not at a precise point.

Finally, one might note that class rule was a useful or even necessary means to advance the level of technology and general culture far beyond what it had been. Primitive societies create neither pyramids nor vast irrigation projects, neither Plato's philosophy nor Euclid's geometry. It required exploitation of the many to give leisure time to a few individuals. A much higher level of technology is required to have leisure time for everyone in a classless society.

Slavery to Feudalism in West Europe

While recent radical (or independent Marxist) debates have restricted the use of the classification of "slavery," the term "feudalism" has been expanded to cover a very wide variety of economies. In fact, "feudalism" is much too loosely applied, since it has been used to cover contemporary northern Nigeria and parts of Latin America as well as tsarist Russia to 1867 and China to 1911! More interesting is the work that has been done toward subclassifications within feudalism. Feudal societies have been classified into evolutionary or progressive feudal structures and devolutionary, stagnant, or regressive feudal structures. For example, West European feudalism led forward to capitalism, yet Byzantine or Arab feudalism had enough different features to lead to dead ends (after a lengthy flowering of very high level cultures). In addition, medieval Russia is a case in which stagnant feudalism is similar to in many respects, and hard to distinguish from, the tributary mode of production.

The discussion of feudalism in this chapter is mainly concerned with the unique case of medieval Europe. It is perhaps the best-known and best-researched case. Yet, there is so little quantitative data or definite knowledge that extremely different views of the period persist. One famous historian, Henri Pirenne (1956), contends that medieval European economic development was determined by the operation of forces external to that society. The official Marxists, on the contrary, have tended to see the development purely in terms of the internal evolution of European society based on conflicts within it. Even the so-called objective facts of medieval history have a different appearance when viewed from these opposing positions.

To illustrate the difference that approach makes, did the Roman Empire fall because it rotted away from within, or was it toppled from the outside? How the mighty Roman Empire declined and the medieval world came into being is a question that has been answered in many ways. The prevailing view used to be that the empire was simply inundated in the fourth and fifth centuries by waves of Germanic barbarian invasions.

Pirenne argues that the Germanic invasions did not interrupt the basic socioeconomic continuity; that agriculture in the Merovingian period (rulers of France, fifth to seventh centuries) followed the Roman pattern; and that the Roman peasant, who was already tied to the land, simply became the serf of the medieval period. Pirenne declares that Merovingian commerce continued to thrive, that trade was brisk with the Byzantine Empire across the Mediterranean, and that Merovingian power was built on the taxes from this commerce. Moreover, the Merovingians still had a certain amount of industry, professional merchants still exported their products, and they even continued to issue the Roman solidus with the emperor's picture on it.

Pirenne finds that "feudalism," defined as a fragmented political-economy based on the independent manor, did not begin until the end of the eighth century (Carolingian period). At that time the Arabs suddenly burst into the Mediterranean, disrupted its commerce, and limited the Franks to a land empire with a northern center of gravity. Only then, as trade declined, was there a tendency toward economic self-sufficiency on the estate of each feudal lord, followed by political disintegration of the central authority in the face of landlord power.

Most Marxists admit that invasions by the Germans and Arabs, as well as the Slavs, Vikings, and Huns, were the catalyst that finally ended the Roman political-economic entity, but they maintain that the underlying process of disintegration began in noticeable degree by the second century (see e.g. Walbank, 1946). The latifundia had almost entirely eliminated the independent peasant through competition based on cheap slave labor. The absentee slaveowners let technique stagnate, while the slaves often revolted or destroyed machinery (so that only the crudest implements and simple one-crop systems could be used). The result was the exhaustion of the land, and the disappearance of the military reservoir of peasant soldiers. Similarly, slave labor in industry meant that it was unprofitable to use complicated machinery, so the benefits of large-scale enterprise were largely lost to the Romans. Since there was little use of large, specialized machinery, and since transport costs were very high, a strong tendency developed for industry to decentralize out to the frontiers, where the army constituted the one mass demand for goods. By the fourth century trade had degenerated, except for a few luxury goods, from international to regional and finally to local commerce.

"Feudalism" or serfdom began to evolve through several paths long before the main barbarian invasions. Whereas the slave was owned in body, the serf was merely bound to some estate to which he or she owed services or a share of his or her produce. The slave was often "emancipated" into a serf in order to obtain more efficient production and more secure military support. The free peasant was "persuaded" to become a serf in order to be protected against imperial taxes as well as against barbarian plunderers. Finally, some of the Germanic tribal members were reduced to serfdom through long reliance on their tribal chiefs for protection and leadership.

While Pirenne dates feudalism from the end of the eighth century, most Marxists place its beginning in approximately the fifth century (the Merovingian reign in France). The Merovingian period was already characterized by self-sufficient estates run by serf labor, a minimum of industry, a balance of trade unfavorable to Europe, and an absence of the formation of new cities. Furthermore, Pirenne gives heavy weight to his evidence that the Merovingian kings kept issuing coins like those of the Roman Empire, whereas it appears that the new coins were issued mainly for prestige value and were more often used as jewelry than money (Cipolla, 1956).

Contrary to Pirenne, most writers argue that Mediterranean trade was thoroughly disrupted in this period, and that trade in Northern Europe had already assumed prominence. The unfavorable balance of trade resulted from the fact that Merovingian commerce in the Mediterranean was mostly limited to the import of a few luxury items from the more advanced East. Moreover, it was the strength of local manorial economies and the self-sufficient decentralized production that, long before the Arab invasions, caused both the decline of international trade and the fall in payment of land taxes to the Merovingian treasury.

In the case of Western Europe one may surely conclude that the transition from slavery to feudalism resulted from internal evolution in that area plus the impact of external events such as the Germanic and Arabic invasions. How much quantitative importance to ascribe the different factors is under continuing debate. But only a dogmatist or theologian would claim that the evolution was the result only of internal or only of external changes. It is perfectly consistent with Marx's view to say that both contributed (the only ''external'' causes that Marx would not admit are supernatural ones).

The Capitalist Model

Capitalism may be defined as an economic system in which one class of individuals (''capitalists'') owns the means of production (''capital'' goods, such as factories and machinery), hires another class of individuals who own nothing productive but their power to labor (''workers''), and engages in production and sales in order to make private profit. These features must now be clarified and their immediate implications seen.

All capitalist effort is directed to selling things in the marketplace. In the conservative view, this is a very favorable feature. The argument is that capitalists must produce what consumers want if they are to sell their goods. Therefore, the market automatically means that the mixture of outputs will tend to conform with the preferences of consumers. Furthermore, they argue that such competition will automatically tend to lower costs and prices toward the minimum level of cost with efficient output, since the inefficient, high-price producers will be unable to sell their goods in the market.

Radicals, on the other hand, point out that the market responds only to preferences based on wealth, that is, the preference of a poor person without money is unheeded. The rich person may satisfy a preference for a palace, while the poor person's preference for food is unfilled and he or she suffers malnutrition. Furthermore, we shall see that production for the market means full employment only so long as there is a demand for all the goods in the market. When there is an overall lack of demand, production and employment decline.

Capitalism characteristically uses "money" as the means of exchange in the market. Conservatives emphasize that the use of gold, tokens, or paper money is a great advance over barter, because the individual can spend a few dollars for one thing and a few dollars for another as he or she chooses. Under barter, the farmer might bring a cow to market, and have to trade the whole cow to the shoemaker for shoes. Since the farmer could use only one or two pairs of shoes, he or she then had to trade the other shoes for other goods, a very complex process.

Radicals certainly agree that money is a useful tool, but they also believe that "money is the root of all evil." On the one hand, that saying refers to the fact that the use of money and the competitive market system normally results in a dog-eat-dog kind of psychology and in robbery, both criminal and "legal" (via exploitation of workers). We shall also see that the use of money opens the door to the possibility of inequality of demand and supply. When one gets money, it may be hoarded, rather than spent. Thus the process of circulation is not always smooth, and the amount of money searching for commodities may be much more or much less than the amount of commodities at present prices.

Another feature of capitalism is the buying and selling in the competitive market of the workers' ability to labor. Conservatives point out that this is a great advance over slavery or serfdom in that workers are free to go where they wish and get employment in any job. Radicals agree, but they add that the worker is also "free" to be fired, and he or she no longer has even the security of a tiny plot of land on the feudal manor. When millions of people are unemployed, the freedom to switch jobs does not appear to be a very useful freedom; it is rather the freedom of the capitalist to hire and fire at will. This job insecurity, plus the knowledge that one is producing for someone else's profit, robs work of its pleasurable "creative" possibilities and tends to produce alienation.

Finally, there is the fact that capitalist production is conducted for private profit. Conservatives tout this feature as meaning that each capitalist will strive for the utmost efficiency, thus lowering costs for all consumers. And, as noted, the capitalist will try to satisfy the preferences of all consumers, at least those who can pay money for their desires. Radicals argue that the private profit motive often means efficiency, not in reducing costs but in milking the consumer, especially when monopoly power allows high prices and high profits. Moreover, production for profit means that if the profit perspective is dim, production is cut back, and mass unemployment results. Many other results of the profit motive might be cited. For example, pollution is a cost to society, but not to the individual firm, so it is left out of enterprise planning considerations. But detail on these points must await later chapters.

The Rise of Capitalism

Pirenne recognizes a vast increase by the eleventh century in international trade, caused by the Crusades. In the Crusades, Western Europe regained the control of the Mediterranean that it had earlier lost to the Moslems. "At the beginning of the twelfth century a new and external impulse affected the economic activity of the Netherlands. Just as the closing of the Mediterranean by Islam had put an end to their relations with the Southern countries, so these were resumed with the revival of navigation there by the Christian countries" (Pirenne, 1929: 40). The new merchants—recruited from the mass of vagabonds, small itinerant merchants, and landless younger sons of peasants—needed new trading posts as well as permanent commercial centers. They constructed large new residential areas, usually around old feudal centers, and these became the towns of the later Middle Ages.

Pirenne argues that the great increase in international trade, in industry, and in the use of money led to the end of serfdom in Italy and Flanders by the thirteenth century. The towns offer a haven for rebellious serfs, who must now be given better terms in the countryside. Moreover, the use of money and the certainty of markets induce the lords to begin to produce for the market and to collect money rents, in order to buy the manufactured products and luxuries offered by the towns and the trade with the East.

Most Marxists, on the contrary, hold that the upswing in European agriculture and industry beginning in the eleventh century was caused primarily by the cumulative effect of new inventions which made available more animal, water, and wind power. These technological improvements themselves resulted from the insufficient supply of labor, which motivated the landlords to find substitutes for human labor. It also resulted from the fact that West European feudalism gave the serf far more reason for initiative—both in making and in using inventions—than was allowed the peasant by Eastern forms of serfdom and slavery. The remnants of slavery were ended about this time because the new methods made it more profitable to use serf or even free labor.

The majority of Marxists argue against Pirenne (and against Paul Sweezy, who took a similar position) that the growth of trade and industry in the cities did not primarily result from the external stimulus of the increased Mediterranean commerce, but rather from the improved agricultural productivity that made available a surplus for the local market of both food and artisan-made goods (see Hilton, 1976). It was from this local trade that the cities arose, more money came into use, goods began to be traded at greater distances, and industry started to be concentrated in the towns.

The improvements in power and transportation made it profitable for the first time to concentrate industry and production on a mass scale for a wide market (as it had not been profitable in the Roman Empire). Thus it is industrial innovation that leads to commercial revolution and not vice versa. Marxists like Dobb (1946) and Kosminsky (1955) admit that Pirenne's concepts of widening market and use of money were important phenomena caused by nascent capitalism. The beginnings of the process, however, they trace to basic agricultural and industrial developments.

Serfdom did not disappear in a simple one-to-one proportion with the widening market. In the twelfth century there was indeed increased industrial productivity, which created a larger marketable surplus and thereby stimulated commercial activity; greater use of money and some switch from services to money rents resulted. There was a tendency throughout the twelfth to fifteenth centuries toward more money rents by the less powerful smaller landlords who could not resist the peasants' demands. But in the thirteenth and early fourteenth centuries there was a "feudal reaction." The increase in profit from marketing in the growing urban areas caused the greater lords to seize some peasant land for their own estates and to demand more services from the serfs. By working the serfs harder, they tried to produce more output in order to make more profits. The peasant revolts were not designed to end some archaic feudal leftovers, but to prevent the imposition of greater feudal burdens.

Marxists and other critics of Pirenne argue that the eleventh to thirteenth centuries saw a great revival of European international trade. They contend, however, that trade had never ceased entirely either in the Mediterranean (Lopez, 1952) or in the North (Postan, 1952), and that its existence and expansion were due in the main to the innovations mentioned above. Furthermore, the Crusades themselves are not viewed as an accidental "external" factor, but as the result of those same internal economic developments.

The Crusades were not undertaken for religious reasons, nor were they due to Turkish molestation of pilgrims, for the Turks continued the Moslem policy of tolerance (Cahan, 1954). Developments on the Moslem side did lead to increased attacks on Byzantium, but the West would have normally sent only token aid, since it had no great love for Byzantium. In fact, because the Italian merchants already had trade with the Moslems, they remained neutral until the first Crusade was almost won. The basic reasons for the Crusades may be seen in the internal developments in France, where they had the most powerful backing. France had been growing stronger, it had more trade relations and interest in the East, and it needed an outlet for social unrest at home. The Venetian oligarchy, which wanted to expand its own Eastern trade and influence, gave additional promotion.

Marxists such as H. K. Takahashi (in Hilton, 1976) have emphasized that there are two roads to capitalism: via the master craft worker or via the big merchant. They argue that only the first way was really revolutionary, because the craft worker represented a new class that made a real break with the feudal rulers, as in England and France. In this process, the craft worker became a craft master, then—after centuries of slow economic expansion—began to accumulate enough wealth to rival the feudal lords. In these areas the increase in capitalist production led to a struggle for power between the old and new ruling classes. This struggle was reflected in ideological battles (fought by such writers as Rousseau, Locke, or Voltaire), political clashes, and finally in actual bloody fighting (such as the English revolution of 1648 or the French revolution of 1789).

By contrast, where the big merchants gained control of industry through the putting-out system (a system in which merchants put out orders for goods to peasants), they worked hand in glove with the feudal lords to bolster the status quo, as in East Europe or Japan. As soon as the merchants accumulated some wealth, they bought land and intermarried with the landholding class. Most Marxists contend—exactly opposite to Pirenne's viewpoint—that a virile bourgeois capitalism never fully developed in the merchant-dominated areas (e.g., Hilton, 1952, or Vilar, 1956).

It is not yet possible to give a fully satisfactory description and explanation of the origins and demise of the feudal economy that characterized medieval Europe. The statistics available for most of the medieval period are so poor that any view of its economic development must be purely speculative. Pirenne, for example, points to the continued use of African papyrus in Europe as proof of his thesis that trade continued at a high level in the Merovingian period. His critics, on the other hand, direct attention to the consumption of pepper in the Carolingian period as evidence that only then did medieval trade reach significant proportions. There are no reliable, quantitative data until a much later period. In spite of the arguments over points of fact, however, the principal differences in interpretation are not rooted in differences in empirical knowledge. All recent writers have had access to approximately the same meager evidence; preconceived dogmas have in part determined the interpretation of these few facts. Obviously, the Marxist method does not require that facts be one way or the other. For example, it suffices to say that European capitalism was born out of European internal evolution and its (mostly exploitative) relations with other continents.

Suggested Readings

References and issues in this chapter have been purposely kept to the early classic works, such as the influential works by Dobb (1946) and Hilton (1976, first ed. 1954). In the 1970s and 1980s there has been a flood of Marxist historical writing on these and other issues, such as the two books by Perry Anderson (1974, 1983) on the ancient and feudal periods. On the Greek and Roman period, see the survey and bibliography in Marylin Arthur and David Konstan, ''Marxism and the Study of Classical Antiquity'' in Ollman and Vernoff (1984). On later historical periods, see the survey and bibliography in Michael Merrill and Michael Wallace, ''Marx and History,'' in Ollman and Vernoff (1982).

EXPLOITATION AND INEQUALITY UNDER CAPITALISM: THEORIES OF VALUE AND DISTRIBUTION

In 1982 the United States government stated that an urban family of four lived in poverty if it received less than $9,862 per year. In that year more than thirty-four million persons received lower incomes than this officially defined poverty level (U.S. Department of Commerce, 1983: 447). That income figure was absurdly low, however, and would more aptly describe a family in a state of desperate destitution.

There are those who argue that the poor have flawed characters and low motivation. A very careful study has disproved this: "Many highly motivated people do succeed in pulling themselves out of poverty—but almost as many of the apparently unmotivated also succeed. . . . We found no significant effects of motives on families' economic outcomes" (Institute for Social Research, 1985: 3). People living in poverty do have lower expectations of the future than other people: "Expectancies, on the other hand, do appear to be related to economic outcomes, but not to cause them; if anything, the causation runs the other way, with the economic situation affecting the expectancy" (ISR, 1985: 3). In other words, if you live in poverty, this may cause you to have a pessimistic outlook for the future.

Inequality

The percentage of total income received by the poorest 20 percent and the second poorest 20 percent has not changed much since World War II. Table 4.1 shows the percentage of total income received by each 20 percent of all families, from lowest to highest, since 1947. In 1983, the

Table 4.1

Income Inequality from 1947 to 1983

Income group	Percentage of income received							
of family	1947	1950	1955	1960	1965	1970	1974	1983
Lowest fifth	5.1	4.5	4.8	4.8	5.2	5.4	5.5	5.0
Second fifth	11.8	11.9	12.2	12.2	12.2	12.2	12.0	11.0
Middle fifth	16.7	17.4	17.7	17.8	17.8	17.6	17.5	17.0
Fourth fifth	23.1	23.5	23.5	23.9	23.9	23.9	24.0	24.0
Highest fifth	43.3	42.7	41.8	41.3	40.9	40.9	41.0	43.0
Highest 5 percent	17.5	17.3	16.8	15.9	15.5	15.6	15.5	17.0

Source: U.S. Department of Commerce, *Statistical Abstract of the United States, 1983* (Washington, D.C.: U.S. Government Printing Office, 1984), p. 387.

poorest 20 percent of families received just 5 percent of all income, while the richest 20 percent of families received 43 percent of all income.

Two conclusions are obvious from table 4.1. First, the distribution of income remains amazingly stable over the years. There is no observable trend toward a decrease in the degree of inequality. Second, on the average for the entire period, the highest 5 percent of income recipients receive almost as much income as the lowest 40 percent combined.

Moreover, these data do not really show the extent of inequality of incomes because they are taken from census reports that use biased data. Rich taxpayers use legal loopholes to report less income, do not respond to census surveys as frequently as other taxpayers, and are counted as having only up to $100,000 (the census does not count above that amount in the annual survey). If true incomes were reported, the higher incomes would be much larger than those shown.

Although there has been no long-run trend in inequality in this century, the inequality of income distribution has increased significantly during the Reagan administration. The Reagan policies and their differential impact are spelled out in detail in Hunt and Sherman (1986: ch. 34). From 1980 to 1984 the median family income of the poorest 40 percent fell $477 in real terms, while the median family income of the richest 10 percent rose by $5,085 in real terms (Edsall, 1986: 23). A study by the Joint Economic Committee (1986) shows that the distribution of wealth is even more unequal than the distribution of income. The study finds that the richest 420,000 U.S. families controlled $3.7 trillion assets in 1983. In other words, just one-half of 1 percent of all families owned 35 percent of total wealth in 1983. This tiny number of super rich families increased their holdings of all wealth from 25 percent in 1962, so the trend is toward greater concentration of wealth. In the same time period, the poorest 90 percent of U.S. families dropped from holding 35 percent to just 28 percent of all wealth. Thus, the rich got richer, while the share of the poor and middle class declined in this period. (Republicans have argued that the study overstates inequality, whereas radicals have argued that it understates inequality. See Dollars and Sense Staff, 1987: 11.)

Income by Source

The most important factor differentiating incomes is their source. Capitalists receive income from owning, whereas nearly all other individuals get their incomes from working. The very wealthy who receive extraordinarily high incomes are almost all capitalists. Table 4.1 gave the figures for the highest 5 percent of income recipients. Included among these are many doctors, lawyers, corporate executives, and so on. Yet the truly wealthy, about 1 percent of the population, are the elite, powerful capitalists.

According to the Federal Reserve (1984), the richest 2 percent of all families own 71 percent of all corporate stock. Only 19 percent of families own any corporate stock. Of all U.S. government bonds, 97 percent are held by just .02 percent of all families. In fact, only 1 percent of all families hold any U.S. government bonds at all.

It is obvious that the top 1 percent of the population, which receives the bulk of the income from ownership, is truly a wealthy power elite. Incomes in this elite range up to highs of over $100 million per year (or more than $270,000 per day, 365 days per year). Among the very wealthy, defined as those individuals with income over $1 million, more than 95 percent of their income (in 1971) came from ownership of property, so these were truly capitalists (See Bowles and Gintis, 1975: 90).

One can also make a rough estimate of the total shares of labor income and property income in the United States. The total amounts of property income and labor income for 1981 are shown in table 4.2 from official data with no adjustments. The official data show that property income was $586 billion or 28 percent of all income. This $586 billion of property income is still badly understated, however, because it is based on what has been reported for tax purposes, so it does not include

Table 4.2

Property and Labor Income (in billions of dollars)

Business proprietor's income	$125
Rental income	$34
Corporate profits before tax	$191
Net interest income	$236
Total property income	$586
Total wages and salaries	$1,494

Source: U.S. Department of Commerce, *Statistical Abstract of the United States, 1983*, p. 423.

Table 4.3

Unreported Individual Income as a Percent of Amount Reportable, by Type of Income, 1976

Type of income	Percent unreported
Wages and salaries	2–3
Dividends	8–16
Interest	10–16
Pensions, annuities, estates, and trusts	12–16
Capital gains	17–24
Self-employment	36–40
Rents and royalties	35–40

Source: Treasury Department, IRS, *Estimates of Income Unreported on Individual Income Tax Returns*, Publication 1104 (9–79) (Washington, D.C.: U.S. Government Printing Office).

the property income that, through tax loopholes, goes unreported. Moreover, as can be seen in table 4.3, Treasury Department Internal Revenue Service audits show that only 2 to 3 percent of wage and salary income goes unreported, whereas up to 50 percent of various types of property incomes goes unreported.

Finally, from table 4.4 it can be seen that wage and salary workers are now the overwhelming majority (83 percent) of Americans. Yet their income share is far below 83 percent. Moreover, labor income is overstated because the labor income data reported by the treasury include all managers' salaries as labor income. For example, in 1982, Frederick W. Smith, chairman of Federal Express, received a total compensation (including salary, bonus, and a commitment for long-

Table 4.4

Evolution of the U.S. Labor Force

Year	Wage and salary workers (percent)	Self-employed (percent)	Managers and officials (percent)
1780[a]	20	80	0
1880	62	37	1
1974	83	8	9

a. The data from 1780 exclude slaves.
Source: Michael Reich, "The Evolution of the U.S. Labor Force," in *The Capitalist System*, ed. R. Edwards, M. Reich, and T. Weisskopf (Englewood Cliffs, N.J.: Prentice Hall, 1978), p. 180.

term income) of $51.5 million; the top four executives of Toys 'R' Us received compensation ranging from $7.7 million to $43.7 million. The twelve highest paid executives each received over $2.5 million in compensation in 1982, while dozens of executives received compensation in excess of $500,000. Thus, by including managers' salaries as a part of labor income, government statistics significantly understate the differences between the incomes of capitalists and workers.

Managers and officials are now a significant 9 percent of the labor force. The 80 percent of the population self-employed in 1780 were mostly farmers. Today the self-employed number only 8 percent, including 2 percent farm owners, 3 percent independent professionals and artisans, and 3 percent self-employed businesspersons. So this 8 percent is what remains of the old middle class; even adding all managers and officials one gets only 17 percent "middle class." This leaves 83 percent in the working class.

But where is the capitalist class? The government data hide the capitalist class. The top corporate executives are hidden among the managers and officials. The biggest millionaire "coupon clippers" are hidden among the self-employed businesspersons. Nevertheless, from the estimates of wealth stated earlier, especially holdings of corporate stock, the entire capitalist class is only about 1 percent of the population.

The Classical Approach

Adam Smith explained price formation through competition in the market. In the market place, sellers and purchasers come together.

Products produced by workers in many regions and many countries flow to each market in one vast network.

Goods flow according to the dictates of profit, where they are demanded; while competition lowers the price to the average profit level. Equilibrium is reached at an average rate of profit in all industries because capital flows to where excess demand has produced high prices and high profits.

Smith interprets this picture to mean that the invisible hand of competition leads to the best of all possible worlds. Some of the problems with Adam Smith's conclusion arise because he (and his followers) ignore a number of important difficulties: (1) demand depends on income but income distribution is very unequal; (2) some workers (and even consumers and small business people) suffer discrimination; (3) workers are exploited; (4) monopoly distorts prices, profits, and allocation; (5) people and commodities do not flow freely between countries; (6) some countries' economies are dominated by others; (7) governments shape and change the market system in the interests of a wealthy, powerful minority; and (8) in the interests of profit-making, giant corporations pollute the environment, produce useless commodities, and produce vast quantities of harmful commodities (from cigarettes to bombs). Each of these problems is discussed in later chapters.

Adam Smith wrote that "labour . . . is the real measure of the exchangeable value of all commodities. The real price of everything, what everything really costs to the man who wishes to acquire it, is the toil and trouble of acquiring it" (1776: 30). Ricardo wrote somewhat similarly that "the value of a commodity, or the quantity of any other commodity for which it will exchange, depends on the relative quantity of labour which is necessary for its production" (1821: 5). Smith presented several other theories along with the labor theory, and Ricardo never completed a consistent presentation of it. The question of their exact views on the labor theory of value is very complex and need not detain us here. What is important is only that one strand of classical thought did favor a labor theory of value, and that Marx seized on that strand as the basis for his work. Other strands of the classical view led to the neoclassical approach.

Adam Smith seems to have two distinct views of profits and wages mixed together in various places. On the one hand, he speaks of wages as equal to the necessary subsistence of the worker; he views the whole product as due to the worker's labor, and thus considers profits as a "residual" surplus after paying wages. On the other hand, he frequently speaks of wages as a cost of procuring labor, and profits as a "cost" of procuring capital.

The notion that profits are a mere residue or deduction from the workers' product led directly to Marx's view of profit as exploitation. The other notion, which was emphasized more in Smith's own work and in the other classical economists, was that profit was a just and natural cost of production. It led eventually to the neoclassical idea of profits as equal to the marginal product of capital.

The Neoclassical Approach

During Ricardo's lifetime, the labor theory of value ruled supreme, but soon after it was challenged by critics and weakened by "supporters." The process of weakening and replacing the labor theory continued from the 1820s to the 1870s.

The main neoclassical "revolution," however, came in the 1870s with Jevons, Menger, and Walras, who emphasized the theory of marginal utility to the exclusion of almost all else. These marginalists saw the problem of economics as the optimizing of production and consumer satisfaction with given amounts of labor, resources, and technology. Hence, they began with the psychological reaction of consumers to commodities, and not with the relationships of human beings, as Marx always did. In fact, several of them consciously aimed at replacing Marx's growing influence (see Meek, 1956: 250). The theory of marginal utility argued the influence of consumer demand on prices. It stated that consumers spend money according to the additional satisfaction (or utility) that they obtain from one additional (or marginal) unit of the products. They concluded that, under pure competition, prices would have to be proportional to the marginal utility of the products.

The Long Run

Alfred Marshall (1890) evolved the concepts of "long-run" and "short-run" time periods. In the short run, production is limited to present capacity because the time is too short for new investment to result in more available capital or greater capacity to produce. The long run is a long enough time for new investment to put more capital goods in place and expand the capacity to produce.

In the long run, says Marshall, the "price" equals the "cost" of production (including an average profit). If profit is above average in one industry because of low prices, capital moves out of that industry so that restricted competition in supply raises prices till they equal costs.

What is the importance of the demand for goods or their utility to consumers in this case? Suppose that for some reason radios suddenly become twice as desirable to consumers. The demand for radios would double at the present price. If we were selling a million radios for a dollar apiece, we could now sell the million radios for two dollars apiece. In the long run, however, two million radios will be built, and the cost per unit for the second million radios will be the same as for the first million radios (because Marshall assumes, as the simplest case, constant costs at any scale). There is then no reason in a purely competitive system for the price to change in the long run (so long as there is no change in the technology of production). Therefore, in the long run, a change in utility or consumer demand will change the amount of production of a particular commodity, and will thereby change the allocation of resources. The change in demand, however, will have no effect on the long-run price (or "value") of that commodity. This is similar to the simplest classical or Marxist case.

The Short Run

In Marshall's "short run," supply can be expanded or contracted within the limits of existing factories and equipment. The cost may vary as supply varies, but for any given supply, it is fixed. As we approach a "maximum" or very intensive use of capacity, the cost per unit tends to increase. Thus, as output rises in the short run, the additional cost per unit must rise. On the other hand, it is a platitude that to sell the higher output, the industry must lower its prices. Thus, as output rises in the short run, the additional revenue per unit must fall. As a result, a point is reached where rising costs per unit and falling prices per unit mean an end to additional profit from additional output; that is, profit is at its highest point and will fall if more is produced. Therefore, output and prices are set at this point where no additional profit is to be made by producing more output. In the short run, then, price is set by both demand and cost conditions. Nevertheless, in the long run price is set by "cost" alone (under certain simplifying assumptions and where "cost" includes average returns to capital).

Marginal Productivity

J. B. Say argued that the capitalist must abstain from consumption in order to invest, so the profit from abstinence is a ''cost'' of production and the capitalist deserves to earn it just as the worker deserves wages. Say's abstinence argument was ridiculed on the grounds that most capitalists are not starving and only invest the excess over their large amount of consumption. Alfred Marshall contended that capitalists must wait for their returns, so the profit from waiting is a ''cost'' of production and the capitalist deserves it just as much as the worker earns wages. This argument also was not very convincing since ''waiting'' does not appear to be a form of labor. But the arguments by Say and by Marshall did lead to the modern theory of marginal productivity in the writings of John Bates Clark (1847–1938). Clark's most important book, *The Distribution of Wealth* (1899), is dedicated to the proposition that workers and capitalists each receive in income exactly what they contribute as their marginal product. In other words, a worker's wage will just equal the additional (or marginal) product that the worker adds to output. Likewise, the profit of the capitalist will just equal the additional (or marginal) amount of product added by the piece of capital that he adds to the productive process.

The argument is just this: Suppose there is a fixed amount of capital (a given factory and machinery). Suppose we ask how many workers should be added by the rational capitalist to maximize his or her profits. Suppose each additional worker adds something to the product, but that each additional worker adds less than the previous one. This is so because there are only so many machines for them to use, so they can add very little beyond the optimum capacity of the given factory. Keeping the same number of machines, as the capitalist adds workers, their additional product will decline. In this case, the capitalist should then continue to add workers until he or she finds the product of the last worker is just equal to the worker's cost or wage. In that case, the last worker makes no additional profit for the capitalist. At that point, the capitalist should hire no more workers. Therefore, the wage will just equal the additional (or marginal) product of the last worker.

Notice that what Clark has arrived at is a rule for the capitalist to follow if he or she wishes to maximize profits. If the capitalist does act this way (and he or she usually does), then it is a platitude that the wage is the same as the marginal product—workers are not hired if they produce a lower marginal product. Clark thought that he had thereby proven that this is a just and ethical distribution of income. Clark does the same thing for profits. In Clark's simple example, each additional machine adds less to the product than the previous machine (because workers and perhaps factory space are limited). In that case, the capitalist should only add machines till the additional product of one more machine will just equal its cost. Beyond that point, more machines give no more profit, so no more machines should be bought. Therefore, the cost of providing an additional machine (whether out of the capitalist's own capital or from borrowed capital) will just equal the value of its additional (or marginal) product. He concludes that what is paid to capital is capital's own marginal product, whereas what is paid to labor is the worker's marginal product. Therefore, there is no such thing as exploitation.

This conservative theory is followed by most of the present textbooks of economics. The most widely used textbook is that written by Paul Samuelson, who says: "After allowing for all depreciation requirements, capital has a net productivity" (1973: 574). By this, he just means that (1) machines as well as labor must be used to produce anything in modern industry, and (2) the use of more machines will increase the product per worker. In this way, he leads into the theory of marginal productivity and specifically endorses Clark's theory of income distribution. He states the basic theory just as Clark did, except that he is a little more careful about the political-ethical conclusions. He still leaves the strong impression that this theory proves that everyone is paid their "just income" according to their contribution.

Radical Critique of Marginal Productivity Theory

There is an enormous, sophisticated literature criticizing neoclassical profit and capital theories (see, e.g., Sraffa, 1960, and Harris, 1978). The most basic criticism, however, is simply that the neoclassicals ignore institutions and class relations, so they confuse the productivity of capital with the productivity of capitalists. Marginal productivity theory may tell us about the production contributions of labor and capital; it says nothing about the contribution of the capitalist. Radicals admit that machines may increase production, that workers need them, and that they increase the productivity of the worker. In that sense Samuelson is right to say that "capital" has a "net productivity." But it is the physical capital that is productive (jointly with the worker) and not the capitalist. The capitalist owns the capital, but he or she is not the machine. The machine does the work (with the worker); the capitalist gets the profit.

The productivity of physical capital goods (created by another labor process in the past) is quite different from the ability of capitalist owners to capture a certain portion of the product as interest or profit. "It is, of course, true that materials and machinery can be said to be physically productive in the sense that labor working with them can turn out a larger product than labor working without them, but physical productivity in this sense must under no circumstances be confused with value productivity" (Sweezy, 1942: 61). In other words, "under capitalism 'the productiveness of labor is made to ripen, as if in a hot-house.' Whether we choose to say that capital is productive, or that capital is necessary to make labor productive, is not a matter of much importance. . . . What is important is to say that owning capital is not a productive activity" (Robinson, 1946: 18). This is clear in the case of a mere coupon-clipper (as most stockowners are today). The fact that some of them may otherwise perform productive labor through their own managerial work (and are paid very high wages for managerial work) is not in contradiction to the fact that they also make money by mere ownership of capital.

Orthodox Marxist Theory

In a capitalist economy, Marx (1867) states, the value of any commodity is determined by the amount of labor embodied in it—including the "congealed" labor embodied in the plant, equipment, and raw materials used up in the process of production. Marx does not "prove" this statement because he assumes agreement with a line of classical thought which, as seen through Marxist glasses, might be stated as follows: Suppose we examine an economy in which each producer is an independent unit, doing his or her own work, hiring no one, and being hired by no one. He or she may produce farm goods, or may hunt for animals, or may do handicraft work.

To begin with the simplest case, assume that the producer also makes his or her own machinery and mines raw materials from scratch, a la Robinson Crusoe. In this case, it is almost a platitude that products exchange according to their labor costs. Adam Smith used an example in which some people hunt beaver while others hunt deer. If it takes on the average twice as long to catch a deer as to catch a beaver, then a deer-catcher will demand and receive two beavers for one deer (or twice as much "money" for a deer as for a beaver).

Suppose a disequilibrium situation in which the market rate of exchange is only one for one, while twice as many labor hours are expended on catching a deer than a beaver. Then the hunters will switch over to catching beaver, because it takes only half the time, yet the reward is equal. As hunters quit catching deer and the supply of deer in the market decreases, competition for the smaller supply must force a rise in the price of deer, till one deer is exchanged for two beavers. Only then will an equilibrium exist, in which it is equally profitable to catch deer as beavers, so that there will be no further switching. Thus, when the system comes to rest, the ratio of prices in exchange will equal the ratio of labor times expended.

If it is necessary to purchase equipment from others, such as a bow and arrows, the answer is still basically the same—although everyone may gain from the greater productivity due to the specialization of labor. If the bow and arrows are offered at a price relatively greater than the labor time bestowed on them, the hunters may go back to making their own bows and arrows. Still, the bow and arrows must be included in the price of deer at the labor cost of making them, regardless of whether they are made by the hunter or someone else.

In the modern case, suppose a society that regularly uses money and is "capitalist" in the sense that there is private ownership of productive facilities, the goal of production is private profit, and capitalists are free to hire and fire workers. In this case, the capitalist supplies capital in the form of factories and equipment, while workers supply the labor power needed for production (here we ignore other classes). The final product must sell for a price equal to the total labor put into it, including the present labor of production plus the labor that went into producing the factories, raw materials, and equipment that were used up in the productive process.

The argument is essentially the same as in the simple economy of independent producers. If the capitalist tries to sell (or exchange) the product at a higher relative price than is proportionate to the labor in it, then other people can produce it for less, either for themselves or to sell in competition with the capitalist. In other words, if the price is above the labor value, so that a profit above average is being made, other capital will flow into the industry and increase its supply until by competition the price falls to the level of its total (labor) value. Yet the capitalist can at least obtain that price because no one can produce it for less. If the price should fall below the (labor) value, profit will be below average, capital will flow out, and supply will drop. Eventually, in the long run, competition will force the price back up to its full (labor) value, and only then will equilibrium be reached.

Marx immediately notes several commonsense qualifications to the "law of value." First, it applies only to labor expended under the usual contemporary technological conditions. If a person produces an automobile by hand, the product will still have a value equal only to the labor necessary to produce it in the usual mass production process. Second, the product must have a utility; labor expended on useless objects does not count. Notice, however, that although utility must be present for any value at all, it does not determine the quantity of value produced. Utility may be a factor determining demand, but if we assume that supply and demand are now balanced and equal, then the quantity of value must be determined by something else, namely, the labor expended. In other words, on these assumptions, the demand will determine the distribution of labor among industries or the amount of each product, but it cannot affect the relative price or exchange ratio of products.

Third, it is assumed that there are constant average costs of production over the whole relevant range—so a higher demand does not affect the labor expended per unit. Fourth, expenditure of more skilled labor will count as some multiple of an hour of average labor expended. The labor expended in "producing" (educating, training) the more skilled worker (for example, an engineer) is greater than that expended in producing an ordinary worker; therefore, he or she passes on to the product a greater value per hour.

Fifth, Marx assumed, as a first approximation, that living human labor and inanimate objects (congealed labor) are used in the same ratio in every product. Otherwise, prices will not be proportionate to labor values, an issue discussed below. Sixth, Marx assumed, as a first approximation, that there is pure and perfect competition, with no monopoly power. Monopoly power will cause prices to deviate from labor values (as shown in chapter 7). Seventh, Marx assumed, as a first approximation, that there is no unemployment and no idle capacity. Unemployment and idle capacity cause prices to drop below long-run equilibrium (as shown in chapter 6). Eighth, Marx assumed, as a first approximation, that government spending and production is negligible and there are no government regulations, except the rules of private property and contract. Government may affect relative and absolute price levels in many ways (as shown in chapter 8). Ninth, it is assumed, as a first approximation, that all the world is one capitalist nation with free flow of labor and trade and capital. International relations may affect domestic prices in many ways (as shown in chapter 9).

The Fundamentalist View

There seem to be in Marx two different views of values and prices that surface at different points in his work. On the one hand, Marx takes for granted the labor theory of value, which he took—and developed—from Ricardo (for Marx's intellectual evolution, see the outstanding analysis in Mandel, 1971). In this view, Marx sees certain inexorable laws of capitalism deriving from the labor theory of value. The notion of such inexorable laws derives partly from the classical economists and partly from Marx's Hegelian tradition. The other view in Marx, which conforms more to the genius of his own historical approach, visualizes prices and wages as the result of human relationships and class conflicts.

Marx's first view, the labor theory of value as the foundation for a set of inexorable laws, is followed by a group often labeled as fundamentalists, since they agree that the fundamentals of political economy are all presented by Marx. Three leading members of this group are Anwar Shaikh (1978), Willi Semmler (1982), and John Weeks (1981), all of whom consider themselves to be "orthodox" Marxists—though they differ among themselves on some more minor points. Thus, John Weeks argues that Marx's work is characterized by the "central role of the law of value and its most important manifestation, the tendency of the rate of profit to fall. This interpretation of Marx's work . . . can be called . . . 'orthodox' Marxism" (p. 7).

The emphasis of Weeks (and Shaikh and Semmler) is on the acceptance and elaboration of the labor theory of value as found in their interpretation of Marx. It is an economic determinist view in that prices, profits, and wages are determined by impersonal economic forces and not primarily by class conflicts. The theory is stated in terms of the technology of commodity production rather than human relations: the value of any commodity is the inherent amount of socially necessary labor embodied in the commodity. Thus, Weeks even claims that Frederick Engels "completely misconstrued Marx's value theory" (p. 8) because Engels emphasized that class conflicts determined profit and wage levels and, therefore, income distribution, whereas Weeks believes that Marx argued only in terms of the inherent value of any commodity, including labor. In Weeks's view, class conflict cannot change what the theory of value has ordained.

The fundamentalists then argue, as Weeks stressed in the quote, that the labor theory of value inexorably leads to a tendency of the rate of profit to fall. This is seen as Marx's central contribution, and the sole cause of economic crises. In understanding U.S. capitalism, as shall be seen in later chapters, fundamentalists downplay any views based on class relations, lack of demand by exploited workers, or extensive monopoly. In this view of economics as a set of impersonal laws of value, coupled with their tendency to downplay messy phenomena like insufficient demand or monopoly power in setting prices, they are remarkably like the neoclassical economists. When asked about the price of a ton of steel, both fundamentalists and neoclassicals will discuss the inherent value of the commodities (including labor) that went into it. Both treat labor as being like any other commodity, and neither discusses the human relationships involved.

Bowles and Gintis (1981) argue that Marx himself, because of his classical and Hegelian background, sometimes remained in the fundamentalist, commodity mode of thought (though he was its strongest critic at other times). Thus, Marx argued for socially necessary labor-time as the value of any commodity on the following reasoning: First, Marx argues that every market exchange (under pure and perfect competition) must be the exchange of two equal values. Second, he contends that the value must be given by something contained in each commodity (1867: 37). Marx goes on to argue that, if two things are being exchanged, there must exist in equal quantities something common to both. The two things must therefore be equal to a third, which in itself is neither the one nor the other (p. 37). What is this mysterious something giving value to all commodities? Marx claims: "This common 'something' cannot be either a geometrical, a chemical, or any other natural property of commodities. . . . If then we leave out of consideration the use-value of commodities, they have only one common property left, that of being products of labor" (p. 37). The abstract and ahistorical approach of this argument (contrary to Marx's usual historical and class approach) has led many radicals (or independent Marxists) to reject this argument—and has led some to reject the whole labor theory of value as wrong or as irrelevant to current conflicts.

Moreover, Marx does not really prove that no other quality is common to all commodities, because he starts with the classic view and does not think it necessary to argue it. Bowles and Gintis contend that Marx was here affected by that same belief in the inherent value of commodities that he so often attacked (and called "commodity fetishism"). "His treatment of the phenomenon of equal exchange may be considered Marx's own flirtation with commodity fetishism" (1871, p. 5). Marx had still not liberated himself completely from the old view of value; he did not follow his own approach of political economy as a science of human, class relations. This commodity approach left Marx open to many neoclassical criticisms, all of which fail if we view the labor theory of value as a class and relational theory of capitalist institutions.

Marx on Income Distribution

Karl Marx's view of income distribution was very different from the classical or neoclassical views. Marx stated that commodities derived their value solely from the labor put into them in the production process. Workers were paid only their means of subsistence. Profit is the "surplus value" or residue of the worker's product that remains after the worker is paid. Marx argued that the capitalist normally makes his or her profit by selling the product at its value, while buying the worker's power to labor or labor power at its value.

Marx's point rests on a very simple distinction, which he claims was overlooked by Adam Smith and most of the classical economists. There is a difference between the value of what the worker produces and the value of the worker's own ability to labor (called "labor power"). The wage of the worker, or the value of his or her labor power, is determined by the labor expended in producing the worker. That labor includes what is necessary for his or her food, clothing, shelter, and education as well as the food, clothing, shelter, and education of her or his family (under the conditions and traditions of the given time and place).

The worker's labor embodied in the final product, however, is much greater than the labor that is required to keep the worker functioning. In other words, a worker produces far more in a day than the wages paid to keep him or her alive and functioning. In Marx's terms, the value produced is much greater than the "necessary value" to pay for the worker's own subsistence. This difference is profit or "surplus value," which reflects the objective fact of excess labor expended by the worker.

Fundamentalist Interpretation of Marx on Exploitation

The fundamentalist or orthodox argument is this:

1. Human labor-power (the capacity to work) is a commodity under capitalism, sold in the market. It is bought and sold like all other commodities at its long-run value, which is the amount of labor-time necessary to produce the worker.

2. The use (or use-value) extracted by the capitalist from this commodity, labor-power, is the expenditure of labor for a given number of hours. Those hours worked may be—and are under capitalism—far more than the hours required to produce the value of the worker (that is, wages). So the difference between the value of the worker (wages) and the value of the product (price) is the surplus value (or profit) going to the capitalist.

This argument is very formal—it is not firmly rooted in institutional and human relations—and has several flaws:

Labor power may be called a commodity if one wishes (that is a semantic or definitional question). But whatever it is called, Bowles and Gintis (1981) are correct that labor power is very different from the usual capitalist commodity in some very important respects relevant to this argument. Labor power is similar to the usual capitalist commodity in that it is bought and sold in the market. This fact often means degradation and alienation of workers and opens the door to unemployment, but it is nevertheless a fact.

Yet labor power differs from most things called commodities in several ways. First, in a pure capitalist system, all other commodities are produced by capitalists. Workers are not produced by a capitalist assembly line. Workers do consume some other commodities, but most of the labor going into the production of a worker is the unpaid love and care of a family.

Second, all other commodities are sold by capitalists in market exchanges governed by impersonal supply and demand. Not only is workers' capacity to work (or labor power) not produced by capitalists, it is not sold by capitalists. The worker's power to labor is sold by millions of workers—though capitalists, once they have bought labor power, may sell services. So the supply conditions of labor power are totally different than those of all other commodities bought by capitalists.

For all commodities, Marx makes the argument that capitalist profit cannot be made by cheating. If a capitalist sells a machine to another capitalist above its long-run value measured in labor hours, then one capitalist makes an extra profit, but the other makes a loss. Therefore, in the aggregate, if one capitalist cheats another, no profit is made by the capitalist class. Yet a capitalist could make a profit by cheating a worker in some sense, so the process of exploitation versus simple cheating must be further clarified.

A Radical (or Independent Marxist) View

The main point of radical value and distribution theory is to understand the exploitation of workers by capitalists, whereas neoclassicals are mainly concerned with relative prices and the allocation of resources. Sweezy (1942) shows that the theory of exploitation requires a qualitative aspect, that is, a general statement of capitalist relations of production and how they lead to exploitation. It also requires a quantitative aspect, that is, how to measure and explain wages and profits within a consistent price theory. Most radicals have a wide range of agreement on the qualitative description of the productive relations causing exploitation but have strong disagreements over how to state a consistent quantitative theory. We begin, therefore, with a qualitative discussion of the relations underlying exploitation.

Productive Relations and Exploitation

All radicals agree that prices, wages, and profits in capitalism reflect the human, social, class relations of capitalism. Neoclassicals, however, begin with the physical marginal products of labor and capital, as if the economy were a purely technical process that could be understood apart from social relations; neoclassical economics assumes that social relations are held constant. Marx's main contribution was not a theory of relative prices, but an explanation of how capitalist relations lead to exploitation. Heilbroner emphasizes the logical distinction that "The conception of surplus value rooted in production is distinct from the labor theory of value, which is an attempt to explain relative prices in terms of labor power. Wage labor can produce a surplus, whatever the source of value, as long as the price of labor power plus used-up materials is less than the price of labor's product'' (1985: 73). Note that the independent Marxist view of exploitation as a class relationship based on unequal, institutionalized power is very similar to the institutionalist view of the economy as a system of power (Samuels, 1979).

Under slavery, it is obvious that slaves are forced—by threat or use of violence—to produce a surplus over their own subsistence that goes to the slave owners. Under feudalism, it is obvious that serfs are coerced—by tradition, religious ideology, and the threat or use of violence—to produce a surplus by working on the feudal lord's land that goes to the feudal lord.

Under capitalism, it is not obvious, but it is still true, that workers are coerced—by economic necessity, where the rules of the game are backed by force—to work for the boss at a real wage (a bundle of goods) that is less than the real output (a larger bundle of goods) of those same workers; that surplus is profit, so the process is exploitation. Under the institutions of private property, capitalists control the means of production and the jobs for workers. Workers, who lack the capital to create their own business, are free to take a job or starve. Today, workers may also go on welfare or unemployment compensation at a low income and a degrading status. The relations of private property—supported by tradition, ideology, law, and force—as well as the threat of unemployment, if one does not work within those relations, are the glue that holds the system of capitalist exploitation in place.

Prices, wages, and profits reflect a system in which workers are paid a certain wage, but the entire product is sold by the capitalist at whatever price it can command in the market. Consumer demand is based on the class income and class behavior of those receiving labor income and property income. The very meaning and amount of prices, profits, and wages are given by these relations, not merely by technical conditions. For example, the cost of production of a product in South Africa will be lower than in the United States—even with the same technology and machinery—because unions are suppressed, prejudice divides workers, and the state is used to oppress the majority of workers. In a planned economy, prices are set by the planners, and wages are set by the planners, so "profits" are simply that part of the product that the government decided to keep when it set wages and prices. In a pure communist economy, there would be no money, no market, no market prices, and no market wages. So the prices of products, wages of workers, and profits of capitalists are the result of a certain set of class relations, certain rules of the game, certain social institutions—and not merely the technical conditions of production.

Wages, Profit, and Class Conflict

It was shown above that the neoclassical view that wages are equal to the marginal product of labor and profit is equal to the marginal product of capital is misleading (and Sraffa, 1960, shows it to be internally inconsistent). It was also shown above that the orthodox or fundamentalist Marxist explanation—wages equal to the socially necessary labor required to produce the goods to be consumed by the worker—is based on the unproven assertion that labor is like all other commodities. But as seen earlier, many radicals (such as Bowles and Gintis, 1981) have shown that labor is very different from other commodities. It differs in three ways: (1) it is not produced by capitalists, but by the family; (2) it is not sold by capitalists, but by workers; and (3) it cannot be merely set in place to be used, but must be persuaded or coerced into working at a particular pace.

What does determine the wage level under capitalism? The total supply of workers is influenced by (a) the amount of population, (b) laws, such as those about child labor, and (c) sociological attitudes, such as those toward women working. Here one must investigate in detail how workers are produced by the family. At any given time, the supply of workers available beyond those now working depends on the level of unemployment; obviously, high unemployment tends to lower wages. Workers and capitalists have very unequal bargaining power, especially an individual worker versus a huge corporation. When workers sell their labor power, the fact of oversupply of labor greatly hinders their bargaining ability. The demand for labor is a derived demand from the consumer and investor demand for all other commodities, which may be above or below the full employment level.

The supply and demand factors describe only the case of pure and perfect competition in the labor market. In reality, there is imperfect and impure competition in the labor market caused by ignorance; immobility; labor unions; the monopoly power of big business and business associations; interference by the capitalist state, from fiscal policy to labor laws; and international barriers. Radicals have also shown that there is a dual labor market, one for high-paid white males and one for low-paid minorities and women (discussed in detail in the next chapter). The actions of unions, business, and government are much affected by public opinion as shaped by the mass media (which are owned by big business). In short, the wage is determined by class power and class conflict, but in given conditions of supply and demand.

Once the wage level is determined, the question is what determines the output per worker. The orthodox Marxist and neoclassical views just assume that a worker's labor power is bought for a given number of hours and is expended at average intensity in that period. But what determines the intensity of labor? A machine will work at a certain maximum load for the lifetime of the machine. In fact, all other commodities bought by capitalists and consumers work within a certain range of intensity given by their technological specifications, so the consumer or capitalist may decide to utilize them anywhere within that range at will. Workers, however, are not machines and may work faster or slower than the average, may resist speed-up, and may go on strike. The fact that a worker's labor power is bought for eight hours does not determine the intensity of labor expenditure per hour.

The average intensity of labor is determined by capitalist attempts to increase intensity and workers' resistance to speed-up. There is a whole large literature (see Braverman, 1974) on the ways used by capitalists to speed up work at a given technology, for example, by Taylorism, which includes precise measurement of minimum job times and setting of norms. The success of capitalist speed-up depends on many of the same factors determining the wage. If there is a weak union and high unemployment (so that workers feel threatened by job loss), then it is possible to intensify labor expenditure per hour. If there is a strong union and full employment, workers may successfully resist speed-up. Thus, labor intensity is determined by relative class power under given conditions of supply and demand.

The institutional setting, that is, the capitalist relations of production, provides the limits within which class conflict determines wages, prices and output, and profits. Given the conditions of demand and supply (including the level of unemployment), class conflict determines wages. Given the conditions of demand and supply (including the level of unemployment), class conflict determines the intensity of labor and the output per worker. Under capitalist institutions and normal relations of class power, the labor (labor-time times intensity) going into the *output of the worker* will be greater than the labor going into the bundle of goods that constitute the worker's wage, thus producing surplus value or profit. Before turning to the quantitative analysis of wages and profits, it is important to remind the reader in detail of how these neat-sounding theoretical relationships have been reflected in the actual, messy history of capital-labor relations in the U.S. economy.

Class Conflict in U.S. Labor Relations

Before the Civil War, the U.S. economy was still dominated by rural, agricultural production and small business; there were few large concentrations of workers. Consequently, unions were weak and usually short-lived. After the Civil War, U.S. capitalism expanded rapidly into the South and the West, industry became large scale, and enterprises with large numbers of workers became commonplace. At the same time, working and living conditions were miserable. For example, in New York City in the 1860s thousands of little girls and boys worked from 6 o'clock in the morning until midnight and were paid only three dollars a week. These conditions brought a spread of individual unions and national federations.

The National Labor Union was a militant federation in the 1860s and 1870s, but it admitted large numbers of professionals and other middle-class individuals. So it turned away from unionism to reform and then quickly died away. In the 1870s and 1880s, the Knights of Labor expanded quickly because of a major, long-term depression, combined with much police brutality toward strikers. After one strike in which police killed twenty men, women, and children, the *New York Tribune* wrote about the strikers: "These brutal creatures can understand no other reasoning than that of force and enough of it to be remembered among them for generations" (quoted in Boyer and Morais, 1970: 69). Anyone could join the Knights, so its middle-class character eventually turned it to currency reform, opposition to all strikes, and a rapid decline of membership.

The American Federation of Labor began in the 1880s and was at first quite militant and socialist oriented. The preface to its first constitution said: "A struggle is going on in the nations of the world between the oppressors and oppressed of all countries, a struggle between capital and labor which must grow in intensity from year to year and work disastrous results to the toiling millions of all nations if not combined for mutual protection and benefit" (quoted in Boyer and Morais, 1970: 90). But the AFL soon gave up the struggle between capital and labor. It became a "business union," trying to win incremental wage increases, paying no attention to larger issues, having high-paid leaders with no militancy, and trying hard to compromise with business.

The biggest and bloodiest strikes of this period were fought by independent unions. The American Railway Union struck the railroads in 1894 but was defeated with violence when the U.S. Army came in to move the trains on the excuse of "protecting the mail." In the early 1900s, the Western Federation of Miners struck against miserable conditions in the Colorado Rockefeller-owned mines but was defeated by the state militia, who used machine guns on some miners' camps. In 1912 a strike by women and children against long hours and low pay in the textile mills of Lawrence, Massachusetts, was led by the Industrial Workers of the World, a radical labor federation.

In the 1930s, wages fell by one-third, while one of every four workers was unemployed. The AFL did little, and it even opposed unemployment compensation. Again, independent unions led some militant strikes. One example was the strike of the West Coast maritime workers in 1934. When they first tried to bargain with the employers, the employers simply fired all the union leaders. Eventually, about thirty-five thousand maritime workers were out on strike, the center of the strike being the Embarcadero at the port of San Francisco. On July 3, 1934, the police decided to break the mass picket lines to allow scabs to work. One reporter wrote, "The police opened fire with revolvers and riot guns. Clouds of tear gas swept the picket lines and sent the men choking in defeat. . . . Squads of police who looked like Martian monsters in their special helmets and gas masks led the way, flinging gas bombs ahead of them" (quoted in Boyer and Morais, 1970: 285). But this was only the preliminary. The pickets returned on July 5 (known as Bloody Thursday), and they were joined by many young people from the high schools and colleges as well as hundreds of other unions members. The police charged, using vomiting gas, revolvers with live ammunition, and riot guns. Hundreds were badly wounded and two workers were killed.

The pickets finally were driven away and the employers thought they had won. But many union locals as well as the Alameda Labor Council called for a general strike. In spite of a telegram from the president of the AFL forbidding any strike, the workers of San Francisco launched a general strike to support the maritime workers and in protest against the killings by the police. The general strike was amazingly successful: "The paralysis was effective beyond all expectation. To all intents and purposes industry was at a complete standstill. The great factories were empty and deserted. No streetcars were running. Virtually all stores were closed. The giant apparatus of commerce was a lifeless, helpless hulk" (quoted in Boyer and Morais, 1970: 287).

During the general strike, labor efficiently allowed into the city emergency food and medical supplies, but nothing else. Thousands of troops moved into the city, but there was no violence; labor simply refused to go to work. The general strike lasted until July 19, when the local AFL officials, refusing to hold a roll-call vote of the central labor council, announced that a majority of the council had called off the strike. The employers, worried about another strike, raised the wages of the longshore workers to 95 cents an hour.

Then in 1935 John L. Lewis, head of the United Mine Workers, led an exodus of the most militant unions out of the AFL to form a new federation, the Congress of Industrial Organizations (CIO). The CIO engaged in many strikes, used many socialists and Communists as organizers, fought the employers tooth and nail, and spread very rapidly. The CIO supported Franklin Roosevelt and the New Deal, which legalized unions (forcing elections when enough workers petitioned), legislated minimum wage and maximum hour laws, and began the social security system. Because of labor militancy and a supportive government, unions grew from 11 percent of all employees in 1930 to 32 percent of all employees in 1950.

Then in the late 1940s and early 1950s, unions came under attack by Senator Joe McCarthy, by the House Un-American Activities Committee, and by new antilabor laws. The Taft-Hartley Act of 1946 weakened unions in many ways, including an anti-Communist oath for union officers. In the hysteria of those days, for example, Clinton Jencks, an organizer in the Mine, Mill, and Smelter Union, was accused of not admitting to being a Communist, tried in a farcical trial, and sentenced to five years in prison. During the many years of trial and the appeal, Jencks suffered personally and the union suffered by loss of his services. Eventually, after much time, expense, and agony, the U.S. Supreme Court held that much of the ''evidence'' was insufficient and unconstitutional.

In the face of such witch hunts, coupled with the cold war ideology, the CIO tossed out its ten most militant left-wing unions in 1949 and merged with the AFL in 1953. The new AFL-CIO compromised with big business, received some gains for its workers in return for no-strike pledges, and supported the cold war. As a result of the decline in militancy, coupled with a generally expanding economy in the 1950s and 1960s, the unions steadily lost strength. Union membership fell from 36 percent of all nonagricultural workers in 1945 to only 18 percent in 1985. This decline has drastically reduced the bargaining power and influence of labor.

This does not mean there are no more class conflicts in the economy.

For example, the *Los Angeles Times* reported that "Striking meat-packers, who have twice blocked roads leading to the George A. Hormel and Co.'s main plant, 'totally took over' when the plant opened Saturday, and one person was arrested, authorities said" (1986: 9). The struggle of labor versus capital continues, but at a lower level than in the 1930s.

Quantitative Measurements of Wages, Prices, and Profits

With a certain amount of labor power employed, Marx (and Bowles and Gintis) emphasizes that how much is produced depends upon the intensity of labor. A worker must come to work for a number of hours, but how much labor she or he does depends on supervision, incentives, how much fear there is of unemployment, and so forth. Employers are always trying to speed up workers, but workers resist. A given amount of labor power with a given intensity of labor (plus the plant and equipment built by past labor) produces a certain value of product, which is the long-run price of production (with the qualifications discussed below). This is a description of production in labor terms, but it could be quantified in other terms as well.

Thus, the class relations of production have determined the revenue from a set of commodities. At the same time, wages are set by the real-world forces of capital and labor, in given circumstances of supply and demand, as shown in detail above. Since the revenue (price times amount) of the goods produced has now been determined, and since the wages of labor have been determined and the cost of the capital goods used up can be calculated, the difference can be found between the revenue and the cost, that is, profit. Profit may thus be described as the surplus of labor contributed to the capitalist above the labor that reproduces the used-up capital goods and the consumer goods used by the workers.

This description, however, pushes under the rug most of the difficult quantitative problems. In the orthodox Marxist view profit only results from current labor. Yet each industry uses different amounts of previous labor in capital goods. Therefore, with the same rate of exploitation of workers (profit to wages of living labor) there will be different rates of profit (profit to wages of living labor plus cost of previous labor embodied in used-up capital). There is a vast literature on how labor values may be "transformed" into prices of production by competition so as to maintain equal rates of profit, as the theory assumes—but technical problems remain behind the elegant mathematical solutions.

A different approach by Piero Sraffa (1960) finds an invariant measuring rod or numeraire in which to measure the value of different commodities through examining the technical relations between commodities, that is, how much of different commodities are used to produce each one. Sraffa uses as a measuring rod a "standard" or "representative" commodity, that is, a hypothetical commodity whose set of inputs have the same composition as its set of outputs. This standard commodity can then be used to measure wages and profits and the amount of capital goods.

This view of price determination, according to Sraffa, eliminates the need for neoclassical economics as well as orthodox Marxist value theory. Sraffa severely criticizes marginal productivity theory on the grounds that "capital" really means a huge number of heterogeneous objects that cannot be added up to talk about a "marginal productivity of capital" in the economy. This "capital" controversy (see Harcourt, 1972) has struck a considerable blow at neoclassical theory at a high level of theory, but the esoteric debate has not affected the teaching of neoclassical theory to masses of students one iota (except for a few cautionary footnotes in more advanced texts).

Marxists welcomed Sraffa's critique of marginal productivity, but some Sraffians used a similar critique against the labor theory of value, pointing out that labor is really very heterogeneous, with many types of labor. Those theorists claim that Sraffa is a better basis for radical political economy than is the labor theory, which should be abandoned (see Steedman, 1977; Bose, 1984). They argue that the labor theory of value is redundant or unnecessary (and perhaps inconsistent). Orthodox Marxists have replied by criticizing Sraffa for having no explicit theory of exploitation and no explanation of wage and profit shares, that is, of being limited to a pure price theory, with no link to the class relations of production. The Sraffians reply that one must begin with a consistent price theory, then one can use the class relations of production—as discussed above—to explain how the net product is divided into wages and profits.

Finally, some theorists (such as Medeo, 1962; Eatwell, 1975; and Roncaglia, 1978) see both theories as consistent ways to explain prices and exploitation. Of the theorists who see the two as consistent, some (such as Bandyopadhyay, 1985) think it best to stick with the more direct price theory in Sraffa and see the labor theory as redundant.

Others (such as Gleicher, 1986) believe that it is still necessary to use the labor theory of value to understand more clearly and spotlight exploitation.

My own view is that radicals have two alternative ways to quantify the relations of exploitation in capitalist economies. Which one is used is partly a matter of the problem and the level of exposition. It is easier to spotlight exploitation using a labor measurement than Sraffa's commodity measure.

From the overall view of radical political economy, as long as there is at least one consistent theory in which one can show how exploitation works, this esoteric debate is not of much additional interest. The fact is that all price theorists, as a first approximation, use such simplified assumptions that they are far, far from reality. They all assume pure competition, no unemployment, no inflation, negligible government economic activity, an isolated economy with no international relations, no discrimination, and no environmental destruction. The greatest contributions of radical (and institutionalist) economics have come by dropping these unrealistic assumptions.

Thus, exploration of low pay and discrimination has led to very fruitful theories of two-level (or dual) labor markets for different groups (see Edwards, Reich, and Gordon, 1978). Exploration of monopoly pricing has led to useful theories of mark-up pricing (discussed in chapter 7). Price behavior under unemployment and/or inflation is discussed in chapter 6, the influence of government on prices in chapter 8, and international influences on prices in chapter 9. The real world of monopoly, recession, inflation, and imperialism is so far from the arid squabbles over price theory that no one has ever tried to "transform" in a precise way the long-run equilibrium prices into prices reflecting all of these real-world facts. The resulting theories would be too complex to be useful.

Suggested Readings

The literature on value theory is technical, complicated, and endless in quantity. After Marx, the classical Marxist account (and easiest to read) is Sweezy (1942). Other classics are Lange (1935) and Dobb (1945). The best history of thought of value and distribution theory is by Hunt (1979); Hunt has one of the clearest explanations of Sraffa's (1960) complex work, as well as an unusually comprehensive chapter on Thorstein Veblen. (Hunt also explains the historical background and class location of each theory.) A very good introduction to value theory is Lichtenstein (1983). There are useful collections of articles by Hunt and Schwartz (1972), Union for Radical Political Economics (1982), and Science and Society (1984–85). There are important books by Harris (1978), Fine and Harris (1979), Roemer (1982), and Marglin (1984), and important articles by Foley (1985) and Wolff, Roberts, and Callari (1982). The most useful single article in preparing this chapter was Bowles and Gintis (1981). Also see an attack on Bowles and Gintis by Ehrbar and Glick (1987). The best work on labor market segmentation is Edwards, Reich, and Gordon (1978), and Braverman (1974) has the pioneering work on the labor process. Most of the history of labor in this chapter is based on the very rich, detailed, and comprehensive history of the U.S. labor movement in the five volumes of Foner (1947–1980). If one reads the references in all of these books and articles, the reader will be busy for at least a year.

— 5 —

PERFORMANCE OF CAPITALISM:
DISCRIMINATION, ALIENATION, AND POLLUTION

Racist and sexist discrimination, alienation of people from their jobs and from other people, and environmental pollution are all evils of modern society. Granted that they all existed in previous societies, to what extent can their present existence be attributed to capitalism?

Racism

Racism is the conviction that minority groups are biologically inferior. Racism is an "ideology" that contains a systematic set of beliefs claiming the superiority of one group to others. Racism is a "prejudice" in that no amount of evidence can shake these beliefs—and even inconsistent beliefs do not bother the true believers.

Adolf Hitler carried racism to its ultimate point in the 1930s, when he proclaimed that white, male, non-Jewish Germans (called "Aryans") were a "master race," superior to all other groups. He created a stereotype, or ideal picture, of all Aryans as big, strong, blond, and of superior intelligence—even though Hitler himself was none of these. His stereotype Jew was small, dark, greedy, and cowardly. His stereotype of all other peoples was likewise physically weak and mentally inferior. In his stereotype, all women were stupid and good for nothing but sex and childbearing; Aryan women were no different but were beautiful as well. Such stereotypes were far more than harmless nonsense; on this basis Hitler killed nearly thirty million Jews and Russians and enslaved hundreds of millions of people, particularly women.

Similarly, slave owners in the U.S. South before the Civil War claimed that blacks were biologically inferior. Stereotypic blacks were stupid and lazy, shuffled their feet when they walked, and liked to sing and dance (to celebrate their happy life as slaves). The stereotype also said that blacks were oversexed. This has long provided an excuse for white men to rape black women, while lynching black men for imaginary rapes of white women. There are still racists who claim that all blacks are mentally inferior. For example, Dr. William Shockley, a white male physicist at Stanford University, claimed in 1973 that in data "from Negro populations with average IQ's of 80 in Georgia and 90 in California . . . each 1 percent of Caucasian ancestry raises average IQ by one point for these low IQ populations" (quoted in United Press, 1973: A-2). So the blood of the "master race" raises intelligence! Yet over and over again anthropologists and psychologists have demonstrated that IQ scores are not dependent on race or physical type, but are dependent on socioeconomic status and cultural background because of the way the tests are designed.

Facts of Racist Discrimination

Black families have much lower income than white families. Because of the victories of the militant civil rights movement of the 1960s, the median family income of blacks was raised from 54 percent of white income in 1964 to 61 percent in 1969. Because of white backlash in the 1970s and '80s black income fell back to 55 percent in 1982. In fact, black family income in 1982 in terms of real purchasing power was considerably below the 1970 level.

In absolute terms the median black family in 1982 earned $13,598, only about 35 percent above the very conservatively defined official poverty level. In fact, 36 percent of all black families in 1982 were below the poverty level. In 1984, according to the Census Bureau, the median wealth (assets minus liabilities) of black families was only $3,397, while the median wealth of white families was $39,135, more than ten times as high.

Black poverty was reflected in deaths of blacks. Infant mortality in 1984 was 19.2 deaths per 1,000 live births for blacks and only 9.7 deaths per 1,000 for whites. A black male could expect to live 65.5 years, but a white male could expect to live 71.8 years. Female life expectancy was 73.7 years for blacks and 78.8 years for whites.

One of the reasons for the number of blacks living in poverty is the job discrimination that results in much higher unemployment rates among blacks than among whites. Decade after decade black unemployment rates are more than double those for whites. In December 1985, for example, black unemployment was 15 percent, compared to 6 percent for whites. Black teenage workers face particularly severe discrimination; their unemployment rate in December 1985 was 42 percent, compared with 16 percent for white teenagers. All of these unemployment figures are official U.S. Labor Department data, but chapter 6 will show that these official data are drastically understated.

Black females are even worse off than black males because they suffer from both racist and sexist discrimination. Whereas the median black two-parent family in 1984 earned $23,418, the median black female-headed family earned only $8,648. Black female adult unemployment in 1983 in a period of recovery was still 17.1 percent, although white female adult unemployment had fallen to 7.9 percent. Most of their poverty, however, was due to the fact that black female family heads were being paid below-poverty wages.

In the political sphere, although blacks comprise 11 percent of the U.S. population, blacks in 1979 comprised only 5 percent of the U.S. House of Representatives (there were no black members of the U.S. Senate). In the same year, blacks made up only 4 percent of state legislatures and less than 1 percent of elected city and county officials.

Another basic area of continuing discrimination is in education. In 1984, in the age group 25 to 34 years old, only 14 percent of blacks had graduated from college, whereas 25 percent of whites had done so. Most blacks who dropped out of school did so because of economic pressures. Even with a college education, blacks face discrimination. The unemployment rate in 1979 for whites with one to three years of college was 6 percent, but it was 13 percent for blacks with the same education. Black college graduates had about the same unemployment rate as white high school graduates.

Finally there is continued job segregation against blacks. Black men and women are overrepresented among poorly paid factory workers and domestic servants. Blacks represent only a very small percentage of highly paid managers, professionals, and administrators.

Black History and Class Structure

Discussion of black history by Baron (1985) and Boston (1985) indicates a useful periodization. Blacks suffered under slavery in the United States until the Civil War. In this period almost all blacks lived in the South on rural plantations as slaves; the few free blacks were an anomaly. A minority of whites owned the plantations and exploited the slaves. The majority of Southern whites were nonslaveholders but did have minor privileges over all blacks.

When the Civil War eliminated slavery (at the cost of thousands of black as well as white lives), the United States became dominated by industrial capitalists, the central government dominated the states, and the North dominated the South. But white landowners in the South were allowed to regain dominance over blacks by the use of violence. So in the first stage of black life under capitalism, most blacks remained in the South as rural sharecroppers, subordinate to the landowners, merchants, and money lenders. Racist laws prevented blacks from voting or from receiving a good education, and segregation was the order of the day.

In 1890, 88 percent of blacks were still in agriculture and domestic service; only 6 percent were in manufacturing, as opposed to 25 percent of whites (see Boston, 1985: 53). By 1930, blacks were still 66 percent in agriculture and domestic service, but 19 percent were now in manufacturing. As late as 1940, three-quarters of all blacks lived in the South, and most were rural (Baron, 1985: 19).

This very slow evolution was suddenly speeded up by the Second World War, which brought about a second stage for blacks under U.S. capitalism. During the war, millions of blacks moved to manufacturing jobs in Southern cities and in the North. By 1960, over 40 percent of blacks were in the North and 73 percent of all blacks were urbanized. Blacks formed a disproportionate share of the manufacturing labor force. Racism, denial of the vote, and segregation (and lynchings) continued into the 1950s. But the new economic and geographical environment allowed blacks to organize. Under pressure of the civil rights movement, the Supreme Court began to loosen racial restrictions in 1954 (*Brown v. Board of Education*), and Congress passed new civil rights laws in the early 1960s.

A third stage has resulted from the combination of the civil rights movement and the further evolution of capitalism. The U.S. economy is now characterized by giant, impersonal corporations and a giant, impersonal government, which provides some welfare support in a degrading manner. The result is formal equality under the law, which has brought into being a black middle class, especially in the service areas and in technical and professional work. Thomas Boston estimates for 1982 that the black middle class is 15 percent of all blacks, whereas the white middle class is 30 percent of all whites (1985: 59). It is important to note that one-eighth of the white middle class is the "old" middle class of retail merchants, farmers, and other self-employed (three million people), with the rest being "new" middle class of management, technical, and professional workers. Among the black middle class, only one-sixteenth is the "old" self-employed group (eighty-one thousand people); so almost all of the black middle class is the "new" group of managers and professionals.

On the other hand, for the mass of blacks, racial discrimination still has terrible effects. There is still a web of urban racism: black and white housing markets, black and white education systems, black and white labor markets.

There is a segmented labor market (see Edwards, Reich, and Gordon, 1978; Attewell, 1984: ch. 2 and 3). The primary labor market has good, permanent, higher paying jobs, with possibilities of advancement. The labor market has temporary, marginal jobs, low pay, no advancement, and much underemployment. Unemployed people are those in jobs way under their qualifications. Most black workers and most women workers are in the secondary labor market, due to discrimination. Moreover, in the 1970s and 1980s there is actually a rising percentage of black workers subject to underemployment, unemployment, and discouraged worker status (not counted in the labor force). Thus, an increasing percentage of black workers have been forced onto welfare, even though it is highly stigmatized in the United States.

What Causes Racism?

The most conservative view now, as always, is that there are inherited biological differences, making blacks (and Mexicans, Indians, Jews, Catholics, and other minorities) intellectually and physically inferior. This inferiority is the cause of their lower income, educational achievement, and so forth. Moreover, they are lazy and like to live in squalor. Because these arguments cannot be validated by any scientific evidence and because refutations do not diminish the prejudice, this view may be left without further comment. Races are, of course, defined by their superficial physical differences, but there are no important biological differences among the races of humankind, much less any inherited intellectual differences.

Most sociologists stress that blacks are not inherently inferior. Many still insist, however, that the problem lies in the minds of blacks and whites. Many assume that all whites have racist attitudes. Many assume that all blacks have attitudes making it more difficult for them to get good jobs, such as a lack of desire (often called a "low aspiration pattern") and limited goals. The traditional sociologists' solution would seem to be that we have to employ an unprejudiced psychoanalyst to change the attitudes of all whites and blacks through therapy.

Radicals agree that most whites have racist prejudices. It is also a fact that a few blacks still have attitudes of inferiority that impede their progress, though most of the reports on black attitudes are myths used to excuse discrimination. It must be emphasized, however, that the discrimination caused by white racism is a thousand times more of a barrier to blacks at present than any remaining black attitudes of inferiority.

But the most important question is, why do these white racist attitudes persist? Hundreds of comparative studies of other societies show that whites are not born with attitudes of racial superiority and blacks are not born with attitudes of racial inferiority. These attitudes are inculcated by society. They are given to children by the older generation in the family; by the educational system (e.g., in stereotypes in textbooks); by the media (e.g., in stereotypes on television, in newspapers, books, and magazines); and by political leaders.

This leads to the next question: Why does the establishment permit and encourage racist stereotypes? Of course, the degree of open stereotyping has been reduced in recent years, but only under the pressure of the civil rights movement. It is the contention of radicals that racism has an important function in supporting the status quo, and that the capitalist establishment benefits from it both directly and indirectly.

Conservative economists, on the contrary, agree with the conservative sociologists that no one benefits from discrimination, that it is merely a matter of irrational and inexplicable tastes or preferences. Conservatives emphasize that discrimination by business is irrational because (so they claim) profits are lost as a result. They argue that if there is discrimination in the economy, then each capitalist is presented with a supply of qualified blacks willing to work for wages below the going wages. Since the capitalist can purchase these workers at lower wages, profits can be increased by doing so. Therefore, capitalists who are willing to hire blacks (below the going wage) will make more profits, whereas those who refuse to hire blacks at any wage will lose profits. Thus the conservative Milton Friedman claims that "a businessman or an entrepreneur who expresses preferences in his business activities that are not related to productive efficiency is in effect imposing higher costs on himself than are other individuals who do not have such preferences. Hence, in a free market they will tend to drive him out'' (1962: 108).

The conservative economists conclude that the capitalists who discriminate do so for irrational reasons and lose money because of the discrimination. They further argue that under pure competition capitalists who discriminate will eventually be put out of business because of their higher costs per unit. Thus competition will tend to end discrimination and push black wages ever closer to white wage levels.

Most liberal economists agree with many of these premises, which flow from good neoclassical economics. They argue, however, that the U.S. economy is characterized by a high degree of monopoly rather than by pure competition. By the exercise of their monopoly power in the labor market and in the commodity market, firms can hold down all wages and pass on to consumers some of the cost of discrimination. In other words, although the liberals agree with the conservatives that racism is an inexplicable attitude, they contend that it costs the capitalist only a little to indulge his or her strange preference. Therefore, they believe it might be a long time, if ever, before capitalism ends discrimination, and so liberals support the passage of legislation to end discrimination.

Radicals, on the other hand, do not believe that capitalists lose money from discrimination or that their attitudes are inexplicable. How could discrimination continue for such a long time if capitalists lose from it? Capitalists gain in many ways from racist discrimination and hence have an interest in continuing it. They gain because racist prejudice divides workers, making unions weaker and resulting in lower wages for all workers; the same division among workers makes capitalist politicians safer from attacks by labor; racist discrimination makes it easy to keep blacks as an unemployed reservoir of cheap labor for boom times; racism provides white politicians with a scapegoat for many social problems; and racism helps inspire soldiers when they are supposed to kill people of other races in foreign wars. As a result, white capitalists as a whole benefit from racism, although white workers as a whole lose from racism.

Radicals maintain that in the pre-Civil War South racism was a useful apologia for slavery, alleviating guilty consciences on the part of slave owners, promoting an easier acceptance of their lot among slaves, and preventing non-slave-owning Southerners and Northerners from interfering. Racism declared that slavery was divinely ordained by God as a benefit to the inferior black. Its first function was to justify economic exploitation.

That function of racism continues today, when apologists contend that black and Chicano workers are poorly paid only because they are inferior workers. More important, to the extent that white workers believe the racist ideology, unions are weakened by excluding black workers—or accepting them reluctantly and preventing them from having equal power. White and black workers have frequently broken each others' strikes in the past, though they are now learning to work together. In the areas of strongest racism and weakest unions, such as the South, black workers' wages are very low, but white workers' wages are almost as low. For this reason, capitalists gain from the prejudices of workers because prejudice allows capitalists to divide and oppress workers.

Another reason that racism is profitable to capitalists is its provision of a handy, but disposable, labor force. If an employer has ten black and ten white workers and must fire half for a couple of months, which will the employer fire? If he is rational and seeks to minimize his labor turnover costs, he will lay off his ten black workers on the assumption that they will be unlikely to get permanent or better jobs elsewhere because of the discriminatory practices of other employers (Franklin and Resnick, 1973: 20). Thus the capitalist can (and does) fire black workers in each recession, easily hiring them back in times of expansion. The capitalist also gains by not having to pay the fringe benefits due workers who stay on the job for a longer time.

Radicals assert that blacks are exploited within the United States, both as an internal colony and as workers. Blacks today constitute about one-third of the entire industrial labor force and an even larger percentage of unskilled manual laborers. Racial discrimination keeps them ''in their place'' as a large pool of unskilled and often unemployed workers to be used to hold down wages in times of high demand for labor; racial prejudice justifies this discrimination. Thus racism is in this respect only an additional apologia for the considerable extra profits extracted at the expense of the lowest-paid part of the American working class.

Radicals maintain that a primary political function of racism is to find a scapegoat for all problems. For example, the white is told that the dirt and violence of the modern city are all due to the black. Similarly,

Hitler told German workers that unemployment was all due to Jewish bankers, and the middle class was told that all the agitation was due to Jewish communists.

Another political function of racism, according to radicals, is to divide the oppressed so the elite can rule. For example, few Americans are more oppressed or exploited than poor white Southerners. But they have usually fought against their natural allies, the blacks. Instead, the poor white has given political support to the wealthy white Southerners who not only monopolize Southern state and local politics but also wield disproportionate influence in Congress because they hold key committee chairmanships and leadership positions by virtue of seniority. The same kind of divide-and-rule tactic is used in Northern cities.

Radicals also claim that racism is a particularly handy tool of imperialism. England especially has long used the strategy of divide and rule: Hindu against Moslem in India, Jew against Arab in Israel, Protestant against Catholic in Ireland. And the United States is quite willing to use the same tactic: Vietnamese against Cambodian, Thai against Laotian. Moreover, "inferiority" (inherited or acquired) is still being given as an excuse for lack of development—where imperialism is the real reason.

Sexism

Just as the ideology of racism relies on stereotypes of blacks, the ideology of sexism relies on stereotypes of women. One stereotype of women is that they are all sentimental, impulsive, emotional, and foolish—not hardheaded, stable, and logical, as in the stereotype of men. For example, former Vice-President Agnew, who was forced to resign because of his criminal activity, says, "Three things have been difficult to tame—the ocean, fools, and women. We may soon be able to tame the ocean; fools and women will take a little longer" (quoted in Amundsen, 1971: 114).

Prejudiced people such as Agnew are not convinced by all the contrary evidence. As an example of how prejudiced stereotyping is much too stubborn for evidence, imagine an employer interviewing a series of people for an executive job. Suppose he possesses the usual stereotype of women. Suppose the first woman is sophisticated and careful before speaking. He thinks: She is too passive and "feminine" for the job. Suppose the second woman objects to something he says. He thinks: She is too aggressive. Suppose the third person is a man: he gets the job. In many real cases like this imaginary one, prejudiced stereotypes are not harmless; they lead directly to discrimination.

Above all, sexist stereotypes are intended to justify the domination of women by men. This is very apparent in a statement by Napoleon Bonaparte: "Nature intended women to be our slaves . . . they are our property, we are not theirs. They belong to us, just as a tree that bears fruit belongs to a gardener. What a mad idea to demand equality for women! . . . Women are nothing but machines for producing children" (quoted in Morgan, 1970: 2). Sexism, or the theory of male supremacy, is an ideology that serves to justify discrimination against the majority of Americans.

Sexist Discrimination

In 1890, women constituted only 17 percent of the labor force, although many more were unpaid workers on farms owned by their husbands. From this period comes the myth that all women are housewives and play no role in the paid labor force. This myth no longer has even a semblance of truth. By 1940 women made up 25 percent of the labor force. In World War II women suddenly became 36 percent of the labor force, then dropped to 28 percent in 1947 as they were pushed out of jobs by returning veterans. Since then, there has been a steady rise: in 1986, women represented 44 percent of the labor force.

A majority of all women (53 percent) in the working ages, from age 20 to age 64, were in the labor force in 1983. Moreover, 58 percent of all working women were married at that time. So most women work at a paid job. And most women workers really have two jobs, a paid job plus the unpaid job of housewife. Even women with small children now work outside the home; by 1979, 54 percent of women with children under 17 were in the labor force.

Working women generally work for the same reason as men—economic necessity. About 42 percent of women workers were single, divorced, separated, or widowed and so had no choice but to work. Women head 12 percent of U.S. families, but about half of families living in poverty.

Why are more and more married women working in paid jobs? Because, with inflation, their wages are more and more necessary to attain a minimum decent standard of living. Women work more if they have more years of education and fewer small children. If one looks at women with the same education (e.g., four years of high school) and the same age number of children (e.g., ages 6 to 17), one finds that the percentage of women working declines as the husband's income level is higher. In fact, 71 percent of all working women are single, divorced, separated, widowed, or have husbands earning less than ten thousand dollars per year and so are working because of dire need.

Because of discrimination most women forced to work outside the home are paid less than male workers receive for the same jobs. The wage gap is large and has been widening in both absolute and percentage terms for many years. The median full-time, year-round woman worker earned only 65 percent of men's median wages in 1955, but this percentage dropped to only 60 percent in 1981. This wage discrimination is true even in specific professions where everyone has high educational qualifications; in 1970 female economists earned 81 percent as much as male economists, and female mathematicians earned 67 percent as much as male mathematicians.

Another factor causing the wage gap is discrimination in promotion. For example, in 1978–79 in all college and university faculties women were 51 percent of the low-paid category of instructors but were only 33 percent of the higher category of assistant professors, only 19 percent of the still higher category of associate professors, and only 10 percent of the highest paid category of professor. Economics is particularly bad: women in 1984–85 were 16 percent of assistant professors in economics, 8 percent of associate professors, and only 3.6 percent of full professors (see American Economic Association, Committee on the Status of Women in the Economics Profession, *Newsletter*, February 1986, p. 6). The same pattern is true of all occupations. For example, women were 90 percent of all bank tellers, but only 19 percent of bank officers.

The largest single cause of the wage gap, however, is the segregation that keeps women out of many high-paying occupations and pushes them into a few low-paying occupations. These low-paying occupations are then relatively overcrowded with the large supply of women workers forced into them, so the employers can continue to pay low wages. Thus in 1980 over 55 percent of all women workers were crowded into just seven occupational groups: clerical worker, retail trade salesworker, private household worker, high school and elementary school teacher, waitress, sewer and stitcher, and nurse. Women constitute over 70 percent of the retail sales force and over 80 percent of the other six occupations. Men, on the other hand, were spread out over a wide range of occupations.

At the other end of the spectrum, women are present in very small numbers in the high-paying occupations and professions. The percentage of women in high-paying jobs did increase in the 1960s, 1970s, and 1980s as a result of the women's movement. Pressure from the women's movement achieved the passage of antidiscrimination laws. Propaganda from the women's movement changed the consciousness of men and women and opened up new vistas on possible careers for women. Even with this movement, which caused large increases in the percentages, women in 1980 were only 4 percent of all engineers, 4 percent of dentists, 7 percent of architects, 13 percent of lawyers (up from 2 percent in 1960), 13 percent of doctors (up from 7 percent in 1960), 1 percent of federal judges, and just 4 percent of the U.S. House of Representatives.

Thus, there are still only small numbers of women in the higher-paying professions. The earnings gap between men and women has continued to increase because most new women workers have gone into the poorest-paying occupations, some discrimination in wages for the same jobs continues, and women are still not promoted as often as men.

What Causes Sexism?

The ideologies of racism and sexism are similar in many ways. Both are based on the supposed inferiority of some groups of human beings to others: "All discrimination is eventually the same—Anti-Humanism" (Chisholm, 1970: 45). Even in the present "enlightened" age, the ideology of sexism continues unabated. Thus the conservative view still justifies lower pay for women: "If a woman were more like a man, she'd be treated as such" (Black, 1970: 37). This view ignores the main point: that millions of women receive less pay for accomplishing exactly the same work as men.

All tests show that men and women are equal in intelligence, although they usually progress at different rates in childhood learning, with women leading in the early years.

Radicals certainly admit that there are physical differences between men and women. With respect to working ability, however, the evidence indicates that male and female workers are equal on the average. In fact, in some primitive societies women normally carry heavier loads than men. The question is one of training and expectations. Listen to the lot of the slave woman of the American South as stated by the great black abolitionist Sojourner Truth: "Look at my arm! I have ploughed and planted and gathered into barns, and no man could head me—and ain't I a woman? I have borne thirteen children, and seen most of 'em sold into slavery, and when I cried out with my mother's grief, none but Jesus heard me—and ain't I a woman?''

In social and sexual matters, it is also not a given, eternal fact that man must always dominate. In some primitive societies men and women appear to have about equal social and sexual roles. This is especially true in societies in which the economic roles of the two are roughly equal in importance, as when women gather wild food and men hunt. In other primitive societies, in which women conduct agriculture and hunting is unimportant, women appear to play the dominant role. If nothing else can be said without controversy, at least modern anthropology makes it clear that there are many types of family organization (including various kinds of group marriages), not just one eternal type in which man dominates.

Only with the coming of "civilization"—meaning economic stratification and the possession of property in land, cattle, slaves, or serfs—do women also become pieces of property. In fact, for purposes of clear inheritance of property the upper class woman in ancient civilizations was very well guarded; only the male could freely violate the theoretical monogamy system. This was the beginning of the double standard.

The particular attitudes of American men and women are carefully inculcated, not inherited. ''Women are taught from the time they are children to play a serving role, to be docile and submissive'' (Goldberg, 1970: 35) by the family, the schools, the media, the church, corporations, and the government—areas in which males are usually dominant.

Who Benefits from Sexism?

As in the case of racism, conservative economists argue that capitalists actually lose by discriminating against qualified women. Such discrimination, they say, means paying men for a job that women could do equally well for less pay. In the words of the Establishment economist Barbara Bergman,

> We come . . . to the allegation, usually made by radicals out to discredit capitalism, that women's subjection is all a capitalist plot. Who benefits financially from maintenance of the status quo? The most obvious beneficiaries of prejudice against women are male workers in those occupations

in which women are not allowed to compete . . . it is not the male workers or their wives who do the discriminating, however. The employers of the male workers (almost entirely males themselves) are the ones who do the actual discriminating, although of course they are cheered on in their discriminatory ways by their male employees. The employers actually tend to lose financially since profits are lowered when cheap female help is spurned in favor of high-priced male help. (1973: 14)

So in her view it is not the capitalists, but only the male workers who gain from discrimination. The poor capitalists, who are actually responsible for the discriminating, lose by it. But why do capitalists in business for profits systematically choose to lose money? She says they lose financially but gain psychologically: "It feels so good to have women in their place." Neither she nor any one else with this view answers the obvious question: If it causes financial losses (even small ones), why hasn't such discrimination tended to decline and disappear under capitalism?

The truth is, according to radicals, that capitalists do not merely gain psychologically, while incurring financial losses, from sex discrimination. On the contrary, capitalists gain from sexism both in power and in profits. Moreover, all workers, male as well as female, lose from sexist attitudes.

How do capitalists make profit from sexism? Obviously they use it as an excuse to pay women lower wages. More important, sexist prejudice divides male and female workers, making it more difficult to organize strong unions. In the United States one of every four men workers is unionized, as compared to only one of every seven women workers. The prejudice of union men is apparent in the fact that women constitute 20 percent of all union members but less than 1 percent of all union executive board members. Even in unions like the International Ladies' Garment Workers' Union, which is over 75 percent female, only a few token women are on the executive board. Furthermore, in the past unions have done little, if anything, for women's specific grievances and have even joined employers in agreements for lower wages and worse job categories for women.

Union men often pay for their prejudices in broken unions and lower wages. For example, "Standard Oil workers in San Francisco recently paid the price of male supremacy. Women at Standard Oil have the least chance for advancement and decent pay, and the union has done little to fight this. Not surprisingly, women formed the core of the back to work move that eventually broke the strike" (McAfee and Wood, 1972: 16).

Because it reduces union bargaining strength, sexism causes lower wages for both men and women.

The evidence shows that in occupations where most of the labor force is female, the pay for both men and women is lower than average, even though the workers in many of those areas have higher qualifications (shown in more education) than the average worker. In most occupations in which women are predominant, women's education is far above the median of U.S. workers, but their wages are far below. Moreover, the same is true of the men in these predominantly female occupations: their education is much above, while their wages are much below, the U.S. median. For example, in 1970 male librarians' educations were 38 percent above the median of all workers, but their wages were only 1 percent above the median; female librarians' educations were 35 percent above the median of all workers, but their wages were 19 percent below the median (Department of Commerce, 1970: table 1). Therefore, sexist discrimination not only hurts female workers but also hurts male workers—and the lower wages produce higher profits.

In addition to weak unions, another reason for low wages in the predominantly female occupations is that women have few other economic options—they are systematically excluded from other occupations and pushed into these. Such segregation causes overcrowding or oversupply in the areas where women are allowed to work, thus lowering wages in these jobs. Some economists admit that males in these occupations will be hurt, but they argue that males in other occupations will have higher wages because the exclusion of women lowers labor supply. Thus they claim that some male workers may gain from sexism. This claim ignores, however, the weakening of unions in all areas and the other unfavorable sociopolitical effects for all workers mentioned below. It might also be noted that the sectors employing mostly white males are often sectors with strong monopoly power, where higher wages are passed along in higher prices to all consumers.

The glorification of housework can also be profitable. In the words of one male advertiser, "properly manipulated . . . American housewives can be given the sense of identity, purpose, creativity, the self-realization, even the sexual joy they lack—by the buying of things" (quoted in Friedan, 1963: 199). Thus advertisers use the sexist ideology to instill "consumerism" in women. The sexist image of the good woman shows her in the kitchen surrounded by the very latest gadgets, with the best cake mix, and made up with miracle cosmetics. Commercials imply that she is a failure if her floors are not the shiniest and her laundry not the whitest in the neighborhood. This image helps business sell billions of dollars of useless (or even harmful) goods.

Sexism is also profitable because women's unpaid work in the home is crucial to provision of the needed supply of labor. Housework is equivalent to about one-fourth of the GNP, though it is not counted in the GNP. If business had to pay women in full to raise and clean and cook for the labor force, profits would be seriously reduced. The labor of women as housewives is vital to industry; there would be no labor force without it, and yet it goes unpaid. Moreover, as a result of their dependent role in the sexist family, some women are socialized to be passive, submissive, and docile workers and are supposed to transmit these values to their children.

The last, but not the least, important profit to capitalism from sexism comes in its increased support for political stability. Much like racism, sexism is also used as a political divide-and-rule tactic. White politicians blame all urban problems on blacks. Secretary of the Treasury Schultz during the Nixon administration blamed unemployment (and accompanying pressure for low wages) on the competition of women workers. Thus conservative politicians try to make women a scapegoat for men's problems so that men do not see in women their natural ally against a system that oppresses them both.

Alienation

We Americans live as alienated strangers to each other and to society as a whole, with the feeling that we are pushed through life by vast social forces over which we have no control. Some problems of alienation are apparent in any large, complex, industrial society. Monopoly capitalism, however, greatly intensifies these problems. The very highly concentrated economic, political, and military power means that a few hundred old, white men make most of the decisions vitally affecting the lives of the other two hundred million people. Is it any wonder that most people feel terribly alone and defensive in such a cold, money- and power-loving society?

It is possible to distinguish at least three different senses in which alienation is found in modern capitalist society (see Marx, 1844). First, the worker is dominated by his or her product. He or she produces consumers' goods, but they are taken away, so that much of his or her life is centered around earning enough money to run after consumer goods. Workers learn to relate to things, such as autos or TV sets, rather than to people. Workers produce producers' goods, which are taken away and become capital, with which a worker is then employed to work. Workers produce military goods, such as atomic bombs, and then they hang over their heads like a Damocles sword, liable to destroy the whole world.

A second meaning of alienation is the separation of workers from their production activity. Workers do not own the means of production with which they work—nor do they own the product of their labor. Thus, their working activity becomes "merely a means to satisfy needs external to it. Its alien character emerges clearly in the fact that as soon as no physical or other compulsion exists, labor is shunned like the plague" (Marx, 1844: 111). The laborer sells his or her labor power as a thing to be purchased on the market. He or she has become dehumanized, a cog in a machine to make profit for someone else.

The worker no longer produces and sells a whole artifact, as in some precapitalist handicraft situations. He or she is therefore bored by the production process and takes no pride in "workmanship" (as Veblen called it). Although the worker must be a small cog in a big machine in any complex industrial society, monopoly capitalism worsens the alienation because the production is carried on solely for the profit of a giant, faceless corporation. This fact also leads to political alienation, since the U.S. government stands to us as a vast and far distant institution, dominated by the large corporation, and dominating over the helpless individual.

A third aspect of alienation follows from the first two: namely, the awful alienation of human from human. The ethic of capitalism is each person for himself or herself, and the only honored goal is money. The result is a "lonely crowd," lack of communication, frustration, crime, and aggression. As long as capitalism and private property exist, the individual must strive by competition to maximize his or her wealth; the competitive view isolates each individual in his or her lonely fortress. This alienation from fellow men and women, linked with a competitive dog-eat-dog drive, gives the United States its high rates of crime, prostitution, gambling, juvenile delinquency, alcoholism, drug addition, divorce, suicide, and mental breakdown.

It comes as no surprise that big crime is linked to big business, both equally intent on making profits. And it is equally no surprise that pornographic magazines and other cultural trash are manufactured solely for profit—why else would anyone produce such stuff? It is also no surprise that advertising expenditures are about three times as high as all our expenditures on higher education taken together. The only surprise in American culture is that any marriages survive under these conditions: where the individual is trained to competition rather than cooperation; where the male is trained to dominate, the female to be beautiful but dumb, and both expect a Hollywood fairyland of perfect lover and companion; where there is stress and tension in modern urban life; where no one stays put long enough to have a secure circle of friends and relatives; where the possibility of nuclear destruction is omnipresent. At the same time as the divorce rate soars, there is much preoccupation with sex today, partly because it seems the only real thing in a world where the old is collapsing and the new not yet built. These conditions are, of course, much worse for low-income and especially for black families.

In some respects the subjective effects of the alienation of human from human make radical organization in America more difficult. The barriers to radicalism include:

> the still-vigorous belief in the possibilities of advancement within the framework of capitalist society. The deepseated acceptance of bourgeois values. . . . The . . . multi-pronged manipulation of the public mind. The heart-breaking emptiness and cynicism of the commercial, competitive, capitalist culture. The systematic cultivation of devastatingly neurotic reactions to most social phenomena (through the movies, the 'funnies,' etc.) . . . the utterly paralyzing feeling of solitude which must overcome anyone who does not want to conform. The feeling that there is no movement, no camp, no group to which he can turn. (Baran, 1950: 82)

On the other hand, an alienated society is not a stable society, so it may radicalize rapidly in some circumstances.

Waste

Radicals and Marxists, especially those who follow the humanist emphasis of the young Marx, do not treat the mere quantitative growth of the national product as the only or even the most important goal of political economy. In the first place, we radicals emphasize the extreme inequality of income distribution as much or more than the problems of aggregate income growth. Secondly, radicals emphasize the composition of national product, the wasteful and harmful uses of it, as well as the very negative noneconomic consequences of the capitalist "automatic market'' pattern of growth.

Waste is defined to mean those activities under capitalism that simply squander resources or use labor and resources to produce products that contribute neither to the present consumption of the populace nor to future growth.

1. Most of the expenditure for advertising gives no information, but is used to convince the consumer that one of two identical products is better. Closely related are huge sales forces (trudging from door to door as well as in stores), costly model changes in style back and forth each year, and ''planned obsolescence,'' the quaint task of engineers to design products so that they will not work after a short time.

2. A high degree of monopoly will be found to result in restriction of output to obtain higher prices. It also means holding back new inventions and innovations to get longer use of present machinery. Thus, monopoly means misallocation of resources, even if the present manipulated consumer preference pattern is taken as the desirable allocation.

3. The still remaining competition is wasteful in other ways. For example, there is unnecessary duplication. Why do we need four banks at a single intersection (as is often the case in American cities)?

4. Capitalist competition is notoriously interested in short-run profit making, so there is little conservation, no care in preserving the natural resource base. ''America was once a paradise of timberland and stream but it is dying because of the greed and money lust of a thousand little kings who slashed the timber all to hell and would not be controlled'' (de Bell, 1970: 31). Of course, this behavior was not individual eccentricity but is inherent in the profit motivation of capitalism.

5. Pollution of the physical environment (see next section) and deterioration of the social environment are normal aspects of capitalist economic growth. ''I am not quite sure what the advantage is in having a few more dollars to spend if the air is too dirty to breathe, the water too polluted to drink, the commuters are losing out in the struggle to get in and out of the city, the streets are filthy, and the schools so bad that the young perhaps wisely stay away, and hoodlums roll citizens for some of the dollars they saved in the tax'' (John Kenneth Galbraith, quoted in Harrington, 1966: 51).

6. Part of the pollution is caused by the overwhelming outpouring of unnecessary and even harmful products, profitable because well advertised. For example, for a long time the cigarette industry was

renowned for both its large advertising expenditure and its very high profit rate.

7. There are also the extreme and even bizarre luxuries of the super rich. Radicals are not against luxury living as an abstract principle. With our present highly unequal distribution of income, however, the extreme luxury living of the few super rich means lack of necessities for many other people. In a world where many children lack sufficient milk, how can one fill a whole pool with milk for a party? And how can ideologists defend such "living" styles as merely necessary incentive for capitalist investment?

8. Considerable chronic unemployment and large-scale periodic unemployment is one of the more spectacular wastes of capitalism. The dry statistics translate into workers with poverty-level incomes and nothing to do, idle factories and products not produced, and "surplus" products (oranges, potatoes) destroyed.

9. Racial and sexual discrimination in America means that the talents of a huge bloc of humanity are wasted and prevented from expression.

10. There is also the incredible harm done to future human resources by allowing poverty to result in ill-fed and ill-housed children, with poor medical care and bad childhood environment.

11. The general alienation of U.S. society causes some of our best students to drop out and causes a significant part of the population to take drugs, or to consume large amounts of alcohol, or to reside in mental institutions. Surely these are wastes of human resources.

12. Overshadowing all the rest in the quantitative amount of wasted resources are the military expenditures of materials, labor, and lives for past, present, and future wars.

Pollution

Before the 1960s pollution was not a major concentration (nor even a footnote) in most works on economics. Our environment, however, has been declining in livability at an alarming pace. Air pollution is making it unsafe to breathe in most American cities. Water pollution is killing fish in rivers and even the life in the oceans (which had been counted as a vast reservoir of food for the future). Animal life and human life are both being hurt by nuclear radiation and pesticides. The worldwide intake of DDT by infants is double the maximum set by the World Health Organization.

All these facts of environmental destruction are recognized equally by liberals and radicals. The two part company, however, over the diagnosis of the problem. What is the cause of this vast pollution? "Who are the destroyers? . . . Who pollutes the air? Who fouls the rivers? Who cuts down the trees, builds houses on the stripped hill-sides? Who poisons the sheep, shoots the deer, oils the beaches, dams, and rivers, dries up the swamps, concretes the countryside? Who bull-dozes homes, builds missile sites, pours poison wastes underground, poison gas overground, slabs over mountain tops, rocks the earth with explosions, scars the earth with stripped mines?" (Johnson, 1969: 1). It is the respectable business person who commits these crimes. Although these problems menace any modern urban and industrial complex, the intensity of the pollution, and the lack of action to stop it, seem directly related to the private profit-making motives of capitalism (and its military arm). "Look at the values which galvanize energies and allo-cate resources in the business system: pursuit of money, enrichment of self, the exploitation of man—and of nature—to generate still more money. Is it surprising that a system seeking to turn everything into gold ends up turning everything into garbage?" (Ramparts, 1970: 2).

The problem is also closely related to the basic characteristic of capitalist society that it expands and promotes private consumption (especially by the rich), but it neglects many needed areas of public consumption. Both problems—the private-profit motivation and the difficulty of public action—may be seen in the facts about smog. Smog is the mixture of smoke and other noxious elements that makes breath-ing so unpleasant and makes the eyes tear in parts of America (for example, in the Los Angeles basin). Most of it is known to be the result of automotive fumes and industrial smoke. Yet it is almost impossible to get any rapid changes, for example, in the auto industry.

On the one side, smog "only" hurts the public and is not a cost directly affecting private profit, so the automobile companies have no monetary incentive to produce new types of smog-free autos, especially because these would require premature scrapping of much of their present plant and equipment. It is easier to spend a few dollars to influence legislatures not to take drastic action. On the public side, even if enough political pressure can get laws enacted in favor of purifying devices, the power of the vested interests involved is so immense that the laws are not enforced by a friendly Environmental Protection Agency.

Private transportation interests have also opposed with tooth and nail all attempts to substitute public transport for private: that is, one electric train carrying five hundred passengers to replace five hundred cars each carrying one passenger, and each adding to smog and traffic congestion. In the radical view, it seems unlikely or impossible that much can be done to eliminate pollution or to expand public substitutes before capitalist private-profit-making is eliminated.

The liberal reformers' view of waste and pollution is really quite different. They may admit that a few unusually greedy capitalists put some harmful products on the market and also cause some pollution from lack of care. But the more "profound" problems, they say, are really too many people for too few resources, and too rapid use of resources and polluting processes by modern and newly developing technology (see, e.g., Erlich, 1970: passim). Thus they argue that if all the underdeveloped world were brought up to the present American standard of living, it would require more than the known world supplies of metals such as copper, lead, and tin.

Moreover, many liberals claim that the most lethal threat is simply lack of food, since supply is limited, while population is doubling every thirty-five years. Hence, they see population and pollution as threats to everyone. In this view, all classes (especially enlightened capitalists) have the same interests in rescuing the environment, conserving resources, and limiting population.

A somewhat different liberal view comes in the vast literature of technocracy. The modern technocratic argument is that, if it were all left to the engineers, technological solutions would be readily available to most of our problems, such as smog. This is a naive view of economics. It is true that engineering solutions already exist to many pollution problems. The problem is that these solutions require massive scrapping of present plant and equipment and massive investment, with no ready hope for profit. In the radical view, only a public framework could handle such a change.

The results of the difference in diagnoses become immediately apparent when one examines proposed solutions. The radical view is that the precondition for eliminating pollution and conserving resources is the abolition of the capitalist private-profit system and its replacement by a socially owned and directed system. The "liberal" part of the Establishment would pass a few reform laws on pollution, restrict output and technology, and limit population, especially among the poor in America and in all the underdeveloped countries. Even with population control, they contend, the underdeveloped countries must understand that resources are too limited for them ever to reach American standards of living, so they should begin to "reorient" and reduce their goals (see, e.g., Erlich, 1970: passim).

Even some radicals have stressed the demand for no more economic growth at all. They argue that the present American national product is enough if waste and pollutants are eliminated, and if there is much more equal distribution of wealth. It is true that every American could be raised out of poverty if the present American production were rationalized and redistributed. But the stress is upside-down. Even in America we can only begin to plan and decide rationally on growth and other goals after the end of capitalism and establishment of a decent, human society. Furthermore, the underdeveloped countries clearly do need a great deal of economic growth.

Suggested Readings

An excellent and comprehensive book on sexist discrimination is by Barbara Sinclair Deckard (1983). A good review of the literature on Marxist feminism is in Omvedt (1986). The best book on racism against blacks is by Michael Reich (1980); racism against Chicanos is best analyzed in Mario Barera (1980).

There is an extremely useful special issue of the *Review of Radical Political Economy* on "The Political Economy of Race and Class," vol. 17, no. 3 (Fall 1985), with outstanding general articles by Thomas Boston and Harold Baron, as well as excellent specialized articles on racial stereotypes by Harry Chang, on white and black women workers by Randy Albeda, on various ethnic women workers by Evelyn Nakano Glenn, on American Indian women by Patricia Albers, on Japanese in America by Robert Yamashita and Peter Park, and on the history of black power in Chicago by Manning Marable (his description of the mayoral race by Harold Washington is fascinating).

The outstanding work on alienation is Bertell Ollman (1971). An excellent pioneering work on pollution and other environmental problems is by Mathew Edel (1973). The most thorough analysis of capitalist waste is by Paul Baran and Paul Sweezy (1966).

The best work on the important area of segmented labor markets is still Edwards, Reich, and Gordon (1978), with a full discussion of the literature in this important area by Attewell (1984). I could only mention segmented labor markets in this book for lack of space, but it is a vital and vigorous area of contemporary political economy.

— 6 —

CAPITALIST CRISES OF CYCLICAL UNEMPLOYMENT

In addition to a considerable long-run level of unemployment, the capitalist system periodically is subject to the peculiar disease of mass unemployment and depression. A time-traveler from the medieval period would find everything upside-down in an Alice in Wonderland world. The traveler would find output dropping and standards of living declining, but she or he could not believe that there were still plenty of factories and workers and bountiful harvests. The traveler would assume that the cause of the severe decline in production is a natural calamity, such as flood or drought, or perhaps the destruction and loss of lives caused by war. How wrong that would be! In these modern capitalist calamities there is no problem of a shortage of supply. On the contrary, there is "overproduction," too many workers, and too much produced relative to the "effective demand" in the market. "Effective demand" means money ready to be spent, not mere desire or need, since the capitalist economy takes no notice of anything but money. And instead of war destruction causing the loss of production and poverty, production for war is often seen as the only solution to unemployment.

Although overproduction seems a strange and even absurd epidemic, its ravages among its millions of human victims are nonetheless very real. It is not merely that thousands of factories are idle and gather dust, but that millions of workers are involuntarily idle and gather frustration. In the Great Depression of the 1930s one out of every four U.S. workers was unemployed by official government statistics. Yet official statistics drastically understate unemployment by ignoring dis-

couraged workers who no longer try for a job. Official unemployment
data also ignore the involuntary reduction of hours to a few hours a
week for many of those who still have a job. In the 1930s, for example,
this part-time unemployment, or less than full-time employment, was
probably visited on another 50 percent of all workers. The remaining
25 percent suffered drastic cuts in wage levels. People traveled from
place to place looking for work, subsisting on private handouts or
government soup kitchens (for the human reaction, see Terkel, 1970).

After the Second World War, there were no more major depressions—due in part to a high level of military production—until 1974.
Periodic "minor" depressions did continue in the 1950s and 1960s
with resulting full-time unemployment of "only" 6 to 8 percent of all
workers (and much higher percentages of unemployed women, black,
brown, young, and elderly workers). In 1975 unemployment rose to 9
percent officially, but actually about 16 percent when "discouraged"
and involuntary part-time workers are added. In 1982 unemployment
rose to over 10 percent officially (or about twelve million workers
unemployed), with two million "discouraged" workers and several
million involuntary part-time workers.

The Possibility of Unemployment

The discussion here is based on the insights of Marx, which foreshadowed most major cycle theories, but it also utilizes some of the findings
of John Maynard Keynes and of Wesley Clair Mitchell. Both Keynes
and Marx began their analyses with attacks on Say's Law, an assumption by which the classical and neoclassical economists denied the very
possibility of insufficient demand or general unemployment. All mone-
tarists and all supply-side economists still believe in Say's Law, so they
do not believe in crises of general unemployment, but only temporary
deviations from equilibrium caused by incorrect government policies
(high taxes or stimulative fiscal or monetary policies)—thus the argument over Say's Law is anything but academic.

Say's Law has been stated in various forms. In its most common
statement, Say's Law holds that "supply calls forth its own demand,"
so there can never be insufficient aggregate demand. The argument in
favor of Say's Law is that any output results in an equal income. When
(and if) that income is spent, it will buy the same amount of output.
This conclusion, while containing a grain of truth as a description of the
"normal" circulation of money and goods, seems to be an unwarranted

generalization from consideration of earlier and simpler societies.

Say's Law must be shown to be inapplicable before one can understand the phenomena of insufficient demand and unemployment in capitalist depressions. Of course, there are business cycle theories that accept Say's Law, but these theories all see cycles only in the supply of output, caused by factors external to the economy and not by lack of demand. On the contrary, it is asserted here that in capitalist economies there is a periodic lack of aggregate effective demand, generated by the internal mechanism of that system.

It is characteristic of the modern capitalist economy that almost all production is directed solely toward its sale in the marketplace. According to most economic historians, this was hardly ever true of earlier societies. In very primitive economies the collective unit of the whole tribe carries on production for the collective use of the whole tribe; there can be no question of "overproduction" of all commodities in this case. Even in the ancient slave empires and in medieval feudalism, the basic production unit was the plantation or manor, which produced mostly for its own self-sufficient existence, though it may have sold a small surplus. In some of these societies there was also a large, though not vital, trade in luxury goods.

In all these earlier societies, since most production was for the immediate use of the economic unit itself, the phenomenon of overproduction was impossible. Thus, the carpenter on the feudal manor would not produce more wagons than the manor would use. It is quite different when Henry Ford produces millions of autos, not for the use of Ford workers, but for sale in the market. It is certainly possible that Ford may produce many more cars than can be sold at a profit in the market. Furthermore, if Ford finds that he cannot sell so many cars at a profit, then he will reduce his production, and some Ford workers will be unemployed.

A second characteristic of modern capitalism is the regular use of money. The defenders of Say's Law always spoke of money as a veil over the process of exchange between two commodities; they held that the "essential" features of the capitalist economic process were the same as in a barter economy. In a barter economy, of course, every supply of goods to the market is at the same time a demand for other goods; there may be too much of single commodity and not enough of another, but there cannot be an excess of aggregate supply over demand. While many features remain the same in a money economy, there is an important difference because money is not only a medium of exchange between commodities, but it may also be withdrawn from exchange and stored away for an indefinite time (as most commodities may not be). Thus, it is possible to have a monetary income in the capitalist economy that is hoarded and not immediately respent for the equivalent supply of products.

A third characteristic of capitalism is that the sole motivation for production is the private profit of the capitalist. Each individual enterprise makes its own plans on the basis of its own estimate of whether it will obtain a private profit by production. It follows that false profit expectations may lead the aggregate of all firms to produce more (or less) than the market will buy. If more is produced than can be sold at a profit, private enterprise will fire workers and reduce its investment spending, thus leading to a depression.

To show analytically the possibility of insufficient demand under capitalism, it is necessary to begin by dividing all spending flows into personal consumption and investment (ignoring, at this point, all governmental and foreign transactions). Excess supply may occur if the value of goods supplied to the market exceeds the planned spending of all consumers and investors. For the moment, let us assume no growth of productive capacity and a fixed money and credit supply. Then it may be argued that if any of last month's income is hoarded, the total of consumer and investor spending will decline, and there will be relative "overproduction" this month.

Suppose one adds the distinction between workers' wages and capitalists' profits (where "profit" includes rent and interest income). If all wages are spent for consumption, then one may further locate the problem in terms of class behavior. Beyond their consumption needs and the profitable investment opportunities, capitalists may have additional money from profits. This excess of saving over investment means less effective demand for goods, so it results in unsold goods or overproduction. It is within this framework that we may construct a theory to account for the recurring depressions and mass unemployment found under capitalism. That there is hoarding of money and unwanted inventories of goods is merely a reflection of the problem; the task is to understand the processes that result in these phenomena.

Production and Realization of Profits

All capitalist profits come out of surplus value, which is that amount of value produced by workers over and above the value of their product necessary to pay their wages. Profits must therefore first be produced by workers in the form of surplus value. If, however, the capitalist cannot sell the product in the market at a price equal to its long-run value, then the capitalist cannot realize the surplus value embodied in the product. Thus, the capitalist still may make no profit or a low rate of profit even though the worker has been exploited. As Marx puts it:

> The creation of . . . surplus value is the object of the direct process of production. . . . But this production of surplus value is but the first act of the capitalist process of production. . . . Now comes the second act of the process. The entire mass of commodities . . . must be sold. If this is not done, or only partly accomplished . . . the laborer has been none the less exploited, but his exploitation does not realise as much for the capitalist. . . . The realization of surplus value . . . is not determined . . . by the absolute consuming power, but by the consuming power based on antagonistic conditions of distribution, which reduces the consumption of the great mass of the population to a variable minimum within more or less narrow limits. (1907, 3:286)

Profits, therefore, may be and are squeezed from two directions at the peak of expansion: (1) by rising costs of production, which may prevent creation of surplus value, and (2) by limited demand, which may prevent realization of surplus value. Some Marxists—and some non-Marxist economists—emphasize only the capitalist's problems in producing surplus value. These are called theories of rising costs, or profit squeeze, or overinvestment (see non-Marxist theories in Haberler, 1960: ch. 3, and a Marxist theory in Boddy and Crotty, 1975). On the other hand, some Marxists—and some non-Marxists economists—emphasize only the capitalist's problems in selling the product or realizing surplus value. These are called theories of overproduction or underconsumption (see non-Marxist theories in Haberler, 1960: ch. 5, and a Marxist theory in Sweezy, 1942). Any complete crisis theory must explain both sides of the nutcracker that squeezes capitalist profits at the cycle peak. Why is profit so crucial in the causation of economic crises? Because profitability determines whether capitalists continue to produce, expand their production through new investment, or cut back their production. Capitalist investment is affected by profits in two ways. First, the total amount of profit realized determines the total funds available for new investment. Second, the expected rate of profit on investment is the prime motive for making any investment at all. Therefore, many cycle theories are devoted to explaining why the rate of profit declines at the peak of expansion and why the rate of profit rises again from the trough of depression.

Problems of Profit Creation
(Rising Wage Costs)

Some conservative theorists, such as Frederick von Hayek, argue that a crisis arises from high costs (see summary in Haberler, 1960: ch. 3). In an expansion, the high level of investment and production leads to a demand for more labor and materials than are available, causing the price of labor and raw materials to rise. Some of Hayek's work also stresses the cost of rising interest rates at the cycle peak. Since it is a high level of investment that leads to rising costs, these are called overinvestment theories.

The heaviest emphasis by overinvestment theorists is usually on the threat to profits from rising wage costs as the economy nears full employment. In wage negotiations employers use this argument to prove that higher wages will lead to less investment and production, and so to unemployment. Therefore, they tell unions to hold down wage requests.

Since the conservative theorists put the whole blame for cyclical depressions on rising wages which "squeeze profits," their solution—which is pleasing to business—is to hold down costs, particularly wage costs. Those who emphasize the rising costs of labor claim that more employment can only come by cutting wages. A standard textbook says, "The general solution to involuntary unemployment is a reduction in real wages until the amount of labor demanded equals the amount supplied" (Leftwich and Sharp, 1974: 249). The notion of solving unemployment by cutting wages conveniently ignores the fact that lower wages mean less demand for consumer goods, which makes it harder for capitalists to realize their profits. Both Marx and Keynes emphasized this fact.

Nevertheless, some radicals agree that every depression crisis is the result of low profits caused by high wages and/or less labor productivity. Thus, two radicals, citing the *Wall Street Journal* as their source, say, "Knowledgeable observers of the labor scene have pointed directly to an increasingly obstreperous labor force as an influence on the decline in productivity during the expansion" (Boddy and Crotty, 1975: 8). Like the conservatives, they argue that high employment levels lead to a militant or "obstreperous" labor force that forces higher wages and lower productivity, thus causing a crisis by "squeezing" profits. Because they stress that a declining "reserve army" of labor (the unemployed) declines in the boom, leading to less profits, their theory may be called the reserve army theory.

The reserve army cycle theory has been spelled out systematically by Goldstein (1985). First, he shows that every cyclical expansion is characterized by accumulation of capital and extensive investment, leading to a declining rate of unemployment. Second, he claims that the falling unemployment strengthens the bargaining power of labor, so there are rising hourly wages and a declining growth of productivity. Third, he argues that the rise in labor costs per unit cannot be passed on in higher prices (though this must depend on demand), so there is a falling rate of profit.

The reserve army theorists correctly emphasize that capitalists may produce profits only by forcing workers to create a surplus value above costs. They do not consider the fact, however, that capitalists must also realize their profits by sales in the market, which require high consumer demand and high wages. In simpler terms, the criticism is that profits cannot be squeezed from only one side at a time; they are squeezed—as in a nutcracker—from both sides. Thus, when Goldstein says that capitalists cannot pass on higher labor costs in higher prices in the crisis, he is right. But the reason is the lack of sufficient consumer demand. The capitalist corporation's dilemma is that it would like both lower wage costs and higher consumer demand.

Marx also acknowledged that, in some extraordinary cases, capitalist investment could be so rapid as to cause a shortage of labor. This shortage leads to high wages, cutting into the rate of profit and causing a crisis. "If the quantity of unpaid labor supplied by the working class, and accumulated by the capitalist class, increases so rapidly that its conversion into capital requires an extraordinary addition to paid labor, then wages rise, and all other circumstances remaining equal, the unpaid labor diminishes in proportion" (1867, 1:620). He goes on to say that this fall in the rate of profit leads to a depression, which causes wages to fall again. Note, however, that Marx calls this an "extraordinary" rise in wages. He also says that such cases have only occurred in exceptional periods, such as the U.S. railway boom of the nineteenth century. Marx emphasized that in most periods of normal capitalist expansion, there is a rising rate of exploitation, that is, profits are rising faster than wages. He makes the point very clear: "The falling tendency of the rate of profit is accompanied by a rising tendency of the rate of surplus value, that is, the rate of exploitation. Nothing is more absurd, for this reason, than to explain a fall in the rate of profit by a rise in the rate of wages, although there may be exceptional cases when this may apply'' (1907, 3:281). Thus, according to Marx, the usual case is that wages rise more slowly than profits in the expansion—so the falling rate of profit at the cycle peak cannot be blamed on rising wages. In a later section, the facts will have to be examined to see whether the wage/income ratio (the wage share) actually rises or falls in an expansion.

Problems of Profit Creation
(Rising Material Costs)

Marx discussed the reasons why there was a long-run trend to a falling rate of profit in the early nineteenth century. He speculated that part of the problem might be a growing amount of capitalist spending on capital goods per worker. But only workers produce profit. Therefore, the rate of profit on total capitalist investment might decline. Some Marxists have tried to turn this view of long-run trends into a theory of cyclical crises.

There are three problems with this approach. First, there is a huge literature challenging the basic theory (see a continuing stream of articles in the *Review of Radical Political Economics*). Second, Marx himself acknowledged that there were many countervailing factors. Thus, in fact, the ratio of capital to labor rose because of labor-saving inventions in the nineteenth century, but there have been mostly capital-saving inventions in the twentieth century. Nor is it clear that the U.S. rate of profit has fallen in the twentieth century. Comparable data in a single series exist only since the early 1930s. The rate of profit was lowest in the Great Depression of the 1930s, rises in every war period, and usually declines when the war is over.

One could argue about exact definitions of the rate of profit (such as including rent and interest to approximate Marx's surplus value). Tests based on all kinds of alternative definitions reveal, however, that they make little difference as to the pattern of rise and fall (Sherman, 1968). There is no long-run trend in the available data, but the rate of profit does rise rapidly in every cyclical expansion and fall rapidly in every cyclical contraction.

The third problem is that no long-run trend can explain the rapid rise of the profit rate in a few months in each recovery. Nor can any long-run trend explain the rapid decline of the profit rate in a few months in the crisis at the cycle peak. When Marx himself turned to explain the falling profit rate in a crisis, he did not refer to his theoretical explanation of a possible long-run trend. Instead, one of the things he did examine was short-run changes in prices of capital goods, affected by temporary excesses of supply or demand.

Marx found that one side of the profit squeeze was the rising cost of capital goods, including plant, equipment, and raw materials. He points out that the rising cost of capital goods is a normal occurrence as capitalists accelerate their demand in an expansion: "The same phenomenon (and this as a rule precedes crises) can occur if the production of surplus capital takes place at a very rapid rate, and its retransformation into productive capital so increases the demand for all the elements of the latter that real production cannot keep pace, and consequently there is a rise in the prices of all the commodities which enter into the formation of capital" (1952: 371).

Not only does Marx point to the rising cost of capital goods in an expansion, he also shows how a fall in the price of capital goods is a very necessary part of the adjustment process of capitalism in the depression (1907, 3:297–99). But Marx wrote over a hundred years ago. Assuming his facts were right then, is he still right now?

There is some dispute, but most of the facts point toward the same process still occurring in most or all cycles. In a careful study of costs and prices, Frederick Mills collected data for many cycles—from the 1890s to the 1930s—on prices of consumer goods, prices of plant and equipment, and prices of raw materials (1946: 132–33). Mills found that in the average expansion period consumer goods prices rose very slowly. He found, however, that prices of plant and equipment rose sharply and raw materials prices rose even further. Because of rapid shifts in demand and slow changes in supply, prices of all capital goods (and especially raw materials) rose more rapidly in expansions and fell more rapidly in contractions than did prices of consumer goods.

In recent business cycles, some changes have occurred since costs seldom decline in recessions. Still it appears that nonwage costs, mainly materials, do tend to rise more rapidly than other prices in expansion and tend to fall more (or rise less) in recessions.

Problems of Profit Realization
(Underconsumption)

So far the problems of profit creation arising from higher costs have been examined. Now it is necessary to look at problems of profit realization, arising from lack of effective demand. Marx emphasized the limited consumer demand resulting from the exploitation of workers. "The ultimate cause of all real crises always remains the poverty and restricted consumption of the masses" (1907, 3:568). Expansions are brought to an end by the limits imposed by class structure:

> The epochs in which capitalist production exerts all its forces are always periods of overproduction, because the forces of production can never be utilized beyond the point at which surplus value can be not only produced but also realized; but the sale of commodities, the realization of the commodity capital and hence also of surplus value, is limited not only by the consumption requirements of society in general, but by the consumption requirements of a society in which the great majority are poor and must always remain poor. (1906, 2:363)

In Marx's day, however, there were already a number of naive "underconsumption" theories, which he attacked and which differ from his own formulation of realization problems. First, it is naive to say that the problem is falling wages. On the contrary, it was true in Marx's day (and is still true today) that the real wage rises throughout the expansion. Marx's more sophisticated point is that profits rise faster than wages, so the *share* of labor usually falls in most of the expansion period.

Second, it is naive to say that the problem is just that workers are exploited, so they can never buy back the product they produce. Some of the product is bought by capitalists for their own consumption and for investment; the real problem is why capitalist demand sometimes fills the gap and sometimes does not. The naive view that emphasizes that workers can never buy back their product often leads to theories of permanent crisis or permanent stagnation. On the contrary, Marx showed that a temporary period of "overabundance of capital, overproduction, crisis, is something different. There are no permanent crises" (1952: 373).

Sophisticated underconsumption theorists, who might be called realization theorists, begin by looking at limitations on consumer demand. In every expansion, they contend that national income rises faster than consumer demand, so the ratio of consumption to income declines. Similarly, in every contraction, consumption declines more slowly than national income, so the average ratio of consumption to income rises. Facts showing the correctness of these assumptions are discussed in a later section.

Why does the ratio of consumption to income rise in expansions and fall in contractions? Most Keynesians attribute it to innate psychological propensities of all people to save more out of rising income and to save less out of falling income. Marx, on the other hand, traced these changes back to the capitalist relations of production. These productive relations ensure that (1) workers have mostly low incomes and capitalists have high incomes, and (2) the increase of workers' wages lags behind the increase of capitalist profits in every expansion.

Therefore, one should consider carefully the differing consumer behaviors of affluent capitalists and lower income workers. As capitalist income rises in an expansion, capitalists consume a smaller and smaller proportion of it. Partly, this is because they still consider their earlier consumption level normal and satisfactory. Partly, it is because the profit outlook has become more optimistic, so they wish to save a larger part of their income in order to invest it in profitable enterprises. In fact, the laws of competition force capitalists continually to expand their capital or be swallowed by their competitors.

Workers, on the other hand, continue to spend almost their whole income on consumption. Since their standard of living was below normal at the bottom of the depression, they use most of their increased income to pay off debts and buy necessities. At any rate, their ratio of consumption to income remains over 95 percent even at the peak of the cycle.

An empirical study by Fichtenbaum (1985) finds that the marginal propensity to consume out of wages (change in consumption/change in wages) is much higher than the marginal propensity to consume out of profits. Therefore, the overall propensity to consume (consumption/ national income) is a positive function of the wage/profit ratio. The higher the national ratio of wages to profits, the higher will be the national propensity to consume. Fichtenbaum used data from 1947 to 1979 and found a correlation of .99 (after adjustment for autocorrelation). He criticizes Blinder (1975), who found no correlation, because Blinder considered only a linear equation and personal income distribution, not the functional distribution between workers and capitalists, which is the important relationship.

Fichtenbaum points out that this hypothesis explains the known tendencies better than other hypotheses about consumption. Thus, in cross-section data, the marginal propensity to consume falls as income rises because the wage/profit ratio falls as income rises. In long-run aggregate time series data, the marginal propensity to consume remains roughly constant because the wage/profit share remains roughly constant.

In the business cycle, there is a declining average propensity to consume (consumption/income) in every expansion. This declining propensity to consume may be explained by a shift of income from workers (with high consumption/income ratios) to capitalists (with much lower consumption/income ratios). Similarly, in every recession or depression, the average propensity to consume rises. This rising propensity to consume may be explained by a shift of income back from capitalists to workers. Thus, a changing rate of exploitation over the cycle provides the clearest explanation of the changing propensity to consume over the cycle.

Realization theorists contend that wages do rise and fall proportionately less than aggregate income, while profits fluctuate more than the total national income. The aggregate data, as will be shown in a later section, demonstrate that the ratio of wages to national income falls in economic expansion but rises in depression.

As a result of the more rapid rise and fall of profits, the ratio of profits to wages changes systematically over the business cycle. Profits rise much faster than wages in expansions, but profits decline faster than wages in contractions. Thus, there is an income shift toward high-income capitalist profits in the expansion and back toward lower-income workers' wages in the contraction. This is a major reason for the declining ratio of consumption in the expansion and the rising ratio of consumption in the contraction.

To avoid confusion, it must be stressed that real wages, profits, consumption, and income all rise in the expansion and all fall in the contraction. But the ratio of consumption to income and the ratio of wages to profits both decline in the expansion and both rise in the contraction. In the expansion workers have rising real income but get a declining proportion of all national income—and vice versa in contraction. At any rate, for realization theorists the expansion is a period of rising exploitation of workers, leading to limited consumer demand.

Consumer demand is more and more limited (as a percentage of income) as the expansion continues, but consumption slowly recovers (as a percentage of income) in the contraction period. The limited consumer demand in expansion leads to lower investment, which sets off a recession. The rising ratio of consumption to income in a contraction eventually leads to more investment, which sets off a recovery.

Capitalists are caught in every expansion between the twin problems of profit creation (rising costs due to overinvestment) and profit realization (limited demand or underconsumption due to limited wages). It is impossible to solve both horns of the dilemma at the same time under capitalism. At the peak of prosperity, the limited consumer demand and the rising cost per unit act together to squeeze profits and choke off economic circulation. At the trough of the depression, the end of decline in consumer demand and the falling costs per unit increase profits and stimulate economic activity.

The theory that depression is caused by both limited demand (underconsumption) and high costs (overinvestment) is a radical one because it shows that cycles of expansion and depression are inevitable under capitalism. Some liberals believe they could prevent depressions by giving higher wages to increase demand, but that ignores the cost problem. Some conservatives would prevent depressions by lowering wages and interest rates, but that ignores the demand problem.

What Happens During Business Cycles

Before turning to a systematic theory of the closing—and opening—of the jaws of the nutcracker on profits, it is necessary to highlight some of the known facts about the cycle, in the tradition of Wesley Clair Mitchell (1951). Mitchell divided the cycle for convenience into nine stages. Stage 1 is the initial trough; stages 2, 3, and 4 are the expansion; stage 5 is the cycle peak; stages 6, 7, and 8 are the contraction; and stage 9 is the final trough.

Mitchell examines each important economic series to see its behavior at each cycle stage relative to its average for the whole cycle. This framework may be used to examine the six cycles from 1949 through 1980 (using U.S. Department of Commerce estimates of the peaks and troughs; for criticism of this dating, see Sherman, 1986).

Within this framework, factual data on some important variables that move with the cycle are shown in table 6.1. The data indicate that real national income rises and falls exactly with the cycle, as does capacity utilization and real gross (nonresidential) investment. Real aggregate consumption rises in expansion and falls till midrecession, but then recovers (because this average includes several very mild recessions). Real total profits and profit rates on capital both rise in much of expansion and fall in much of contraction, but they lead the cycle turning point at both the peak and trough. Interest rates on short-term

Table 6.1

Procyclical Behavior, Six Cycles Average, 1949–1980
(change from stage to stage, per quarter, as percent of cycle average)

Stages	Trough		Peak				Trough	
	1–2	2–3	3–4	4–5	5–6	6–7	7–8	8–9
National income	.54	.51	.31	.20	−.22	−.60	−.32	−.08
Capacity utilization	.63	.49	.09	.01	−.92	−1.60	−1.04	−1.20
Consumption	.41	.37	.32	.23	.05	−.30	−.03	.27
Gross investment (nonresidential)	.25	.66	.52	.46	−.11	−.91	−.74	−.87
Profits	.97	.56	.12	−.08	−.94	−1.47	−.51	.44
Profit rate on Capital	.78	.28	−.20	−.40	−1.15	−1.67	−.71	.20
Interest rates	−.82	.42	1.24	2.00	.21	2.45	−.58	−6.43

Source: All data from U.S. Department of Commerce, with definitions, sources, and derivation given in detail in Howard Sherman and Gary Evans, *Macroeconomics: Keynesian, Monetarist, and Marxist Views* (New York: Harper and Row, 1984), pp. 142, 163, 170, and 198.

business loans are also mostly procyclical, but they lag at the peak and trough turning points.

Table 6.2 shows some important series with a countercyclical movement. It reveals that both unemployment and the ratio of consumption to personal disposable income (average propensity to consume) fall during every stage of cyclical expansion and rise during every stage of cyclical contraction. Both the ratio of consumption to national income and the ratio of wages to national income fall in the cyclical expansion and rise in the cyclical expansion, but they lead considerably at the peak and wages/national income also leads at the trough.

Contrary to the reserve army theory, the wage share (wage to national income) and unemployment move in the same direction in most of the business cycle. They do, however, move in opposite directions before the cycle peak.

Finally, in table 6.3 the data on income distribution and productivity are examined more carefully for the 1970s. To understand this table, some definitions are useful. It will always be the case mathematically that

$$\text{wages/national income} = \frac{(\text{wages/total hours})}{(\text{national income/total hours})}$$

Table 6.2

**Countercyclical Behavior, Six Cycles Average, 1949–1980
(change from stage to stage, per quarter, as percent of cycle average)**

Stages	Trough		Peak				Trough	
	1–2	2–3	3–4	4–5	5–6	6–7	7–8	8–9
Unemployment	−1.36	−1.79	−.59	−.19	3.28	5.18	5.18	4.55
Consumption/personal disposable income	−.04	−.03	−.02	−.04	.03	.02	.02	.09
Consumption/national income	−.17	−.15	0	.02	.25	.29	.29	.34
Wages/national income	−.18	−.01	.09	.10	.27	.28	.07	−.07

Source: All data from U.S. Department of Commerce, with definitions, sources, and derivations given in Sherman and Evans, *Macroeconomics*, pp. 143, 146, 198.

This relationship can be simplified by pointing out that, by definition, "wage share" means wages/national income, "hourly wage" means wages/total hours, and "productivity" means national income/total hours of labor. All of these concepts are in real terms, not money or nominal terms. Thus, we can rewrite the awkward expression above to say that

$$\text{wage share} = (\text{hourly wages})/(\text{productivity})$$

Notice that, in national income terms, Marx's rate of exploitation equals profits/wages or the profit share/wage share. So the rate of exploitation always moves the same way as the profit share but always moves opposite to the wage share. It makes no difference, therefore, whether one discusses the profit share or the wage share or the rate of exploitation.

For convenience, the wage share is discussed here—and is conceptualized as hourly wages divided by productivity. Table 6.3 shows that (in these cycles) the wage share falls for three periods of expansion (stages 1 to 2, 2 to 3, and 3 to 4). Why? The wage share falls because hourly wages rise more slowly than productivity, thus increasing the capitalist's share of the product and reducing the worker's share of the product. Productivity rises—though more and more slowly—because of industrial innovations, closer approach to optimal use of capacity, and less overhead workers (guards, bookkeepers) per unit of product. Hourly wages rise more slowly than productivity because capitalists

Table 6.3

Wages and Productivity, Two Cycles Average, 1970–1980
(change from stage to stage, per quarter, as percent of cycle average)

	Trough		Peak				Trough	
Stages	1–2	2–3	3–4	4–5	5–6	6–7	7–8	8–9
Wage share	−.16	−.05	−.04	.05	.21	.61	.10	−.03
Hourly wage	.14	.12	.03	−.07	0	.03	−.06	−.16
Productivity	.29	.16	.07	−.12	−.20	−.54	−.16	.20

Source: All data from U.S. Department of Commerce, with definitions, sources, and derivations given in Sherman and Evans, *Macroeconomics*, p. 193.

own the increased product, so workers must bargain for it. Wages are changed only in a new contract, and capitalists resist higher wages, usually with the help of the media and the government.

The declining wage share and a rising use of capacity lead to a higher profit rate for the first four-fifths of expansion. But the falling wage share (or rising rate of exploitation) also spells trouble in the future on the demand side because it causes the average propensity to consume (consumption/income) to decline.

Table 6.3 also shows, however, that in the last period of expansion (stages 4–5) the wage share rises at least in the average of these cycles. The naive underconsumptionists cannot fit this into their theory; they assume that the wage share is always negatively correlated with production growth—so by their theory the wage share should fall for the whole expansion and rise for the whole contraction. A naive reserve army theory predicts, on the contrary, that the wage share rises whenever unemployment is falling (the two are negatively correlated); but their theory is contradicted by the fact that the wage share falls in four-fifths of expansion, when unemployment is falling. Sophisticated reserve army theorists such as Boddy and Crotty (1975) argue that falling unemployment will cause a rising wage share only with a long time lag. This formulation is logically compatible with the facts, but the long time lag makes it less persuasive and less useful as a tool.

All radicals and Marxists can agree at a general level that the wage share (and, therefore, the rate of exploitation) is determined by class conflict of labor and capital, within certain conditions of supply and demand. These conditions are reflected in expansion and contraction of production and in rises and falls in unemployment. Given the long-run power of the opposing classes, the wage share appears to be a function of both the degree of unemployment and the expansion or contraction of production. These two factors pull the wage share in opposite directions. Rising unemployment reduces workers' bargaining power, so it reduces the wage share. Rising production usually means productivity rising faster than real wages, so it reduces the wage share. But unemployment and production almost always move in opposite directions, so they pull the wage share in opposite directions. Which is dominant at a given phase of the cycle determines the actual movement of the wage share.

Key Relationships in the Cycle

The following may be summarized as the key relationships in the business cycle:

1. Investment changes set off the recession and also set off the recovery. Investment is a lagged function of the rate of profit. The profit rate is a leading indicator, whereas investment does not turn till the cycle turning points.

2. The propensity to consume (consumption/income) is a lagged function of the wage share (or the wage/profit ratio or the rate of exploitation).

3. The wage share is a lagged function of the unemployment rate and the level of production.

4. The short-run profit rate is mainly a function of the profit share (reflecting the rate of exploitation) and the degree of capacity utilization. Capacity utilization, of course, depends on consumer and investment demands.

Expansion and the Nutcracker Crisis

In most of the expansion (usually the first four-fifths), production and income are rising, capacity utilization is rising, and consumption and investment are rising. Profits and profit rates are rising rapidly because both capacity utilization and the profit share are rising. On the other hand, unemployment, the propensity to consume (consumption/income), and the wage share (wages/national income) are all falling. Unemployment falls because it is a lagged function of production. The wage share declines because productivity is rising more rapidly than real wages. The propensity to consume declines mostly because the wage share of income declines.

During the first four-fifths of expansion, profits rise not only because demand is rising and because productivity rises faster than wages, but also because other costs are low. Raw material costs remain very low in the first stage of expansion and rise very, very slowly in the first half of expansion. Interest rates lag, so interest rates are very low and actually fall in the first stage of expansion; then they start rising slowly. Thus, for much of expansion, consumer demand rises at a fair rate, while costs are low and rising very slowly. Hence, the jaws of the nutcracker flop open and profit rates rise rapidly.

Eventually, in the last fifth of expansion (stages 4–5), there is a crisis. The crisis is shown by a declining rate of profit—which leads to declining production and investment after the peak. How does this happen?

On the demand side, the declining propensity to consume (caused, with a time lag, by a falling wage share) eventually leads to limitation of demand—so aggregate consumption rises very, very slowly in the crisis (stages 4–5). But limited demand is only one side of the nutcracker, so it can never lower the profit rate by itself. What happened on the supply or cost side?

In the crisis period, the usual phenomenon is that the wage share rises because productivity rises more slowly than real hourly wages. In the two cycles in table 6.3, however, the wage share rises because productivity falls more rapidly than hourly wages in this period. Hourly wages declined at the peak of these two cycles because demand for labor did not keep up with a rising labor force (as more people were attracted to the labor market) and because of antilabor government controls and restrictive fiscal policy. Productivity declined more for many reasons, including bottlenecks and shortages, labor militancy and resistance to speedup, and no more improvement of the ratio of overhead workers to product.

In the same crisis period—in stages 4–5—raw material prices are rising very rapidly because supply of raw materials has grown less than demand. Interest rates are rising more rapidly than at any other time because speculation becomes frantic before the peak.

Thus, in the crisis, consumer demand is limited; it grows only minutely, as a result of the long previous fall in the average propensity to consume. At the same time, in the crisis, labor costs per unit are rising because productivity is falling faster than wages; raw material costs are rising faster than finished goods prices; and interest costs are rising. Hence, the jaws of the nutcracker close, and profits and profit rates are squeezed. After a lag of a couple of quarters, production and investment decline, setting off a recession or depression. Whether there is a mild recession or a severe depression usually depends on whether there is a monetary and credit panic, that is, whether the financial system survives or collapses (see Wolfson, 1986).

Depression, the Opening of the Nutcracker, and Recovery

The recession or depression is symmetrical in behavior to the expansion, but everything happens in reverse. In most of the contraction, production and income are falling, capacity utilization is falling, and consumption and investment are falling. Profits and profit rates are both falling rapidly because both capacity utilization and the profit share are falling. On the other hand, unemployment is rising, the propensity to consume is rising, and the wage share is rising.

Unemployment, of course, rises because it is a lagged negative function of production. The wage share rises because productivity is falling faster than real wages (at this point, the effect of declining production has a stronger impact than the effect of rising unemployment). The propensity to consume rises because the wage share rises.

During most of the contraction, profits fall, not only because demand is falling and because productivity falls faster than wages, but also because other costs remain high for quite a while. Raw material costs remain high at the beginning of the contraction, then start to fall slowly. Interest rates lag, so interest rates are still very high and actually continue to rise in the first stage of contraction; then they start to fall slowly.

Thus, for much of contraction, consumer demand declines, while costs are still high and falling only slowly. Hence, the jaws of the nutcracker continue squeezing profits, and the profit rate falls rapidly. Eventually, in the last part of the contraction, the ground is laid for recovery. The imminence of recovery is foreshadowed by the leveling off or even a rise in the rate of profit. How does this miracle occur?

On the demand side, the rising wage share causes, with a time lag, a rising propensity to consume, which eventually leads to a slow in the decline or a slight rise in consumption. But rising consumer demand cannot by itself guarantee an opening of the nutcracker or a rise in profits. Demand is only one side of the nutcracker; what about the costs of supply?

At the end of the contraction in these two cycles, the wage share declines (or the profit share rises) because the hourly wage is still declining while productivity actually rises. Hourly wages decline because of the continuing decline in production and rise in unemployment. Productivity rises somewhat because there are no more bottlenecks and shortages, labor militancy declines, and there are more overhead workers per unit of output.

At the same point in the trough of the contraction, raw material prices are falling very rapidly because demand falls far faster than supply of raw materials. Interest rates are also falling rapidly because there is no demand for loans, due to the poor profit outlook.

Thus, in the trough of the contraction, consumer demand has reached a floor and may be inclining upward—as a result of the long improvement in the average propensity to consume (which was due to the lagged effect of the wage share). At the same time in the trough of the contraction, labor costs per unit are falling because wages are still falling, though productivity is rising a little. Raw material costs are falling faster than finished good prices. Interest rates are falling. Hence, the jaws of the nutcracker open again. Profits and profit rates begin to rise. After a time lag, production and investment rise, setting off a recovery.

It should be stressed that this is only a first approximation to a theory of the actual crises of the present U.S. economy. A more complete treatment would have to discuss the role of money and credit in detail, the role of monopoly power (chapter 7), the role of government (chapter 8), and the international relationships of the modern world (chapter 9). Two examples may illustrate the extent of modifications in the model caused by these factors. First, the profit rates of monopolies and competitive businesses have very different cyclical patterns. Second, government has both set off cyclical downturns and helped cause cyclical upturns (such as the minirecession of six months in 1980, caused by Jimmy Carter's policies). For a far more complete treatment of the business cycle, see Sherman and Evans (1984).

Suggested Readings

The article by Fichtenbaum (1985) on consumption is outstanding. Much of the recent radical literature on crises is surveyed very clearly by Attewell (1984). For a quite different and interesting approach to crises, see Aglietta (1979). Philip Klein (1986) has a very useful critique of the macroeconomic approaches of Robert Lucas and Milton Friedman. The best study of Marx's views on the role of money in crises is by Crotty (1985). An excellent presentation of both theories and data on money and credit in the business cycle is Wolfson (1986). For excellent data on unemployment, see Ginsburg (1983). The best recent collection of empirical work on economic crises is an entire journal issue by the Union of Radical Political Economics (1986).

— 7 —
MONOPOLY CAPITALISM

An outstanding book by Baran and Sweezy (1966) sets out the thesis that we live in a period in which the U.S. economy is dominated by huge monopoly capitalist corporations. They show that monopoly has more market power, higher prices, and higher profit rates than small competitive firms. They contend that monopoly has more political power, creates more waste, produces more pollution, and alienates more people than small competitive firms. They explore the role played by monopoly in maintaining racism and sexism. They point out that U.S. monopolies form the core of most multinational corporations, through which they control the destinies of many nations.

This overwhelming power of monopoly is disputed by most neoclassical economists. The neoclassicals contend that monopoly is not very extensive; most of the economy is competitive. Some argue that there has been little or no increase in monopoly since the early 1900s; competition always tends to end monopoly in the long-run. They assert that, even where monopoly exists, the economy acts as if it were roughly competitive.

A group of fundamentalist Marxists agrees with the neoclassical view, arguing that monopoly power is not pervasive, and that competition continues to rule the capitalist economy. For example, John Weeks writes that ''The monopolies that stalk the pages of Baran and Sweezy have no existence beyond the works of those authors'' (1981: 164). In addition to denying the existence of much monopoly, Weeks stresses competition and claims that Baran and Sweezy believe that ''competition has been virtually eliminated'' (p. 150).

In reality, Baran and Sweezy argue that fierce competition continues among the giant corporations and between them and the small firms, but they contend that the forms of competition have changed. The monopolies do not compete by lowering prices, but by more advertising, more services to customers, and sometimes better quality (or, at least, new, different-looking products). Baran and Sweezy argue that price behavior and profit performance are very different under monopoly capitalism than under a purely competitive model. The fundamentalists, however, argue that competition eventually restores competitive prices and levels profit rates toward equality (see Semmler, 1982; Glick, 1985).

What makes two groups of Marxists oppose each other so vehemently over these issues? The reason appears to be that each group sees the logic of the other group sinking it back into the viewpoint of neoclassical economics and the politics of liberalism, rather than socialism. The monopoly capital theorists (Baran and Sweezy and others) believe that the dominance of the giant, oligopoly corporations is the reality of our present economy, and that this reality means the extreme intensification of the evils of capitalism, including inflation, depression, and exploitation. Whenever they hear someone say—as liberal economists are always doing—that monopoly may be bad but is not so important as you think, or that its effects on prices and profit rates are temporary, or that competition will win in the long run, they immediately see the usual neoclassical approach. The neoclassical approach leads to the conclusion that a few reforms of the antitrust laws will easily get rid of monopoly; then a renewal of competitive capitalism will reduce or eliminate inflation, depression, and exploitation. The monopoly capital school would disagree with both aspects of this argument: competitive capitalism cannot be restored and, even if it were restored, competition will not eliminate exploitation or unemployment.

The fundamentalists look at the same liberal argument and come to very different conclusions about the main danger to a radical perspective. The liberals stress that many evils are caused by monopoly power, but that it is temporary, and once the country gets back to competitive capitalism, everything will be wonderful. The fundamentalists agree that monopoly power is temporary and competition is the rule—but they stress that Marx's analysis of competitive capitalism shows that this system causes exploitation, crises, and so forth. They are afraid that if Marxists base their critique on monopoly, then Marxists will accept the liberal argument that competitive capitalism is wonderful.

Since the fundamentalists believe that monopoly has not changed many of the rules, and that competition does win in the long run, this would mean that the whole liberal argument was basically correct. Of course, since the monopoly capital theorists do not believe that competitive capitalism is wonderful, they find it hard to understand the worry of the fundamentalists.

This is a case of lack of communication between Marxists, but it is also a case of very strongly different methodologies—for example, the importance of always beginning with Marx's categories versus the importance of always beginning with today's reality. Since the whole approach is so different, no amount of careful definition or empirical measurement will resolve the differences.

The Increase of Monopoly Power

As late as 1860, small farms and small businesses produced most of U.S. output. After the Civil War had wiped out the slave owners, the capitalist class had no more rivals for the power to rule. The Northern industrialists ran the government through the Republican party and used government power to penetrate into the South and the West. For example, huge parcels of land, equal in total to more than many European countries, were given to the railroads. At the same time, technological improvements made a much larger scale of production more profitable, so there was strong motivation to expand. Furthermore, improvements in transportation and communication made nationwide firms quite feasible.

By 1929, the two hundred largest manufacturing corporations held 45.8 percent of all manufacturing assets. Except for a slight decline in the Second World War (when medium-sized corporations did very well), this index of overall concentration has been rising steadily. The share of the two hundred largest manufacturing corporations rose from 47.1 in 1949 to 54.8 in 1959 and to 60.7 in 1984 (see Blair, 1972: 64; Penn, 1976: 3; U.S. Department of Commerce, 1986: 524).

Some of this increase in concentration was due to internal growth of the largest corporations, and some of it was due to mergers. Since 1950, one out of every five of the one thousand largest manufacturing corporations has been swallowed by an even larger giant. The nature of these mergers has changed over time. In the 1890s and the 1900s, there was a wave of horizontal mergers, that is, mergers between competitors in the same industry. In the 1920s and the 1930s, there was a wave of vertical mergers, that is, mergers between a manufacturer and its suppliers or its retail dealers. There has been only a very small increase in horizontal and vertical concentration in recent decades. But there has been an enormous wave of conglomerate mergers in the late 1960s, 1970s, and 1980s, that is, mergers of unrelated firms. These conglomerate mergers have not been limited to manufacturing but have occurred in every sector of the U.S. economy.

By 1963, before most of the conglomerate mergers, just four firms had over half the sales in 40 percent of U.S. manufacturing industries. In another 32 percent of U.S. industries, just four firms had between 25 and 50 percent of all sales. Only in 28 percent of the industries were less than 25 percent of the sales controlled by four firms (see Blair, 1972: 14). These data on concentration are very impressive, but they still greatly underestimate the concentration of economic power.

One problem is that the census industries are too broadly defined; that is, they include products that are not substitutes and do not compete. This reduces the reported degree of concentration. On the other hand, the reported concentration is increased by not including international competition. Adjusting for these two contrary biases, and some other less important biases, Shepherd (1970: 274) found that in most industries concentration is higher than reported. A concentration ratio may be defined as the percentage of total industry sales controlled by four firms. In 1966, the unadjusted concentration ratios were lower than the adjusted ratios in all major industry groups except one. The changes were substantial: for example, the adjusted ratios rose from 16 to 46 in lumber, and from 32 to 64 in petroleum and coal products.

Second, each of the one hundred largest conglomerates controls some of the biggest firms in several industries, so their power goes far beyond the recorded concentration ratios. Using the census definition that best fits economic theory, there are 1,014 individual manufacturing industries. The concentration ratio was defined earlier by the percentage of sales controlled by the four largest firms in each of these industries. Yet, in a majority of the manufacturing industries, at least one of the four largest firms in that industry is controlled by a large conglomerate (see Blair, 1972: 53–54). By large conglomerate is meant one of the one hundred largest firms in all of manufacturing.

Third, there are many interlocking directorates among the largest conglomerates, so one person sits on several boards to oversee their collusion or cooperation. In 1965, the 250 largest corporations had a total of 4,007 directorships, and 5 men held 6 each. There are also

Table 7.1

All U.S. Corporations, 1977

Size of assets	Number of corporations	Amount of assets (in $ millions)	Percent of corporations	Percent of assets
Less than $100,000	1,274,318	$ 40,593	57.0%	1%
$100,000-$500,000	650,754	149,072	29.0	3
$500,000-$5 million	269,301	353,199	1 2.0	6
$5 million–50 million	38,262	580,012	1.6	11
$50 million–250 million	6,443	662,666	0.3	12
Over $250 million	2,239	3,563,433	0.1	67
Total	2,241,317	$5,348,974	100.0%	100%

Source: U.S. Internal Revenue Service, *Preliminary Report, Statistics of Income, Corporation Income Tax Returns for 1977* (Washington, D.C.: U.S. Government Printing Office, 1981).

various groupings of corporations; for example, large blocks of stock in one group are held by the Rockefellers, whereas large blocks of stock in another are held by the Du Ponts.

Furthermore, banks are interlocked with many industrial corporations to form other important groups that work in a unified manner. Within the banking system itself, there is concentration of assets. In 1968, there were 13,775 commercial banks. Of these, a mere 14 banks (not 14 percent, but just 14) held 25 percent of all deposits. The 100 largest banks held 46 percent of all deposits (see Committee on Banking and Currency, 1968: 5).

In addition to the industrial and banking sectors, the traditional small business sector of farming has become steadily more concentrated. Although the decline in the number of farms began in the late nineteenth century, there were still 6.8 million U.S. farms in 1935. Fifty years later, after millions of bankruptcies, there were only 2.2 million farms by 1985. Furthermore, giant corporate farms, constituting just 1.2 percent of the total number, produced 63.5 percent of all net farm income in 1985. If this trend continues, there will be only a little over a million U.S. farms in the year 2000—and just 50,000 will produce 75 percent of all income (Schoenbaum, 1986: B6).

Finally, it is necessary to examine all U.S. corporations, including all sectors of business. Table 7.1 shows the most recent available data. The corporations below $5 million in assets include 98 percent of all corporations (2,194,373 corporations), but they have only 10 percent of all corporate assets. The corporations above $250 million in assets include only one-tenth of 1 percent of all corporations (2,239 corporations), but they hold 67 percent of all corporate assets,

All of this data leads to the conclusion that economic concentration among U.S. corporations is very high. Aggregate economic concentration among U.S. corporations, as defined by the percentage held by the one thousand largest corporations, increased considerably in the 1970s. Industrial concentration, defined as the percentage of sales held by the top four in each industry, is much less clear in its trend, but did show a slight average increase in the last available data (though even this is controversial and depends on definitions). With these facts in mind, one can examine some of the reasons for increasing concentration of U.S. corporations.

The Reasons for Monopoly

The fundamental cause of the emergence of the giant corporation is the economy of scale to be derived from large-size production units. Large-scale production turns out cheaper goods by using more specialized machinery, more specialized workers, and mass production assembly lines. Given this situation, competition causes monopoly. "The battle of competition is fought by cheapening of commodities. The cheapness of commodities depends, ceteris paribus, on the productiveness of labor, and this again on the scale of production . . . it always ends in the ruin of many smaller capitalists, whose capitals partly pass into the hands of their conquerors, partly vanish" (Marx, 1867: 686–87). The large firm has the technology to sell at a lower price while making more profit. In addition to improved technology based on the economies of scale, there are other reasons for the greater profitability of huge firms such as General Motors. These firms grow internally or by merger far beyond the technologically necessary minimum because they wish to exercise monopoly power over the market. With small competitors eliminated or dominated, the few remaining giant firms can restrict output and set higher prices to make higher profit rates. Moreover, they can plan with more certainty over a longer period of time with less risk.

This elimination of risk and uncertainty entails not only control of their own industry's output but also control (or ownership) of suppliers, control (or ownership) of dealers and outlets for the finished product, vast nationwide advertising, and link-up with banks and other financial sources. In addition to nationwide advertising and control of retail outlets, there are other economies of scale in selling. For example, Litton Industries maintains a flock of ex-army officers, so they can sell to the Pentagon "more efficiently" than the small companies it bought up could do alone. With these motivations, there is no clear upper limit to desirable size. The motto seems to be "the bigger the better."

Prices and Profit Maximization

What is the effect of monopoly on the price structure? The essence of the monopolist's position is his or her ability to keep competitors out of the market by greater efficiency, or by control of natural or financial resources, or by control of patents, or by any other legal or illegal methods. Thus, monopoly can charge what the market will bear, and there are only limited competitive mechanisms to bring monopoly's higher profit rates back down to the average rate of profit in all industry.

Although the monopoly firm can make a higher than average rate of profit, the firm cannot make profit out of thin air. Total profit still remains within the limits of the total surplus value produced by the working class. Of course, in terms of the labor theory of value, monopoly power means that prices deviate still further from the values of particular commodities. One way to rescue the labor theory of value is by arguing that monopoly does not affect aggregate prices or aggregate profits, but only redistributes the aggregate profits. "The monopoly price of certain commodities would merely transfer a portion of the profit of the other producers of commodities to the commodities with a monopoly price" (Marx, 1907: 1003). From a given amount of aggregate profits (or surplus value), monopolists may take away part of the profits of small businessmen and small farmers by their competition for the consumer dollar, or by their power to buy raw materials and food at low prices and sell finished goods at high prices to these small entrepreneurs. Marx, however, immediately qualifies this statement by admitting that monopolists may also increase the total surplus. They may do this by using their power to raise prices or to restrict money wages so as to lower the workers' real wages.

Whereas Marx thus retains clear, objective limits to monopoly power, various superficial radicals have seen no limits, except demand, to the monopoly power to raise prices. For a long time, radicals said very little about the quantification of monopoly prices. An orthodox Marxist writer of the 1950s merely wrote that monopoly prices are determined "in the manner with which we are nowadays made familiar in every economics textbook" (Meek, 1956: 292).

The modern neoclassical textbooks give the following account. Monopoly price and quantity of production are set by the monopolist, but to maximize profits, the firm can only set the quantity at the point of greatest difference between total revenue (determined by demand) and total cost. Once the quantity is set, even a monopoly can only sell at a price determined by the demand at that point. The difference from competition is that the quantity supplied is set lower so that the price is higher, and, therefore, the short-run rate of profit is higher than average. The long-run rate of profit remains higher because capital cannot freely enter the industry. (Later it will be seen that the neoclassical theory is not as useful as a mark-up theory in explaining some recent price phenomena.)

The giant corporation today is still an engine for maximizing profits as were the individual enterprises of an earlier period, but it is not used merely as an enlarged version of the personal capitalist. There are two differences: (1) it has a much longer time horizon, and (2) it is a much more rational calculator.

Having said that much, the dogmatic notion that every corporate decision is made in terms of immediate dollars-and-cents returns must be avoided. It is certainly true that a corporate management may sacrifice short-run profits to the security of their market control, to the growth of their company, and even to the somewhat vague concept of "prestige." Thus, prices are not always set as high as the market will bear. One could say that they maximize a multiple set of objectives. Equally well (since the difference is only semantic), one could emphasize that each of the other objectives is merely a rational way of achieving maximum "long-run" profits, so that is really the sole objective.

The large corporations do prevent price competition, although they compete through alleged quality differences and advertising. With no price competition, sellers of a given commodity (and its close substitutes) have an interest in seeing that the price or prices established are such as to maximize the profits of the group as a whole. In other words, each product is priced as if it were sold by a single monopoly corporation. This is the decisive fact in determining the price policies and strategies of the typical large corporation. And it means that the appropriate price theory of an economy dominated by such corporations is not competitive price theory, but monopoly price theory. What economists have hitherto treated as a special case is the general situation!

It is true that there is little open collusion in the United States because of the antitrust laws. Yet some kind of tacit collusion probably exists to a large degree in most industries. This tacit collusion reaches its most developed form in what is known as "price leadership." It is a mutual agreement for common interests in which no formal communication is necessary. In this situation, when one firm raises or lowers the price, if it is in the interest of all the others, they will follow. If they do not follow, the firm that made the first move will rescind its initial price change. It is this willingness to rescind if an initial change is not followed that distinguishes the tacit-collusion situation from the price-war situation. So long as all firms accept this convention, which is really nothing else but a corollary of the ban on price competition, it becomes easy for the group as a whole to feel its way toward the price that maximizes the industry's profit. There is the qualification that in theory pure monopoly prices move upward or downward with equal ease, whereas that is not the case today. If one seller raises the price, this cannot possibly be interpreted as an aggressive move. The worst that can happen to that firm is that the others will stand pat and it will have to rescind (or accept a smaller share of the market). In the case of a price cut, on the other hand, there is always the possibility that aggression is intended, that the cutter is trying to increase its share of the market by violating the taboo on price competition. If rivals interpret the initial move in this way, a price war with losses to all may result. Hence, everyone is more likely to be careful about lowering than raising prices. Under the present situation of oligopoly, in other words, prices tend to be stickier on the downward side than on the upward side, and this fact introduces a significant upward bias into the general price level in a monopoly capitalist economy.

Who Controls the Corporation?

Liberals agree that monopoly is an evil aspect of capitalism, but they believe the evil can be ended without ending capitalism. Some rely on stricter enforcement of the antitrust laws. Others admit that the law is plainly inadequate on the basis of all our experience but claim that the giant corporation is changing internally, so as to eliminate automatically most of its negative qualities while remaining large. Galbraith (1967), whose description of monopoly capitalism is otherwise excellent, is the leading spokesman of this latter view.

Galbraith says there is a great contradiction between the notion that the modern corporation is mostly controlled by the management and that the modern corporation nevertheless ruthlessly tries to maximize profit for the stockholders. Furthermore, he argues that the most important factor of production is no longer capital, but the specialized talent of scientists and technologists. Therefore, he claims that real power passes from stockholders and top management to the members of the technical structure (scientists and technicians). Moreover, the members of the technical structure do not get the profits that they are supposed to maximize. Since the technical structure supplies talent, not capital, why should they worry about the return to capital? He says that the modern corporation has power to shape society, but this power has been used to serve the deeper interests or goals of the technical structure, for this structure possesses the power.

Galbraith agrees that a few hundred giant corporations control the market, regulate output and prices, and exercise enormous political control. Yet by a wave of his hand he eliminates class conflict and puts the control of the corporation in the hands of all scientists and technically skilled workers. He then finds that they manage the corporation in the best interests of all society (this has been called the "soulful corporation" view). In other words, Galbraith is very critical of capitalism, especially in the tremendous centralization of the means of production, but nevertheless is apologetic in the sense that he concludes that the "industrial system" has actually solved (or is solving) its problem.

The liberal view, as expressed by Galbraith, seems to ignore the real position of modern corporate management. In the first place, the fact that so many top executives hold stock means their motivations cannot possibly be inconsistent with profit-making. For example, twenty-five General Motors officers in early 1957 owned an average of 11,500 shares each. They might not be able to affect policy even with that amount of stock in General Motors, yet each one owned roughly a half million dollars in the company, so their motivation was anything but nonprofit-directed. Moreover, a larger proportion of managers hold stock than any other group, and there are more of the managerial group in the stockholding class than any other group (see Kolko, 1962: 13).

Galbraith, of course, argues that it is not the motivation of the managers but the motivation of the technostructure that is decisive. Still, the goals of the technostructure would be the same as those of the managers, namely, survival of the firm, its growth, its independence from outside control. All these demand profit making. More importantly, it flies in the face of reality to think that the technicians control the corporations. The managers hire and fire the technicians, and not vice versa. In the end it is the boss, rather than the hired hand, who makes the decisions (and will use expert advice only to make more profitable decisions).

Monopoly and Instability

When monopoly or oligopoly became the predominant forms of business enterprise in the 1890s and 1900s, many reformist socialists such as Eduard Bernstein predicted that careful planning by these large firms would end the periodic depressions of capitalism. Of course, if all competition were eliminated and there were only one big firm in each industry, then the business cycle might disappear; it would at least have an entirely different manifestation from what we know today. This, however, has never happened. In most industries there are a few large firms with most of the assets and sales, but a very large number of small firms continue in business. There is still violent competition between small firms and large firms within the same industry, between large firms with products that are substitutes, and between all firms for the consumers' dollar. It can hardly be said that a situation of long-run industrial planning has replaced competition even if a few large firms do such planning for themselves. In this environment it is easy to understand why the prediction that the advent of trusts and oligopolies would completely eliminate the business cycle has proven false. On the contrary, the following sections show that price and profit behavior of the economy under monopoly capitalism greatly increases the dangers of instability.

Monopoly Power and Administered Prices

In the Great Depression of the 1930s (and in the smaller depression of 1938), Gardiner Means (1975) found what he called "administered" prices in the monopoly sector. In the more concentrated industries, Means discovered, prices were not set in a competitive market but were carefully administered or set in the best interests of the monopolies. He found that the competitive prices changed frequently, but that the administered or monopoly prices changed very seldom.

More specifically, prices in the competitive sector registered large declines in the depression contractions, but the administered prices in

Table 7.2

Price and Production Behavior in Depression, 1929–1932

Industry	Decline (as percentage of 1929 figures)	
	Prices	Production
Motor vehicles	12%	74%
Agricultural implements	14	84
Iron and steel	16	76
Cement	16	55
Automobile tires	25	42
Leather and leather products	33	18
Petroleum products	36	17
Textile products	39	28
Food products	39	10
Agricultural commodities	54	1

Source: National Resources Committee (under the direction of Gardiner Means), *The Structure of the American Economy* (Washington, D.C.: U.S. Government Printing Office, 1939), p. 386.

the monopoly sector declined very little. Means defines the competitive sector as the 20 percent least-concentrated industries whereas the monopoly sector is defined as the 20 percent that is most concentrated. From 1929 to 1932, prices in the more competitive sector fell 60 percent, but prices in the monopoly sector fell only 10 percent. A few prices in the monopoly sector even rose a little in the face of the Great Depression.

In the expansion of 1933 to 1937, competitive prices rose by 46 percent whereas monopoly prices rose only 10 percent. In the depression of 1937 to 1938, competitive prices fell again by 27 percent whereas monopoly prices fell only 3 percent. Monopoly prices are clearly more stable and are very resistant to the decline of demand during depressions. It will be shown that the stability (or increase) of monopoly prices is achieved at the expense of large price declines for small and competitive business, lower purchasing power for consumers, and high unemployment of workers.

Table 7.2 shows that even in the Great Depression the industries with great monopoly power lowered their prices very little. They kept prices from dropping farther only by reducing their production by very large percentages. In contrast, the more competitive sectors had no choice but to let their prices be forced down by lack of demand. Production in the competitive sector declined less, because the lower prices brought

Table 7.3

Expansion Amplitudes of Prices in Monopoly and Competitive Sectors

Dates of expansion	Prices in monopoly sector	Prices in competitive sector
October 1949–July 1953	13.6%	11.1%
May 1954–August 1957	11.0	4.6
April 1958–April 1960	2.1	3.0
February 1961–December 1969	8.3	16.3
November 1970–November 1973	10.2	23.4

Note: Expansion amplitude means rise from trough to peak as a percentage of cycle average.
Source: Kathleen A. Pulling, "Market Structure and the Cyclical Behavior of Prices and Profits," Ph.D. dissertation, University of California, Riverside, 1977, p. 194.

greater demand. The monopoly sector thus held up its prices (and profit per unit) at the expense of great decreases in production and large-scale unemployment. The competitive sector lowered production less, fired fewer workers, but suffered much greater declines in prices and profits per unit. A highly monopolized economy is thus more apt to produce high rates of unemployment in every decline.

Data for more recent business cycles show similar patterns, becoming most dramatic in the 1975 depression. The competitive sector is defined as all those industries in which concentration of sales by eight firms is under 50 percent. The monopoly sector is defined as all those industries in which concentration of sales by eight firms is over 50 percent.

The *expansion amplitude* of a price index is defined as its rise from initial trough to cycle peak as a percentage of its average level over the cycle. The average expansion amplitudes for all the prices in the monopoly sector and for all the prices in the competitive sector are given in table 7.3 for five recent expansions.

The results for the two cyclical expansions of 1949–1953 and 1954–1957 are somewhat unusual in that prices in the monopoly sector rose faster than prices in the more competitive sector. In the three later expansions, 1958–1960, 1961–1969, and 1970–1973, the prices in the more competitive sector rose faster than prices in the monopoly sector. This is the same pattern as in the expansion of 1933 to 1937. It will usually be the case that, in expansions, prices in the more competitive sector rise somewhat faster than prices in the monopoly sector. The reasons for this behavior are discussed in the next section.

Table 7.4

Contraction Amplitudes of Prices in Monopoly and Competitive Sectors

Date of contraction	Prices in monopoly sector	Prices in competitive sector
November 1948–October 1949	− 1.9%	− 7.7
July 1953–May 1954	+ 1.9	− 1.5
August 1957–April 1958	+ 0.5	− 0.3
April 1960–February 1961	+ 0.9	− 1.2
December 1969–November 1970	+ 5.9	− 3.0
November 1973–March 1975	+ 32.8	+ 11.7

Sources: Price changes for 1948–1959 and 1957–1958 from Robert Lanzillotti, Hearings before the Joint Economic Committee of the U.S. Congress, *Employment, Growth and Price Levels* (Washington, D.C.: U.S. Government Printing Office, 1959). Price changes for 1969–1970 from John Blair, "Market Power and Inflation," *Journal of Economic Issues* 8 (June 1974): 453–78. Price changes for 1960–1961 and 1973–1975 from Kathleen Pulling, "Market Structure and the Cyclical Behavior of Prices and Profits."

Of most interest, however, are the relative price behaviors in recent contractions. As noted earlier, average prices for all sectors have behaved differently in recent contractions than in all previous recessions or depressions. They have risen instead of falling, so depression and unemployment no longer guarantee an end to inflation. For this reason, significant inflation has been continuous since 1967, though at different rates. The inflation began in the "normal" way with the spending during the Vietnam War, but its persistence through periods of falling demand indicates a new kind of animal. How much of this new phenomenon is associated with the competitive sector, and how much with the monopoly sector?

Table 7.4 reveals that the pattern of the 1948 recession was the same as in the 1929 and 1937 depressions. In all three cases, monopoly prices declined a little whereas competitive prices declined an enormous amount. In the 1954, 1958, and 1961 recessions, the first indications of the new stagflation behavior appear. Competitive prices decline as usual, although by a small amount, but monopoly prices actually rise in the recessions, although again by a small amount. The new situation is very clear in the 1970 recession, in which competitive prices decline by a significant amount, whereas monopoly prices rise by a considerable amount.

Price data on the 1973–1975 depression indicate that monopoly prices rose in the depression by an astounding percentage. This very large price increase throughout the now-dominant monopoly sector caused even competitive prices to show a small rise in the depression for the first time on record. This undoubtedly caused great disruption in the competitive sector, decreased production, increased bankruptcies, and increased unemployment.

A very useful study by Schervish (1983) finds that oligopolies support their prices by drastically lowering their output and employment. Thus, over the average cyclical contraction, unemployment rose from peak to trough by 48 percent in the monopoly sector (p. 179). In the competitive sector, on the other hand, firms are forced to reduce their prices when demand declines, but this allows them to suffer a smaller decline in output and employment. Thus, over the average cyclical contraction, unemployment rose from peak to trough by only 10 percent in the competitive sector.

Explanation of Monopoly Price Behavior

In all recessions before the 1950s, prices fell. That behavior was predictable and easily explained by traditional economic theory. Neoclassical theory leads one to expect that falling demand will cause both output and prices to decline. By reducing supply and also reducing prices to sell more of the supply, the amount of output supplied is brought back into equilibrium with the demand in each industry.

Neoclassical theory does not predict rising prices (inflation) in the face of falling demand. Yet that has been the fact in the monopoly sector in the recessions of 1954, 1958, 1961, 1970, 1975, 1980, and 1982. Of course, neoclassical theory would admit that firms with monopoly power can always set prices higher if they wish to restrict their supply enough to do so. But why, in the face of falling demand, should monopolies find it profitable to reduce their production so drastically as to actually increase prices?

In most of the monopoly sector a single large firm in each industry sets prices; other firms just follow this price leader. These large corporate price leaders mostly follow a policy of marking up their price at a certain margin of profit added on to their price level. This procedure of mark-up pricing (sometimes called cost-plus pricing) by the large corporations has been confirmed by a large number of empirical investigations (see articles cited in Eichner, 1973).

The giant corporations do not maintain their short-run profit by setting prices as high as possible at any given moment. Rather, they set prices with a profit margin that will ensure their long-run maximum growth—that is, enough profit to meet fully their expected needs for growth and expansion. Each large corporation sets a target profit level based on its previous earning record and the record of the other leaders in its industry.

What happens if a giant corporation finds its sales revenue falling in a recession? The firm will try to regain enough revenue to reach its target profit by higher price mark-ups in the remaining sales. This process has been illustrated very well in an arithmetic example by Wachtel and Adelsheim:

> For example, say a firm operating in a concentrated industry has direct costs (raw material and labor) of $200 per unit of output and sets its profit markup above direct costs at 20 percent, therefore selling the product for $240 per unit and making a profit of $40 per unit. Let us say the firm has a target level of $40,000; to realize this profit level it will have to sell 1,000 units at $240 per unit. Now we have unemployment and a recession which causes the volume of sales to fall, say, to 950 units. But if the firm still has a target level of $40,000, which it wishes to attain, it will have to raise its prices to slightly over $242 per unit. . . . It does this by raising its percentage markup over costs to 21 percent compared to the previous 20 percent. Having increased their profit per unit, the firm now achieves its target profit level, but the resultant manifestation in the economy is the simultaneous occurrence of inflation and unemployment. (1976: 1)

This illustration assumes little or no further decrease in demand when the price is marked up. But Wachtel and Adelsheim point out that their conclusion—that monopolies will raise prices in a recession by implementing these policies—holds true even if the price increases cause some further decreases in demand. Of course, even the tightest monopoly or oligopoly will lose some customers from any price rise, but most of them have a strong enough market control—and a strong enough image from advertising—that they will not lose many customers. Just how high a price they can set is a function of their degree of monopoly power, a power that is roughly reflected in their high degree of industrial concentration, but has other aspects as well.

More specifically, their degree of monopoly power over price has three main constraints. First, if the industry raises its price (led by the price leader), how many customers are willing or able to switch to a substitute product? Second, if the price is raised and if this leads to a higher profit margin, how many new firms will be able to enter the industry, that is, how high are the barriers to entry to such new entrants? Third, what is the realistic likelihood of any government intervention if the price gouging becomes very obvious?

It follows from this mark-up or cost-plus behavior that such oligopoly firms do not change their prices as frequently as competitive firms. Even if there is a rapid price and cost inflation, these firms usually keep one price for quite a time, while attempting to gain good will and increasing their share of the market. If costs rise, they will raise their prices only high enough to make their usual profit margin above costs. Thus, there is considerable evidence that in periods of business expansion and rapid inflation, it is the prices of the more competitive firms that rise rapidly from day to day.

In a recession, however, the small, competitive firms are immediately forced to drop their prices as demand falls (since no one of them can restrict the industry supply) regardless of the effect on their profit rates. Not so the large, oligopoly firms. In the recession, if their costs remain the same (as they do in physical terms over a wide range of output), then they can and will adjust their prices so as to maintain total profits as near constant as possible. Of course, that entails extra reduction of production and unemployment of many more workers than in a similar competitive industry, but that is not their worry.

Monopoly and Profit Rates

If our economy operated under pure and perfect competition, then capital would flow immediately from areas of low profit rates to areas of high profit rates. It follows that the rate of profit would be equal in all industries. The rate of profit, however, is not equal in all industries. It is consistently higher in industries with greater monopoly power.

Once again, define a *concentration ratio* as the percentage of industry sales controlled by the eight largest firms. The ratio for each industry group is a weighted average of the ratios in each of its component industries. The monopoly sector is defined as all those industry groups over 50 percent concentration in all the census years from 1949 to 1973, whereas the more competitive sector is all those groups under 50 percent concentration in all the census years from 1949 to 1973. The rate of profit used here is the percentage of profit to sales in each industry group. Other studies have found the exact same results when the rate of profit is defined as the percentage of profits to owner's capital or to all capital (including borrowed capital,

Table 7.5

Monopoly Power and Profit Rates, 1972

Industry Group	Concentration ratio	Profit rate
Monopoly Sector		
Motor vehicles	88%	8.7%
Tobacco	87	11.3
Instruments	65	13.9
Primary nonferrous metals	64	5.6
Electrical machinery	62	7.1
Primary iron and steel	56	5.0
Chemicals	55	11.3
Petroleum and coal products	55	8.3
Average		8.9%
More Competitive Sector		
Food	49%	4.7%
Paper	47	6.8
Textiles	46	4.7
Leather	41	5.1
Fabricated metals	39	6.5
Apparel	33	4.3
Lumber	31	8.0
Furniture	29	6.7
Printing and publishing	29	8.7
Average		6.2%

Source: U.S. Federal Trade Commission data on profits and U.S. Census Bureau data on concentration, compiled by Kathleen Pulling, ''Cyclical Behavior of Prices and Profits.''

see, e.g., Sherman, 1968: ch. 3).

Table 7.5 shows the results for 1972. The average rate of profit on sales for the monopoly sector (over 50 percent concentration) was 11.2 percent for the average of the years from 1949 to 1973. The average rate of profit on sales for the more competitive sector (under 50 percent concentration) was only 6.2 percent for the average of the years from 1949 to 1973 (see Pulling, 1977; 1978).

Why does the monopoly sector have higher profit rates than the competitive sector? In the first place, monopoly power means the ability to restrict supply and keep prices higher than in the competitive sector. The higher prices mean lower real wages for all worker-consumers. The profits of small, competitive business and farmers are also hurt by monopoly prices to the extent that they must purchase producer goods from the monopoly sector. Some large firms in the monopoly sector also have extra market power as large buyers of commodities from small competitive business, forcing down the prices charged by these small suppliers.

Large firms in the monopoly sector may also have extra power in the labor market, so they may add to profits by buying labor at a rate lower than the average wage. This factor may, of course, be somewhat offset by trade union action. In the modern world, wages are not automatically determined by supply and demand in the market. They are determined by the bargaining strength of capital and labor (under given conditions of supply and demand), with monopoly capital usually in the stronger position. Workers are thus squeezed from both sides by monopoly. On the one hand, the monopolies can pay lower money wages by exerting their power in the labor market. On the other hand, monopolies can charge workers higher prices as consumers.

Additional monopoly profits come from lucrative government military contracts, which are financed from the workers' tax money, thus again increasing total profits. Extra-high returns from foreign investments abroad also add to monopoly profits; that is, profits are extracted from workers in foreign countries. In summary, monopolies or oligopolies make profit far above the average rate in several ways: selling at higher prices to consumers, thereby lowering the real wage; selling at higher prices to small business and farmers; buying at lower prices from small business and farmers; buying labor power at lower wages from workers; selling to the government at higher prices; and buying labor power and materials at lower prices in foreign countries. Through these relatively high prices and low costs (always relative to a competitive firm in the same situation), the monopoly or oligopoly firms extract more profits from the worker-consumer-taxpayer here and abroad; they also transfer some profits from small business and farmers to themselves.

Table 7.6 shows the profit rate on the capital investment of all stockholders averaged for the years 1956 through 1975. Each group of corporations is shown by the size of total assets, from the smallest (below a million) to the largest (over a billion). The relationship in table 7.6 is very clear. The profit rate on investment rises monotonically as the size of the corporation increases.

The fact that the profit rate rises with size is explained by all the reasons given earlier for the fact that the profit rate rises with monopoly power. To a large extent, large size means monopoly power—though

Table 7.6

Long-Run Profit Rate on Investment for All U.S. Manufacturing Corporations, 1956–1975 Average

Size (by assets)		Profit rate (profit before taxes divided by stockholders' capital)
$0–	$1,000,000	3.7%
1,000,000–	5,000,000	5.3
5,000,000–	10,000,000	6.7
10,000,000–	50,000,000	7.4
50,000,000–	100,000,000	8.1
100,000,000–	1,000,000,000	8.8
$1,000,000,000	and over	11.7

Source: U.S. Federal Trade Commission, *Quarterly Reports of U.S. Manufacturing Corporations* (Washington, D.C.: U.S. Government Printing Office, 1956–1975).

there are industries where there are so many giant firms that the concentration ratio by four or eight appears low, and there are industries small enough for a medium-sized firm to have monopoly power. Moreover, when we examine behavior by size alone, this eliminates some of the distortion of the concentration ratios caused by one conglomerate's controlling subsidiaries in a number of different industries. The large size also directly affects profitability through economies of scale in production, in distribution, and in nationwide advertising. The large manufacturing corporation may also own its own natural resources. Moreover, the large corporation may have much cheaper access to finances either by its credit rating or by a direct tie-in with a financial institution.

Monopoly Profit Rates Over the Cycle

We have seen that the large monopoly corporations have higher profit rates in the long run than small competitive firms. We have also seen that, in expansions, the large monopoly firms raise their prices more slowly in order to increase their share of the market. In contractions, the large monopoly firms keep their prices from falling or actually raise them; whereas competitive firms have to reduce prices or raise them much, much less than the monopolies. Given this difference in price conduct, what is the difference in performance of profit rates in the two sectors over the cycle? Table 7.7 shows the cyclical amplitudes of the

Table 7.7

Amplitudes of Monopoly and Competitive Profit Rates

Cycle	Monopoly sector		Competitive sector	
	Average expansion	Amplitude in contraction	Average expansion	Amplitude in contraction
1949–1954	32.1	−30.8	45.8	−56.9
1954–1958	21.6	−41.3	32.1	−47.8
1958–1961	33.5	−28.6	36.6	−47.1
1961–1970	25.0	−35.1	49.0	−32.3
Average	28.0	−34.0	−40.9	−46.0

Source: Federal Trade Commission data compiled by Kathleen Pulling, ''Market Structure and Cyclical Behavior of Prices and Profits.''

monopoly and competitive profit rates.

In table 7.7, the monopoly sector includes all major industry groups with concentration ratios greater than 50 percent in all of the Census of Manufactures years, 1954, 1958, 1967, and 1972. The competitive sector includes those groups of less than 50 percent in all the same years. An expansion amplitude measures the increase from trough to peak as a percentage of the cycle average. The contraction amplitude is the final trough minus the peak as a percentage. The profit rate is the total profit divided by sales (but very similar results have been found using the profit rate on capital). All manufacturing corporations are included in the groups examined.

It may be seen quite clearly that the profit rates in the more competitive sector normally rise and fall more violently than profit rates in the monopoly sector—which parallels their price behavior. Profit rates in the more competitive sector of manufacturing rose faster than in the monopoly sector in four out of four expansions from 1949 to 1970. And profit rates in the more competitive sector fell further in three out of four contractions.

If one examines the cyclical amplitude of profit rates by size of corporation, the pattern is very similar. Table 7.8 reveals that the profit rates of the larger corporations rise less in expansions and fall less in contractions than the profit rates of the smaller corporations. When these findings are combined with the similar findings of table 7.7 on monopoly and competitive sectors, the conclusion is that the profit rates of large monopoly corporations are far more stable than those of small competitive corporations.

Table 7.8

Amplitude of Profit Rates by Size

A. Average of Three Cycles, 1949–1970

Asset size	Expansion amplitude	Contraction amplitude
(lower limit)	+83%	−83%
$250,000	+39	−55
$1 million	+37	−52
$5 million	+28	−27
$100 million	+22	−27

B. Cycle of 1970–1975

Asset size	Expansion amplitude	Contraction amplitude
$0	+87	−22
$1 million	+36	−24
$5 million	+22	−13
$10 million	+27	−18
$50 million	+29	−10
$100 million	+12	−5
$250 million	+13	−8
$1 billion	+22	−5

Note: Profit on sales of all U.S. manufacturing corporations.
Source: Federal Trade Commission, *Quarterly Financial Reports of Manufacturing Corporations* (Washington, D.C.: U.S. Government Printing Office, 1949-1976).

Why do the large monopoly corporations have more stable profit rates in both boom and bust? First, they attempt to set their prices so as to maintain a stable profit rate. Second, their monopoly power allows them to set their prices at those levels. They maintain those prices in contractions by restricting their production (and employment). In expansion, they raise prices only slowly while rapidly increasing their production (and employment) to obtain or keep a high share of the expanding market. Third, the costs per unit of the largest corporations remain fairly constant over a wide range of output below full capacity. The unit costs of small corporations rise rapidly when they drop below optimum capacity. Fourth, the unchanging interest burden of small as compared to large corporations is greater both because they pay higher interest rates and because they borrow a higher percentage of their capital. Fifth, and very important, the small corporations have all their eggs in one basket (with no reserves) whereas the large conglomerates are very diversified, with some investments in industries that may happen to grow despite a contraction (and an ability to shift reserve capital from one area to another).

It appears that the increased monopolization of the economy does mean stability in the sector of high monopoly power, but further destabilizes the competitive sector. And the instability of the competitive sector is the prime factor setting off each new crisis of overproduction and contraction.

Monopoly and Waste

Production does not reach optimum efficiency below some crucial size. Thus, the increase in importance of large firms does mean that most of the economy has the ability to produce at lower costs than ever before. Of course, the very large firms also have disproportionately larger research facilities and hold a very large proportion of all unexpired patents. Therefore, they have the most potential for efficiency improvement. Moreover, many investment projects are simply too large for small firms.

On the other hand, the large, entrenched firm stands to lose most by the obsolescence of present machinery. It also loses most from such product improvements as will reduce the number of units that the customer need buy—for example, a longer-lasting light bulb. Therefore, if the large firm has an oligopoly position and faces no serious competitive pressure for improvement, it may hide away and not use many important new inventions. Oligopoly power may also be used to restrict supply in order to maintain prices. Oligopolies will expand production as rapidly as possible only in the unusual periods of unlimited demand, such as the Second World War. Monopoly capitalism has paradoxical effects on innovation; it has a rapid rate of technological progress but retains a large amount of technologically obsolete equipment.

Moreover, it has been shown that the existence of economic concentration may have increased the severity and possibly the number of depressions because of its destabilizing effects on the remaining small businesses. If this is so, then unless it has had a fully offsetting effect in increasing growth during prosperity, it would seem that this is another reason why the net effect of oligopoly may be to lower the rate of economic growth. This is not to say, of course, that breaking up large firms into smaller units would increase economic growth. Reduction of the American economy to small firms only would certainly cause a major decrease of economic efficiency, in addition to its probable negative effects on investment.

The rate of growth (and waste) under monopoly capitalism is also affected by the fact that the sales effort has greatly expanded. From being a relatively unimportant feature of the system, it has grown to the status of one of its decisive nerve centers. Impact on the economy is outranked only by militarism. In all other aspects of social existence, its all-pervasive influence is second to none. In an economic system in which competition is fierce and relentless, but in which the small number of rivals rules out price cutting, advertising becomes to an ever-increasing extent the principal weapon of the competitive struggle. There is little room under atomistic competition for advertising, whereas in monopoly it is one of the most important factors in the firm's survival. Relatively large firms are in a position to exercise a powerful influence upon the market for their output by establishing and maintaining a pronounced difference between their products and those of their competitors. This differentiation is sought chiefly by means of advertising, trademarks, brand names, distinctive packaging, and product variation. If successful, it leads to a condition in which the differentiated products cease, in the view of consumers, to serve as close substitutes for each other.

Several studies have demonstrated that advertising involves a massive waste of resources, a continual drain on the consumer's income, and a systematic destruction of the consumer's freedom of choice between genuine alternatives (see Baran and Sweezy, 1966: 122ff.). Furthermore, advertising in all its aspects cannot be meaningfully dealt with as some undesirable excrescence on the economic system which could be removed if we would only make up our minds to get rid of it. Advertising is the very offspring of monopoly capitalism, the inevitable by-product of the decline of price competition; it constitutes as much an integral part of the system as the giant corporation itself. The economic importance of advertising lies not primarily in its causing a reallocation of consumers' expenditures among different commodities, but in its effect on the magnitude of aggregate effective demand and thus on the level of income and employment. In other words, it generates useless expenditures, both by capitalists and by consumers, that soak up part of the "overproduction" of monopoly capitalism.

Advertising affects profits in two ways. The first effect is the fact that part of advertising and other selling expenses are paid for through an increase in the prices of consumer goods bought by productive workers. Their real wages are reduced by this amount, and profit is correspondingly increased. The other effect is that some capitalists make profits from the business of advertising. At the same time, advertising constitutes an expense for other capitalists. Thus, advertising costs redistribute profits from one capitalist to another. Some individuals living off profits are deprived of a fraction of their incomes in order to support other individuals living off profits, namely those who derive their incomes from the profits in the advertising industry itself.

A main function of advertising, perhaps its dominant function today, is to wage a relentless war on behalf of the producers and sellers of consumers' goods, against saving and in favor of consumption. Actually, much of the "newness" with which the consumer is systematically bombarded is either fraudulent or related trivially, and in many cases even negatively, to the function and serviceability of the product. Moreover, there are other products introduced that are indeed new in design and appearance but serve essentially the same purposes as old products they are intended to replace. The extent of the difference can vary all the way from a simple change in packaging to the far-reaching and enormously expensive annual changes in automobile models.

Furthermore, most research and development programs, which constitute a multibillion dollar effort in the United States, are more closely related to the production of salable goods than to the much touted mission of advancing science and technology. For example, yearly changes in automobile styles are enormously expensive, amounting sometimes to 1 to 2 percent or more of gross national product (see Baran and Sweezy, 1966: 128–29). Yet these style changes have helped very little toward safety, durability, or reduction of gas consumption— GM and Chrysler are still fighting attempts to make them follow the laws on reduction of gas consumption (though they are still way behind the Japanese). When we include not only automobiles but all consumer goods, the total amount of waste from all the time and effort devoted directly and indirectly to selling products under monopoly capitalism must considerably lower the potential rate of economic growth.

Not only does monopoly capitalism greatly increase the waste of capitalism, but it raises pollution and environmental destruction to a new level. In the competitive model, apologists could claim that what was produced was according to the consumers' preferences, so pollution was merely an unfortunate by-product of public demand (an "external diseconomy''). These unfortunate by-products of public preferences could be handled by some minor public action in beautifying the environment. Under monopoly capitalism the ''preferences'' are manipulated and directed toward whatever products are most profitable to produce. Therefore, under monopoly capitalism ''environmental damage becomes a normal consequence of the conflict between the goals of the producing firm and those of the public'' (Galbraith, 1970: 477).

Suggested Readings

In addition to the works by Blair, Pulling, Shepherd, and Baran and Sweezy cited above, there is an extremely useful book on monopoly by Bowring (1986). There is also an interesting left-post-Keynesian discussion of monopoly and macro instability by Sawyer (1982). The relation of finance to industrial capital is described in Kotz (1978). An excellent survey of the literature on the theory of monopoly capitalism is by Foster (1986).

— 8 —

CAPITALISM AND THE STATE

There are three different views among economists and political scientists concerning how the U.S. government is shaped and operates.

Conservative View of Government

Milton Friedman, in his *Capitalism and Freedom* (1962), makes explicit his assumption that the economic system of capitalism tends to produce a perfect political democracy. Friedman contends that the capitalist system is an economic democracy because anyone can start a business and because consumers vote with their dollars on what shall be produced. This economic democracy of capitalism is the perfect base for a political democracy because it does away with all interfering bureaucrats. Thus, the United States enjoys a political democracy based on capitalism. Every citizen has an equal vote. Every citizen has an equal right to publish a newspaper or own a TV station without interference or censorship.

The Friedman position has frequently been criticized. "Anyone" cannot start a business in the United States because most people do not have the capital to start a business. Consumers vote with their dollars, but consumers with a million dollars outvote consumers with a thousand dollars by a thousand times. Consumer votes reflect the enormous inequality of our society, so a few can "vote" successfully for mink coats and Cadillacs whereas many do not have enough votes for sufficient milk and shoes for their children.

Less than 1 percent of Americans control a majority of corporate stock. One thousand corporations control two-thirds of corporate assets. Those thousand corporations make most of the economic decisions in the United States on hiring and firing workers, what products to produce, where to locate, and what prices to charge. Those thousand corporations are controlled by boards of directors who are mostly old, white, and male. Most directors are on several boards, so the total number of directors on these boards constitutes a remarkably small number of decision makers. In this sense, the United States is an economic oligarchy, a small number of decision makers selected only because of their wealth.

Moreover, this economic oligarchy has not produced a perfect democracy. Although all citizens may have a vote, their political power is not equal but is weighted by their wealth, as described in detail later. Nor is there equal freedom of the press. Most citizens cannot publish a newspaper or own a TV station because this requires millions of dollars. Thus, it will be argued that capitalist economic power places severe limitations on political democracy, even in the few capitalist countries where the forms exist.

As evidence that capitalism leads to political democracy, conservatives like Friedman argue that political democratic forms do exist in the capitalist countries of North America, Western Europe, and Japan. They emphasize the fact that the so-called socialist countries of Eastern Europe, the Soviet Union, China, and Cuba have undemocratic forms of government. They ignore, however, the contrary evidence. The overwhelming majority of all capitalist countries are political dictatorships. These countries—mostly developing countries in Asia, Africa, and Latin America—are either military dictatorships or one-party dictatorships. These capitalist countries with dictatorships, such as Chile, are no more democratic than many so-called socialist countries, such as China. There have also been dictatorships in developed capitalist countries, such as Japan, Germany, and Italy. Moreover, there are some countries with self-defined socialist governments, such as France or Sweden, that have democratic political processes.

Conservatives like Milton Friedman do make some major exceptions to the rule that the U.S. government serves the best interests of everyone. Government makes many mistakes. For example, government may reduce the money supply, causing the Great Depression of the 1930s, and may repeat this mistake periodically, causing recessions. Or government may increase the money supply too rapidly over many years, causing inflation. The mistakes are usually made by misguided liberal governments. Liberals act for political gain based on the short-run interest of corrupt unions or of the lazy unemployed. Conservative economists claim that the actions of liberal governments hurt everyone in the long run, including even union members and the unemployed (e.g., by easy money leading to inflation).

It is natural for conservatives to think that misguided government itself is the cause of most macroeconomic problems because they believe Adam Smith's theory that competition in the market produces the highest quality, the best mix, the most productivity, and the most growth. They also believe Say's law that in an unregulated market aggregate demand must always adjust to aggregate supply in the private sector. As everyone knows, this results in their view that the best government role in the economy is no government role. One should note, however, that the conservatives have many, many exceptions to the rule that less government is better. The exceptions include a huge military complex, a large police force, harsh sentences for not following social dictates (e.g., smoking marijuana), prohibiting some choices (e.g., women's choice of abortion), punishment for dissenting views (e.g., anti-Communist oaths), and welfare payments to business (e.g., subsidies to tobacco growers). The economic exceptions, which allow conservative governments to practice a great deal of active intervention, are all based on "remedying previous liberal mistakes," for example, reducing the taxes of the rich, ending welfare, giving more money to police and military.

The Liberal View: Keynesians and Pluralists

Liberal economists like John Maynard Keynes tend to reject the extreme Adam Smith view of automatic optimal behavior by private business, and they reject Say's law, so they do believe there are many inequities and many macro problems generated by capitalism. They fervently hope and believe that government can and will solve these problems.

In the liberal view, Herbert Hoover simply lacked the knowledge of how to eliminate unemployment, which liberal economists can now furnish the government. Liberal economists, therefore, tend to be much greater defenders of the virtues of government and its programs than are conservative economists. They implicitly accept the popular American myth that the U.S. government results from a perfect democracy and serves the best interests of everyone. If pushed, they will agree that some politicians (like Ronald Reagan) serve "special interests." They strongly defend the notion, however, that all such "political" problems should be left to political scientists (in spite of the all-important role of government in the U.S. economy) and should not be considered by economic theory.

The dominant school in American political science is the liberal pluralist school. The pluralists assert that the U.S. government is not a class dictatorship but a democracy reflecting many different interest groups, and that power is not held by one group but plurally by many groups. They assert that the "power structure of the United States is highly complex and diversified (rather than unitary and monolithic), that the political system is more or less democratic . . . , that in political processes the political elite is ascendant over and not subordinate to the economic elite" (Rose, 1967: 492). Notice that in arguing for the proposition that America is democratic in nature, the pluralists find it necessary to emphasize that political power is to a large degree independent of and superior to economic power. The reason for this insistence is that economic power is so extremely unequally distributed. If political power exactly followed economic power, the degree of inequality would leave little to be called "democracy."

The interest groups discussed by the pluralists are very different from the classes discussed by Marxists. Pluralists have a long list of interest groups, including not only rich and poor, debtors and creditors, unions and big business, but also advocates of gun control and the National Rifle Association, women's rights groups and antifeminist groups, Protestants, Jews, Catholics, and so forth. The pluralist view is that all of these compete in the political arena. The democratic process chooses representatives from among them all according to their success with the voters. The resulting government compromises and reconciles all the competing interests.

For those pluralists who stop at this point, it is a complex way of arriving at almost the same conclusion as the simplistic view that the U.S. government serves everyone's interests. Most sophisticated pluralists, however, do go somewhat further. They ask why one group is more successful than another. Most of those asking this question more or less agree that economic power has something to do with the political results. (For a powerful critique of pluralism by a former pluralist, see Lindblom, 1977; for an excellent Marxist critique, see Miliband, 1969.)

The Radical or Marxist View

Radicals recognize that one cannot study political power without studying economic power, and vice versa. The most vulgar and dogmatic Marxists go to the other extreme, arguing that economics determines everything and that politics is completely subordinate. They love to quote one line that Marx and Engels wrote in *The Communist Manifesto*: "The executive power of the modern state is simply a committee for managing the common affairs of the entire bourgeois class." In the literal, dogmatic interpretation, this statement says that freedom of speech does no good, that elections can change nothing, that workers can have no influence and can achieve no major reforms in capitalism. Marx himself had a very sophisticated and complex view of political sociology (see Avineri, 1968; Draper, 1977; Szymanski, 1978; and Carnoy, 1984). It is a view quite different from some of the vulgarized versions that often pass for Marxism. Where vulgar Marxists usually speak of only two classes fighting for political power, every one of Marx's own analyses—including detailed political studies of France, England, Germany, and the United States—specified numerous subclasses, remnants of classes, in-between or middle classes, and strife between factions of a single class. Where vulgar Marxists assume that capitalist governments bear a one-to-one relation to the economic interest of "the capitalist class," Marx shows that governments do have a certain limited autonomy from the dominant class and that politics represent a tangled skein of long-run and short-run interests of a wide variety of different classes and different factions within classes.

To begin with, Marx argues that there are two aspects to the origin and functioning of the state. He uses the term *the state* to mean all the power structures of government (everything from the police functions to the propaganda functions of "public relations" personnel). Marx contends that one source of the origin of state power was the need for control of some common functions in the interest of the whole community; for example, in ancient Egypt it was necessary to control the Nile and irrigation. A second source of the origin of state power was the need by the ruling class, as in ancient Egypt, to hold down and repress the slave class in order to exploit the slave's labor. All U.S. government functions today still have these two aspects: common functions for the community and class functions for the ruling class. For example, the building of highways serves the whole community, but the question of which highways and how many highways is largely determined by the profit goals of the automobile industry and the construction industry (both of which maintain huge lobbies at the federal and state levels).

Marx was also very critical of theorists who insist that there always has been and always will be an elite of rulers and an oppressed mass of ruled. Marx and Engels were among the first to take seriously the findings of anthropology that many primitive societies are built around the extended family or clan, have no government in the modern sense, and certainly no police or other repressive forces. Marx said that this absence of a repressive state was due to the fact that there was no class division. People were elected for temporary leadership of community functions, but there was no need for repression because there was no exploited class.

The goal of Marxists is a communist society in which there will again be no classes, no ruling elite, voluntary cooperation by all, and no repressive state machinery. As the first step in this direction, Marx advocated democratic socialism as the only consistent form of democracy. He pointed out that capitalist states have the forms of democracy in the political sphere, but that the dictatorship of a small number of capitalists in the economic sphere extends their power in substance to the political sphere as well. Socialism means a society of democracy in substance as well as in form because the democratically elected government will own and control the economy. This direction over the lives of the people is taken away from a few capitalists and exercised by all of the people (that is, the working class).

Official Marxists argue as if the capitalist class directly runs the government of capitalist countries. Marx, on the contrary, emphasized that the actual day-to-day running of the government is usually left to a specialized group (politicians, employed in the same way that engineers are employed) and that capitalist control is indirect. Nor is the control exercised by a conspiracy, but by the built-in structural features of the whole system and its institutions. Marx emphasized in his writings a long list of means by which capitalists exercise control. These means are mostly indirect and mostly accomplished by peaceful propaganda and economic means.

The Marxist Debate on the State

Marxists and other radical economists have recently spent a great deal of time debating a proper theory of the state because: (1) Stalinism distorted and prevented reasonable discussion on the left for many decades; (2) the state is growing much more powerful in the United States, Japan, and Western Europe than it was; and (3) dictatorship prevails, not only in most underdeveloped capitalist countries, but also in all of the so-called socialist countries. These debates are discussed briefly here, but they are discussed in detail with great clarity in Carnoy (1984).

Instrumentalism

The simplest Marxist view is known as "instrumentalism." It sees the state as a direct instrument of the ruling class, using the state for its own benefit. It argues that capitalist wealth is used to gain many of the key positions in the state for members of the capitalist class. Since this is a very simplistic view, no known Marxist radical scholar in the United States or Western Europe admits to owning it. It is sometimes alleged that William Domhoff (1967) holds this view because he does trace the interrelationships of the ruling class in various spheres of activity and argues that there is indeed only one ruling class. Domhoff, however, specifically states that he is not an instrumentalist because he does not focus solely on the role of the capitalist elite. Rather, he sees the political sphere as one of class struggle and says that this is basic to his analysis. Domhoff has analyzed labor laws in this perspective and sees a complex three-way relation between labor, business, and government.

Gramsci

To see how the strong Marxist reaction against instrumentalism has evolved, one must begin with Antonio Gramsci (1971, written in the 1920s). Gramsci argues that the most important weapon of capitalist dominance is the "hegomony" of bourgeois values and ideology. He sees the state as a key factor in supporting bourgeois hegemony. Thus, the state is viewed as something more than a mere instrument of violence, as is often stressed in official Marxism. Gramsci's spotlight here is on thought and how the state affects thought and how thought affects the state; he disowns any simplistic economic determinism. It is through the culture (or superstructure) that the ruled come to accept a conception of the world put forth by the rulers. And it is this conception that keeps the rulers in power. This emphasis on spelling out the importance and the details of the ideological process is the most vital contribution of Gramsci.

Structuralism

Althusser (1971) argues that political economy should not study human psychology, but social structures. The function of government is to reproduce and protect the relations of production. The state has a repressive apparatus consisting of the government, army, police, courts, prisons, and so forth. Yet the state also has ideological functions (a la Gramsci). The state operates to support capitalist ideology through the educational system, political parties, trade unions, the legal system, churches, the media, and the cultural system (even though most of these are formally separate from the state).

Poulantzas's early work (1969a) is also structuralist, arguing that the state is part of the class relations of production. The state, through its laws and ideology, isolates workers into individuals to prevent working class consciousness; it also uses patriotism to instill a national consciousness. The state is both a product of class struggle and a shaper of class struggle (but it is not itself a place of class struggle). Poulantzas's later work (1978) argues that the class struggle also takes place within the state apparatus.

There have been further contributions to the debates by Poulantzas (1969b) and Miliband (1973; 1977) as well as contributions by E. Atwatter, Claus Offe, and James O'Connor, all reported in detail in Carnoy (1984). One may summarize the literature by saying that the long decades of Soviet domination and stultification of Marxist theory of the state have suddenly given way to a blossoming of huge amounts of discussion in Western Europe and the United States. The debates are still underway to shape a new independent Marxist or radical view of the state, but they have certainly not yet been resolved. Some specific issues may now be examined in detail.

The Conflict Between Capitalism and Democracy

Perhaps the best answer to Milton Friedman's argument that capitalism is an excellent foundation for democracy is provided in a book by Bowles and Gintis (1986). They point out that capitalism means the rule of a small elite in the economy—and that capitalism keeps spreading to new realms, such as preparation of food by restaurants and fast food places rather than in the family. They point out that democracy means the rule of all the people—and that democratic processes keep spreading into new realms, such as suffrage for women or workers' control of enterprises. Thus there is a conflict between capitalism (control by a small elite) and democracy (control by all the people).

The conflict has been reflected in the fear expressed by the rich that, in a democracy, the propertyless majority might vote to take over the economy and the wealth. Thus, in the nineteenth century most countries with "democracy" restricted voting to those people with a certain amount of property. Also, the U.S. system of checks and balances was partly designed to prevent rash actions by the democratic majority. In the last fifty years the U.S. government has also placated the majority by welfare spending and employment stimulation.

Bowles and Gintis further point out that economic wealth gives power over jobs, investment, and the media, which leads to extra political power for the elite. Finally, since capitalists control investment, they can have a capital strike or threaten it unless policies favorable to capital are enacted. These issues are examined in detail below.

The Importance of Class

The radical view emphasizes that economic inequality does lead to political inequality. The institutions of the United States are democratic in form, but not in content, because of differences in economic power. Thus, a millionaire who owns a newspaper chain has only the same formal political rights as an unemployed poor worker, but surely their actual political influence is very different. Domhoff discusses

> the existence of a national upperclass that meets generally accepted definitions of social class . . . that this upperclass owns a disproportionate amount of the country's wealth and receives a disproportionate amount of its yearly income, and that [its] members . . . control the major banks and corporations, which . . . dominate the American economy . . . that [its] members . . . and their high-level corporation executives control the foundations, the elite universities, the largest of the mass media, . . . the Executive branch of the federal government . . . regulatory agencies, the federal judiciary, the military, the CIA, and the FBI. (1967: 10–11)

The radical hypothesis is that class interests play a major role in political behavior; the most powerful economic class, the capitalist class, dominates the political system; most of those elected are capitalists or, more importantly, subservient to capitalist interests; and the outcomes of the political process are mostly favorable to the capitalist class because of (a) their domination of the process and (b) the structural features that set the limits of policy (see, e.g., Domhoff, 1967; 1970; 1978; 1979; Parenti, 1977; Szymanski, 1978).

Two mainstream political scientists, Irish and Prothro, summarizing a great deal of empirical data, say that "class, whether determined by personal feelings or by educational and occupational status, is an essential concept for understanding political differences" (1965: 175). Of course, a great many other socioeconomic factors affect political differences, including racial and religious background, friends and community, union membership (obviously related to class), family tradition, and upbringing in one political ideology or party affiliation. Family influence has been emphasized in a study that found that 80 percent of American voters cast their first vote for the same party as their parents did (ibid.: 170). Furthermore, the amount of education, which is partly determined by class, has a striking effect on opinions, changing them quite significantly (ibid.: 174).

Class differences affect political behavior in many ways, of which the most obvious is voting behavior. Using the crudest indicator of class, the income of individuals, a leading liberal sociologist found that "More than anything else the party struggle is a conflict among classes . . . the lower income groups vote mainly for the parties of the left, while the higher income groups vote mainly for parties of the right" (Lipset, 1963: 234). One study shows that in 1980 in the U.S. presidential election, Ronald Reagan received only 32 percent of the votes of the poor (lowest 10 percent of income recipients), 43 percent of the lower middle income group (11–30 percentiles), 57 percent of the middle income group (31–60 percentiles), 64 percent of the upper middle income group (61–90 percentiles), and 75 percent of the votes of the richest group (top 10 percent) (Edsall, 1986: 23).

How Economic Power Determines Political Results

We have seen that an individual's political behavior is strongly influenced by class background. But that leads to a puzzle. If a majority of the people are in the the working class and everyone has one vote, how is it that parties favorable to the working class do not win every election? How come government policies usually do not represent working class desire, but the overwhelming influence of the capitalist class? More precisely, given formal democracy and capitalism, exactly how does the extreme economic inequality tend to be translated into inequality of political power?

In the first place, there is the simple fact that the degree of political participation tends to vary with class background. "The average citizen has little interest in public affairs, and he expends his energy on the daily round of life—eating, working, family talk, looking at the comics [today, TV], sex, sleeping" (Irish and Prothro, 1965: 165). More exactly, in a 1964 study, 86 percent of those identified as middle class voted, but only 72 percent of the working class voted (and that percentage has declined since then). Similarly, 40 percent of the middle class had talked to others about voting for a party or candidate, but only 24 percent in the working class had. Among the middle class people interviewed, 16 percent gave money to a political cause, 14 percent attended political meetings, and 8 percent worked for a party or candidate; in the working class, figures on the same activities were only 4, 5, and 3 percent (ibid.: 38).

Thus, political participation of all kinds rises in the capitalist class and middle class but drops in the working class. Some of the reasons are obvious. Lower-income workers have less leisure time, less money above minimum needs, and more exhausting jobs. Furthermore, detailed studies show that the workers' lower participation also reflects less knowledge of how important the issues are because of less education and less access to information. The same studies show more "cross pressures" on workers—for example, the racial antagonisms that divide and weaken their working class outlook (ibid.: 193). By far the best study of U.S. voting from a critical perspective is the definitive book by Walter Dean Burnham (1982).

Unequal political power is also achieved by control of the "news" media. Even if the average worker "had an interest in politics, he would have great difficulty getting accurate information; since the events of politics unfold at a great distance, he cannot observe them directly, and the press offers a partial and distorted picture" (ibid.: 164). Even the quantity of news is limited. Although 80 percent of Americans read newspapers and 88 percent have TV, political news is only 2.8 percent of total newspaper space and less on TV (ibid.: 183).

If the quantity of political news is deplorable, the quality is abysmal. The first problem is that only one view is available to most people because of the increasing concentration of newspaper ownership. In 1910 some 57 percent of American cities had competing daily newspapers, but in 1980 only 3 percent had competing dailies. Furthermore, news media tend to have a conservative bias for three reasons. First, they do not want to offend anybody. Second, they especially do not want to offend major advertisers, all of whom are big businesses. Third, and most important, "since the media of communication are big businesses, too, the men who control them quite naturally share the convictions of other businessmen" (ibid.: 184).

Unequal political power is also caused by the vast difference in the influence of different pressure groups according to their economic power. Of course, pressure groups employ lobbyists who persuade and bribe members of Congress as well as those in the executive branch, including presidents. The largest lobbies in Washington represent the military contractors and the oil companies. Yet lobbying is nowhere near as important as other means mentioned here.

Furthermore, advertising is now a vital component of politics: "Pressure groups . . . are now spending millions of dollars every year on mass propaganda. Not only broad groups like the National Association of Manufacturers, but even individual companies maintain elaborate bureaucracies to sell 'correct' ideas on general policy questions along with favorable attitudes to the company" (ibid.: 249). The largest amount of political contributions now comes from political action committees, mostly set up by corporations.

The vast amount of business advertising reinforces the general ethos of capitalism. It says that material luxuries are the highest priority and implies that everyone can have them. A certain percentage of advertising is also specifically devoted to political issues, as seen earlier. Yet all advertising is counted as a "cost," so it can be deducted from income when computing taxes. Of course, labor unions are not allowed this tax deduction for political advertising.

Specifically, the unequal distribution of economic power means a very unequal distribution of the power to control political parties and their choice of nominees, as well as to influence elections. Thus, in America the capitalist class has a very disproportionate power in campaigns. Two other pluralist writers state that "because campaigns are exceedingly costly, the wealthier a person is, the more strategic his position for bringing pressure to bear on politicians" (Dahl and Lindblom, 1953: 313).

There is nothing new about this situation. In 1900, Senator Boise

Penrose said to a meeting of business people: "I believe in a division of labor. You send us to Congress: we pass laws under . . . which you make money . . . and out of your profits you further contribute to our campaign funds to send us back again to pass more laws to enable you to make more money" (quoted in Green, 1972: 7–8). The only thing that has changed is the amounts of money involved.

By 1980, many candidates for the House of Representatives were spending over $500,000; and many candidates for the Senate, over $3 million. In total in the 1980 election, $250 million was spent in the presidential campaign, and $300 million was spent electing people to Congress, including $60 million spent directly by corporate political action committees. Moreover, the influence of money on elections has become still more crude and obvious as politicians hire professional advertising or public relations firms to campaign for them. Whom you can hire and how much they will do depends on how much money you are willing to spend. During the 1970s several legal reforms ostensibly designed to reduce the political power of the rich by restricting the size of the political contributions of wealthy individuals were enacted. These reforms have greatly increased the political power of large corporations. Whereas in the past a relatively small number of capitalists would each give hundreds of thousands of dollars to the candidates they believed would best promote their interests, now they organize political action committees (PACs). In a corporate PAC, all of the corporation's executives, managerial personnel, and major stockholders are asked to give up to five thousand dollars a year. A large corporate PAC can raise hundreds of thousands of dollars each year. In 1975 there were a few dozen corporate PACs; by 1987 there were several thousand.

Thus, by 1987 the emphasis in financing political campaigns had shifted from a relatively few extremely wealthy individuals to a few thousand corporate PACs. There are, of course, also labor union PACs. The *New York Times* reported, however, that in the 1980 congressional elections there were 1,585 corporate and commercial or trade PACs that contributed $36 million to their candidates whereas 240 labor organizations contributed $13 million to theirs (*New York Times*, August 4, 1981: 12). Clearly, the corporate PACs are enormously more powerful than the labor PACs, and this is reflected in the very conservative, antilabor Congress that was elected in 1980. The imbalance between the influence of business and labor is, however, understated by those figures. In politically conservative regions such as the South or the intermountain West, labor is weak, and business need spend relatively little to maintain its dominance. In states where the populace is less conservative, and labor is stronger, business spends proportionately more. In 1982, for example, in the elections in California, business outspent labor by more than a 7 to 1 ratio (*Riverside Press-Enterprise*, October 7, 1982: A–7).

To influence political decisions, big business can threaten to open or close plants in a particular congressional district. Business can give a member of Congress free time on radio or television or a free plane ride. In addition, there are about five thousand full-time lobbyists in Washington, about ten for each representative (and many are former members of Congress or good personal or business friends of members of Congress). Except in emergencies, lobbyists do not directly buy votes. They merely serve as the main channel for the largest campaign contributions; buy lunches and dinners; and supply petty cash, credit cards, profitable investment opportunities, legal retainers to members of Congress (most of whom are lawyers), lecture fees, poker winnings (members of Congress always win), vacations, and fringe benefits ranging from theater tickets to French perfume. The two largest lobbies are the oil interests, with corporate income of billions of dollars because of special tax loopholes, and the military armaments industry.

Another line of control of considerable importance in the modern United States is the private foundation, which spends money to support education and research. Naturally, the big businesspeople who set up such foundations have some say over the content of the education, propaganda, and research on which their money is spent. Moreover, many of these foundations get direct help from government, at least in their beginnings, and many of them are closely connected with the espionage and intelligence network (see Wise and Ross, 1964).

Class Background of Political Leaders

Because of their disproportionate political influence, individuals of the capitalist class have a disproportionate percentage of the top political positions. From 1789 to 1934, fathers of U.S. presidents and vice-presidents were 38 percent professionals, 20 percent proprietors and officials, 38 percent farm owners, and only 4 percent wage earners or salaried workers (Irish and Prothro, 1965: 39). Similarly, fathers of U.S. senators in the period from 1947 to 1951 were 22 percent professionals, 33 percent proprietors and officials, 40 percent farm owners, and only 4 percent wage earners or salaried workers. Finally, fathers of members of Congress (House of Representatives) in the period 1941–1943 were 31 percent professionals, 31 percent proprietors and officials, 29 percent farm owners, and only 9 percent wage or salary workers (ibid.: 39).

Data for 1978 show that 153 of the 435 members of the House of Representatives had financial ownership of wealth of over $100,000, not including ownership of houses, automobiles, jewelry, insurance policies, or retirement funds. With regard to special interests (in conflict with their impartial lawgiving), 150 representatives have speculative real estate investments, 107 own parts of banks, large numbers own stock in top defense contractors, oil and gas industries, radio and television industries, and airlines and railroads (all of these data were taken from statements filed with the House Committee on Official Conduct, 1978). Thus very wealthy men, with fortunes ranging from many tens of thousands of dollars up to the figure of slightly under three million dollars listed for Representative Pierre Du Pont, sit in Congress.

What are the sources of their wealth? A total of 102 members of Congress held stock or well-paying positions in banks or other financial institutions; 81 received regular income from law firms that generally represented big businesses. Sixty-three got their income from stock in the top defense contractors; 45, in the giant (federally regulated) oil and gas industries; 22, in radio and television companies; 11, in commercial airlines; and 9, in railroads. Ninety-eight members of Congress were involved in numerous capital gains transactions.

In the executive branch, upper-income, business-oriented individuals have had a majority of all the important positions throughout U.S. history. This includes members of the cabinet, their assistants and department heads, and heads of most regulatory agencies. They quite naturally, with no conspiracy, tend to consult big businessmen and business groups as experts (such as the Committee for Economic Development or the Council on Foreign Relations). Wealthy families have also contributed a majority of federal judges, top military men, and top leaders of intelligence agencies. Finally, it should be noted that there is much crossing over at the top: Former generals often become corporate executives, and corporate executives often get to be cabinet members.

The results of the importance of wealth in getting elected, as well as the effects of wealth on ideological outlook, can be seen clearly in table 8.1. In 1978, there were at least twenty-one millionaires in the Senate

Table 8.1

Wealth and Ideology in the U.S. Senate, 1975

Wealth group	Senators in group	Average liberal rating by ADA, 1975
Under 50,000	5	92%
$50,000-$250,000	30	59
$250,000-$500,000	18	53
$500,000-$1 million	4	53
$1 million or more	21	29

Source: Ralph Nader study, reported in Jim Chapin, "The Rich Are Different . . . ." *Newsletter of the Democratic Left* (November 1976): 3. The results are for seventy-eight senators for whom questionnaire or other data were available; no data on twenty-two.

but only five senators whose total wealth is below $50,000 (though this lowest category includes 99 percent of Americans). The table also shows an inverse relation between wealth and a liberal political outlook. The poorest senators (not very poor) were given a liberal voting rate of 92 percent by the Americans for Democratic Action (ADA), but the ADA gave only a 29 percent liberal voting record to the twenty-one millionaires. These results fit almost too well with a vulgar Marxist economic determinism. There are certainly many exceptions; for example, Senator Edward Kennedy is both a millionaire and very liberal. Personal financial disclosures now required by law indicate the number of millionaires in the Senate has increased to thirty-five.

The Structural Bases of Control

Unlike the simplistic notion of a conspiracy by a small number of nasty capitalists, it has been emphasized here that the very structure of capitalism means that wealthy capitalists have the means to hire most lobbyists, to do most advertising, to make the largest political contributions needed to buy candidates, and—quite naturally—control the flow of information in the press, the radio, and on television. In addition, the capitalist structure constrains the policy options of any government, even one elected with a strongly working-class base and honest intentions.

For example, when Chrysler Corporation started to go bankrupt in

1980, the U.S. government gave it a welfare handout in the form of loan guarantees. If public ownership is ruled out as a solution, then the only thing to do with a large corporation going bankrupt is to put it on public welfare. The alternative is a large downward pull on the economy. It is not surprising that a capitalist-oriented government rode to the rescue (though Chrysler's competitors did not cheer the action). What seems at first glance to be a surprise is that the lobbying in favor of welfare to Chrysler was led by a very liberal union, the United Auto Workers. Yet if a socialist solution is ruled out, the UAW position makes good sense. If Chrysler goes down the drain, tens of thousands of UAW members would lose their jobs. Given the reality of heavy unemployment under capitalism, there is no guarantee that they would soon get other jobs.

This case could be multiplied a thousand times. Very liberal members of Congress and very liberal unions frequently support welfare in the form of subsidies to corporations in their localities. For example, all the liberals in Congress from Hawaii support subsidies to the sugar companies in order to keep jobs for sugar workers. Some unions resist environmental controls for corporations in their industry because of fear of losing jobs. These are real political facts of life, and they cannot be changed as long as the structure of capitalism exists.

Even where a government, such as the socialist government of Allende in Chile, was committed to ending capitalism, the structural facts are a barrier to transition. As soon as some part of industry was nationalized, a great deal of capital fled the country, with a naturally depressing effect.

These structural constraints apply very strongly and clearly in the realm of macroeconomic policy. John Maynard Keynes stressed the need for "business confidence" to maintain investment and get out of a depression. Business confidence is achieved by policies that give tax cuts to business, shift income distribution toward the wealthy, cut spending programs that would help the poor, restrict union wage increases, and so forth. Given the structure of capitalism, it is perfectly true that there will be no new investment—and consequently high unemployment—if business is not confident of making profits. High profit rates are the only road to prosperity under capitalism, but one must remember that this requires policies designed not only for high rates of exploitation of workers, but also policies to ensure that workers have enough income to buy the mass of commodities embodying the high profits.

Qualifications to the Class Analysis

So far, these radical theses have been stated: (1) class differences determine much of political behavior, (2) the wealthy capitalist class has a disproportionate amount of political power, to the extent that (3) it occupies or controls most key political positions, and (4) the structural features of capitalism put narrow constraints on policy, forcing it to be procapitalist. Now it is necessary to turn to some very definite qualifications to these theses.

First, although the capitalist class has a strong influence on Congress, the Congress is not fully controlled or dominated by the capitalist class. The direct representation of the capitalist class is disproportionate, but still a small minority (Domhoff, 1967: 111–14). Influence must rather be exerted indirectly through pressure from the executive branch, paid lobbyists, and big campaign contributions to the parties and candidates. Second, although strongly influenced by the capitalist class, most state governments and most city governments are not controlled or dominated directly by that class (ibid.: 132–37).

Third, although the old middle class of independent small-farm owners, small businesspeople, and self-employed artisans is no longer the vast majority but only a tiny percentage of the labor force, U.S. society has not polarized into two classes with no middle. In addition to low-paid manual workers, there is a very large and growing percentage of high-paid professional and technical workers—a "new working class" (or "new middle class" if you prefer) of engineers and teachers and such. Even though they are workers in a purely economic sense, they see themselves mostly as middle class, and their political behavior follows that pattern to some extent. On the other hand, teachers and even college professors are now organizing and even striking in some places, so that the behavior of at least some of the new working class approximates that of the old working class rather than the old middle class.

Fourth, although the capitalist class controls some areas of government and strongly influences others, "the control is not complete; other groups sometimes have their innings, particularly when these groups are well organized and angry" (Domhoff, 1969: 277). Thus, farmers won reforms in the late nineteenth century against monopoly pressures, and angry workers won many reforms in the New Deal of the 1930s. The power of numbers and organization can defeat the power of money in some extraordinary circumstances.

Fifth, there is disagreement and factionalism within the capitalist class. "Nor is the power elite always united in its politics; there are long-standing disagreements between its moderate and conservative wings" (ibid.). They disagree partly because of opposed interests. Thus, most large corporations benefit from and favor military spending, but a significant minority does not benefit from it and is opposed to much military spending. The large corporations also have major tactical disagreements over the best way to handle current macro problems.

Sixth, business people and those who follow their view in government do not always have a perfect grasp of their own best interests: "To read case studies of specific decisions is to be aware that lack of information, misunderstandings, and personality clashes may lead to mistakes on issues that must be decided in a hurry" (ibid.). Thus, no one should predict that government policy will always represent an optimal solution from the capitalist view. (For a catalogue of idiotic decisions and mistakes of the Reagan administration, see Stockman, 1986.)

Seventh, critics of the class analysis sometimes point out that in the United States there are real conflicts over policies, that decisions are made by shifting coalitions, that these coalitions usually include some worker or farmer organization. True, but "the shifting coalitions are dominated . . . by members of the American upperclass" (Domhoff, 1969: 3). Thus, one cannot simply say that a certain group of small capitalists decides government policy. On the contrary, there appear to be several conflicting capitalist groups, and some of them are loosely allied with some farmer or worker groups. But the ruling coalition does always end up dominated by a major capitalist group—though, as in the New Deal, it may have to grant many reforms to its coalition partners.

Eighth, "most businessmen are not part of the group that controls the government" (ibid.: 154). Certainly, most businesspeople are small businesspeople and have little, if any, more power than workers or farmers. A ruling coalition may sometimes include small business, but it is usually dominated by a small group of big capitalists. In fact, the U.S. economy is dominated by very large corporations, exercising vast amounts of monopoly economic power and political power.

Last, the political behavior of individuals is guided at any given time by many factors besides pure economic motivations. A politician may simply be power-hungry rather than consciously acting in favor of class interest. If a white male worker is infected with racism, he may vent his anger at bad conditions against black workers rather than against the capitalist owner.

Feedback Mechanisms of Political Control

It has been seen how—with many qualifications—extremely unequal economic power tends to lead to extremely unequal political power in the United States. On the other hand, once the state apparatus is controlled via economic power and economic structure, it may then function as a feedback mechanism to secure political power more firmly. Thus, the Egyptian slaveholders (including the pharaoh and priests) used their control of the state apparatus—the police, army, courts—to control the slaves by laws supported by force. Similarly, given a large measure of political control by those with the most economic power in America, the wealthy naturally tend to use the government apparatus to strengthen their power. Thus, the police or the National Guard or the army may be directly ordered to support "law and order" by force, as law and order is interpreted by those with political control. Many, many times in American history police or even soldiers have shot down American workers trying to strike for better conditions; police have even been used in the 1980s against the relatively conservative construction workers. Most courts have always cooperated by issuing injunctions against strikes by labor unions.

There is also that means of feedback control that is a mixture of propaganda and force, namely, the various espionage and information agencies. These include in America the Central Intelligence Agency, Defense Intelligence Agency, National Security Agency, Army Intelligence, Navy Intelligence and Research, and the Federal Bureau of Investigation. "By 1964 the intelligence network had grown into a massive hidden apparatus, secretly employing about 200,000 persons and spending billions of dollars a year" (Wise and Ross, 1964: 4). This so-called invisible government is still only an instrument of political power, but it does exert its own semi-independent, malevolent influence once it is activated, especially in foreign policy—such as the secret sales of arms to Iran and the illegal sending of the profits to the contra rebels in Nicaragua. Frequent publicized scandals have taught us that its corruption and paid agents reach down into every private organization; one outstanding case was the subsidized foreign activities of the AFL-CIO.

Another important feedback is the use of the prestige of the state. Thus, while police try to break a strike by construction workers, the president tells the nation that their wages are too high. Every department of the government, particularly the military, also does its own massive advertising in favor of business and government policies, particularly military spending.

Education is the last avenue of feedback control considered here. Children are brought up to believe in the righteousness of a value system that preserves the status quo. Even if one looks at university boards of regents and trustees, it is astounding to find that they are almost wholly composed of capitalists, corporate lawyers, military officers, and their wives. Much of the funding (and direction) of research comes from military expenditure. The important schools of law and business administration take the capitalist system for granted and work to improve (or have their students improve) its efficiency—mainly in the making of private profits.

Finally, if all else fails, the capitalist class may use outright repression or even force and violence to prevent governments from using drastic anticapitalist macro policies. Many countries have suffered from military coups and ended with military dictatorships. In a very large number of the underdeveloped countries of the "free" capitalist world, there are now such dictatorships, mostly dedicated according to their leaders "to the protection of democracy." Also in the twentieth century a number of semideveloped capitalist countries (Spain, Italy, Portugal, Brazil, Chile, Greece) and at least two developed capitalist countries (Nazi Germany and Japan) have had fascist or military-fascist dictatorships. In most cases, they were instituted because of the threat that the Left might win power in a peaceful democratic election (or, in Spain, after such an election). In these cases, the feedback control of vested interests is manifested directly through the dictatorship of an extreme right-wing individual or party (though they may claim to be anything but a class dictatorship).

Much of this chapter has emphasized how economic power allows the capitalist class an enormous influence on even the most democratic of political processes. Nevertheless, it must be stressed that a liberal democratic process is not the same as a Fascist or military dictatorship, either politically or in macroeconomic policies. As long as there is a liberal democratic political process, it allows the working class to exercise its influence and to win very significant reforms. Thus, Bowles and Gintis (1982) emphasize that most democratic freedoms have been won and retained by the struggles of the working class, with much resistance by the capitalist class. There is always a potential or actual conflict between the popular participation in the liberal democratic process and the control of the economy by a small group of capitalist owners.

Economic Behavior of the Capitalist State

The class basis of the capitalist state and some of its political feedback mechanisms have been examined; now it is necessary to examine those feedbacks of the political system that affect the economic structure. In general, the main function of capitalist government is to preserve private property through laws and force, otherwise known as preservation of "law and order."

Effects of Government

Although there is no question that extreme inequality exists in the United States, liberals argue that the inequality is much reduced by higher tax rates on the rich, welfare payments to the poor worker, subsidies to the poor farmer, and public education for the poor. Thus, Paul Samuelson asserts that the U.S. government has reduced income inequality, though he admits that it has not been much of a change: "The welfare state, through redistributive taxation and through educational opportunity . . . has moved the system a bit toward greater equality" (1973: 804). Radicals object to this conclusion on several grounds.

First, radicals present the facts of income distribution. These facts show that there was very little overall change in income distribution between 1910 and 1977; the share of the poorest 20 percent of the population has actually declined; and the share of the richest 20 percent has fluctuated, going down very slightly by 1970, but rising throughout the 1970s and 1980s. Therefore, in spite of many promises by liberal U.S. government administrations, there has been no reduction of inequality since 1910. In fact, since 1980 the Reagan administration has systematically increased inequality.

Second, the main function of the system is the preservation of "law and order," which means that police and armies and courts and prisons all protect the private ownership of the vast fortunes of the rich. Government thus preserves capitalist control of land and factories.

Third, radicals have shown that the administration of every program from taxation to welfare has been such that the rich have benefited more and the poor less than the law would seem to indicate at first glance. The following sections discuss each program in detail.

Taxation

It is certainly true that the income tax rate rises as income rises; in theory, at least, individuals in the higher income brackets not only must pay more taxes but also must pay a higher percentage of their income in taxes. Indeed the top theoretical tax rate used to be 90 percent; it was 70 percent before Reagan's tax cuts and then fell to 50 percent; but it will be 28 percent under the 1986 tax reform.

In practice rich taxpayers find many loopholes that allow them to pay much lower tax rates. Thus in 1969 the highest tax rate was an apparently confiscatory 90 percent, but the tax rate paid by all taxpayers with incomes reported over $1 million was actually only 34 percent of their reported income, and—if one includes all the income they are not required to report—the rate was actually only 20 percent of total income.

One large loophole is the tax-free bond. The interest on federal bonds cannot be taxed by states, and the interest on municipal bonds cannot be taxed by states or by the federal government. Of course to make a significant amount of money from bonds a very large investment is necessary, and bonds are typically sold in large lots that only the rich can afford. Other loopholes include homeowners' preferences, depreciation allowances, and depletion allowances (especially gas and oil). The money that flows through tax loopholes is now called "tax expenditures," that is, money not collected but going instead to the tax avoiders and the corporations because of the loopholes written into the tax laws. The best study of the tax expenditures is by Peterson (1985), which reveals how much they benefit the wealthy. He shows how the conservative counterrevolution of the Reagan administration has enormously increased these benefits to the wealthy. Thus, Peterson finds that tax expenditures were 31 percent of total federal taxes in 1979, but rose to 49 percent by 1983 (p. 617). Tax expenditures for the corporations rose from 63 percent of their taxes paid in 1980 to 108 percent in 1983—or, for every dollar collected, $1.08 is not collected. Even though the rich (over $100,000 income level) are only 1.7 percent of all taxpayers, they receive 15 percent of all tax expenditures.

Also important to the perpetuation of income inequality in the United States is the fact that the federal income tax amounts to only 40 percent of all taxes and is the only tax that is progressive to even a slight extent (progressive means that the tax falls more heavily on the upper-income groups). The other 60 percent of taxes are mainly regressive in that they fall more heavily on the lower income groups. Most of the regressive taxes are state and local, such as the sales tax and the property tax. In terms of percentages these fall much more heavily on lower- and middle-income groups than on the rich. For example, a tax on gasoline or telephone service is spread rather equally among the population; therefore these taxes take a much higher percentage of a poor person's income. Thus, the burden of state and local taxes is definitely regressive. The lower one's income, the higher the rate at which one pays these state and local taxes.

In addition, a large amount of taxes are paid in the form of compulsory contributions by workers to the social security system. These taxes are highly regressive because there is a maximum tax. After the rich person receives income above the point at which the maximum tax is incurred, the remainder of his or her income becomes tax free.

When all kinds of taxes—federal, state, and local—are added together, the proportionate burden on the poor seems to be actually larger than on the rich. Although the rich pay a larger total of taxes, the percentage of their income going to taxes is actually less than the percentage of poor families' income going to taxes. In fact, in 1967 the richest 5 percent of taxpayers had 15 percent of all income before taxes; but they had 17 percent of all income after all federal, state, and local taxes were paid (see Pechman, 1969: 113). From all evidence, it would appear that taxes in the mid-1980s are even more inequitable.

In the last forty years, the tax burden has actually been moving from rich capitalists to all workers. In 1944 corporate income taxes were 34 percent of all federal revenue, but corporate taxes had fallen to only 6 percent of federal revenue by 1984. At the same time, social security taxes (paid mostly by workers) rose from 4 percent of federal revenue in 1944 to 29 percent in 1974. In the 1970s and 1980s, the social security taxes were rising faster than any other form of taxes.

The greatest windfall for corporations, however, came with the Reagan tax cuts of 1981. The result of the Reagan counterrevolution— the combination of an onslaught against welfare spending (see below) plus the giveaway of more tax expenditures to the rich—has been a significant change in income distribution. From 1980 to 1984, the average real disposable income going to the poorest fifth of U.S. citizens declined by 8 percent, whereas the average real disposable income going to the wealthiest fifth of U.S. citizens rose by 9 percent (Peterson, 1985: 635).

A tax reform was passed in 1986 that ends some loopholes but also reduces tax levels for the wealthy. Therefore, the final result of this reform for income distribution will take some years to be clearly determined.

Welfare

Because the present tax system does not redistribute income toward more equality, the question is whether welfare programs have a significant effect in that direction. In the first place, expenditures for welfare have been fairly small. In 1968 welfare spending under all federal, state, and local programs was only $26.9 billion. This included public aid, unemployment payments, workmen's compensation, health and medical programs, public housing, and educational aid to low-income students. These payments do help the poor somewhat, but the effect is small; they do virtually nothing to alter the relative positions of the poorest or the richest segments of society. Moreover, this $26.9 billion for welfare represented only 3.82 percent of all personal income in 1968. Therefore, although it could improve the lot of a few people, it could not change things very much.

What has been the historical trend of welfare payments? In 1938, welfare payments were 6.7 percent of personal income; in 1950, welfare was down to 3.86 percent; in 1960, it was down a little more, to 3.31 percent. In 1968 it was 3.82 whereas in 1983 it was 4.6 percent. These figures reflect the general state of the economy. In 1938 unemployment was very high and poverty was widespread. By 1968, the rate of unemployment as well as the poverty rate had improved. Between 1968 and 1983, however, the economic situation deteriorated. Thus, the 4.6 percent in 1983 does not reflect liberalized welfare payments— on the contrary the Reagan administration discontinued or reduced the funding for many programs—but an increase in the number of unemployed and poor people. In the early years of the Reagan administration, the persons below the poverty line rose from 13 percent in 1980 to 15 percent in 1983.

Interestingly, this pattern of small welfare effects and no significant reduction in income inequality over many decades also holds true for the capitalist countries of Western Europe. Even in Denmark and Sweden, where taxation and welfare programs are supposed to be extremely progressive, there has been little change in income distribution (after taxes and welfare) for several decades.

In the social and economic conditions of a private enterprise economy, there is a belief that one works only if one has to work. Thus U.S. welfare programs are very carefully designed to assist those who cannot work—children, the old, the blind. Very little welfare income goes to those who work hard but are paid low wages (who constitute about half of the poverty group) because that might lower their "incentive." A few programs give the low-paid worker minimum health and education so that he or she is able to work, but these programs are very careful to avoid providing any food, clothing, or shelter. This philosophy of welfare leads to extreme degradation of welfare recipients. To "motivate" the working poor to ever greater effort, welfare recipients are kept in such a pitiful, dehumanized condition that anyone would rather work, even at the most disagreeable jobs and at the lowest pay.

The dole a welfare recipient receives is grossly insufficient for even the barest subsistence livelihood. Moreover, in return for this insignificant sum the individual loses many basic civil rights supposedly guaranteed to everyone. The single woman supporting a family on welfare, for example, must permit welfare workers to search her house and subject her to a demeaning interrogation to ascertain whether her personal sexual conduct is proper and fitting. This is only one of many ways welfare recipients are degraded and dehumanized. It is absurd to argue that programs like these will ever eliminate poverty.

Farm Subsidies

The rural poor have suffered the post pathetic poverty. For most of the twentieth century the incomes of small-farm owners and farm workers have lagged far behind other U.S. incomes. For that reason, liberals have persuaded Congress to pass various bills aiding farmers with subsidies. What has been the practical effect of these subsidies?

First, the high economic concentration among the business firms engaged in farming should be noted. At present the richest 7 percent of all farms produce 56 percent of total agricultural output. The poorest 66 percent of all farms produce only 9 percent of farm output. Concentration in agriculture has greatly increased in the period since subsidies were initiated.

Second, the farm support programs benefit mainly the richest farmers and provide very little support for the poorest farmers. The poorest 20 percent of farms get 1 to 5 percent of subsidies while the richest 20 percent of farms get 50 to 60 percent of subsidies.

Third, it appears in fact that the net result of the farm program has been to increase the percentage of total farm income going to the richest farmers and to decrease that going to the poorest farmers. Thus not only do most of the benefits go to the richest farmers, but their share of the subsidies is higher than their share of the presubsidy income, so the disproportionate subsidies increase even further the extreme inequality in farm income.

The discussion up to this point has shown the effects of the farm programs on farmers who own their own farms. There is a fourth factor: What are the effects on farm workers, who own nothing but their labor power? The answer is very simple. The main farm programs provide farm owners—mainly on the largest, richest farms—price supports to maintain prices at a certain level above costs, and payments to keep some land out of production in order to reduce the supply of farm goods. No money from these programs goes to farm workers. In fact the program may hurt farm workers to the extent that the programs pay to keep land out of production, thereby increasing unemployment. "The State pays the owners of farm property not to produce, but pays virtually nothing to farm workers who become unemployed as a result of this dole to property owners" (Wachtel, 1971: 12).

The net result of this program—to help farm workers not at all, to help poor farmers slightly, and to help rich farmers very much—is not at all surprising. Indeed it represents the continuation of a consistent pattern in U.S. history. Large corporations have always been the ones helped by government subsidies. In the nineteenth century, for example, three-fourths of all railroad construction was paid for by the government, and huge amounts of land were given to the railroads. Merchant shipping today receives large subsidies. Largest of all is the amount the government gives business for "research and development" ($17 billion in 1969 alone) both directly and indirectly through academic institutions. President Reagan has recommended giving military contractors over $25 billion for research and development just for the "Star Wars" project, that is, military weapons in space.

An amusing book by David Stockman (1986), former director of the Office of Management and Budget under President Reagan, reveals a lot about the political process whereby subsidies are given to rich farmers and other businesses. Stockman is a right-wing ideologue who really believes that the U.S. government should do no spending, except massive military spending. He was successful in eliminating or reducing many subsidies to poor women and children (such as school lunch programs and nutrition for expectant mothers), but he hit a stone wall when he attacked business subsidies. For example, the U.S. government subsidizes tobacco, even though it is harmful to health. The tobacco industry forced an extension of it through Congress, and President Reagan signed it because it was supported by Senator Jesse Helms. Helms supports Reagan; the tobacco industry sees to it that Helms is elected. Stockman is shocked by these violations of the free market, but he should not be surprised; capitalist corporations are for the free market only when they themselves are not helped by government subsidies and regulations.

Education and Inequality

Government-subsidized education is often thought to decrease the inequality of incomes. "The government gives free education to all," goes the argument, "so anyone can improve his or her station in life by going to school for a longer period."

Clearly there is a significant positive correlation between amount of education and level of income. On average, the more education a person has the higher will be his or her income. In large part, however, more and better schooling is the effect of having a high income—and to some extent individuals from high-income families may get high-income jobs merely because their parents own the businesses in which they work.

Children of richer parents receive more schooling largely because their parents can afford to keep them in school longer than poor parents can. They can pay high tuitions in private schools that admit students even with low grade averages. Even in the public universities, where the tuition may be much lower or nonexistent, there are still living expenses. Many students must drop out of college or are unable to enroll simply because they have no money on which to live while in school.

Furthermore, children of richer families have a better chance to do well in school and learn more. Opportunities and encouragement provided in the home and community are much more likely to produce highly motivated children who know how to study. Cultural background is very important in performance on IQ tests and college entrance examinations. These examinations, which purport to test general ability, in reality are designed to conform to middle-class, white, urban experience. A student from a poor or rural background will lack the necessary cultural references to understand the questions or have any intuition of the answers. This has been proven again and again, but the tests are still used. They determine which "track" (discussed below) an elementary student is put into, and they determine who enters college. Thus it is no surprise that only 7 percent of all college students come from the poorest 25 percent of all families.

Another condition that hurts students from poor families and helps those from richer families is the fact that schools in different areas receive very different amounts of money. Central-city slum schools often are given less money per student and almost always attract less competent teachers. Suburban township schools are apt to receive more money per student and attract better teachers.

Students in elementary and high schools are put into different tracks. One track is vocational training, which prepares the poor for manual labor. Another track, college preparation, prepares students from upper-middle-class and richer families for college, so that they can move into high-income jobs (so that their children can go to college, and so forth). In elementary schools it is often called ability grouping of the bright and the stupid. But the degree of ability is determined by IQ tests that are not objective measures of innate intelligence but, as noted previously, discriminate on the basis of class background.

The tracking system exists both within and between high schools. Within some high schools, counselors push the poor and minority groups into vocational training and the rich into college preparation. Within others, such pushing is hardly necessary because of the vast differences among schools. Schools in the black slums provide only basic, or vocational, training. Schools in the richest areas give only college preparation. These different tracks are enforced both formally by the tests given and informally by counselors and teachers.

It may be concluded with certainty that our educational system does not reduce inequality from generation to generation. On the contrary, the richer students have more opportunities to obtain a good elementary and high school education, to be accepted into college, to remain in college, and therefore to be hired at a high-income job after college— and then to send their own children to college. Thus the educational system seems to transmit inequality from one generation to the next.

(The best detailed study of the education system is Bowles and Gintis, 1975.)

History of U.S. Government Fiscal Activity

The U.S. government has always aided the economic activities of big business; railroads were given much economic aid even before the Civil War. Between 1850 and 1871, the U.S. Congress gave away 175,350,000 acres of choice public lands to the railroads—a gift to private enterprise of taxpayers' property worth about $489 million in the valuable dollars of those days. In addition, in the same period, the government had granted the railroads $65 million in special low-cost credit (see Fite and Reese, 1965: 330).

Thus, throughout the period during which American capitalism was developing into an industrial giant, the government was instrumental in providing the institutional and economic framework in which profitable business could be conducted. Private enterprise profited handsomely as taxpayers subsidized many of the business and industrial ventures that helped provide these necessities. The economic role of government that most directly influences the level of output, income, and employment is its taxing and spending of money, or fiscal policy. During most of American history the prevailing economic philosophy was that taxes should be used only to finance necessary government expenditures. It was thought to be an unsound financial practice for governments to borrow money. If a balanced budget, in which expenditures equaled taxes, could not be achieved, it was thought to be preferable to have taxes exceed expenditures so that any debts incurred in the past could be retired. Only the Great Depression and the World War II experiences forced a change in this policy. The trend since that time has been for government spending to rise much more rapidly than taxes.

Federal government spending in the United States in 1929 was only 1 percent of GNP. In 1930–1940, as the New Deal responded to the Depression, it had increased to 4 percent of GNP. With World War II government spending rose to the incredible height of 42 percent of GNP in 1944. After the war it fell somewhat, but it bounced up again in the Korean War, so federal spending averaged 11 percent of GNP in 1945–1959. In 1960–1970, partly owing to the Vietnam War, federal spending averaged 13 percent of GNP, about two-thirds or more being military (see Cypher, 1973).

After the Vietnam War, federal spending for goods and services (mostly military) declined. But it rose again in the 1980s under the Reagan administration. In 1982, all federal spending for goods and services was still only 8.4 percent of GNP, but military spending alone was 5.8 percent of GNP, so all federal nonmilitary spending for goods and services was only 2.6 percent of GNP! There is also state and local spending, which had risen to 13.2 percent of GNP in 1982, a major increase from earlier decades.

Finally, the federal government also made transfer payments amounting to 16.4 percent of GNP. These transfer payments among citizens included huge subsidies to big business, subsidies to large farms, a small amount of welfare payments to the poor, unemployment compensation to individuals, payments of interest on government bonds to rich bondholders, and payments of social security pensions to people who have paid social security taxes.

Fiscal Policies and Social Priorities

There are three different policy views of what government discretionary fiscal policy ought to be. The most conservative economists, such as Adam Smith or the contemporary Milton Friedman, argue that no discretionary fiscal measures are needed. The government should stay out of the economy. Friedman agrees with Adam Smith that the less government the better. He attributes many of our economic problems to too much interference with private enterprise, which would otherwise automatically adjust to all situations in a near-perfect manner. To the extent that conservatives admit any need for government policy, they say that only monetary measures are necessary. Conservatives favor measures affecting the money supply (via interest rates, for example) rather than any fiscal measures of spending or taxation because they feel that monetary measures do not directly interfere with business. They view an adequate money supply merely as one of the prerequisites for a private enterprise economy. Other prerequisites that they believe government should provide include police and armies to maintain ''law and order,'' primarily to protect private property from its domestic and foreign enemies.

Contrary to the liberal view that government spending can employ workers and increase demand, Friedman (1982) contends that ''Government spending does not increase employment. First, government spending has increased for the last 25 years, but so has unemployment. Two, government spending just takes money from private people who would have spent it, so there is no net increase in demand for labor.'' As to his first point, it may only prove that the private sector performed so poorly that even more government spending is needed. As to the second point, it is shown below that money for spending may be borrowed from the rich (who might not spend it) or it may simply be printed.

The second, the liberal, view is that of such economists as John M. Keynes or the contemporary Paul Samuelson. Liberals admit that capitalism has real problems, such as general unemployment and inflation. Liberal Keynesians argue that adequate government measures of increased or decreased taxation are necessary to correct these problems. Franklin Delano Roosevelt (1944) argued that every American has the "right to a useful and remunerative job in the industries or shops or farms or mines of the Nation.'' Since Roosevelt, most liberals have favored full employment policies.

With a large government in the picture, Keynesians argue that something can be done about either unemployment or inflation, assuming we do not have both at the same time. If there is unemployment—because supply is far above demand—then the government can add to demand in one of two ways. It can directly increase government spending, which is a component of demand, and/or it can lower taxes, which increases the income available to be spent for consumer or investor demand.

On the other hand, if there is inflation because demand is at too high a level (perhaps because of vast government military spending), then the government can reduce demand in one of two ways. First, it may lower the level of government spending. Second, it may raise taxes, which reduces the amount people have left over for consumer or investor spending. These are the simple mechanics of fiscal policy; we shall now proceed to its problems.

Liberals used to maintain that spending and taxation measures can always successfully bring about full employment with stable prices. Some of them now, however, define full employment as "only" 4 or 5 percent unemployment and stable prices as "only" 2 or 3 percent inflation per year. Others, including Samuelson, simply admit that ending inflation and getting full employment at the same time is one little thing not yet solved by establishment economists: "Experts do not yet know . . . an incomes policy that will permit us to have simultaneously . . . full employment and price stability'' (Samuelson, 1973: 823).

The radical view was expressed by Karl Marx or the contemporary

Paul Sweezy. Radicals argue that problems like periodic unemployment are deeply rooted in the capitalist system and cannot be cured by any amount of monetary or fiscal measures. They contend that the U.S. economy has reached full employment only during major wars. In normal peacetime years, they believe unemployment and/or inflation is the usual state of capitalism. In 1986, with the largest deficit spending in history, the U.S. economy still had 7 percent official unemployment. Radicals argue that the necessary drastic fiscal measures cannot be taken by capitalist governments because powerful vested interests oppose each such step, aside from military spending.

Even if one accepts liberal Keynesian estimates of the proper aggregate amounts of spending and taxation, the problem remains: Which spending? Whose taxes? Suppose it is agreed to spend the large amounts of money necessary to maintain full employment. Many outlets that would be socially beneficial conflict with the vested interests of large corporations or wealthy individuals. Larger welfare payments tend to raise the wage level; while government investment in industrial ventures or in public utilities tends to erode monopolistic privileges. The issue is the political constraints to economic policies.

One popular cure for depression is reduction of taxes to allow more money to flow into private spending. Given the composition of the U.S. government, however, tax cuts always end up benefiting mainly the rich and the corporations. Even in the liberal Kennedy administration, the taxes of the poor were reduced very little and of the rich very much, resulting in a redistribution of income to the members of the wealthy class. In fact, on the excuse of stimulating investment, corporate income taxes have declined from 40 percent of net Federal revenue in 1945 to only 6 percent in 1985. Especially in a depression, however, the wealthy will not spend their increased income. The consumption of the wealthy remains at adequate levels even in a depression, and they have no desire to invest in the face of probable losses. Hence the political restriction as to who gets the tax cuts makes this policy economically ineffective.

In the years immediately after World War II, the problem was to spend $15–20 billion annually. This might have been an agonizing social and political issue except for the advent of the cold war. Dollars for cold war armaments did not violate any vested interests. Military spending is considered an ideal antidepression policy by big business for three reasons. First, such expenditures have the same short-run effect on employment and profits as would expenditures on more socially useful projects. Second, military spending means big and stable profits, whereas welfare spending may shift income from rich taxpayers to poor recipients. Third, the long-run effect is even more favorable because no new productive equipment is created to compete with existing facilities.

During the past forty years, the main change has been that the necessary addition to the income stream by deficit spending has risen to at least $200–300 billion a year. If it were politically possible, the whole amount could be spent on useful public commodities, such as housing or health or education, rather than on military waste. These useful types of public spending are not politically feasible in such large amounts, however, as long as the U.S. government is dominated by big business. Private developers fight public housing. Private power companies fought the cheap public electricity of the Tennessee Valley Authority. The American Medical Association opposes free public health care. And some private interests oppose any constructive public project.

The rich see expenditures on hospitals and schools as subsidies to the poor for things that the rich can buy for themselves out of their own pockets. Proposals to increase unemployment compensation or lower taxes paid by the poor encounter even greater resistance because they would transfer income from the rich to the poor. Likewise, billions could usefully be spent in aid and loans to the less developed world, where poverty and human suffering are so widespread. That, however, could be passed on a massive scale only over the bodies of hundreds of members of Congress, who represent well the wishes of their self-interested constituents and have no concept of the long-run gain to world trade and world peace. If any of these measures are to some extent allowed, it is only after a long political fight, certainly not promptly enough to head off a developing depression.

One could list, one by one, all the areas in which powerful vested interests stand in opposition to the satisfaction of some of the nation's most basic social needs. These interests will not tolerate government competition with private enterprise, measures that undermine the privileges of the wealthy, or policies that significantly alter the relative distribution of income. They therefore tend to oppose all government nonmilitary spending—except direct business subsidies.

Military Spending vs. Welfare Spending

From all of the facts just given, one must conclude that constructive spending on a large scale is opposed by too many special interests to be politically feasible. Only large-scale military spending brought the United States out of the Great Depression of the 1930s, and only large-scale military spending has kept the United States out of a major depression. Liberals like Samuelson are much more complacent: he says mass unemployment and galloping inflations are things of the past. He asserts that these are ancient problems that are solvable and have been solved: "For example, however true it might have been in the turn-of-the-century era of Lenin . . . , it is definitely no longer the case in the age after Keynes that prosperity of a mixed economy (i.e., capitalism plus government) depends on cold-war expenditures and imperialistic ventures" (1973: 823). It is a fact, however, that our economy has boomed by spending immense sums of money to kill the people of Vietnam, Nicaragua, Granada, and so forth. How would Samuelson replace that crutch to the economy? He says: "Does building missiles and warheads create jobs . . . ? Then so too will building new factories, better roads and schools, cleaning up our rivers, and providing minimum income-supplements for our aged and handicapped" (p. 824) Certainly it is true that jobs could be created in all these constructive ways rather than the destructive ways of warfare. But—and it is a big but—we are talking about government spending, so we must remember that vested interests will obstruct programs that might harm them. Yet for the government to build new factories means direct competition with private industry. For the government to build schools means to take money from rich taxpayers and transfer it to the education of poorer citizens. To clean up the rivers means both more use of tax money and forcing private industry to spend money on purifying its wastes. Giving to the aged and handicapped means again adding taxes and shifting income to the poor. The political reality is that vested interests oppose each of these programs with violent rhetoric and successful political pressure.

Paul Samuelson says that radicals have asked, "Politically, will there be as much urgency to spend what is needed for useful, peacetime full-employment programs as there is urgency and willingness to spend for hot- and cold-war purposes?" And he answers, "It was proper to ask this question back in the 1950s. But . . . experience since then has shown that modern electorates have become very sensitive to levels of unemployment that would have been considered moderate back in the good old days. And they do put effective pressure at the polls on their government" (pp. 824–25). But, in the first place, the pressure is only to get jobs—not necessarily to get welfare rather than warfare jobs; so both Republican and Democratic administrations continue military spending to avoid unemployment and do not do large amounts of constructive spending. Moreover, instead of reducing the level of unemployment at which government should be sensitive and alarmed, as Samuelson predicted, the Carter administration and Reagan administration have made much higher levels of unemployment commonplace.

In the second place, Samuelson just assumes that "the people" make our governmental decisions, but it was seen earlier that the dominant power in governmental decision making in the United States is big business. Even the liberal administration of John F. Kennedy vastly increased military spending, invaded Cuba, and expanded the Vietnam War. The liberal Lyndon Johnson administration further expanded the Vietnam War on a vast scale. The reactionary Reagan administration has had the largest military build-up in history in peacetime!

Keynesian liberals fail to see the political constraints that make military spending the only allowable solution to unemployment. The political nature of the problem has become even more apparent in the inflationary situation of the past twenty years. The Korean and Vietnam wars caused so much government demand for military supplies that inflation resulted, prices rising especially in 1950–1953 and 1967–1981. To cure inflation the simple Keynesian prescription is to increase taxes and reduce spending.

But whose taxes; which spending? Major increases in taxes on the wealthy are not easily passed by our government. And there is not that much room for further taxes on the poor and the middle class without provoking rising discontent. So it is easier to reduce government spending. But not military spending; politicians and spokespersons for industry and the military continue to convince the nation that these are absolutely necessary. Thus welfare spending is cut. Already a tiny percentage of the American government budget, welfare has nevertheless been cut further as a tool to fight inflation. Hence the burden of inflation has fallen on the common man and woman in the forms of rising prices, rising taxes, and falling welfare spending all at the same time.

The question of social and political priorities often boils down to a conflict between the genuine needs of the majority versus the desires of the tiny minority that possesses immense economic and political power. The majority of Americans need more education, health, and welfare; but a powerful minority favors military spending.

The Military Economy

To measure the full extent of the military impact on the economy, one must recall that the U.S. Department of Defense is the largest planned economy in the world today outside the USSR. It spends more than the net income of all U.S. corporations. By 1969 it had 470 major and 6,000 lesser installations, owned 39 million acres of land, spent over $80 billion a year, used 22,000 primary contractors and 100,000 subcontractors—thus directly employing in the armed forces and military production about 10 percent of the U.S. labor force. Some key areas of the economy are especially affected. As early as 1963, before U.S. entry into the Vietnam War, studies show that 36 percent of the output of producers' durable goods were purchased directly or indirectly by the federal government, mostly for military use (data discussed in Melman, 1970).

How did the U.S. economy come to have such a huge military sector? Of course in World War II the United States had an enormous military production. It was assumed by every policy maker, including economists and businesspersons and political leaders, that the United States would mostly disarm after the war. It was also assumed that this would lead to a depression; therefore every possible solution was considered, with most analyses leading to the sole suggestion of renewed military spending. It was in this atmosphere that the cold war was born; it provided every possible increase in military spending. In fact, since the United States had a monopoly of atomic bombs, the USSR was very unlikely to be aggressive. Moreover, Soviet foreign policy was mostly very cautious and conservative (so much so that revolutionaries in other countries accused them of betrayal for not supplying arms). Therefore the armaments spending justified by the cold war rhetoric was not militarily necessary. It was utilized, as in Southeast Asia, to protect U.S. investments abroad but also in large part to support the U.S. economy at home. In both world wars the industrialists dictated to the government exactly how the procurement process should be run, completely dominated the Department of Defense, and made enormous rates of profit. This condition has continued ever since.

How big is U.S. military spending? It certainly includes all Department of Defense spending, but it goes considerably beyond that. How far is controversial, but the most careful study to date (by James Cypher, 1973) includes half of all "international affairs" spending, veterans benefits, atomic energy and space appropriations (all military-related) and 75 percent of the interest on the public debt—since at least 75 percent of the debt was used to pay for wars. (Most of the data used in the rest of this chapter are from the outstanding study by Cypher.) Other military activities, on which it is too hard to get exact data, are major parts of the budget for research and development, the CIA, and other intelligence agencies—and of course the deaths, wounds, and alienation of young Americans. For the five quantifiable items in military spending, Cypher adds up the grand total of $1.7 trillion from 1947 through 1971—enough to buy our entire gross national product for 1969 and 1970. Similarly, Department of Defense spending was listed at "only" $127 billion in 1980, but if one includes the military items cited by Cypher, then it came to $223 billion.

Yet this amount of direct military spending (even if it included the things we cannot quantify) still underestimates the impact of military spending on the U.S. economy. There is a very large indirect or secondary effect on additional consumer goods from the spending of those who receive military dollars and on additional investment in plant, equipment, and business inventories by military industries. Economists measure the secondary effects of military spending by the government multiplier, which measures the ratio of the total increase in all spending to every dollar of increase in government spending. Estimates of the multiplier from military spending range from about $1.85 to $3.50 of total spending for every dollar of military spending.

The most important measure of military spending is as a percentage of our gross national product (GNP). For the whole 1947–1971 period, direct military spending averaged 13.2 percent of GNP. Now if one is quite conservative and assumes a multiplier of only 2, it is apparent that direct and indirect military spending accounted for the demand for 26.4 percent of GNP. This means that if military spending and its indirect effects had not been present in this whole period and all other things had been the same (which is very unlikely), we would have had a depression greater than that in the 1930s—when unemployment was 24.3 percent. Of course, military spending has not disappeared, but grew again in the 1980s under President Reagan. Total Department of Defense spending (with none of the additions calculated by Cypher) was a record $263 billion in 1983. The Reagan administration proposed to spend two trillion dollars on the military in its second term in office.

How Much Profit in Military Contracts?

Why is big business normally happy with such a high level of military spending? On the aggregate level, we saw that it is used to protect U.S. investments abroad, to get the economy out of recessions, and to prevent a major depression; but there is an additional incentive for the individual defense contractor. This incentive is based on the fact that the rate of profit is very high in military production and that most of these profits go to a few very large firms. Almost all military contracts go to some 205 of the top 500 corporations, and just 100 of them get 85 percent of all military contracts.

There are some studies of military profits, but all of them understate the profit rates. In reporting to the government, the military firms overstate their costs—and since they do not operate under competition, but in a cozy relation with the Pentagon, they probably overstate costs more than most firms. Thus they allocate costs of other parts of their business to military contracts and add in all sorts of other unrelated costs. Some have even tossed in the costs of call girls to influence governmental inspectors (called "entertainment" in their accounts). They also make many hidden profits through the use of complex sub-contracting procedures to subsidiaries, unauthorized use of government-owned property, and getting patents on research done for the government.

Still, a study by the General Accounting Office (GAO) of the U.S. government has definitely spelled out their high profit rates (see Cypher, 1973: ch. 5). First the GAO asked eighty-one large military contractors by questionnaire what their profit rates were for 1966 through 1969. The replies, which were limited by self-interest, still admitted an average profit rate of 24.8 percent—much higher than nonmilitary profits in the same industries. But spot checks showed that these profit rates were still very much underreported. So the GAO did its own audit of the books of 146 main military contractors. The study found that the profit rate of these merchants of death was a fantastic 56.1 percent rate of return on invested capital.

Suggested Readings

The best critique of pluralism is by a former pluralist, Lindblom (1977). Two excellent surveys of all the literature are Carnoy (1984) and Szymanski (1978). A thorough study of Marx's political thought is by Draper (1977). The fullest empirical data are in Domhoff (1967; 1970; 1978; 1979), and there is excellent data on middle-class politics in Openheimer (1985). An outstanding study of both the data and the literature on the state under capitalism is Bowles and Gintis (1986). Tom Gervasi (1984; 1986) has written two good books on Soviet and U.S. military spending. There is a good article on the state and the economy by John Miller (1987). On local government policies, see the excellent book by Gottdeiner (1987). For light reading, one should read the very revealing book by the right-wing David Stockman (1986) on the U.S. budget process.

— 9 —

CAPITALISM, IMPERIALISM, AND UNDERDEVELOPMENT

Has there always been imperialism? Certainly, there has been colonial occupation and plunder since the days of the ancient Egyptians and Persians. The phenomena of modern imperialism, however, are quite new and different. The radical, Marxist definition of "imperialism" (Lenin, 1915) emphasizes that the internal environment of modern imperialism is monopoly capitalism, which only became predominant in Western Europe and the United States in the 1880s and 1890s—so imperialism in the modern sense dates from that period. Furthermore, modern imperialism utilizes not only plunder and unequal trading, but especially vast amounts of international investment.

Definitions are arbitrary, of course, but the main characteristics of what we call imperialism—international trade and investment dominated by the giant corporations of a few countries—are the key to the modern world. Emphasis on these characteristics helps to explain why the change from outright colonial control to "independence" in most of the underdeveloped world made much less difference than most liberals expected. While the forms have changed, the essential structure of imperialism persists, and the colonies have become neo-colonies.

Facts of Economic Underdevelopment

There are at least two generally accepted definitions of an underdeveloped country: one based on an economic index and the other based on certain distinguishing characteristics. The economic index that is generally used is average income per person (gross national product divided by the number of the population). Over 50 percent of capitalist countries fall into the "low income" category of less than $410 a year (World Bank, 1984: *ix*).

The word "underdeveloped" is used here because it is in common usage. Its connotations, however, are very misleading. For example, there is no correlation between the level of income and the level of cultural or social development. Obviously, ancient Greece or Egypt or China had very highly developed cultures with very low average income levels. Furthermore, an average may hide wide disparities in individual incomes. For example, Kuwait has one of the highest levels of average income per head; but most of the income is concentrated in the hands of a few very rich persons, and there is an enormous gulf between the very rich and the very poor. The high level of average income per head in Kuwait is solely the result of the oil resources of that little country, and, therefore, one cannot assume that the country is highly developed in an overall sense.

Dissatisfaction with the use of a single, purely economic measure of development has led some students of the subject to suggest a definition of underdevelopment based on several distinguishing characteristics of underdeveloped countries. The commonly found characteristics of underdeveloped countries are a relatively low income per person, a relatively high proportion (often 60 percent or more) of the population engaged in agriculture, a relatively low level of technology used in production, a relatively low level of education, and a relatively low level of capital formation. This definition still leaves more than 50 percent of the population of the capitalist world in countries that can be classified as underdeveloped.

Among capitalist or capitalist-dominated countries in the lowest category, with extraordinarily low income per person, mostly agrarian, and lacking in technology, education, or capital, fall India, most of Asia, and most of Africa. Slightly better off in income, but still very underdeveloped in all other indices, are most of Latin America, North Africa, Indonesia, and the Philippines. Countries that are still very poor but are more developed in some aspects include a few Latin American countries, Greece, and Spain. Countries with the highest category of income, and well developed in many aspects include Australia and New Zealand, Japan, most of Western Europe, and Canada and the United States (Kuwait and Qatar are also listed as high-income countries, but these are tiny areas sitting on top of oil wells with most of the income going to a small elite.)

In the advanced capitalist countries it is true that workers' wages have grown greatly in the last hundred years. But conditions in most of the capitalist world—its poorest, underdeveloped part—are still miserable, and incomes remain at incredibly low levels. In fact, many of the Third World countries are not only below poverty, but below subsistence levels. "Two thirds of the inhabitants of the underdeveloped countries of the Third World do not get the essential minimum of 2,500 calories per day; the expectation of life for many of them is less than half that in the highly developed countries" (Jalee, 1965: 8).

The gap between rich and poor is reflected in the fact that in 1964 two-thirds of the world's population produced only about 25 percent of world output. At the same time the United States alone (with only 6 percent of world population) produced about 30 percent of world output. Furthermore, the gap is getting larger; Marx might say the underdeveloped capitalist countries (or Third World inhabitants) are more and more relatively impoverished.

Griffin and Gurley (1985: 1115) contend that in the last thirty-five years, most Third World countries have had a growing national product. Yet the Gross Domestic Product (GDP) per person is still rising more slowly in the underdeveloped countries than in the more developed countries. In the developed capitalist countries the percentage rates of growth of GDP per capita have been 3.9 (1960–1973), 2.1 (1973–1979), and 1.5 (1980–1985). But the rates of growth of GDP per capita in the underdeveloped countries have been 3.7 (1960–1973), 2.0 (1973–1979) and 0.7 (1980–1985) (World Bank, 1984: 36). Thus, the gap in production per person is still growing between the poorest countries and the richest countries.

Overpopulation?

Many of the evils of capitalism are blamed, incorrectly, on overpopulation. If this apologia for the status quo is said to apply to the advanced capitalist countries, how much more is it said to apply to the underdeveloped capitalist countries. It is asserted as an axiom, which only crude and biased radicals could deny, that people in the underdeveloped countries are hungry because there are too many people. Proof: Just look at the vast number of poor and starving people, as in India. Thus that sophisticated and unbiased scholar, Robert S. McNamara (former president of Ford Motor Company, former U.S. secretary of defense, former head of the World Bank) asserted that "the greatest single obstacle to the economic and social advancement of the majority of the peoples in the underdeveloped world is rampant population growth" (1970).

The important point to note about McNamara's ideology is that it tells hungry people that the "greatest single obstacle" to their development is their own animal sexual desires. The function of this ideology is thus identical to that of the theory that underdevelopment is due to racial inferiority, the laziness and/or stupidity of "the natives." It provides the perfect defense against the suspicion of these peoples that their problems are due to antiquated social systems, rapacious ruling classes, and imperialism.

If one turns to the facts, there is no evidence that high population density is the prime cause of underdevelopment. More precisely, there is no statistically significant correlation between high population density and low income per person (Baran, 1957: 237–48). On the contrary, many countries with high incomes per person also have high population densities. For example, Belgium has 816 people per square mile; West Germany, 624; and the United Kingdom, 588. India has only 406 people per square mile, and most of the underdeveloped countries have much lower population densities.

Another related "theory" of underdevelopment claims that the underdeveloped nations are all those who by accident have relatively few natural resources on their territories. Yet 69.1 percent of the exports of the underdeveloped countries in 1980 were minerals, fuels, and crude materials (United Nations, 1985: *iii.*). In fact, most of their raw materials are taken away to the advanced capitalist countries and are there manufactured into finished goods (some of them being sold back at a high profit to the underdeveloped countries).

In the radical view, therefore, the main obstacles to development are not natural or biological factors inherent in the underdeveloped countries, and not sexual desires and procreation, laziness, low intelligence, or lack of natural resources. The obstacles are in the present social class relationships: the fact that all the peasants' and workers' surplus over immediate needs is extracted from them by the landlords, moneylenders, tax collectors, and foreign corporations. The problem, as shown below, is that the native ruling classes use their high incomes for luxury consumption, while most of the enormous profits of foreign corporations are removed from the country altogether.

As a result there is a lack of capital for investment in development. The lack of capital (and lack of nonhuman power per person) is correlated with low income per person (Baran, 1957: 246). The lack of capital means not only little construction, but also little new equipment and little technological improvement. It also means few funds available for education and training, let alone research. The lack of capital also means that millions of workers cannot be employed at a sufficient rate of profit, so they are left unemployed or underemployed. Thus, it is the social relations (and their consequences) that are the real obstacles to development.

As an example, let us take the attempts at technological revolution in farming in several underdeveloped countries. In this "green revolution" new types of grains have been introduced, especially in India and Pakistan (see Griffin, 1972). They have brought much higher yields, so that the technical barrier to feeding the population seems to be falling. To make efficient use of the new processes and output, however, requires large mechanized farms. Indeed, small peasants are being evicted in growing numbers to make way for large agricultural enterprises. The dispossessed peasants are swelling the ranks of the unemployed in the cities. At the same time, complaints are heard from the large farm owners that there is overproduction of grain relative to the small money demand of the poor. Thus, the socioeconomic relationships form a barrier to technological development.

Theories of Imperialism

Imperialism (see survey by Griffin and Gurley, 1985) is domination by one country over another to benefit the imperialist country (see early theories by Hobson, 1902; Hilferding, 1910; Lenin, 1915). In Lenin's view a new type of imperialism began in the 1870s and reached a peak about 1900. All territory was controlled by various strong capitalist powers. Its characteristics were a merger of bank and industrial capital into finance capital, the export of capital abroad, and militarism. Capitalists fight to expand and to redivide the world. Export of capital occurs because there is no profitable outlet in the imperialist country. Lenin is followed by Nicolai Bukharin (1917), Sweezy (1942), and many others.

Harry Magdoff (1969; 1978) finds an older type of imperialism with commercial capitalists characterized from 1450 to 1650 by plunder and piracy, from 1650 to 1770 by slavery and extraction of raw materials, and from 1770 to 1870 by remaking the colonial world for capitalism. In 1870–1914 England was dominant. There were struggles to redivide the world in World War I and II. From 1945 to the present, the United States is mostly dominant.

Rosa Luxemburg (1913) argued that capitalists must expand or collapse. Workers have a constant level of consumption, so capitalists always need new markets. Although Luxemburg has some elements of truth, most writers believe she is far too extreme and overstated.

Sweezy (1942) says that the dominance of finance capital was a passing stage. Now there are giant multinational monopoly corporations. Why is imperialism so urgent? According to Sweezy, imperialism means more profit; it holds back the impact of falling domestic profit; and there is a need for raw materials.

There is a big difference between the early and later writers on one point. Lenin and Marx believed that capital flows to underdeveloped countries. Sweezy, Baran (1957), and Magdoff find that capital flows to the developed countries—because profit is greater than investment! This issue is investigated below.

Most radicals (such as Baran) see imperialism as having enormous negative effects on underdeveloped countries. Surplus flows out by means of plunder, unequal trade, and profit on investment; it causes distortion because the economy is only export oriented; and the economy is mostly limited to primary agriculture and raw materials.

Neoclassical economists often cite the benefits of colonialism. First, there is a market in capital and labor. On the contrary, radicals argue that there is much slavery and forced labor. Second, there is free trade, everyone gains—the Third World has a comparative advantage in agriculture and minerals. On the contrary, radicals argue that there is unequal trade. Also, the result of export trade exclusively in agricultural products and minerals is no industrialization. Third, capital flows cause growth. But radicals argue that the surplus from investment flows out! Even in the eighteenth century England got 8–10 percent of its income from the underdeveloped countries. Surplus flows out of the underdeveloped countries in the form of cheap exports, cost of colonial administration, a large police force and large army, and luxury consumption. So there is economic dependency, and economic dependency leads to political dependency. But there is a weak internal ruling class, so the military often takes over, and their rule depends on foreign capitalist support. Thus dependency theorists such as Frank (1967), contrary to Marx, argue that capitalism is a motor of growth in imperialist countries but is a barrier in the Third World.

Baran (1957) stresses that the main problem is not the size of the surplus. There is plenty of surplus, contrary to neoclassicals who see a low level of production and a low surplus, but the surplus flows out and/or is not used for growth. Also, Baran says that much of the potential surplus is not actually produced; for example, there is unemployment, unproductive labor, and wasteful labor, such as production of alcohol and tobacco.

Many radicals in the 1970s and 1980s have found that the Third World is not all stagnating, but that some countries are growing rapidly, even under capitalism (see de Janvry, 1981: 18–22). There is even some growth of manufacturing, though most of it is assembly, not production.

Unequal Exchange

Early radical theories argued that the terms of trade tend to go against the less developed countries (Prebisch, 1962). Neoclassicals argue that less developed countries will change their composition of output as supply and demand determine. Radicals contend the production set-up is relatively immobile and cannot change.

Arghiri Emmanuel (1972) says that unequal exchange means more labor hours for less. Capital is mobile, but labor is not. Labor is cheap in the poor countries. The criticism (by Bettleheim in an appendix to Emmanuel) is that exploitation is not mainly in exchanges between countries, but between classes in production—so don't whitewash the Third World ruling class by blaming exploitation only on the advanced capitalist countries.

The World System View

Marx mostly expected that the present backward countries would follow the same path as the developed, that industrial capital would triumph over merchant capital, that only the industrial proletariat could and would lead the revolution, and that the advanced capitalist countries would first reach socialism. Wallerstein says those predictions are mostly wrong; he notes that Marx himself noted many qualifications and exceptions. He argues that in the late Middle Ages in West Europe the crisis of feudalism led to the new system of capitalism by which the elite restored their ability to extract surplus value. "The new system consolidated itself in Europe [by about 1650] and went on from there to take over the world, in the process eliminating all alternative modes of social organization and establishing a single division of labor throughout the globe for the first time in human history" (1985: 389).

Wallerstein says that the capitalist world system extracted surplus value from workers (and peasants) and sent most of it to the "so-called core areas of this world economy, essentially by means of unequal exchange mechanisms that gave the advantage to upper strata in core areas at the expense of smaller numbers of upper strata in the peripheral areas" (p. 389). Contrary to early Marxist expectations, he finds that the backward countries remained underdeveloped, that merchant capital remained in control, that workers in the advanced capitalist countries did not become revolutionary, and that socialist revolutions came first in the less developed countries. Since these peripheral countries call themselves socialist, but remain part of the capitalist world system, the revolutions eventually lead back to some new form of capitalism—which view is discussed critically in the next part of this book.

According to Wallerstein, capitalism has brought moral and "material regression" to most of the people of the world. His assertion, however, that capitalism has caused Third World economies to contract is very questionable. He asserts that capitalism will only be overthrown when it has further disintegrated all over, so that revolutions may be more or less simultaneous by all the oppressed peoples of the world (also a very questionable prediction).

Obstacles to Development

What keeps a country in an underdeveloped condition? It is a truism to say that growth would be faster if underdeveloped countries had more capital, more technology, and more education and training. In fact, for many underdeveloped capitalist countries the problem is not a low rate of growth of income per person, but no per capita growth at all. The aggregate income does not grow much faster than (and maybe not as fast as) the population. Moreover, a complete change is needed from a rural, agrarian economy to an urban, industrialized economy. The issue, then, is how to begin to develop, how to start from little or no growth at all, and how to change the whole economic structure.

The argument here is that the obstacles are mainly institutional: an internal ruling class spends much of its income on luxuries and spends government revenues on unnecessary public monuments or military expenditures; foreign trade is on very poor terms, and the wrong items are imported for development; and foreign investment is in the sectors least useful to development, with high profits sent abroad (see Dobb, 1967: part 2). Notice that this is quite opposite to most nonradical views. Some, we have seen, argue that the trouble is sex and too much population, or laziness, or stupidity.

Others argue a vicious circle in which poverty is the main cause of poverty: "The poor are considered the victims of their poverty. . . the poor society has nothing with which to buy growth. Having less than enough for its current needs for food, clothing and shelter, it has nothing for investment" (Galbraith, 1962: 25–26). One wonders how the impoverished Soviet Union ever developed without foreign aid. The theory is a good apologia for the status quo. What are some real obstacles to development?

Internal Class Structure

Let us begin with the internal obstacles to development created by the social systems within the underdeveloped countries. The typical situation finds millions of peasants engaged in subsistence farming, obligated to pay high rents to landlords, high interest to moneylenders, and high taxes to local and national governments. From his or her small net product, the peasant usually pays more than half to meet these obligations (Baran, 1957: 165). The peasant retains hardly enough for bare subsistence and has none left for major improvement or investment.

The landlords and moneylenders spend much of their share of the surplus taken from the peasant in conspicuous luxury consumption. If they reinvest any, their extreme conservatism prompts them to invest in more land or to send it to some safe foreign country; little if any is invested in industry. (The best discussion of the misuse of the surplus in underdeveloped countries is by Lippit, 1985. Also see Thomas, 1974.) The governments are mostly dominated by a small elite of wealthy landlords and merchants (in turn, often foreign-dominated), so they have little motivation to invest government funds in constructive projects—in fact, the advent of industrial capitalism would lose this elite their present power. Most government revenue is spent on military goods and services for the purpose of internal repression. Governments spend some on showcase projects, such as new sports arenas, or—as in Venezuela—in beautification of the capital city. The little that is spent constructively is usually for roads or ports to serve the needs of foreign investors.

One liberal view holds that the best panacea would be land reform, which would turn over the full ownership of their plots to the peasants, eliminating rents and landlords completely. The problem is that splitting up the estates into many small plots would make investment and technical progress even less likely. The peasant would still have very little income and would tend to consume it all. The plots of land would be too small for the application of modern technology. This was exactly the case in the thorough-going Soviet land reform of 1917, which created 26 million tiny farms. The Soviets also discovered a tendency for competition to ruin the small farms and recreate large landholdings.

A related view holds that the main obstacles to progress in the Third World are the semifeudal forms and holdovers in the countryside. The key issue is again considered to be land reform to bring these countries at least into the age of capitalism. Although the problems of land reform are clearly important, this view probably gives too much weight to the few remaining leftovers of earlier systems. Throughout Latin America and much of the Third World, the web of capitalism reaches through the foreign enterprises in the ports and main cities via the native merchants and traders right down to the local landlords and moneylenders. In most of the underdeveloped areas agriculture is in fact highly commercialized, so that more commercialization and more capitalism does not seem to be the answer (Frank, 1967).

A study by Alain de Janvry (1981) explains how the complex alliance of industrial bourgeoisie and landed semifeudal elites dominates many countries in Latin America. He demonstrates how, together, they hold back political and economic progress in Latin America to preserve their own interests in the status quo.

Lippit (1978) shows that China was perhaps the world's most developed country in the thirteenth century but was one of the least developed by the twentieth century. The reason was not mainly foreign imperialism, but was mostly a class structure that determined an unproductive use of surplus. He finds no signs of development in the nineteenth century, so the West could not hold it back. Elements of the ruling class are merchants, landlords, government officials, and gentry. Lippit says that gentry, who get their surplus from the peasants, are really the only ruling class; the others are aspects of it (landowning, mercantile, money lending, a few big businesses, official position, and so forth, all being additional functions of some members of the gentry).

Lippit concludes that ''Both in industry and agriculture, the production relations of late imperial China were marked by a fairly complete separation between large-scale owners and production processes. The path to profit was not the improvement of production, but command over the social processes whereby the direct producers were relieved of the surplus they produced . . . the system worked well from the standpoint of the gentry, providing them with wealth and status; there was no reason why they should want to change it, and indeed they did not want to do so'' (1978: 305-306). He finds that the gentry opposed modernization because of the threat to their position, fostered an ideology that was hostile to new scientific inquiry (pushing only an education in the classics), were hostile to change, and helped maintain the status quo.

With respect to the government in underdeveloped countries, Griffin and Gurley argue that ''Orthodox economists . . . assume that the state is essentially an even-handed institution [with no class bias] which attempts to maximize [utility for everyone]. . . . If welfare is not in fact maximized, this must be because policy mistakes have been committed . . . the radical economist is likely to regard [these 'mistakes'] as a deliberate attempt to improve the position of particular interests'' (1985: 1122-23). Thus, the government policies holding back development in some countries—no land reform, no tax reform, misallocation of credit only to the largest firms—reflect the dominant class interests. Hence the orthodox cost-benefit analysis from the viewpoint of the whole society is useless because the dominant class and its government will ignore it—and the exploited have no power to put it into operation.

In education policy, for example, most Third World countries give large money subsidies to universities, but much less to elementary schools and high schools. If more went to the lower grades, society as a whole would greatly benefit from the reallocation of resources. But children of the ruling class benefit most from university educations and get high-paying positions as a result, while the poor never get that far. So the disproportionate funding of the universities is retained because ''from the point of view of those who control the government, there is no misallocation of resources'' (ibid.: 1124).

Colonialism and Neocolonialism

From the fifteenth to the nineteenth centuries Europeans slowly took over the rest of the world. They plundered, enslaved, and ruled so as to extract the maximum from their subjects, all in the name of God and the spread of Christianity. Such havoc was created that ancient and culturally advanced civilizations disappeared, as in Peru and West Africa, and progress was set back hundreds of years by the destruction of native industries, as in India.

On the other side, the plunder was so great that it constituted the main element in the formation of European capital and provided the foundation for prosperous trade and eventual industrialization. "The discovery of gold and silver in America, the extirpation, enslavement and entombment in mines of the aboriginal population, the beginning of the conquest and looting of the East Indies, the turning of Africa into a warren for the commercial hunting of black-skins, signalised the rosy dawn of the era of capitalist production" (Marx, 1967: 823). It is important to remember always that the West industrialized with the help of loot from imperialism. By contrast, the present underdeveloped countries not only do no plundering of others, many of them are still being plundered.

By the end of the nineteenth century, almost all the present underdeveloped countries were under the colonial rule of the more advanced countries. The imperialist countries invested in the colonial countries at astoundingly high profit rates, primarily because of a cheap labor supply and an enforced lack of competition. The capital was mainly invested in extractive industries, which exported raw materials to the imperial country. In the imperial country, the cheap raw materials were profitably turned into manufactured goods, part of which were exported back (tariff-free) to the colonial country.

The tariff-free imports of finished goods from the imperial country generally completed by competition the destruction (often begun by plunder) of the manufacturing industries in the colonial country. An example of this destruction may be seen in colonial India, especially in its textile industry: "Foreign trade statistics best show the effects of 'deindustrialization.' India, still an exporter of manufactured products at the end of the eighteenth century, becomes an importer. From 1815 to 1832 India's cotton exports dropped by 92 percent. In 1850, India was buying one quarter of Britain's cotton exports. All industrial products shared this fate. The ruin of the traditional trades and crafts was the result of British commercial policy" (Bettleheim, 1968: 47).

The development of the colonial areas was thus held back by the imperialist countries, while the development of the imperialist countries was greatly speeded up by the flow of plunder and profits from the colonies. The exception is Japan, since Japan did escape colonialism. Thus, it was able independently to industrialize and develop its own advanced capitalism, alone among the countries of Asia, Africa, and Latin America, because the others had all been reduced to colonies and had their further development prevented.

From 1890 to the Second World War was the peak period of colonialism, when all the world was divided among the West European and North American powers. In the late 1940s and 1950s a new era began, with formal independence achieved by hundreds of millions of people throughout Asia and Africa—as a result of struggles unleashed by the impact of two world wars, the Russian and Chinese revolutions, and the long pent-up pressures for liberation. The day of open colonialism is over (except for southern Africa), but the pattern still holds by which the former colonial countries export food or raw materials. In fact, the underdeveloped countries are often dependent mainly on exports of just one product, and they still import most of their finished goods. Foreign investment still dominates their industries. Moreover, most foreign capital invested in the less developed countries still goes into raw materials extraction, in spite of the recent spread of some foreign investment to manufacturing in certain countries. Because of the continuance of the underlying colonial economic pattern, many radicals call this situation "neocolonialism," in spite of formal political independence.

The point is that imperialism has changed in form, is supposed to smell better, but is still imperialism. On the one side are all the underdeveloped and newly "independent" countries, still under foreign economic domination, still facing all the old obstacles to development. On the other side are the advanced capitalist countries, still extracting vast profits from the dependent Third World. The imperialist group includes all those who extract profits by trade and investment. Thus, it includes most of West Europe, Japan, and the United States. Most imperialist control now comes through economic and monetary penetration, not direct occupation. The control ranges from blatant forms such as subsidies and military supplies to highly complex monetary agreements.

It should also be noted that the economic control is often not direct, but built up in a complex pyramid. For example, some American companies directly invest in Northeast Brazil. More control of that area, however, is achieved through American domination of major Brazilian companies in the South, which in turn buy control in companies in the Northeast area. Still more control is achieved through American domination of some West European companies, which in turn own some major Brazilian firms, or which directly own some of the local firms in the Northeast area (Frank, 1967).

The most urgent world issue today is the relative impoverishment of the vast neocolonial areas of the world. This is the breeding ground of wars of liberation from imperialism, all of which eventually tend to escalate under current circumstances into "limited" wars between the statist and capitalist blocs.

Methods of Neocolonialism

In addition to economic penetration, the methods of neocolonial subjugation extend from propaganda to assassination to coups d'etat by foreign-supported forces. One should also mention direct military force. In the Reagan administration, the United States has invaded Grenada, mined the harbors of Nicaragua, supported the use of force to overthrow Angola, and bombed Libya. Short of that, treaties guarantee military bases (such as Guantanamo Bay in Cuba) and even grant exclusive rights to Western information services such as the U.S. Information Agency. Sophisticated imperialists naturally prefer control by propaganda in the broadest sense to armed intervention (the U.S. image has suffered under the Reagan administration). Under the category of imperialist propaganda, certainly, one must include the vast flow of Hollywood movies, Western books, and Western news services to the neocolonial areas. Another important agency of imperialist propaganda is the activity of missionary religious sects. The older ones would seem laughable and anachronistic in the twentieth century world of science. New ones with new techniques, however, are better prepared to attack the neocolonial world. These include Moral Rearmament, Jehovah's Witnesses, and even some forms of Zen Buddhism.

Closely akin is the evangelism, well subsidized by the CIA, of some American labor unions. American unions split the world unity of labor unions after the Second World War, and even then found their new restricted group of allies too far left. In international affairs American unions are one of the most reactionary forces, wielding major economic strength and utilizing a vast flow of money to buy propaganda and friends. Nor should the effective propaganda use of the U.S. Peace Corps be overlooked. If all other propaganda means fail, the CIA itself is clearly willing to use thirty pieces of silver in the case of important leaders (see Nkrumah, 1965: 245–50).

Finally, it should be stressed that the single most effective form of imperialist propaganda is prejudice, including the inflaming of racial, religious, and nationalist prejudices. By this disgusting means, imperialism has successfully practiced divide and rule in many areas. Instead of fighting imperialism, Jews fights Arabs, Catholics fight Protestants, Hindus fight Moslems, and so forth. Each is told that the other is the cause of their troubles, that the other is inferior, and anything else to prevent their unity. Yet is is the disunity fostered by racism that mortally weakens the position of both sides against imperialism.

Racism also operates to prejudice the working class of the imperialist country in support of military ventures against other peoples. At the end of the nineteenth century a leading European "socialist" could write: "Only a conditional right of savages to the land occupied by them can be recognized. The higher civilization ultimately can claim a higher right" (Bernstein, 1899: 179). Essentially the same racist thought was used to justify the attempt of Hitler's Aryan master race to conquer the world.

When beating the drums of war, racism is often called "patriotism." Such patriotism was used to justify the massacre of women and children in Vietnam by machine guns or by napalm. One general called for open provision of prostitutes (naturally, Vietnamese women) to men at American Post Exchanges, all in the name of patriotism (Thomas, 1969: 1). "Patriotism is an acceptance of national immorality" (Pauling, 1964).

Foreign Trade

The colonial era left the economies of the underdeveloped countries very dependent on foreign demand, and consequently very sensitive to the foreign business cycle of expansion and depression. It is also a fact that international investments and trade in primary products (that is, in raw materials, both agricultural and mineral) show the greatest fluctuations. Since the Third World countries are very dependent on foreign investment and exports of primary products, their economies show enormous fluctuations as a result of forces beyond their control.

By the end of World War II, this dependence was recognized in the underdeveloped countries. The government of Ceylon stated: "The economy of Ceylon depends almost entirely on its export trade in tea, rubber and coconut products. . . . About 80 percent of the people are employed directly or indirectly in the production and handling of these exports" (United Nations, 1949: 42). The government of Burma said explicitly that "the most important source of unemployment in Burma is a decline in prices of raw materials caused by the depression generated elsewhere" (ibid.).

In the forty years since the end of World War II, the dependence of the former colonial countries on exports of agricultural goods and raw materials has remained. Thus, in 1980 the Third World countries had 79 percent of their exports in food, mineral fuels, and crude materials (United Nations, 1985: *iii*).

On the other hand, in 1980 the developed capitalist countries had 75 percent of their exports in machinery and equipment, chemicals, and other manufactured goods (ibid.). Thus, the Third World countries remain primarily suppliers of raw materials, while the advanced capitalist countries are industrialized suppliers of manufactured goods to the world. Very frequently a raw material is exported relatively cheaply from the Third World to the developed capitalist countries, then comes back to the underdeveloped countries as part of an expensive manufactured commodity. The pattern of unbalanced production and dependence continues.

Foreign Investment

Many economists, radicals and nonradicals alike, have argued that the profits of the advanced capitalist countries have been dependent on the constant expansion of new opportunities for investment abroad. During a depression, a country may have an intense desire to find or conquer new markets for goods and capital exports. Although England actually did this at times before about 1870, this easy road to recovery has seldom been open since then. On the contrary, in the whole period since about 1870, the net flow of capital has been into the imperialist countries.

Foreign investment is very large today. Yet it can no longer be said to play an important role as an outlet for an investment-seeking capital surplus. The reason is that the returns on it are greater than the new investment each year. Indeed, except possibly for brief periods of abnormally high capital exports from the advanced countries, foreign investment must be looked upon as a method of pumping capital out of underdeveloped areas, not as a channel through which capital is directed into them. Even in the years between 1870 and the First World War, England's income from overseas investment far exceeded its capital exports. Thus, in the years 1870 through 1913, net export of capital totaled 2.4 billion pounds, while income received from foreign invest-ment came to 4.1 billion pounds (Cairncross, 1953: 180).

At any rate, in the present stage of mature imperialism, the situation is that the export of capital is exceeded by foreign earnings of the imperialist countries. The profit (and interest) payments from the un-derdeveloped countries to the imperialist countries are greater than the flow of investments (and loans) going the other way. The reason for this phenomenon is quite simple. Suppose the United States invests (net) $100 million in Latin America each year. Suppose the profit rate is 25 percent. By the fourth year $400 million has been invested, so total profit is $100 million. In the fifth year total profit is $125 million, which is greater than the yearly investment of $100 million.

This hypothetical example is mirrored in reality. Thus, for the entire period 1950–1975, the U.S. direct investment outflow was a total of $68.4 billion. In the very same period, investment income receipts flowing into the United States from direct investments were $110.6 billion. Hence, the U.S. economy gained $42.2 billion from abroad in that period in receipts minus costs (U.S. Council on International Economic Policy, 1977: 167).

The picture is far more striking, however, when one divides the flows between U.S. investments in the developed and underdeveloped areas (Magdoff, 1969). For example, in 1950–1965 in the developed area of Europe, U.S. corporations invested $8.1 billion but received back only $5.5 billion to the United States. In the same period, howev-er, in the underdeveloped Third World, the situation was very different. In Latin America in those years American corporations invested $3.8 billion but extracted in income $11.3 billion, for a net flow of $7.5 billion from that area to the United States! Similarly, in Africa and Asia in the period 1950 through 1965 American corporations invested only $5.2 billion, while transferring to the United States $14.3 billion of profits, for a net flow of $9.1 billion to the United States.

These data on investment flows reflect the fact that rates of return are much higher in the underdeveloped Third World countries than in the developed capitalist countries. The rates differ greatly over time, but the higher rate area remains the same. In 1970, for example, U.S. rates of return on investment (income/average capital invested) were 21 percent in the underdeveloped countries and only 10.5 percent in the developed countries. In 1974 the rate of return was 13.3 from the developed, but 52.2 from the underdeveloped. In 1984, the rate of return was 9 percent from the developed, but 13 percent from the underdeveloped (U.S. Department of Commerce, 1971–1985).

Two facts are blatantly obvious from the above data: the rate of profit on U.S. investments abroad is higher in the underdeveloped than in the advanced capitalist countries; and the underdeveloped neocolonial countries generously make a good-sized net contribution to U.S. capital accumulation. In other words, since the flow of profit out is more than the flow of investment into the underdeveloped countries, the net effect of the present situation is not a help to their development, but a drain on their capital.

Not only is aggregate investment less than the profit extracted, but the pattern of investment is very imbalanced. The U.S. Department of Commerce figures show that in Latin America, Asia, and Africa, a large majority of all U.S. investment is in the extractive industries, especially petroleum. Thus, most foreign investment does not help the underdeveloped countries to industrialize, but only helps to deplete their raw materials. Only in Europe and Canada is the majority of U.S. investment in the nonextractive industries, mostly manufacturing, although there is a recent trend for more U.S. investment in manufacturing (or at least assembly of parts) in some of the underdeveloped countries.

Multinational Firms

The form of surplus extraction has been changing since the Second World War. It used to be that most investment was in the form of loans or stock purchases in existing companies or the setting up of brand new companies (with or without native participation). Today, the capitalist corporation simply sets up branches of its own firm or completely subordinates satellite firms. The day of the multinational firm is here.

The very dramatic example of Standard Oil of New Jersey typifies the trend. By 1962 Standard Oil of New Jersey had 33 percent of its assets abroad, 20 percent of its assets being in Latin America and 13 percent in Europe and Asia. Furthermore, the importance of these areas is shown by the fact that Standard Oil's profit on equity amounted in the United States to only 7.4 percent, but its rate of profit in Canada and in Latin America amounted to 17.6 percent and in Europe and Asia, 15 percent.

Not only does the giant multinational firm operate equally well here and abroad, but its board of directors (and its control) usually has an inseparable mixture of financial and industrial interests. "One can no longer today speak of either industrialists or bankers as the leading echelon of the dominant capitalist classes'' (Baran and Sweezy, 1966b: 18). In the fantastic size and complexity of their structure, which includes both finance and industrial capital, and the multiplicity of their interests, which includes both domestic and foreign sales, the giant corporations of today are very different from either earlier banking or earlier industrial interests.

Through the multinational corporations, American capital thus directly owns a large chunk of West European industry, and the capitalists of all the imperialist countries together own the major industrial enterprises of the underdeveloped countries. "There are no reliable figures for the Third World as a whole which measure the extent of foreign economic intervention, but it is certain that many, perhaps even most, of the industrial undertakings of the underdeveloped countries are foreign-owned or controlled" (Jalee, 1965: 22). A careful investigation of one important neocolony concludes that "foreign capital can . . . be said to share the control of the Indian economy with domestic capital on what is very nearly a fifty-fifty basis" (Bettleheim, 1968: 47).

It should also be stressed that most of these multinational firms are none other than our old friends, the few largest American corporations. In 1966, more than half of American profits from abroad went to just sixteen firms, all among the top thirty according to the *Fortune* listing (see MacEwan, 1970). Moreover, these profits were not a small sum, even relative to total American profits. By 1980, 24 percent of total U.S. corporate profit came from investments abroad (U.S. Department of Commerce, 1981).

One of the most important recent trends is the differential growth of domestic U.S. sales and sales abroad. The "sales abroad" do not include export sales, but are only the sales of the affiliates and subsidiaries of American corporations in foreign countries. This means that the United States is able to compete abroad not only by exports, but even more importantly by production of its subsidiaries within those countries. This trend is reflected in the fact that the sales of American-owned plants abroad rose by 140 percent in the last ten years, while exports from the United States went up by only 55 percent. The expansion can also be seen in the fact that in 1961 only 460 of the thousand largest U.S. companies had a subsidiary branch in Europe, but in 1965 over 700 of them had a branch in Europe (Baran and Sweezy, 1966b: 40–46). All the largest American firms are on the road to being truly multinational, to think from a viewpoint based on their worldwide investments. Therefore, they are not merely interested, like the earlier industrialists, in the export of commodities nor, like earlier bankers, in the export of capital. Rather, many of them have some of their major assembly plants in foreign countries, and they export a great deal from those subsidiaries in foreign countries.

In 1966 a study found that seventy-one of the top U.S. corporations averaged over one-third of their whole employment abroad (Heilbroner, 1971). Adding the multinationals of other capitalist countries, it now appears that approximately one-fourth of all capitalist production is in overseas plants (Turner, 1971). In fact, the foreign subsidiaries of many U.S. multinational firms are already large-scale exporters to the market in the United States.

As noted earlier, this especially means that profits can be transferred around within the corporation from a subsidiary in one country to the subsidiary in another. Therefore, we can no longer trust the reports of total profit remittances from the colonial areas to the United States as more than a general indicator. The total profits of an entire corporation are the crucial point, and they often include hidden profits in one subsidiary by reason of another selling to it more cheaply, or hidden losses in one subsidiary by reason of another selling to it more expensively than market price. For example, it appears that bauxite production in Jamaica, Surinam, and Guyana yielded to American corporations in 1961 a rate of profit of 26 to 34 percent. Yet this does not really give the total picture. Much of their costs "on materials and services" turn out to be exceedingly high payments to American corporations, also subsidiaries of the same major corporate group, at very high prices.

It follows that "the multinational companies often have conflicting interests when it comes to terms, export subsidies, foreign investment, etc." (Turner, 1971: 29). They are absolutely united, however, in desiring that as many nations as possible should have laws and institutions that are favorable to the unhampered development of private capitalist enterprise. Thus, there is much intracorporate conflict over economic details, but there is no conflict over the main political and strategic issues concerning the defense of imperialism.

Neocolonial "Aid"

Liberal economists favor foreign aid as a means to increase the growth of underdeveloped countries. But many radicals (such as Griffin and

Gurley, 1985) say that most aid is channeled into luxury consumption or government bureaucracy or police or military spending to help repress people. Even the total amount is very limited. By the mid-1980s, the percentage of foreign aid was certainly less than 1 percent of the national income of the countries giving the aid, so it could not be considered much of a burden. And also, unfortunately, it is not much of a help.

As seen earlier, the private investment part is itself more than offset by the profit and interest returns on the investments. The small public aid does not even offset the capital extracted by imperialism. That public aid which is nonmilitary and in the form of official donations or grants may be of some help, but it is not a large total amount. Even this ''help'' has extreme qualifications in that it is used to bolster repressive governments, to subsidize foreign investments, ''to subsidize foreign imports which compete with national products, to introduce technology not adapted to the needs of underdeveloped countries, and to invest in low-priority sectors of the national economies'' (Dos Santos, 1970: 233).

One type of ''help'' comes from the developed capitalist world in the form of loans. These loans, that is, the external debt of all the underdeveloped countries, have risen from $90 billion in 1972 to $462 billion in 1981 (United Nations, 1985: 330). The ratio of debt to GNP in all of the underdeveloped countries rose from 13 percent in 1970 to 27 percent in 1983 (World Bank, 1984: 31). At the same time, of course, the amount of principal and interest kept rising. In 1972, the principal repayment was $5 billion and the interest payment was $2 billion. In 1981, the principal repayment had risen to $31 billion and the interest payment rose to $29 billion. Thus, the interest is now almost equal to the principal, and the two together are a very large burden for the Third World. These payments are now so high that they threaten bankruptcy to many underdeveloped countries and crisis to the banks of the developed capitalist countries. Thus, loans are not a big help and are causing a crisis of repayment, while other nonmilitary aid has been small and very selective. The basically political nature of this aid is clear: ''Bilateral Public Aid, by far the most important, brings political servitude and economic subjection. It is given, received and applied in such a way as to strengthen business circles in the country giving it, and the local oligarchies in the country receiving it. International public aid is dispensed by international agencies dominated by the imperialist countries. It is technically better applied than bilateral aid but is, nevertheless, subject to one fundamental cause: anti-communism'' (Jalee, 1965). Certainly, one cannot find any specialist in foreign relations today who would claim that international public aid is given by any of the imperialist countries for purely charitable purposes. Obviously, it is given, and openly defended as such, for direct purposes of political domination and/or military support against the Soviet bloc or against native liberation armies.

It is the declared policy of all the U.S. agencies (for example, the Agency for International Development) that the countries that receive the aid shall use it primarily to beef up the private enterprise sectors of their economies, and shall not use it for public investment, which is often the most necessary in these countries for rapid development. Obviously, the aid of the United States is directed to help the profits of U.S. firms and to shore up these countries against communism and is not given for any pure, idealistic reason. In fact, the American aid agencies point out: ''(1) Foreign aid provides a substantial and immediate market for U.S. goods and services. (2) Foreign aid stimulates the development of new overseas markets for U.S. companies. (3) Foreign aid orients national economies toward a free-enterprise system in which U.S. firms can prosper'' (Magdoff, 1969: 13).

The U.S. Agency for International Development boasts that ''private enterprise has greater opportunities in India than it did a few years ago . . . fertilizer is an example of a field which is now open to the private sector, and was not in the past. This is largely a result of the efforts which we have made, the persuasion that we along with other members of the consortium have exerted on the Indian government'' (Committee on Foreign Affairs report, 1968: 185). A more blatant case of political pressure occurred in Brazil, where American aid fell from $81.8 to $15.1 million from 1962 to 1964 because the United States disliked the Goulart government. When ''good'' reactionary military officers overthrew Goulart, American aid jumped to $122.1 million in 1965 and $129.3 million in 1966 (Agency for International Development, 1967).

Nor are all the rewards of foreign aid purely ideological and in overseas areas. Just as the aid agencies claim, large parts of U.S. business benefit directly from the foreign aid program. Thus, 24.4 percent of U.S. exports of iron and steel products are financed by the U.S. Agency for International Development. Similarly financed are 30.4 percent of fertilizer exports, 29.5 percent of railroad equipment exports, 11.5 percent of nonferrous metal exports, and 5 to 10 percent of the U.S. exports of machinery and equipment, chemicals, motor vehicles and parts, rubber and rubber products, and textiles (Hyson and Strout, 1968: 71). Teresa Hayter (1971) concludes that foreign aid is in part a subsidy for multinational corporations because it raises demand for their products, finances infrastructure in the Third World, and avoids payment crises so that Third World countries can continue paying profits and interest.

Cheryl Payer (1974; 1982) shows how the World Bank and the International Monetary Fund act as agents of the multinationals. The IMF and World Bank threaten Third World countries to get them to denationalize, to support private enterprise and the use of the market, end price controls, and favor stability over growth (thus creating unemployment).

The Importance of Imperialism to the United States

Although everyone admits the importance of U.S. foreign investment and trade for the rest of the world, many economists consider that the effects of foreign trade and investment for the United States itself are negligible. This seems to be a misconception. It is true that our total exports normally are a small percentage of our gross national product and that our foreign investment is normally a small percentage of our domestic capital investment. The whole brunt of the argument for some pages previously, however, is the point that of very great importance today are the actual holdings of the United States through the means of multinational corporations which have branches in foreign countries (that is, the cumulative effect of all past investment). To emphasize this point once more, it may be noted that the ''goods produced in enterprises owned by U.S. corporations in other countries now exceed 100 billion dollars yearly, or three times the annual export of goods from the United States'' (Hymer, 1970: 244).

To find the total sales of U.S. corporations to foreign countries, one must add together exports and production of U.S. firms abroad. To make the most conservative estimate, some amount of double counting must be eliminated, since there is a certain type of overlap. If this is done, it is still found on the most conservative basis that the foreign market is something like 40 percent of the domestic market for U.S. corporations (Magdoff, 1969). Moreover, we saw above that the profit rate on U.S. foreign investment is much higher than the domestic rate, and that profits on foreign investment have averaged over 15 percent of total corporate profits for the last two decades. We also mentioned that some raw materials from abroad are vital and not obtainable in the United States.

Finally, we note the impact of military spending on the United States. Most U.S. military expenditures at home and abroad are directed to the aims of imperialism: protecting raw materials, foreign markets, commercial routes, spheres of influence of U.S. business, and U.S. investment opportunities (as well as capitalism in general). When one adds together the profits from U.S. foreign trade, from U.S. foreign investment, and from the military production to "defend U.S. interests," these profits come to about 25 to 30 percent of all profits. Recalling that most military and foreign profits go to the same few giant corporations, one begins to have some idea of the importance of American international relationships.

Imperialism and War

Capitalism has always shown its aggressiveness in the international arena. Capitalist nations and their colonies have always been arranged in pyramid style, where the largest dominate the medium sized and the medium sized dominate the small ones. What has changed over time has been mostly the positions of leading capitalist countries in the international arena. From 1815 to 1914 the British Empire played a dominant, completely superior role to any other capitalist country. Germany, however, developed industrially at a much more rapid rate, so it soon demanded as its "right" a larger share of the colonial spoils than it had. The clash of the two countries (and their allies) over redivision of the colonies seems to have been the major cause leading to the First World War.

The Second World War might also be termed a clash of two sets of imperialist powers, each seeking added wealth and power. Yet it was also something more because of the fascist ideology of one group, because of the participation of the Soviet Union, strong conflicting social forces within many advanced capitalist countries, and the beginnings of armed national liberation movements throughout Asia. It did, indeed, result in an expansion of various forms of statism or socialism in a third of the world, as well as struggles for independence over half the world.

In the capitalist sector, the defeat of the fascist powers left the United

States the single dominant force. Moreover, there was no complete American demobilization and demilitarization such as occurred for the most part after the First World War. The reason is that the United States, as the dominant imperialist power, now attempts to maintain a clear military superiority as well as an economic superiority.

It maintains this military superiority both through the vast system of alliances in which it is the dominant power and through its own very much enlarged armed forces. According to official (underestimated) U.S. data, the North American (mainly U.S.) share of military expenditures was 28 percent of all military expenditures in the world (U.S. Arms Control and Disarmament Agency, 1985: 4). The real rate of growth of North American (mainly U.S.) military expenditures from 1981 to 1983 was an amazing 7.5 percent a year. The Reagan administration has proposed a total military expenditure of $2 trillion for its second four years.

One major reason for this tremendous amount of armament is the need of control over the vast American empire. Notice in this connection that the decision to fight for a given area does not depend on the profits to be made from that area alone, but even more on its military-strategic importance to the structure of imperialism in a wider area. "Understood in these terms, the killing and destruction in Vietnam and the expenditure of vast sums of money are not balanced in the eyes of U.S. policy makers against profitable business opportunities in Vietnam; rather they are weighed according to the judgment of military and political leaders on what is necessary to control and influence Asia, and especially Southeast Asia, in order to keep the entire area within the imperialist system in general, and within the United States sphere of influence in particular" (Magdoff, 1969: 14-15).

A secondary reason for armament is the need or desire to oppose liberation movements and to oppose socialism. The third reason for armament is the fact that military expenditure is especially helpful to capitalism. It is unlike almost any other type of government expenditure in that it does not compete with any sort of private production. Furthermore, "the military plays the role of an ideal customer for private business, spending billions of dollars annually on terms that are most favorable to the sellers. Since a large part of their acquired capital equipment has no alternative use, its cost is commonly included in the price of the end product. The business of producing arms is therefore virtually risk free, in spite of which the allowable profit rates include a general margin for a mythical risk factor" (Baran and Sweezy, 1966b:

207). Thus, the capitalist class tends to be strongly in favor of military spending, though particular capitalists may oppose any specific action or tactic.

Whereas education and welfare may redistribute some profits to the working classes, militarization works in the opposite direction. Not only does it provide high rates of profit, but it also tends to kill "everything progressive and humane" and to "foster all the reactionary and irrational forces in society" (Baran and Sweezy, 1966b: 209). We saw in an earlier section that suddenly during a war the whole nation is made highly patriotic and chauvinist overnight by the vast outflowing of propaganda; and that patriotism kills off all reform, let alone radical sentiment for change in the society. Not only are the military and the capitalist class in favor of increased military spending; a large portion of the population is really convinced of the continued need for military spending. Only in the exceptional case of the Vietnam War was a large part of America roused into opposition, many being radicalized by this exposure to one violent example of imperialism. Even a part of the capitalist class opposed it, mainly on tactical grounds (impossible to win, causing too much inflation).

Enough military spending may stave off a major depression; but, under conditions of monopoly capitalism, the increased military expenditure may also lead to significant inflation, less welfare spending, and aggravation of all social problems. Moreover, if the choice is between depression and war escalation (to get steadily increasing military spending), surely it is better to face directly the economic problems of depression than to have chronic "limited wars" and to run the risk of complete nuclear destruction. After nuclear destruction, there can be no saving the world. After the beginning of an economic depression, it is certainly possible to fight for a rational economic system that would get us out of the depression immediately and restore prosperity.

We may now make a clear evaluation of the costs and benefits of imperialism and militarism to the imperialist country, using the United States as the example. Military production and military service increase employment, assuming we begin with major unemployment. If not, as in the Vietnam War, military spending leads to inflation. The large corporations make large profits on foreign investment. The flow of capital to the imperialist country (the excess of returns from foreign investment over current investment), however, must have a negative effect on domestic profits and employment through the competition of more capital.

The public at large, the taxpayer, pays the direct costs in money terms. In addition to money, more than forty-five thousand Americans were killed in Indochina, and more than five times that many were wounded. (About one million Vietnamese civilians have been killed, but that is presumably not a cost to the United States.)

The necessary climate of racism against the ''inferior'' Indochinese also worsened racism at home during the Vietnam War. The Korean War led to repression of civil liberties in order to limit opposition to the war. There are also attempts to curb inflation in wars by cutting all welfare spending so there are large costs to the poor. For the public as a whole, therefore, the costs in blood and money are vast and outweigh any slight benefits.

For the largest corporations, however, the balance is very different. They do pay some added taxes for the war, but they are able to pass on most of these to consumers and workers. They do have some higher costs from inflation, but their own prices rise faster. We saw that the sum of profits from military production and profits from foreign investment is about 25 to 30 percent of all corporate profits. (Of course, there are also many small corporations and some large ones that participate neither in foreign investments nor in military production, and who therefore tend to oppose military adventures).

Furthermore, the hundred largest corporations receive more than half of that very large amount of profit. For them it is the difference between depression and very high profit rates. Therefore, for the giant corporations the benefits of the military-imperialist effort clearly outweigh the costs. Since these same corporate interests are dominant in the capitalist state, it is no wonder that militarism and imperialism continue to be American policy, regardless of the tremendous cost to the American people.

Militarism and military actions are the ''inevitable'' tendency of imperialism. The American people have the power, however, if they will exercise it, to change the government, to end imperialism, militarism, and wars. Even short of that, the situation is very different from the beginnings of the two World Wars. Within the capitalist world, America is so militarily dominant (though it faces enormous economic competition) that conflicts over imperialist spoils cannot conceivably come to the point of major warfare. Between the leading capitalist and statist powers, one hopes that even the blindest ''statesmen'' on both sides recognize that all-out nuclear and biological warfare would cause the extinction of all human life on Earth within a few hours or days. Of course, increasing stockpiles of weapons by many countries make "accidental" war ever more likely.

We are still left with wars between the imperialist countries and the neocolonial countries, as the latter fight for their liberation. The question is whether these will remain "limited wars" or escalate to become the Last World War. World public pressure, and especially American and West European public pressure, can at least limit these wars and make the liberation of the neocolonial peoples as quick and peaceful as possible.

The Cure for Underdevelopment

The cure for underdevelopment is socialism (with democracy). Even liberal writers now recognize the appeal of socialism in the underdeveloped countries (such as Heilbroner, 1963). Socialist ownership means the end of foreign domination, the end of profit-outflow, and the concentration of resources and wealth on development. The problem is whether socialism (with democracy) can come peacefully or not in the Third World. The obstacles are internal reactionary power and foreign imperialism.

Suggested Readings

Almost all the references in this chapter are worth reading. In addition, the best survey is Griffin and Gurley (1985). An interesting predecessor of the world systems analysts is Cox (1964). A very good case study on Korea (Foster-Carter, 1985) reveals a lot about underdevelopment. Another good survey is by Attewell (1984: ch. 5). Two good articles on debt are by Magdoff (1986) and MacEwan (1986). An outstanding article on the spread of international interdependence and instability is by MacEwan (1984). An excellent book surveying views of imperialism is by Charles Barone (1985).

PART
III
STATISM

— 10 —

THE STATIST MODE OF PRODUCTION

Radical or independent Marxist analysis always begins with an analysis of the relations of production among classes in the society under examination. In the case of the Soviet Union, there is an enormous literature asking what type of productive relations exist in it. Is it socialist or capitalist or something else?

Semantic Issues vs. Real Issues

A scientist may use any definition, since definitions are created by human beings in order to communicate about particular problems. A scientific definition should merely be the most useful or fruitful concept of a phenomenon, that is, the one leading to the most successful research. If, as shown below, the Soviet Union cannot usefully be called socialist or capitalist, then it could be called something else, such as the X form of productive relations.

Some groups of orthodox Marxists argue the purely semantic question of what to call the USSR, but the real question is how does it work, how does it perform, and where is it going. Some official Marxists seem to think there is a ''correct'' definition—given by Marx or Lenin or Stalin or Mao or some other authority—but this confuses reality with sacred words.

The semantic question is important mainly because of propaganda. Official Marxists believe that the Soviet Union is a wonderful place, so it should be given the name ''socialism,'' which is a mark of approval in most of the world (and on the Left in every country). Most radicals, however, believe that the Soviet record is very mixed, with Stalin's mass murders and repression being the single most negative factor against modern socialism. Whatever the USSR may be, most radicals see it as the opposite of their vision of socialism, which is humane, peaceful, reasonable, and so forth.

Thus, most radicals define socialism so as to exclude the Soviet Union and Eastern Europe. Since socialists have a well-developed critique of the evils of capitalism, there is a tendency to call the Soviet Union some form of capitalism. It has been called state capitalism, bureaucratic capitalism, collective capitalism, in transition to capitalism, on the road to capitalism, and even capitalism. Before defining it and discussing how it operates, let us turn briefly to the previous radical literature on this subject (the best summary of which is in Griffin and Gurley, 1985, whose footsteps are followed here part of the way).

What Is the Soviet Union?

There are three main radical positions: (1) the USSR is a type of capitalism, (2) the USSR is socialist or near socialist, and (3) the USSR is neither socialist nor capitalist.

The USSR Is Capitalist

The Maoists, at one point in their history, argued that the USSR is capitalist, though they tried to protect Stalin to some extent because Stalin was their symbol of aggressive class struggle. Thus, Martin Nicolaus (1975) claimed that the USSR was socialist in Stalin's period, though Stalin made "mistakes," pushed too excessive a rate of growth, and restored some petty bourgeois incentives and inequality. But Khrushchev-Brezhnev ended socialism, set out on the road to capitalism, and reached "state monopoly capitalism." This system is led by a bureaucratic-monopoly-bourgeoisie. This new bourgeoisie has seized control of the Communist party, restored capitalism, and put the economy on an aggressive war footing.

Similarly, Bettelheim (1976a; 1976b; 1978; 1985) says that the Bolshevik view always suffered from "economism," a viewpoint that downplays class struggle and emphasizes only increased production in the transition to socialism. But without class struggle, the revolution failed and the USSR became "state capitalist." This means there is an elite that controls capital or the means of production, though they do it through the state. He argues that each Soviet firm is in practice separate and competitive, and that the system has business cycles. Thus, it is the same as capitalism.

The USSR Is Socialist

The basic argument against Nicolaus and Bettelheim and all others who call the USSR capitalist is that they prove too much. If the word "capitalist" has any meaning, then a capitalist economy should have the characteristic performance of capitalist economies, such as cyclical unemployment. But the USSR behaves very differently than capitalist economies, so how can it be called capitalist?

The defenders of the Soviet Union have seized on this weak point to argue that the Soviet Union is not capitalist. For example, Laibman (1983) argues that the USSR has no capitalist social structure because there are no capitalists, it has no unemployment and is always at full employment (a very strong point), and the ruling groups cannot give power over capital to their children. Similarly, Szymanski (1979) points out that Soviet wages are not set by the market, but by the plan, and that no one gets income simply by ownership of capital. In pointing out that the Soviet Union is very different from the U.S. economy, they are on solid ground—so their conclusion that the USSR should not be called capitalist is persuasive.

But Laibman and Syzmanski go much farther. They each claim that the Soviet Union is socialist because workers control power through the Communist party, workers nominate candidates, and criticisms are allowed in the media. These arguments about political democracy in the USSR are, however, totally incorrect. The fact that hundreds of thousands of people were murdered by the Soviet state under Stalin is proof enough of the lack of democracy. The only criticisms allowed in the Soviet press are of people already on their way out of power. There is no prior discussion, let alone criticism, of most major decisions, such as the invasion of Czechoslovakia in 1968. The only nominations allowed are those approved by the higher echelons. In summary, the top party bosses have power over the workers and everyone else, not vice versa.

If the definition of socialism includes exercise of political power by the working class, then the Soviet Union is not socialist.

The USSR Is a Backward Socialism

Trotsky (1937) saw the USSR as a "transitional" form, not a set of socialist relations of production. The USSR was backward and isolated, so it created a huge bureaucracy with inefficient planning. Socialism requires a democratic tradition, a high level of production, and a simultaneous revolution in many advanced capitalist countries. A backward socialism, isolated in one country, will be "deformed," but Trotsky still called it socialism because he hoped to recapture and reform the Soviet Union.

Mandel (1982), a follower of Trotsky, agrees with Trotsky that the USSR is a "bureaucratically degenerated workers' state." Mandel says the Soviet Union is in "transition" from capitalism to socialism, so it is neither the one nor the other.

Since the Soviet Union has been around for seventy years, to claim that it is still transitional is neither persuasive as propaganda nor useful as science. To say it is transitional does not tell us how it works.

Eastern Europe Is "Actually Existing Socialism"

Bahro (1981) has an analysis of Eastern Europe that similarly sees "actually existing socialism" as different from a genuine socialism. He claims that Eastern Europe took the noncapitalist road to industrialization. But the working class was too weak to control the difficult industrialization process, so the Communist party and the state bureaucrats controlled it in the USSR and in Eastern Europe. Bahro, writing in East Germany, painted a graphic picture of a strict hierarchy in the government and in the economy, so there is no governing role for the working class. Bureaucratic rivalry, not profit, is the driving force of the economy, so there are frequently economic decisions that appear to be irrational from a profitability view, though the decisions are rational within a framework of bureaucratic rivalry. Such decision making causes alienation, environmental destruction, and ever-rising material desires. Bahro has clearly spelled out a new and unique political-economic system, for which "actually existing socialism" was merely a euphemism.

China in "Transition"

Communist China has existed for thirty years, so it is a functioning economic system. Nevertheless, changes since Mao have been so drastic that the word "transition" is somewhat more reasonable in this case than the others. There are, however, two diametrically opposed views of where it is transitioning from and to.

Bettelheim (1978) argues that Maoist China was on the road to socialism, though there were many capitalist leftovers in ideology and even in productive relations. Since Mao, however, China is regressing along the road back to capitalism. Thus, the new rulers stress the market over central planning, production over class struggle, and petty bourgeois monetary incentives over equality and social nonmonetary incentives.

On the other side, Selden and Lippit (1982) contend that Maoism prevented socialism by exaggerating class struggle, making grievous economic errors, holding back workers' living standards, and—above all—creating a new hierarchy over the workers. They believe that the new Chinese leadership is back on the road to socialism. There is a moderate policy that goes more slowly but does not alienate workers, allows better living standards, and builds a more democratic political process. They would describe China as in "transition" to socialism.

Neither Capitalism nor Socialism

Sweezy (1980; 1985a; 1985b) argues that the USSR is neither capitalist nor socialist. The capitalists were pushed out in 1917–18. But the workers have not achieved power. In the 1920s there arose a new ruling stratum of political bureaucrats and economic managers. The Communist party in the 1920s chose rapid economic growth over all else, including a downplaying of equality. Thus, a society grew with a large bureaucracy, a managerial elite, inequality, and political dictatorship. Hence the USSR is not "socialist." Yet there are no capitalists, central planning is important, and there is full employment. In his continuing debate with Bettelheim, Sweezy emphasizes that Soviet firms are controlled by the central authorities and the central plan, they do not make basic decisions, and there is no competition between firms. Yet the major tendencies of capitalism result from the competitive drive for profits by the competing firms. Hence the USSR is not capitalist.

In addition to Sweezy's view, there is a large body of literature discussing in detail the new class structure in the USSR. This class structure will be discussed in chapter 12.

A Definition of Socialism

Socialism has often been defined too narrowly by official Marxists and others (including this author in some previous writing) to mean merely government ownership of the means of production. But that is a very misleading definition that does not catch the meaning of generations of socialists. Government ownership of all the land of Egypt existed in one sense under the pharaohs—and that is not what we mean. Socialists have always fought to extend democracy from the political sphere to the economic sphere. *Socialism means economic democracy.* It means that a few autocrats should not run a huge enterprise.

Socialism means that the society and economy should be run by the people, at different levels of decentralization. For example, international airlines should be controlled by a democratically elected world government. Purely local enterprises should be run by a democratically elected committee of their workers or by a local government or by some combination of both.

Socialism, in the meaning of economic democracy, obviously does not exist in the Soviet Union. A self-chosen political leadership selects economic planners, who tell managers what to do, and managers tell workers what to do. All major political and economic decisions in the USSR are decided by a small group of men (with no women). On some issues there is prior public discussion and on some issues there is not, but the same small group makes the final decision. That is not political democracy and it is not economic democracy; so, on my definition, which reflects the goals of most socialists, it is not socialism.

Socialism is defined here as a set of productive relations (and productive forces) that are democratically run by workers or by all citizens, so that it is impossible to have a class of exploiters and a class of exploited. As long as there is a small group at the top of the economic pyramid who are not democratically chosen, it is possible—and likely—that there is a class of exploited workers, as well as an exploiter class (whether capitalists or Politbureau members).

A Definition of Statism

Statism is a set of productive relations (and productive forces) characterized by control by a small, self-selected group through the political apparatus, while there is a very large class of controlled and exploited workers. This definition should be scientifically useful because it indicates some of the most important ways in which statism is similar to and different from capitalism. (It is also useful as propaganda for socialists because it says that the Soviet-type economies are "statist," not socialist.)

As they are in capitalism, workers under statism are alienated, undemocratically controlled, and exploited—as will be shown in chapter 12. Unlike capitalism, however, control of the productive forces is obtained by control of the political structure. In the Soviet Union, the economy is to a large degree planned and controlled by the central political structure.

Socialism is similar to statism only in the negative feature that private capitalist ownership of major enterprises is not allowed. But socialism means democratic control of the economy, whereas statism is undemocratic.

Operation and Evolution of Statism

So far, these societies have merely been given a name, statist, but the real question is: what is their structure and how do they operate? Chapter 11 describes the historical circumstances giving rise to statism. Chapter 12 analyzes its class structure. Chapter 13 considers the relation between the class structure and the state under statism. Chapter 14 discusses the economic performance of centrally planned statist societies. Chapter 15 discusses the economic performance of statist political economies that make widespread use of the market. Chapter 16 looks at the performance of statist societies in other aspects, including pollution, discrimination, alienation, and imperialism.

Suggested Readings

Socialism and Democracy is published by the Research Group on Socialism and Democracy, Ph.D. Program in Sociology, P.O. Box 375, Graduate Center, 33 West 42nd Street, New York, New York 10036–8099; it is a very useful journal with an immense amount of bibliography.

There are a number of useful articles on statism and socialism in a special issue of the *Review of Radical Political Economics* 13, 1 (Spring 1981). Obviously, one should also read the survey by Griffin and Gurley (1985). Another very interesting and useful survey is by Kelley (1985). An outstanding book on both capitalism and statism is by

Horvat (1982), though I disagree with his characterization of Yugo-slavia as socialist.

Perhaps the best single book on the relation of the economic and political structure of the statist mode of production is Brus (1975). On the history of the statist political structure, there are three beautifully written books by Isaac Deutscher (1965; 1966; 1967).

— 11 —

ORIGINS OF STATISM

Radical critiques and visions of socialist utopias have existed for several centuries, but the first serious attempt to produce a comprehensive radical social science was made by Karl Marx. Karl Marx was born in 1818 in Trier, Germany. Although his family wished him to be educated as a lawyer, he chose to obtain his doctorate in philosophy. Because his views were already "too liberal," the German government prevented the young Marx from obtaining a job in a German university. Perhaps if the witchhunters of that day had not been so careful, Marx would have settled down to become a brilliant, but eventually forgotten, German professor. Nevertheless, Marx carried the imprint of the predominant Hegelian philosophy throughout his life; for example, he made a modified form of Hegel's concept of alienation the basis of his humanist critique of society.

Marx turned to journalism and ran a liberal newspaper for a time, until he was exiled to France for his republican ideas. In Paris, Marx learned the views of the French socialists and the tradition of the French Revolution. His conversion to socialism was also aided by his friend, Frederick Engels, who reached a socialist position before Marx. Eventually the French government also decided that Marx was too radical for it, and he was exiled to Belgium. He returned to Germany to take part in the revolution of 1848. When that revolution failed, Marx emigrated to England. He spent most of his life there, from 1849 until his death in 1883.

In London, Marx spent several decades studying classical political economy, from the works of Adam Smith to those of Ricardo and

Malthus. In addition, he read the reports of the factory inspectors and made much use of the official parliamentary investigations.

Thus the intellectual heritage of Marxism was derived from three main sources: German Hegelian philosophy, French revolutionary socialism, and English classical economics. Marx fused these divergent views into one unified social science.

1848 to the Paris Commune

After the collapse of the 1848 revolution, Marx led the inactive life of the political exile for many years. In 1864, however, he joined with British trade unionists and some French and Belgian unionists, as well as certain sects of anarchists, to form the First International (officially called the International Workingmen's Association). The International did succeed in coordinating the efforts of unionists in several countries, in preventing strikebreaking by workers of adjoining countries, and in giving support to the revolutionary nationalist movements of Poland and Italy. The International also supported the North in the American Civil War against the slaveholders. In this action it succeeded in rallying large numbers of British workers against the views of the British government and the conservative ruling classes, who might otherwise have intervened on the side of the South.

The First International lost much of its strength in intense factional struggles. The socialists, led by Marx, and the anarchists, led by Bakunin, clashed over basic theoretical and tactical issues. How disciplined should the workers' movement be? Is a state apparatus necessary after the revolution? On the other side, Marx had to debate with conservative unionists, who wanted less interest in revolution, and more attention to bread-and-butter issues.

Although the International was already in decline, the final blow was the advent of the Paris Commune, which split its ranks wide open. In 1871 when the French armies had been defeated by the Germans, Napoleon III was dethroned and a republican government came into being. The republican government, however, was quite reactionary, and also was unpopular because of its forced concessions to the Germans. The Parisian populace then took matters into its own hands and elected its own government, the famed Paris Commune. An overwhelming majority of the delegates were socialists, though not members of the Marxist International. The Commune lasted but a few months and then was drowned in blood by the reactionary French government. All Europe was aghast at the red Commune of Paris, and just as horrified were the respectable British unionists who constituted the base of the International in England. When Marx wrote a flaming defense of the Commune, the end of the International was made certain. The International formally died in 1876.

The Paris Commune to the Russian Revolution

Marx continued working and writing until his death in 1883. The early 1880s witnessed at the same time the beginnings of strong Socialist parties in France, Germany, and much of Western Europe. In spite of much initial persecution, the German Social Democratic party eventually came to be a very large and highly respectable party. The various Socialist parties together formed the Second International in 1889.

Although the Second International continued to use revolutionary Marxist language, the content of its actions grew less and less revolutionary as its member parties grew more and more respectable. The various socialist parties of Europe and the United States drew large numbers of votes, ran their own newspapers, controlled most of the trade union apparatus, and acquired many vested interests in the continued operation of capitalist society. During the 1890s the chief spokesman of orthodox socialism was Karl Kautsky, who used suitable revolutionary language while defending a peaceful evolutionary view of socialism.

Kautsky was challenged from the right by Eduard Bernstein. Bernstein contended that the Socialists continued to repeat Marx's revolutionary phrases, but that in reality they pursued a much more practical policy of gradual reforms. Bernstein wished to explicitly revise Marxist theory to make it accord with the new reformist practice (hence the labels "revisionist" or "reformist"). He believed that things were slowly getting better even under capitalism, and that democratic parliamentary pressure by Socialists would lead to a very gradual evolution toward socialist ideals.

Kautsky answered in orthodox Marxist language that a "revolution" was necessary to introduce full socialism against the opposition of the old ruling classes. The Socialist parties then interpreted "revolution" to mean a fundamental social change, but assumed it could be achieved through a majority in parliament by democratic means. So in practice they continued a policy of gradual reforms by gradual election victories. By the 1920s the official Socialist parties came to accept almost all of Bernstein's revisionist position. In fact, at the present time the major

West European Socialist and Labor parties no longer advocate complete public ownership in industry, much less revolution to achieve it.

As the official Socialist parties swung to the right, there arose a left opposition, which became ever more vocal and important. It was led by such striking personalities as V. I. Lenin and the fiery Rosa Luxemburg, whose powerful oratory moved thousands of workers. Lenin and Luxemburg agreed that real revolutionaries needed practical action as well as Kautsky's revolutionary words and gestures. They emphasized that imperialism was leading to war, and that the Socialist parties must take united revolutionary action in that case.

In 1914 when the First World War broke out, the Second International was put to the test. The question was whether the socialists of all countries would stand together against the war, or whether the socialists of each country would support their own ruling class against the opposite group of countries. The Second International flunked its test and thereafter was terminated in all but name. Officially it has continued to this day, but in practice it split into warring groups: the German and Austrian Socialists fought against the British and French Socialists, while each of the Socialist parties split into right, center, and left factions. The right wing supported its own government in each of the warring countries. The center was pacifist, advocating a negotiated end to the war. The left wing of the Socialist parties continued to advocate workers' revolution against each government. The left wing eventually split off to form a Communist party within each country.

In 1917 the Russian Revolution broke out. Its first phase was the so-called February Revolution of March 1917, which put the liberals and moderate socialists (called Mensheviks) into power. The Russian peasants were represented by the Socialist Revolutionary party, which stood for a populist type of agrarian socialism. In November 1917 there occurred the famous October Revolution (October on the old Russian calendar) led by the Bolsheviks, who had constituted the left faction of the socialists in Russia, and who later were to be called the Communist party.

Under the leadership of Lenin, the Bolsheviks attempted to transform Russia into a "socialist" country. Their attempt was opposed not only by the forces of reaction, but also by all the old Socialist parties. As a response, Lenin in 1919 gathered the Communist parties of the world into the new Third International or Communist International, called, for short, the Comintern. (An excellent history of the Communist movement is Claudin, 1975.)

The Russian Revolution to the Death of Stalin

In the 1920s, especially after Lenin's death in 1924, the Communist party of the Soviet Union divided into a "left" faction under Leon Trotsky, a "right" faction under N. I. Bukharin, and a "center" faction under Joseph Stalin. Of course, right and left here are only relative and somewhat misleading. All factions considered themselves to be revolutionaries and good Communists. All of them denied any "revision" of Marx or Lenin, but each argued that their opponents were revisionists. (But what is a revisionist? Lenin, for example, made more fundamental additions to Marx than anyone else who claimed to be a Marxist. Does that make him a revisionist?)

All factions agreed on industrialization of the Soviet Union and advocacy of world socialist revolution, but with very different tactics and emphasis. Bukharin (joined by Stalin for some years) advocated a firm alliance with the peasantry, eventual enrichment of the peasants through private trade, and cautious industrialization through moderate taxes and investment. On this basis, socialism would slowly be built in one country, the Soviet Union, which would eventually serve as a powerful support for the world revolution.

Trotsky, on the contrary, advocated rapid industrialization by taking the necessary resources from agriculture, even if most peasants were temporarily displeased (the details of this economic debate are discussed later in this chapter). Trotsky also wanted to commit this rapidly growing industry of the USSR to the all-out support of the world revolution, even at the risk of temporarily losing control of the USSR itself. The point is that Trotsky did not believe the USSR could achieve full socialism without the success of the socialist revolution in the advanced countries.

After a struggle lasting from 1924 to 1928, Stalin won undivided power. Trotsky was exiled in 1928 and murdered in Mexico in 1940. The other old Bolshevik leaders continued to work under Stalin's direction until they were mostly killed in the purge trials of 1936 to 1938. During the Stalin era, Trotsky's followers became a small sect, the Bukharinites disappeared, and the Soviet Union was rapidly industrialized. The industrialization was carried out on the basis of restricted consumption enforced by extreme repression. Thus, it should be no surprise that the result was not socialism, but rather statism, a new type of class society.

After 1928, Stalin ruled alone until his death in 1953. He ruled not only the Soviet Union but also the other Communist parties of the world, including the new rulers of Eastern Europe. In theory, the Comintern was dissolved in 1943, but in practice Stalin continued to direct the other parties with an iron fist. Only Tito of Yugoslavia dared to defect in 1948. Stalin kept the other Communist parties in line partly by means of the new Communist Information Bureau (or Cominform), set up in 1947.

Soon after he took power, Stalin transformed Marxism-Leninism into a divinely given rigid doctrine. Only Stalin could make new interpretations, which he did only to suit his needs, with little regard for theoretical niceties. All dissent was met with prison or murder, and silence descended on the theoretical stage. Through his hold on foreign Communist parties, and through their position in each country, Stalin dominated international Marxist thought from about 1926 to 1953, when he died. This was a period of utter sterility in Soviet Marxist thought, with few major contributions, either by those who idolized Stalin or by those who hated him. No serious attention was paid to Western social science, except to criticize it.

After the Death of Stalin

Even when Stalin was laid to rest in 1953, he was still venerated in Red Square with Lenin. The Communist leaders, always with the exception of Tito, continued to act in Stalin's image with apparently iron discipline and a monolithic face toward the outer world. In 1956, however, Khrushchev, who was then the leader of the Soviet Union, disinterred the old bones of Stalin along with the old ghosts of Stalinism. He achieved popularity at the Twentieth Congress of the Communist Party of the Soviet Union by denouncing the evils and murders of Stalin's day and promising a new era of freedom. His denunciation of terror and dogmatic thinking had a thrilling and profoundly traumatic effect on Communist intellectuals the world around. Many of them escaped from the heavy chains of Stalin's irrational and dogmatic orthodoxy. Many proclaimed a renaissance of Marxist thought and began to take seriously Marx's injunction to "doubt everything." The frozen thinking of the Stalinist bureaucrats was challenged from many sides at once.

De-Stalinization, however, went far beyond what Khrushchev had anticipated. Eastern Europe took Khrushchev's teachings to heart and showed a restless independence. Poland in October 1956 ousted its own Stalinists and established a more liberal Communist regime under

Gomulka, barely avoiding the violence of civil war in the process. Poland continued to have internal Communist rule, however, though with much freedom of discussion, and largely followed the leadership of Soviet foreign policy. Finally, the pot boiled over in Hungary in November 1956. A brief attempt at a more tolerant Communism, followed by widespread organized opposition stretching to the extreme fascist right, led to the bloody intervention of the Soviet army.

The genie of independent thought, once unleashed, was not easily put back into the bottle. The Italian Communist leader, Togliatti, voiced the thoughts of many when he said that this was to be an era of "polycentrism," that is, of many divergent national paths to socialism. The many rumblings within the Communist movement were kept under cover for some years but then broke into the open in 1959 with the leftist defection of tiny Albania. Albania, with the friendly hand of one billion Chinese, thus formed a balance against right-swinging Yugoslavia.

There were constant ideological arguments between the Soviet and Chinese parties. The crucial point of no return in the split came in 1960, when Khrushchev went from words to deeds by recalling from China all Soviet technicians (and their blueprints and plans). Finally in 1963 came an open break between the Chinese Communists and the Soviet Communists. To some extent, the split reflects the fact that the Chinese are still attempting to break the chains of economic underdevelopment while the Soviets are now a developed industrial power.

Last but not least, in 1968 the Czechoslovak people lifted their heads, ousted the old leadership, and began to build a socialism with a human face. This was the most important experiment in democratic Communism to date. It was led by Alexander Dubcek and the Czechoslovak Communist party to their eternal credit. It was crushed by the Soviet army to its eternal shame in August 1968 before it had a chance to build a new structure.

Communists, themselves, are thus divided among "right" and "left" today. The labels used here are very confusing. Is it "right wing" to advocate more democracy, and "left wing" to advocate Stalinist dictatorship, or vice versa? What should we call the new breed of radicals who advocate both full socialism and full political democracy? They cannot be called social democrats because they do call for an immediate and complete socialist revolution. Yet they cannot be called Communist if that refers only to the Stalinists who are in favor of political dictatorship. Those who advocate both political democracy and a completely socialist economy should be called "Democratic Socialists" or even "Democratic Communists."

The Viewpoint of U.S. Sovietologists

At least until recently, most U.S. experts on the Soviet Union merely labeled it "totalitarianism." But this label tells us little and is misleading in that the Soviet Union is very different than the fascist regimes, who were totalitarian in every way. A very interesting book by Stephen Cohen (1985) criticizes this view and shows how it originated with little thought during the worst of the cold war in the 1950s.

Cohen finds that most Sovietologists assume that Lenin laid the basis in the early 1920s for a totalitarian system, while Stalin merely carried out Lenin's wishes. Cohen shows, on the contrary, that there was a very major change in Soviet Communist theory and ways of thinking—as well as behavior—from Lenin to Stalin. Both Marx and Lenin assumed a very democratic socialist society, with political processes based on the democratic forms of the Paris Commune of 1871. Stalin, however, elaborated a new theory and established a new, undemocratic process, while claiming continuity from Marx and Lenin.

The essence of the orthodox Sovietologist view is that the Soviet leadership always held a rigid totalitarian view and that explains their totalitarian behavior. On the other hand, the essential point of Cohen's view is that early Bolshevik ideas allowed for democracy. The change made by Stalin was revolutionary, presenting an apologia for dictatorship. It was Stalin's new view that led to—and supported—a dictatorial practice in the USSR.

Cohen seems clearly correct with regard to the major ideological change of the late 1920s, which he illuminates very well and in detail. What he does not explain, however, is why this change took place. Like the rest of U.S. Sovietologists, his explanation of political change is limited to the realm of ideas. To understand why ideas change, one must delve into the changes and trends in socioeconomic relations, as shown in chapter 2 of this book. That is attempted in the next section.

Similarly, Cohen criticizes those who believe that Stalin's planned, centralist, and "totalitarian" methods were the inevitable way to industrialize, given the Leninist outlook. Cohen argues that Bukharin's more gradual, market-oriented path was also feasible, and he notes that more use of the market is now being considered seriously by the Soviet leadership. Cohen, however, does not consider the actual socioeconomic situation on the eve of the debate over industrialization. As shall be seen below, that real situation severely constrained what ideas would be feasible economically or politically at the time.

Soviet History and the Origins of Statism

The Soviet Union has had the longest experience with a planned economy, but it has been saddled with a political dictatorship for the entire period. Is the one the "cause" of the other? Currently, there are three different answers deriving from three basically opposed interpretations of Soviet history. Some critics of socialism argue that there has been one of the world's worst dictatorships in the Soviet Union, and that dictatorship is the necessary result of central planning and socialism (and the Sovietologists see planning as one result of Communist ideology). The official Marxists (the descendants of Stalinism) argue that the Soviet Union has had the world's most wonderful democracy and that perfect democracy is the result of socialism. The independent Marxist view is that the Soviet Union suffered from a terrible dictatorship (as well as economic overcentralization), but that this was due to unique historical circumstances and not the socialist economy.

Of course, no iffy question in history can be answered with much certainty, but one can attempt to pick out the various ideological and objective factors that produced and maintained the Soviet dictatorship. Among the preconditions for emergence of dictatorship were poverty, serfdom till very late, and destruction of much of the urban working class in the violent events of war and revolution. Among reasons for maintenance of the dictatorship are economic backwardness and the industrialization drive, and the class interest of the ruling class in maintaining the system. Some of these points are obvious or have been already discussed, so their consideration will be very brief.

Preconditions of Dictatorship

Poverty. When (as in tsarist Russia) people live in grinding poverty, direct needs—and not political democracy—are the main goals.

Serfdom. Official serfdom ended in Russia in 1861, but situations similar to the serf and lord relation persisted in some areas till the revolution and made local democracy impossible.

Illiteracy. Illiterate people lack an important tool for democratic participation. There was over 80 percent illiteracy in Russia in 1917.

Lack of democratic tradition. Prerevolutionary Russia was an absolute autocracy for most of its history, headed by the tsar, strongly military and imperialist in nature, and supported by a feudal landowning nobility. Ideas of political democracy came very late to Russia, and for some time after the French Revolution they influenced only the few intelligentsia. A small degree of parliamentary political democracy was practiced only from 1906 to 1917, and, then, the Russian Duma or parliament was neither very popular nor very effective. There was thus very little theoretical or practical experience with democracy among the Russian people.

An underground political movement. West European socialists before 1917 expected the proletarian "dictatorship" to be simply the majority rule through elections in the form of a victory of a Socialist party or parties. The Russian Marxists, operating within the confines of tsarist autocracy, appear to have developed a more restricted and somewhat different attitude toward democracy from an early date. Lenin, speaking for the Bolshevik faction of the Russian socialists, emphasized by the early 1900s the leading role of his party (which eventually became the Communist party). The party was not to wait until the masses spontaneously found their way to socialist ideas, but should lead down the road to the truth. This notion of a monopoly on "the truth" was later to be a principal weapon of the Stalinist dictatorship.

Furthermore, the Russian Marxists were forced to pursue an illegal conspiracy by the repressive laws of the tsarist government. Therefore, they instituted a very strict discipline within the party, were not always able to hold elections for top officers, but always enforced orders from the top down. In theory, the Leninist leadership argued for "democratic centralism," which meant democratic election of central officers plus strict obedience to orders from the elected officers. Tsarist repression made democratic election impossible, but the central officers still demanded strict obedience to orders (and no criticism). This tradition, by which the party led the masses and the top leaders directed the party, was necessary to action and harmless to individual freedom before the 1917 Revolution. Since anyone could leave the party without harm, the party could only lead by persuasion, and party discipline could only be voluntary self-discipline. Few revolutionaries thought about how differently this might operate when the party became the all-powerful ruling party of the government, with persuasion changed to censorship and coercion, while voluntary discipline became external control or opportunistic fawning on leaders.

Conditions Leading to Dictatorship

War and revolution. The First World War included vast human misery in Russia and suspension of any normal liberties. Then the Russian Revolution of October 1917 resulted in a government of "soviets" or councils of workers, peasants, and soldiers, led by the Communist party (Bolsheviks). At first, the Communist party ruled in alliance with the Left Socialist Revolutionary party, which mainly represented the poor peasantry. Within a month after the revolution, the first step against political democracy was taken when all the parties (and all the newspapers) advocating capitalism or monarchism were banned. This was partly explained as a temporary measure during the violence of the revolution and attempts at counterrevolution. Yet it was also given more dangerous meaning as a "natural act of proletarian dictatorship."

Then two months later the Constituent Assembly was dispersed because, it was said, the attitude of the people had greatly changed (and the dominant Socialist Revolutionary party had split), so that the elections to the assembly were now outdated. This was a reasonably democratic argument, except that new elections to the assembly were not called then or ever. The further argument was given that the soviets were more democratic in nature than a parliamentary assembly. The soviets were councils representing soldiers, industrial workers, and farmers. Since the owning classes were to be dispossessed, they would eventually also be part of the working classes, so eventually everyone could vote for the soviets (as has been the case since 1936). Furthermore, in 1917–1918 all the various socialist parties still participated in the soviets. Therefore, except for the exclusion of the capitalist and monarchist parties, the soviets, it was said, would eventually turn out to be a democratic instrument like the assembly.

Within a few more months, however, as the civil war grew in intensity and bitterness, the other socialist parties were also prohibited from the soviets to a large extent. Even this further measure of political restriction could be defended in the terrible conditions of the time—a single, poor, and exhausted workers' state standing alone against formidable domestic enemies and massive foreign intervention. "The danger begins only when they make a virtue of necessity and want to freeze into a complete theoretical system all the tactics forced upon them by these fatal circumstances'' (Luxemburg, 1918: 79).

In theory, it has long been the Marxist view that when a democratic election threatens to bring a socialist majority into office, the ruling capitalist class will attempt to launch civil war violence to stop socialism. The classic examples were Russia and Spain, while other examples were Guatemala or Brazil. Furthermore, these examples illustrate the willingness and ability of foreign capitalists to intervene in this era of imperialism. The issue of a violent or peaceful transition to socialism is of vital importance to the present discussion because a peaceful transition may help create an environment favorable to democratic development. All democratic forms tend to fall by the wayside during any violent and rapidly changing civil war. After the bitterness of civil war, it is not easy to let the opposition immediately reenter politics.

The long and bloody civil war in the Soviet Union (worsened by foreign intervention) made immediate initiation of widespread political democracy very unlikely. The civil war killed off many Communists and killed and dispersed much of the old working class. In fact, the number of industrial workers shrank from a small 2.6 million in 1917 to a minute 1.2 million in 1920. Furthermore, the unpopular measures necessary for warfare alienated many former supporters. As a result, the few surviving old Bolsheviks felt as if they were a tiny remnant defending a beseiged fortress. "Beseiged fortresses are hardly ever ruled in a democratic manner'' (Deutscher, 1967: 31).

Foreign intervention. It is certainly true that a large number of foreign capitalist countries intervened militarily against the Soviet Communists in the years 1918–1921 (including the United States, England, France, and Japan). Furthermore, the blockade of the Soviet Union was continued for many years. Foreign threats never ceased until they culminated in the devastating Nazi invasion. This was followed by the cold war, the threat of the nuclear bomb, and the renewal of attempts at economic blockade by the United States (against both the Soviet Union and Eastern Europe). Against China the United States has also applied military intervention, nonrecognition, and severe economic blockade. The same interventionist policies have been applied against Cuba.

These circumstances do partly make political democracy objectively more difficult in these countries. They are also used, however, as a rationale for repression by some of the ruling elements in these countries, just as Joe McCarthy used the Korean War as an excuse for repression in America, and just as Nixon-Agnew used the Vietnam War as an excuse for more repression in America (and each side points to repression in the other country as a reason for its own repression).

Reasons for Maintenance of the Dictatorship

A great many of the underdeveloped countries, from China to Algeria, have tended toward both state ownership of the means of production and dictatorial one-party control of political life. Why should economic backwardness generate both planning and dictatorship? These are countries mostly filled with a raging desire for rapid economic growth. Yet they are also largely poor, agrarian countries with little modern industry and lacking in buildings, equipment, skilled workers, or experienced managers.

Many radicals view central planning as a useful instrument of industrialization in the underdeveloped countries. For one thing, there are few educated and experienced planners, so the central government can best make use of them, whereas many decades might be required for the voluntary emergence of bold, private entrepreneurs. Furthermore, the total lack of capital in the underdeveloped countries could most easily be remedied by governmental control of resources. The government could tax the rich, gather the small savings of the poor, and expropriate foreign profits, in order to invest by itself in new factories and equipment.

It is thus clear why planning may be chosen as an instrument to overcome backwardness, but why does backwardness unfortunately also generate one-party dictatorship? The reason lies within exactly the same set of circumstances.

The Soviet people may have been convinced of the desirability of rapid economic growth. Yet the Soviet leadership and their economic planners soon found that there is a conflict between rapid long-run growth and immediate consumption. Concretely, they found that to gather the resources necessary to build industry means to take food away from the mouths of the farm population. Excluding foreign investment, there was simply no other source of capital. For very rapid industrialization, it was necessary to take from the farms the food and raw materials for export, food for the feeding of the new industrial working class, and raw materials as the basis for the manufacturing processes themselves.

We shall see below that Stalin solved the resource problem by forcefully putting the peasantry into collective farms from which the entire surplus could be taken. At the cost of a long stagnation or drop in living standards, naturally accompanied by violent resistance to the regime among much of the farm population, Stalin succeeded in putting heavy investments for several years into basic industrial capital and education of a whole new working class. Such a sudden and unpopular transformation (unpopular to the peasant majority) could not have been accomplished without a dictatorship. The only historical issue is whether the Soviet industrial transformation could have been made a little more slowly and with democratic consent.

Although there have been major setbacks, the Soviet Union has increased political freedom since Stalin's death. The Soviet Union has now progressed to the stage where it has a large industrial base capable of generating sufficient surplus within itself to facilitate continued rapid growth of production as well as increasing satisfaction of consumer needs both in cities and on the farm.

The intensive education of a large part of the Soviet population has now provided that population not only with scientific knowledge, but also with a minimum of liberal arts education. Even with a generous helping of propaganda, this education makes it capable of using and demanding a wider democratic process.

Stalinism was thus a phenomenon of social transition and not (as its adherents and also most Western anti-Communist Sovietologists once maintained) "the quintessence or the final shape of the postcapitalist or socialist society. The very success that Stalinism attained in changing and modernizing the social structure of the USSR turned it into an anachronism and made de-Stalinization a historic necessity" (Deutscher, 1957: 10).

The conclusion is that political dictatorship in the Soviet Union resulted from the Russian tradition, the underground political tradition, civil war, foreign wars (and encirclement), and economic backwardness; not because of socialism, but in spite of socialism. In an advanced economy, one may still argue (or hope) that a socialist system will provide a better environment for political democracy than does capitalism.

Early Economic Development Under Statism

Marx predicted socialism in the advanced capitalist countries, with the assumption that there would be an educated, working-class majority and a large, highly concentrated industry. He assumed that the working class would democratically run the economy, that planning would be efficient, that full employment could reduce hours and raise wages. Instead, according to Griffin and Gurley (1985), "socialist" revolutions occurred in less developed countries, with a small percentage of urban workers, high illiteracy, no democracy, little industry, and a low standard of living. "Socialism had to be constructed on the foundations of poverty" (Griffin and Gurley, 1985: 1127).

The whole period of the 1920s in the Soviet Union was witness to a violent debate on methods of rapid initial development. Immediately after the revolution, from 1918 to 1921, the Soviet government had practiced the policy called "war communism." Under that policy, all enterprises and all trade were nationalized, central directives tried to cover all economic activity, and food was simply requisitioned from the peasantry. In 1921 Lenin led a "temporary" retreat to the New Economic Policy (NEP), which allowed a return to the use of the market to sell peasant goods, and a return to private enterprise for merchants and small businessmen.

After Lenin died in 1924, the left wing of the Communist party, led by Trotsky, took the view that the NEP must be quickly ended and a transition made to the rapid growth of socialist industry. They considered it necessary to build large-scale industry on the basis of modern technology, but they also considered it necessary for such modern technology to be extended into the countryside by the fullest encouragement of agricultural cooperatives to replace the tiny peasant farms. Yet Trotsky considered that the international political situation would prevent such a development until the revolution could spread to more advanced economies, capable of furnishing political support and economic aid to Soviet Russia. In this context, he denied "the possibility of socialism in a single country." Trotsky argued instead that "the contradiction inherent in the position of a worker's government functioning in a backward country where the large minority of the population is composed of peasants, can only be liquidated on an international scale in the arena of a worldwide proletarian revolution, [and that] the real growth of the socialist economy in Russia can take place only after the victory of the proletariat in the more important countries of Europe" (Dobb, 1966: 178).

Although Trotsky was the main proponent of the notion that socialist industry could not really expand rapidly in the Soviet Union until after the revolution triumphed in Europe, he nevertheless was also the main proponent of the attempt to industrialize as rapidly as possible, while recognizing the difficulty of accomplishing this under the existing conditions. (In fact, it seems that Trotsky later came to believe that economic growth was possible under these conditions, but that such forced industrialization would lead to harsh political dictatorship over the proletariat.) The argument in favor of the all-out expansion of industry at the expense of agriculture came to be the principal economic plank of Trotsky's opposition faction in the party. He conceived that it was unfortunate but true that rapid industrialization under the existing circumstances could only come at the expense of the peasantry. Furthermore, he argued strongly that such industrial expansion could be achieved only by detailed and comprehensive economic planning under the direction of the state planning commission.

The more systematic economic analysis of the left-wing position was most clearly stated by the very original Soviet economist, Preobrazhensky (1926). Preobrazhensky spoke of the need for ''primitive socialist accumulation.'' Marx had described ''primitive capitalist accumulation'' as the period in which ''capitalist'' countries first acquire the initial capital for rapid industrialization. They acquire most of it by piracy or colonial plunder or the slave trade, or some other means of extraction from other countries. Primitive socialist accumulation, according to Preobrazhensky, means the accumulation of capital for socialist industry from ''the surplus product of all presocialist economic forms.'' Of course, when a socialist revolution happens in an advanced capitalist economy, the primitive accumulation will be completed by the revolutionary acquisition of all large firms. In a relatively underdeveloped economy, however, there is little to take over, so the problem is one of constructing industry from scratch.

Where could capital be obtained? The Soviet Union in the 1920s had neither the desire nor the strength to engage in the imperialist plundering of other countries. It was also impossible to obtain large foreign loans or investments. Most foreign governments still backed the return of the pre-Soviet government or even the tsars. Moreover, they feared that the Soviets might confiscate any new loans and investments just as they had done the old. At any rate, they were more willing to hinder Soviet development than help it.

Thus, the Soviet Union would have to develop solely from its own meager resources. Preobrazhensky argued that up to half of all the profits of Soviet trade and industry were going into private hands under the NEP. He advocated nationalizing these enterprises so as to increase the profits available for government investment in industry. Yet Preo-brazhensky pointed out that Soviet industry was still so small that, even including private profits, the internal reinvestments of its surplus product (above workers' wages and replacement costs) would mean only minute amounts of new capital each year. A "big push" in investment was necessary, however, to create new factories in the many related industries all at once. Without this initial surge of capital creation, development could never get off the ground, let alone gain momentum.

Since sufficient capital could not be obtained from foreign countries or from the infant Soviet industry, the only remaining possibility was to extract it from agriculture. In agriculture, presocialist private ownership prevailed. In fact, in 1928 there were still twenty-six million private farms in the Soviet Union. The left wing urged that the agricultural surplus be extracted by high taxes, and by setting high monopoly prices on the industrial goods that farmers must buy (which amounts to the same thing as taxation of the product of the private farmers).

The right wing of the Communist party, led by Bukharin, criticized this policy on several grounds. First, they argued that it would not succeed because the farmer would either cut back production or use his or her ingenuity to hide the products, and either consume the products right on the farm or sell them on the black market. Second, Bukharin argued that such a harsh policy would break the vital political alliance between the workers and the farmers.

Third, Bukharin presented his own policy, which he believed would reach the same goal more easily. He had been impressed by the results of the NEP, which had allowed freedom for private trade and private agriculture. Under the NEP, large-scale industrial output had tripled from 1920 to 1924, although this was reconstruction and not new expansion. So Bukharin recommended more of the same, allowing the farmer to prosper and grow rich. Eventually he would use moderate taxes on the farmer to build industry, while very gradually forming voluntary farmer cooperatives to end the rule of rich farmers. In his own words, Bukharin wrote: "The ideologists of Trotskyism believe that a maximum annual transfer from peasant agriculture into industry secures the maximum rate of development of industry in general. But this is clearly incorrect. The maximum continued rate of growth will be experienced . . . when industry will advance on the basis of rapidly growing agriculture (Spulber, 1964: 260).

Another right-wing writer, Rykov, expressed the idea that industry would eventually acquire the capital for expansion simply out of the continually increasing turnover of goods traded between agriculture and industry.

Preobrazhensky and Trotsky countered with three arguments. The political argument was given that the right-wing policy would strengthen the rich farmers and thereby weaken the Communist political base. Furthermore, the Left argued that their own policy of rapid industrialization would eventually result in an increased flow of manufactured consumer goods to the villages, which would finally solve the scarcity problem and peasant dissatisfaction once and for all. Finally, they claimed that small amounts of resources drawn very gradually from agriculture would never get industry moving on a basis of self-sustaining expansion (because of the necessity for an initial "big push" to development).

Stalin, leading the center faction, first joined with the right to defeat the left and to exile Trotsky. Then he swung over to an ultraleft program and used the remnants of the left to help defeat the right wing. Finally, when Stalin became sole ruler, he "solved" the problem.

Stalin claimed that industry had recovered the prewar level by 1926 and had surpassed it by 18 percent in 1927. Whereas industry was doing well, in agriculture the total harvest was barely above prewar. Thus, the crucial grain production was only 91 percent of prewar production, and the marketed surplus of grain was only 37 percent of prewar surplus. He concluded that collectivization was necessary: "The way out is to unite the small and dwarf peasant farms gradually and surely, not by pressure but by example and persuasion, into large farms based on common, cooperative cultivation of the soil, with the use of agricultural machines and tractors and scientific methods of intensive agriculture" (quoted in Dobb, 1966: 222). He defended this sudden policy shift by arguing that conditions had changed considerably since the last party congress, that now the peasants were in a mood favorable to collective farming, that the party was now strong and capable enough to lead the change, and that industry was now enough developed to supply the new collective farms with sufficient machinery and tractors. Whether this argument was true or merely politically convenient, the Fifteenth Party Congress (packed with Stalin's supporters) agreed "to build the industrialization program upon the introduction of large-scale farming on cooperative lines as its cornerstone."

Stalin's solution to economic development was bloody and costly, but it did accomplish its objectives. He "persuaded"—by coercion and violence—the unwilling farmers to give up their private farms and livestock and to join collective farms. These collectives were supposed to be cooperative ventures, but they were actually under strict central control. It should be noted that the earlier proposals by Bukharin had only casually mentioned peasant cooperation and collectives, and even Trotsky had thought of the process as a very long and gradual one, not an overnight collectivization. Thus, until Stalin acted in favor of collectivization in 1928, no one else had seriously considered it as more than a minor component in raising the marketed agricultural surplus. Even Stalin started very slowly and only intensified the program in later years as a result of unforeseen emergencies.

Stalin's "persuasion" to collectivize, which began in earnest in the fall of 1929, was marked by a civil war in which large numbers of peasants were killed or exiled to Siberia for resisting collectivization. Farmers slaughtered livestock, and crop production fell. Yet Stalin succeeded in three objectives. First, he eliminated the rich farmer and strengthened his regime politically. Second, the large size of collectives eventually allowed the introduction of machinery and more efficient farming (though they were anything but efficient in the first few years). Third, and this was most important, in spite of the lower total production, the collective farms apparently—by official data—increased the amount of grain actually marketed and available for government use as "capital."

According to official data, procurements of grain doubled from 1928–29 to 1930–31. Then, despite the terrible famine in 1931–32, procurements actually increased slightly. There has been an extensive debate on whether and how much the agricultural surplus did increase; the official data are strongly questioned and the literature is reported extensively in three articles by James Millar (1970; 1974; 1978) and by Ellman (1975).

Whatever the agricultural surplus actually was, it would have been impossible to achieve as much if the peasants had not been collectivized. But in collective farms and under strict government control, they were no longer in position to withhold grain either for speculation or for their own use. The government levied upon the farms so-called obligatory deliveries—in effect, a tax in kind—which had first claim on whatever output was produced. The amount of deliveries was based on the number of acres owned by the farm or in cultivation. Thus, it did not matter how much the farm produced, or whether or not there was a famine; the state's share remained stable since it was based on acreage, not output. The state did pay the farms for these deliveries, but at a fraction of their true cost of production, not to mention the high prices at which grain products were eventually sold in state stores. It was this tax in kind that provided the bulk of the "capital" for the industrialization drive of the first two five-year plans.

How can farm products become capital? First, note that some farm products, such as industrial crops and raw materials, are directly useful in industry. Second, farm products can be exported in exchange for machinery. Third, and most important, farm products can be used to feed industrial workers while they build new factories and basic utilities (or infrastructure). Fourth, food must be sent to those other rural areas that specialize in the production of nonedible industrial crops and raw materials.

Farmers then constituted the majority of the Soviet population, as in most underdeveloped countries. Stalin's solution therefore amounted to keeping most of the population at a very low level of consumption, while using their "surplus" product for investment purposes. Since investment reached 25 to 35 percent of national income, this naturally resulted in a very rapid economic growth. Once industry got underway, the problem became a little easier since more of industry's own resources could be reinvested for further expansion. This meant high profits and restriction of wages, again postponing the increase of current consumption, though this time at the primary expense of the urban worker.

Obviously, this model of economic development not only presumes heroic sacrifices in present consumption initially and for many years to come, but it implies a need for one-party dictatorship. No people will freely vote for such unpopular and drastic development measures. Only a one-party dictatorship allowing no opposition could possible enforce these "temporary" measures for the development of an "infant" economy. But, one wonders, who decides when the infant is grown up enough to restore democracy?

Summary of the Causes of Statism

The recipe for statism requires that one begin with an undemocratic, underdeveloped country. Russia in 1917 was ruled by an autocratic tsar, had a landed nobility, very low productivity in agriculture, a tiny industrial base, and an illiterate and very poor peasantry as 80 percent of the population. A socialist revolution came in the midst of a world war, followed by a civil war and foreign intervention. The revolutionaries were a political party that had spent most of its life as a small, persecuted, highly disciplined, underground group. They suddenly took power in a hostile world.

In a country that was devastated, with much of the former urban working class killed or dispersed, the main business was development. After a long debate, the Communist party under Stalin chose to develop rapidly, using resources taken by force and coercion from the peasantry, 80 percent of the people. Under these circumstances, a violent dictatorship was inevitable.

Statism may be defined as a state-owned economy (whether centrally planned or decentralized), controlled by a party dictatorship. The next chapter examines the class structure of the actually existing statist mode of production in the Soviet Union.

Suggested Readings

On the Communist movement, read Claudin (1975). On the development of the Soviet Union, see Isaac Deutscher (1965; 1966; 1967); also see Zimbalist and Sherman (1984). On the development of statism in Eastern Europe, see Brus (1975). On the development of China, see Lippit (1987).

— 12 —
CLASS STRUCTURE OF STATISM

The most useful definition of a class is with respect to exploitation, that is, the extraction of surplus labor (see Wolff and Resnik, 1986); a class may be exploited or it may be an exploiter. Official Soviet Marxists claim that, in this sense, there are no classes in the Soviet Union. They claim that there are only workers, divided into nonantagonistic strata; there are manual workers, intellect workers, and farm workers, none of whom exploit one another. Similar claims are made by official Marxists in China and Eastern Europe.

Exploitation, Power, and Ownership Under Statism

If classes are defined by legal ownership of the means of production, then there are no classes in the Soviet Union. Aside from the collective farms, all means of production are owned by the Soviet government.

Obviously, a small group of people holds political power in the Soviet Union, while most people have little or no political power. But that fact by itself is of little help in analyzing Soviet class structure since it is equally true of many, very different countries, for example, the small group with political power in Chile. Classes are not defined by political power, though one can analyze which class holds the ruling power.

If, however, one combines the facts that (a) the means of production are owned by the Soviet government and (b) the Soviet government is controlled by a relatively small group, then one is close to the beginning of an understanding of the class structure. Given the Soviet system, those who exercise political power automatically exercise economic power as well.

In the Soviet system, wages and salaries are set by political decree, not by the market. Therefore, those with political and economic power set their own wages and salaries—or have some impact on setting those salaries. In Soviet theory, all wages and salaries are paid according to the labor that is accomplished, so there is no exploitation. But it would be naive to think that the people at the top set their own salaries merely to reflect their labor expenditure. We shall return to this point below.

It is also the case—even according to official Soviet analysis—that the average Soviet worker has extracted from him or her a certain amount of surplus labor, that is, labor expended above the necessary labor going to produce their own individual consumption of goods and services. This does not prove exploitation; it must be true of any modern economy. The surplus labor, extracted from the Soviet working class, is—in the official view—supposed to go to (a) creation of new means of production to expand the economy, and (b) collective consumption by the whole population, such as parks.

Whether or not there is exploitation depends on the answer to two questions. First, is there also a third part of the surplus labor of workers going to pay the salaries (and fringe benefits) of top Soviet officials beyond the remuneration due to the labor of those officials? Second, does the ruling elite of the Soviet Union control expenditures on new investment and collective consumption for its own purposes, or does the average Soviet worker have an equal say concerning that expenditure?

Surplus Labor to the Ruling Class

It has been noted that the people at the top of Soviet society set their own salaries. These salaries have three components. First, the official salary itself is several times higher than the average wage. Second, there are many important fringe benefits, including chauffeurs and automobiles, specialized health treatment, special luxury stores, and summer homes in the countryside. Third, there are large additional, secret sums of money.

There are no exact data on the secret incomes of Soviet leaders. In neighboring Czechoslovakia, however, when President Novotny was pushed out of power, an investigation by the new government was undertaken to examine his finances. During the investigation, Novotny returned thirteen billion crowns, which he claimed he had received by mistake (see Zimbalist and Sherman, 1984: 282).

Thus, it appears that the top Soviet leaders do receive the surplus labor of others as part of their own remuneration. Since they receive surplus labor, their own remuneration may be far above what their own labor produces. That surplus labor is extracted from the exploitation of the Soviet working class.

But the total amount of surplus labor transferred directly from Soviet workers to the Soviet ruling class is very small by U.S. standards (the reasons and data are discussed in the next section). The main distributional issue in the Soviet Union is the use of the huge surplus labor product that goes to investment and collective consumption. As noted earlier, there is nothing wrong or exploitative per se in such uses of the surplus product. If workers agree that some of their surplus labor shall go to build a swimming pool for everyone in their enterprise to use, that is obviously not exploitation. If all Soviet workers agree that 10 percent of GNP—coming from their surplus labor—should be invested in new plant and equipment, that is not exploitation.

The problem in the Soviet Union is that workers do not make these decisions. Self-selected leaders decide on the entire allocation of the surplus labor. Suppose a small, dictatorial group decides that a large amount of workers' surplus labor shall be used to build nuclear bombs rather than hospitals. Is that exploitation?

It would certainly seem that extraction of surplus for purposes dictated exclusively by the ruling class is exploitation just as much as the extraction of surplus labor directly into the pockets of the ruling class. Both forms of exploitation depend on ruling class control of the Soviet political process and political control of the means of production. Under statism, one can separate politics from economics even less than under capitalism.

Strata of the Ruling Class

There are four main hierarchies in the Soviet Union: the Communist party, the government apparatus, the economic pyramid, and the military. Within the Communist party, the top functionaries (such as in the Politbureau) have enormous power and are appointed rather than elected—though there are "elections" after the decision is made. There are also powerful officials in the government, such as the Council of

Ministers and their deputies. The economic pyramid is ruled by a small group of economic planners at the top (responsible to the government and party leaders) plus some powerful directors of sectors and very large enterprises. The military is, of course, completely hierarchical, with the top generals also being party leaders in some cases. In each of the four hierarchies, orders flow downward, while some information flows upward. At the top are fifty to a hundred people who control all four hierarchies and frequently transfer from one to the other. These people get high salaries, huge fringe benefits, and probably enormous secret income. Thus, their income levels approximate those of the top U.S. capitalists, when considered relatively to each of the two societies.

Below the very top Soviet group, there are another 100,000 to 200,000 Soviet officials who have high salaries and huge fringe benefits (with perhaps some illegal income). The total income, however, of each of these high Soviet officials is still far below that of most U.S. capitalists, both absolutely and relatively to their societies.

One U.S. study finds that the Soviet "elite" were only 0.2 percent of all gainfully employed Soviet citizens or only 220,000 people (Bergson, 1984: 1085). The "elite" are defined in this study as those who receive at least 3.1 times the average wage or at least 5.7 times the minimum wage. These 220,000 include most enterprise directors, party officials, government officials, top military officers, and some professionals.

Since the total number of the Soviet rich is perhaps a tenth of the U.S. number, and since their average income is much lower than the U.S. capitalist's average income, the total amount of surplus labor going into individual pockets is much lower in the Soviet Union than in the United States. The reason is that exploitation for individual wealth is more difficult in an economy where it appears to flow directly from raw political power (really, control of the means of production) than from private investments of funds (really, control of the means of production).

On the other hand, the top Soviet members of the ruling class probably have far more power of social decision-making (over jobs, investment, and allocation of goods and services) than does the U.S. capitalist class. This is because, in their normal role, the Soviet leaders directly control all of the levers of political decision-making and economic decision-making—and economic decisions are highly centralized. Taken together, U.S. capitalists do control jobs, investment, and allocation of resources in the private sector, but the decisions are more decentralized (though a fairly small number of capitalists control the thousand largest corporations that own a majority of the U.S. assets). U.S. capitalist control of political decisions, such as military spending, is more indirect and is limited in certain ways.

Mobility

The U.S. ruling class is more secure than the Soviet ruling class, both for themselves and for their children. If a U.S. capitalist loses or gives up an executive job, he or she retains wealth and status. The wealth may continue to increase through ownership of the means of production. Even power may be retained and exercised without an executive position. Furthermore, U.S. wealth can be passed on to children, limited only by the ineffective inheritance laws. Given a million dollars, a child possesses economic power, will be given a good education, and may easily attain executive decision-making power—as well as some amount of political power if he or she wishes.

In the Soviet Union, on the other hand, power and wealth adhere to a particular official position. If you lose the position, then you lose all your power. If your power is lost, then your income disappears. Wealth is soon gone because it is not capital that is invested for a profit. So the Soviet ruling class is, as individuals, less secure than the U.S. ruling class.

Since power and wealth cannot be directly inherited, and all positions are supposed to be by merit, education is more of a key to success in the USSR than in the United States. It is illegal to pay money to gain entrance to a Soviet university, but children of the elite do usually have the advantage of a greater access to culture as they are growing up, so a higher proportion of them do well in secondary schools and a higher proportion of them are admitted to universities.

One study finds that "specialists," those with secondary or higher education, are 14 percent of the whole Soviet population (Bergson, 1984: 1086). The children of specialists, however, constitute from 31 percent to 51 percent of the various Soviet universities in the survey. The study notes that specialists' children enjoy (a) a better cultural and learning environment at home than nonspecialists' children on the average, (b) special tutoring, and (c) perhaps some payment of bribery in admissions in a few cases.

The children of the top twenty thousand Soviet leaders do not hold the same jobs and are not usually at the same rank as their parents (see Nove, 1975: 615-38). If one goes much lower, however, to examine the top 10 percent of all Soviet income receivers, one does find that their children are also usually somewhere in that category. Thus, it can be concluded that top leadership is not hereditary; but that the bulk of the officials, managers, and higher placed professionals do give their children enough moral and monetary support—and perhaps good connections—that those children also usually land good jobs.

One survey finds that these children of the upper income groups do have good positions on average, but it stresses the point made above that they lack the security of American capitalists: "Tenure in such positions, however, for them [children of the Soviet elite] and for the less elevated but still comfortably privileged, is at the pleasure of those who hold real power; and the strictly private resources that allow the rich in capitalist systems to enjoy privileged lives whoever is in power, to participate in or withdraw from public life at will, are not theirs to command" (Connor, 1979: 258). One may conclude that: (1) there is no rigid, hereditary hierarchy; (2) anyone can move up in the statist countries by merit, with education being of great importance; (3) but ordinary workers seldom move into the top 10 percent; and (4) a few children of the top 10 percent become top leaders, while most of the top 10 percent do get their children into the same strata.

Strata of the Soviet Working Class

Historically, the Soviet revolution equalized incomes to a great extent in the 1920s. During 1928 to 1953, Stalin created wide differences of income among workers (not to speak of the very high incomes of the top leaders) to act as a goad to harder work in the industrialization drive. After Stalin, the leadership recognized that the initial industrialization had been completed, so such wide differences were no longer helpful— and might have great negative affects among lower paid workers. At the same time, the populace wanted more freedom and less sacrifice. So, incomes were equalized again by raising the lowest levels, while keeping the higher levels from rising as fast.

The Soviet working class presents a wide spectrum of income and status differences, from highly paid artistic and sports stars to very low paid menial workers. The top 10 percent of Soviet families, mostly the highest strata of the working class (but also including the relatively tiny ruling class) have an average income three to five times higher than the bottom 10 percent (see Yanowitch, 1966; 1977). But the ratio of income of the top tenth to the bottom tenth declined in the 1960s and 1970s, so Soviet income distribution has been becoming more equal (see McAuley, 1977; Nove, 1982).

The available data are not very clear as to the incomes of the Soviet elite, but there are data as to the incomes of the Soviet working class. Thus, in 1961 the top 10 percent of Soviet wage and salary workers earned four times what the bottom 10 percent earned (Bergson, 1984: 1063). The decline in inequality is measured by the fact that in 1981 the top 10 percent of wage and salary workers earned only three times what the bottom 10 percent earned. By comparison, in the United States in 1975 the top 10 percent of wage and salary workers earned four times what the bottom 10 percent earned. So there appears to be somewhat less inequality within the Soviet working class today than the U.S. working class, but the main differences in income inequality between the two countries come in the much greater wealth of the U.S. elite.

One overall estimate, with considerable guess work and limited data, finds that a standard measure of inequality (the Gini coefficient) for the pretax income of all households in the United States was .376 in 1972 (Bergson, 1984: 1070). The same measure of inequality for the pretax income of all urban households in the USSR was only .288 in 1972–1974, reflecting significantly less inequality.

It is also very important to remember that there are far more free public goods and services in the USSR than in the United States. Thus, the real income distribution in the USSR is always much more equal relative to the United States than the distribution of money income.

It is worth emphasizing that in the U.S. economy, the large-scale poverty comes mainly from unemployment or part-time unemployment, while the immense fortunes come from private profit, rent, and interest. In the USSR, there is no unemployment and there is no private profit, rent, or interest. So almost all income differences represent differences in pay scales for labor services—plus the small number of the ruling class who receive surplus labor of others. Among actual employed workers, the USSR income distribution is somewhat more equal than, but in the same range as, the U.S. distribution. But without unemployment at one end and vast private profit at the other end, the overall USSR income distribution is far more equal than the U.S. distribution.

Within the Soviet working class, there are important differences between skilled and unskilled workers. Besides more income, the skilled workers have more education (and their children have more education), more cultural activities (the top 20 percent of workers read one to three books a week), and participate more in community affairs, including local politics (see Zimbalist and Sherman, 1984: 288, for details). On the other hand, there is considerable upward mobility—a little more than in the United States—from unskilled to skilled worker, and even higher if one gets a good education.

Managers in Statist Society

In the United States, there is a considerable radical literature on the managerial strata and their class location (see, e.g., Ehrenreich and Ehrenreich, 1979). What goes under the title of manager in the official U.S. data—about 8 percent of the labor force—is a very mixed bag. Most are merely low-paid supervisors, expending labor power like any other worker. Some are middle-level managers, with good salaries and some power, perhaps being neither workers nor capitalists. A few are high-level executives, with large incomes from capital investment, and also large salaries (usually profits pretending to be wages, for tax reasons).

Soviet "managers" cover the same wide spectrum. There are many poorly paid supervisors. At the top, in regional- and ministerial-level organizations, are people who are part of the ruling class. But when one says "manager," one normally means the head of a Soviet enterprise, who is neither an ordinary worker nor a member of the top Soviet leadership.

The Soviet manager faces a very different set of problems than does the U.S. manager. The U.S. manager is mainly concerned with demand for the company's goods and services. The normal environment is lack of demand, unemployed labor, and unutilized capacity. Therefore, many U.S. managers have a background in marketing or in finance. If a U.S. manager has a college degree (and some do not if they have the right connections), then it may be in business administration or accounting or finance.

On the contrary, the Soviet manager normally has no problem with demand, but spends all of his or her time on the technical problems of increasing supply with limited resources. The normal environment is shortage of labor, shortage of capital, and shortage of raw materials. Almost all Soviet managers have college degrees, and most are in engineering, which is the most prestigious profession. (For more details on Soviet managers, see Zimbalist and Sherman, 1984, ch. 10).

Unlike U.S. managers, the Soviet manager does not own any of the enterprise. On the other hand, there are very strong incentives to produce because a large bonus results from meeting and surpassing the plan, and a manager will soon be demoted for poor performance. Soviet managers work very hard to meet the plan goals, but they often use dubious means to do so (see chapter 14).

Trade Unions Under Centrally Planned Statism

Trade unions in a centrally planned statist economy create many para-doxes and contradictions. On the one hand, in Russia and in most countries before the revolution, the Communist party was closely linked to the unions, so there is a tendency to make the unions all-powerful after the revolution. On the other hand, after the revolution it is claimed that the workers own the whole economy and control every enterprise, so there is a tendency to say that unions are completely unnecessary. If there are no antagonistic classes and no conflicts in production, then what is the function of unions?

A debate about unions raged in the USSR in the 1920s (see Deut-scher, 1950). One side wanted the unions to be independent and run the economy. The other side wanted the unions to be part of the govern-ment. A compromise was reached in which the unions would be inde-pendent, but would "cooperate" with the government. In practice, unions were a source of opposition in the early 1920s. Then under Stalin the union leaders were ousted and replaced by loyal Stalinists. For thirty years the major function of the unions was to push workers to produce more output. In the late 1950s and 1960s with anti-Stalinism dominant, the unions had relatively free elections of local union offi-cers and saw their task as advocates for and protection of workers. In the 1970s and 1980s unions have been more tightly controlled, but they continue to support the grievances of individual workers against man-agers. Although there have been wildcat strikes, no official union has ever led a strike—and wages are set by central decree.

In Poland, the official unions were always viewed as alien to the workers, and workers have had a long history of protest strikes (ignor-ing or opposing the official unions). In 1980, a protest over higher prices led to an independent union movement known as Solidarity. The dramatic rise and fall of Solidarity is briefly described in Zimbalist and Sherman (1984, ch. 10) and is described in a moving and enlightening narrative in Singer (1981). For more than a year, Solidarity grew into a broad movement of millions of Polish workers fighting for traditional trade union rights and for broader democratic rights for all citizens. Then it was suppressed by imposition of martial law.

The important point about the confrontation between Solidarity and the Polish government is that it revealed a sharp conflict of interests and ideology between the working class and the government. After this violent clash, no one in Poland could believe the myth that the statist government represents the working class; on the contrary, it is clearly a dictatorship over the working class.

Suggested Readings

The most important books and articles mentioned in this chapter are Bergson (1984), Connor (1979), Deutscher (1950), McAuley (1977), Nove (1975; 1982), Singer (1981); Yanowitch (1966; 1977), and Zimbalist and Sherman (1984).

— 13 —

STATISM AND THE STATE

So far, this part of the book has defined the statist mode of production (after examining all the alternative concepts), examined briefly the evolution of statism, and investigated the class structure of statism. Here, the role of the state in such societies is examined in greater detail, beginning with the question of the desirability of democracy, the probability of democracy under central planning and government ownership, the reasons why the Soviet Union lacks democracy, the effect of the market on democracy in Hungary, the implications of workers' councils in Yugoslavia, and the need for institutionalized democratic safeguards.

The Desirability of Democracy

If the definition of "socialism" is difficult, that of "democracy" is almost impossible. A few general notions are given here, to be further developed in the rest of this chapter. Roughly, political democracy is defined as some degree of control of the government by the majority of the people through various means. In practice, according to the Marxist Maurice Cornforth, it means the ability of those not in office to "question, check and control the policies of office-holders, and confirm them in, or dismiss them from office" (1969: 260). While this view corresponds to some commonsense notions, it does not answer a great many questions. For example, should democratic rights protect the minority as well as the majority? Should democratic procedures be applied to the work center, farm, factory, or university as well as the whole government?

Marx stated that the state under socialism would take the form of a dictatorship of the proletariat. "Between capitalist and communist society lies the period of the revolutionary transformation of the one into the other. To this also corresponds a political transition period in which the state can be nothing but the revolutionary dictatorship of the proletariat" (1930, 2:33–34; also see Draper, 1962). The "dictatorship of the proletariat" is Marx's conception of a socialist democracy, a more democratic government than that which can exist under capitalism. In socialism all economic and political power must pass to the working class (or "proletariat," including farm workers, industrial workers, and intellectual workers). Therefore, until the former capitalist class has been economically eliminated, the working class majority must exercise its "dictatorship." At a minimum, Marx assumed this dictatorship would mean complete political democracy *within* the proletarian majority.

In Marx's terminology "dictatorship" is not used in its superficial political sense, to mean an authoritarian government (like Stalin's); but rather in a sociological sense, to mean the domination of a class. For example, in ancient Athens there was a democracy of all "citizens"— that is, of all slaveholders—but a dictatorship over the slaves. In modern American capitalism there is a democracy of all factions of the capitalist class, but a dictatorship over the working class (although the workers may exert a great deal of pressure on the capitalist state). Similarly, Marx expected a democracy of the working class to exert a dictatorship over their former masters, the capitalists, until the capitalists would disappear completely.

Specifically, during his lifetime Marx was able to point to the Paris Commune as an example of a socialist democracy (or a "dictatorship of the proletariat"). In the Commune there were a large number of conflicting political parties, with the full structure of democratic elections, right of recall, freedom of speech, and so forth. Marx wrote that "the Commune was formed of the municipal councillors, chosen by universal suffrage in various wards of the town, responsible and revocable at short terms" (1948: 4). The capitalist representatives voluntarily withdrew from the Commune, but this still left a large number of socialist parties, of whom the Marxists were a very small minority. Thus, Marx certainly did not expect a one-party dictatorship *over* the workers as the content of a future socialist democracy (or proletarian dictatorship).

V. I. Lenin emphasized that the capitalist class would violently resist a socialist majority. Thus the socialist revolution could only be carried through by a violent upheaval (a realistic appraisal in tsarist Russia). Yet after the revolution Lenin also foresaw that the "dictatorship of the proletariat" would be a government by the peasant and working class majority operating through democratic processes. Though civil war might automatically outlaw the capitalist political parties, Lenin specifically endorses the example of the Paris Commune with its multiplicity of "socialist" parties. He writes that in the Commune, "representative institutions remain. . . . Without representative institutions we cannot imagine democracy, not even proletarian democracy" (1917: 41).

Although Lenin endorsed representative democracy, his view on democracy has some basic ambiguities. Lenin distinguishes an earlier period after the revolution and a later period. In the initial period after the revolution, Lenin sees the need for certain dictatorial methods by the "socialist" state. The opposing capitalist power must be crushed. Former capitalists cannot vote or participate in politics. The infant socialist state must have full police and military powers to defend itself. In fact, Lenin dispersed the Constituent Assembly and did not convene another. The soviets were restricted in their franchise and only socialist parties could participate. Yet Lenin also zealously protected the rights of the minority in the Communist party and encouraged free debate.

In the long run, after "socialism" has been achieved and there is a transition to "communism," Lenin predicts a very different situation. Lenin defines "socialism" to mean public ownership plus income paid according to work done. He defines "communism" to mean public ownership plus income according to "need," which has been interpreted in the Soviet Union to mean that all public goods and services are to be free (at zero price). Lenin agrees with Engels' prediction that under communism the state will slowly disappear or wither away. The argument is that the state only exists to repress the exploited class and protect property. Under communism there is no exploited class and no need to protect property—therefore, no state. But Lenin goes on to argue that democracy is merely a form of the state. If there is no state, there can be no democracy. As a result, there is no place in Lenin's argument for democracy under socialism or communism. In the first period, there can be no democracy because the militant state must protect the transition to socialism—and later, socialism—by any means. In the second period, there can be no democracy because, under communism, there is no state. These views, which Lenin never expressed dogmatically except during the revolution itself, were taken up and expanded by Stalin into a rigid dogma, as a justification for dictatorship and a strong state.

Stalinist Ideology

After Stalin had consolidated his power in the late 1920s, there was a sharp break with the past socialist practice, and an insidious change in socialist ideology. In practice, instead of a political democracy of the working class, the "dictatorship of the proletariat" came to mean a dictatorship over the working class by one party (the Communist party) and over the party by one man (Stalin, particularly after 1935). We leave for later the question of how and why this happened. Here we are concerned with the "arguments," if they may be dignified by that name, in favor of the Stalinist position presented by Stalin and his followers.

The Stalinists did in practice glorify the single leader (the "cult of personality" still prevalent in some Communist countries), but they never really argued for this in theory because it is so blatantly opposed to the whole Marxist tradition. They did, however, present arguments in favor of one-party rule. First, they claimed that even after the civil war ended, the class struggle became ever more violent in the socialist Soviet Union. Therefore, a multiparty system was a luxury that could not be afforded. Apparently, even today the defeated capitalists still have so much strength that they could sneak back into political power if other political parties were allowed. When it is pointed out that the capitalists and rich peasants were eliminated in the Soviet Union by the mid-1930s, it is argued that they would make up for weakness by all-out desperation. In addition, and perhaps most convincingly, Stalin raised the potent specter of foreign espionage and foreign help for the capitalist side. There was anti-Soviet intervention by fourteen capitalist countries in 1917 and continued attempts to instigate counterrevolution ever since that time.

The second Stalinist argument was the reverse of the first. It is said that there is no class struggle in socialism and no opposing interest, therefore, no need for more than one political party (why even one?). The working class (urban and rural) is the only class left in society, the Communist party represents the working class and the Politbureau represents the Communist party. One of the faithful Stalinists in the United States, W. Z. Foster, writes: "The existence of many political parties in capitalist countries . . . merely signifies that the class struggle is raging. . . . In a fully developed socialist country, inasmuch as all the people's interests are fundamentally harmonious, there is a proper place for only one political party, the Communist Party" (1953: 271).

Of course, the perfect harmony and increasing disharmony arguments do seem to contradict each other. If there are no more opposing interests, then why does the Soviet constitution have to prohibit other parties? If there are still opposing class interests, then there is not perfect harmony—although Stalin tried to answer this by claiming that all the hundreds of thousands of Communists executed were "foreign agents." By using both arguments at once, Stalin forgot Lenin's distinction of two time periods—he merely gives a caricature of both of Lenin's analyses and applies them both to the present.

Opposing interests have been found in socialism, however, not just by the critics, but by such a revolutionary Marxist as Mao Zedong. Mao (1957) argues that even in socialism there are conflicts or "contradictions" between farm workers and industrial workers, between manual workers and intellectuals, and between individuals and the government bureaucracy. Although Mao himself experimented with allowance of more open opinion in China only for a short time in 1957, by 1986 there was again a struggle over political democratization in China (see Mann, 1986).

Radical View of the Desirability of Democracy Under Socialism

Most U.S. radicals believe that political democracy is a useful and important instrument to improve society, and that it could operate more meaningfully for the workers under socialism than under capitalism. This view of political democracy is founded on an anti-elitist view of mankind's potential. Fascists, elitists, and racists hold that one leader or one God-given elite or one race among men, such as the "Aryan race," is superior to all others. They hold that some, such as Jews, blacks, Chinese, and anyone else convenient to attack, are especially inferior. It follows that the elite by birth, and especially their leader or "Fueher" (Hitler—or Stalin?), should rule, and the majority of inferiors should merely accept commands.

Independent Marxism completely rejects these assumptions of racial or class inequality. Most propaganda for such assumptions stems from ulterior motives of justifying exploitation, as for example when the Southern slave owners tried to argue that blacks are inherently inferior.

Instead, we emphasize education and cultural environment in determining performance. Modern anthropology shows that if any two large groups are given equal opportunities and motivation for learning, they will perform equally on the average.

Most U.S. radicals do not argue that political democracy is good because of an eternal ethical imperative. It is merely the best means toward the end of the greatest happiness for the greatest number of people (specifically, the working class). The socialist humanist position is that political democracy serves a very useful function in improving society. Since the position is not an absolute one, they are quite willing to admit that there may be periods of war or revolution in which political democracy is difficult or impossible.

They can never agree with official Marxists, however, who argue that democratic political processes are unnecessary or harmful under socialism. Some "Marxist" writers have wrongly generalized from Cuban experience (see, e.g., Morray, 1965). They correctly argue that Cuba is under attack from the United States, and that all previous elections in Cuba were frauds. These writers conclude that all elections are "phony," that all the processes of democracy are a mask for reaction, and that no socialist country can allow any democracy while capitalism exists anywhere. Instead of democratic safeguards and processes, there is a vague rhetoric about mass participation in carrying out Fidel Castro's decisions. It is true that Cuba has gained much in democracy by increased mass participation since the revolution, true that the prerevolutionary Batista press was corrupt, true that Batista elections were a fraud, and true that Cuba is under siege by the United States. But that does not mean that elections and freedom of the press are bad on principle and should be permanently abolished.

Leaving aside special circumstances (such as in Cuba), radicals argue that political democracy within the working class is necessary to make socialism work better than without it. It has been seen that social ownership without political democracy means an elite in control of the means of production, able to reinstitute the exploitation of the workers to some extent. Thus democratic forms may help workers restrain the bureaucratic elite. Beyond that basic point, however, one may argue some more specific advantages.

Democratic processes would at least guarantee a peaceful succession to power, unlike the bloody conspiratorial fighting of Stalin and Trotsky or Khrushchev and Beria. Leadership in that period was selected by the physical elimination of all opponents. In the post-Stalin era physical violence has gone out of fashion, but rival leaders are still eliminated by a power struggle within the narrow confines of the Central Committee, a body small enough to be subject to personal log-rolling and self-perpetuating recruitment procedures.

Second, and closely related to the first point, is the necessity for political democracy to help restrict personal power drives. Socialist bureaucracy is by nature all-powerful, and there have been many cases of personal corruption in the Soviet Union at the local and regional levels as well as in national administration (for example, using public bricks and public labor to build an official's house). Since a bureaucracy in socialism is so important, the free criticism of it—including the very highest officials—is more important than ever. This principle is recognized by official Soviet theory, but it is not recognized in practice. The top Soviet leadership is never open to criticism of its policies or personal behavior; and criticism by an organized opposition is strictly prohibited.

Third, it is necessary to have a nonviolent process for criticism of tactical and strategic errors made by the leadership. "Freedom only for the supporters of the government, only for the members of one party—however numerous they may be—is no freedom at all. Freedom is always and exclusively freedom for the one who thinks differently. Not because of any fanatical concept of 'justice' but because all that is instructive, wholesome and purifying in political freedom depends on this essential characteristic" (Luxemburg, 1918: 69).

In theory the Soviet Union is very much in favor of criticism, but in practice the Stalin era witnessed a process that was inevitable once begun. Criticism was allowed, but not criticism of the top leadership; political campaigns were allowed, but only by the Communist party. In the end, any criticism of the Communist party (or of Stalin) was considered a crime against the Soviet state or against socialism. Yet no leadership is perfect, and this process has undoubtedly reduced the efficiency of the Soviet administrative apparatus—and, more important, prohibited open expression of public preferences. The present leadership still prohibits dissent on most issues. In foreign policy this was evident in the harsh treatment of Soviet citizens who opposed the invasion of Czechoslovakia.

Finally, there are objective clashes of interest in socialism that should be expressed in the political process (recognized even by Mao Zedong as noted above). Assume even that all remnants of capitalism, including individual handicraft workers and individual or cooperative farmers, have been replaced by complete public ownership. The short-run interests of the individual worker do often conflict with the long-run interests of the whole society. For example, all state planners tend to take a long-run view that favors the relatively greater expansion of the means of production rather than goods for immediate consumption. Individual Soviet citizens may have a very different view concerning the division of new investment between producers' goods and consumers' goods, but in a centralized socialist economy this influence can only come through the political process.

Class and Democracy in Socialism

What about Lenin's argument that after the revolution, in the first phase there must be a revolutionary class dictatorship, not democracy, while in the second phase, communism, there are no classes, no state, and no democracy? Lenin's argument had a powerful grip on most Marxists for many decades. Then it was directly assailed by Carrillo (1978), who stated the Eurocommunist view. Lenin's view arose out of the situation in Russia in 1917, but Carrillo reflects modern Western Europe and the experience of Soviet tanks crushing workers' revolts in Hungary and Czechoslovakia (and indirectly in Poland).

First, Carrillo argues that there need not be a revolutionary dictatorship because there may be a peaceful, democratic transition to socialism. Russia in 1917 had a state apparatus run by a small elite and an army run by the same small elite, a tiny professional class, vast illiteracy, a small urban working class, and a repressive autocracy. Modern Europe is different in every way. In Western Europe, the state apparatus is run by millions of workers, there is a huge professional class, the urban working class is very large, literacy is almost universal, and the army is a mass army. There are struggles within the media as to the propaganda line; there are struggles within the state as to class interests; and there may be struggles within the army over what direction to follow in a crisis (for example, in the U.S. Army in Vietnam).

Moreover, we are no longer talking about poor, backward economies where the class struggle is desperate over a very limited pie, but affluent economies where there is greater freedom for maneuver and compromise. Thus, Carrillo sees possible peaceful democratic evolution in Western Europe, Japan, and the United States. He does not, however, claim that this view applies to Latin America, Asia, and Africa, because they resemble Russia of 1917 more than Europe of

1987. It is for this reason that the label "Eurocommunism" has a theoretical as well as geographical justification.

Carrillo thus concludes that democracy would flourish in Western Europe after a peaceful transition to socialism—so Lenin is wrong about democracy being impossible in the first phase of socialism. But Carrillo also believes that Lenin is wrong to say that democracy must be nonexistent (because the state is nonexistent) in the second or communist stage. Carrillo agrees with Lenin that the repressive state apparatus—police, courts, armies, prisons—can and should disappear as socialism evolves. If there is no need for one class to oppress another, then, the need for this state apparatus disappears, that is, the state, in this sense, withers away. Note how different the Soviet evolution has been, where the state apparatus has grown stronger rather than disappearing; this is one reason it is reasonable to call the USSR "statist" rather than "socialist."

Lenin, however, also agrees with Frederick Engels that the administration of people will be replaced by the "administration of things." Lenin does not develop this theme fully because it would contradict his notion that the need for democracy disappears. The "administration of things" refers to the fact that under socialism as under capitalism roads and hospitals must be built and trains must run on time. In fact, everyone knows that the socialist state must make many more decisions than the capitalist state. For example, major investment projects are private under capitalism but should be collectively determined under socialism.

If one really acknowledges the need to administer things on a vast scale, then democracy is more important than ever. Carrillo concludes: "There seems to be no doubt that also in the maximalist [Leninist] conception of the disappearance of the State, and its replacement by what is called the 'administration of things,' that administration will be carried by human beings, and not by the things themselves, and will give rise to new forms of democracy" (1978: 90). Of course, one can define the state to mean only organs of repression and not administrative agencies—but that is only a semantic sleight of hand, not an analytic argument.

Socialism requires a constructive effort of society (the administration of things) to plan, control, and improve the economic and social progress of society. If decisions are not made democratically by the representatives of the majority of the people, then they will be made by a small, self-selected group. Hence, the necessity of a democratic process, including multiparty elections and civil liberties for all opposition.

The Probability of Democracy in Socialism

Is political democracy more or less likely in socialism than in capitalism? To these important questions there are a variety of answers among both anti-Marxists and Marxists. Some of the major theoretical positions will be explored in the following sections, and the facts of Soviet and East European history will be used as a test of the theories.

The Critics

All the critics of socialism have argued that any attempt at marriage between socialism and democracy can only end in violent divorce, that socialism is only compatible with political dictatorship. The critics now argue on the basis of experience that in all areas of "socialism" there is also dictatorship. Thus the USSR, Eastern Europe, Cuba, and China all claim to have socialist economies, but they all have political dictatorships. Moreover, many of the underdeveloped countries, such as Guinea or Syria, seem to show similar trends toward both "socialism" and dictatorship. Can all these areas be shown to have other or special characteristics such that their dictatorships may not be the results of "socialism"?

The critics have also argued, long before the present world situation, that the functioning of a planned economy is such as to make dictatorship more likely. In the first place, there is the physical difficulty of disseminating ideas in opposition to the government. If the government owns all radio, television, newspapers, and book publishing, how can ideas contrary to the government ever get a hearing? In a capitalist democracy, at least, each person may have the formal right to spread any ideas if that person has the money to do so. Then even a whole group of very poor people might together find enough money to print a newspaper or publish a book on a modest scale.

In the second place, and more profoundly, under the heading of functional problems comes the fact that the government leaders under central planning must control not only the means of propaganda, but the whole economy. This enormous economic power may, to take a leaf from Marx's writings, be used to achieve complete effective political control. It means the power to hire and fire individuals, or to prevent an individual from getting any job. This is a much greater control over livelihoods than the most powerful single group of capitalists could have in view of the millions of other corporations and businesses that may offer jobs. Such economic power also means that vast resources of the nation may be diverted into the treasury of the ruling party for all-out advertising and influencing of all individuals.

The Radical View

Before 1917 it seems that almost all socialists from Marx to Kautsky argued or assumed that democracy is quite compatible with socialism (and even Lenin assumed a parliamentary republic). In fact, they believed that one of the main arguments for socialism is that it constitutes economic democracy, a necessary extension of political democracy, and an addition of effective freedom to the "merely formal" freedoms of a capitalist democracy. Moreover, the early socialist parties were all closely tied into the fight against monarchy or for the extension of political democracy; for example, they fought against Prussian and tsarist autocracy and for the extension of voting rights to all citizens including women (and ethnic minorities). Recently, it has been argued that it is capitalism that is in direct conflict with political democracy (see Bowles and Gintis, 1982). Capitalism means rule of the economy by a tiny minority, whereas political democracy means rule by the majority on all social decisions, which may include the economy. Capitalists now mostly fight against extension of democracy, whereas working class parties fight for it.

Socialists argue that effective freedom of the press in capitalism is limited to the few newspaper magnates who control these very big businesses. On the contrary, in socialism public ownership would mean more equal economic power for everyone, would guarantee everyone the job security and leisure time to participate in politics, would mean there could be no millionaires to buy votes, and would mean an equal access of everyone to the means of propaganda (with guarantees of minority rights).

In socialism, the majority of the people would extend their control to the economy through their majority control of the political process. In concept, political democracy and socialism were thus inseparable. In early socialist writing, however, the mechanics of "everyone" controlling the economy and "everyone" controlling the government by means of "everyone" (or even all "workers") participating in political life were not worked out in any detail. The difficult problems were hardly conceived, let alone squarely faced, before the time that "socialist" governments really came into existence. Most socialists seem to have merely assumed that the formal political and democratic processes would continue to operate as always, but with more life and with effective meaning for the great majority when the small minority of capitalists would be deprived of economic control.

Origins of Soviet Dictatorship

If socialism should lead to increased democracy, why did the socialist revolution in the Soviet Union lead to a statist dictatorship? This question was answered in great detail in chapter 11, so the answer need only be briefly summarized here. The precondition for development of statism is an undemocratic, underdeveloped country. Russia in 1917 was ruled by an autocratic tsar and had a landed nobility, very low productivity in agriculture, a tiny industrial base, and an illiterate and very poor peasantry as 80 percent of the population. How did the transition to statism occur? A socialist revolution came in the midst of a world war, followed by a civil war and foreign intervention. The revolutionaries were a political party that had spent most of its life as a small, persecuted, highly disciplined, underground group. They suddenly took power in a hostile world. Why was the dictatorship continued and maintained? In a country that was devastated, with much of the former urban working class killed or dispersed, the main business was development. After a long debate, the Communist party under Stalin chose to develop rapidly, using resources taken by force and coercion from the peasantry, 80 percent of the people. Under these circumstances of rapid, forced development, a violent dictatorship was inevitable. Statism and dictatorship in the USSR were caused by a specific historical situation. When socialism comes to the advanced capitalist countries, there is good reason to expect that it will expand and deepen democratic processes.

The Ruling Class and Dictatorship

The previous chapter described a Soviet ruling class that controls the surplus and exploits workers at least to some extent. No ruling class likes to give up such a privileged position.

There are two contradictory tendencies in modern Soviet society. On the one hand, the improved level of communication and education and the more relaxed pace of industrialization make more political democracy possible and useful. On the other hand, increasing industrialization has resulted in a vast, entrenched, and conservative bureaucracy (though an increased democratization might reduce their influence). The result is that the USSR is still "a stratified society, with a deep chasm between the ruling stratum of political bureaucrats and economic managers on the one side and the mass of working people on the other" (Sweezy and Huberman, 1967: 11). Yet democratic pressure from below and recognition from above of bureaucratic inefficiency have resulted in much widening of the area of formal political freedoms since Stalin's death.

First, there is some evidence that, in addition to the General Secretary and the Politbureau, the more numerous Central Committee members are now more fully involved in the decision-making process. Second, even the Supreme Soviet has shown a little more life and has developed a functioning committee system. Third, Stalin's police terror has been denounced, the number of political prisoners reduced perhaps 90 percent from the hundreds of thousands once held, due process increased, and there have been no political executions. But Soviet progress toward more democracy, which was considerable in Khrushchev's period, declined to almost nothing under later leaders—and regressed in some periods. In the late 1980s, both economic and political reforms are again being seriously considered.

Market Statism and Democracy

Many conservative writers argue that use of a market mechanism in the economy automatically results in political democracy. But most capitalist, market countries in the world are dictatorships. The confusion comes because the Soviet Union is associated with both central planning and dictatorship. Poland, Hungary, and Czechoslovakia all have made attempts at greater democracy and greater use of the market, but their attempts at democracy were ended by Soviet tanks or Soviet threats. This does not prove, however, that democracy and the market go together.

In fact, Hungary and Yugoslavia both make very widespread use of the market, but are still political dictatorships. Yugoslavia does have enterprise self-management, run by elected workers' councils. The notion of workers' self-management, the election of workers' councils (or some other name for a managing body) to run the enterprise, has a long history. Especially in France many workers have favored it under the name ''syndicalism'' or industrial democracy. Even in America we have long had the Socialist Labor party, a small sect that advocates industrial democracy or workers' self-management as the panacea to all social evils.

Yugoslavia certainly has the forms of economic democracy at the enterprise level. There is some question about the content because ordinary workers participate much less than managers and professionals (the details are in chapter 15). It is obvious, however, that this attempt to give workers collective control over decision making in the enterprise does contribute to the democratic process (see the detailed discussion of democracy and self-management by Dahl, 1985).

It is quite different, nevertheless, to claim that local workers' control of enterprises ensures democracy at the national level. It does not. Yugoslavia does have some formal representation from workers' councils in higher assemblies. The fact is, though, that Yugoslavia has some degree of democracy in each firm but has a one-party dictatorship at the national level—albeit the national party is somewhat weak and much less oppressive than in the Soviet Union.

Many East European intellectuals believe (and some have stated it strongly to me in private conversations) that a market socialism would allow for more democracy than does central planning. Most of their worries about the undemocratic effects of central planning are the same as those of the conservative critics of planning (such as Hayek), but they add a factor from their East European experience. They argue that the Communist party automatically exerts influence (and power) over all of economic life through the central planning mechanism. Central planning also means control over everyone's jobs and control over the means of propaganda. They believe that use of market socialism would automatically reduce the power of the Communist party to interfere in everyone's life.

Yet the conclusion is not so obvious as a generalization. As noted above, Hungary and Yugoslavia are still one-party dictatorships even though they use the market (and there are plenty of dictatorships in market capitalist countries). The two facts, that Hungary and Yugoslavia (a) make use of the market and (b) are less repressive than the Soviet Union, may both be due to historical situations that weakened the Communist parties of both countries.

It is true that central planning puts enormous power in the hands of a central government, but all governments already have enormous power. The question remains control of the central government. That is partly a question of democratic safeguards being institutionalized, as discussed in the next section. As to control of jobs and control of propaganda, use of the market is certainly one way to decentralize that control, but other safeguards are also possible. The various possible institutional safeguards are discussed in the next section.

Institutionalized Democratic Safeguards

After Stalin's performance, it should be impossible for any Marxist to maintain that elimination of the capitalist class also eliminates any need for democratic safeguards. It appears that socialism may be one necessary condition of democracy, but it is not a sufficient condition. In addition, we need the institutionalized democratic safeguards, which some capitalist countries have, but which are rendered ineffective by capitalism. "The point of the socialist critique of 'bourgeois freedoms' is not (or should not be) that they are of no consequence, but that they are profoundly inadequate, and need to be extended by the radical transformation of the context" (Miliband, 1969: 167). In the context of a publicly owned economy, what freedoms must be put into institutionalized democratic safeguards?

First, a multiparty system (or, at least, a multifaction system of a single party) is necessary to allow for peaceful succession of leaders, for organized criticism of the known bureaucratic excesses, and for more representation of popular interest, such as in the question of the immediate expansion of consumer goods. Whether there need be several parties, or some kind of nonparty system, cannot be decided abstractly but must depend on the greatly differing national traditions and conditions of different countries.

There have been as yet few cases where political democracy has allowed a clear-cut decision between capitalism and socialism. Where socialism is the major issue, as in France and Italy, political democracy under capitalism tends to break down (in Germany it led to fascism). It is more realistic to acknowledge that in a certain sense there must be an implicit pre-election agreement for capitalism or for socialism by all parties in normal times. Democratic processes are excellent for making incremental decisions; it is far more difficult to make revolutionary decisions by a democratic process.

The confusion is in thinking that if political democracy does not serve the function of deciding between capitalism and socialism, it serves no function. In the United States capitalism is assumed and is not at issue in elections. Nevertheless, political democracy serves the ruling capitalist class in several functions. First, it allows criticism of capitalist tactics and strategy by more "liberal" capitalist factions. Second, personal corruption in government is limited by the criticism of the opposition party. Third, it produces some degree of leadership and legitimate succession in government by a nonviolent method.

In the Soviet Union public ownership is assumed and is not at issue in the political process. Even one study of anti-Soviet emigres from the USSR finds that almost all of them admit that they were in favor of Soviet public ownership before they went abroad (see Bauer, Inkeles, and Kluckholn, 1956: 262). Nevertheless, there is great need for expansion of political democracy there for all the reasons discussed above. There is still needed a formal apparatus openly guaranteeing political democracy and preventing retrogression to an era like the Stalin period (which is always a real threat).

Second, even if there is more than one political party in socialism, the ruling party may exert enormous control over the means of propaganda, the radio, television, books, and newspapers. Even without censorship, public ownership seems to imply political control. Two different ways may be used to avoid this one-party control of all propaganda, which would otherwise make democracy impossible in practice. One way is used in England where the British Broadcasting Company (BBC) is compelled by law to allot a certain amount of time to opposition views. This could be extended to use of newspapers and other media. The law might require subsidies to the opposition by free use of facilities and other services.

A second way, used for a short time in Poland and proposed in Czechoslovakia, is to allow nonprofit, cooperative ownership of some means of propaganda by any willing group. For example, control of a newspaper or radio station might belong to the writers or readers or listeners, such as the Pacifica Foundation's stations in the United States. In this limited sense, use of the market by cooperative, nonprofit media is a very good idea.

There is also the problem that the ruling political party—even if democratically elected—would control all jobs under centralized socialism. One useful mechanism to prevent misuse of this power is the institution of civil service (with certain regularized procedures for hiring and firing), as it is widely used in countries such as England and the United States. The other mechanism is economic decentralization of an economy, so that public jobs are determined quite separately in each enterprise.

If democratic safeguards are ignored in statism, the result is a dictatorship over the working class, political persecution from mild to violent and bloody, and a loss of economic efficiency as well as general governmental corruption and inefficiency. If the society is not in a crisis caused by rapid economic development or very powerful foreign pressures, it is possible for a socialist economy (as was observed in Czechoslovakia in 1968) to have much wider democratic participation than capitalism. Thereby it may increase its efficiency in functioning, increase expression of public preferences, and generally improve workers' welfare.

A few very tentative conclusions may be drawn from this chapter. First, institutionalized democratic safeguards are necessary under socialism to help the working class maintain control of "its own" government and to prevent a statist dictatorship. These democratic procedures and safeguards may differ widely in different countries. Second, with such safeguards and with the added features of public ownership and more equal distribution of income and property—even when balanced against the enlarged bureaucratic corps—socialism may claim in theory to be expected to be more democratic and responsive to working class needs than any capitalist democracy. Third, this comparison holds only for capitalist and socialist systems of the same level of development. Socialism in economically backward countries tends to be backward in many ways, including the political dimension. Instead of socialism, underdeveloped countries tend toward statism. Fourth, any socialist economy still has unequal distribution of personal private property and an accompanying state apparatus; therefore, its democratic potential is still limited. Yet socialism, of which there is still no example, may produce democratic participation far beyond that of capitalist "democracy." Finally, at the present time, it is still the case that all the statist societies, whether centrally planned or market economies, lack a democratic political process. Because they lack democracy, they cannot be called socialist. Socialism can emerge only on the basis of democracy, but a more thorough-going democracy can only be imagined on the basis of a socialist economy.

Suggested Readings

In addition to the references in the chapter, there is a collection of readings mostly on the Soviet state by British social scientists edited by Harding (1984). There are also useful articles on the Chinese state by David Goodman (1984) and on the Yugoslav state by Sharon Zukin (1984).

— 14 —

CENTRALLY PLANNED STATISM

The Soviet Union has a centrally planned economy, controlled by a self-chosen group of leaders. In a pure centrally planned economy, all prices, outputs, and choices of technology would be decided by central planners under the direction of the government. In fact, many Soviet decisions are made at the regional level, in lower economic agencies, or at the enterprise level. Central planners create a plan, usually with several variants, but the central political leaders make the final planning decisions and control the economy.

Capitalist Unemployment Versus
Statist Shortages

Under capitalism considerable unemployment is a fact of life, rising in depressions and falling in expansions, but always present. All kinds of goods and services are usually available in abundant supply if one has the money. Supply usually exceeds demand at the present price.

Under centrally planned statism, on the contrary, there is usually full employment, but the demand for many goods and services exceeds the supply at the present price. Thus, there are shortages, long lines of consumers waiting to buy scarce goods, and desperate attempts of producers to procure supplies. An article by Lebowitz (1985) and two books by Kornai (1980; 1982) describe this situation in great detail.

Full Employment and Shortage Under
Central Planning

Why is there full employment under central planning? First, the aggregate investment at least equals the aggregate saving. This is because the same agency (the central planning agency) does both the saving and the investment. The planners are always trying to get as much saving as possible in order to invest as much as possible. There is no demand problem because the planners themselves set the investment demand, and they set the consumer demand by determining wages and salaries.

Second, the socialist political movement that produced statism in the USSR promised full employment. Soviet and East European workers consider full employment one of the main achievements of "socialism." It is politically impossible to be against full employment in these countries.

Third, the USSR and Eastern Europe practice taut planning, that is, planning with at least 100 percent of all factors employed. The political leaders are always demanding more, so such planning is a fixed goal for the planners. Moreover, there are many reasons why individual managers may not make use of all of their workers at once and may hoard skilled labor until it is necessary to use it. Thus, one function of central planning is to make sure that all factors are being used.

Fourth, this planning system (especially in its undemocratic context) results not in full employment, but in over full employment. By "over full" employment is meant that the Soviet system attempts to employ more people than there are—and more machines and factories than there are. It is this over full employment caused by taut planning that leads to shortages.

By definition, over full employment means there is a shortage of labor. There is also a shortage of machines, raw materials, and factories because the plan calls for more of each than exist. Finally, since labor and capital are diverted away from production of consumer goods and services into investment, there are also shortages of these consumer commodities.

Given an economy of shortages, there are many obvious implications. The effects include the following: (1) inflationary pressures; (2) difficulties in meeting the plan for lack of necessary materials,; (3) less incentive to work than otherwise (because there is no unemployment and because there are few things on which to spend); (4) attempts by managers to go around the rules in order to get the things needed for production; (5) sellers don't worry about the quality of their goods, because they can sell anything; (6) consumers will buy anything regardless of quality, and they feel at the mercy of sellers; (7) enterprises will also buy any supplies regardless of quality—their insatiable demand leads them to hoarding; and (8) buyers (including consumers and firms) must wait a long time to get things, conduct long and painful searches to find things, and substitute one item for another (most of these points are made in the excellent article by Lebowitz, 1985, reviewing the book on shortages by Kornai, 1980).

Planning and the Growth Problem

The following sections examine the relation of growth to shortage, growth to the investment/consumption ratio, fluctuations in the rate of growth, and the actual rise and fall of Soviet growth rates as a case study in statist growth.

Growth and Shortage

The statist economies tend to be engaged in a continuous drive to produce at a maximum rate of growth, partly due to the attitudes of the political leadership. Political leaders press planners to make their plans as ambitious as possible. Planners produce very taut production plans that use every available resource and then some. These overambitious plans cause shortages of resources as firms attempt to meet the plans. The over-ambitious plans also cause shortages of consumer goods, since some resources are directed away from consumer goods to investment goods. Prices must rise because workers are fully employed and have plenty of income to buy the consumer goods and services that are available and still have leftover money.

The mounting evidence of shortages, however, induces planners to attempt to expand industry still further and faster (according to Lebowitz, 1985). By attempting to expand industry even faster, planners create additional shortages. Thus, shortages lead to greater growth efforts and greater growth efforts lead to more shortages. Obviously, these are short-run shortages. High growth rates will eventually expand output, though growth may never catch up to expectations.

The good side of high planned growth rates is full employment, since the planned growth always keeps ahead of actual labor available. The bad side of it is that the shortages lead to inefficiency.

Fluctuations in Growth Rates

In the Soviet Union and Eastern Europe, the rate of economic growth has shown relatively regular fluctuations for the last thirty years (see, e.g., Goldmann and Kouba, 1969: 41). What are the causes of these fluctuations? A centralized bureaucracy, goaded by an impatient political leadership, creates impossibly ambitious plans that cannot be fulfilled. More specifically, overoptimistic planning leads to supply bottlenecks and shortages of vital resources. Excessive investment in new projects periodically leads to a lack of the basic raw materials necessary to complete these projects. Thus, these countries frequently witness a large number of uncompleted construction projects. The rate of growth declines because these partly finished factories cannot yet produce anything.

Eventually, the planners recognize this situation because new productive capacity and output fail to reach the planned targets. They are then forced to reduce new investment projects, so that the old ones can be completed. This relaxation of the investment pace is often sudden and uncoordinated, so it may even further lower the growth rate by confusion and by reduction of all investment. Nevertheless, the reduction of the number of construction projects eventually eases the disproportions and shortages, brings material supplies into balance with investment demands, and allows completion of existing construction projects. This makes possible a new balanced expansion.

Success of the new expansion produces higher growth rates once more. This again leads to overoptimism, "overplanning," new disproportions, and a new slowdown. Thus, the cycle repeats itself again and again, being caused apparently by "subjective" mistakes by politicians and planners. It is, however, the objective fact of an overcentralized planning structure in a statist dictatorship (which does not allow free criticism) that leads to these recurrent "mistakes."

Length of the Cycle

The length of the growth cycle under statism is based mainly on the construction time and gestation period of new investment. A new wave of investment causes excess demand and shortages on the supply side. The period of reduced growth lasts until the new investment is completed; it is usually completed only after the forced slowdown on further investment has made supplies available. The new capacity in turn increases supplies, further aiding expansion. The length of the period of high growth rates is based on the time for the new capacity to reach full use, the time for the data to reflect that increase, and the time for overoptimistic planning to lead to new bottlenecks and shortages.

Inventory investment has a reinforcing effect on the cycle because when the economy is overheated, firms attempt to hoard supplies; but when things are going more smoothly, the hoarding is reduced. Also, in the smaller countries of Eastern Europe, the cycle is further complicated by foreign trade, since imports become a desperate necessity in periods of greatest shortage, whereas exports can only be increased when higher growth is resumed.

In spite of certain superficial similarities, the fluctuations in growth of output in the statist countries are fundamentally different from the capitalist business cycle. Capitalist business cycles have usually been more drastic in effect, normally resulting in an actual decline in output and employment, while the cycles in the statist countries usually mean only reduced growth with continued full employment. More important, the fluctuations in capitalism are characterized by lack of demand, where the lack of demand is due to relations of exploitation. The fluctuations under statist central planning are manifested in shortages and supply-side bottlenecks, where the shortages are due to overcentralized planning and an undemocratic political system.

Growth: Investment versus Consumption

One of the most vital problems for statist societies has been the determination of how much of the relatively scarce supply of capital should be used to help increase immediate consumption and how much should be used for more long-range increase of producer goods to expand the economic base. This problem has been vehemently debated in the USSR since the 1920s. The official Soviet ideology includes the "laws" that socialism has planned and proportional development, that socialism produces for social need, and that investment always grows faster than consumption in socialism. An excellent article by Magdoff (1985) shows that these and other so-called laws are a mixture of propaganda, obvious truisms, and confusion.

To understand the problem more scientifically, it may be useful to state the identity that:

$$\text{output} = \text{output/capital} \times \text{capital} \tag{1}$$

This equation makes the obvious point that the more capital there is and the more that is produced per unit of capital, the higher will be the output. We can also state a truism involving the rate of growth (change in output/output). Thus:

change in output/output = (change in output/change in capital)
$$\times \text{ (change in capital/output)} \qquad (2)$$

In other words, the rate of growth is determined by the increase in capital times the increased output obtained from an increase in capital. Now increase in capital is, by definition, the same thing as investment. So it may be said that one way of looking at the rate of growth is to examine investment and the product obtained from the investment.

It is very hard to change the product obtained per unit of investment, since that is determined by technology and scientific advance, education and training of more workers, and discovery of new raw materials. Therefore, most Soviet policy battles rage around issues of finding new investment capital. Stalin argued that the growth of investment must always be greater than the growth of consumption if there is to be smooth economic growth. That is false, as is shown by the simple algebra of growth demonstrated above. Yet it it true that, all other things being equal, a higher ratio of investment to current output will raise the rate of growth.

Even the principle that a higher ratio of investment in the society will mean a higher rate of growth is true only under certain circumstances and within certain limits. First, if there is too much output shifted from consumer needs to investment, then consumers will be very unhappy, may create slowdowns in production, and may take other actions against the state. Second, the productivity of that new capital depends not only on workers, but also on new raw materials and new technology. Third, it has been noted above that an excessive amount of investment will leave many construction jobs idle for lack of raw materials and/or skilled labor, so a too high rate of planned growth may lead to a lower rate of actual growth.

There is no economic rule for the optimum ratio of consumption to investment. This is rather a question that has been fought out on the political field. It depends on one's pragmatic and ethical decision about the importance of current consumption versus long-run building of the economy. In a democratic socialist society, this would be the prime question discussed by and decided by the society through democratic procedures and free discussion. Everyone should decide together how much of social output should go into building factories versus consumer goods, for example, shoe machinery versus shoes. When the Soviet leadership decided on an all-out industrialization drive at the expense of current consumption, they reduced incentives and efficiency, and they set up the circumstances for a rigid dictatorship silencing opposition to that drive.

Rise and Fall of Soviet Growth Rates

Soviet economic growth rates were among the highest that the world has ever seen from the 1930s through the 1950s (except for the years of the Second World War). From 1950 to 1980, the Soviet economy grew at least twice as fast as the U.S. economy (see Zimbalist and Sherman, 1984: ch. 6). Why did the Soviet economy grow so fast? Most important, perhaps, is the fact that it did not suffer from unemployment, but had full employment of both workers and capital goods in that whole period. Second, central planning also meant that the USSR was able to gather savings together and reinvest about 30 percent of national income every year for some years. This is a far higher ratio of investment to income than most capitalist economies have ever been able to generate. Finally, the planned Soviet economy has consistently invested major resources in education, science, and research and development of new technology. Numbers of people employed in the USSR in research and development are far higher than in the U.S. economy.

Central planning has thus meant full employment, high rates of investment, and plentiful funds for basic research. Yet Soviet growth rates have been falling since the 1950s. What accounts for this decline?

Some of the decline has resulted from success. One effect of Soviet industrialization and urbanization has been declining population growth. Second, another effect of the greater urban sophistication and success in building an industrial base has been a greater demand for immediate production of consumer goods and a reduction of the urgency of further rapid growth. As a result, some resources have been shifted from investment to consumption. So this part of the decline was a voluntary change in planning desired by the population. Third, the cold war has also meant continuing diversion of resources from investment into military spending. These three factors account for much of the decline in the amount of new labor and new capital added each year in the Soviet Union.

Of more concern are those systemic factors that have caused a slowdown in the growth of productivity. Central planning tends to leave managers with an incentive to produce immediate growth, but disincentives to innovate for the long run (this problem is explained below). In the early years, the Soviet Union was still way behind other countries in technology, so it could simply borrow technology. As it gets closer to the technological frontier, it must generate more of its own innovations, so this factor has become more important. Second, central planning has a harder and harder time making optimal decisions as the complexity of the economy grows over time. It is better suited to the initial task of mobilizing all resources for an all-out industrialization drive than it is for the more delicate task of running a modern industrial economy, which requires millions of decisions. Under central planning, the lack of optimal decisions tends to be revealed in the existence of shortages everywhere.

Third, there is a growing contradiction between the Soviet relations of production and the potential growth of its forces of production. As defined in the first chapter of this part, the Soviet relations of production are based on the political control of the economy by a small group of self-appointed leaders. These relations of production hold back progress by stifling scientific thought and research by ideological barriers and by censorship; making arbitrary decisions contrary to the economic good, but not allowing the criticism that could correct these decisions; and reducing the earlier revolutionary enthusiasm of Soviet workers to a routine and sullen alienation from participation in work improvements.

Planning and the Balance Problem

It was shown earlier that Soviet planning does lead to full employment, but the tendency to attempt to produce more than is possible leads to relative shortages of most things and inflationary pressures. In this section the problem of aggregate balance is examined in detail, followed by the problem of balance between industries.

Aggregate Balance: Inflationary Pressure

Soviet prices rose by 7 times their initial level in the 1930s, that is, from an index of 100 in 1928 to 700 in 1936. Then, in the Second World War, prices rose to an index level of 3,895. What caused the inflation and shortages of the 1930s and 1940s?

The USSR planned an incredibly rapid growth of investment in the 1930s and pushed all-out for military growth in the first half of the 1940s. The excessive growth plans of these two sectors meant a scramble by managers to buy any available raw materials, capital, and labor.

As a consequence, the price of each of these investment goods rose very quickly.

Workers were shifted from production of consumer goods to production of investment goods and military commodities. Workers were given higher wages. As a result, workers had a lot of money to spend, but very few consumer goods were being produced. Therefore, the prices of consumer goods also rose.

Since "wages" (including salaries and bonuses) are the only form of consumer income, the condition for an aggregate equilibrium is that wages must equal the sum of the prices of all consumer goods. The problem is that total wages are greater than consumer goods. Let W be the wage rate, N be the number of workers, P be the price level, and Q be the quantity of goods supplied. Then:

$$WN > PQ \tag{3}$$

One may think of a fixed number of workers, part of whom are shifted from consumer products to investment products and military products. Suppose N_c is the workers in consumer goods, N_i is the workers in investment goods, N_m is the workers in military production, P_c is the price of consumer goods, and Q_c is the quantity of consumer goods supplied. Then::

$$WN_c + WN_i + WN_m > P_cQ_c \tag{4}$$

One way to state the problem is that workers earn high salaries producing plant, equipment, and military products but must spend their wages for food, clothing, and shelter.

Some complicating secondary factors also need to be considered. First, Soviet consumer goods include a large sales tax (T_s), so that may be added to the price side of the equation. Second, workers must pay some rather small personal income taxes (T_p), so that must be subtracted from wages available for spending. Third, personal saving (S) must also be subtracted from the wages available for spending. So the full equation looks something like this:

$$WN_c + WN_i + WN_m - T_p - S > P_cQ_c + T_s \tag{5}$$

This is how the problem looks to Soviet planners. What can they do to get balance and end inflationary pressure? Obviously, they can increase the quantity of consumption at the expense of investment (assuming that military spending is fixed); they have done that in recent years, but it reduces growth. They can reduce wage rates or increase personal taxes or increase sales taxes, but all of those are very unpopular. They may try to raise saving by higher interest rates or social pressures, but this is a tiny item. Or they may do nothing and have long lines of consumers and shortages—which is part of the present solution. In the long run they may try to increase the product per worker by adding more capital, more education, and better technology. In the short run, however, research and education also require resources.

Industrial Balance

Every industry requires inputs of others. For example, steel requires iron, coal, construction of new mills, and so forth. All of these inputs must be coordinated with the outputs available from other industries. The Soviets try to balance the needs or uses for each industrial product with the resources going into it. Thus, for the steel industry, they must calculate the following balance sheet:

Balance for Steel

Needs	Available
Exports	Imports
Increases in inventories	Decreases in inventories
Uses by:	Production in:
Other industries	Region 1
Consumers	Region 2
	.
	.
	.
	Region N

Frequently, the total of urgent needs and uses is greater than the existing resources can produce. Then, Soviet planners must urge managers to overcome the shortages by producing more outputs with no more inputs—a difficult task. Otherwise, they must eventually cut back on the outputs of some highly desirable final goods.

The Problem of Efficiency

The problem of producing most efficiently in a centrally planned statist economy will be discussed in the following aspects: (1) efficiency and prices, (2) efficiency and information, (3) efficiency and shortage, (4) efficiency and statist political institutions, and (5) efficiency of statist planning versus market capitalism.

Efficiency and Prices

Even in a centrally planned economy, prices have several very important functions. The price of labor (wages) balances the supply and demand for labor in each skill, each region, and each enterprise, helping to determine where workers will live and work and what skills they will acquire. Under central planning, in theory there is only one employer. In practice, however, since there are acute shortages of skilled workers relative to demand, managers compete fiercely against each other.

Second, the price of consumer goods must balance their demand and supply at each retail outlet. If there is not enough supply of a good to satisfy consumers at the going price, there are going to be shortages and long lines. Third, as shall be seen below, the actions of managers are affected by the price of producer goods.

Finally, the decisions of planners will be determined by relative prices of goods. To be efficient, planners must decide an optimal ratio in which different goods and services will be produced, for example, the ratio of production of automobiles to houses. This ratio should be based on consumer preferences, which may be expressed in prices. To be efficient, planners must also decide an optimal ratio in which inputs should be used in each industry, for example, the ratio of use of oil to electricity. This ratio should be based on the relative cost to society of the different inputs at present technology, which may be reflected in prices.

Some antisocialist economists, such as Ludwig von Mises (1935), have argued that prices in a market economy do represent preferences and technologically given cost ratios. Since only a market will generate such prices, the true price ratios cannot be known in a centrally planned economy. Therefore, all central planning is irrational and inefficient. This theory is incorrect because planners do not need market-generated prices; they simply need three types of information (see, e.g., Lange, 1938).

First, they must know relative consumer preferences, including preferences of individual consumers, industrial units, and government units. Second, they must know what resources are available, including capital goods, workers, and raw materials. Third, at the present level of technology, they must know what combinations of resources will produce what outputs. With this information, planners may produce a set of "shadow prices" (prices for planners' use only, not market prices), which can then be used to generate a rational, efficient, and optimal plan.

Efficiency and Information

The criticism has been made that it is enormously difficult to describe all of the output and price relations of a centrally planned economy, let alone compute the optimal answers (see Hayek, 1935). There are millions of products, so it would take millions of equations to describe the economy. It would take an army of planners to collect all of the necessary information. It would take another army of planners to do all of the computations.

One answer to this criticism is the improvement of techniques for planning and the use of faster and faster computers. The Soviet Union has attempted to follow this path to some extent, but it is a very difficult road to efficiency. Defenses of planning (such as Dobb, 1955: 55-93) emphasize that optimal efficiency under planning may be an impossible goal, but no more so than in the highly wasteful monopoly capitalist system. It has also been emphasized, as discussed earlier, that planned economies do better in terms of full employment and that they have higher growth rates than the capitalist countries.

A second type of answer is to argue that a truly socialist country could be decentralized (see Lange, 1938) and make use of the market. The USSR has attempted some decentralization, but it has not been very successful in the attempt, as shall be seen below. This road to optimal efficiency by decentralization has been taken by Hungary and Yugoslavia, whose degree of success is discussed in the next chapter.

Efficiency and Shortage

The centrally planned economies tend to have over full employment and therefore have shortages relative to demand. This economy of shortages has many negative effects on efficiency (see Lebowitz, 1985). Since consumers will buy most anything, retail sellers don't have to worry about quality. Since firms will also buy most anything, sellers of producers' goods and services also do not worry about quality. Buyers must accept poor quality, or wait a long time, or search for substitutes. In this situation, hoarding is rational, which increases the shortages.

According to Granick (1983), workers under statism not only expect full employment but assume that they will have a job in the local area, that they will not be dismissed, and that they may continue working at a fairly low labor intensity. But if workers cannot be dismissed or transferred, this makes managers much less interested in innovations. Thus, the rate of industrial innovations remains low and productivity growth is slow.

Managerial Incentives and Efficiency

Under full employment and central planning, with large bonuses for fulfilling or overfulfilling a plan, managers have a strong incentive to appear to produce a lot of goods, but they have no worry about quality because anything can be sold. Managers also have few worries about efficiency because incentives to produce far outweigh disincentives for high costs. The following problems have been noted with respect to Soviet managerial efficiency (for details, see Zimbalist and Sherman, 1984: 316–19):

1. Withholding or slanting information. Soviet managers cannot submit absolutely false figures because there are many lines of control from above. They can and do, however, withhold some information and slant information, such as what month something was actually produced. Thus, planners are led astray.

2. Easy plans. The manager slants the information about capacity and bargains for an easier plan than the plant can actually accomplish. Thus, the plan appears to be overfulfilled, but it is not optimal.

3. Poor quality. The temptation is to produce as much as possible by ignoring any controls for quality.

4. Few styles. Since they can sell almost anything, Soviet managers have an incentive to produce as few styles of a good as possible because that makes production easier.

5. Easiest mix. Similarly, among different types of goods, the Soviet manager will choose the easiest kind to produce, regardless of consumer desire. In the shortage economy, consumers will grumble,

but they will buy anything.

6. Illegal means of supply. Given the shortages, Soviet managers use every means—including bribes and persons known as pushers—to obtain supplies. These illegal or semilegal purchases must disrupt central planning.

7. Hoarding supplies. Given the shortages, a rational Soviet manager will hoard supplies for the future, thus aggravating the shortages.

8. Hoarding labor. The same argument applies to the hoarding of skilled labor.

9. Resistance to innovation. All of the above are ways in which the system of centrally planned statism seriously reduces efficiency at any given time. But the system also reduces dynamic efficiency, that is, economic innovations that would increase efficiency. One reason is that Soviet managers view innovations as risky because innovations may reduce output for some months during the transition. Soviet managers often have a short time horizon because their bonuses are based on monthly production figures and because they are frequently transferred to new jobs.

Another reason why innovations are impeded is the fact that a democratic environment of open and free discussions is an absolute necessity for scientific progress, which is the basis for technological innovation. Yet the statist countries are undemocratic and do not allow free discussion of all subjects. Recently, the Soviet leaders have learned that scientific discussion must be encouraged in a freer atmosphere, yet there are still many bureaucratic obstacles and limits to discussion in some fields. Also, the fact that Soviet education is conformist toward existing ideas is not helpful to scientific progress.

Reforms and Continuing Contradictions

Growth rates declined in the Soviet Union in the late 1950s and early 1960s, probably due to the fact that central planning has more and more trouble, given the increasing complexity of the economy. The planned economy of Czechoslovakia suffered an actual decline in 1962. At the same time, Yugoslavia decentralized and seemed to be successful.

As a result the Soviet leadership authorized a fairly open debate on economic reforms in 1962–1965, centering on decentralization and incentives to managers (for a survey of the literature on Soviet and East European reform, see Koont and Zimbalist, 1983). An economist named Evsei Liberman was chosen to lead off the debate. He suggested the profit rate as the main criterion of manager's performance. His idea was not merely to reward for physical output, but to force managers to pay attention to costs and efficiency.

In 1965 official reforms were made in the Soviet Union and soon thereafter in the rest of Eastern Europe. In the Soviet reforms, three important changes were made (as well as several others of less importance). First, a large number of indexes of the manager's performance were abolished, leaving three main ones: sales, physical output, and profitability. Second, capital was to come in large part from banks, with interest paid on the loans. This would prevent managers from treating capital as a free good by wasting it or hoarding it. Third, firms were allowed to retain a percentage of profits for bonuses in order to increase incentives. Firms would also retain some profits for reinvestment in order to allow more local decision making.

What has happened since 1965? Because the reforms apparently gave more power to managers, they were resisted and sabotaged by middle-level state bureaucrats and middle-level party leaders. And as the reforms ran into problems, they were modified, mostly in the direction of more central power, though not always.

First, more indexes of managerial performance were added—each bringing more central control—but not as many indexes as before the reforms. Second, interest is being charged Soviet firms, but not enough to have much practical effect. Anyway, a losing Soviet firm is always bailed out by subsidies. Third, although decentralized investment was allowed to increase for a while, it has now decreased again.

But the reform movement ebbs and flows. It depends on the emergence of real problems, such as declining growth rates, as well as the balance of power resulting from political fights among different groups. There has been tremendous ferment since 1965, with new ''reforms'' every year, so many that firms have trouble adjusting to each new change. By 1987, it appeared that the forces of reform were again ascendant—but their direction is still unclear in the Soviet Union. It is worth noting that the planned economy of China has been moving rapidly toward more use of the market.

Contradictions of Statist Central Planning

Why has there been so much effort put into reform in the USSR and apparently very little to show for it? The problem is that the Soviet leaders do seriously wish to decentralize decision making, but they do not want to abandon central planning in favor of the market—and that is a contradiction! Every economy needs coordination, for example, the number of rubber automobile tires and the number of automobiles must be coordinated. But there are only two ways to coordinate the economy: one is some form of conscious central planning and the other is automatic adjustments by competition in the market place. There is no other way. If the Soviets let the rubber tire factories and the automobile factories each make their own decisions (but with no market), then there will be no balance between products.

Thus, every time the Soviets move toward decentralization, they run into problems and retreat toward centralization. This contradiction between the reforms and the planning system is reflected in many concrete conflicts and tensions. First, the manager would like to achieve high quality to satisfy individual and industrial consumers. If all of your consumers are satisfied, then your superiors are more likely to be happy with you even in the Soviet system. So even without a monetary incentive for quality (and there are now some of these), the Soviet manager certainly prefers to produce good quality rather than bad. But the central plan allocates raw materials and labor, so changing production mixes may be impossible under the plan, unless it is done illegally.

Second, the manager wishes to choose the optimal, most efficient technology in order to lower costs. But the plan specifies types of raw materials, machines, and labor allocated to the factory. Thus, it is impossible to change technology, even if the manager is encouraged to do so.

Third, the reforms make profitability a very important index of managerial performance, so managers certainly want to maximize profits. But the central planners set prices, often in an arbitrary manner, not reflecting costs or collective and consumer preferences. Therefore, achievement of maximum enterprise profitability may not achieve the greatest social profitability, considering social benefits and social costs. Since it is prices that are incorrect, the calculation of profits will be incorrect even if external costs, such as pollution, are given a price and included. It is an extraordinarily difficult job, however, to set 10 or 20 million prices in a rational manner without using some market mechanism.

Fourth, because the prices are arbitrary, the Soviet enterprise does not have enough information to make good decisions. Yet, because of the enormously complex economy, central planners also do not have enough information to make good decisions.

Why do the Soviets not make more use of the market? Partly, it is because they recognize the problems that capitalist market systems have—and they do not want those problems. Partly it is because they have a one-party dictatorship. The top leaders could possibly retain their dictatorial power in an economy making wide use of the market—witness Hungary or Yugoslavia or any of the dictatorships in capitalist countries. But the thousands of middle-level Communist party leaders and middle-level government bureaucrats would suddenly lose much of their power. At present, they interfere at all levels of economic direction as well as day-to-day enterprise direction. If the manager were truly free to follow the market, their power to interfere would be ended. Thus they resist and make it close to impossible for top leaders to really reform the system by extending use of the market. This could change if top leaders face enough of an economic crisis.

Another way to state the most basic contradiction of centrally planned statism is that it is committed to "public" ownership of the means of production, but there is no democracy. Thus, in the Soviet Union, public control of the economy means control by a small elite. This class relationship of production holds back the development of the forces of production in many ways. The resistance of most of the elite to meaningful market reform has already been noted. Continued centrally set arbitrary prices as well as continued central control of supplies of labor and raw materials and machinery are quite contradictory to the reform idea of more local control over quality and technology, contrary to the local need for information, and contrary to the possibility of using enterprise profitability as a good indicator of performance.

Furthermore, the one-party dictatorship's control of society and the economy severely restricts economic progress, holding back technological development. As noted above, technology depends on science, and science depends on the free exchange of ideas, which is severely restricted in the Soviet Union both by censorship and by bureaucratic control of scientific institutions.

Even the discussion of economic reform operates under severe constraints because of the dictatorship. Thus, even the formulation of optimal reforms, especially market reforms, is difficult or impossible.

The political dictatorship makes it difficult to criticize inefficiency. Inefficiency by important officials is criticized only after they are removed or about to be removed. An example is the Soviet nuclear industry where safety was pronounced excellent by top officials. So it could not be criticized until after a disaster occurred. The same penchant for secrecy and central control, without any criticism, makes progress in the nuclear industry—or any other industry—very difficult. So, again, the conclusion is that the statist, centrally planned mode of production is holding back the forces of production.

Suggested Readings

The book by Zimbalist and Sherman (1984) provides seven chapters of detailed analysis of the Soviet planned economy, as well as lengthy chapters on the evolution of the Cuban planned economy and the evolution of the Chinese planned economy (as well as recent new directions). It also lists plenty of additional literature on the subject. The article by Lebowitz (1985) and the book by Kornai (1980) are notable for their focus on the shortage problem in planned economies.

There is a good article on inflation in planned economies by Nuti (1986). Grosfeld (1986) has written a good article on investment cycles in planned economies. There are some mainstream articles on Soviet growth by Gomulka (1986), Desai (1986), and Kantorovich (1986). An excellent collection of the views of various China experts is that edited by the Bulletin of Concerned Asian Scholars (1983). Also on China, the book by Lippit (1987) is outstanding.

— 15 —

MARKET-ORIENTED STATISM

The term "market statism" is rather awkward sounding, but it does accurately denote a statist society that makes predominant use of the market rather than central planning. Statism has been defined as state control of the economy, with control of the state by a small elite. All statist societies make some use of the market; for example, even the USSR uses a labor market and a consumer market, though they operate somewhat differently than U.S. markets because of the role of the state.

Two statist societies, Hungary and Yugoslavia, make very extensive use of the market. In Hungary, the state clearly controls the means of production and appoints a manager in all of the larger firms; though, as discussed below, all of the smaller firms have managers appointed by a board including worker representatives. Yet the manager in Hungary is told to maximize profits in the market, not to follow a central plan. In Yugoslavia, each enterprise is collectively owned by its workers, but within limits (for example, they may not sell the whole enterprise). The workers in Yugoslavia appoint a manager who is supposed to maximize profits in the market, not to follow a central plan. In both Hungary and Yugoslavia, in spite of the market, the state still controls the overall direction of the economy, and the state itself is still controlled by a small elite—hence the name "market statism."

Origins of Market Statism

On the theoretical side, Oscar Lange (Lange and Taylor, 1964) wrote in the 1930s on the problems raised against centrally planned socialism.

He argued that one could have the best of all worlds in a market socialism. The means of production are publicly owned and the central planners decide overall investment policy as well as appointing managers. But the manager decides what to produce and how to produce. Managers set the price of consumer goods according to supply and demand in the market, following traditional neoclassical rules of profit maximization.

On the practical side, the cooperative movement has a long history of attempts to organize enterprises owned by their workers and self-managed, or managed by a manager appointed by the workers. Specifically, in Eastern Europe in the 1960s the severe problems encountered by central planning led to a rethinking of the relation of plan and market. The Hungarian reforms went the farthest toward the market, but others were close behind. Yugoslavia followed a somewhat different road: having been excommunicated from the Soviet bloc in the late 1940s, it made drastic reforms very early. In the late 1980s, China had begun to explore market solutions very seriously, and even the Soviet Union is contemplating greater use of the market.

Hungary

Hungary is a small country (eleven million people) with very few natural resources, so it is primarily dependent on international trade. Therefore, high quality is very important for its competitive position. This is one factor that turned Hungary from central planning toward a decentralized, market-oriented economy.

Hungary attempted to democratize in 1956 but was prevented from doing so by Soviet troops. Yet the resulting government soon committed itself to extensive economic reform, partly to gain popularity. Hungary instituted several partial reforms from 1957 to 1965, then made a sweeping reform in 1968. There have been three periods so far in the history of the Hungarian reforms.

First Period, 1968-1972

Under the 1968 reform, the state uses macroeconomic controls and price controls, but the physical output targets for each firm are purely advisory. The state still owns the firms, but each manager is an autonomous director, basing her or his decisions on profitability.

In other words, Hungary has abolished central planning as a system of commands. No orders are given as to outputs of goods and services. There are no allocations and no rationing of materials. Hungarian planning is "indicative" or advisory. The market decides allocation and outputs. The market, however, is regulated by the planners so as to coax enterprises to do what the planners desire. The regulatory aspects include: (1) macroeconomic fiscal and monetary policies, (2) direct allocation of some new investments, (3) direct control of public utilities and infrastructure, and (4) some influence and direct controls over prices, wages, interest rates, and exchange rates.

The manager is appointed by the government but is then supposed to maximize profits. The manager's bonus is based on profitability, so this is an avenue of control. There is some conflict in goals because the manager is supposed to be free to make any decision, yet the manager is hired and fired by the central planners. To give the enterprise more decentralized decision-making power it would be necessary to move in the Yugoslav direction, in which the manager is appointed by the workers' council in the enterprise.

Workers in Hungary do receive bonuses based on the profitability of the enterprise. Most workers' income, however, comes from regular wages and salaries. There are centrally determined wage scales, covering each type of labor and skill-grade of labor.

For the enterprise manager to make rational market-oriented decisions, prices must be determined by pure and perfect competition or by perfect computation. There were to be three kinds of prices under the Hungarian reforms. First, a large and increasing sector was to have prices freely set by the manager. Second, there was a lot of inflationary pressure in the previous shortage economy. To prevent inflation, some essential sectors of the economy continued to have their prices set by the central planners. Finally, some important but less essential sectors had their prices set by the manager, but within minimum and maximum bounds set by the central planners.

This also meant that managers were free to make some decentralized investments. For some years, enterprise investments rose rapidly, even going beyond the planned investment targets.

At the same time, competition was severely limited in its scope because of the commitment to full employment. Full employment policies meant that inefficient, failing firms were not allowed to go bankrupt but were saved by state subsidies. Thus, some economists perceived a trade-off between efficiency and full employment (see Kornai, 1980b).

To increase incentive, managers and workers were given direct bonuses out of profits. But this meant that high-profit firms paid much higher wages and salaries; many managers got bonuses ten to twenty times the average wage. This inequality of income, caused by competition, was constrained by the desire for income equality. Therefore, the Hungarian state guaranteed minimum wages, while heavily taxing wages above the average. There was thus perceived to be a trade-off between equality and incentives (again, see Kornai, 1980b).

Another problem was that competition was limited; no change was made in the industrial structure. The Hungarian economy is highly concentrated, with only 702 enterprises in 1979, so domestic competition is very limited. The international market, however, does enforce quite a bit of competition. In addition to the large state enterprises, there are also many private cooperatives, which have a significant percentage of output and trade.

Finally, a step was taken toward self-management by allowing workers to elect shop stewards. The shop stewards were given some influence over decisions on wages, production, reinvestment, and enterprise welfare programs.

Because of the influence of competition in the market, even though regulated and imperfect, every traveler has observed that Hungarian stores are well-stocked and—at the higher prices—there are few shortages. There is also some evidence, however, of substantial inflation and unemployment as a result of the change to a market-oriented economy.

Most observers considered the reforms to be a great success because the annual growth rate of national income in Hungary rose very significantly in the early 1970s. Yet the continuing problems, mentioned above, allowed a counterattack to develop.

Second Period, 1973-1978

The counterattack was led by middle-level state and party bureaucrats, who were losing power because they no longer had control over economic decision-making. According to Marer (1986), there was also some resistance to the reforms by the heads of some of the large industrial firms. They gained much more freedom of decision making under the reforms. On the other hand, they lost their security, that is, subsidies from central planners with whom they had close ties. Now they must prove themselves by competition in the market, by which one could win big bonuses but one could also fail.

Janos Kornai wrote:

> The majority of directors of large enterprises are ambivalent: they resent the paternalistic center and would like real independence, including opportunities to independently export and import, to set wages and prices, etc. They get upset about the complexity and perpetual changes in the "regulators" [i.e., price and wage controls, import and export controls, etc.]. But at the same time they note with satisfaction that the state responds to their pressure and in case of financial difficulties, helps them out, and would not like to lose the security this provides. (Quoted in Marer, 1986: 288)

Because of the opposition of some directors and bureaucrats, and because some problems were perceived, the reform process was halted for five years. One problem particularly stressed was the need for central intervention to help Hungarian firms in foreign trade, which absorbs a large part of Hungarian production.

Third Period, 1979–1984

By 1979, it was felt that the early reforms were consolidated and more reforms were the only way to overcome continuing problems. The new reforms attempted to bring about greater competition by changing the old industrial structure. For example, 25 giant enterprises were broken up and were replaced by 332 smaller enterprises between 1980 and 2983. Many new, small state enterprises and small cooperative enterprises were created.

Considerably more freedom was given to enterprises in setting prices—for which real competition was a prerequisite. By 1980, about two-thirds of all prices were allowed to fluctuate freely in the light of market conditions. Moreover, domestic prices would be the same as foreign export prices, thus strengthening the influence of foreign competition.

Since these prices now reflected supply and demand, profits became a more meaningful category. Thus, the performance of managers could be more accurately evaluated by profitability. The use of the same set of prices for domestic and foreign trade also meant that managers could be given more freedom in the conduct of foreign trade—since their profits would better reflect their performance.

The number of personnel in central planning was cut because the importance of the central plan had greatly diminished. The meetings that had taken place between enterprises and their superiors for "plan coordination" were abolished.

In the first period of reform, decentralized investments by firms expanded so rapidly that they caused shortages. In the second period, decentralized investment was sharply curtailed. Now, the firms do about half of new investment, while the center does the other half (see Nove, 1983). The investment by the center thus remains a powerful weapon of macro control.

The changing structure of Hungarian enterprise has produced four main types. First, in public utilities that maintain the infrastructure (power, water, etc.) and in defense industries, the firms are still centrally controlled, pay all of their profits into the government budget, and receive subsidies as necessary; managers are government-appointed. Second, most large state enterprises are run by the manager plus an enterprise board; the board is composed half of management representatives and half of elected worker representatives. Smaller enterprises are run by a general assembly of the workers; these are more like a U.S. producers' cooperative, but they do not legally own the firm, nor do they have the right to sell all of its assets (so these cooperative enterprises are similar to the Yugoslav model). Finally, some tiny private enterprises are allowed, strictly constrained as to size.

Conclusions for Political and Economic Reform

What has been the relation of political reform and economic reform in Hungary? It has made clear that decentralization means loss of some power for party and state officials. In the first place, some political liberalization and open debate is necessary before decentralization; that did happen in Hungary. Second, detailed intervention is prohibited. Thus, managers are now not so easily controlled, so they have more freedom of maneuver and perhaps more power vis-à-vis party and state. Third, decentralization has brought into the open these and other opposing interests, such as consumers versus sellers. These opposing interests make more obvious the need for political openness and free debate. Hungary, today, is more open than it was, but it still has one-party control.

How successful has Hungarian economic reform been in stimulating better economic performance? Galasi and Sziraczki (1985) have evaluated performance in the three different periods. In the first period,

1968-1971, the national income rose at an excellent 5.7 percent a year, while inflation in consumer prices was only 1.0 percent a year. In the second period, 1972-1978, while reform paused, the excellent growth continued, with national income growing at 5.8 percent a year; but inflation rose to 3.6 percent a year, an unwelcome portent. In the third period, 1979-1984, with renewed decentralization and greater competition, growth of national income fell to 0.8 percent a year, while inflation grew to 7.4 percent a year. Consumer prices grew faster than nominal wages, so real wages fell by 0.7 percent a year.

Interestingly, this period of stagflation—the combination of stagnation and inflation—did not lead to unemployment. Since the government is committed to full employment, workers remained on the job, but real wages were allowed to fall. Since enterprises continue to expect that the government will not allow them to go bankrupt but will subsidize them in emergencies, they continue to hire more workers in spite of insufficient demand for goods or stagnating productivity. "Under socialism, where the cost of labor does not influence the level of employment, economic stagnation manifests itself in a decline in real wages, as prices rise faster than money wages, rather than in open unemployment" (Galasi and Sziraczki, 1985: 216).

It appears that Hungary has moved a long way from central planning toward the use of market competition. It is, however, still a highly regulated market economy, so it still behaves differently on a macro level than a capitalist market economy in some respects. It also appears that, as it has moved from central planning to the market, it has lost some of the problems of central planning (for example, there are no shortages in the stores); but it has gained some of the problems of a market economy (for example, inflation and falling real wages in some periods). It is much too early to reach a final sort of judgment on the Hungarian experiment.

Arguments For and Against Workers' Councils

Hungary has decentralized its economy and has made considerable use of the market. There is a vision and long tradition among some socialists, however, that goes far beyond decentralization and managers maximizing in the market. The essence of this socialist dream is a set of producers' cooperatives in which the workers manage themselves. This issue of workers' control of the local firm is analytically quite different from the issue of letting the local firm make its own decentralized decisions rather than follow central orders. A firm may make its own decisions (based on the market), but that does not answer the question of whether it is controlled by the workers or by the center.

In Hungary, the top 20 percent of firms by size mostly have state-appointed managers. The other 80 percent of Hungarian firms have 50 percent worker representation on a management unit that advertises for, hires, and fires managers.

In Yugoslavia, there is a system of self-management of all firms by elected workers' councils. The workers' councils are elected by all the workers of the enterprise. They hire a manager in conjunction with the local government. The workers' councils make basic decisions, with the help of the manager, as to prices, output, technology, and use of all income for investment or for wage distribution. The workers' councils are even represented in one chamber of the Yugoslav congress, called the Council of Producers.

A sophisticated theoretical explanation and defense of workers' councils has been written by a Yugoslav economist, Branco Horvat (1976). Horvat argues on economic and political grounds the need for decentralization in order to eliminate an inefficient and dictatorial centralized bureaucracy. He concludes that we must, therefore, substitute decisions by workers' councils for decisions by central planners.

The specific advantages of workers' councils claimed by Horvat and others are: First, by reducing the role of the central planning bureaucracy as well as the economic role of the Community party apparatus, there is a better foundation for socialist political democracy. Second, since the workers control their own economic activity, there is less alienation than under central control. Third, since workers divide the profits of the enterprise (after taxes and investment), they will have more incentive to work and will take more initiative in innovation. Fourth, because the enterprise competes in the market, it will be more efficient than under central planning.

The disadvantages of workers' councils have been brought out by many writers. In the first place, workers' councils may be inequitable, that is, they may distribute income to a group of workers, not on the basis of individual or group effort alone, but on the basis of an accidentally better endowment (in resources, facilities, and technology) of the enterprise.

Second, the workers' council system may develop antisocial interests in that the individual enterprise may charge monopoly prices and distribute the monopoly profits to its own workers at the expense of the rest of society. The problem of monopoly is especially difficult in Eastern Europe because there is a tendency to merge all firms in each industry for ease of central planning. For example, in Czechoslovakia in 1967 all manufacturing was concentrated in just seven hundred enterprises!

Third, democracy might be better achieved by political democracy at the national level, which could direct central planning toward social aims. The proponents of workers' councils do not seem to realize that any decision making at local levels, for example, decisions on income distribution, must reduce national decision-making powers. There is a built-in political and economic conflict in a system of self-managed firms between local collectives' interests and those of the national working class. They also overlook the possibility that purely economic efficiency might be as easily gained by decentralization without workers' councils—for example, by putting enterprise decisions in the hands of state-appointed managers, as in the large enterprises in Hungary.

Fourth, to attack "bureaucracy" meaningfully means not just reducing central planners, but attacking all those with privileged positions in statism. Yet the workers' council system allegedly would result in more differentiated income and in very high incomes for a few groups of skilled workers. This income inequality again means less political democracy. The Yugoslav income spread is now about five to one.

Fifth, use of the market and material incentives means not only more economic and political inequality, but also more bourgeois psychological behavior and more alienation from other people. This means moving ever farther away from the socialist and communist ideals of a cooperative society.

Workers' Councils Without the Market?

A theoretical confusion that seems to lurk in the approach of many contemporary radical writers is the notion that a society can eliminate the central planning bureaucracy but can also eliminate the decentralized market mechanism. The central bureaucracy is attacked for its disproportionate economic privileges and consequent disproportionate political power, while the market is attacked for creating inequality and alienation. Both criticisms have an element of truth. Well and good! But, pray tell, how do you eliminate both at the same time? The real, not imaginary, world shows in a modern industrial economy millions of difficult economic decisions interrelated in a complex web. Either competition in the market must make most of these decisions or a very large bureaucracy must make them.

If an economy was all run by workers' councils, with no use of the market, there would be chaos. How would anything be coordinated? For example, if a workers' council in the auto industry decided to build a million automobiles, where would it obtain the necessary 4 million rubber tires? Suppose the workers' council producing rubber tires decided to produce only 2.5 million tires; that would leave a gap of 1.5 million tires. But there is no market, so there is no automatic supply and demand mechanism to encourage the production of the other 1.5 million tires. If there is also no central planning, then there is no higher agency to determine that the 1.5 million tires must be produced.

If there are to be workers' councils with some power, that implies decentralization. But decentralization implies a market mechanism for coordination. Thus, when one dreams of an economy of producers' cooperatives, so that there is economic democracy within each firm, one must also assume a market economy. Yugoslavia went in this direction, with all of the problems that accompany a market economy.

Evolution of the Yugoslav System

The Yugoslav Communists, led by Tito, emerged victorious and very popular from World War II. They immediately introduced a planned, statist economy, very similar to the Soviet economic system. But Tito used his immense popularity to resist Soviet efforts to dominate the politics of Yugoslavia. As this resistance was intolerable to Stalin, Yugoslavia was excommunicated from the Soviet bloc in 1948.

As a result of this historical development, the Yugoslav government began experimenting with workers' control or self-management in 1950. It was in part an attempt to gain popularity for the government in the face of Soviet attack. Under the new system, workers elect a workers' council, which runs the enterprise.

The enterprises are still owned by the nation, but the council decides on what and how to produce, sets prices, and disposes of profits. The council may do almost anything except sell the whole enterprise. The enterprise works in a setting of market competition, rather than plans and orders from above. The remaining economic plans of the central government are considered as merely indicative guidelines, not orders. The government is supposed to use macroeconomic policy (like any capitalist government), but to leave microeconomic decisions to the firm.

In the 1950s, the government set very high tax levels, so it, rather than the firm, received most of the profits and made over 60 percent of new investment. But in 1965 Yugoslavia went even further; it lowered tax rates, so the firms kept most of the profits. By 1967, firms were making over 80 percent of new investments. Thus the main direction of the economy was left in the hands of the firms rather than the central government.

In the 1950s the central government also exercised considerable price controls in order to prevent inflation. In the 1965 reforms, most price-setting power was given to the firm, to be exercised in the competitive market. Thus most prices came to reflect supply and demand.

The evolution of the Yugoslav system is interesting with respect to the relation of the market and the workers' councils. While Yugoslavia was still a planned economy, the workers' councils were introduced to give the workers a greater say in the governance of the enterprise. But under central planning, there is very little for the enterprise to decide, so workers were not interested in investing their time with so little real power. The protests of workers then led to the firm being given more power. This greater power to the decentralized firm over decisions led to the greater and greater use of the market.

Advantages of Yugoslav Self-Management

Yugoslavia claims that it has the best of both worlds, both competition and socialism. Because it is decentralized and practices market competition, its economy should be much more efficient than the overcentralized Soviet economy—and the virtues of competition are praised in Yugoslavia along the lines argued by Adam Smith. It is certainly true that the Yugoslav economy has far less bureaucratic interference than the USSR. The Communist party of Yugoslavia still runs a one-party government, but it is a relatively weak central government. Regional and local governments may sometimes interfere in the economy, but they do no comprehensive planning. Thus, most of the economic problems caused by excessive central planning in the USSR are absent in Yugoslavia.

On the other hand, Yugoslavia claims that it has socialism with democratic workers' control at the firm level. Thus Yugoslav theorists claim that they have reached the socialist goal of economic power residing with the workers, while both private capitalists and government bureaucrats are eliminated from economic decision-making. There are periodic elections in every Yugoslav enterprise, in which the workers elect the ruling council, which appoints the management.

Any profits are divided as the workers' council decides. Thus the socialist goal of no private profit has been reached. The council may decide to reinvest the profits (beyond taxes) or may decide to distribute the profits as bonuses to the workers. Income distribution is, therefore, fair, and exploitation has been abolished in the official view.

Moreover, since the workers have full control of the profits, workers should be more highly motivated than in a capitalist-run firm or in a centrally planned firm. Workers have the incentive, not only of their wages, but also of contributing to enterprise profits, which are also theirs. Thus, they claim that the incentive problems of centrally planned economies have been eliminated.

Problems of Yugoslav Self-Management

It has been argued by some critics that Yugoslavia has the worst of both worlds, the evils that accompany the market as well as the evils of statism. The first problem is that workers' participation in the self-management process is limited. Some workers do not vote for their representatives, many are bored with meetings, and many do not see themselves really affecting the process. As a result, some elections may be dominated by the organized activities of the trade union or Communist party leaders (like organized groups in all countries). Also, due to levels of participation, blue collar workers are very much underrepresented on the workers' councils, while white collar and technocratic workers are overrepresented.

A second problem is that a high level of economic concentration drastically limits competition (though there is foreign competition). In 1977 the 130 largest firms in manufacturing and mining had 70 percent of all sales and 48 percent of all employment (see Zimbalist and Sherman, 1984: 429). Some economists from "socialist" Yugoslavia have even come to the United States to study U.S. antitrust laws, though the U.S. laws have been very ineffectual. Even neoclassical economists do not claim that the market can perform wonders if the industrial structure is mostly oligopolistic. Firms using monopoly power may put local workers' interests above the social interest.

A third problem is that the high economic growth rate of the 1950s and 1960s has declined, while unemployment has risen. Unemployment averaged around 12 percent from 1977 to 1980. Yugoslavia is integrated with Western Europe to a sufficient degree that it is affected by recessions in that area, especially because it cannot then export its surplus workers. Some of the many migrant Yugoslav workers have been forced back to Yugoslavia.

Fourth, inflation has increased to high levels in Yugoslavia. The annual rate of price inflation was only 1.5 percent (1956–1964), rose to 10 percent (1965–1975), then to 15 percent (1976–1980), and finally to 35 percent (1981–1983). Such rates of inflation are very disruptive to the economy as well as to the lives of ordinary people.

Fifth, Yugoslavia has had increasingly unequal income distribution. Its income distribution is more equal than U.S. distribution and about on a par with Sweden. Sweden has one of the most equal income distributions of any capitalist country, but it is still less equal than most of the centrally planned economies. The Yugoslav system of profit-making firms means that some firms in good locations or affluent regions may make a lot of profit, while those firms in poor locations or poor regions may make little profit. Again, this points to the clash of interests between one region or one firm versus the national interest. Moreover, the ratio between the highest and lowest paid workers in a firm is sometimes twenty to one. Thus, income distribution is not equal and may be getting less equal in "socialist" Yugoslavia.

Sixth, there are Yugoslav complaints that managers have too little power for efficient management. There have been allegations that Yugoslav managers are not professional enough because workers' councils refuse to hire university graduates, perhaps to hire their own friends or perhaps because university graduates "cost too much."

Finally, the system of competition for profit tends to produce very competitive and very materialistic attitudes among the people. Yugoslavia seems farther than ever from the socialist goal of a loving, cooperative people.

Decentralization and extensive use of the market in Hungary and Yugoslavia have clearly avoided or eliminated the problems of central planning. At the same time, market statism has restored some of the problems of market capitalism. For example, Yugoslavia suffers from oligopoly, inequality, alienation, unemployment, and inflation.

Suggested Readings

The works of Kornai (e.g., 1980b) and Horvat (e.g., 1976) give interesting views from inside Hungary and Yugoslavia. An interesting and very useful book on planning and the market is by Brus (1972). Ellen Comisso's work (1979) on workers' control is highly recommended. Deborah Malenkowitch (1983) has an excellent article on Yugoslav self-management. For more detail on Hungary and Yugoslavia and other bibliographic references, see Zimbalist and Sherman (1984: ch. 15 and 16). Two excellent articles on Hungary are by Paul Marer (1986) for the U.S. Joint Economic Committee and the inside view by two Hungarians, Galasi and Sziraczki (1985). Derek Jones (1985) has written a clear evaluation of producer cooperatives in Poland. Charles Sperry (1985) explores the virtues of the producer cooperatives at Mondragon, Spain. Christopher Gunn (1984) has a very useful book on worker-run firms in the United States. There is an entire issue of the journal of the Association for Comparative Economic Studies (1986) on market socialism and cooperatives, with several useful articles including an outstanding one by Branco Horvat.

— 16 —

PERFORMANCE OF STATISM: POLLUTION, DISCRIMINATION, ALIENATION, AND IMPERIALISM

This chapter analyzes the performance of statism in its most important noneconomic aspects, beginning with waste and pollution.

Waste in the Soviet Union

The Soviet Union does not have aggregate unemployment. There is, however, some amount of "frictional unemployment," which could be lessened by more rapid retraining of workers for new jobs. Furthermore, there are some workers who are formally employed but who are doing not much of anything because of bureaucratic inefficiency in assignments.

More important are the inefficiencies in planning caused by lack of sufficient information at the center and lack of sufficient trained manpower and machines to perform all the necessary calculations. First, the plan often commands enterprises to do more than is physically possible, leading to excess demand, inflation, and growth fluctuations. Second, there is often imbalance between various sectors and industries, so that an enterprise is held back from meeting its target because of a lack of key inputs. Third, some resources (labor, capital, and materials) are incorrectly allocated at the margin to enterprises and industries with a lower social priority than others that could use the same resources. Finally, one may add the inefficiencies of Soviet managers in carrying out the plan. All of these problems were discussed in chapter 14.

Insofar as exploitation exists in the Soviet Union, some of the luxury living of the elite may be condemned as waste, but this is minute compared to the similar waste in the United States. There is a certain amount of propaganda in favor of the present ruling leadership, but this is much less than the resources spent in political campaigns in the United States. Although there is now some informative economic advertising in the USSR, there is little or none of the wasteful competitive advertising so abundant under capitalism.

There is still some amount of racial and sexual discrimination in the USSR. The waste of human resources in the Soviet Union as a result of such discrimination is, however, perhaps less than in the United States. There is some pollution in the Soviet Union, but probably less than in the United States. Unfortunately, the Soviet Union does spend about as much on military production as does the United States.

Pollution in the Soviet Union

No experts, least of all Soviet writers, deny that there is some amount of pollution and lack of conservation in the Soviet Union. Although there are no aggregate data, some of the more important of a long list of officially admitted incidents are as follows:

1. Careless crop-dusting with pesticides, killing much bird life.

2. Dumping of sewage and industrial wastes into many rivers and lakes (with a great outcry over pollution of Lake Baikal), killing the fish and making the water unusable for drinking or recreation.

3. Cutting of forests to the point where there is not enough growth to hold back the soil when it rains, creating shifting sands in some areas and vastly increasing silt in rivers and lakes.

4. Lack of selective cutting that would preserve forests as a future resource; the lack of forest cover has also reduced animal life.

5. Lack of sufficient purification equipment in industrial plants.

6. Taking over agricultural land by industry.

On the other side, the Soviet Union has taken the lead in passing laws against pollution and in favor of conservation. As early as 1918 and 1919, laws were passed to protect forests and national monuments, to restrict hunting, to protect fish, and to stop industrial contamination of water resources. In the 1930s and 1940s, however, the emphasis on rapid industrialization meant neglect of conservation and increased pollution. The Russian Republic finally passed an excellent conservation law in 1960. The whole Soviet Union introduced a stiffer conservation and antipollution law in 1968 (*Current Digest of the Soviet*

Press, 1968). Moreover, in 1963 the State Sanitary Inspection Service was given the authority to veto all future blueprints for construction projects and design norms.

The laws are not bad, but the enforcement has been far from perfect. The reasons why the Soviet Union has so far had less pollution than the United States are not so much the law or enforcement, but technical and institutional factors. In the first place, the Soviet Union has a lower population density and a lower level of economic development, both making for lower levels of destruction and pollution. Second, the Soviet Union has far fewer gas-burning automobiles. Third, the Soviet Union does have comprehensive planning, both for new cities and for new factories. Finally, the Soviet Union has public ownership and no private profit motive in industrial production. Two excellent articles by McIntyre and Thornton (1974; 1978) substantiate the positive effects of planning and public ownership on pollution control.

Since no one makes private profit from production, why is there any resistance to conservation and control of pollution? There *is* resistance, both from managers and from some higher agencies. The manager's bonus (and promotion) depends on producing maximum output at minimum cost. Until the 1960s, penalties for polluting or unnecessarily destroying natural resources were negligible compared with the rewards for meeting production targets.

Unlike in the United States, higher economic agencies can directly order the manager to take conservation and antipollution steps. Unfortunately, they are also under enormous pressure to produce goods, and the pressure for conservation has been much less important until recently. "Any expense that detracts from the performance of the Soviet factory in the region similarly detracts from the economic performance of the overall region. Therefore, political and party officials frequently find themselves more in agreement with the polluters than with the conservationists" (Goldman, 1967: 9). Only agencies separate from the task of economic production, such as the State Sanitary Inspection Service, can give undivided loyalty to conservation in the Soviet Union.

Thus one Soviet problem has been to create a single strong conservation agency from the many different agencies that have been partly concerned with it in the past. Another problem has been to give the conservation agencies real teeth, that is, legal power to supervise all economic activity, and to intervene directly against destruction or pollution. Moreover, the conservation agencies need enough personnel to enforce the laws effectively.

Since the Soviet government owns and runs industry, their pollution problem is even more directly political than the U.S. problem. Whereas in the United States the obstacle to sanitation and conservation has been profit-hungry corporations, in the Soviet Union it has been a bureaucracy devoted to more and more production at a high human cost—a bureaucracy led by a self-perpetuating leadership without much democratic control. Nevertheless, the lack of private enterprise has led to more conservation and less pollution in most sectors.

The Soviet Union's worst performance has been in the area of nuclear pollution. The Soviet Union had the world's worst nuclear disaster at Chernobyl in 1986. The problems in the Soviet nuclear industry clearly reflect both overcentralized planning and lack of democracy. Thus, Medvedev writes: "The nuclear disaster at Chernobyl happened not so much because there was no second containment structure around the reactor, not because the reactor was poorly designed, but because there is no free and democratic discussion in the Soviet Union" (Medvedev, 1986: 16).

Medvedev points out that all of the decisions on construction and design were made centrally. Because of the lack of democracy, the three top planners in the field are now ages eighty-four, eighty-six, and eighty-eight. The Soviet scientists have not been allowed sufficient contact with their foreign colleagues. The central planners concentrated on nuclear production over nuclear safety to the extent that there was no special state committee on nuclear safety till 1986. Thus, the decision not to have a second line of containment resulted from central planning with limited debate. Although there were public objections, the center decided to put nuclear power stations near big cities, and further debate was cut off. Because of the strict censorship, there was a time-lag before a public alarm was given.

One may conclude that lack of a private profit motive helps prevent pollution in the Soviet Union. On the other hand, inefficient central planning under a bureaucratic, dictatorial state greatly increases pollution in the Soviet Union.

Population and Statism

Marx called the Malthusian theory of people breeding like rabbits a slander on the human race. Radicals emphasize that the evils of poverty—both in the advanced capitalist countries and in the colonial and semicolonial countries—are not primarily caused by too much population, but are social diseases caused by too much exploitation and profit making. In the history of capitalism the improvement of technology has greatly surpassed the rise of population, so further tremendous increases in the product per capita could be achieved if they were not held back by the institutional barriers imposed through the capitalist and imperialist systems. The Soviet economists have gone much further than Marx: they declare that more workers simply mean more output, and that "socialism" solves all economic problems, so no degree of population growth can ever be a problem in any statist country.

Even if one accepts the idea that Soviet statism can ensure a high rate of growth of output, this does not prove that the rate of growth per person could not be higher if there were less population growth. In other words, additional workers may add to the total product, but surely a point could be reached where the number of workers grows faster than the amount of capital. In that case, each additional worker has less capital with which to work, so he or she will add to the product less than the previous average. It may still be true that more population means greater absolute growth of product, which is good for military and prestige purposes. Nevertheless, more population also means a much slower growth of output per worker, so it constitutes a heavy drag on the improvement of individual welfare. China seems to have recognized this in practice with a significant birth control drive (through propaganda and availability of contraceptive devices), though with very hesitant theoretical recognition of the problem.

Racism and Statism

The Soviet Union inherited a nation filled with discrimination and bigotry of Russians against all the smaller non-Russian nationalities, the opposite anti-Russian sentiment by the other nationalities, plus intense hatred (and even physical pogroms or mass killings) by all against the Jews. To the credit of the Soviet government, it ended pogroms; prohibited all official discrimination; pursued a policy of equal opportunity in jobs, education, and all other needs; and conducted official propaganda against all chauvinism, especially condemning anti-Semitism. A traveler in the USSR says: "One of the difficulties encountered in earlier postwar years in convincing Soviet people (including nonreligious, younger Jews) that anti-Semitism exists in the USSR at all is that they know from their own experience how vastly it has declined'' (Mandel, 1967a: 188).

The Soviet government especially made an important effort to bring the most underdeveloped non-Russian (and mostly nonwhite) areas rapidly toward economic equality even at the sacrifice of some growth in more developed areas (mostly Russian). Many pro-Soviet writers have reported that ''the USSR continues today to put more money per capita each year into health, education, housing, and economic development in the former czarist colonies than into Russia proper, for the purpose of closing the tremendous gap that existed between them'' (ibid.: 189). This view has now been supported in a systematic non-Marxist study, which found that ''more resources have been devoted to industrialization in the seven (middle eastern) republics than would be warranted by any economic calculation, capitalist or socialist'' (Nove and Newth, 1967: 46).

Under Stalin, however, there did continue to be much real (though more hidden) anti-Semitism. For leading political jobs Stalin tended to favor Russians over Jews and other nationalities of the Soviet Union (though he did keep several Jews, Armenians, and Georgians in top offices, and he himself was a Georgian). In the great purges of the 1930s a disproportionate number of Jews were killed, but that is probably because they contributed a disproportionate number of the politically active individuals. At times, Stalin seemed to use anti-Semitism as a political weapon against his enemies. And at the very end of his life, it seems that the arrest of several Jewish doctors was to be the beginning of a whole new bloody purge. Furthermore, Stalin in 1948 ended the previously large-scale facilities for Jewish cultural life. The attack included the closing down of Yiddish theaters, imprisonment of writers, and suspension of publication of almost all periodicals and books in Yiddish.

In the Soviet Union today no schools or classes or even textbooks in the Yiddish language exist. From the amount of continued use of Yiddish by Soviet Jews, it is clear that this was not a voluntary suspension. The present Soviet government, however, has allowed resumption of publication of one Yiddish newspaper, one Yiddish bimonthly magazine, and has published some books in Yiddish.

On the other hand, the distance from the position of black people in the United States may be seen in the economic and educational status of Soviet Jews. In 1961 Jews were 1.1 percent of the population. They were, however, 8.5 percent of professional writers and journalists, 10 percent of college professors, 33 percent of personnel in the film industry, 10 percent of scientists, 10 percent of judges and lawyers, 16 percent of doctors, 7 percent of musicians, artists, and actors, and 3.3 percent of college undergraduates. On the other hand, in the political sphere only 0.5 percent of the members of the government at all levels are Jews (see Mandel, 1967b: 46–70). Furthermore, although the sociopolitical situation is now qualitatively improved for Soviet Jews (with the absence of terror), there is still a residue of popular anti-Semitic sentiment, and there are still very few Yiddish cultural facilities. There is no official propaganda against anti-Semitism. Similarly, in Eastern Europe, "given our countries and their history, it is straining credulity to imagine that anti-Semitism disappeared overnight: it is not discreditable that it exists; what is discreditable is that it is not being combatted" (Schaff, 1970: 224).

There is also a vast amount of very intensive "anti-Zionist" propaganda, which may easily be interpreted as anti-Jewish propaganda—and may be so interpreted by most Russians. In addition, some "antireligious" propaganda against Judaism is strongly anti-Semitic. Thus, the problem of anti-Semitism was not caused by one crazy dictator, and the tendencies are still present in the whole social organism (though there are countertendencies also present).

One cause of anti-Semitism is the leftovers of prejudice from tsarist Russia. More basic are the facts of continued bourgeois psychology as to which groups get what income and of continued differential political power used for individual advancement. The point is that under statism—especially in nondemocratic political conditions—anti-Semitism can still be a profitable tool to certain political leaders. Only with some democratic control over leaders and with less income inequality could the conditions for completely ending anti-Semitism and other racism finally be established.

Sexism Under Statism

Women in tsarist Russia were badly oppressed; had few if any rights, either political or economic; had to obey their husbands in all matters; could not get a divorce; and were considered inferior to men in most ways (although literature depicted some strong-minded heroines among the educated women). The revolution changed all this. Article 122 of the Soviet Constitution (1936) says that "women in the USSR are accorded equal rights with men in all spheres of economic, cultural, political, and other public activities."

Women fought in the revolution, and there was a considerable women's liberation movement. In November 1918, a Soviet women's conference was held in Moscow with 1,147 delegates, including many peasant women. In 1918, also, the Central Committee of the party established a women's section of the committee composed of women to push women's liberation. Most of the Soviet Union in the 1920s remained agricultural, and most peasants stuck to a traditional subservient role for women. As late as 1933 an American woman in the Soviet Union wrote: "On a motor trip I visited many cottages in outlying villages; the women stood while the men sat down and ate; kept their heads bent and their hands folded, not speaking until they were spoken to" (Winter, 1933: 101).

The Soviet government in the 1920s propagandized for equal rights, allowed freedom of divorce, legalized abortion, and pushed for women's liberation in many ways, even helping women to remove the veil in Central Asia. Marriages and divorces could be registered by a simple postcard, but many intellectuals did not register at all, feeling that registration of marriage was "too bourgeois."

With the five-year plans, Stalin wanted to aid industrialization with a more regimented society, including a stable family and more difficult divorce, and by higher population growth rates, through encouraging children, ignoring birth control, and making abortion illegal. Stalin abolished the women's section of the Central Committee in 1929. The government declared that "so-called free love is a bourgeois invention and has nothing in common with the principles of conduct of a Soviet citizen. Moreover, marriage receives its full value for the State only if there is progeny" (Commissariat of Justice, 1939). These authoritarian and puritanical trends were not reversed again until after Stalin's death.

The Soviet Union is now far more urban than rural, has a high degree of education, and has ceased the all-out industrialization drive. In 1975, over 83 percent of all women between sixteen and fifty-four years old were in the labor force (see McCauley, 1981: 34). Furthermore, women are 63 percent of all specialists with a secondary education, and they are 53 percent of all professionals with higher education. Therefore, the role of women has drastically changed in many ways. For example, the largest-circulation magazine in the Soviet Union today is *Rabotnitsa* (The Working Woman). Moreover, the Soviet Union does have a vast system of low-cost or free child-care facilities; legal dissemination of birth control information and devices; legal and universally available abortion; equal pay for equal work; acceptance of women in all professions; equality before the law; divorce at will; and an insignificant rate of prostitution.

On the other hand, in the professions in which women predominate, for example, medicine and teaching, the pay is much less than in those in which men predominate, for example, engineering. Thus, women are 75 percent of all physicians (who have low pay), but only 33 percent of all engineers (who have high pay). There is sex segregation in blue collar jobs. Moreover, it is still the case that men are expected to enter the higher paid professions, because the man is supposed to support the family. Men predominate overwhelmingly at the top level of all professions. Even in teaching, for example, women are 72 percent of teachers, but only 32 percent of principals. There are few women (8 in 1982) among the 319 members of the Central Committee and only one woman in the Soviet Council of Ministers, although women are 27 percent of the deputies in the not-too-important Soviet Congress (or Supreme Soviet).

Women are helped to keep their jobs by an adequate system of maternity leaves in all industry. Women are allowed eight weeks prenatal and eight weeks postnatal leave at full pay. They may also choose to take their annual paid vacation (two to three weeks) immediately after the postnatal leave, and an additional three months unpaid leave if desired.

Just before the revolution, women made up only 25 percent of all university enrollment. Since the revolution, the number of girls and boys in grades one through ten is equal except for the more backward republics, where girls leave school at an earlier age than boys. Through the tenth grade, the curriculum is uniform for both sexes. Beyond that grade the percentage of women tends to decline. Still, 53 percent of all medical students and even 25 percent of all agricultural students are women.

In 1933, women with a degree of *kandidat* (close to our Ph.D.) were very close to zero percent. In 1968, they received 31 percent of all *kandidat* degrees. In 1967, women were 20 percent of associate professors and 9 percent of the highest academic ranks (full professor or member of Academy of Sciences).

Marriage still presents many traditional male-female problems, including the attitude of men that the woman should do all the housework after she returns from the day's work (although educated men under age thirty-five do much more housework than the average). The basic problem of the Soviet woman, in spite of her equal opportunities for education and occupation, is that male supremacy still keeps her doing about three times as much housework as the man (even though her outside job is often equal in toil). The resistance of women is showing up partly in a skyrocketing divorce rate. Divorce is most frequent among the intelligentsia.

It is also true that Soviet women still have many fewer household appliances and poorer services for the household than American women. Some Soviet women have complained of sexual oppression from lack of sufficient services, such as child-care centers (better than in America, but still inadequate) and laundries (worse than in America). Some progress has been made in helping the housewife in recent years. The USSR made three hundred washing machines in 1950, but five million in 1969. Seating capacity of restaurants rose 80 percent from 1960 to 1969. The retail sales force per head of population has risen one-third since 1960.

The first Soviet thesis on sex attitudes in forty years appeared in 1968 (Golod, 1969). Among other things, this thesis notes that 47 percent of undergraduate, unmarried women had had intercourse, although only 38 percent approved of premarital sex. In a sample of white-collar people, 90 percent of men and 81 percent of women approved of premarital sex if the experience was with a loved one. Of the men, 60 percent thought premarital sex with an acquaintance (not loved) was permissible for themselves, but only 14 percent of the women thought so.

Concerning the double standard, 30 percent of the men thought that it was all right for a woman they love to have sexual relations with others; 48 percent of the women okayed it for a loved man. The survey showed that, although the double standard is dying out, men are still "more liberal toward their own sexual behavior than toward that of women, and women are more liberal toward male sexual behavior than toward their own" (Golod, 1969: 13).

Soviet sexual morality in the 1980s nevertheless demands of young people continence until marriage, associating sex only with children and a family. Extramarital affairs are frowned upon. The cult of virginity is once again glorified. And some women still choose to marry the man with the most material wealth.

Men and women have equal rights in marriage. Prior property remains owned by the individual. Property acquired after marriage is communally owned. Soviet sociological surveys find most spouses saying they married for love, few for material reasons, and less than 1 percent because children would otherwise be born out of wedlock (Mindlin, 1967). Of course, there is much less real equality in the rural areas, with women still being harassed for loss of virginity.

The history of divorce law shows some changing Soviet views. Immediately after the revolution and in the 1920s and 1930s divorce was free and automatic when requested. In 1944 Stalin made divorce complicated and expensive, although incompatibility was still the usual grounds. The family then became a sanctified institution, not to be easily dissolved. In 1955 and again in 1965 divorce was made a little simpler and a little less expensive.

Stalin's 1944 law also had ended the father's obligations to children born outside marriage. Before that time, the father's obligations to all children were the same. In 1968 a new law gave the single mother the right to receive a state allowance, and the right to place the child in an institution to be brought up at the state's expense if the identity of the father is not established (and the mother is once again entitled to child support if the father's identity is established).

Immediately after the revolution, birth control information was made free and available. This was done in spite of continued firm opposition to Malthusian overpopulation theories. Lenin wrote: "The freedom of medical information and the defense of the elementary democratic rights of men and women citizens is one thing. The social theory of neo-Malthusianism is something else" (1918: 5). The point is that the overpopulation theory is often a mask and rationale for poverty and exploitation in the capitalist countries and for imperialism in the underdeveloped countries. It is a problem, but of much lower priority than the abolition of capitalism and imperialism. Under socialism birth control aids the mother to plan her life as she pleases and helps keep down population growth. In most instances, the lower population growth means greater goods and services to the individual with less total pollution (and less total national product, but the smaller national product hurts only military potential and national prestige).

In 1936 Stalin radically changed the policy. Birth control by contraceptives was still legal, but discouraged (especially by very low production of contraceptives for at least two decades). Stalin also in 1936 banned all abortions not medically necessary. He began a policy of subsidies increasing with the number of children, designed to increase population so as to provide more labor for industrial expansion. Under Stalin, a doctor performing an abortion was imprisoned for two years and the woman was subject to public censure for the first offense and fined three hundred rubles for a second offense.

In 1955 Khrushchev repealed the ban on abortions. Abortions were made legal and free for working women, cost five rubles (about $4.50) for housewives and students, and two rubles (about $1.80) for farm women. The abortion rate has been quite high, especially because contraceptives, such as the diaphragm or the pill, have been almost impossible to get (remember that the top planners are mostly men). Apparently, a major increase in the production of contraceptives in the last few years has finally started, mostly because of alarm over the abortion rate. As a result of all birth control methods the number of children per woman in the USSR has been steadily dropping, so the present official Soviet line is worry over declining population.

Alienation

The problem of alienation under statism has many facets, and each has given rise to different, partially contradictory theories. The old dogmatic Marxist theory espoused by Stalinists said that all alienation is due to capitalist ownership of the means of production and exploitation of the workers. Since "socialism" is by definition an economy in which the workers (represented by the state) own the means of production and their product, alienation must disappear. This theory has been negated by long experience of alienation in countries that Stalinists have considered "socialist." An East European philosopher admits sadly that "the course of socialist revolution has shown that the various forms of alienation do not automatically disappear with the abolition of the institution of private ownership of the means of production" (Schaff, 1965: 196).

Private ownership of the means of production is a major cause of alienation under capitalism, but it is not the only cause. The fact that private ownership is a major cause of alienation is brought out in some evidence on the favorable effects of the British nationalization of a few industries. It has been found that the British nationalization of the coal mines—even though they are run by independent boards under ultimate parliamentary control without much workers' participation—has nevertheless reduced strife and alienation in the mines (see Jencks, 1969).

The dogmatic view taken by the defenders of capitalism admits that alienation exists under capitalism but argues that it must also exist in any industrialized society. Marxists—beginning with Marx—have always acknowledged that any industrialized society up to and including socialism will be plagued by certain problems of alienation inherent in the work process of industry. There is the fact that one must work for a living; being a necessity, it is difficult to make it a joy. There is the fact that much work is dirty or routine or dangerous. There is the fact that a hierarchy is needed from the worker to the foreman to the manager in order to supervise and ensure the orderly progression of the work process. There is the fact that above the enterprise in a planned economy it is necessary to have a large bureaucracy of planners and administrators to make and carry out the plans. There is the fact that with present technology almost all workers (except a minute number of artisans and creative workers) make only a small part of their product. Marx himself stressed this point of the division of labor and the specialization of workers to one very detailed process, with its crippling effect on human mental and physical processes. The problem exists as well under statism. "Unfortunately, the technical aspects of the problem cut across all systems—for example, work on an assembly line is inherently the same regardless of government" (Schaff, 1965: 135). Democratic socialism may, of course, consciously try to choose less alienating technologies, but that is not easy. The end of exploitation through private ownership of the means of production does drastically lessen one source of alienation. The point of serious Marxists is only that other causes still persist (an excellent study of alienation in Hungary is Haraszti, 1977).

It is also true that all the present statist economies illustrate the common causes of alienation. They all continue to use money, there is continued wage differentiation, continued unequal income distribution, continued consumer markets, continued private ownership of consumer goods, and continued labor markets in which labor power is bought and sold. All of these are necessary and understandable at the present level of technology, but they also assume and continually reinforce the old commercial psychology. The psychology of getting rich, the dog-eat-dog mentality, and so forth, cannot be eliminated so long as these institutions exist, although social propaganda can begin to reduce them (and many aspects of psychology have changed somewhat in the Soviet Union). If some day an economy is instituted with no wages or prices for consumer goods, then perhaps this psychology might begin to change radically.

In the existing statist societies there is also the additional problem that historical conditions of economic and political backwardness resulted in the dismal type of Stalinist dictatorship over the workers:

"Overcentralization, the over-expansion of the role of the State, not only had a harmful effect on the development of socialist democracy, but distorted and pushed toward alienation the productive activities of people too" (Almasi, 1965: 126). A democratic socialism may greatly reduce alienation, but that cannot yet be proven because the existing statist societies have mostly been run as dictatorships, with special privileges for a small elite.

There is finally the question of what kind of statism is to exist, how much plan and how much market, moral or material incentives, collective or individual incentives—and how each of these forms affects alienation. On the one side are those who argue that economic planning by society, with the elimination of as much as possible of the market, will reduce commercial psychology and allow people to cooperate in production for social use rather than for profit. They consider that this is central to the socialist vision and quote Marx and Engels on the change from the anarchy of the market to the freedom of a society that is consciously planned.

On the other side are many East European Marxists who agree on the need for broad social planning but argue that its vast overextension into everyday details for each plant has created a bureaucratic monster. "The ideology of market socialism sees the roots of alienation in bureaucratic manipulation of men both in economic and in political life" (Rychetnik, 1968: 216). The practical point here is the need for decentralization and use of the market to reduce bureaucracy; and perhaps for workers' participation in economic decision-making at the enterprise level (as is the case in Yugoslavia, and to some extent in Cuba, Hungary, and China).

As pointed out in the section on market statism, however, any increase in local decision-making does carry the danger that the local collective may enrich itself at the expense of the rest of society, as with monopoly profits from high prices. Moreover, any increase in local decision-making does lessen the area of democratic decision-making at the national level. To this extent, therefore, decentralization and worker participation may increase commercialization and alienation from that source.

Furthermore, the introduction of the market focuses the manager and the worker more on individual, material incentives—with bonuses reflecting enterprise profitability. Obviously, any Marxist must be in favor of increased moral and collective incentives as circumstances allow. It is not clear, however, that the old Soviet system of output targets, with managers and workers under immense pressure to meet the target by any means legal or illegal, was any less conducive to a psychology of individualism.

It is one thing to argue for an increased area of free goods and purely moral incentives to work. It is quite a different thing to argue for centralized planning of day-to-day decisions by bureaucrats as being better than decentralized decisions at the enterprise level with the aid of the market. As stated above, it is simply a chimera to think that an advanced economic system can operate with neither a market nor a central-planning bureaucracy. No third way of economic decision-making has been invented. One must choose some combination of these evils. This does not affect the earlier conclusion that it is still possible greatly to reduce alienation, given a democratic socialist society.

Statism and Imperialism

Socialists have always claimed that capitalism and the private profit motive are the main cause of imperialism. As to whether a statist country could be imperialist, there are only a few limited experiences and very little theory. Let us investigate a few cases.

The Soviet Union and East Europe

There can be no doubt that, in the years immediately following the Second World War, the Soviet Union removed a certain amount of resources from Eastern Europe without giving equal resources in payment at the same time. There was some direct plunder and military reparation, especially from East Germany and other formerly fascist countries. Joint companies were established with Soviet predominance in control and Soviet exploitation of profits from these countries. There were also extremely unequal trade agreements that amounted to further reparations. And interbloc agencies, such as the Council for Mutual Economic Aid, were used to control East European development along lines favorable to the Soviet Union rather than lines optimal for the countries involved.

On the other hand, the Soviet Union bore the main brunt of the fascist assault and did liberate most of Eastern Europe by itself. Its contribution to the defeat of fascism was made at enormous cost, twenty million dead, a third to a half of industry and housing destroyed. The Soviet Union thus viewed most of the resources taken from Eastern

Europe as very minor and totally inadequate repayment for the cost of liberation, especially since most of the resources were taken from the countries on the fascist side such as East Germany and Hungary. Moreover, the reparations levels were reduced or completely forgiven after a few years for some countries. The joint companies were all eventually abolished.

At present, the Soviets are taking no outright plunder from East Europe. At present, there are no more joint companies and no other form of Soviet investment in Eastern Europe. Allegations of economic imperialism are based mostly on the pattern of trade. The pattern of trade is alleged to have resembled neocolonialism in some areas. For example, it is argued that the Soviet Union sold Rumania finished industrial goods and bought from Rumania raw materials (mainly petroleum) and agricultural goods. On the other hand, it must be said that Soviet trade with the more industrialized areas, such as Czechoslovakia and East Germany, was quite different in pattern.

The Rumanians particularly objected to the fact that the Soviets tried to use Comecon (the Council for Mutual Economic Aid) to enforce the existing pattern over a long period. The Soviet idea sounded innocuous enough; it was that planning should be extended from countries to supranational planning via the Comecon agency. The Soviets then argued on the fine-sounding economic principle of comparative advantage, namely, that each country should concentrate on what it could produce best at the present time. In practice, however, this meant that Rumania and Bulgaria would concentrate on raw materials and agricultural goods forever. Thus, these countries opposed the idea and called for freedom of trade. Not unexpectedly, the Czechs and East Germans, who would concentrate on advanced industrial machinery, thought more highly of it. The Rumanian argument was based on the usual view of underdeveloped countries that all countries should develop fully in a well-rounded way, and that one cannot say just on the basis of present production what they should specialize in in the long run.

In addition to the pattern of trade that was enforced for a short while, the Soviets have clearly also practiced political domination in East Europe. They have encouraged their own puppets, overthrown governments by force, and maintained long-term occupying armies.

Soviet Costs, Benefits, and Motivations

The Soviet Union cannot be considered imperialist in the capitalist sense, since it has no private enterprises making profits from exploitation of other countries. The public firms engaged in foreign trade may still make some extra profits out of unequal treaties imposed on East European countries, but these are small amounts in terms of aggregate Soviet incentive to imperialism, and no Soviet individual makes private profit from foreign trade. On the contrary, like any occupying power, Soviet costs of keeping Eastern Europe in control to any extent are probably much higher than their current extra profits from unequal foreign trade. Since the benefits are not concentrated in a small group, as in the large capitalist firms, it is hard to attribute Soviet control of East Europe to economic imperialism.

The reasons for Soviet interference and efforts at control stem more from their political, bureaucratic, and military sectors. No Soviet citizen can criticize military spending or foreign policy decisions. The political monopoly, with a heavy component of high military officers involved in policy decisions, considers how to expand and consolidate its own position, domestically and abroad. "While the expansionist capitalist dynamic is absent in the Soviet Union, the bureaucratic-militaristic dynamic is very present indeed. . . . Thus, while the Soviet Union lacks an imperialist dynamic that springs from its economic organization, it does not lack an expansionist dynamic which reflects the needs of its establishment to consolidate its world position" (Papandreou, 1970: 49).

This political-bureaucratic-military dynamic could be seen in the Soviet invasion of Czechoslovakia in 1968. The bureaucracy chose not to understand how any socialist country could legitimately take a road different from the Soviet road. The military seemed to think of it in terms of their "need" for a protective wall of utterly subservient countries against the designs of German and American imperialism (but would Czechoslovakia be "needed" in a nuclear war?). The political leaders seemed most concerned lest the Czechoslovakian democratization process might spread to other countries and even to the Soviet Union.

The same political-bureaucratic-military dynamic took place in Afghanistan. Once the Soviet Union was drawn into the civil war on the side of the Communist government, withdrawal would mean that the USSR loses face and that their partisans in Afghanistan might be slaughtered. Note that the reasoning is very similar to U.S. political-military reasoning in Vietnam.

There have been clashes between China and Vietnam. There has been an occupation of Cambodia by Vietnam. Both result from the conflict between China and the USSR. This is the problem of conflicts arising between developed, affluent statist nations, such as the USSR, and poor, underdeveloped statist nations, such as China. There are naturally differences in the degree of militancy of psychological attitudes, in domestic development policies, and in willingness to take international risks. The underdeveloped China of the 1960s resembled in revolutionary fervor and militant dogmatism the early Soviet Union of 1917–1921 (but it would be unrealistic to expect China to stay so revolutionary when its economy matures and affluence spreads). Moreover, there is a real material question at issue. What amount of aid should the advanced socialist country give the poor socialist country? Contention over this issue was one of the bases of the split between the Soviet Union and China.

Of course, the Soviet political-military dynamic was also in evidence in the split, with a Soviet demand for political obedience. The Chinese, though, reflected the same kind of political-military outlook, demanding recognition of Mao as the direct heir of Lenin and Stalin and "return" of certain territories from the Soviet Union.

Finally, the conflicts among the statist countries have been intensified by survivals of virulent nationalist chauvinism. Marxism has always been optimistic on this score: "National differences and antagonisms between peoples are already tending to disappear more and more. . . . The rule of the proletariat will efface these differences even more" (Marx and Engels, 1948: 28). These brave words of 1848 have so far not come true. Instead, our century has seen nationalism and racism used as a tool by all the forces of reaction, such as German fascism or American imperialism. Moreover, sad to tell, Soviet leaders have appealed with very little disguise to Russian chauvinism against China, while the Maoists have used Chinese chauvinism against the Soviet Union.

Suggested Readings

On Soviet sexist discrimination, see the critical books by Lapidus (1978) and McCauley (1981). A good book on alienation in Hungary is by Haraszti (1977). An excellent article on the extent of pollution in the USSR is McIntyre and Thornton (1974); although much has changed since they wrote, one should begin with their article because they emphasize the real differences (as well as the similarities) in pollution under the two different systems.

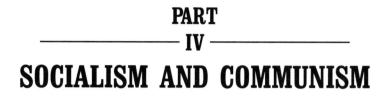

PART IV
SOCIALISM AND COMMUNISM

POLITICAL ECONOMY OF FEASIBLE SOCIALISM

Alec Nove (1983) has raised the question as to what kind of socialism is actually feasible at the present time. Although one can argue about his answers, his detailed list of particular questions is excellent. For the purposes of this book, the questions may be regrouped into three sets of issues. First, what kind of political and economic structures will produce the most democratic content? Second, what degree of planning or market should be used to ensure the best solution in terms of micro problems (such as efficiency) and macro problems (such as full employment and stable prices)? Third, what degree of government control versus workers' control of enterprises produces the best result in terms of democracy, efficiency, macro balance, and environmental protection? Given the choices under the first, second, and third questions, what should be the role of trade unions? The attempt here is to indicate the questions and the constraints as clearly as possible, not to give definitive answers.

Democracy Under Socialism

The socialist vision includes democracy in political processes and democracy in the economy. Let us first look at political processes.

Political Democracy

Even if all capitalists are extinct, there will still be many conflicts of interest and of judgment in a socialist society, which must be resolved democratically. For one thing, the different strata of the working class—farm workers, industrial workers, white collar workers, professionals, and managerial personnel—will all tend to have somewhat different interests and views. To represent their interests and articulate their views, political parties (more than one!) will be required. A lone individual cannot make himself or herself heard by all of society. Political parties are needed for an organized debate on social issues, as well as an organized choice of representatives.

Should representatives be chosen by geographical area or by enterprise or both? That question is quite secondary (in contrast to the question of having some kind of representation) and can only be answered on the basis of each country's past history and traditions.

If they are working in government enterprises, should workers all have some kind of civil service status to protect their rights? Certainly, most should be covered, but (a) merit must still be the basis for promotion and demotion and must be considered as a trade-off to protection (again, different in every country); and (b) those in top executive positions should probably be subject to hiring and firing at will by the government, so as to set policy in a unified way. How many people are "top executives" will have to be determined.

Should the media be run as government enterprises or as nonprofit cooperatives? This is wrongly posed as an either-or question. There is no reason that both types could not exist. Government-owned media require an elaborate set of procedures to guarantee opposition rights to media time. But an even better guarantee is to allow any group of persons to set up their own media cooperative to put out news and opinions as they see fit. All media should be nonprofit to prevent commercial considerations from governing their behavior; people in the media would still be receiving wages and salaries for their work.

Economic Democracy

Different visions of socialism encompass two different mechanisms of economic democracy. One mechanism is the control of enterprises by the government, where the government is democratically elected. A second mechanism is the control of enterprises by the workers (all employees) in each enterprise through duly elected representatives. The two may also be combined in various proportions, with different degrees of control in various enterprises by the government and the workers. This, again, must differ by the history and traditions of each country and by circumstances, particularly the level of development.

Arguments for Workers' Control. Given our history and traditions, most U.S. enterprises would probably be under employee control in a U.S. form of "socialism." (What is being discussed here is how to define "socialism," and it might be best for U.S. conditions just to call it "economic democracy.") There is at present considerable receptivity to employee control in U.S. politics—though many instances of "employee control" seem to be euphemisms for management control when the details are examined. When this book speaks of employee control, what is meant is one vote for each employee in the election of the board of directors. The board would then hire and fire the manager, would decide wages and salaries, and would use and distribute profits as it wishes.

This arrangement would extend economic democracy to the enterprise. Employee control could also be extended to nonprofit organizations, such as hospitals and universities, though the details would be somewhat different. The main argument is that the benefits of democracy should extend to the workplace.

If all firms were employee-controlled, this would eventually destroy all large private fortunes. Thus, it would automatically mean an end to all exploitation of workers and a far more equal distribution of income than at present. The lack of large private fortunes and the more equal distribution of income would give a much firmer foundation to political democracy, which would no longer be controlled by private wealth.

If an enterprise is controlled by its employees, this means that they receive all net profits (beyond taxes and reinvestment) in the form of bonuses. If employees know that they will receive the profits of the enterprise, then this should greatly improve their incentive to produce and innovate. Unlike capitalism, profits would not go to private owners. Unlike central planning, profits would not go to government. Thus, the incentive problem is solved.

Similarly, in terms of efficiency, employees (workers and managers) on the spot would make better informed decisions than absentee owners or distant government planners. Thus, efficiency would also be improved.

Arguments for Public Control and against Employee Control. Public control means control by the democratically elected representatives of all the people. It has been argued that democracy should mean control by all of the people in an area, rather than any particular group, even the workers in an enterprise. Obviously, both types of control—by all of the people and by all the workers in an enterprise—are aspects of democracy.

The issue is not which is more democratic; the issue is that the interests of a particular group of workers may diverge from the public interest. For example, workers in an employee-run firm may wish to push prices upward if the firm has a monopoly, an action that helps them but has a negative effect on the rest of society. An employee-run firm may wish to produce as much as possible, without worrying about environmental pollution or being willing to spend the necessary amounts on antipollution devices.

The other set of problems would arise if the employee-run firms (often called a self-managed firm) operated in a market system. In that case, the system would be subject to all of the evils that arise from any market system. It is shown below that employee-run firms must operate in a market system.

Markets, Planning, and a Third Alternative

In chapter 14, the many problems and weaknesses of central planning were exposed. In all of part II and in chapter 15, the many problems and weaknesses of the market—both under capitalism and under statism— were exposed. After looking at these problems, some radicals have concluded that neither central planning nor the market is a good system. Their solution, in a variety of forms with different details, is to have all firms controlled exclusively by the employees and to have each firm do its own planning in voluntary cooperation with all other firms.

Such a notion, however, is utopian and impossible (as demonstrated very clearly by Alec Nove, 1983, and many other writers). One cannot get rid of both central planning and the market because there will then be no coordination between units and the economy will collapse. To understand this argument, imagine that the United States has just two hundred thousand enterprises, all run by employees.

Two cases are possible. First, each firm decides to do its own plan without consulting other firms. In that case, if an automobile-producing firm decides to produce one million automobiles, it requires a certain amount of steel and it requires four million rubber tires. But there is no guarantee at all that the requisite amount of steel and the required four million tires will be produced and delivered to it. In this case, the initial result is chaos. After that, the likely result is that firms will have to resort to barter to get needed supplies—as well as consumer goods for their workers. Since the barter will be very complex and awkward, eventually a market system will develop with all of its advantages and disadvantages.

In the second case, suppose that all two hundred thousand employee-operated firms do wish to cooperate with each other. Each region would have to elect representatives and the representatives would have to meet. They would eventually have to make detailed decisions about who is to produce what. No matter what terminology is used to describe the process, this is central planning. It is a very democratic form of central planning, but the result would still be central planning.

Thus, the necessary result of hundreds of thousands of enterprises producing things is that their decisions must be coordinated either by a market or by a central plan—or else there is chaos. There is no third alternative. Of course, some combination is possible, as outlined below.

Debate on Market vs. Plan Between Nove and Mandel

Some of the issues have been highlighted in a debate between two excellent writers, Alec Nove (1983; 1986) and Ernest Mandel (1986). Nove argues that the distortions and inefficiencies of the Soviet economy are caused by central planning, not by the control of a bureaucracy and privileged strata. Nove contends that any modern industrial economy has millions of products and billions of interdependencies, so central planning cannot be efficient. Therefore, he concludes in favor of market socialism.

Mandel argues that the capitalist countries illustrate the evils of the market with large firms (with planning inside the firm only). The capitalist market economies not only exploit workers but have vast number of unemployed workers and unused factories in every recession. The Soviet economy has bureaucratic planning, that is, dictatorship plus government ownership plus central planning. Mandel favors democratic planning, that is, public ownership and central planning plus a democratic political system. He claims that democratic planning would work much better than bureaucratic planning.

Since there is no system with democratic central planning, Nove cannot prove his statement that the problem is central planning rather than dictatorship. On the other hand, since it does not exist, Mandel cannot prove that democratic planning will be efficient. The theoretical arguments indicate that both overly centralized planning and dictatorship help cause Soviet economic problems, but the two effects are not easily separable.

Nove further argues that democratic planning is impossible in some senses because 200 million people cannot meet and decide anything. Of course, democratically elected representatives can decide broad priorities, but even elected representatives cannot decide the best technology to produce diapers or steel. Mandel, however, contends that if democratically elected representatives set broad priorities, then planners could do a better job than capitalist firms (for example, in preventing unemployment and pollution, or constructing an electric grid for the whole western United States).

Nove argues that central planners cannot instruct firms in enough detail. For example, if glass is planned in tons, then it will be too thick and heavy. If glass is planned and ordered in square meters by central planners, then firms will tend to make it too thin. Mandel says there may be problems, but they will be a lot less than those of capitalist monopoly firms. Mandel stresses central control of macro decisions and a few vital micro decisions.

A Combination of Central Planning and Markets

In all of the part on capitalism (part II) and in chapter 15 (on market-oriented statism), the problems of the market were explored. Some of the worst economic problems are unemployment, monopoly, and pollution. Note that other problems of capitalism, particularly exploitation of workers, would not be present in a market system of employee-run enterprises. A market system of employee-run enterprises, however, would be subject (as shown by Yugoslav experience) to cyclical unemployment and to periods of inflation. Yugoslav enterprises also show a tendency to attempt to charge monopoly prices. Furthermore, if it would cost money to prevent pollution, then Yugoslav firms tend to follow the U.S. example by creating pollution rather than spending the money to stop it.

When one enumerates the problems of a market system, central planning sounds attractive. Yet central planning does a poor job of making efficient micro decisions on technology and output for each of the hundreds of thousands of firms. This poor performance is caused by lack of information, bureaucratic inefficiency, the difficulty of calculating all of the millions of optimal outputs and prices, and the inherent difficulty of setting exactly the right incentives to get managers to make the proper operational decisions to follow the plan.

The problems in central planning of efficiency and incentives are best overcome by allowing each enterprise to be run by an employee-elected board with power to hire and fire managers, set prices, and decide outputs within a competitive market framework. How, then, may the problems of the market be overcome?

To avoid unemployment, a central plan—arrived at by democratic debate—should specify total new investment. How does the plan become operational? One way is to use monetary and fiscal policy to influence employee-run firms. A second way is for the government (local, state, or national) to invest directly in new firms. Only through planned control of investment can the human misery of unemployment be avoided. Sufficient taxes can be collected from firms to ensure that the government has funds for new investment without inflation.

No person should be involuntarily unemployed. If a person cannot find work with a worker-managed firm, then she or he must be able to demand work with the government. Local, state, and national governments would need some arrangement between themselves on providing jobs. If the planners control investment properly, however, there should be no one unemployed in the first place.

One alleged problem of full employment has been raised in Eastern Europe. If an economy is at full employment, it is alleged that workers are lazy and undisciplined because a worker who is fired can always get a new job. One answer is that most people do not want to go through the trauma of being fired and hunting for a new job even if it is relatively easy to find a new job. More important, if full employment means that workers are more relaxed at work, then this is a worthwhile result even if some loss of productivity is involved. Part of the goal of a good society is people being happy at their jobs.

The problem of monopoly can be met by direct government control of prices in all firms with significant monopoly power in the market; this means government regulation and/or control of prices in the top one thousand firms in the United States. To facilitate government regulation of prices and other government regulations (for example, safety regulations), there should be a government representative on the board of each large firm. Such a public representative would ensure open books and disclosure of all information to the public. When all firms are run by their employees and the government controls monopoly prices, there is no reason to break up a large firm unless it is inefficient.

Pollution could be controlled two ways. One way is the present type of regulations. Another way is to give the government representative on the large firms incentive to resist actions that might cause pollution. For example, the government representative's bonus could depend in some part on reductions of pollution.

In summary, the suggestion is for some combination of employee self-managed firms in a market system—along with government ownership of a few vital sectors (with employee participation), government planning and control of much new investment, government monetary and fiscal policy, government regulation of safety and pollution, government control of monopoly prices, and government representation on all boards of directors of firms (all with the assumption of political democracy). The exact balance between employee self-management in the market and government planning will be different in every country at every time. The tendency is to say that employee-run firms make micro decisions in the market while governments make macro decisions through planning. But exactly how these two different processes of decision making can or should fit together will be the subject of much research and debate in every concrete case.

The Level of Government Planning

What level of government (local, regional, or national) should do the necessary planning and regulation? For both democracy and efficiency, the lowest possible level is the best choice. But what is possible depends on the type of industry.

Local municipal governments will normally plan, regulate, or own their own public utilities, such as gas and power and water. To the extent, however, that these are based on regional networks or resources, then the state or region may have to play the leading role. Health care and educational care may perhaps be located at state or regional levels, but with national regulations and support to ensure quality.

At the national level, there must surely be planning and control of railroads to operate as a national unit. Telephone and telegraph may also be most sensibly planned at the national level, with some international controls.

In most of the above cases we are talking about natural monopolies that may not and should not be left to the market, so they must be subject to planning. How employee representation on their boards of directors can or should mesh with government planning requires much thought. Note that some institutions leave some functions to the government unit, while other functions are left to the employees. For example, the state of California sets the levels of faculty salaries in the University of California, but curriculum and programs are decided by the faculty. So the proper combination of employee control versus government control may be solved in one of two ways: (1) how many representatives each has on a single board of directors or (2) how much power each separate body (employee board or government unit) has over different functions.

International Controls

Some industries would seem to be best directed at the international level. For example, air travel is international. Nuclear power is too dangerous to leave to local or national control. Military supplies ought to be produced only internationally, so they are given only to peace-keeping and police forces. What is required is an international governmental unit in each case with international employee representation.

Only rudimentary international economic controls now exist in a few areas. Is it utopian to talk of international economic controls or planning? One could argue that it is more utopian to expect that the present situation of warring nations (several with power to destroy the whole world) could last forever.

It has been observed that "World government in some form is both possible and imperative if the human race is to be saved from suicide" (Schuman, 1967: 230). Since many nations have awesome weapons that could wipe out the whole human race, and since most governments show few signs of rational behavior, it seems obvious that humanity will eventually be destroyed unless there is an effective world government. That government should control all the means of force and violence in the world.

Not only is a world government a necessity for survival, but it has also become an economic necessity. The world clearly has an integrated economy today, with products coming from all over to all over. My shoes may be from Italy, my clothing from Hong Kong, my car from Japan; yet each of those areas needs certain things from the United States. Multinational firms do business in a score of countries at once.

Tourist travel is important all over the world. Yet there are all kinds of political barriers to international economic activity, tariffs and quotas, confusion and crisis caused by over a hundred different currencies, and no real international control of international economic crises. Moreover, as long as there are different governments, the economic drain from military spending is an unbelievably enormous sum.

But it will not be easy to have a democratic and socialist world government. The prerequisite is that all the major powers, beginning with the United States and the Soviet Union, must have democratic and socialist governments. That is the only peaceful road to a democratic and socialist world government; and it is impossible to form such a government by violence.

Are Trade Unions Necessary Under Socialism?

Are trade unions necessary under socialism? There is an old argument that under socialism the workers are the public and the public are the workers. So, if an enterprise is run by the public, the workers in it are working for themselves. Therefore, they do not need a union because their interests are identical with their employers, namely themselves. In truth, however, the workers in each enterprise do not have exactly the same interests as the general public. Workers in a public enterprise may be paid more, less, or the same as comparable workers. If their pay is less, or believed to be less, than comparable workers, then the workers in an enterprise may wish to protest. A collective representative, that is, a trade union, is then necessary to make the protest, to negotiate, or even to strike if the demands are not met. In addition to pay, there are many other issues, such as working conditions, that require a trade union for effective representation.

Similarly, suppose that all enterprises are run by employee cooperatives, with elected representatives to an employee board of directors. It may then be argued that no unions are necessary because the board represents all of the workers. That argument is also false. The board may heavily overrepresent managerial and clerical workers and underrepresent production line workers. Since they do not always have the same interests, the production line workers may need a union to protest the actions of the board. Furthermore, not all workers may choose to vote in board elections, and those elected to the board may sometimes distance themselves from the rest of the workers. There are thus many situations in which the majority of workers may feel that their interests are not correctly represented, so they need some other vehicle to protest these actions.

Even with a union, a minority of workers may feel that their interests are not well-represented, so there may be a wildcat strike without union authorization. Sometimes, if it is felt that the union's elections were fraudulent for one reason or another, even a majority of workers may consider a wildcat strike necessary. This has been the case in the United States in many instances. It has also sometimes been the case in Yugoslavia, in which all firms are producer cooperatives. Thus, not only are unions necessary, but it is impossible to prohibit any kind of strike without trampling on workers' rights and workers' most basic needs for expression.

Finally, there are not only collective grievances, but there are many types of individual grievances possible either in a public enterprise or in a producers' cooperative. An individual worker may be sexually harassed. An individual worker may have a bad relationship with a supervisor. An individual worker may be treated unfairly for many different reasons. It is therefore necessary to have a grievance procedure in every enterprise, and—because individual workers have little power— it is necessary for the worker to be represented by the trade union.

For all of these reasons, trade unions will continue to be necessary for the foreseeable future under any type of socialism. It may be noted that the Soviet Union and the eastern European countries do have trade unions. The problem in these statist countries is that the unions (a) are dominated by the Communist party and are part of the state apparatus and (b) are concerned with greater efficiency rather than protection of employee interests. What is needed are unions that are independent and primarily devoted to employee interests.

Suggested Readings

The book on feasible socialism by Nove (1983) is very thoughtful and is good for forcing socialists to think about difficult issues. Nove has been criticized by numerous authors, including Anderson (1983), Mandel (1986), and Chattopadhyay (1986). Brown (1985, ch. 17 and 18) also raises some good questions on the transition to socialism and a democratic society but does not give many helpful answers.

— 18 —
POLITICAL ECONOMY OF
FEASIBLE COMMUNISM

Marxism divides the postcapitalist era into two stages (Marx, 1930). The first stage is ''socialism,'' in which there is public ownership of the means of production, but wages are paid according to the amount produced by the worker. The second stage is ''communism,'' in which there is still public ownership, but workers receive goods according to ''need.''

There are, however, as many interpretations of the word ''need'' as there are of ''communism.'' One view of full communism is that of the utopian socialists. Bellamy (1887), in *Looking Backward*, thinks of full communism as meaning equal wages for everyone. The equality of wages is, in his view, the way to achieve the minimum needs of all individuals.

The most common Marxist view visualizes neither equal wages nor rationing, but rather a complete absence of money, prices, and wages. Under pure communism, ''free'' goods would be produced under public control and ownership, and consumed by everyone according to his or her desires. The communist goal would include elimination of poverty, but it also stresses the need for a noncommercialized cooperative society. It would eliminate the present money-grubbing, competitive psychology.

The need for free goods and services is very clear in U.S. society, particularly in the health sector. For example, a new drug (AZT) may help patients with the dread disease called AIDS. But the new drug is being sold with a 1,000 percent profit by a drug company because, it says, it may soon be replaced by a newer drug. Whatever the excuse, this means that many poor patients may not be able to afford it (see Jacobs, 1987: 1). This situation is barbaric; someday, people will be incredulous that a person could die solely for lack of money.

The Problems and the Model

Assume an economy with public ownership, central planning, and central commands to producers, but no wages and no prices. Critics of this model of pure communism allege that three major problems are unsolvable (see Wiles, 1964). First, at zero price for all goods, demand would be infinite, since human desires are infinite. Therefore, no supply could ever be enough to meet the demand. Second, at zero wages and with no penalty for indolence, labor, it is alleged, would lack sufficient incentive to work, since humans are by nature lazy. Third, without rational prices there can be no optimal planning. Hence, communism would be very inefficient.

Assuming contemporary attitudes to work, it may be admitted that the first two objections are accurate enough to make full communism impossible at present. The utopian answer has always been that these attitudes will change, that women and men will be willing to work for the social good alone, and that desires may be voluntarily limited to some "reasonable" finite amount. Obviously, if attitudes were to change in this way, the first two objections to full communism would vanish. But this is not a very interesting assumption because it is only a wish.

What is interesting is to know whether partial communism is compatible with present worker and consumer attitudes. By partial communism is meant an economic system where 80 to 90 percent of all goods and services are free. It is claimed below that this system is workable and that it would achieve almost all the political and social advantages usually alleged in favor of full communism.

The Problem of Abundance

Socialists have always assumed a great increase in production under socialism as a prerequisite to communism. They assume efficient planning, increased education and research, no unemployment, no wasteful advertising, no monopoly misallocation, no military spending, and so forth. These arguments need not be evaluated here because it is important to examine the objections to communism on their own grounds.

Certainly, fantastic productivity increases make the supply problem easier, but they would still not meet infinite demand. To be realistic, we should assume only the rate of growth of labor productivity currently found in the United States or the Soviet Union.

In addition to the material achievement of very high labor productivity, official Marxist theorists assume changes in subjective behavior with respect to both willingness to work with no personal economic goal and willingness to avoid pure wasteful or conspicuous consumption. Soviet and Chinese leaders sometimes talk as if these changes in human nature could be achieved by propaganda alone. That is not credible in terms of any social science, and certainly is not credible in Marxism, which always emphasizes the importance of the economic base. It is quite another thing to say that, after there is a very high level of abundance, a large sector of free goods, and the reduction of labor hours to four or five a day, it may be possible to change "human nature."

Assume extreme acquisitiveness on the commodity demand side and extreme indolence on the labor supply side. Are foreseeable advances in productivity sufficient to institute full communism? Suppose we begin with a pure socialist economic model according to which public ownership is the only mode of ownership, most goods are sold for money, and wages are highly differentiated. Some Soviet goods and services, such as health and education, are already free. The Soviet leaders claim that these free goods amount to more than 20 percent of the real Soviet wage, but the true percentage is quite debatable. It must be emphasized that the economics of communism is the economics of affluence. Thus, with its much larger material base, the United States could start with a much larger percentage of free goods (skipping socialism to that degree). Conversely, China cannot immediately have a large free-goods sector except by drastic rationing of those goods, with high prices and high taxes on the remaining goods.

The argument here is that, whatever the present sector of free goods and services in the statist countries, they could—if that were honestly desired by the political leadership—expand the free-goods sector more rapidly than is usually admitted by most economists. Suppose a socialist economy in which there is public ownership of all enterprises. Suppose that initially 10 percent of all consumer goods are distributed free of charge. Suppose that its output of consumer goods doubles every twenty years. Suppose, finally, that this country decides to pursue a strict policy of no money-wage increases, but uses the entire increase in productivity to increase the output so as to reduce the prices of selected consumer goods. Within a relatively short time, such an economy could have a very significant proportion of free consumption.

Suppose that in 1990 the aggregate consumption of goods and services in that economy is, say, 100 billion dollars, and that the money income is 90 billion dollars. Assume in that year 10 percent free consumption, or 10 billion dollars of free consumer goods (here "goods" means goods and services). If we assume that it is possible to double the output of consumer goods in twenty years, this means 200 billion dollars of consumer goods at constant prices in the year 2010. Assuming no wage increases (where this is the only source of income), there is still only 90 billion dollars' income in 2010. But this leaves 110 billion dollars of consumer goods unsold, all of which may be distributed free. Thus, with no inflation or higher taxation, the percentage of free consumer goods could rise to 55 percent in that year. On the same assumptions, the free-consumption sector would be 78 percent by the year 2030. Yet the economic assumptions here (a 10 percent initial free-goods sector, and twice as many consumer goods in twenty years) are reasonably conservative for many countries. Only the political assumptions (real willingness to hold down money incomes and increase free goods) are radical.

To accomplish this economic transition gradually means to lower the prices of basic necessities slowly, while noting the reaction (the "elasticity") of demand to price changes. It is even possible to specify which goods should first be made free without causing economic disruption. One of the criteria must be fairly inelastic demand, so that falling prices do not greatly increase demand. A related criterion is that the free products should not be substitutes for those still on sale, otherwise the increase in demand for the free goods might be much greater than predicted on the basis of their previous use.

Luckily, these two criteria only exclude luxury goods and admit on the whole all consumer necessities. Obviously, in the continuing expansion of the free public goods sector, each marginal choice is a vital and controversial social decision. It would be imperative to make it as democratically as possible.

Economics and Psychology

The communist dream and the arguments supporting the change from a socialist to a communist economy seem to be satisfied sufficiently by the provision of a free supply of basic consumer necessities (with prices remaining on luxuries). Free consumer necessities may be sufficient because the point of the change is to increase socialist consciousness and the feeling for social cooperation and to remove the ethos of competition. If all the basic necessities are free, and one need no longer work in order to earn a living, eventually there would probably be a large change in the basic attitudes toward work and consumption, regardless of whether wages were still paid and luxury goods still cost money. An economy of 80 percent free goods would also mean most other noneconomic advantages claimed for full communism (see below).

With the retention of prices for luxury goods, however, a communist economy may be established without asking workers and managers to act as if their psychological attitudes had progressed far beyond the actual "human nature" imposed by the current economic base. To hope that revolutionary propaganda and education alone can permanently (beyond a temporary enthusiasm following a successful revolution) provide a sufficient basis for a change in human nature is unscientific and utopian. In other words, neither workers nor managers will change their competitive, egotistic economic behavior until after the material and institutional conditions are changed. A socialist economy, in which payment for consumer necessities is required, reinforces and produces competitiveness in people every day—it is not a leftover from capitalism. As long as we have a money economy, and money is necessary to meet one's needs, most people will continue to fight and struggle for money. Only when all consumer necessities have been free for some time under communism would any social scientist, Marxist or otherwise, expect that acquisitive behavior might begin to diminish very considerably.

It would, of course, be a very crude and inaccurate economic determinism to claim that there can be no changes in the ideological outlook of most people until a whole, completely new structure of society is actually in existence. For example, in the Soviet and Chinese cases, ideology toward collective work and consumption has slowly changed. Certainly many people must have advanced toward a communist consciousness even under capitalism or there never would have been a socialist revolution. Moreover, the peoples of the statist countries do take for granted that a large proportion of the product will be in collective consumption rather than private goods. The only point is that Chinese managers, for example, are not saints. They are far from working purely for love of humanity; nor would that be expected in a situation where long, hard working hours are required and where many goods and services are still in very short supply.

Obviously, socioeconomic conditions and psychological outlooks intertwine, mutually affect each other, and generally move together. Communism requires as prerequisites changes in material conditions, changes in economic structures, and changes in consciousness. The only warning is that one must not expect miraculous changes in average consciousness overnight far in advance of structural changes and material conditions. Thus, it is not fair to expect Chinese managers to act on the whole differently than their incentive structure directs them. Nor can one expect that new communist-type attitudes will fall from the skies and allow us to establish a brand new society of voluntary cooperation with no struggles and no resistance to basic structural changes.

Balance of Supply and Demand

Peter Wiles maintains that it is impossible to have full communism if it means no rationing through prices and no physical rationing (1964: 348). He maintains that one or the other is necessary. His argument may be correct with regard to the immediate introduction of 100 percent free goods. Yet, the point really is that, while keeping supply and demand in equilibrium, one could gradually eliminate prices and rationing for, say, 80 percent of goods in the foreseeable future. Demand would be limited by keeping aggregate wages constant, while labor would be allocated by the same differential wages as before.

The official Marxists like to discuss the psychological conditioning that inclines people to make fewer, more "reasonable demands." It was pointed out above, however, that basic consumer attitudes cannot be expected to change as a result of propaganda. Yet attitudes may change eventually as a result of changed conditions. If 80 percent of consumer goods are free, there may be some decrease in the desire to keep up with the Joneses and, generally, less conspicuous consumption. After all, conspicuous consumption is designed to impress others, and one cannot do that by consuming free goods. Furthermore, purely wasteful use by delinquents should also disappear as a new generation takes such free goods for granted—especially if one begins with basic necessities. Even the anticommunist Wiles admits that, given present attitudes toward work and consumption, the "rational" consumer of Western economics (1) has physical limits on the food, clothing, and shelter he or she can use, and (2) wants some leisure from consuming.

Even at zero price in money terms, an individual's demand must be limited for particular goods because time as well as money must be spent on the purchase and consumption of goods and services. For example, health services and education both require much time to consume. Even food requires time to find in stores, to prepare, and to eat. This is one reason why even the very rich buy limited amounts of many desirable things.

It may be suggested that very low prices should be kept on basic necessities to prevent mischievous waste by children or teenagers. Low prices, however, may mean more administrative cost than revenue. For example, in the case of buses, removing fares altogether would lessen the work of bus drivers. Yet how many people will ride in buses just for fun if the reduction of prices is gradual? After a product is free for some years, it is more likely to be taken for granted. In any case this is not a crucial point.

Finally, if 80 percent of consumer goods are free, the other 20 percent might be distributed mainly by monetary means. In some small sectors we may even wish to use physical rationing or a combination of physical and monetary rationing. For example, even at a fairly high level of affluence, some expensive items like trips to other stars might be rationed.

The Saving Ratio

The upshot of the above discussion is that a wide area of purely communist distribution could be achieved in a practical way in the near future without an extraordinary rate of growth. In fact, there is no reason to expect a communist society to pursue growth in a feverish manner. For one thing, the rate of saving should be democratically decided in a communist society. The question must be decided by everyone, not by a few giant corporations or an elite bureaucracy, because dissatisfaction would easily reveal itself in the decision of individuals to do less work or no work, since basic sustenance is guaranteed.

Moreover, at a reasonably high level of affluence, further advances become less urgent. One winter coat may be vital, two, less so. At a high level of consumption and automation, there may only be temporary and specialized reasons for further growth. Furthermore, one can assume that cultural advance and family planning will tend to produce a stable population. Finally, as artistic sensitivity increases, and as the current commercialization of culture is finally reduced by institutional change, one may perhaps expect a stronger desire for leisure time than for growth of material goods.

Full Employment

If the economy were a fully communist one in which labor was completely voluntary and unpaid, then there would clearly be no problem of full employment. Suggestions can always be made as to useful projects, so that willing hands can always be employed. Moreover, if a worker sees no useful projects, then he or she can remain at leisure without any harm whatsoever, assuming that all goods are free.

Assume, however, that one is dealing with an economic model in which only 80 percent of all goods are free (mainly the basic necessities of life), but in which many luxury goods are not free. Furthermore, assume that there are still differentiated wages for workers. In this model of an impure communism, one may still conclude that there should be little problem of unemployment, provided there is central planning of all investment. With central planning of investment, the situation is really identical to that of centrally planned socialism. Namely, since the same agency is doing all investment and presumably all saving (or at least controls all savings), there can never be a problem of excess savings. Rather, as is shown empirically in the history of the Soviet Union, the problem tends to be the opposite, namely, overfull employment and shortage. The planners continuously conceive of many more possible projects than they have investment funds with which to complete them.

The Incentive Problem

The classic attack on pure communism is that, if all goods are free, there is insufficient incentive to work. Suppose, however, that there is a gradual change, with only a half percent of consumer goods per year passing from the monetary to the free goods sector. It seems unlikely that at some point the ordinary worker would suddenly stop working. It may still be argued that she or he will gradually reduce her or his effort. Even at an 80 percent free goods level, however, differentiated wages (which could be used to buy the remaining, priced luxury goods) would probably be a more than sufficient incentive for those who still need such incentives.

This assertion is not easy to prove because incredibly little research has been done on the relation of material incentives to willingness to work. What evidence there is indicates, though, that "within any one culture differential money rewards are of limited importance in transforming a less industrious workman into a more industrious one" (Dahl and Lindblom, 1953: 154). The evidence indicates, in particular, little relation of industrial innovation to monetary rewards, but rather to noneconomic factors like temperament and intelligence. Even a very cautious liberal treatise concludes "that incentive problems do not invalidate the case for adjustments in the direction of equal income shares" (ibid.: 161). Surely, one may extrapolate that incentive problems do not invalidate the case for a high percentage of free public goods.

The incentive problem is much easier to solve if there is a very high level of production per labor hour, so that each worker needs to work only a few hours a day. If automation continues at a rapid pace, and the first goal is only a gradual approach to 80 percent communism, then reduction of working hours can be sufficiently met within the foreseeable future. Hours of labor have declined astoundingly in the last hundred years.

The trend toward automation makes it likely that an ever larger part of the population will devote itself to advanced scientific and creative work. In that case, one can assume that there would be much greater willingness to work for the good of society. After all, once assured a basic minimum wage, most scientists today probably work more for the joy of what they are doing than for any amount of income. The same would certainly be true of artists, even today. Thus, although everyone may be guaranteed a minimum standard of living, most people would probably continue to do a large amount of productive labor. This would be especially true if there were a vast amount of leisure time. Even today, there is certainly some question about how much leisure time one really wants, what one can do with it, and how much time one can simply fritter away. It seems much more likely that one would want to begin to do something constructive even if there were no constraint to do so.

Certainly, then, given only 80 percent free consumer goods with differentiated wages and prices on luxury goods, rewards would be offered to workers, managers, or scientists who invented or applied new industrial processes. Furthermore, if the amount of leisure time is greatly increased, one would assume that this factor plus the increase in scientific education should assure a great deal more research than ever before. Moreover, the barriers to the use of innovations that have arisen from rigid central direction in the Soviet economy—that is, the unwillingness of managers to take risks that might result in a short-run decline of their bonuses—should be reduced when managers have much less to fear from demotion or bonus reduction.

There is, nevertheless, the problem of incentives for the reluctant worker. Suppose that there is some significant percentage of workers with such inclinations that they are simply unwilling to do any work whatsoever, when they are provided with all the basic necessities of life free of charge. Should there be a reward and punishment system for such workers? If someone simply says: "I will not go to work for the society," then certainly some social and economic pressure could be brought to bear. In the first place one would assume that in such a society there would be a great deal of social pressure by friends, neighbors, and relatives to do some amount of work. After all, we are only talking here about four or five hours a day!

It is easy to conceive of other punishments and rewards. In purely economic terms, the individual refusing to do any work will not receive wages. Therefore, he or she will not be able to buy any of the remaining 20 percent of consumer goods (mainly luxury goods). Presumably, that will be a goal for those workers who continue to have present-day attitudes toward work and consumption. More extreme economic or even criminal penalties—such as those that Soviet writers on communism sometimes imply—violate the basic humanist goals of a communist society. Nor are these penalties of great use to society. The fact is that those workers who would be so unwilling to give the minimum amount of labor (such as four hours a day) would probably be of such poor quality that society would miss very little by not having their work.

Optimal Planning Without Prices

Assume that a very wide range of consumer goods, say 80 percent, are free: they have no prices (or their price is zero). Assume also that there is public ownership, and that wages are still paid according to the amount of work done. The wages can only be used to buy the remaining 20 percent of consumer goods (mostly luxury goods). If 80 percent of consumer goods have no prices, can there be any optimal planning?

Suppose in the first case that there is central planning. For the remaining consumer goods with prices, the situation has not changed from that obtaining under planned socialism. For goods and services with no market the planners must simply gather information on the three things needed for the usual optimal programming: first, marginal preferences for the outputs; second, all the alternative technologies (as sets of input-output coefficients); and third, the available resources. With these data, optimal programming can find the output combinations and technologies producing the maximum output. (They can also then solve the dual programming problem to find shadow prices. The shadow prices are prices set in accordance with the planned optimal outputs; they are used in this model solely within the planning organs for accounting and planning purposes only.)

For priced consumer goods, mostly luxury goods, there is still a market with consumer choice. Since, however, the long-run supply is set by a government monopoly, the prices in the market only make short-run supply and demand equal. They are not long-run "rational" prices, that is, they do not directly tell us the degree of long-run scarcity of resources or the consumer preferences at equilibrium prices. The planners could get an indication of preferences if they know that the current prices are above or below long-run equilibrium prices. In any event, they could use resources where the rate of profit is highest. Such planning, however, is still very complex, and the current prices give only the smallest part of the data. Calculating the long-run equilibrium prices or costs is a very difficult problem in this case, for which a great mass of information is needed. Hence, under planned socialism (even with a consumer goods market), it may be easier to collect the direct information about demands, technologies, and resources, so that planners can calculate maximum outputs or minimum costs.

Market (Decentralized) Communism and
Optimal Choice

Is not "market communism" a contradiction in terms? Certainly, full communism implies no wages and no prices, no competitive markets for any type of commodity or for labor. Even 80 percent communism implies that there is a zero price and no market for 80 percent of all consumer goods. It must be emphasized, however, that "decentralized communism"—with the continued use of a market for luxury goods and all producer goods—is no contradiction.

How can a manager make decentralized optimal decisions if there is no market price on the output? Suppose that managers are given the rule to maximize profit and are told to set outputs and technologies on that basis. Suppose also that the manager receives a bonus according to the enterprise rate of profit and gives bonuses to the workers on that basis or other appropriate criteria. The wages and bonuses are used to buy luxury goods. If the luxury goods are 20 percent of all consumer goods, then the total wage bill must be fixed to equal the prices of just that 20 percent. Furthermore, producer goods continue to be sold for money. Thus, in the sectors of luxury goods and producer goods, prices can continue to be set by competition in the market—as under market socialism.

This still leaves difficult questions for the sector in which consumer goods are given away free. How do firms plan rationally in that sector? Where do firms get the money to pay for labor and for producer goods in that sector? The best institutional solution would be for the central government to pay the firm a price per unit. The central government can then give away the goods through local outlets. This system allows the consumer goods firm (producing "free" goods) to have the money to pay for the labor and the producer goods they need in the market.

Tentative Conclusions on a Communist Economy

The economic arguments against free goods were examined and found wanting. "It seems possible that those who would deny the eventual possibility of communist distribution tend to underestimate the growing technological potential for the creation of abundance; to overestimate the insatiability of innate consumer needs; and to underrate the possible changes in man's approach to work and life" (Turgeon, 1963: 164).

An economy of 70 or 80 percent free consumer goods seems possible, with little or no loss in performance. A gradual increase of the free goods and services sector, with careful attention to elasticities of demand, should make it possible to maintain equilibrium of supply and demand for all products, assuming present rates of productivity increase in the United States or the Soviet Union. Second, a gradual increase of free goods and services combined with continued wages to pay for the remaining priced (luxury) goods should present few new incentive problems. Third, with the use of accounting prices for free goods and services (derived from optimal programming processes), optimal planning can continue to function as well as under socialism. Moreover, the planning can be centralized or decentralized as preferred, assuming the accounting prices are paid to the enterprise managers by the government.

Political Aspects of Pure Communism

Marx and Engels expected that the advent of payment according to need (or free public goods and services) would mean the end of socioeconomic classes, and the classless society would witness a withering away of the state as the need for it disappears. By definition, what is meant by the withering away of the state is the disappearance of all the oppressive and violent sides of government, namely, the end of police, prisons, courts, and armies. Yet this does not mean that government in the more general sense disappears. There may no longer be administration by force over human beings, but there is certainly economic administration, the administration of things, the planning for all society for the allocation of resources, and even the allocation of labor (though the plans are presumably followed voluntarily). This is a very different question, and it must be expected that economic administration will increase during the period of communism, though it will henceforth work on noncoercive principles.

We can talk about a classless society only when we begin to reach a society of great abundance, a society in which at least the bulk of goods are freely given to the population according to their need. Only in this case, as we approach full communism, can we expect some change in the political and social aspects of society. In this situation it certainly is reasonable to expect that the need for courts, police, prisons, and armies will die away. Certainly, if one can take all the property that one wants at any given time, at least all the food, clothing, and shelter one wants, then the need, desire, and reason for a great deal of crime and aggression certainly vanishes. The basic thought behind the doctrine of the withering away of the political functions of the state is that the apparatus of force will become superfluous the moment there is no longer a privileged class which must defend its property and interests, if necessary by force, or by the constant threat of force.

Since, however, administration and social decision-making are very extensive, the need for political democracy is very great. Because there are few, if any, differences in wealth, the actual equality of power—and possibility of democracy—should be greatly increased over any previous society.

Ecology and Pollution

Some pollution is the unavoidable consequence of modern industry and can only be reduced by further technological advances. Much pollution, however, is avoidable and may be traced to private greed under capitalism. Under statism there has also been some avoidable pollution because (1) planners in underdeveloped economies have concentrated on output growth without regard to its social costs, and (2) managers are given incentives to produce, and there are only slight penalties for pollution. Under communism (even 80 percent communism) an affluent, socially planned society may have less compulsion for growth, more concern for human and social costs, such as prevention of ecological destruction. With the focus off rapid growth and with much less drive for their own private economic gain, managers under communism are more likely to take measures to preserve the ecology as well as to produce output.

Racism

Radicals oppose the Freudian view that humans are and always will be aggressive wolves toward their fellow humans. Neither do we believe that all human beings are born "good" and then corrupted by social institutions. Rather, human beings are not born with any social nature, either greedy or aggressive, loving or giving. Human psychology is shaped by the environment, specifically the social environment.

Racism, then, has resulted from certain factors in the social environment, particularly vested economic interests that profit from it under capitalism, and vested political interests that have found it a useful tool in statist countries. When these interests—and the domestic and international conflicts and frictions generated by them—have been eliminated under communism, it is possible that the remnants of racism will be slowly defeated (but even then it will take a continuous and conscious social effort).

Sexism

Sexism is like racism in that it is an ideology caused by a certain social environment, and it can be largely eliminated by drastic changes in that environment. Under capitalism discrimination against women is profit-able to monopoly capital. Under Soviet statism, for all its other weak-nesses, the absence of economic profitability from sexism (and the recognition of the social gain from full use of the economic potential of women) has meant an improvement in equality in both education and jobs. The sexist ideology, though, still seems dominant among most Soviet men. Soviet women have an equal burden of industrial work, but they also do almost all the housework in most families. Soviet women are still excluded from many top positions.

Communism (even 80 percent communism) should help break down remaining sexist attitudes. Social planning can emphasize a vast in-crease of household services by public enterprises. These would in-clude free or cheap (but high quality) child-care centers, restaurants, and highly automated cleaning services. All these services mean that the mother or father can be liberated from chores to the extent she or he wishes.

Communist free distribution of basic goods and services would also liberate women from going into marriages for material gain (and would end a reason for subservience within marriage). It would make divorce easier when desirable, since most contested divorces revolve around property rights. On the other hand, to the extent that some marriages run into trouble through economic squabbles or the economic pressures of insufficient income, communism might allow more stable relation-ships. Of course, diminution of the importance of private property would also make more feasible communal living arrangements for several adults and children, but that does get into a realm of utopian speculation.

Alienation

Communism means an end to exploitation and alienation of the work-er's product by economic or political means. But what about the alienation caused by the detailed, tedious demands of the work pro-cess? Marx and Engels expected that in the communist era there would be less distinction between intellectual and manual labor, that everyone would do some of each. A Soviet science fiction writer predicts that, on the basis of automation and a high level of physical and mental training, it will be "possible for a person to change his profession frequently, learn another easily, and bring endless variety into his work so that it becomes more and more satisfying" (Yefremov, n.d.: 62). This prediction is greatly exaggerated, but it has some slight basis in modern technological trends, in the sense that automation means that industry needs more highly skilled and more intellectually trained workers in large numbers. As the trend continues, perhaps everyone will know how to do certain of the simple tasks necessary to control automated machinery (for three to four hours a day), but will also have time for creative effort beyond that.

World Government

A communist economy—even 80 percent, not to speak of full communism—presupposes a united, peaceful world as both cause and effect. On the one hand, how could a wide sector of free goods exist in one country and not in the others? The poor would want to migrate there; tourists would want to take the goods away—already people go to countries with free health services just to use them. Moreover, a high degree of communism could only be practical with no drain for military spending—not to speak of the conflict between training people to be decent human beings and training them to be killers. Furthermore, if the use of force and violence by the state is to wither away, that implies first and foremost an end to the military. Can anyone imagine a real reduction of racism, sexism, and alienation while international conflicts exist and are accompanied by virulent nationalism and "patriotism"?

On the other hand, perhaps the most important argument for communism is that it would end the main causes of war. Imperialism cannot exist in the face of the availability of free goods and services. To bring the underdeveloped countries up to the level needed for communism will require a wide flow of aid without strings from the advanced countries. At the same time in the advanced countries no small groups of people could make economic (or political) gain from the domination of other countries. Thus, such an economy makes possible a united world.

Humanity seems to be in an awful race that must be decided in a relatively short time. It is possible that increasing levels of environmental pollution and wasteful use of resources could kill most of us within less than a century. It is also possible that increasing production and spread of nuclear weapons could end in a holocaust, killing most or all of us within the next few years or decades. Yet it is barely possible that we will first reach a worldwide democratic, socialist, or communist human society, which could end the possibility of disaster and open the way to truly human development.

Suggested Readings

By far the best fictional account of the possibilities and problems of a pure communist society (from a feminist point of view) is *The Dispossessed*, by Ursula Le Guin (1974).

REFERENCES

Adams, Robert M. (1965) *The Evolution of Urban Society*. Chicago: Aldine.

Addis, Laird (1968) "The Individual and the Marxist Philosophy of History," in *Readings in the Philosophy of the Social Sciences*, ed. May Brodbeck. New York: Macmillan.

Agency for International Development (1967) *U.S. Economic Assistance Programs*. Washington, D.C.: GPO.

Aglietta, Michel (1979) *A Theory of Capitalist Regulation*. London: New Left Books.

Almasi, Miklos (1965) "Alienation and Socialism," in *Marxism and Alienation*, ed. Herbert Aptheker. New York: Humanities Press.

Althusser, Louis (1971) *Lenin and Philosophy and Other Essays*. New York: Monthly Review Press.

Amin, Samir (1985) "History and Unequal Development," *Science and Society* 46:201–208.

Amundsen, Kirsten (1971) *The Silenced Majority*. Englewood Cliffs, N.J.: Prentice Hall.

Anderson, Perry (1974) *Lineages of the Absolute State*. London: New Left Books.

————. (1983) *Passages from Antiquity to Feudalism*. London: New Left Books.

————. (1983b) *In the Tracks of Historical Materialism*. London: Verso.

Arestis, Philip, and Thanos Skouras (1985) *Post Keynesian Economic Theory*. Armonk, N.Y.: M. E. Sharpe.

Associated Press (1986) "A Little Less 'Super Rich,'" *Los Angeles Times* (August 22).

Association for Comparative Economic Studies (1986) "Colloquium on Participatory Economics and Politics," *Journal of Comparative Economics* 10 (March).

Attewell, Paul (1984) *Radical Political Economy Since the Sixties*. New Brunswick: Rutgers University Press.

Avineri, Shlomo (1968) *The Social and Political Thought of Karl Marx*. Cambridge: Cambridge University Press.

Bahro, Rudolf (1981) *The Alternative in Eastern Europe*. New York: Schocken.

Bandyopadhyay, Pradeep (1985) "Value and Post-Sraffa Marxian Analysis," *Science and Society* 48, 4 (Winter): 433–48.

Baran, Paul (1950) "Marxism and Psychoanalysis," *Monthly Review* (July): 82–86.

————. (1957) *Political Economy of Growth*. New York: Monthly Review Press.

Baran, Paul, and Paul Sweezy (1966a) *Monopoly Capital*. New York: Monthly Review Press.

————. (1966b) "Notes on the Theory of Imperialism," *Monthly Review* 17 (March).

Barera, Mario (1980) *Race and Class in the Southwest*. Notre Dame: Notre Dame University Press.

Baron, Harold (1985) "Racism Transformed: The Implications of the 1960s," *Review of Radical Political Economics* 17 (Fall): 10–33.

Barone, Charles (1985) *Marxist Thought on Imperialism*. Armonk, N.Y.: M. E. Sharpe.

Bauer, Raymond, Alex Inkeles, and Clyde Kluckholn (1956) *How the Soviet System Works*. New York: Random House.

Becker, Gary (1957) *The Economics of Discrimination*. Chicago: University of Chicago Press.

de Bell, Garrett (1970) "Introduction," *The Environmental Handbook*. New York: Ballantine.

Bellamy, Edward (1887) *Looking Backward*. New York: New American Library, 1960 edition.

Bergman, Barbara (1973) "Economics of Women's Liberation," *Challenge* (May-June).

Bergson, Abram (1984) "Income Inequality Under Soviet Socialism." *Journal of Economic Literature* 22 (September): 1052–99.

Bernstein, Edward (1899) *Evolutionary Socialism*. New York: Schocken Books, repub. 1961.

Bettleheim, Charles (1968) *India Independent*. New York: Monthly Review Press.

————. (1976a) *Economic Calculation and Forms of Property: An Essay on the Transition Between Capitalism and Socialism*. New York: Monthly Review Press.

————. (1976b) *Class Struggles in the USSR: First Period, 1917–1923*. New York: Monthly Review Press.

————. (1978) *Class Struggles in the USSR: Second Period, 1923–1930*. New York: Monthly Review Press.

————. (1985)"The Specificity of Soviet Capitalism," *Monthly Review* 37 (September): 43–55.

Bhaskar, Roy (1978) *A Realist Theory of Science*. Atlantic Highlands, N.J.: Humanities Press.

————. (1979) *The Possibility of Naturalism*. Brighton, Sussex: Harvester Press.

Black, Angus. *A Radical's Guide to Economic Reality*. New York: Holt, Rinehart, and Winston.

Blair, John (1972) *Economic Concentration*. New York: Harcourt, Brace, Jovanovich.

Blinder, Alan (1975) "Distribution Effects and the Aggregate Consumption Function," *Journal of Political Economy* 83 (June).

Bobbio, Norberto (1979) "Gramsci and the Conception of Civil Society," in *Gramsci and Marxist Theory*, ed. Chantal Mouffe. London: Routledge and Kegan Paul.

Boddy, Raford, and James Crotty (1975) "Class Conflict and Macro-Policy," *Review of Radical Political Economics* 5 (Spring).

Bordaz, Jacques (1959) "First Tools of Mankind," *Natural History Magazine* 68 (January-February): 1–15.

Bose, Aron (1984) "Modern Marxian Political Economy," in *What Is Political Economy? Eight Perspectives*, ed. David Whynes. New York: Blackwell.

Boston, Thomas D. (1985) "Racial Inequality and Class Stratification," *Review of*

Radical Political Economics 17 (Fall): 46–71.

Bowles, Samuel, and Herbert Gintis (1975) *Schooling in Capitalist America*. New York: Basic Books.

————. (1977) "The Marxian Theory of Value and Heterogeneous Labor," *Cambridge Journal of Economics* 2.

————. (1981) "Structure and Practice in the Labor Theory of Value," *Review of Radical Political Economics* 12, 4 (Winter): 1–27.

————. (1982) "The Crisis of Liberal Democratic Capitalism," *Politics and Society* 11:51–93.

————. (1986) *Democracy and Capitalism*. New York: Basic Books.

Bowring, Joseph (1986) *Competition in a Dual Economy*. Princeton: Princeton University Press.

————. (1982) "The Dual Economy: Core and Periphery in the Accumulation Process in the United States." Ph.D. dissertation, University of Massachusetts, Amherst.

Boyer, Richard O., and Herbert Morais (1970) *Labor's Untold Story*, 3d ed. New York: United Electrical Workers.

Braverman, Harry (1974) *Labor and Monopoly Capital: The Degradation of Work in the Twentieth Century*. Monthly Review Press.

Brodbeck, May, ed. (1968) *Readings in the Philosophy of the Social Sciences*. New York: Macmillan.

Brown, Michael Barratt (1985) *Models in Political Economy*. Boulder: Lynne Reiner Publishers.

Brus, Wlodzimierz (1972) *The Market in a Socialist Economy*. London: Routledge and Kegan Paul.

————. (1975) *Socialist Ownership and Political Systems*. London: Routledge and Kegan Paul.

Bukharin, Nikolai (1917) *Imperialism and World Economy*. New York: Monthly Review Press, repub. 1973.

Bulletin of Concerned Asian Scholars, ed. (1983) *China from Mao to Deng: The Politics and Economics of Socialist Development*. Armonk, N.Y.: M. E. Sharpe.

Burnham, Walter Dean (1982) *The Current Crisis in American Politics*. New York: Oxford University Press.

Burns, Arthur (1964) *Frontiers of Economic Knowledge*. Princeton: Princeton University Press.

Cahan, C. (1954) "Introduction to the First Crusade," *Past and Present* 6 (November): 6–30.

Cairncross, A. K. (1953) *Home and Foreign Investments, 1880–1913*. Cambridge: Cambridge University Press.

Carling, Alan (1986) "Rational Choice Marxism," *New Left Review* 160 (November-December): 24–62.

Carnoy, Martin (1984) *The State and Political Theory*. Princeton: Princeton University Press.

Carrillo, Santiago (1978) *Eurocommunism and the State*. Westport, Conn.: Lawrence Hill.

Caudwell, Christopher (1971) *Studies and Further Studies in a Dying Culture*. New York: Monthly Review Press.

Chattopadhyay, Paresh (1986) "Socialism: Utopian and Feasible," *Monthly Review* (March): 40–53.

Cheney, Edward (1927) *Law in History and Other Essays*. New York: Harper and Row.

Childe, V. Gordon. (1950) "The Urban Revolution," *Town Planning Review* 21:3–17.

————. (1951) *Social Evolution*. London: Watts.

Chisholm, Shirley (1970) "Racism and Anti-Feminism," *The Black Scholar* (January-February).

Cipolla, C. M. (1956) *Money, Prices, and Civilization in the Mediterranean World*. Princeton: Princeton University Press.

Clark, J. B. (1899) *The Distribution of Wealth*. Clifton, N.J.: Augustus Kelly, reprint, 1966.

Claudin, Fernando (1975) *The Communist Movement; From Comintern to Cominform*. 2 vols. New York: Monthly Review Press.

Cohen, G. A. (1978) *Karl Marx's Theory of History*. Princeton: Princeton University Press.

Cohen, Stephen F. (1985) *Rethinking the Soviet Experience*. New York: Oxford University Press.

Commissariat of Justice (1939) *Sotsialisticheskaya Zakonnost*, no. 2.

Committee on Banking and Currency, U.S. House of Representatives (1968) *Commercial Banks and Their Trust Activities*. Washington, D.C.: GPO.

Committee on Foreign Affairs, House of Representatives (1968) *Hearings on Foreign Assistance Act of 1968*. Washington, D.C.: GPO.

Committee on Foreign Relations, U.S. Senate (1966) *Some Important Issues in Foreign Aid*. Washington, D.C.: GPO.

Connor, Walter D. (1979) *Socialism, Politics, and Equality: Hierarchy and Change in Eastern Europe and the USSR*. New York: Columbia University Press.

Cornforth, Maurice (1969) *The Open Philosophy and the Open Society*. New York: International Publishers.

Cox, Oliver C. (1964) *Capitalism as a System*. New York: Monthly Review Press.

Crotty, James (1985) "The Centrality of Money, Credit and Financial Intermediation in Marx's Crisis Theory," in *Rethinking Marxism*, ed. Stephen Resnick and Richard Wolff. New York: Autonomedia.

Current Digest of the Soviet Press (1968) 20, 30 (August).

Cypher, James (1973) "Military Expenditures." Ph.D. dissertation, University of California, Riverside.

————. (1981) "The Basic Economics of 'Rearming America,'" *Monthly Review* (November): 11–17.

Dahl, R. A., and C. E. Lindblom (1953) *Politics, Economics, and Welfare*. New York: Harper and Row.

Dahl, Robert (1956) *A Preface to Democratic Theory*. Chicago: University of Chicago Press.

————. (1985) *A Preface to Economic Democracy*. Berkeley: University of California Press.

Dalton, George (1964) "Economic Theory and Primitive Society," in *Cultural and Social Anthropology*, ed. Peter Hammond, pp. 96–115. New York: Macmillan.

Deckard, Barbara Sinclair (1983) *The Women's Movement: Political, Socioeconomic, and Psychological Issues*. New York: Harper and Row.

Desai, Padma (1986) "Soviet Growth Retardation," *American Economic Review* 76 (May): 175–80.

Deutscher, Isaac (1950) *Soviet Trade Unions*. New York: Oxford University Press.

————. (1957) *Russia in Transition*. New York: Coward-McCann.

————. (1965) *Trotsky*. 3 vols. New York: Vintage.

————. (1966) *Stalin*. New York: Oxford University Press.

————. (1967) *The Unfinished Revolution*. New York: Oxford University Press.

Dewey, John (1939) *Logic, the Theory of Inquiry*. New York.

Diesing, Paul (1982) *Science and Ideology*. New York: Aldine.

Dobb, Maurice (1945) *Political Economy and Capitalism*. New York: International Publishers.

————. (1946) *Studies in the Development of Capitalism*. London: George Routledge, ch. 2.

————. (1955) *Economic Theory and Socialism*. New York: International Publishers.

————. (1966) *Soviet Economic Development Since 1917*. New York: International Publishers.

————. (1967) *Capitalism, Development, and Planning*. New York: International Publishers.

Dollars and Sense Staff (1987) "Scandal at the Fed: Doctoring the Numbers on Wealth Concentration," *Dollars and Sense* 125 (April): 10–11, 22.

Domhoff, G. W. (1979) *The Powers that Be*. New York: Random House.

————. (1978) *Who Really Rules?* Santa Monica: Goodyear Publications.

————. (1970) *The Higher Circles*. New York: Random House.

————. (1969) *C. Wright Mills and the Power Elite*, ed. Domhoff and Ballard. Englewood Cliffs, N.J.: Prentice-Hall.

————. (1967) *Who Rules America*. Englewood Cliffs, N.J.: Prentice-Hall.

Dos Santos, Theotinos (1970) "The Structure of Dependence," *American Economic Review* 60 (May).

Draper, Hal (1977) *Karl Marx's Theory of Revolution*. New York: Monthly Review Press.

Eatwell, John (1975) "Mr. Sraffa's Standard Commodity and the Rate of Exploitation," *Quarterly Journal of Economics* 89, 4 (November): 543–55.

Edel, Mathew (1973) *Economies and the Environment*. Englewood Cliffs, N.J.: Prentice Hall.

Edsall, Thomas (1986) "More than Ever, the Electorate Is Polarized on Economic Lines," *Washington Post National Weekly Edition* (January 6).

Edwards, Richard, Michael Reich, and David Gordon, eds. (1978) *Labor Market Segmentation*. Lexington, Mass.: Heath.

Ehbbar, Hans and Mark Glick (1987) "The Labor Theory of Value and Its Critics," *Science and Society* 50 (Winter): 464–78.

Ehrenreich, Barbara, and John Ehrenrich (1979) "The Professional-Managerial Class," in *Between Capital and Labor*, ed. Pat Walker. Boston: South End Press.

Eichner, Alfred (1973) "A Theory of the Determination of the Mark-up Under Oligopoly," *Economic Journal* 83 (December): 1184–99.

Elliott, John (1986a) "Modeling Technological and Institutional Change in Karl Marx's Theory of Capitalism." *Journal of Economic Issues* 20 (June): 403–12.

————. (1986b) "On the Possibility of Marx's Moral Critique of Capitalism," *Review of Social Economy* 44 (October): 130–45.

Ellman, Michael (1975) "Did the Agricultural Surplus Provide the Resources for the Increase in Investment in the First Five Year Plan?" *Economic Journal* (December): 859–64.

Elster, John (1985) *Making Sense of Marx*. New York: Cambridge University Press.

Emmanuel, Arghiri (1972) *Unequal Exchange*. New York: Monthly Review Press.

Engels, Frederick (1884) *The Origin of the Family, Private Property, and the State*. New York: International Publishers, reprint, 1942.

England, Richard W. (1986) "Ecology, Social Class, and Political Conflict," in *Economic Processes and Political Conflict*, ed. R. W. England. New York: Praeger.

Erlich, Anne and Paul (1970) *Population, Resources, and Environment*. San Francisco: W. H. Freeman.

Federal Reserve (1984) "Survey of Consumer Finances 1983," *Federal Reserve* (September and December).

Ferman, Louis, Joyce Kornbluh, and J. Miller, eds. (1968) *Negroes and Jobs*. Ann Arbor: University of Michigan Press.

Feuer, Lewis (1969) *The Conflict of Generations*. New York: Basic.

Fichtenbaum, Rudy (1985) "Consumption and the Distribution of Income," *Review of Social Economy* 43 (October): 234–44.

Fine, Ben, and Laurence Harris (1979) *Rereading Capital*. New York: Columbia University Press.

Fite, G. C., and J. E. Reese (1965) *An Economic History of the United States*, 2d ed. Boston: Houghton Mifflin.

Foley, Duncan (1985) "On Prices of Production in a General Model of Production," *Contributions to Political Economy* 4 (March): 25–36.

Foner, Philip (1947–1980) *History of the Labor Movement in the United States*. 5 vols. New York: International Publishers.

Forde, Daryll, and Mary Douglas (1967), in *Tribal and Peasant Economies*, ed. George Dalton. Garden City, N.Y.: Natural History Press.

Foster, John Bellamy (1986) *The Theory of Monopoly Capitalism*. New York: Monthly Review Press.

Foster, William Z. (1953) *History of the Three Internationals*. New York: International Publishers.

Foster-Carter, Aiden (1985) "Korea and Dependency Theory," *Monthly Review* 37 (October): 27–34.

Foucault, Michel (1972) *The Archaeology of Knowledge*. New York: Harper Colophon.

Frank, Andre Gunder (1967) *Capitalism and Underdevelopment in Latin America*. New York: Monthly Review Press.

Franklin, Ray, and Soloman Resnick (1973) *The Political Economy of Racism*. New York: Holt, Rinehart, and Winston.

Friedan, Betty (1963) *The Feminine Mystique*. New York: Dell.

Friedman, Milton (1962) *Capitalism and Freedom*. Chicago: University of Chicago Press.

————. (1968) "The Methodology of Positive Economics," in *Readings in the Philosophy of the Social Sciences*, ed. May Brodbeck. New York: Macmillan.

————. (1982) "Government Spending," speech on CBS-TV. January 8.

Friedman, Milton, and Rose Friedman (1979) *Free to Choose*. New York: Harcourt, Brace, Jovanovich.

Comisso, Ellen (1979) *Workers' Control Under Plan and Market*. New Haven: Yale University Press.

Galasi, Peter, and Gyorgy Sziraczki (1985) "State Regulation, Enterprise Behavior, and the Labor Market in Hungary," *Cambridge Journal of Economics* 9:203–19.

Galbraith, John Kenneth (1962) *Economic Development*. Boston: Houghton Mifflin.

————. (1967) *The New Industrial State*. Boston: Houghton Mifflin.

————. (1970) "Economics as a System of Belief," *American Economic Review* 60 (May): 469–78.

————. (1973) "Power and the Useful Economist," *American Economic Review* 63 (March).

Gervasi, Tom (1984) *America's War Machine*. New York: Grove Press.

————. (1986) *The Myth of Soviet Military Supremacy*. New York: Harper and Row.

Giddens, Anthony (1981) *A Contemporary Critique of Historical Materialism*. Berkeley: University of California Press.

Ginsburg, Helen (1983) *Full Employment and Public Policy: The United States and Sweden*. Lexington, Mass.: Lexington Books.

Gleicher, David (1986) "The Ontology of Labor Values," *Science and Society* 49 (Winter): 463–70.

————. (1983) "A Historical Approach to the Question of Abstract Labour," *Capital and Class* 21:97–122.

Glick, Mark (1985) "Monopoly or Competition in the U.S. Economy?" *Review of Radical Political Economics* 17:121–27.

Goldberg, Marilyn (1970) "The Economic Exploitation of Women," *Review of Radical Political Economics* (Spring).

Goldman, Marshall (1967) *Controlling Pollution*. Englewood Cliffs, N.J.: Prentice-Hall.

Goldmann, Joseph, and Karel Kouba (1969) *Economic Growth in Czechoslovakia*. Prague: Academia.

Goldstein, Jonathon (1985) "The Cyclical Profit Squeeze: A Marxian Microfoundation," *Review of Radical Political Economics* 17 (Spring/Summer): 103–28.

Gollobin, Ira (1986) *Dialectical Materialism*. New York: Petras Press.

Golod, S. I. (1969) "Sociological Problems of Sexual Morality," transl. in *Soviet Sociology* (Summer).

Gomulka, Stanislas (1986) "Soviet Growth Slowdown: Duality, Maturity, Innovation," *American Economic Review* 76 (May): 170–74.

Goodman, David (1984) "State Reforms in the People's Republic of China," in *The State in Socialist Society*, ed. Neil Harding. Albany: State University of New York.

Gosta Esping-Anderson, Roger Friedland, and Eric Olin Wright (1976) "Modes of Class Struggle and the Capitalist State." *Kapitalistate* 4–5 (Summer): 186–220.

Gottdeiner, Mark (1987) *Decline of Local Politics*. Newberry Park, Ca.: Sage.

Graff, J. de V. (1967) *Theoretical Welfare Economics*. London: Cambridge University Press.

Gramsci, Antonio (1971) *Selections from Prison Notebooks*. New York: International Publishers.

Granick, David (1983) "Central Physical Planning: Incentives and Job Rights," in *Comparative Economic Systems: An Assessment of Knowledge, Theory and Method*, ed. Andrew Zimbalist. Boston: Klower-Nijhoff.

Green, Mark (1972) *Who Runs Congress?* New York: Bantam.

Griffin, Keith (1972) *The Green Revolution: An Economic Analysis*. New York: UNRIFD.

Griffin, Keith, and John Gurley (1985) "Radical Analyses of Imperialism, the Third World, and the Transition to Socialism," *Journal of Economic Literature* 23 (September): 1089–1143.

Grosfeld, Irena (1986) "Endogenous Planners and the Investment Cycle in the Centrally Planned Economies," Comparative Economic Studies 28 (Spring): 42–53.

Gunn, Christopher (1984) *Workers' Self-Management in the United States*. Ithaca, New York: Cornell University Press.

Haberler, Gottfried (1960) *Prosperity and Depression*. Cambridge: Harvard University Press.

Habermas, Jurgen (1984) *The Theory of Communicative Action*. Vol. 1. Boston: Beacon Press.

Hahnel, Robin, and Howard Sherman (1982) "Income Distribution and the Business Cycle," *Journal of Economic Issues* 16 (March): 49–73.

Hamilton, David (1970) *Evolutionary Economics*. Albuquerque: University of New Mexico Press.

Haraszti, Miklos (1977) *A Worker in a Workers' State*. Harmondsworth: Penguin.

Harcourt, G. C. (1972) *Some Cambridge Controversies in the Theory of Capital*. Cambridge: Cambridge University Press.

Harding, Neil, ed. (1984) *The State in Socialist Society*. Albany: State University of New York.

Harrington, Michael (1966) "Reactionary Keynesianism," *Encounter* 26 (March).

Harris, Donald J. (1978) *Capital Accumulation and Income Distribution*. Stanford: Stanford University Press.

Harris, Marvin (1968) *The Rise of Anthropological Theory*. New York: Thomas Crowell.

———. (1985) *Cultural Materialism*. New York: Random House.

Hayek, F. A., ed. (1935) *Collectivist Economic Planning*. London: Routledge and Kegan Paul.

Hayter, Teresa (1971) *Aid as Imperialism*. Hardmondworth: Penguin.

Heilbroner, Robert (1963) *The Great Ascent*. New York: Harper and Row.

———. (1971) "The Multinational Corporation and the Nation-State," *New York Review of Books* (February 11).

———. (1985) *The Nature and Logic of Capitalism*. New York: W. W. Norton.

Hilferding, Rudolf (1910) *Finance Capital*. London: Routledge and Kegan Paul, repub. 1981.

Hilton, R. H. (1952) "Capitalism—What's in a Name?" *Past and Present* 1 (February): 32–44.

Hilton, R. H., ed. (1976) *The Transition from Feudalism to Capitalism*. London: New Left Books.

Hindus, Maurice (1961) *House Without a Roof*. Garden City, N.Y.: Doubleday.

Hirsch, Joaquin (1978) "The State Apparatus and Social Reproduction," in *State and Capital*, ed. Holbway and Sol Picciotte. London: Edward Arnold.

Hobsbawm, Eric (1964a) "Introduction," in Karl Marx, *Pre-Capitalist Economic Formations*. New York: International Publishers.

———. (1964b) *Social Evolution*. London: Watts.

Hobson, J. A. (1902) *Imperialism: A Study*. Ann Arbor: University of Michigan Press, repub. 1965.

Hodgson, Geoff (1986) "Behind Methodological Individualism," *Cambridge Journal of Economics* 10 (September): 211–24.

Horowitz, David (1971) *Radical Sociology*. San Francisco: Canfield.

Horvat, Branco (1961) *Towards a Theory of Planned Economy*. Belgrade: Yugoslav Institute of Economic Research, trans. 1964.

———. (1982) *The Political Economy of Socialism*. Armonk, N.Y.: M. E. Sharpe.

Hunt, E. K. (1979) *History of Economic Thought: A Critical Perspective*. Belmont, Calif.: Wadsworth.

———. (1983) "Joan Robinson and the Labor Theory of Value," *Cambridge Journal of Economics* 7 (September-December).

Hunt, E. K., and Jesse Schwartz, eds. (1972) *Critique of Economic Theory: Radical Essays*. London: Penguin.

Hunt, E. K., and Howard Sherman (1986) *Economics: An Introduction to Radical and Traditional Views*, 5th ed. New York: Harper and Row.

Hymer, Stephen (1970) "Comment on Imperialism," *American Economic Review* 60 (May).

Hyson, Charles, and Alan Strout (1968) "Impact of Foreign Aid on U.S. Exports," *Harvard Business Review* (January-February): 71.

Institute of Social Research (1985) "Economic Mobility," *ISR Newsletter* (Autumn).

Irish, Marian D., and James W. Prothro (1965) *The Politics of American Democracy*. Englewood Cliffs, N.J.: Prentice-Hall.

Jacobs, Paul (1987) "Medi-Cal to Make New AIDS Drug Available," *Los Angeles Times* (March 24).

Jalee, Pierre (1965) *The Pillage of the Third World*. New York: Monthly Review Press.

de Janvry, Alain (1981) *The Agrarian Question and Reformism in Latin America*. Baltimore: Johns Hopkins University Press.

Jencks, Clinton (1969) *Men Underground: Working Conditions of British Coal Miners since Nationalization*. San Diego: San Diego College Press.

Johnson, Josephine W. (1969) "Who Is Really Uprooting This Country?" *New York Times* (May 10).

Joint Economic Committee, U.S. Congress (1986) *The Concentration of Wealth in the United States*. Washington, D.C.: GPO.

Jones, Derek (1985) "The Economic Performance of Producer Cooperatives Within Command Economies: Evidence for the Case of Poland," *Cambridge Journal of Economics* 9:111-26.

Kanth, Rajani (1985) "The Decline of Ricardian Politics: Some Notes on Paradigm-Shift in Economics from the Classical to the Neo-classical Persuasion," *European Journal of Political Economy* 1-2:157-87.

Kantorovich, Vladimir (1986) "Soviet Growth Slowdown: Econometric vs. Direct Evidence," *American Economic Review* 76 (May): 181-85.

Kaplan, Abraham (1964) *The Conduct of Inquiry*. San Francisco: Chandler.

Keiusinen, Otto, ed. (1961) "Introduction" to Karl Marx, *Pre-Capitalist Economic Formations*. New York: International Publishers.

Kelly, Kevin D. (1985) "Capitalism, Socialism, Barbarism: Marxist Conceptions of the Soviet Union," *Review of Radical Political Economics* 17 (Winter): 51-71.

Keynes, John Maynard (1936) *The General Theory of Money, Interest and Employment*. New York: Harcourt-Brace.

Klein, Philip (1986) "Institutionalism and the New Classical Economics," *Journal of Economic Issues* 20 (June): 313-24.

Kolko, Gabriel (1962) *Wealth and Power in America*. New York: Praeger.

Koont, S., and A. Zimbalist (1983) "Incentives and Elicitation Schemes: A Critique and an Extension," in *Comparative Economic Systems: An Assessment of Knowledge, Theory and Method*, ed. Andrew Zimbalist. Boston: Klower-Nijhoff.

Kornai, Janos (1980) Economic of Shortage. 2 vols. Amsterdam: North-Holland.

———. (1980b) "The Dilemmas of a Socialist Economy; the Hungarian Experience," *Cambridge Journal of Economics* 4.

———. (1982) Growth, Shortage, and Efficiency. Berkeley: University of California Press.

Kotz, David (1978) *Bank Control of Large Corporations in the United States*. Berkeley: University of California Press.

Kosambi, D. D. (1965) *Ancient India*. London: Routledge and Kegan Paul.

Kosminsky, E. (1955) "Feudal Rent in England," *Past and Present* 7 (April): 12-36.

Krupp, Sherman (1965) "Equilibrium Theory in Economics," in *Functionalism in the Social Sciences*, ed. Don Martindale. Philadelphia: American Academy of Political and Social Science.

Kuhn, Thomas (1962) *The Structure of Scientific Revolutions*. Chicago: University of Chicago Press.

Laibman, David (1983) "The 'State Capitalist' and 'Bureaucratic-Exploitative' Interpretations of the Soviet Social Formation: A Critique," *The Communist*.

Lakatos, Imre, and Alan Musgrave, eds. (1970) *Criticism and Growth of Knowledge*. New York: Cambridge University Press.

Lange, Oscar (1935) "Marxian Economics and Modern Economic Theory," *Review of Economic Studies* 2 (June): 189–201.

————. (1938) *On the Economic Theory of Socialism*. Minneapolis: University of Minnesota Press.

Lange, Oscar, and F. M. Taylor (1964) *On the Economic Theory of Socialism*. New York: McGraw-Hill.

Lapidus, Gail W. (1978) *Women in Soviet Society*. Berkeley: University of California Press.

Latsis, Spiro J. (1976) *Method and Appraisal in Economics*. New York: Cambridge University Press.

Le Guin, Ursula (1974) *The Dispossessed*. New York: Avon.

League of Nations (1945) *Report of the Delegation on Economic Depression, Economic Stability in the Post-War World*.

Lebowitz, Michael (1985) "Kornai and Socialist Laws of Motion." *Studies in Political Economy* 18 (Autumn): 39–67.

Leftwich, Richard, and Ansel Sharp (1974) *Economics of Social Issues*. Homewood, Ill.: Irwin.

Lekachman, Robert (1973) "The Conservative Drift in Economics," *Transaction* (Fall).

Lenin, V. I. (1915) *Imperialism: The Highest Stage of Capitalism*. New York: International Publishers.

————. (1917) *State and Revolution*. New York: International Publishers, repub. 1932.

————. (1918) *The Woman Question*. New York: International Publishers.

Lichtenstein, Peter M. (1983) *An Introduction to Post-Keynesian and Marxian Theories of Value and Price*. Armonk, N.Y.: M. E. Sharpe.

Lichtman, Richard (1982) *The Production of Desire: The Integration of Psychoanalysis into Marxist Theory*. New York: Free Press.

Lindblom, Charles E. (1977) *Politics and Markets*. New York: Basic Books.

Lippit, Victor (1978) "The Development of Underdevelopment in China," *Modern China* 4 (July): 251–328.

————. (1985) "The Concept of the Surplus in Economic Development," *Review of Radical Political Economics* 17 (Spring-Summer): 1–20.

————. (1987) *The Economic Development of China*. Armonk, N.Y.: M. E. Sharpe.

Lipset, Seymour (1963) *Political Man*. Garden City, N.Y.: Doubleday.

Lopez, R. S. (1952) "The Trade of Medieval Europe in the South," *Cambridge Economic History* 2:159–63.

Los Angeles Times (1986) "Strikers 'Totally Take Over' Hormel Gates" (February 2), part 1.

Lustig, Jeffrey R. (1982) *Corporate Liberalism: The Origins of Modern American Political Theory, 1890–1920*. Berkeley: University of California Press.

Luxemburg, Rosa (1913) *The Accumulation of Capital*. London: Routledge and Kegan Paul, repub. 1951.

————. (1918) *The Russian Revolution*. Ann Arbor: University of Michigan Press, repub. 1961.

McAfee, Kathy and Myrna Wood (1972) "Bread and Roses," in *Female Liberation*, ed. Roberta Salper. New York: Knopf.

McAuley, Alastair (1977) "The Distribution of Earnings and Incomes in the Soviet Union," *Soviet Studies* 27 (April): 227–31.

————. (1981) *Women's Work and Wages in the Soviet Union*. London: Allen and Irwin.

MacEwan, Arthur (1970) "Comment of Imperialism," *American Economic Review* 60 (May).

————. (1984) "Interdependence and Instability: Do the Levels of Output in the Advanced Capitalist Countries Increasingly Move Up and Down Together?" *Review of Radical Political Ecnonomics* 16 (Summer-Fall): 57–80.

————. (1986) "International Debt and Banking," *Science and Society* 50 (Summer): 177–209.

McIntyre, Robert, and James Thornton (1974) "Environmental Divergence: Air Pollution in the USSR," *Journal of Environmental Economics and Management* 1 (August): 109–20.

————. (1978) "On the Environmental Efficiency of Economic Systems," *Soviet Studies* 30 (April): 173–92.

McNamara, R. S. (1970) "Introduction" to *Economic Development and Population Growth: A Conflict?*, ed. H. Gray and Shanti Tangri. Lexington, Mass.: D. C. Heath.

Magdoff, Harry (1978) *Imperialism: From the Colonial Age to the Present*. New York: Monthly Review Press.

————. (May 1970) "Militarism and Imperialism," *American Economic Review* 60 (May): 237–42.

————. (1969) *The Age of Imperialism*. New York: Monthly Review Press.

————. (1985) "Are There Economic Laws of Socialism?" *Monthly Review* 37 (July-August): 112–27.

————. (1986) "Third World Debt," *Monthly Review* 37 (February): 1–10.

Malenkowitch, Deborah (1983) "Self-Management and Thirty Years of Yugoslav Experience," *The Aces Bulletin* 25, 3 (Fall).

Mandel, Ernest (1971) *The Formation of the Economic Thought of Karl Marx*. New York: Monthly Review Press.

————. (1982) "The Class Nature of the Soviet Union," *Review of Radical Political Economy* 14 (Spring): 55–67.

————. (1986) "A Critique of Market Socialism," *New Left Review* 159 (September-October): 5–38.

Mandel, William (1967) "Decline of Anti-Semitism in the USSR," in *The U.S.S.R. after 50 Years*, ed. Samuel Hendel and Randolph Braham. New York: Knopf.

————. (1985) *Soviet but Not Russian*. Palo Alto: Ramparts Press.

Mandel, William, ed. (1967) *Russia Re-Examined*. New York: Hill and Wang.

Mann, Jim (1986) "Talk of Political Reform Begins to Flower in China," *Los Angeles Times* (June 23): 1.

Mao Tse-tung (1957) *On the Correct Handling of Contradictions Among the People*. New York: New Century Publishers.

Marcuse, Herbert (1961) *Soviet Marxism*. New York: Vintage.

————. (1964) *One Dimensional Man*. Boston: Beacon Press.

Marer, Paul (1986) "Economic Reform in Hungary: From Central Planning to Regulated Market," Joint Economic Committee, U.S. Congress. *East European Economics*. Washington, D.C.: GPO.

Marglin, Stephen A. (1984) *Growth, Distribution and Prices*. Cambridge: Harvard University Press.

Marr, William, and Baldew Raj (1983) *How Economists Explain*. New York: University Press of America.

Marshall, Alfred (1890) *Principles of Economics*. New York: Macmillan, repub. 1953.

Marx, Karl (1844) *The Economic and Political Manuscripts of 1844*. New York: International Publishers, trans. and repub. 1964.

————. (1867) *Capital*. Vol. 1. Chicago: Charles H. Kerr, repub. 1906.

————. (1904) *A Contribution to the Critique of Political Economy*. Chicago: Charles H. Kerr.

————. (1906) *Capital*. Vol. 2. Chicago: Charles H. Kerr.

————. (1907) *Capital*. Vol. 3. Chicago: Charles H. Kerr.

————. (1930) "Critique of the Gotha Programme," in *Selected Works of Marx and Engels*. Moscow: Foreign Languages Publishing House.

————. (1948) *The Civil War in France*. New York: International Publishers.

————. (1952) *Theories of Surplus Value*. New York: International Publishers.

————. (1968) *Theories of Surplus Value*. Moscow: Progress Publishers.

————. (1973) *Foundations of the Critique of Political Economy*, trans. Martin Nicolaus. New York: Vintage.

Marx, Karl, and Frederick Engels (1948, written 1848) *The Communist Manifesto*. New York: International Publishers.

Mead, Margaret (1971) *Sex and Temperament in Three Primitive Societies*. New York: Dell.

Means, Gardiner (1972) "The Administered-Price Thesis Reconfirmed," *American Economic Review* 67 (June): 292–306.

————. (1975) "Inflation and Unemployment," in *The Roots of Inflation*, ed. John Blair. New York: Burt Franklin.

Medeo, Alfredo (1972) "Profits and Surplus Value," in E. K. Hunt and Jesse Schwartz, *A Critique of Economic Theory*. Harmondsworth: Penguin Books.

Medvedev, Zhores (1986) "Chernobyl Won't Stop Soviet Economic Power," *In These Times* (May 28-June 10).

Meek, Ronald (1956) *Studies in the Labor Theory of Value*. New York: International Publishers.

Meek, Ronald L., ed. (1953) *Malthus: Selections from Marx and Engels*. New York: International Publishers.

Meiksins, Peter (1986) "Beyond the Boundary Questions," *New Left Review* 157 (May/June): 101–20.

Melman, Seymour (1970) *Pentagon Capitalism*. New York: McGraw-Hill.

Miliband, Ralph (1969) *The State in Capitalist Society*. New York: Basic Books.

————. (1973) "Poulantzas and the Capitalist State," *New Left Review* 82:83–92.

————. (1977) *Marxism and Politics*. London: Oxford University Press.

Millar, James (1970) "Soviet Rapid Development and the Agricultural Surplus Hypothesis," *Soviet Studies* 22 (July): 77–93.

————. (1974) "Mass Collectivization and the Contribution of Soviet Agriculture to the First Five Year Plan," *Slavic Review* 33 (December): 750–66.

————. (1978) "A Note on Primitive Accumulation in Marx and Preobrazhensky," *Soviet Studies* 30 (July): 384–93.

Miller, John (1987) "Crisis Theory and the Expansion of the State," *Research in Political Economy* 10:25–47.

Mills, Frederick (1946) *Price-Quantity Interactions in Business Cycles*. New York: National Bureau of Economic Research.

Mindlin, I. (1967) "The Old in the New," in *American and Soviet Society*, ed. Paul Hollander. Englewood Cliffs, N.J.: Prentice-Hall.

Mises, Ludwig von (1935) "Economic Calculation in the Socialist Commonwealth," in *Collectivist Economic Planning*, ed. F. A. Hayek. London: Routledge and Kegan Paul.

Mitchell, Wesley C. (1951) *What Happens in Business Cycles*. New York: National Bureau of Economic Research.

Mongait, A. L. (1961) *Archaeology in the USSR*. Baltimore: Penguin, first pub. 1955.

Morgan, Robin, ed. (1970) *Sisterhood is Powerful*. New York: Vintage.

Morray, J. P. (1965) "Marxism and Democracy in Cuba," in *Marxism and Democracy*, ed. Herbert Aptheker. New York: Humanities Press.

Nash, Manning (1967) "The Organization of Economic Life," in *Tribal and Peasant Economies*, ed. George Dalton. Garden City, N.Y.: Natural History Press.

Nicolaus, Martin (1975) *Restoration of Capitalism in the USSR*. Chicago: Liberator Press.

Nkrumah, Kwame (1965) *Neo-colonialism: The Last Stage of Imperialism*. New York: International Publishers.

Norman, Richard, and Sean Sayers (1980) *Hegel, Marx, and Dialectic: A Debate*. New Jersey: Humanities Press.

Nove, Alec (1975) "Is There a Ruling Class in the USSR?" *Soviet Studies* 27 (October): 615–38.

————. (1982) "Income Distribution in the USSR," *Soviet Studies* 34 (April): 286–88.

————. (1983) *The Economics of Feasible Socialism*. London: Allen and Unwin.

————. (1986) *Socialism, Economics, and Development*. London: Allen and Unwin.

Nove, Alec, and J. A. Newth (1967) *The Soviet Middle East*. New York: Praeger.

Nuti, D. M. (1986) "Hidden and Repressed Inflation in Soviet-Type Economies," *Contributions to Political Economy* 5 (March): 37–82.

Offe, Claus (1975) "Theses on the Theory of the State," *New German Critique* 6 (Fall): 137–47.

Ollman, Bertell (1971) *Alienation*. New York: Cambridge University Press.

————. (1973) "Marx and Political Science," *Politics and Society* 3 (Summer).

Ollman, Bertell, and Eduard Vernoff (1982) *The Left Academy*, vol. 1. New York: McGraw-Hill.

————. (1984) *The Left Academy*, vol. 2. New York, McGraw-Hill.

Omvedt, Gail (1986) "Patriarchy: The Analysis of Women's Oppression," *The Insurgent Sociologist* 13 (Spring): 30–50.

Openheimer, Martin (1985) *White Collar Politics*. New York: Monthly Review Press.

Orans, Martin (1966) "Surplus," *Human Organization* 25 (Spring): 24–32.

An Outline History of China (1958). Peking: Foreign Languages Press.

Papandreou, Andreas (1970) *Man's Freedom*. New York: Columbia University Press.

Parenti, Michael (1977) *Democracy for the Few*. 2d ed. New York: St. Martin's Press.

Pauling, Linus (1964) Speech at a meeting of the Ethical Culture Society in Pasadena, Calif. (January 19).

Payer, Cheryl (1982) *The World Bank: A Critical Analysis*. New York: Monthly Review Press.

————. (1974) *The Debt Trap: the IMF and the Third World*. New York: Monthly Review Press.

Pechman, Joseph (1969) "The Rich, the Poor, and the Taxes They Pay," *The Public Interest* 17 (Fall): 113–37.

Penn, David (1976) "Aggregate Concentration," *Anti-Trust Bulletin* (Spring): 1–15.

Peterson, Wallace C. (1985) "The U.S. 'Welfare State' and the Conservative Counterrevolution," *Journal of Economic Issues* 19 (September): 601–42.

Pirenne, H. (1929) "The Place of the Netherlands in the Economic History of Medieval

Europe," *Economic History Review* 2 (January): 40–61.

————. (1956) *Economic and Social History of Medieval Europe*. New York: Harcourt Brace.

Planty-Bonjour, Guy (1967) *The Categories of Dialectical Materialism*. New York: Praeger.

Popper, Karl (1958) "Prediction and Prophecy in the Social Sciences," in *Theories of History*, ed. Patrick Gardiner. New York: Free Press.

Postan, H. (1952) "The Trade of Medieval Europe: The North," *Cambridge Economic History* 2:159–63.

Poulantzas, Nicos (1978) *State, Power, Socialism*. London: New Left Books, trans. 1980.

————. (1969A) *Classes in Contemporary Capitalism*. London: New Left Books, trans. 1975.

————. (1969B) "The Problem of the Capitalist State," *New Left Review* 58:67–78.

Prebisch, Raul (1959) "Commercial Policy in the Underdeveloped Countries," *American Economic Review* 49 (May): 251–73.

Preobrazhensky, E. A. (1926) *The New Economics*. Oxford: Clarendon Press, repub. 1965.

Pulling, Kathleen (1978) "Cyclical Behavior of Profit Margins," *Journal of Economic Issues* 12 (June): 1–24.

————. (1977) "Market Structure and the Cyclical Behavior of Prices and Profits." Ph.D. dissertation, University of California, Riverside.

Ramparts (1970). "Editorial," *Ramparts* (May): 2.

Reagan, Michael (1963) *The Managed Economy*. New York: Oxford University Press.

Redfield, Robert (1953) *The Primitive World and Its Transformations*. Ithaca: Cornell University Press.

Reich, Michael (1980) *Racial Inequality, Economic Theory, and Class Conflict*. Princeton: Princeton University Press.

Reichenbach, Hans (1951) *The Rise of Scientific Philosophy*. Berkeley, University of California Press.

Ricardo, David (1821) *Principles of Political Economy and Taxation*, ed. P. Sraffa and M. Dobb. Cambridge: Cambridge University Press, republished 1953.

Robinson, Joan (1946) *An Essay on Marxian Economics*. New York: St. Martin's Press, repub. 1960.

Roemer, John (1982) *A General Theory of Exploitation and Class*. Cambridge: Harvard University Press.

Roncaglia, Allesandro (1978) *Sraffa and the Theory of Prices*. New York: Wiley.

Roosevelt, Franklin D. (1944) "State of the Union" Message to Congress. January 11.

Rose, Arnold (1967) *The Power Structure*. New York: Oxford University Press.

Rychetnik, Ludek (1968) "Two Models of an Enterprise in Market Socialism," *Economics of Planning* 8, 3.

Sahlins, Marshall D. (1965) "On the Sociology of Primitive Exchange," in *The Relevance of Models for Social Anthropology*, ed. Michael Banton, pp. 142–57. New York: Praeger.

Ste. Croix, Geoffrey (1985) "Class in Marx's Conception of History," *Monthly Review* (March).

Samuels, Warren (1977) "Technology vis-a-vis Institutions: A Suggested Interpretation," *Journal of Economic Issues* 11 (December): 867–95.

Samuels, Warren, ed. (1979) *The Economy as a System of Power*. 2 vols. New Brunswick: Transaction Books.

Samuelson, Paul (1973) *Economics*. 9th ed. New York: McGraw-Hill.

Sawyer, Malcolm C. (1982) *Macroeconomics in Question: The Keynesian-Monetarist Orthodoxies and the Kaleckian Alternative*. Armonk, N.Y.: M. E. Sharpe.

Schaff, Adam (1960) "Marxist Dialectics and the Principle of Contradiction," *Journal of Philosophy* 57 (March).

—————. (1970) *Marxism and the Human Individual*. New York: McGraw-Hill, first publ. 1965.

Schervish, Paul G. (1983) *The Structural Determinants of Unemployment*. New York: Academic Press.

Schoenbaum, David (1986) "It's No Pizza Parlor, It's the Family Farm, and It's Going, Going . . . " *Los Angeles Times* (June 17).

Schuman, Frederick (1967) "The USSR in World Affairs," in *The USSR After 50 Years*, ed. Samuel Hendel and Randolph Braham. New York: Knopf.

Schwendiger, Herman and Julia (1974) *Sociologists of the Chair: A Radical Analysis of the Formative Years of North American Sociology, 1883–1922*. New York: Basic Books.

Science and Society (1984–85) "The Theory of Value: A Symposium," *Science and Society* 48, 4 (includes articles by Mohun, Carling, Seking, Bandyopadhyay, and Laibman.)

Selsam, Howard, and Harry Martel (1963) *Reader in Marxist Philosophy*. New York: International Publishers.

Semmler, Willi (1982) "Competition, Monopoly, and Differentials of Profit Rates," *Review of Radical Political Economics* 13 (Winter): 39–52.

Shaikh, Anwar (1978) "An Introduction to the History of Crisis Theories," in Union for Radical Political Economies, *U.S. Capitalism in Crisis*. New York: Monthly Review Press.

Shen Ping-yuan (1969) "A Discussion of Formal Logic and Dialectics," translated in *Chinese Studies in Philosophy* 1 (Fall).

Shepherd, William B. (1970) *Market Power and Economic Welfare*. New York: Random House.

Sherman, Howard (1968) *Profits in the United States*. Ithaca: Cornell University Press.

—————. (1986) "Changes in the Character of the U.S. Business Cycle," *Review of Radical Political Economics* 18 (Spring-Summer): 190–204.

Sherman, Howard, and Gary Evans (1984) *Macroeconomics: Keynesian, Monetarist, and Marxist Views*. New York: Harper and Row.

Sherman, Howard J., and James L. Wood (1979) *Sociology: Traditional and Radical Perspectives*. New York: Harper and Row.

Singer, Daniel (1981) *The Road to Gdansk*. New York: Monthly Review Press.

Skocpol, Theda (1979) *States and Social Revolutions: A Comparative Analysis of France, Russia, and China*. New York: Cambridge University Prss.

Skocpol, Theda, ed. (1984) *Vision and Method in Historical Sociology*. Cambridge: Cambridge University Press.

Smith, Adam (1776) *The Wealth of Nations*. Modern Library, repub. 1937.

Sperry, Charles W. (1985) "What Makes Mondragon Work?" *Review of Social Economy* 43 (December): 345–56.

Spulber, Nicholas (1964) *Foundations of Soviet Strategy for Economic Growth: Selected Soviet Essays, 1924–1930*. Bloomington: Indiana University Press.

Sraffa, Piero (1960) *Production of Commodities by Means of Commodities*. Cambridge: Cambridge University Press.

Steedman, Ian (1977) *Marx After Sraffa*. London: New Left Books.

Stigler, George (1959) "The Politics of Political Economists," *Quarterly Journal of Economics* (November).

Stigler, George, and J. K. Kindahl (1970) *The Behavior of Industrial Prices*. New York: National Bureau of Economic Research.

Stockman, David (1986) *The Triumph of Politics*. New York: Harper and Row.

Sweezy, Paul (1942) *Theory of Capitalist Development*. New York: Monthly Review Press, repub. 1958.

————. (1961) "Toward a Critique of Economics," *Monthly Review* 21 (January): 1–12.

————. (1980) *Post-Revolutionary Society: Essays*. New York: Monthly Review Press.

————. (1985a) "After Capitalism, What?" *Monthly Review* 37 (July-August 1985): 98–111.

————. (1985b) "Rejoinder," *Monthly Review* 37 (September): 56–61.

Sweezy, Paul, and Leo Huberman (1967) "50 Years of Soviet Power," *Monthly Review* 19 (November).

Szymanski, Albert (1978) *The Capitalist State and the Politics of Class*. Cambridge, Mass.: Winthrop.

————. (1979) *Is the Red Flag Flying? The Political Economy of the Soviet Union*. London: Zed.

Terkel, Studs (1970) *Hard Times: An Oral History of the Great Depression*. New York: Pantheon.

Thomas, Clive (1974) *Dependence and Transformation: The Economics of the Transition to Socialism*. New York: Monthly Review Press.

Thomas, David, Brigadier General of the U.S. Army in Vietnam (1969) Reported in *San Francisco Chronicle* (October 24): 1.

Thompson, M. W. (1961) "Transator's Foreword," in A. L. Mongait, *Archeology in the USSR*. Baltimore: Penguin.

Trotsky, Leon (1937) *The Revolution Betrayed*. New York: Pathfinder.

Tullock, Gordon (1971) *The Logic of the Law*. New York: Basic Books.

Turgeon, Lynn (1963) "Future Levels of Living in the USSR." *Economics of Planning*.

Turner, Louis (1971) *Invisible Empires*. New York: Harcourt Brace Jovanovich.

Union for Radical Political Economics (1982) "Modern Approaches to the Theory of Value," *Review of Radical Political Economics* 14, 2 (Summer) (includes articles by Hunt, Fischer, Foley, Lipietz, Hodgson, Shaikh, Ernst, and Laibman).

————. (1986) "Empirical Work in Marxian Crisis Theory," *Review of Radical Political Economics* 18 (Spring-Summer): *passim*.

United Nations, Department of International Economic and Social Affairs (1985) *United Nations Statistical Yearbook, 1982*. New York: United Nations.

————. (1959) *The International Flow of Long-Term Capital and Official Donations, 1951–1959*.

————, Department of Economic Affairs (1949) *National and International Measures for Full Employment*. New York: United Nations.

United Press (1973) *Press-Enterprise* (October 23).

U.S. Arms Control and Disarmament Agency (1985). Washington, D.C.: GPO.

U.S. Congress, House Committee on Official Conduct (1978) "Financial Disclosure," *Congressional Quarterly* 36 (September 2): 2311–66.

U.S. Council on International Economic Policy (1977) *International Economic Report of the President*. Washington, D.C.: GPO.

U.S. Department of Commerce (1960) *United States Business Investments in Foreign Countries*. Washington, D.C.: GPO.

————. (1970) *1970 Census of Population*, Subject Report PC(2)-7A, *Occupational Characteristics*. Washington, D.C.: GPO.

————. (1983) *Statistical Abstract of the United States*. Washington, D.C.: GPO.

————. (1986) *Statistical Abstract of the United States, 1986*. Washington, D.C.: GPO.

Vilar, P. (1956) "Problems of the Formation of Capitalism," *Past and Present* 10 (November): 15–39.

Wachtel, Howard (1971) "Looking at Poverty from a Radical Perspective," *Review of Radical Political Economics* (Summer): 12.

Wachtel, Howard, and Peter Adelsheim (1976) "The Inflationary Impact of Unemployment Price Markups During Postwar Recessions, 1947–1970," U.S. Joint Economic Committee, *Hearings*. Washington, D.C.: GPO.

Walbank, F. W. (1946) *The Decline of the Roman Empire in the West*. London: Cobbett Press.

Wallerstein, Immanuel (1985) "Marx and Underdevelopment," in *Rethinking Marxism*, ed. R. Wolff and S. Resnick. New York: Autonomedia, 1985.

Walras, Leon (1874) *Elements of Pure Theory*. Homewood, Ill.: R. D. Irwin, transl. 1954.

Weeks, John (1981) *Capital and Exploitation*. Princeton: Princeton University Press.

Westergaard, John, and Henrietta Resler (1975) *Class in a Capitalist Society: A Study of Contemporary Britain*. New York: Basic Books.

Wilbur, Charles, and Kenneth Jameson (1983) *An Inquiry into the Poverty of Economics*. Notre Dame: University of Notre Dame Press.

Wiles, Peter (1964) *The Political Economy of Communism*. London: Basil Blackwell.

Winter, Ella (1933) *Red Virtue*. New York: Harcourt, Brace.

Wise, David, and Thomas Ross (1964) *The Invisible Government*. New York: Random House.

Wolff, Richard, and Stephen Resnick (1986) "Power, Property, and Class." *Socialist Review* 86, 16 (March-April): 97–124.

Wolff, Richard, Bruce Roberts, and Antonio Callari (1982) "Marx's (not Ricardo's) Transformation Problem: A Radical Reconceptualization," *History of Political Economics* 14, 4: 564–82.

Wolfson, Martin H. (1986) *Financial Crises*. Armonk, N.Y.: M. E. Sharpe.

World Bank (1984) *World Development Report 1984*. New York: Oxford University Press.

Wright, Eric Ohlin (1978) *Class, Crisis and the State*. London: New Left Books.

Yanowitch, Murray (1966) "The Soviet Income Revolution," in *The Soviet Economy*, ed. Morris Bernstein and Dan Fusfeld. Homewood, Ill.: Irwin.

————. (1977) *Social and Economic Inequality in the Soviet Union*. White Plains, N.Y.: M. E. Sharpe.

Yefremov, Ivan (no date) *Andromeda*. Moscow: Foreign Languages Press.

Yunker, James (1986) "In Defense of Utilitarianism: An Economist's Viewpoint," *Review of Social Economy* 44 (April).

Zimbalist, Andrew, and Howard Sherman (1984) *Comparing Economic Systems*. Orlando, Fla.: Academic Press.

Zinn, Howard (1970) *The Politics of History*. Boston: Beacon Press.

Zukin, Sharon (1984) "Yugoslavia: Development and Persistence of the State," in *The State in Socialist Society*, ed. Neil Harding. Albany: State University of New York.

INDEX

Advertising, 132; effects on profits, 181–82

Afghanistan, 360

Africa, 301; and colonialism, 235–36; and foreign investment, 241; income, 225; and political democracy, 185

Agency for International Development, 245

Agnew, Spiro, 122, 275

Alameda Labor Council, 108

Albania, 269

Alienation, 129–31; and communism, 390–91; in Hungary, 356; in the Soviet Union, 344–61; under statism, 355–58; in the United States, 133

Allende, Salvador, 200

American Economic Association, 3, 28–29

American Federation of Labor (AFL), 107, 109

American Federation of Labor and Congress of Industrial Organizations (AFL-CIO), 203

American Railway Union, 107

Americans for Democratic Action (ADA), 199

Angola: and neocolonialism, 237

Antitrust laws, 166

Aquinas, 27–28, 30

Aristotle, 30

Army Intelligence, 203

Asia, 301; and colonialism, 235–36; and foreign investment, 241; income, 225; and political democracy, 185

Asiatic mode of production, 71–73

Austria: and socialist parties, 266

Automation, 384. *See also* Science; Technology

Bahro, Rudolf, 258

Baran, Paul, 230

Belgium, 263; underdevelopment in, 227

Bergman, Barbara, 126–27

Beria, 299

Bernstein, Eduard, 168, 265

Bilateral Public Aid, 244

Blacks. *See* Racism

Bolsheviks, 46, 256–57, 266, 267, 270, 273

Bowles, Samuel: emphasis on labor intensity, 110–12

Brazil, 204, 274; imperialism in, 236; and neocolonial aid, 245

Brezhnev, Leonid, 256

British Broadcasting Company (BBC), 309

British Revolution, 62

Brown v. Board of Education, 117

Bukharin, Nicolai, 228, 267, 270–71, 279

Bureau of Labor Statistics (BLS): price indexes, 22

Burma: and foreign trade, 238–39

Business cycles, 149–55, 177–80

Canada: income, 225

Capitalism: capitalist model, 80–82; and class conflict, 57–58, 59, 107–10; classical approach to, 90–92; competition, 132; conflict with democracy,

ABOUT THE AUTHOR

A graduate of the University of California, Los Angeles, Howard J. Sherman received an M.A. in Economics from the University of Southern California, a Jur.D. in Law from the University of Chicago Law School, and a Ph.D. in Economics from the University of California, Berkeley. He has taught at a number of distinguished universities, and he is now Professor and Chair of Economics at the University of California, Riverside.

A frequent contributor to scholarly journals, Professor Sherman is the author of a number of notable books, among them: *Macrodynamic Economics* (1965), *Elementary Aggregate Economics* (1966), *Profits in the United States* (1968), *Radical Political Economy* (1972), *Stagflation* (1976), and *Comparing Economic Systems; A Political-Economic Approach* (1984, co-authored with Andrew Zimbalist). He is a founding member of the Union of Radical Political Economics and has twice been a member of the Board of Editors of the *Review of Radical Political Economics*.